THE SALVAGE

JAPANESE AMERICAN EVACUATION
AND RESETTLEMENT

The Salvage

By Dorothy Swaine Thomas

WITH THE ASSISTANCE OF

Charles Kikuchi and James Sakoda

UNIVERSITY OF CALIFORNIA PRESS

Berkeley and Los Angeles · 1952

UNIVERSITY OF CALIFORNIA PRESS
BERKELEY AND LOS ANGELES
CALIFORNIA

❖

CAMBRIDGE UNIVERSITY PRESS
LONDON, ENGLAND

PRINTED IN THE UNITED STATES OF AMERICA
BY THE UNIVERSITY OF CALIFORNIA PRINTING DEPARTMENT

PREFACE

I_N 1946, the University of California Press published *The Spoilage*, by Dorothy Swaine Thomas and Richard S. Nishimoto. Publication of *The Salvage* completes the plan, announced at that time, for a two-volume work on social aspects of the wartime evacuation, detention, segregation, and resettlement of the Japanese American minority. As stated in *The Spoilage:*

The first volume analyzes the experiences of that part of the minority group whose status in America was impaired: those of the immigrant generation who returned, after the war, to defeated Japan; those of the second generation who relinquished American citizenship. It is, thus, concerned with the short-run "spoilage" resulting from evacuation and detention; the stigmatization as "disloyal" to the United States of one out of every six evacuees; the concentration and confinement of this group in the Tule Lake [Segregation] Center; the repressive measures undertaken by government agencies, including martial law, incarceration and internment; the successive protest movements of the group against these repressions, culminating in mass withdrawal from American citizenship. . . .

The second volume will include analysis of the short-run "salvage," i.e., the experiences of that part of the minority whose status in America was, at least temporarily, improved through dispersal and resettlement in the East and Middle West. This group includes one out of three of the evacuees who left the camps [by the end of December, 1944] to enter new areas as settlers, many participating directly in the war effort." (p. xii.)

The Spoilage was a case history, focused upon the disorganizing effects of the evacuation-detention crisis of 1942 and of the administrative effort to assess the "loyalty" of the detained evacuees and to segregate the "disloyal" in 1943. Its primary data were day-by-day records, obtained over a three-and-a-half-year period by participant observers and field workers on the staff of the Evacuation and Resettlement Study, and these were supplemented by copious contemporary documents (surveys, questionnaires, petitions, minutes, and so on) from evacuee or administrative sources. Because of possible implications for policy formation, it was considered desirable to publish an analysis of this "continuing process of interaction between government and governed" as promptly as possible. The authors of *The Spoilage*, therefore, did not attempt to place the segregation phase of the evacuation-detention crisis in historical perspective or to delineate social and demographic base lines.

The Salvage is focused upon evacuee migration from War Relocation Authority camps to the Middle West and East during 1943 and 1944. Its primary data are derived from official censuses of evacuees, from transcripts of segregation transfers and of leave permits, from participant observation, and from interviews with resettlers in the Chicago area. To develop a context for analyses of these primary data and to provide a historical frame of reference and a prewar base line for placing the evacuation-detention crisis in perspective, data from a variety of secondary sources are utilized in Part I. Wherever possible, the period of reference is from the turn of the century to 1945. The first ten sections chronicle the main political events and administrative actions that impinged upon the Japanese American minority group during the course of immigration and settlement; define group trends and intragroup differentials in demographic, economic, and cultural terms; and piece together fragmentary data bearing on social organization and political orientation. A section on forced mass migration includes a summary of *The Spoilage* as well as statistical analysis of the differential incidence of segregation; and a section on selective resettlement evaluates the factors that facilitated and impeded resettlement and culminates in statistical analysis of the nature and extent of demographic, economic, and cultural selection in the outmigration from WRA camps during 1943–1944.

Part I deals with mass phenomena; Part II with the train of individual experience as exemplified by career-lines and life histories. The section on social demography synthesizes the results of the historical, institutional, and statistical analyses of Part I and provides a frame of reference for Part II. The next section describes how the experiential records were obtained and outlines their content, and the section following defines the basis of selection. Detailed life histories are presented of fifteen resettlers, whose prewar careers covered the range and represented most of the types of occupations open to second-generation Japanese on the West Coast, and who came from diverse communities of origin and family backgrounds. Each of these histories indicates how an individual lived his life within the context delineated in Part I and complements the treatment of mass phenomena by adding specificity of detail, emphasizing the continuity of experience, and portraying the subjective (attitudinal) as well as the objective (behaviorial) aspects of experience.

The authors of *The Spoilage* acknowledged indebtedness to a large number of individuals and organizations whose encouragement, support, and coöperation were essential to the launching of the Evacuation and Resettlement Study. (*Ibid.,* p. xiv.) The author of *The Salvage* reaffirms this indebtedness and is especially grateful for the continued generosity of the Rockefeller, the Columbia, and the Giannini Foundations; for the coöperation of the War Relocation Authority; and for assistance received from the Universities of California and of Pennsylvania.

Like the authors of *The Spoilage,* the author of *The Salvage* drew heavily upon the work of colleagues and research assistants on the Evacuation and Resettlement Study. Of the two whose names appear on the title page of this volume, Charles Kikuchi prepared the first draft of all of the life histories used in Part II, and James Sakoda was primarily responsible for collecting, evaluating, tabulating, and analyzing details of the characteristics of approximately 24,000 evacuees whose statistical histories are synthesized in Part I. Richard S. Nishimoto, coauthor of *The Spoilage,* gave invaluable advice and prepared

several basic economic analyses. Research reports by Frank Miyamoto, Tamotsu Shibutani, and Togo Tanaka were used extensively. Donald Kent helped select and abridge the life-history
material; Daphne Notestein prepared most of the charts; Georges
Sabagh, Everett Lee, and Himeko Nichols, among others, helped
on the statistical phases; and Louise Suski, Mary Wilson, and
Helen White were the principal secretarial assistants.

Finally, it must be stressed that the data in Part II of *The
Salvage* represent the contribution of hundreds of "resettler-
hours" by the fifteen Nisei whose abridged life histories are
utilized; and that purposeful selection of these fifteen documents
was possible only because scores of other resettlers made similar
contributions to the Evacuation and Resettlement Study. We
are grateful for their willingness to relive, "for the record," the
traumatic period following Pearl Harbor, to reconstruct the
details of family and community background, and to particu-
larize their experiences and attitudes with so few reservations.

D. S. T.

Philadelphia, Pennsylvania
October 15, 1951

CONTENTS

PART I

Patterns of Social and Demographic Change

PART II

The Course of Individual Experience

x   CONTENTS

CHARTS

Part I

PATTERNS OF SOCIAL AND DEMOGRAPHIC CHANGE

Introduction

In 1880, there were fewer than 200 alien Japanese in the United States. Between 1885 when Japan legalized labor emigration and 1924, when Oriental exclusion was incorporated in the Immigration Act of the United States, more than 200,000 Japanese aliens entered this country as direct migrants from Japan, and thousands of others were admitted as secondary migrants from Hawaii. By 1940, cumulative admissions of Japanese aliens had probably exceeded 300,000, and at least 125,000 children had been born to Japanese parents residing in the continental United States. But the net result of half a century of immigration and of three decades of family building, as shown in the census of 1940, was only 47,000 Japanese aliens and 80,000 American-born descendants. And, as of 1940, almost 90 per cent of this total Japanese American population of 127,000 lived in the four western states of California, Washington, Oregon, and Arizona.

During the spring and summer of 1942, the Western Defense Command ordered the exclusion of all persons of Japanese ancestry from the whole of California, from the western third of Washington and Oregon, and from the southern quarter of Arizona. For a short period, voluntary exodus with free choice of destination outside the exclusion areas was permitted and even encouraged. So much hostility developed in the receiving areas, however, and so few evacuees were able to find destinations for themselves that by the end of March, 1942, voluntary evacuation on an individual basis was superseded by controlled mass evacuation. Centers, originally set up for "reception" or "assembly" purposes to provide temporary refuge for the displaced evacuees were superseded by more extensive, barbed-

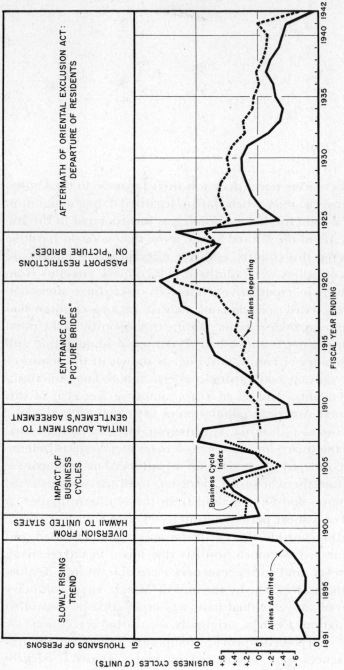

Chart I. Japanese immigration to and emigration from continental United States, by fiscal years, 1891–1942, and index of United States business cycles, by calendar years, 1900–1906. (See Appendix, tables 1 and 2. Note that business cycles index, though referring to calendar years 1900–1906, is plotted for fiscal years ending 1901–1907.)

wire-enclosed camps, called "relocation projects" but designed for war-duration occupancy. During the summer and fall of 1942, more than 110,000 evacuees were moved under federal supervision from homes and assembly centers to relocation projects.

In December, 1944, orders excluding the Japanese from the West Coast were rescinded and the evacuees were free to return to their former homes. But, by this time, one in three had migrated eastward from camps to American communities outside the exclusion areas or had entered the armed services, one in six was confined in a segregation center for the "disloyal," and the population remaining in relocation projects had dwindled to 62,000. In the frame of reference to be developed in the following sections, these three groups are defined, respectively, as the *salvage,* the *spoilage,* and the *residue* of a historical process culminating in evacuation and resettlement. This process is appraised and, where possible, analyzed quantitatively in terms of the social demography of the prewar period, the impact upon disparate population segments of the forced mass migration that followed exclusion from the Pacific Coast, and the selective nature of wartime dispersal from relocation projects.

Immigration and Settlement[1]

Year-by-year variations in the course of migration between Japan and the continental United States are shown in Chart I, in the series of alien admissions which were recorded first in 1890–1891 and in that of alien departures for which records are available only from the fiscal year 1907–1908.

Although Japan's abandonment of a two-century long seclusion policy in 1868 eased restrictions on free movement from the country and an edict in 1885 removed barriers to labor emigration, the number of aliens entering American ports before

[1] The main sources used in the discussion of Japanese immigration are H. A. Millis, *The Japanese Problem in the United States,* Macmillan, New York, 1915; Y. Ichihashi, *Japanese in the United States,* Stanford University Press, 1932; E. K. Strong, Jr., *The Second-Generation Japanese Problem,* Stanford University Press, 1934; U.S. Congress. Senate. *Reports of the Immigration Commission, Immigrants in Industry, Japanese and Other Immigrant Races in the Pacific Coast and Rocky Mountain States,* 61st Congress, 2d Sess., S. Doc., 85, Part I, Washington, 1911.

the turn of the century oscillated only slightly around a slowly
rising trend, from a level of about 1,000 a year in the early
'nineties to not much more than 2,000 a year toward the end
of the decade. During this early period, Hawaii, rather than the
continental United States, was the destination preferred by
Japanese emigrants,[2] and the sharp rise in admissions to the
mainland in 1900 reflects a fortuitous diversion to San Francisco
of Hawaiian-bound immigrants whose ships were turned away
from Honolulu because of an outbreak of bubonic plague in
the Islands. Between 1901 and 1907, the curve of admissions
ebbed to troughs of 4,000–5,000 and rose to a crest of almost
10,000, in response to the slackening and quickening of the
demand for labor on the West Coast, and during these years,
as Chart I indicates, there was a striking covariation in curves of
immigration and of American business cycles. From 1908 on-
ward, however, the limits of fluctuation in admissions were set
primarily by political restrictions.[3]

Following the establishment of territorial government and
the abolition of contract labor in Hawaii, secondary migration
from the Islands to the continent began to assume numerical
importance. The bulk of secondary and direct migrants alike
sought California as a destination, and though the numbers
involved were still small in the first few years of the twentieth
century, the increasing tempo of the movement stimulated demands for complete cessation of immigration. Boycotts and other
discriminatory measures were instituted against the resident
Japanese in many California localities and in 1906, the San
Francisco School Board passed a resolution requiring all Japanese then in the public schools to attend a segregated school for
Orientals. Denouncing the action as a "wicked absurdity," President Theodore Roosevelt "finally persuaded the School Board

[2] There are no accurate statistics on the movement of Japanese between Hawaii
and the mainland. We have used estimates, from the sources cited in footnote 1
above, based on various reports of the Commissioner General of Immigration and
of the Board of Immigration of Hawaii.

[3] A positive relationship between business cycles and immigration had been, and
continued to be, characteristic of wave after wave of European migrants to the
United States. (See Harry Jerome, *Migration and Business Cycles*, National Bureau
of Economic Research, New York, 1926.)

to rescind its resolution on the understanding that the President would bring Japanese immigration to an end."[4] In March, 1907, Roosevelt issued a proclamation, prohibiting remigration to the continental United States of Japanese laborers who had received passports to go to Mexico, Canada, and Hawaii, and in the same year the Japanese government agreed to undertake measures to end direct immigration of Japanese laborers to the United States. Under this, the "Gentlemen's Agreement," Japan would issue passports only to "such of its subjects as are non-laborers or are laborers who, in coming to the continent, seek to resume a formerly acquired domicile, to join a parent, wife, or children residing therein, or to assume active control of an already possessed interest in a farming enterprise located in this country."[5] Following enforcement of the Agreement, admissions fell from an annual level of 10,000 in 1907–1908 to about 2,500 in each of the two following years, and return-migrants to Japan numbered some 5,000 annually.

The renewed upswing that began in 1910 and culminated in 1920 reflected an unexpectedly enthusiastic response of Japanese settlers to the Agreement's provision permitting entry of relatives, and the liberal interpretation immigration officials made of the somewhat ambiguous provision. Husbands who had left their wives and children in Japan now sent for them, and bachelors made hurried trips to their native villages, married, and brought their brides to America. Soon a more economical method of family-building became popular: relatives and friends in the mother country helped find brides for Japanese living in the United States, photographs were exchanged, and, if the arrangements proved mutually agreeable, marriage vows were

[4] R. L. Buell, *Japanese Immigration,* World Peace Foundation Pamphlets, Vol. VII, Nos. 5–6 (1924), p. 287.

[5] The Agreement was not published. The above interpretation is that of the Commissioner-General of Immigration. (See *Annual Report of the Commissioner-General of Immigration for the Fiscal Year ended June 30, 1909,* p. 121.) This interpretation is worded ambiguously. A clearer statement is that of Ambassador Hanihara to Secretary of State Hughes in a letter dated April 10, 1924, *viz.* "The Japanese government will not issue passports good for the Continental United States to laborers, skilled or unskilled, except those previously domiciled in the United States, or parents, wives, or children under twenty years of age of such persons." (Buell, *op. cit.,* p. 359.)

taken by proxy, and bachelors were thus spared the inconvenience and expense of trips to Japan. Until 1920 passports were freely issued to "picture brides."

As the influx of women[6] gained momentum, the birth rate rose. There were repeated protests against the "alarming increase" of the Japanese American population until Japan discontinued the practice of issuing passports to "picture brides." The number of alien arrivals dropped sharply after 1921, and return-migrants again exceeded immigrants, but regional groups persevered in their demands for complete cessation of Japanese immigration. "Finally, the Immigration Act of 1924 was passed (effective July 1, 1924), giving California what she wanted. . . . This act abrogated . . . the Gentlemen's Agreement and provided for the exclusion of all aliens ineligible to citizenship."[7] Among those ineligible on racial grounds were the Japanese, and with the enforcement of the Act, their immigration to the United States was effectively ended. After a short-lived rush to beat the deadline, arrivals declined sharply. Immigrant settlers who had failed to call their wives and children from Japan were no longer free to do so. Visas were now issued only to visitors, students, treaty merchants, and similar classes, and to returning residents. It was this last class which accounts in large measure for the slowly rising trend in arrivals from 1925 to 1930, but the increase was too slight to offset the drainage of alien Japanese from this country, and a negative balance in the population movement between the United States and Japan persisted to the eve of World War II.

Settlement proceeded slowly, and at no census year did Japanese immigrants and their descendants represent as much as 3 per cent of the total population of any one of the states. About

---

[6] Females accounted for close to 40 per cent of all arrivals in the upswing from 1910 to 1920, and more than three-quarters of them were wives of residents. The proportion of females in the total fell slightly to 35 per cent in the next four years, and fewer than three out of five of them were classified by Immigration authorities as wives. [Calculations based on U.S. Immigration reports which include immigration to Hawaii.]

As Strong pointed out female immigration "would undoubtedly have dropped very materially in a short time anyway. About twelve thousand more in 1925 would have supplied all the Japanese bachelors with wives." (*Op. cit.*, p. 86.)

[7] Strong, *op. cit.*, p. 48.

three-quarters of the 2,000 aliens enumerated as residents of the United States in 1890 settled near ports of entry in California or Washington. The other quarter, consisting mainly of students and businessmen, dispersed widely, passing through the mountain states toward the eastern seaboard. By the end of the next decade, tendencies both to dispersal and concentration were apparent. The movement to eastern states did not keep pace with immigration. Only one in twenty-five aliens was recorded as an eastern resident in the 1900 census, and 21 per cent of the total were enumerated in the intermountain states—many of them in Montana and Colorado. On the Pacific Coast, Washington expanded its proportion from 18 to 23 per cent of the total alien residents, and Oregon, with 10 per cent, emerged as an important area of absorption. After 1910 dispersal practically ceased, and settlement became more and more concentrated on the Pacific Coast; within the Pacific Coast area, in California; and within California, in Los Angeles and vicinity. In 1900 California's share of the country's alien Japanese was 42 per cent, and in 1920, 63 per cent. By 1940 the California proportion had risen to almost 75 per cent, with Los Angeles City accounting for no less than 25 per cent.

In the continental United States 44,000 Japanese aliens were added by 1910 to the 24,000 who had settled by 1900. There was an increment of only 14,000 in the next decade, and in the intercensal periods, 1920–1930 and 1930–1940, there were decrements of 11,000 and 23,000, respectively. The maximum foreign-born population of 80,000 was reached in 1920, and the drop to 47,000 in 1940 represented a decline of almost 40 per cent in the course of twenty years.[8]

Decreases in the number of immigrant settlers were, for a time, more than offset by increases in the number of their

---

[8] Hawaii's aliens, increasing by immigration from Japan but yielding later to the pull of the mainland, as well as to return migration, showed even narrower margins. The base of 56,000 aliens in 1900 was augmented by less than 4,000 in the next decade, and by less than 1,000 between 1910 and 1920; and diminished by 12,000 and 11,000, respectively, in the next two intercensal periods. Thus, Hawaii, which had started in 1900 with a cohort of Japanese immigrants more than twice as large as that of the mainland, had by 1940 some 10,000 fewer Japanese alien residents.

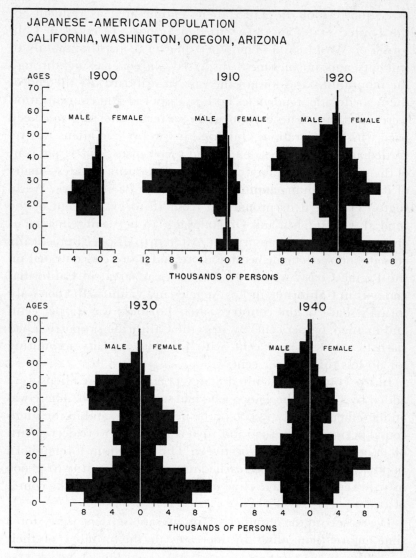

Chart II. Age-sex structures of the Japanese American population in California, Washington, Oregon, and Arizona, by decades, 1900–1940. (See Appendix, table 4.)

descendants. In 1900 there were fewer than 300 American-born Japanese, and their increase of about 4,000 in the next decade was only one-tenth as great as the corresponding increment of immigrant settlers. During the next decade the absolute growth of the second generation was double that of the first, and the ratio of American-born to foreign-born was almost one to three by 1920. In 1930 the two generations were approximately equal, at about 70,000 each. By 1940, the American-born had outstripped the immigrant group and, totaling 80,000, were two-thirds again as numerous as the 47,000 aliens. Their rate of growth, however, had not been sufficient to stabilize the size of the minority group as a whole, and the total Japanese population in the United States declined from 139,000 in 1930 to 127,000 in 1940.

Demographic Transitions

Concomitant with shifts in the numerical importance of immigrant settlers and of their American-born descendants were far-reaching transformations in age-sex structures, as shown in Chart II. At no census from 1900 to 1940, did the age-sex structure of the Japanese American population attain the form either of the classical, tapering pyramid, characteristic of the increasing population of the mother country or of the bulging pyramid with eroded foundation, characteristic of the areas of settlement. They were always unstable and transitional between the Oriental and the Occidental patterns. Their irregularities and imbalances recapitulate immigration history and at the same time suggest the extent and rapidity with which the Japan minority was assimilating Western population patterns.

The structure of 1900 consisted almost exclusively of young males: it had no foundation of children, no apex of old people, and a barely discernible number of females. By 1910 the male lateral had increased enormously and was covering a greater age-range, the female lateral had begun to swell, and a narrow base of children was forming. The 1920 structure, with its wide base of children, its large segment of potential reproducers, and its tapering apex implied future development of the true pyramid toward which populations with high natural increase tend. By 1930, however, the foundation had contracted sharply and by 1940 the age-sex "pyramid" consisted of a series of bulges and hollows. The attenuation of the foundation had sharpened even further, and age-classes 0–4 through 15–19 now formed a "pyramid-in-reverse." Ages 30–34 were markedly deficient for males and females alike, and there was another hollow class for males at ages 45–49. Both laterals had primary modes within the age-group 15–19, whereas there were secondary modes for males at 50–54 and for females at 40–44 years of age.

The structures of 1900 and 1910 show the immediate effects of age-selective immigration of laborers prior to the Gentlemen's Agreement; those of 1920 and of 1930, the changes that followed the influx of picture brides. The structure of 1940, while still reflecting the timing, magnitude, and selective force of these great waves of immigration, reveals also the transformation caused by transition to patterns of high survival and controlled fertility and by reversals of the migration balance.

Even in 1920 the Japanese in America were superior to the Japanese in Japan in their ability to survive, their advantage—as measured by expectation of life at birth—amounting to some eight years. They were, however, inferior to the whites on the Pacific Coast, the expectation of life at birth of Japanese males being 51 compared with 56 for whites; and for females, the Japanese expectancy was 50 years whereas that for whites was 59. During the next two decades, their transition to the high-survival pattern proceeded so rapidly that by 1940 the expectation of life at birth for males had increased from 51 to 63 years and for females from 50 to 67 years—approximately the level then attained by whites in the Pacific Coast states.

The crude birth rate of Japanese Americans rose sharply after 1910, and in California reached a maximum of 68 per 1,000 population in 1920—a rate four times as high as that of the whites. Popular fear of "invasion by immigration" gave way to concern over the "phenomenal fecundity" of the settlers. State Senator J. M. Inman, for example, interpreted the birth level of 1920 to mean that "all Japanese women in California between the ages of of 15 and 45 are bearing children at the rate of one every other year,"[9] and J. S. Chambers, writing in 1921, predicted that there would be 150,000 American-born Japanese in California "in ten years" and that "by 1949" they would "outnumber the white people."[10] Other observers, noting the unusual concentration of females in the childbearing ages, took issue with these alarmist conclusions. For example the State Board of Control pointed out that "among the Japanese . . . most of the adults are comparatively young and of the family-raising ages, while among the whites . . . there is necessarily the usual proportion of elderly persons."[11]

But even if measured by rates that are independent of the age distribution, the fertility of Japanese Americans in the early 1920's was extraordinarily high. For example, the gross reproduction rate—the number of daughters imputed to the average woman passing through the childbearing ages, on the assumption of a continuation of current age–specific fertility rates—was 3.4 for Japanese Americans in 1920. This was one-third again as high as the gross reproduction rate of 2.6 for Japan in 1925 and three times that of the rate for West Coast whites in 1920. By 1940 the rate for the Japanese in Japan had declined only slightly to 2.1, but that of the Japanese Americans on the West Coast, falling to 1.1, had practically converged with the rate of 1.0 for whites in the same area.

The margin between immigration of Japanese to the United States and emigration of Japanese from the United States was consistently a very narrow one after 1908. Many arrivals were canceled by departures, and the migration and remigration of a relatively small number of highly mobile people inflated the figures of both immigration and emigration without any effect on numbers of settlers. During the years 1908–1914, 97 out of every 100 alien arrivals were offset by alien departures, whereas from 1915 to 1924 the ratio was 86 departures to every 100

[9] *The Grizzly Bear,* "THE TIME HAS ARRIVED TO ELIMINATE THE JAPS AS CALIFORNIA LANDHOLDERS." June, 1920, p. 4.

[10] J. S. Chambers, "The Japanese Invasion," in *Annals of the American Academy of Political and Social Science,* Jan., 1921, p. 36.

[11] State Board of Control of California, *California and the Oriental,* Sacramento, 1922, p. 37.

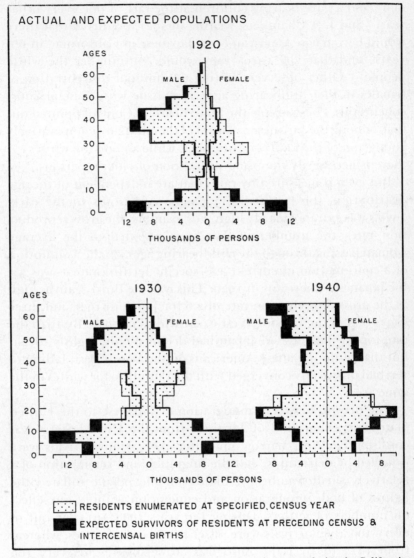

ACTUAL AND EXPECTED POPULATIONS

RESIDENTS ENUMERATED AT SPECIFIED, CENSUS YEAR

EXPECTED SURVIVORS OF RESIDENTS AT PRECEDING CENSUS & INTERCENSAL BIRTHS

Chart III. Age-sex structures of the Japanese American population in California, Washington, Oregon, and Arizona, by decades, 1920–1940, compared with structures expected on the basis of survivors of residents at preceding census and of intercensal births. (See Appendix, table 9. Note that all ages over 65 are cumulated at ages 65–69.)

arrivals.[12] After 1924 when there was a consistent net migratory loss, departures per 100 arrivals numbered 146. Included in the currents and countercurrents of migration were appreciable numbers of repeaters, who visited and revisited the mother country after their initial immigration to the United States. Thus among the foreign-born evacuees enumerated by the War Relocation Authority in 1942, no fewer than 40 per cent had returned to Japan and remigrated to America at least once, and about one in ten had made three or more trips to Japan.[13]

As suggested by Chart III, return migration to Japan was selective of aging immigrants in general and of males in particular. So heavy were the losses of the middle-aged and the old that males enumerated in the age-groups 50–59 in 1920, in 1930, and in 1940 were only three-quarters as numerous as those expected as survivors of males aged 40–49 who were enumerated in 1910, 1920, 1930, respectively. Correspondingly, the deficit of those 60 years of age and older amounted to a third or more of the expected survivors of residents aged 50 and older, ten years earlier. Although percentage divergences between expectation and enumeration were, in 1930 and in 1940, almost as great for older females as for comparable age-ranges of males, the absolute losses of males aged 35 years and older were almost twice those of females. This discrepancy was due, in the main, to the departure of alien bachelors who, after the immigration restrictions of 1920 and 1924 became effective, found it difficult to establish families in America. Return migration to Japan between 1920 and 1940 depleted their ranks by 50 per cent or more, while the comparable migratory loss of those who had married and established families in the United States before 1924 was only of the order of 15 per cent.[14]

---

[12] The increase in numbers directly attributable to net migration was much less for the Japanese than for other immigrant groups. On the basis of data presented by W. F. Willcox (*International Migrations* II, National Bureau of Economic Research, New York, 1931, pp. 88–89) the ratios of total alien departures per 100 total alien arrivals for 1908–1914 and for 1915–1924 were computed as 49 and 54, respectively.

[13] United States, Department of the Interior, War Relocation Authority, *The Evacuated People*, Washington, 1946, p. 84.

[14] Expected survivors, at each census, of residents aged 5–9 and over, at the preceding census, were estimated by applying 10-year survival coefficients derived from life-tables constructed for the Japanese population as of 1920, 1930, and 1940. (See Appendix table 9.) The procedure used is essentially that described and evaluated by E. P. Hutchinson in D. S. Thomas, *Research Memorandum on Migration Differentials*, Social Science Research Council, New York, 1938, App. C2.

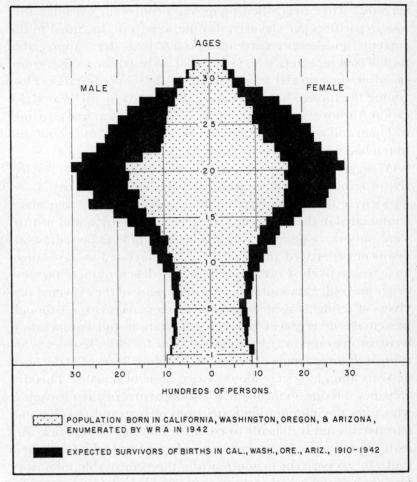

AGES

MALE　　　　　　　　　FEMALE

30

25

20

15

10

5

-1

30　　20　　10　　　0　　　10　　20　　30

HUNDREDS OF PERSONS

□□□ POPULATION BORN IN CALIFORNIA, WASHINGTON, OREGON, & ARIZONA,
ENUMERATED BY W R A IN 1942

■■■ EXPECTED SURVIVORS OF BIRTHS IN CAL., WASH., ORE., ARIZ., 1910-1942

Chart IV. Age-sex structure of Japanese American evacuees, 32 years of age and younger in 1942, who were born in California, Washington, Oregon, and Arizona, compared with structure expected on the basis of survivors of births to Japanese in these states by years, 1910–1942. (See Appendix, tables 10 and 11.)

Chart III suggests also a heavy migratory loss of young children, in the discrepancy between the "expected" survivors of births to Japanese parents in the Western states, decade by decade, and the number of children of Japanese ancestry actually enumerated in decennial censuses. Thus at least 28 per cent of the expected survivors of the birth cohorts of 1910–1919 had been "lost" through migration, and corresponding deficits in the expected number of children under 10 years of age in 1930 and 1940 (birth cohorts of 1920–1929 and 1930–1939) amounted to 24 per cent and to 16 per cent, respectively.[15] To some extent, these losses represented the family component in the stream of return migration to Japan, that is, the dependent, American-born children who accompanied their immigrant parents to the homeland. To a greater extent, however, they probably reflected the practice—initiated during the early family-building days and culminating in the 1920's—whereby many immigrant parents, who themselves remained on the West Coast as workers or entrepreneurs, sent one or more of their young children to Japan for foster care and education. An appreciable proportion of the Japan-educated American-born Japanese came back to their own native land, particularly during the 1930's. By 1942 they numbered almost 10,000 and represented one in seven of the American-born Japanese of California, Washington, Oregon, and Arizona. That the majority were still in Japan at the outbreak of World War II is suggested by the cumulative deficits to January 1, 1943, in survivors of annual birth cohorts from 1910 through 1942 in the four western states. These averaged 18 per cent for the cohorts of 1928–1942 (the survivors of which were under 15 years of age at the end of 1942), but more than 40 per cent for the cohorts of 1910–1927 (aged 15–32 in 1942) and exceeded 50 per cent for several of the single-year cohorts within the latter range. (See Chart IV.)

By 1942 when the Japanese were evacuated from the Pacific Coast, bimodality was a striking characteristic of their age-sex structure, as shown in Chart V. The modes differentiate the population sharply in terms of nativity, generation, and citizenship: *Issei,* the foreign-born, first generation immigrants from *Nisei,* literally the "second generation" but including, by usage, all of the American-born[16] except the Japan-educated *Kibei,* a

---

[15] The "expected" American-born population under 10 years of age at each census was computed by the application of appropriate survival coefficients to births for each year during the preceding decennium. (See Appendix tables 10 and 11.)

[16] Among the American-born, a third generation (*Sansei*) was beginning to assume importance: at the end of 1942, 88 per cent of the American-born under 3 years of age were of native or mixed parentage, compared with 25 per cent of those aged 3–19, and less than 2 per cent of those 20 years of age or older. (Births to Japanese, by nativity and parentage, in the four western states, 1940–1942, were collated with data on parentage of American-born evacuees, by sex, for ages under and over 20, to obtain an estimate of *Sansei.* See Appendix table 6.)

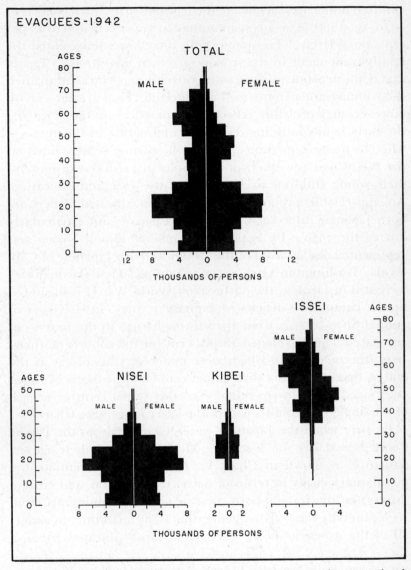

Chart V. Age-sex structures of Japanese American evacuees by generational-educational classes, 1942. (See Appendix, table 5.)

marginal class comprising the regained fraction of the cohorts of young children earlier lost to Japan.[17] Nisei and Kibei, being American-born, held American citizenship. Issei, however, could not become American citizens by naturalization,[18] and with few exceptions, foreign-born Japanese were aliens. In 1942 the median age of Nisei was 17 years, of Issei males 55, and of Issei females 47. Kibei were divided about equally above and below 26 years of age, with more than 80 per cent of them crowded into the narrow range of ages between 20 and 35 years and only 6 per 1,000 younger than 15.

The significance of these age disparities of the 1940's was vividly anticipated by a writer in the vernacular press around 1920. Commenting on the birth rate of this period, he says:

What invites our attention is the great discrepancy in age between the father and the babe. In many cases the father is a half-old man of fifty, while his children are only four or five years old. When the latter reach the age of twenty the former will be approaching the grave, if not actually in it. Time will come when our community will be made up of weak, half-dead old men and immature and reckless youths. Who will guide the young men and women of our community twenty years hence? There is no answer.

It is true that the "Gentlemen's Agreement" permits the parents in this country to send for their sons and daughters in Japan that are under age, and we see a small influx of boys and girls in their teens into our community. . . . Our community of twenty years hence will have to depend on these few young newcomers of today. These are a most precious handful. . . . They form the link between the decaying age and the immature youth, and twenty years hence they will serve as the bridge over an inevitable and dangerous gulf in our community.[19]

Agricultural Adjustments

The early Japanese immigrants entered the rural labor force of the Pacific Coast and intermountain states as seasonal or as casual workers. In many activities and localities they merely replaced

---

[17] Kibei are, by definition, American-born Japanese who had had some education in Japan and then returned to America.

[18] See pp. 43–44, below.

[19] *Hoku-Shin-Juho,* San Francisco, undated, cited by R. E. Park, *The Immigrant Press and its Control,* New York, Harper & Brothers, 1922, pp. 163–164.

the aging Chinese who had been "gap-fillers—assuming the menial, petty and laborious work which white men would not do."[20] In some they were themselves soon replaced by Mexicans and by newly arrived immigrants from southeastern Europe. The number employed on the railroads, in the mines, and in the lumber industry began to decline by the end of the nineteenth century, but the number engaged in agriculture increased markedly throughout most of the first decade of the twentieth century and kept pace with population change up to 1940.

By 1908–1909, two out of every five of the Japanese immigrants who had settled in the western states were engaged more or less continuously in farming operations, and "among those who became railroad laborers and miners, there . . . [was] a strong 'back current' into agricultural pursuits, especially in California."[21] By the time the Gentlemen's Agreement had become effective, they had penetrated almost all of the intensive branches of California agriculture and were already a major element in the seasonal labor supply. To paraphrase the Immigration Commission's summary of the situation at that time: the Japanese numbered 4,500 out of 6,000–7,000 handworkers employed in the beet industry during the thinning season, and "predominated and controlled" the handwork in the beet fields of all except three districts in the state. They were "the most numerous race" engaged in grape picking. They did "practically all of the work" in the berry patches, and "much of the work" on truck farms near the cities. They did "much of the seasonal work in most of the deciduous-fruit districts," and in Southern California they comprised more than 50 per cent of the total number of citrus-fruit pickers during the busy spring months.[22]

At first they worked in small, unorganized groups, "but as their numbers increased and they were more extensively employed, they soon became organized into 'gangs' under leaders or bosses."[23]

---

[20] M. R. Coolidge, "Chinese Labor Competition on the Pacific Coast," *Annals of the American Academy of Political and Social Science,* Sept., 1909, pp. 120–121.

[21] Millis, *op. cit.,* p. 79.

[22] *Reports of the Immigration Commission* (U.S. Congress, Senate, *op. cit.*), pp. 62, 64 *passim.*

[23] *Ibid.,* p. 62.

Bosses channeled their gangs to localities where their services were in demand, and, under their auspices, various organizations were developed. Ichihashi described "typical cases of these Japanese labor organizations" as follows:

In 1892 [a Japanese immigrant] took with him a dozen of his countrymen to Watsonville, California, and worked on a farm in the district, he acting as their "boss." His employer gave him a "bunkhouse" in which to lodge his men. But soon other Japanese appeared in the district, and their number kept on growing. Whereupon [the boss] effected in 1893, what he called a "club" for these Japanese by renting a house and having each man pay annual dues of $3, for which he was allowed to cook his meals or lodge at the club or both whenever he was out of work. In time this club became a general rendezvous for the Japanese in the district, and when employers needed extra hands they went to the club and secured the men they wanted. . . . [Other clubs were organized.] Each club had a secretary whose function it was to find jobs and arrange them so that its members could work most advantageously. His compensation consisted of a five-cent commission collected from each man per day, but he had no fixed salary. When the demand for men was more than the members could supply, he sought outsiders, who obtained jobs by paying him the same commission, . . .

When the season of the district began to slacken, the "outsiders" first withdrew, and some of its members also migrated whenever it was found advantageous to work elsewhere. To assist these migratory members, the secretary . . . often arranged with employers of such districts for the employment of his men . . . [or] communicated with the bosses of such localities, who were more than glad to furnish the information because they had to secure a labor force fluctuating with the seasonal needs of their respective districts. . . .

[There were also] the so-called "Japanese camps." . . . In the Santa Clara Valley [for example] . . . the term "camp" was applied by the local farmers to the headquarters where they could secure Japanese laborers to work for them. These headquarters were in all cases bunkhouses of the cheapest sort managed by the local Japanese bosses. . . . The bosses received orders from the local farmers for so many men, and distributed them accordingly, receiving for this service a five-cent commission from each man for each daily job but charging nothing to the employers. . . .

Larger farmers, as a general rule, kept in permanent employment, what they styled "Jap bosses" who were paid from $40 to $60 a month, varying widely with the size of farms. . . . The Japanese bosses possessed a knowledge of the whereabouts of Japanese laborers and succeeded in gathering together the men needed by their employers. . . .

All the employer needing "help" had to do was simply to telephone or write to a club or a camp to tell his Jap boss how many men were necessary; he then settled wages to be paid to the men with the labor-supplying agent, to whom money was paid, and he, in turn, paid the men after deducting a commission, except in the case of the Jap boss.[24]

For some years bosses offered the services of their gangs at rates well below prevailing wages. Before 1900 underbidding of Chinese was said to be "very general," and in some localities day rates for Japanese were only half of the prevailing rate for Chinese. At the same time, their underbidding of white laborers was "all but if not quite universal." By 1908–1909, however, they were reported to have "ceased to greatly underbid other laborers," and their wages were estimated to have risen by more than 50 per cent in fifteen years.[25]

After the turn of the century, tenancy and sharecropping arrangements began to supplant the boss-gang system, and in California Japanese-leased farms increased in total acreage from fewer than 4,000 in 1900 to 60,000 in 1905 to 177,000 in 1910.[26] Some of the tenants continued to operate as bosses and to supply own-

---

[24] Ichihashi, *op. cit.*, pp. 172–175.

[25] *Reports of the Immigration Commission* (U.S. Congress, Senate, *op. cit.*) p. 63.

[26] We have used data reported in the *Japanese-American Yearbook* cited by Millis (*op. cit.*, pp. 137–138), by Ichihashi (*op. cit.*, p. 184), and by the Immigation Commission. The Commission evaluated the data for 1909 as follows: "The agents of the Commission were able to check these figures in several localities and found them to be fairly satisfactory, except that in some instances not all holdings were reported. The figures presented, therefore, should be regarded as somewhat smaller than the proper figures would be." (*Op. cit.*, pp. 76–77.) Millis, under whose direction the Immigration Commission reports were prepared, however, later decided that "these figures and the growth of Japanese farming indicated by them are exaggerated. . . ." (*Op. cit.*, p. 132.) In spite of biases, they probably give a more accurate picture than the U.S. Census, which failed to enumerate many of the farms operated by sharecroppers and contract tenants. Thus, the census for 1910 showed only 99,254 acres owned or operated by Japanese for the whole United States, while the *Japanese-American Yearbook* reported almost 195,000 acres in California alone including 37,000 under contract tenancy, and over 50,000 under share tenancy.

ers with the extra labor required during busy seasons. This, in turn, facilitated the spread of tenancy, for owners having no Japanese tenants found it "increasingly difficult . . . to obtain desirable laborers of that race."[27] In some areas, the tenants cleared, drained, and leveled waste land and reduced it to cultivation. They installed pumping plants and introduced irrigation systems. They transformed land from extensive farming to the more profitable intensive cultivation of vegetables, berries, and fruits, and they pioneered in developing new crops. They accepted inferior housing—often constructing rude shelters on the leaseholds or utilizing the "Asiatic bunkhouses," which had been erected for seasonal laborers, for their own families. Above all, they paid high rents, "such high rents, in fact, that leasing his land [gave] the owner a better return than farming it himself, allowance being made for the diminished risk."[28]

In general, the Japanese operated very small holdings[29] and specialized in types of farming that required little capital outlay. Although their dealings with Caucasian firms were often on a cash basis, many of them received liberal advances for operating and marketing expenses from the large shippers and packers. At the same time, they bought food and other necessities on credit from Japanese firms, kept their wage bills low, and drew heavily on the unpaid labor of wives and children. When failures occurred, they bore heavily on the Japanese merchants who had extended credit and made for an unstable financial structure in many of the Japanese communities.

Tenancy continued to increase—for the most part profitably— until 1913, when, with the passage of the first of California's alien land laws, Japanese aliens could no longer legally purchase land or hold leases for terms exceeding three years. An Initiative Act in 1920 and a statute in 1923 restricted even short-term leases

[27] Millis, *op. cit.*, p. 141.

[28] *Idem.*

[29] "In 1910, 38.9 per cent [of all California farms] contained 100 acres and over. The average was 316.7 acres. Most of those held by Japanese, however, [were] small. Almost an eighth of those investigated by the Commissioner of Labor [in 1909–1910] contained less than five acres, more than one-fourth less than ten acres, . . . and only 14.3 per cent, one hundred acres and over. The average . . . [size] reported by the Census was only 54.7 acres." (*Ibid.*, p. 144.)

and proscribed sharecropping and shareholding in agricultural corporations.[30]

Strict enforcement of the land laws would have driven the Japanese back to the status of laborers or out of agriculture altogether, for the vast majority of tenants and owners were foreign born, and their American-born children were still too young to exercise citizenship rights. But these laws were inherently difficult to enforce, and they were extensively, continuously, and collusively evaded.[31] Farms were bought or operated by aliens who acted as guardians of their minor American-born children; land was leased under names "borrowed" from older Japanese American citizens; and corporations were formed for the sole purpose of undercover leasing of land. Tenants sought legal refuge by assuming the permissible status of farm managers, foremen, and laborers. In these and other evasive practices the Japanese had the active coöperation of the many Caucasian ranchers, shippers, and merchants to whom their tenancy was profitable and expedient. In the few cases which were brought to court, it was difficult to obtain and introduce evidence of "criminal conspiracy," and defendants could refuse, on constitutional grounds, to testify about their citizenship status.

Evasion became less necessary and less frequent during the 1930's, when appreciable numbers of Nisei came of age and could appear openly as owners of or leaseholders for the parent-operated enterprises. The increase in the number of Japanese "manager-operated" farms from 113 in 1920 to 1816 in 1930 suggests the probable extent of evasion that followed the 1920 and 1923 laws. Correspondingly, the expansion in the number of tenant-

---

[30] Most of the restrictions were phrased in a "backhanded fashion." The laws affirmed rights to aliens who could become naturalized citizens, and denied them to aliens "ineligible to citizenship." The latter class, of course, included the Japanese. The laws did not mention "agricultural lands" but denied rights to "real property" except for purposes "prescribed by any treaty." The only treaty then existing between Japan and the United States (that of 1911, which was abrogated in 1940) secured the Japanese in rights to own and lease certain sorts of buildings and to lease land for residential and commercial purposes only. (See D. O. McGovney, "The Anti-Japanese Land Laws of California and Ten Other States," *California Law Review*, March, 1949, pp. 7–60.)

[31] See Strong, *op. cit.*, pp. 212–213, and E. G. Mears, *Resident Orientals on the American Pacific Coast*, Chicago, 1928.

operated farms from 1,580 in 1930 to 3,596 in 1940 may be more apparent than real, reflecting in many instances the assumption of tenant status by citizens on farms operated by their alien fathers under some legally permissible status. The fact that the total number of Japanese-operated farms was approximately the same in 1920 and in 1940 indicates that the foothold in agriculture was maintained in spite of legal restrictions.[32] (See Appendix, table 12.)

Japanese farmers in California participated in the general shift of intensive agriculture to the southern vegetable-growing areas, and in 1940 one in three of their farms was located in Los Angeles County. Concomitant with this shift, and as a result of their well-established patterns of specialization and intensification, they obtained virtual monopolies in the production of many of the important truck crops. During 1941, for example, they produced 90 per cent or more of all snap beans grown in the state for marketing, of spring and summer celery, of peppers, and of strawberries; and 50 to 90 per cent of the artichokes, snap beans for canning, cauliflower, fall and winter celery, cucumbers, fall peas, spinach, and tomatoes. Operating only 3.9 per cent of all farms, and 2.7 per cent of all the cropland harvested, on holdings that averaged only 44 acres in size compared with a state total of 230, they were then producing between 30 and 35 per cent by value of all commercial truck crops grown in California.[33] Their place in the state's agricultural economy seemed assured.

Japanese agricultural operations in Washington were similar in many respects to those in California. The farms were small and represented insignificant proportions of the total acreage under cultivation in the state. They were highly localized, almost

---

[32] Data collected by the Japanese Association of America (*Zaibei Nippon-jin Shi*) show that there was, in 1929, over twice as much acreage under ownership and tenancy as the corresponding figures from the U.S. Census for 1930 indicate. They suggest that the drop in 1930 was "real," though greatly magnified by Census reports. The tremendous recovery between 1930 and 1940 was, however, not "real," in the sense that most of these farms had been held all the time by the Japanese. There was, in fact, some loss rather than gain in acreage during the depression of the 1930's.

[33] U.S. Congress, House, Select Committee Investigating National Defense Migration, *National Defense Migration, Fourth Interim Report*, 77th Congress, 2d Sess., Washington, 1942, pp. 117–118.

half of them being in Seattle's hinterland, the White River Val-
.ley. They specialized and intensified, and their productive contribution in a few truck crops reached similar monopolistic
proportions.

Getting a foothold in Washington agriculture had, however,
been more difficult. There was no ready-made labor demand of
the sort existing in California, where the withdrawal of the Chinese had coincided with a tremendous expansion of intensive
agriculture at the height of Japanese immigration. Restrictions
on alien land ownership were embodied in the Washington state
constitution as early as 1889, and strengthened by statute and
procedural devices for enforcement in 1921.[34] Anticipation of
further restrictions, comparable to those in California, may well
have accounted for the increase in farms operated by "managers"
from 5 in 1920 to 180 in 1930. As in California, there was approximate equality in the total number of farms operated in
1920 and in 1940.

Urban Enterprise

Entrance to the urban labor force in California was often
achieved by way of domestic service. In this sphere as in agriculture, the early Japanese immigrants found an active demand
created, in part, by a decline in the number of available Chinese.
Many of the more ambitious worked for room and board in
Caucasian households to learn English and to familiarize themselves with American ways while devoting part of their time to
classes and study. Known as "schoolboys," they became a prominent feature of the San Francisco life of the early twentieth
century.[35] Others obtained full-time, highly remunerative work
as cooks, butlers, and houseboys for the upper classes. But the

---

[34] The Washington restrictions on ownership differed from those in California
in that they were not "exclusively racial" in their discrimination. (McGovney,
op. cit., p. 43.) The proscribed classes were *all* aliens who had not, in good faith,
declared intention to become United States citizens. Since Japanese could not
become declarants the restrictions made it impossible for them, as well as for
other groups racially ineligible to citizenship, to own land.

[35] Many who later became proprietors spent their first years in America in
domestic service or other menial work. Of 439 business men interviewed by Immigration Commission investigators in 1908–1909, less than one-sixth engaged in
business on their own account as their first gainful occupation in this country.

greatest number entered service on a contract basis as "day work-ers" for middle-class households. Through employment offices established in Japanese boardinghouses or behind shops, day workers were "on call" for a great variety of jobs, including house-cleaning, window washing, laundry, cooking, and gardening. During the housing boom of the 1920's, the demand for garden-ing services expanded rapidly, and through the advantages of group organization and family enterprise, the Japanese almost monopolized this type of work in the Los Angeles metropolitan district and in the suburban areas around San Francisco.[36]

The Japanese alone . . . made an organized effort to meet the de-mands of those in need of temporary and irregular service and in California especially a large number [were] thus occupied. . . . By organization to meet this need of service, perhaps the Japanese . . . added more to the comfort of the housewives who [did] not keep reg-ular servants than to the comfort or profit of any other group in the population.[37]

Trade and nondomestic service enterprises developed along two lines: (1) proliferation of small businesses designed to meet the needs of the ethnic group, and (2) specialization in a few activities catering to the general public. The demand for Japa-nese-operated enterprises was acute among the newly arrived immigrants and the rural laborers. Many of them spoke little English and were unfamiliar with American ways. They found it difficult to obtain service in Caucasian-operated hotels, lodging-houses, restaurants and barber shops, and they were denied access to places of public recreation. To meet their immediate needs, Japanese-operated lodginghouses, hotels, restaurants, and food

One-third had started in domestic or personal service, one-fifth as farm laborers. *Reports of the Immigration Commission* (U.S. Congress, Senate, *op. cit.*) p. 34.

According to Ichihashi, *op. cit.*, p. 109, the "schoolboy" job originated during the 1880's, when some young Japanese who had come to America to attend eastern universities "had to remain where they landed at San Francisco and earn their living there. These worked in families and tried to get an education at the same time."

[36] Gardeners are not isolated in U.S. Census tabulations. They are included in both the "domestic service" and in the "agriculture" category in the industrial classification; among "proprietors and managers" and "unskilled laborers" in the occupational classification.

[37] Millis, *op. cit.*, pp. 53-54.

shops sprang up in many localities, and around this nucleus, laundries, cobbler shops, bathhouses, pool halls, and other service enterprises and recreational facilities were established. With the arrival of wives from Japan, many of the immigrants sought living quarters in or on the periphery of these trade-service centers, and "Little Tokyos" thus developed in most of the larger cities.

A few service enterprises operated by Japanese for Japanese were in existence as early as 1890 in San Francisco and Seattle. For some years, especially after 1904, "the number of places of business increased considerably more rapidly than the Japanese population."[38] By 1909 there were about 500 Japanese establishments in San Francisco, Seattle, and Los Angeles;[39] scores of others in Sacramento, Fresno, Portland, and Tacoma, and "a few . . . in almost every town of importance near which [Japanese were] employed."[40] Their proliferation and range are suggested by the fact that in San Francisco alone Japanese then operated 76 shoe stores and cobbler shops; 52 cleaning, dyeing, and tailoring establishments; 51 hotels, boarding and lodginghouses; 17 restaurants serving American and 33 serving Japanese meals; 42 art and curio shops; 18 barbershops; 13 bathhouses; 19 laundries; 37 grocery and food shops; 28 pool and billiard parlors; 24 employment agencies; and a variety of other small enterprises.

[38] *Ibid.*, p. 58.

[39] Data on number and kinds of business enterprises in San Francisco, Seattle, and Los Angeles, cited here and elsewhere in this chapter, were obtained from the following sources:

1909, all three cities: *Reports of the Immigration Commission* (U.S. Congress, Senate, *op. cit.*) p. 100.

1928, Los Angeles   :   W. T. Kataoka, "Occupations of Japanese in Los Angeles," *Sociology and Social Research*, Sept.–Oct., 1929, pp. 53–58.

1929, San Francisco :   Ichihashi, *op. cit.*, p. 131 (Based on *Japanese-American Yearbook*, 1929.)

1930, Seattle   :   S. F. Miyamoto, *Social Solidarity Among the Japanese in Seattle*, Bulletin of the University of Washington, Dec. 1939, p. 73. (Based on business census of North American Japanese Association.)

1936, Seattle   :   Our tabulation from *Hoku Bei Year Book*, 1936.

1939, Los Angeles   :   Our tabulation from *Rafu Shimpo Year Book and Directory*, 1939–40.

1939, San Francisco :   Our tabulation from *Nichi Bei (Japanese-American) Directory*, 1940.

(See appendix tables 13A, 13B, and 13C)

[40] *Reports of the Immigration Commission* (U.S. Congress, Senate, *op. cit.*) p. 99.

In general their plants were small and their equipment meager. Workers formed partnerships and there were few wage employees. A single enterprise often performed several functions, for example, according to the Immigration Commission: labor contractors, in addition to running employment agencies, "almost invariably" operated hotels and boardinghouses "as a further source of profit and as a means of assembling laborers," and frequently conducted provision and supply stores as well. Billiard and pool halls and cigar stores were often connected with barbershops, and bathhouses were operated behind barbershops or laundries or in boardinghouses.[41]

An appreciable proportion of the Japanese-operated establishments in Los Angeles, the majority of those in San Francisco and Seattle, and almost all those in many of the smaller cities continued for some years to cater exclusively to the ethnic group. But the demand for Japanese services and products began to be adversely affected when the Gentlemen's Agreement was enforced in 1908, and the potential market was narrowed further after Japan stopped granting passports to picture brides in 1920, and again when Oriental exclusion was enacted in 1924. Stabilization of employment and the growth of the tenant class in agriculture had a depressing effect on those urban enterprises which depended upon a floating population. And as the maturing second generation increased in numbers, consumer preference tended to shift to American goods and services. Consequently, numbers of small ethnocentered businesses failed after World War I and particularly during the 1930's, and many of the survivors broadened or attempted to broaden their bases of operation to serve a wider public.

The early history of Japanese-operated businesses and services directed toward meeting the needs of the general public is one of stormy opposition from competing Caucasian-operated enterprises, from organized labor, and from anti-Oriental pressure groups. The opposition was most intense and most successful in restraining Japanese competition in the restaurant and laundry businesses in San Francisco, and the pattern of agitation that

[41] *Ibid.*, p. 101.

developed there was later imitated in other spheres of activity and in other localities.

After the San Francisco earthquake and fire of 1906, there was a sudden upsurge in demand for consumers' goods and services to meet the needs of laborers who had come from other areas to clear debris and help rebuild the city. In response to this demand, the number of Japanese-operated restaurants serving "American food" increased in a single year from 8 to 30. Operating on a modest scale, these restaurants came into direct competition only with nonunion "cheap eating houses charging '15 cents up' for meals." Nevertheless, they were soon "strongly opposed by organized labor," some of them "became an object of attack by rioters" and "several of the proprietors suffered serious loss because of destruction of property or loss of their patrons or both."[42] According to investigators for the Immigration Commission, the Japanese were undercutting only slightly on cash wages. They did, however, have other tangible advantages over their competitors because of their partnership arrangements, the long work day served by partners and family members and required of their few paid employees, the perquisites such as lodging which they provided the workers, and the greater cleanliness and attractiveness of the food they served the public. At the request of the powerful "Japanese and Korean Exclusion League," and motivated also by fear of eventual Japanese competition in higher class restaurants, the Cooks and Waiters Union, in coöperation with a number of others, instituted a successful boycott in October, 1906, and by the end of 1908 the number of Japanese-operated restaurants serving American meals had declined from 30 to 17.

Laundries met the same type of opposition, and for many of the same reasons. They had increased in number from 8 in 1904 to 18 in 1909, but with the exception of one mechanized establishment, they were in competition only with nonunion French-operated hand laundries where cash wages were only slightly higher than those paid their own employees. But again, the longer working day, the advantages of group organization, the paucity

---

[42] *Ibid.*, p. 200.

of wage laborers, and the perquisities provided made it possible
to undercut on the prices charged the consumer. According to
the Reports of the Immigration Commission, there always had
been "more or less agitation in San Francisco against the Japanese laundries," and there was "a general feeling of opposition
among the working classes towards the Japanese." This opposition became organized in March, 1908, with the formation of
the Anti-Jap Laundry League by members of the Laundry Driv-
ers' Union. The League organized a campaign directed toward
"reducing the number of the patrons" and toward "preventing
them from obtaining supplies and becoming equipped as steam
laundries." The opposition was rationalized on the grounds that
if Japanese laundries were "equipped with modern machinery
while maintaining their lower wage scale and working longer
hours, their competition would become a serious matter." Agents
of the Anti-Jap Laundry League followed Japanese collectors
and reported the names of patrons, who were "corresponded with
and personally visited and an appeal made to them to patronize
laundries conducted by and employing the white race." The
League advertised extensively, appealed to various organizations
for aid in maintaining the boycott, and for some years succeeded
in preventing supply men from selling equipment to Japanese
laundries.[43]

Largely because of the effectiveness of labor opposition, San
Francisco became a dead-end area for most Japanese enterprises.[44]

[43] *Ibid.*, pp. 193–196, *passim.*
For example, the following poster was displayed on billboards in San Francisco,
Berkeley, Alameda, and Oakland:

The Jap Laundry Patrons.
Danger!
Yellow competition,
Fostered by the white man's money,
Is the ammunition that will
Orientalize our City and State.

[44] There had been notable expansion in early years in the shoe repairing business,
where the Japanese artisans, highly organized among themselves, competed with
unorganized foreign-born whites, and there were 72 small-scale cobbler shops in
San Francisco by 1909. Most of the proprietors derived additional income from the
operation of agencies and boardinghouses for domestic day workers and were able
to undercut on prices, but the number of such establishments declined to 23 in
1929, and to 12 in 1939. "The Japanese cobblers succumbed before the onslaught
of chain systems as have other small retailers in many lines." (Ichihashi, *op. cit.*,
p. 135.)

The only types of business that did not decline in number between 1909 and 1939 were cleaning and dyeing establishments and Oriental art goods shops. The former required little capital and were eminently suited to family enterprise, where the wife did the repair work and pressing, and the children helped out after school. They never came into serious conflict with white competitors, and their number increased steadily from 52 in 1909 to 114 in 1929 to 122 in 1939. Oriental art goods stores required heavy investment, employed a relatively large sales personnel, and came into competition only with similar Chinese-operated enterprises. They increased in number from 42 in 1909 to 54 in 1929. Although they suffered serious reverses during the depression of the 1930's, and after 1937 were the objects of informal boycotts initiated by their Chinese competitors, 51 of them were still operating in 1939.

The San Francisco pattern of restraint was applied only sporadically and far less effectively in Seattle and Los Angeles, where the relative weakness of their labor unions made it difficult to organize latent opposition against the Japanese.

In Seattle the Immigration Commission reported lower-than-average prices, appreciably greater cleanliness, and more attractive service in Japanese restaurants than in comparable establishments operated by whites. "The perceptible difference has been sufficient to attract many white patrons in spite of the odium attaching among certain classes to patronizing Japanese restaurants." A general boycott "ceased after a few months without seriously injuring their business," and though "many of the unions" resolved that their members should not patronize Japanese restaurants and in some instances imposed penalties when they did, "the effect [was] evidently not great, for many union as well as nonunion men [were] numbered among the patrons."[45] Japanese-operated restaurants catering to the general public not only held their own but increased in number from 36 in 1909 to 42 in 1936.

In spite of some opposition, Japanese-operated grocery stores in Seattle increased during the same period from 26 to 138. As

---

[45] *Reports of the Immigration Commission* (U.S. Congress, Senate, *op. cit.*) pp. 283–284 *passim.*

early as 1909 about three-fifths of their patronage was from whites, in spite of the fact that the stores were then almost all located in the Japanese quarter. By the end of 1941 according to the Japanese American Citizens League, one in six of all Seattle grocery stores was Japanese operated, and almost all of them were located outside the Japanese community. These included several large establishments which employed five or six clerks each, but most of the stores were small-scale enterprises that depended on occasional "extra help for delivery and general work in the store."[46]

There was a similar trend in the Seattle hotel business. Even in 1909, "two or three" of the 72 Japanese-operated hotels and lodginghouses were catering exclusively to whites, and in about half of the others from 10 to 20 per cent of the roomers were white.[47] By 1941 almost two-thirds of all hotels in Seattle were being operated by Japanese. Most of these were small enterprises, the average capacity being 60 rooms. In general, the premises were held under lease, the operator owned only the equipment and furniture, and the business was "profitable only if operated by the manager and his wife, with the aid of the family and a minimum of outside help."[48]

In Los Angeles attempts to restrain Japanese competition were similarly ineffective. For example, the Immigration Commission reported a "Gentlemen's Agreement" between laundrymen and machinery-supply houses "to the effect that the latter shall not furnish equipment of any kind to the Japanese,"[49] but the boycott had little support, and several of the laundries soon became mechanized.

Business of various types expanded rapidly in Los Angeles just before and after World War I. Millis reported that the num-

---

[46] U.S. Congress, House, Select Committee Investigating National Defense Migration, *National Defense Migration*, Hearings, 77th Congress, 2d Sess., Pt. 30. Washington, 1942, p. 11,460.

[47] *Reports of the Immigration Commission* (U.S. Congress, Senate, *op. cit.*) p. 288.

[48] This estimate is by the Japanese American Citizens' League (U.S. Congress, House, *National Defense Migration,* Hearings, *op. cit.*, p. 11,459), which reported 206 hotels and 56 rooming houses. A representative of the First National Bank however estimated "181 hotels, rooming houses, and small apartments . . . conducted by the Japanese." (*Ibid.,* p. 11,418.)

[49] *Reports of the Immigration Commission* (U.S. Congress, Senate, *op. cit.*) p. 228.

ber of establishments had increased by "fully fifty per cent" between 1909 and 1914, and the amount of capital invested and business transacted by "perhaps two hundred percent," that some of the general stores were "very good ones indeed," that barbershops had expanded in some cases "from two to four or more chairs," that two "first-class tailoring establishments" and "two very good hotels" had appeared, that the latter were "patronized by others as well as by Japanese," and that several of the boardinghouses were in very good buildings and were well furnished.[50] By 1928, there were almost 1,800 Japanese-operated enterprises in Los Angeles, compared with fewer than 500 in 1909. By 1939 the total had risen to 2,300. All of the important increases were in enterprises serving the general public. About three-quarters of the more than 300 hotels and lodginghouses operated in 1939 were patronized by non-Japanese. Restaurants serving American meals had increased fivefold since 1909. Cafés serving "Chinese food" to the general public numbered no less than 48 in 1928 and 75 in 1939. Florist shops and nurseries selling plants and shrubs at both wholesale and retail had become numerically important.

The most notable expansion was in enterprises marketing agricultural produce—an expansion that paralleled the rapid growth of Japanese farming in the southern counties and linked the urban economy closely with the agricultural.

Before World War I farmers sold directly to consumers at roadside stands or to retailers in the city markets, and there were few Japanese wholesalers in the produce markets.[51] By 1939, however, 149 Japanese-operated wholesale establishments were listed in Los Angeles. These included middlemen who took fruit and vegetables on consignment, firms specializing in interstate commerce, jobbers who bought produce from other houses and resold to retailers, and "stall merchants" who operated fleets of trucks, made the rounds of Japanese farms every evening, and trans-

---

[50] Millis, *op. cit.*, pp. 73–74, *passim.*

[51] The Immigration Commission did not classify wholesale produce firms separately in its reports. That several were in existence in 1909 is, however, apparent from reports of the Japanese Association of America (*Zaibei Nippon-jin Shi*, pp. 201–205).

ported the daily harvest of fruit and vegetables to the city markets for sale to the retailers. During 1941 Japanese wholesalers in the two Los Angeles markets were estimated[52] to have handled more than 60 per cent of the total amount of business, and to have grossed $26,500,000. Unlike most Japanese American enterprises these were large-scale establishments, employing numbers of wage or salary workers. Of the 20 firms operating inside the markets in 1940, six were estimated to have had an annual business exceeding $1,000,000 each, eight to have grossed between $500,000 and $750,000 each, and the remaining six to have been somewhat below the $500,000 level. They were said to have employed on the average 30, 20, and 12 persons per firm and to have distributed profits to each of several partners per firm of $10,000 to $50,000, $10,000 to $20,000, and $5,000 to $15,000 for the three size classes, respectively.[53]

Retail developments were also impressive, and the number of fruit-and-vegetable enterprises increased from 20 in 1909 to 203 in 1928, and exceeded 300 in 1939.[54] In these businesses the Japanese adapted the country roadside stand to the urban setting. They used family help to the maximum, required long hours and "split shifts" of their unorganized employees, and themselves gave unstintedly of their time. They were thus able to apply labor intensively in the planning and buying of fresh produce, in the constant care required to reduce wiltage and wastage of these highly perishable products, and in the meticulous attention to details necessary for attractive arrangements and display. They undercut on prices and put employers who were dependent largely on wage labor at a competitive disadvantage. They intro-

[52] Statement by Sam Minami (U.S. Congress, House, *National Defense Migration*, Hearings, *op. cit.*, p. 11,723).

[53] These estimates were reconstructed by an officer of the Los Angelees Junior Produce Club. They refer to the year 1940. (Letter to R. S. Nishimoto, October, 1946.)

[54] *Rafu Shimpo Yearbook*, from which we made our tabulations for 1939, combined fruit and vegetable stores with grocery stores. Through a name-by-name checking of the lists we estimate the former at 309. The Japanese Association of America, however, reported the number of fruit and vegetable stores in 1939 as 410 (*Zaibei Nippon-jin Shi*, p. 867.) A much higher estimate for 1941, that is, 1,000, was given by Sam Minami, Business Manager of the Los Angeles Junior Produce Club, but his estimate apparently covered the whole county of Los Angeles. (U.S. Congress, House, *National Defense Migration*, Hearings, *op. cit.*, p. 11,724.)

duced "fruit stands" into small neighborhood stores, built up chains, and obtained fruit-and-vegetable concessions in Caucasian-operated markets. By the 1930's they predominated in the retail vegetable trade in Los Angeles and in many other southern communities, and the Japanese-operated fruit stand, with its attractive displays, fresh produce, and low prices was the featured department in many of the supermarkets in this area.

Occupational Mobility

Penetration of the urban economy was not accompanied by an exodus from agriculture. According to the Immigration Commission's estimates, approximately 40 per cent of the Japanese immigrants in the western states in 1908–1909 were "more or less continuously" engaged in agriculture, and according to the 1940 census, 42 per cent of the Japanese then employed in the California and Washington labor force were in farming occupations. During the three decades between the Immigration Commission's investigations and the 1940 census, however, the structure of the Japanese agricultural labor force underwent a radical transformation. In 1908–1909 almost all farm workers were aliens, but in 1940 two in five were American citizens. At the earlier date only one in six was an owner, tenant, or manager of farm property,[55] but at the later date, two-fifths of all the males and almost half of those who were foreign-born held entrepreneurial or managerial status. Females and children were unimportant elements before World War I, but on the eve of World War II females comprised one-fifth of the agricultural labor force and one in four of all Japanese employed on farms was an unpaid worker in a family enterprise.

The situation in respect to family labor was especially noteworthy. Whereas only 6 per cent of the total agricultural labor force in California and Washington were Japanese, more than 27 per cent of all unpaid family workers were from this ethnic group. For every 100 Japanese farmers and farm managers, indeed, 70 family members were recorded in the census as working, on a nonwage basis, in family enterprises. The contribution of

---

[55] Reports of the Immigration Commission, (U.S. Congress, Senate, op. cit.) p. 61.

Nisei and Kibei to Issei-operated farms was probably even greater than census data suggest, for in addition to the 3,000 American-born Japanese officially reported as "unpaid family laborers" in agriculture, thousands of young children worked on the family farms before and after school and during vacations without ever appearing in labor-force statistics.

Although 58 per cent of the Japanese were in urban occupations, they represented not quite 1 per cent of the employed nonagricultural labor force in California and Washington in 1940. Their distribution by specific occupational groupings is shown in Charts VI and VII in terms of the usual hierarchical arrangement of occupations, where the highest socioeconomic ranks are assigned to professionals and to other white-collar workers, intermediate ranks to the skilled-labor category, and lowest ranks to semiskilled and unskilled laborers and to domestic servants. Their most marked concentrations, compared with the general population, were in domestic service, in unskilled labor generally, and in the proprietor-managerial class; and they were notably deficient in the higher professional and white-collar ranks and among skilled laborers.

Occupational differentials are, of course, partly a function of differing age-sex structures and of rates of labor-force participation. Immigrant Japanese were much older, and American-born Japanese much younger, on the average, than was the general employed population of the Pacific Coast states. Disproportionate numbers of the first generation were working beyond the usual age of retirement from the active labor force, disproportionate numbers of second generation were remaining in school beyond the usual age of taking up a career, and disproportionate numbers of urban Japanese females, both first and second generation, were employed outside the home, compared with the Caucasian majority group. The present comparisons of Japanese and of the general population in Charts VI and VII are designed to be free of the biasing effects of some of these interfering variables. (See notes to Appendix, table 14.) In these charts, each sex-nativity group among the Japanese is compared with a "population norm," representing the occupational distribution that this sex group in the general population would have had in terms of its own age–specific occupational rates if its age structure had been identical with that of the Japanese group under comparison. Thus, the norms in Chart VI show the occupational distributions of relatively old segments of the general population, whereas

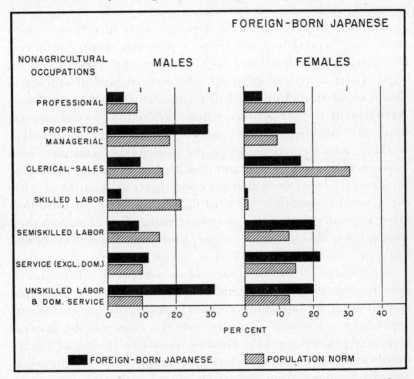

Chart VI. Distribution of foreign-born Japanese males and females, 14 years of age and older, employed in nonagricultural pursuits in California and Washington, 1940, by major occupational classes, compared with age-adjusted sex-specific norms for the total population of these states. (See Appendix, table 16.)

those in Chart VII are based on distributions of younger elements. For each sex-nativity class, the Japanese exceeded the population norm in the proportion of proprietors and managers, the difference being greatest for foreign-born males. The pattern of overrepresentation at the lowest level of unskilled labor and domestic service is, similarly, manifested in all four groups but is most marked for American-born females and foreign-born males. The skilled-labor deficiency distorted both nativity groups of Japanese males, and underrepresentation at the professional level was common to all four nativity-sex classes. Contrary to the pattern for other classes, American-born males exceeded their population norm in proportions at the clerical-sales level, and

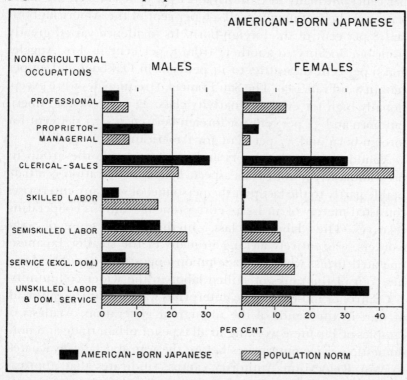

Chart VII. Distribution of American-born Japanese males and females, 14 years of age and older, employed in nonagricultural pursuits in California and Washington, 1940, by major occupational classes, compared with age-adjusted sex-specific norms for the total population of these states. (Appendix, table 16.)

foreign-born females were overrepresented among semiskilled laborers.

Concentrations in the domestic-service category were especially noteworthy. One in every seven of all Japanese in the nonagricultural labor force in California and one in seventeen of those in Washington were domestic servants in 1940. In California, domestic service was the modal occupation for American-born girls, accounting for almost 40 per cent of those employed in nonagricultural pursuits, whereas in Washington, with 25 per cent so employed, it was their second most frequent occupation. It absorbed few of the foreign-born women in Washington (4 per cent) but many in California (21 per cent), and in the latter state, numbers of men as well—6 per cent of the American-born and 8 per cent of the foreign-born. Its incidence varied greatly from one locality to another: from 5 per cent in Los Angeles and 6 per cent in Seattle, to 14 per cent in Oakland and 39 per cent in San Francisco. The San Francisco frequencies were exceptionally high for every sex-nativity class: 23 per cent for American-born and 34 per cent for foreign-born males, 51 per cent for foreign-born and 57 per cent for American-born females.[56]

Abundance of proprietors and managers gave the group its predominantly middle-class aspect. This concentration is attributable partly to the fact that the personnel of so many enterprises consisted merely of an Issei "entrepreneur" and his coöperating relatives. The "laboring class," in the narrow sense of wage workers, was entirely lacking in many of the smaller Japanese-operated firms, whereas trade-union opposition kept the Japanese out of the ranks of skilled labor in the wider community.

Control of most Japanese enterprises was still, at the outbreak of war, in the hands of the immigrant generation. Analysis of samples of Japanese working in all types of urban trade and non-domestic service enterprises before the war and later evacuated to War Relocation Authority camps,[57] indicates that approximately half of the Issei in San Francisco, Los Angeles, and Seattle were self-employed, but that the comparable proportions for Nisei were only 9 per cent, 17 per cent, and 24 per cent, and for

[56] Computed from data in U.S. Bureau of the Census, 16th Census of the United States, 1940, Population, *Characteristics of the Nonwhite Population by Race.* Washington, 1943, pp. 108–109.

[57] Data on the status of Nisei and Kibei, compared with Issei, were obtained by analyzing a sample of employment histories from the WRA census of 1942. The sample was selected by location in camp, corresponding roughly to prewar address, with date of reference as April, 1940. It was limited to persons born in 1921 or earlier, and excluded agricultural workers, gardeners, domestic servants, and persons not in the labor force. The total of 3,216 records analyzed were distributed as follows: *San Francisco,* 548 Issei, 263 Nisei, 126 Kibei; *Los Angeles,* 883 Issei, 476 Nisei, 201 Kibei; *Seattle,* 456 Issei, 215 Nisei, 48 Kibei. (See Appendix tables 17A, 17B, and 17C.)

Kibei 25 per cent, 22 per cent, and 21 per cent, respectively, for the same three cities. Only in the retail fruit-and-vegetable business in Los Angeles and in the grocery trade in Seattle had appreciable numbers of second generation attained independent status. In each of these two branches of urban trade, approximately one in three of the Japanese entrepreneurs was American born, and in the former the absolute number of Kibei about equalled that of Nisei.

Generational differences in employment status are, again, partly a function of age. The paucity of Nisei at ages when middle-class economic independence is normally achieved meant that many parents were carrying on family enterprises beyond the normal retirement age. But youth was not the only factor retarding Nisei entrepreneurship. Issei had attained status by long hours of arduous work and by dependence on family help. Assumption of responsibility for the family enterprise would, in many cases, have meant an intolerable personal burden for Nisei, and the perpetuation of a way of life incompatible with American standards. Their vocational preferences were strongly oriented toward majority-group patterns, but they had had little success in reaching their goals. Analysis of the WRA sample shows, indeed, that, as of 1940 almost half of the Nisei employees in trade and nondomestic service enterprises in San Francisco and over half of those in Los Angeles were working in a single type of Japanese-operated firm: Oriental art goods stores in the former, fruit stands in the latter. Not even one in ten Nisei was working for a Caucasian-operated firm in either San Francisco or Los Angeles, and only two in every ten were so employed in Seattle. Thus, the concentration of Nisei males at "white-collar" levels—as shown by United States Census data (Chart VII)— may be interpreted to mean that many of those classified in the proprietor-managerial group were in fact working in secondary positions in the larger, Issei-controlled enterprises, and that most of those classified in the clerical-sales category were, similarly, working for other Japanese. The few who had progressed beyond the limits of the Japanese business community were, for the most part, on low rungs of the urban occupational ladder and held the less desirable jobs. A small number were working for Caucasian firms that solicited Japanese patronage. A few typists, stenographers, bookkeepers, stock clerks, and mail-order house salesmen had found employment outside the ethnic community, but rarely in any capacity that required contact with the general public. Outlets for Nisei trained for the professions were limited. Doctors, dentists, lawyers, and optometrists usually served the needs of other Japanese and rarely succeeded in obtaining Caucasian clientele or connections with Caucasian-operated institutions, either public or private. Engineers, accountants, teachers, and social workers found it almost impossible to practice the skills they learned. On the other hand some technicians, for example biochemists and dieticians, were working in the fields for which they had been trained, and there was little discrimination against nurses. Several hundred clerical workers and a few persons classified at higher levels had received state civil service appointments in California, and a small number had entered Federal civil service.

Kibei marginality extended also to matters of occupational preferences and economic adjustments. Some Kibei, especially among those whose education had been completed or largely obtained in America, were indistinguishable from Nisei in outlook, goals, accomplishments, and frustrations. A few, economically and socially advantaged, had achieved a superior integration of the two cultures and had obtained positions of responsibility in firms engaged in international trade or in governmental agencies. But compared with Nisei, most Kibei were linguistically and culturally handicapped, and their superiority in age had not greatly facilitated a rise to the entrepreneurial level. The setting in which their parents had reached this level had changed, and unlike the Issei, the Kibei had not been exposed to decades of accommodation to minority status. An appreciably greater proportion of them than of Nisei were working for other Japanese, and they were disproportionately in agricultural rather than in urban pursuits, in manual rather than clerical activities.

In the main, Japanese immigrants had, at the outbreak of the war, made more satisfactory economic adjustments than had their children. About half of the farming group had moved up the agricultural ladder to become owners or managers or tenant-operators, and in the whole nonagricultural labor force (including domestic service), at least one in three was self-employed. But, with exceptions of the sort noted above, Nisei and Kibei were, in many respects, back where their parents had started.

Sociopolitical Orientation

Japanese immigrants were described in the Immigration Commission Reports of 1908–1909 as living in but as no integral part of the community.[58] Their integration had been and continued to be retarded by many forces and circumstances: by ineligibility to American citizenship and the necessity of maintaining political allegiance to a foreign power; by the paternalistic attitude of the Japanese government and of its consular representatives toward Japanese nationals residing abroad; by economic discrimination and social segregation imposed by the whites on the West Coast; by the self-sufficiency of their ethnocentered communities and the strength of their organizations; by their failure to master the English language; and by their adherence to an alien religion.

Their ineligibility to American citizenship stemmed from the racial restrictions of the Naturalization Act of 1790 in which acquisition of citizenship by naturalization was limited to "free white persons." An act of 1870 extended the privilege to "aliens of African nativity and persons of African descent." Amendments and revisions of this act removed racial barriers for American Indians, for Filipinos, for Chinese, for "persons of races indigenous to India," and for persons who possessed, "either singly or in combination, a preponderance of blood" of one or more of some of these classes or as much as one-half blood of these and "some additional blood" of others.[59] But the Japanese were consistently declared by judicial interpretation to be racially ineligible for naturalization, and this interpretation was confirmed by the United States Supreme Court in 1922.[60] For a short period—

---

[58] *Reports of the Immigration Commission,* (U.S. Congress, Senate. *op. cit.*) p. 166.
[59] McGovney, *op. cit.,* p. 11.
[60] *Ozawa v. United States* 260 U.S. 1-8.

between 1935 and 1937—Japanese aliens who had served in the
armed forces of the United States during World War I were
allowed to apply for naturalization.[61] This was the only important
exception to the rule that persons of Japanese "blood" born on
alien soil were ineligible to citizenship in the United States, whatever their qualifications or however long their period of residence.

Ineligibility to citizenship was a constant reminder of the racial
prejudice of the dominant group, and it became an increasingly
serious threat to the collective security of the minority group.
During the course of the Immigration Commission's investigations "a comparatively large number of the farmers and the business classes expressed a desire to become naturalized and expressed
regret at the discrimination against persons who do not belong
to the white race." The economic aspect became especially important after the passage of California's first antialien land law in
1913. The statute of that year and more stringent regulations in
1920 and 1923 declared in effect that aliens ineligible to naturalization had no rights whatsoever to real property—other than
those secured by then-existing treaties—whereas all other aliens
had the same rights as citizens.[62] Between 1917 and 1925 seven
other states enacted legislation similar to California's, with variations on relatively minor points,[63] and in 1924, ineligibility to
citizenship provided the legal basis for Oriental exclusion in the
United States Immigration Act. The seriousness of the citizenship
issue was emphasized by vigorous protests of Japanese diplomats,
by boycotts in Japan, and by critical comments in the Japanese
press, bearing especially on the discriminatory aspect of exclusion.[64]

On the West Coast complaints against discrimination were
channeled to the Japanese consulates, where they usually received
prompt and sympathetic attention. The consul thus became the

---

[61] Aliens otherwise ineligible to citizenship were made eligible by an act of
Congress (U.S. 49 Stat., 397–398) passed in June, 1935, if (a) they had served in the
U.S. armed forces between April 6, 1917, and November 11, 1918, and had been
honorably discharged, and (b) they were permanent residents of the United States.
A small number of Issei obtained citizenship under this act before the deadline,
which was set at January 1, 1937.

[62] McGovney, op. cit., p. 26.

[63] Ibid., pp. 7–8.

[64] See Buell, op. cit., pp. 314–315.

recognized guardian of immigrant welfare and a "symbolic substitute for the nation and the Emperor" whom he represented.
"For the Japanese immigrants, lacking the right of franchise as
they [did], the strength of the Japanese consular office . . . in no
small measure compensated for their lack of citizenship."[65]

In view of their anomalous position in the United States, it is
not surprising that the Japanese, perhaps more than any other
immigrant group, regarded themselves as sojourners in this country. At the time of the Immigration Commission's investigations
in 1908–1909, a majority of all classes interviewed either expected
to return to Japan or were undecided about their future place of
residence. The proportions indicating that they had decided to
become permanent residents of the United States were, however,
highest among those who had "succeeded in rising from the ranks
of the laboring classes." Thus 40 per cent of the farmers—"most
of them tenants"—and 38 per cent of the businessmen—"most of
them small shopkeepers"—who were interviewed, stated that they
expected to remain permanently in this country, contrasted with
13 per cent of the city wage earners and 8 per cent of the farm
laborers. Conversely, 76 per cent of the farm laborers and 53 per
cent of the city wage earners but only 27 per cent of the farmers
and 24 per cent of the businessmen expected "sooner or later to
return to their native land," whereas the proportions expressing
themselves as still "in doubt" were 38 per cent of the businessmen,
34 per cent of the farmers and of the city wage earners, and 16 per
cent of the farm laborers.[66]

Renewal of the incentive to return after the restrictive legislation of the 1920's is suggested in the results of a census conducted
by the Japanese Association in Seattle in 1925. Of 2,000 family
heads from whom information was obtained, no one was then
willing to say that his family "definitely" would not go back to
Japan, 13 per cent indicated that they would like to return but
had no prospect at the time, 24 per cent reported definite inten-

---

[65] Miyamoto, *op. cit.*, pp. 112–113.

[66] These percentages were computed from data in the *Reports of the Immigration
Commission* (U.S. Congress, Senate, *op. cit.*) p. 29. The numbers "reporting complete
data" used as the bases for the percentages were as follows: businessmen, 442; city
wage earners, 427; farmers, 327; farm laborers, 414.

tion of returning, and 63 per cent said they were still "undecided." Commenting on these data in 1939, Miyamoto concluded that, though they were "indicative of the general Japanese frame of mind" at the time the census was taken, "an increased attitude toward settling permanently in the United States . . . [had] penetrated a large part of the community in the thirteen years since that census," but that "the significant point is the extremely slow recession of the feeling that America is just a place to make money, and that Japan is really home."[67]

The isolation and segregation of Japanese immigrants from the life of the general American community were repeatedly emphasized in the Immigration Commission Reports. In many ways, the Japanese lived and worked under conditions "different from those of the non-Asiatics." In agriculture and in other occupations where group organization prevailed, bosses managed all the business affairs and most other interracial contacts for the laborers, and it was customary for "Japanese quarters or 'bunkhouses' to be located away from the homes of other races." Independent farmers had "little intercourse with other races in matters other than of business," and even their business relations were greatly limited by the facts that they usually employed Japanese laborers and made most of their purchases at Japanese stores. There was the same pattern of segregation "in a more modified form" in the cities, and Japanese quarters, "though not as distinct in their boundaries as the 'Chinatowns,' usually [came] to be sharply defined." Although the many urban Japanese who worked in domestic and personal service were thrown into direct contact with whites, employment of this type usually carried with it "an inferior rank, with its limitations." Segregation in living quarters and at work and limitation of employment opportunities were alike attributed to "an attitude of opposition to this race taken by the 'white' races." In many cases, this was "more than a negative refusal of association," having taken "organized form" in some communities and in others resulting in "open violence." In the western states marriage with whites was either prohibited, as in California, or else prevented by "strong popular sentiment." In

---

[67] Miyamoto, *op. cit.*, p. 86.

most localities the Japanese were not welcome in public places of recreation and were not accepted in community organizations. They were "racially ineligible" for membership in practically all fraternal orders. "The only organizations other than religious in which they as well as white persons" were members, were "of a business nature."[68]

Concomitant with segregation and exclusion from American community life, the immigrants developed strong organizations within their own communities. In most settlements the Japanese Association, which included in its membership most of the farmers and businessmen and some of the laborers from surrounding areas, became the focal organization. The first Association was organized in San Francisco in 1900 "at the time of the threatened outbreak of bubonic plague, when the Japanese and Chinese, being Asiatic races, were dealt with in a different manner from other races. . . . When the crisis due to the fear of bubonic plague ended, the organization was continued in existence because of the strong anti-Japanese movement which had sprung up in San Francisco. Upon the renewal of this agitation in 1905, the Association was reorganized and extended its activity to the entire State of California. Local associations were soon organized in no fewer than 33 different places,"[69] and by 1908–1909, there were Japanese Associations "in every urban center where the Japanese [had] settled in any considerable number." They received recognition from the consular offices and were used by them "to some extent as administrative organs, as, for example, in the issuing of certificates of various kinds and in related matters."[70]

The prestige conferred by consular recognition made Japanese Associations a powerful force in immigrant communities. On behalf of the consulates the Associations collected statistics of all kinds and took business censuses. They "certified status" of resident aliens who wished to bring in their wives, children, or parents from Japan. They processed applications for deferment from military service in Japan, which was compulsory for all male na-

---

[68] *Reports of the Immigration Commission*, (U.S. Congress, Senate, *op. cit.*) pp. 160–164 *passim*.

[69] *Ibid.*, p. 220.

[70] *Ibid.*, p. 164.

tionals of draft age including not only immigrant aliens but also those among the American-born who held dual citizenship. They were responsible for implementing the provisions of Japan's nationality laws, both in registering the American-born as "dual citizens," and later, in canceling the Japanese nationality of such citizens upon application from the principals or their guardians.[71]

The social and meliorative activities of Japanese Associations involved almost every immigrant individual and family. As the Immigration Commission Reports expressed it, the aims of the Associations were "general and vague"; they did whatever came to hand, and they interested themselves in whatever concerned the Japanese. For example, the San Francisco Association hired plain-clothes men to protect the immigrants against violence during periods of severe agitation against them, and the Fresno Association "was instrumental in closing the oriental gambling dens and houses of prostitution located in that city." In many localities they were, similarly, "of great value in promoting morality and orderly living as well as in preserving harmony between conflicting interests."[72] They were on the alert to meet the changing needs of immigrant communities. They developed programs for adult education, emphasizing Americanization, and they translated and interpreted American news items and documents for the Issei. At the same time, they promoted Japanese language schools for Nisei. They directed the settlers in matters where concessions to

[71] When Japan authorized emigration in 1885 it was, "with the stipulation that the emigrant should never lose allegiance to the Mikado." In 1916, however, "Japan enacted an Expatriation Law providing that a Japanese acquiring another nationality [might] lose Japanese nationality by petitioning the Minister of Foreign Affairs." If he were over 17 years of age, however, he had first to perform military service for Japan or be specifically exempted from it. (Buell, op. cit., p. 281.) Moreover, according to Japanese nationality laws, children of Japanese nationals were Japanese citizens, irrespective of place of birth. Since American nationality law bestowed American citizenship upon all children born on American soil, irrespective of ancestry, Nisei automatically became dual citizens until the 1916 law. In 1924, a new Japanese law—effective December 1, 1925—provided that a Japanese who had acquired another nationality by birth in certain specified countries, including the United States, automatically lost Japanese citizenship unless he declared his intention of retaining that nationality. The same law provided for renunciation of Japanese citizenship, at will, by the Japan-born living in these same countries if they retained the nationality of the foreign country. (Strong, op. cit., p. 141.)

[72] Reports of the Immigration Commission, (U.S. Congress, Senate, op. cit.) pp. 164, 220.

the American public seemed advisable, for example, they recommended abandonment of the "picture bride" practice, and advised immigrants "not to work so hard as to cause their neighbors to criticize them, and to create some leisure for self-development."[73] They assisted the indigent who wished to return to Japan. Their members visited sick Japanese in hospitals and cared for graves in cemeteries where Japanese were buried. They gave banquets honoring the aged, the mothers, the distinguished. They acted as arbiters among businessmen, cleared up misunderstanding about contracts, and promoted Japanese and immigrant business interests in the American community. They contributed to American welfare and patriotic societies, and during the 1930's they also collected funds for the Japanese war effort in the Orient. They sponsored tours for Nisei in Japan and promoted the return to America of those among the second generation who had been sent to Japan for education, arranging special steamship rates for Kibei and in some cases financing their passages and assisting them in finding jobs. They encouraged higher education for Nisei, publicized honors conferred upon them, and acted as the "watch-dog for any cases of juvenile delinquency, that they might be publicized as a moral lesson to other children."[74]

Farmers and businessmen united in trade associations "to limit competition among themselves or to protect themselves from injury by others and to further their own interests,"[75] and other organizations "of a general and benevolent and social nature" sprang up. Among the latter were the prefectural societies (*kenjinkai*) which included as members immigrants originating in the same prefecture (*ken*) in Japan and served "in some degree as a center of the social life of the Japanese." No fewer than 27 prefectures were represented in San Francisco by as many prefectural societies in 1908–1909, and there were "24 in Seattle, 12 in Los Angeles, 8 in Sacramento, and smaller numbers in other communities."[76] By the 1930's there were 34 different *kenjinkai* in Los

[73] Statements by officers of the Japanese Association cited by R. E. Park and H. A. Miller, *Old World Traits Transplanted*. New York, Harper & Brothers, 1921, p. 179.
[74] Miyamoto, *op. cit.*, p. 116.
[75] *Reports of the Immigration Commission*, U.S. Congress, Senate, *op. cit.*, p. 131.
[76] *Ibid.*, p. 164.

Angeles and "half-a-dozen in Santa Maria Valley, San Luis Obispo, and Lompoc."[77]

As described by Miyamoto, a *kenjinkai* was, on the informal side, "a social gathering of people from the same prefecture, having, therefore, a common background of memories, speech, and customs that [offered] the members of the group an intimacy which they [could] not feel with people from other *ken*." The local organizations held frequent business and social meetings, and their spectacular annual picnics drew together immigrants from many communities on the West Coast. They were useful in providing intermediaries for arranged marriages and in facilitating the investigation of family lines. On the formal side they functioned "in the much more significant capacity of mutual aid, giving help to those members who [were] financially embarrassed by illness, death, or a lack of economic means."[78] They acted as *ad hoc* employment agencies and introduced new arrivals in the community "to those members of the association who might be able to offer employment; usually a *kenjin* [that is, a person from the same *ken*] got the first chance of employment . . . other things being equal." They coöperated with the Japanese Association in the latter's tours for Nisei in Japan and they, too, facilitated the return to America of the Japan-educated second generation. In some localities they arranged loans for Kibei who were willing to enter agriculture and might thus become successors to farms operated by the aging Issei.[79]

Immigrant organizations expanded and proliferated and, as of 1920, the Japanese were described, in the Carnegie-sponsored *Studies of Americanization,* as "the most efficiently and completely organized among the immigrant groups" and as "not at all equaled" by any other foreign language minority in "the work of accommodating themselves to alien conditions."[80] In Seattle there were at that time "40 public and social institutions . . . 14 schools and religious organizations . . . 13 newspapers and maga-

---

[77] F. Fukuoka, *Mutual Life and Aid Among the Japanese in Southern California with Special Reference to Los Angeles,* M.A. thesis, unpublished, University of Southern California, 1937.

[78] Miyamoto, *op. cit.,* p. 118.

[79] Fukuoka, *op. cit.*

[80] Park and Miller, *op. cit.,* pp. 168, 180.

zines." And in San Francisco 111 "Japanese cultural institutions" were listed—most of them within the boundaries of an area of half-a-dozen blocks. These included 27 prefectural societies, 15 churches or religious organizations, 18 schools, 8 clubs, 2 women's patriotic societies (branches of American organizations), 7 newspapers, 1 boy scout troop, 2 consular offices, 4 branches of the Japanese Association, and 27 different types of economic organizations.[81]

A similar listing, as of 1940, showed 161 instead of 111 Japanese organizations in San Francisco and included 27 prefectural or similar "geographical" societies, 20 Buddhist and 19 Christian churches or religious groups, 14 schools (most of them Japanese language schools), 1 students' club, 18 clubs fostering Japanese hobbies and sports (calligraphy, tea ceremonial, fencing, wrestling, and so on), 5 clubs devoted to American sports (golf, tennis, and so on), 3 "social" clubs, 3 mothers' clubs, 2 boy scout troops, 4 social welfare groups, 11 offices of Japanese or vernacular newspapers and periodicals, 6 Japanese nationalistic societies, 1 society directed toward the promotion of international harmony, 2 branches of the Japanese American Citizens League, 1 branch of the Japanese Association, 1 consular office, and 23 economic organizations.[82]

Between 1920 and 1940 many of the Nisei businessmen and farmers joined "junior associations" which were usually sponsored by the more powerful Issei economic organizations, but efforts of the older generation to organize "junior auxiliaries" of *kenjinkai* for the second generation met with limited success. A number of spontaneous groupings of Nisei, composed of students, athletes, or persons having similar political, artistic, or "social" interests, did, however, emerge during this period. Two of these loosely knit groups—one starting in San Francisco in 1918 and the other in Seattle in 1921—were the precursors of the Japanese American Citizens League, which by 1940 had 50 chap-

---

[81] *Ibid.*, pp. 171–173.

[82] The listing for 1940 is from our own tabulation from *Nichi Bei (Japanese-American) Directory*. An earlier edition of this directory was the basis for the tabulation cited from Park and Miller.

ters and 5,600 paid-up Nisei members.[83] The San Francisco group, which started as a "post-collegiate Nisei study group," disbanded because of lack of interest and support in 1922. In contrast the Seattle group, which from the beginning had had strong Issei backing and was for a time an adjunct of the Japanese Association, became increasingly powerful. Recognizing that "sustained organization existence depended necessarily upon older generation support," the San Francisco founders asked the Japanese Associations in California to select representative Nisei delegates for a meeting which effected a new, statewide organization in 1923. In 1929 the Seattle and California organizations merged, and in the following year the Japanese American Citizens League was formally organized on a national basis.

In many localities JACL chapters were primarily social in orientation and, particularly in the rural areas and smaller cities, directed their energies toward sponsorship of picnics, talent revues, oratorical contests, dramatic and musical presentations, and similar activities. In the larger cities and in their "national" conferences, however, their interests developed increasingly along three lines (1) political pressure against discriminatory legislation; (2) promotion of "public relations" by interpreting the Japanese to the larger community; and (3) education of the second generation in Americanism.

In some of their protective activities, JACL chapters joined forces with the Japanese Association and even attempted to obtain the intervention of the Japanese consuls, for example, in connection with the bombing of Japanese farmers' homes in the Salt River Valley of Arizona in 1934 and during a period of interracial tension in the Tulare County farming region of central California in the following year. For the most part, however, they emphasized the franchise as a protective device and made a direct approach to representatives of the American government. As early as 1931 JACL members lobbied successfully in Washington for an amendment to the Cable Act, making it possible for Nisei women married to Issei to regain or retain American

---

[83] The remainder of this section is based on a manuscript history of the Japanese American Citizens League, prepared by Togo Tanaka for the Evacuation and Resettlement Study, 1944.

citizenship. They played an important role in the campaign to bring about passage of the Oriental Veterans Citizenship Act in 1935; and in 1936 they obtained "recognition of passport" for Nisei who had traveled abroad, thus facilitating reëntry to America without passport-inspection delays. In California they lobbied periodically against legislative restrictions on land ownership, against antialien fishing bills, and against segregated schools. They instituted local campaigns against restrictions on the use of public swimming pools and recreational facilities and against segregation in theaters. They took a strong and consistent stand against dual citizenship and urged Nisei to expatriate from Japanese citizenship and to pledge undivided allegiance to America. At the same time, they were sympathetic to the development of Japanese language schools, and when Japan invaded Manchuria, "JACL assumed the burden of speaking for Japan's case to the American public." Between 1937 and 1939 the organization shifted to a stand of neutrality in regard to the Sino-Japanese conflict and after 1939, concomitant with the development of strong anti-Japanese sentiment in the United States, not only abandoned neutrality but coöperated actively with American intelligence agencies in evaluating the loyalty of members of the Japanese community. "By 1940–1941, all of the national officers of the JACL [were said to have] come into personal contact with Federal investigative agencies. Similarly, district and local chapter leaders found themselves increasingly approached by representatives of not only Federal but state and local law enforcement agencies."

Language and Communication

According to the Immigration Commission Reports of 1908–1909, the Japanese had a much higher standard of literacy in their native language than did Chinese, Mexican, and most south and east European immigrants on the West Coast, when comparison was limited to those employed in the same industries and at the same kind of work. They had made relatively rapid progress in acquiring a speaking knowledge of English, being consistently superior not only to Chinese and Mexicans but also to the most recent arrivals among many of the European groups. The progress of those who had been in this country for a longer period of time had, however, been somewhat less rapid than that of the south and east Europeans of comparable length of residence. The relative retardation of these older residents was attributed largely to the fact that the extent to which Europeans associated with English-speaking "natives" increased with their period of residence whereas there was "little change in the course of time of the clannish conditions" under which Japanese immigrants lived and worked.[84]

There were significant intragroup differences. For example, the following proportions[85] of Japanese males who had had less than five years' residence in the United States were reported as speaking English: 95 per cent of the self-employed in city trades and services and 86 per cent of those in agriculture compared with 79 per cent of the wage earners in city trades, 59 per cent of those in agriculture, and 42 per cent of those in other rural occupations. Corresponding proportions for males with five to nine years' residence in the United States, were, in the same order of occupation and urban-rural residence, 97 per cent, 96 per cent, 84 per cent, 73 per cent, and 57 per cent; and for those with ten or more years' residence, 99 per cent, 98 per cent, 91 per cent, 84 percent, and 67 per cent. In all classes in which females were sufficiently numerous to permit comparison with males, the for-

---

[84] *Reports of the Immigration Commission,* (U.S. Congress, Senate, *op. cit.,*) pp. 149–151, 158.

[85] These percentages were computed from data in the Immigration Commission Reports (*Ibid.,* pp. 145–147). We included as "urban" wage earners those employed in laundries, canneries, and in the miscellaneous category; as "other rural," those employed in mining, smelting, and transportation. The following table shows the number of cases on which the percentages were based:

Occupational class	Years in the United States		
	Under 5	5 to 9	10 or over
Self-employed			
City trades	100	206	152
Agriculture	263	373	211
Wage earners			
City trades	1,134	708	255
Agriculture	3,479	1,984	578
Other rural	1,585	915	208

mer were greatly inferior to the latter. The several contrasts were explained "partly by the different classes represented in the different groups, partly by the possibility of association with the members of other races, and partly by the possibility of attendance at school." Thus the student class was concentrated in city trades and services and entered the rural labor force only for seasonal work in agriculture and in canneries. Females had had a "lower standard of education" in Japan than had males, and few of them belonged to the student class in the United States; they did not take employment as servants and thus did not come into much contact with whites, and "not finding it urgent to know English in order to be successful," they had not so frequently attended night classes for the study of English. Although schools established primarily for "imparting a knowledge of English" were numerous, most of them were in the large cities, and the majority of the pupils were "recent immigrants . . . gainfully employed, largely in domestic service." The number of these schools—thirty-three—and "the many Japanese who attended them at an earlier time when many immigrants were arriving" were considered "the best evidence of the ambition and eagerness of the members of this race to learn western civilization." Comparison with other groups suggested that "no adult immigrants in the West, unless it is the Hebrews, [showed] as great a desire to learn the English language."[86]

The patterns and differentials noted by the Immigration Commission in 1908–1909 were still apparent more than two decades later when Strong and his associates at Stanford University conducted field studies in Japanese communities in six California counties. Of approximately 3,700 foreign-born Japanese included in their survey, the following proportions had spent more than half a year studying English at day or night schools: 45 per cent of urban males, 28 per cent of rural males, 25 per cent of urban females, and 5 per cent of rural females. For males, there was an inverse relationship between the amount of time spent studying English and age, the time spent by those who were then more than 60 years of age being "almost nil." Females had "de-

[86] *Ibid.*, pp. 147–148, 152–153 *passim*.

voted far less time to the study of English" and showed no significant age differential.

Strong emphasized that attendance at school did not "measure very accurately the amount of English acquired by these immigrants," inasmuch as "it was customary for many years for the newcomers to obtain positions as servants in American homes in order to acquire the language." The extent to which they expressed preference for the use of English or Japanese might, however, indicate "in a rough way . . . greater ability in the one than the other." But "only a handful of the Japan-born men and women," that is, 3 per cent and 2 per cent respectively, preferred English to Japanese. There was "a somewhat greater preference for English" among those living in the cities than among those from country districts, but "little or no relationship between preference for English and length of residence in this country" except for the fact that "no Japanese who had been in this country 35 years or more preferred English to Japanese."[87]

Highly literate in the Japanese language as they were, and having imperfect knowledge of English, many more Issei turned to the Japanese or to the vernacular than to the American press for information and viewpoints about local, national, and international affairs.

The first small Japanese language newspaper was established in San Francisco in 1892, and the *Japanese-American News* (*Nichi-Bei*), which became one of the major vernacular dailies, began operations in that city in 1897. A few years later, *Nichi-Bei* opened a branch office in Sacramento to report the local events in that area, and this movement was followed by other papers in various places.[88] In 1908–1909 the Immigration Commission enumerated "4 Japanese daily newspapers published in San Francisco, 3 in Los Angeles, 1 in Sacramento, 2 in Seattle, and a few elsewhere," which, along with a few weekly and monthly publications in the same cities, presented "Japanese and American news from the Japanese point of view."

---

[87] E. K. Strong, Jr., R. Bell, *et al.*, *Vocational Aptitudes of Second-Generation Japanese in the United States*, Stanford University Press, 1933. Pp. 115–118. These percentages were based on the following numbers: urban males, 819; rural males, 875; urban females, 665; rural females, 683.

[88] S. Washizu, article in the *Japanese-American News* (*Nichi Bei*), undated. Cited by R. E. Park, *op. cit.*, pp. 280–286.

Among households investigated by the Immigration Commission "the number of Japanese subscribing for no newspaper [was]
much smaller than that of the Italians and Portuguese," and the
number of publications taken was "very much larger." In both
these respects, the Japanese were said to compare "favorably with
the households of north European immigrants." However, "a
far larger percentage of the publications subscribed for [were]
printed in their native language in the case of the Japanese than
in the case of the city and farm households of most of the other
races investigated." Among the Japanese there were, again, significant urban-rural differences: only 2 per cent of the urban,
but 28 per cent of the rural households subscribed to no newspaper; 40 per cent of the urban but only 6 per cent of the rural
subscribed to one or more publications printed in English; and
58 per cent of the urban, and 66 per cent of the rural households
subscribed to publications printed only in the Japanese language.[89]

In 1918 there were "44 Japanese papers, according to students
of the press." San Francisco was then "the center of intellectual
life, and of commercial and official relations with the home country," and its dailies had editorials and articles on such topics as
Americanization and reconstruction. In Los Angeles—"the newest Japanese center"—the vernacular papers were "full of gossip,
sensation and fiction," and they circulated widely in the surrounding agricultural settlements. "The stream of travel and
commerce" that poured into Seattle kept "the interest in Japanese news alive," and there, as in San Francisco, the cosmopolitan
press flourished, though newspapers in the smaller settlements,
like those then in Los Angeles, dealt almost exclusively with local
gossip.[90]

Concomitant with discriminatory legislation—just before and
after World War I—the vernacular press was "greatly exercised
in regard to the anti-Japanese movement on the coast and it
[recorded] any manifestation of feeling against the Japanese."[91]

---

[89] Percentages computed from data in the *Reports of the Immigration Commission*, (U.S. Congress, Senate, *op. cit.*), p. 159. These percentages were based on 332
urban and 490 rural households.

[90] Park, *op. cit.*, pp. 295, 151–152.

[91] *Ibid.*, pp. 154–155.

As Kusama described the situation: "A little account printed in the American press was translated at length . . . with an additional write-up by the editors. (The items so gathered were not confined to the local events but were collected from all over the state and country.) By so editing, the papers gave the impression that every American was active in promoting the anti-Japanese movement and [that] the items printed were events taking place simultaneously when they covered [in fact] a period of a week or two."[92]

By the 1930's almost every immigrant household was reached by one or more of the vernacular publications. In Seattle according to Miyamoto who wrote in 1939, "only a minimum of first-generation Japanese" read the American dailies, and the vernacular press had "an almost uncontested supremacy" in forming Issei opinion. By that time Seattle's two papers were covering "with unabated avidity all the important news to be had about the Oriental crisis," and since July, 1937, there had "not been a day . . . when the war news was not the most important item on the front page." Their effect was apparent "in the solid attitude of the community in support of the program to which the Japanese government [had] committed itself in China, and the vigorous and bitter attacks that the people [made] against the American newspapers. . . . In this regard . . . the Japanese newspapers, in conjunction with the Japanese consulate . . . sponsored a program of educating the second-generation Japanese concerning the 'true' conditions behind this conflict" and admonished parents "to interpret the Japanese newspapers to their English-speaking sons and daughters so that the latter [might] correctly state the case to the larger American public." In an effort to attract second-generation readers, it eventually became necessary "to give over one of their daily eight pages to an English section." The major part of every edition, however, was given over "to discussing matters which [were] largely Japanese, from the editorial down to the novelette." The organizational activities of the community were reported in great detail, as were "all the births,

---

[92] S. Kusama, document, cited by R. E. Park, *op. cit.*, p. 155.

marriages, deaths, and other events which [went] to make up the body of the community's daily conversation."[93]

The development of the vernacular press in Los Angeles was, in many respects, similar to that in Seattle. In 1941 three dailies were being published in "Little Tokyo." Each was primarily a Japanese language medium, with a supplementary English section of one or two pages. The Japanese sections were staffed by Issei with the help of an occasional Kibei, and the English editors were Nisei. According to an account by Tanaka, policymaking was, in all three newspaper offices, "in the hands of conservative men with fairly characteristic Japanese antipathy toward any views favorable to Soviet Russia." Moreover, the term *aka* (Communist) was used opprobriously against "those who actively campaigned to unionize hotel and restaurant employees and fruit stand workers" and was "directed sharply against the occasional Issei who spoke out or wrote about the 'militarism' of Japan. . . . The political ideology of Japan in the late 'thirties found reflection in the controlling leadership of the vernacular dailies in Los Angeles, and a strong conscious identity with the fortunes of Japan in the military venture in China was the keynote of front-page editing."[94]

The combined circulation of the three Los Angeles dailies reached 17,000 in the prewar years. There was a good deal of overlapping in subscription lists, and it was estimated that "the average Japanese family in Southern California subscribed to two out of the three newspapers." In general, the vernacular press constituted the chief source of immigrant political opinion and "exerted an influence greater than is generally attributed to the press in American life." By 1941 the Japanese and English sections were serving two different audiences. "The parents turned to the Japanese section, the children to the English." The content of the two was often quite different and, just before the outbreak of war, divergencies in editorial policy and in the handling of political reports were especially noteworthy.

---

[93] Miyamoto, *op. cit.*, pp. 119–121.

[94] The description of the Los Angeles vernacular press is from a manuscript prepared by Togo Tanaka for the Evacuation and Resettlement Study, 1944.

Two distinct phases mark the period between 1937 and 1941. From July 7, 1937, when Japanese and Chinese troops clashed at Loukia-chow Bridge in North China bringing Japan's invasion and the start of the conflict in the Far East, through July two years later when the United States State Department announced intent to abrogate the Treaty of Trade and Commerce of 1911 with Japan, there was fairly close coöperation between English and Japanese sections of the vernacular dailies. The Japanese sections fed the English departments with dispatches from Tokyo. The English section's function in this period came to be well defined: (1) interpret properly for Nisei the "true aims" of Japan in her efforts to establish permanent peace and justice in Asia and (2) help the American newspapers understand this point of view by giving them the facts, pointing out to them that they were being "flooded with clever Chinese propaganda." From some-time in August, 1939, after American-Japanese tensions had culminated in the announcement of treaty abrogation, however, the Japanese vernacular newspapers of Los Angeles began to acquire traits of a dual personality. The ideological gap between Japanese and English sections gradually widened until, by fall of 1941, the two departments were editorially committed on differing sides of two potential belligerents. The Japanese sections had stuck by Japan, the English sections had gone American.

In 1929 the San Francisco forerunner of the Japanese American Citizens League launched an all-English semimonthly publication, the *Nikkei Shimin*, which shortly changed its name to the *Pacific Citizen*. Its prewar development and policies are analyzed by Tanaka, as follows:

The early editorials in *Nikkei Shimin* and *Pacific Citizen* stimulated interest in and set the groundwork for the organization of the Japanese American Citizens League. "Join the Citizens League for your own Protection" became a slogan, and the paper urged the establishment of a central organization, with "binding ties and tangible benefits accruing to the membership." From the beginning, it was self-consciously American, and within Japanese communities it came to symbolize American education among the Nisei. It consistently opposed dual citizenship and urged Nisei to expatriate from Japanese citizenship and to register and vote in American elections. Although nonpartisan in policy, there is, during the early thirties, evidence of leanings to the conservative right. Rugged individualism and capitalism were idealized, and private enterprise, in the form of small businesses, was encouraged. It refrained from openly endorsing candidates for political office, deviating from this position only in implied opposition to political figures charged with discriminatory anti-Japanese records.

In the course of time, the *Pacific Citizen* gave increasing expression to the view that Issei, as well as Nisei, should regard themselves as permanent residents of the United States and urged them to follow the pattern of other new immigrants and cease looking back to their native land as a place to which they planned to return. It committed the JACL movement to this position, in contrast to the sojourner attitude of most Issei organizations. At the same time, it subscribed to the prevalent concept that a good Japanese education in the language schools was as important as a thorough American public school education in preparing Nisei for the role of builders of a bridge of understanding across the Pacific.[95]

Language schools, which served the dual purpose of teaching English to immigrant children and Japanese to Nisei, were already in existence by 1908–1909 in San Francisco, Los Angeles, Sacramento, and Seattle.[96] The San Francisco school was described in the Immigration Commission Reports as follows:

There is . . . a school the object of which is to teach Japanese children born in this country the use of their mother tongue, and something of the history and institutions of Japan, and to assist children born in Japan and recently arrived in this country in learning English in order that they may be less handicapped in the classes of the public schools.[97]

Because few Japanese children entered this country as immigrants, there was no continuing need for privately organized English language schools. On the other hand the rapid increase in the number of American-born, American-educated children after 1908 stimulated the demand for instruction in the Japanese lan-

---

[95] Analysis of the role of the *Pacific Citizen* is based on a manuscript prepared by Togo Tanaka, for the Evacuation and Resettlement Study, 1944.

[96] *Reports of the Immigration Commission* (U.S. Congress, Senate, *op. cit.*), pp. 219, 246, 267, 300.

[97] *Ibid.*, p. 152.

guage, as a means both of strengthening the attenuating lines of communication between parents and children and of reinforcing the control of the Japanese community upon the second generation. By 1920 there were 40 Japanese language schools in California and appreciable numbers in the other western states, whereas Hawaii, with its larger Japanese population and longer period of settlement, had no less than 163 such schools with 20,000 students in attendance. In both Hawaii and in California, they became "one of the focal points of criticism for outspoken patriotic groups interested in Americanization." In 1920 the Hawaiian legislature passed an act "regulating foreign-language schools and placing them under the supervision of the Department of Public Instruction," and a section was added to California's school law in 1921, "closely modeled on the Hawaiian law." In 1927, however, a Supreme Court decision declared the Hawaiian law unenforceable, and two and a half months later the Attorney General of California "ruled the California law invalid in the light of the Supreme Court decision."[98]

In California almost all language school teachers were Japan-educated Issei, and almost all textbooks were imported from Japan and drew their illustrations from Japanese events, personalities, and concepts. Between 1921 and 1927 the State School Department specified standards for the content of permissible texts—emphasizing Americanization—and required the teachers to be "conversant with English." According to Bell, the language

---

[98] Reginald Bell, *Public School Education of Second-Generation Japanese in California*, Stanford University Press, 1935, pp. 19–20.

According to A. W. Lind, in *Hawaii's Japanese*, Princeton University Press, 1935, pp. 22–24, the language-school issue "did much to accentuate the anti-Japanese sentiment, particularly in the vocal portions of the community" in Hawaii, during "the seven years of bitter controversy over this issue." He points out that "the Japanese language schools had actually been in existence some twenty-five years, and prior to this sudden outburst of feeling, had received the unofficial sanction, if not the official blessings, of both the American and the Japanese community.... Once the issue had been resolved by the United States Supreme Court decision in 1927, no further legal obstacles were placed in the way of the Japanese language schools, which continued to offer instruction in Japanese language and etiquette until the outbreak of World War II. The peak of language-school attendance was reached in 1934, when 41,192 children, or approximately 85 per cent of all children of Japanese ancestry who were of school age, received some instruction every school day in the language school; by 1941 the ratio of attendance had dropped to 74.5 per cent."

school associations "complied as rapidly as possible with the law requiring registration of schools and qualifying of teachers and adopted the approved text books."[99] But between 1927 and the outbreak of war there were no legal restrictions, and procedures varied greatly from one locality to another.

The number of Japanese language schools in California increased from 40 in 1920 to 248 in 1934 to 261 in 1940.[100] In some localities all, and in most others the overwhelming majority, of the Nisei attended these schools, and for many of them daily attendance at Japanese language schools paralleled the whole course of their training in American public schools. As described by Bell in the early 1930's:

Among the common sights in those parts of California where Japanese communities exist are straggling groups of little Japanese children walking slowly home along the streets or highways at four-thirty or five o'clock in the afternoon. The observer is puzzled, for the public schools have been out for two hours or more. Inquiry brings the information that they have been attending, since school hours, the Japanese-language schools, whose primary purpose is, as their name implies, to teach the Japanese language, the language ordinarily of their homes and their churches. The schools are held in church basements, parish houses, parsonages, Japanese community halls, or special language-school buildings. Teachers are employed by local Japanese boards of trustees. Regular, graded instruction is given in Japanese language and literature and in reading, writing, and speaking Japanese.[101]

Some Nisei were sent to Japan to be educated for much the same reasons that others were required to attend language schools. In other cases the children were sent as precursors of parents who intended sooner or later to return to the home country. But in the main the movement was based on short-run economic considerations. The small family enterprises, which had proliferated both in agriculture and in urban trades and services, called for the active participation of the wife of the owner or operator. Sending a young child to Japan freed the mother for

[99] Bell, op. cit., p. 24.
[100] Japanese Association of America (Zaibei Nippon-jin Shi), pp. 469, 483–493.
[101] Bell, op. cit., p. 17.

this essential "unpaid family labor" and was, under the circumstances, often less expensive than rearing him in America. Correspondingly, calling the Japan-educated child back to America was motivated, in many cases, by the economic requirements of the family enterprise as well as by family and ethnic sentiment.

The magnitude of the Kibei migration to America during the 1930's, concomitant with the marked decline in the proportion

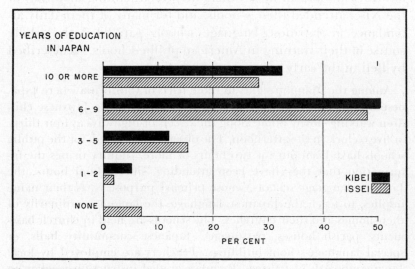

Chart VIII. Distribution of Kibei and Issei evacuees, 1942, by years of education in Japan. (See Appendix, table 19.)

of children sent to Japan, suggests that even though sojourner attitudes persisted, increasing numbers of the Issei on the West Coast had become residents-in-fact if not settlers-by-intention. Of the 9,800 Kibei enumerated in the War Relocation Authority's census of 1942, only 35 per cent had returned to the United States before 1930, and almost 40 per cent of them came between 1935 and 1941.[102] Although they were American-born American citizens, they had, on the average, had far fewer opportunities to assimilate American ways than had their alien parents. Not only had they spent a greater proportion of their lives in Japan

[102] As computed from a table showing the "last year attended school in Japan." (*The Evacuated People,* U.S. Department of Interior, *op. cit.,* p. 88.)

than had the resident Issei, but they had also been more thoroughly schooled in that country. As Chart VIII shows, 50 per cent of the Kibei, compared with 48 per cent of the Issei, had had 6–9 years' education in Japan, and 33 per cent of the Kibei, but only 28 per cent of the Issei, had attended school there for at least 10 years. Conversely, 8 per cent of the Issei, but only 5 per cent of the Kibei, had had fewer than 3 years' education in Japan. Only 6 per cent of the Issei, however, had completed their education in American schools, compared with 26 per cent of the Kibei, and an additional 10 per cent of the latter were still attending schools on the West Coast at the outbreak of war.

Religious Differentials

Appreciable numbers of the immigrants had had contact with Christian missionaries before leaving Japan, and the Japanese settlers on the West Coast were the objects of extensive proselytizing through "home missions." As described by La Violette:

When the immigrants arrived, Christian missionaries became active among them and were of great assistance in getting them started in American life. The missionaries taught them English, found jobs for them, helped plan for marriages, acted as counsellors, tided them over the slack periods of employment, and, in general, taught them about our ways of living. The missionaries in Japan had advised the immigrants to call on certain people, and for these services the Japanese felt deeply indebted.[103]

Nevertheless, most of the Japanese immigrants continued to prefer Buddhism to Christianity. The Immigration Commission reported, as of 1908–1909, that "the majority of those who [took] an interest in religious work [adhered] to the Buddhist faith";[104] Strong's survey in six California counties in 1930 yielded a proportion of 77 per cent Buddhists among the Japan-born;[105] and in the War Relocation Authority's 1942 census of evacuees from

[103] F. E. La Violette, *Americans of Japanese Ancestry*, The Canadian Institute of International Affairs, Toronto, 1945, p. 46.

[104] *Reports of the Immigration Commission* (U.S. Congress, Senate, *op. cit.*), p. 166.

[105] E. K. Strong, Jr., *Japanese in California*, Stanford University Press, 1933, p. 169.

California, Washington, Oregon, and Arizona, 69 per cent of the Issei expressed preference for Buddhism.[106]

As of 1908–1909 none of the twelve Buddhist temples on the West Coast included "natives or Europeans" in their membership,[107] and in 1940, of an estimated 56,000 Buddhists in the United States, 55,000 were said to be of Japanese ancestry.[108] Almost all the American sects were branches of organizations centered in Japan, and their priests customarily came over from the home country for relatively short periods of service.[109] Whereas American Buddhism soon adopted many of the formal practices of the Japanese Christian congregations, it adhered more closely than did the latter "to the traditional customs of Japan, particularly the rituals in connection with life crises," emphasized the basic ideas of ancestor worship, and "by its very nature [oriented] the members of its congregation towards Japan."[110]

Acceptance of Christianity did not, in and of itself, imply integration into the larger American community, since all of the major denominations on the West Coast segregated their Japanese members. As described in the Immigration Commission Reports, Christian missions had been instituted by 1908–1909 in "every community where any considerable number of Japanese [had] settled," including "practically all of the urban centers." No missions had been established "in several of the rural settlements. . . . In some such cases, a few Japanese who [had] accepted the Christian faith . . . united with local churches on an equal footing with the white members, but such instances [were] comparatively rare." Wherever missions existed, they were "for Japanese alone, a recognition of a difference between them and other races and a condition which [lessened] their value as an assimilative force."[111] In the course of time a few Japanese Christian

[106] *The Evacuated People,* U.S. Department of the Interior, *op. cit.,* p. 79.

[107] *Reports of the Immigration Commission* (U.S. Congress, Senate, *op. cit.*), p. 163.

[108] War Relocation Authority, *Community Analysis Report No. 9,* May 15, 1944. "Buddhism in the United States" (Mimeographed)

[109] Kosei Ogura, *A Sociological Study of the Buddhist Churches in North America with a Case Study of Gardena, California Congregation,* M.A. thesis, unpublished, University of Southern California, 1933, p. 34.

[110] Miyamoto, *op. cit.,* p. 104.

[111] *Reports of the Immigration Commission* (U.S. Congress, Senate, *op. cit.*), p. 163.

churches achieved independent status, but most of them continued up to the war to be operated by the home-mission branches of the various denominations. Their Japanese pastors conducted most of the services in the Japanese language, and their activity programs "from athletics to large conferences" were described by La Violette as "essentially Japanese" in sponsorship, support, and attendance. Not infrequently, however, a white pastor or layman was associated with the Japanese pastor, and church workers and teachers from the larger community sometimes served as leaders of discussion groups, as speakers at conferences, and as participants in other programs.[112] Thus, in spite of the fact that the contacts so engendered were with very limited segments of the American community, they provided a basis for interracial association that had no counterpart in Buddhist congregations.

As of 1930, though Japanese Americans as a group were still predominantly Buddhist, there were marked differences between the first and second generations and between rural and urban residents. In Strong's analysis of the religious preference of approximately 3,000 Japan-born and 1,000 American-born Japanese residents of California who were 14 years of age and older, Buddhist proportions were at maxima among the Japan-born residents of country districts, accounting for 80 per cent of the males and 84 per cent of the females, and at minima of 32–36 per cent among the American-born living in urban areas. Correspondingly, the proportions of Christians were at maxima of 59 per cent for females and 53 per cent for males among American-born urban residents, and at minima of 11–12 per cent for Japan-born residents of country districts.[113]

The over-all proportion of Buddhists was still high, and the sociodemographic differentials were still pronounced in 1942. Charts IX and X show the preference patterns for 48 regional-generational-occupational-sex groups, comprising the 24,000

---

[112] La Violette, op. cit., pp. 46–48, passim.

[113] Computed from data in Japanese in California (Strong, op. cit., p. 170). The totals in each of Strong's categories were as follows: Japan-born residents of city districts, males 887, females 710; Japan-born residents of country districts, males 917, females 696; American-born residents of city districts, males 226, females 230; American-born residents of country districts, males 294, females 208.

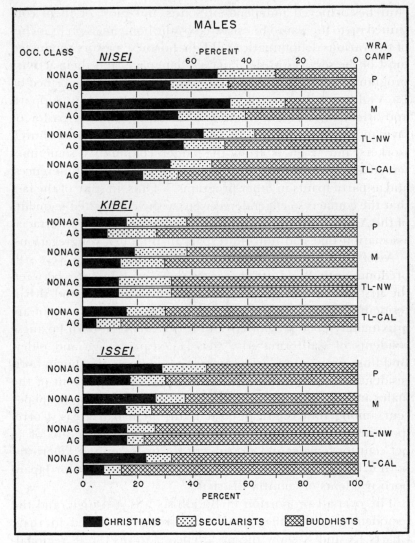

Chart IX. Distribution of male evacuees, 17 years of age and older, in selected WRA camps, 1942, in generational-educational and prewar occupational classes by religion. (See Appendix, tables 20A and 20B. Note that P=Poston, Camp I; M=Minidoka; TL-NW=Northwesterners at Tule Lake; TL-C=Californians at Tule Lake.)

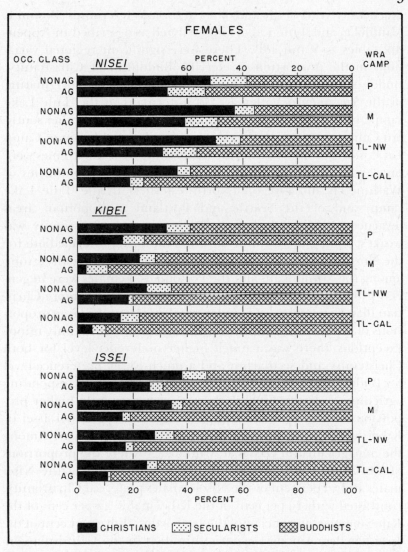

FEMALES

Chart X. Distribution of female evacuees, 17 years of age and older, in selected WRA camps, 1942, in generational-educational and prewar occupational classes by religion. (See Appendix, tables 20A and 20B. Note that P=Poston, Camp I; M=Minidoka; TL-NW=Northwesterners at Tule Lake; TL-C=Californians at Tule Lake.)

evacuees 17 years of age and older in three WRA camps (Poston I,
Minidoka, and Tule Lake) and analyzed as described in Appendix tables 20A and 20B. There were significant regional variations in the proportions preferring Buddhism or Christianity,
Buddhist proportions being highest among evacuees originating
in the Sacramento Valley area (Californians in the Tule Lake
camp), lowest among those from Los Angeles and the other southern California communities from which the population of Camp
I at Poston was drawn. Intermediate between these extremes were
prewar residents of the small cities and rural communities of
Washington and Oregon (Northwesterners in the Tule Lake
camp) and of the Seattle and Portland metropolitan areas
(evacuees at Minidoka camp). Preference for Christianity was
weakest among the Californians in Tule Lake, intermediate for
the Northwesterners in the same camp, and about equally strong
among the Minidokans and the Postonians. Females were in general proportionately both more Buddhistic and also more Christian than were males—a paradox resulting from the large proportions of the nonreligious in all classes of males. With only minor
exceptions, there was a much higher preference-level for both
Christianity and secularism and a much lower preference-level
for Buddhism among nonagricultural than among corresponding
agricultural classes. Finally, there were consistently higher proportions of Christians among Nisei than among either Issei or
Kibei of the same regional-occupational-sex groupings. Among
the nonagricultural classes at Minidoka—where the proportions
of Christians were, in general, high—54 per cent of the Nisei
males and 57 per cent of the Nisei females preferred Christianity,
contrasted with 19 per cent of the Kibei males, 22 per cent of the
Kibei females, 26 per cent of the Issei males, and 34 per cent of the
Issei females. Among the agriculturalists in the California contingent at Tule Lake—where the preference pattern was overwhelmingly Buddhist—22 per cent of the Nisei males and 19
per cent of the Nisei females preferred Christianity, compared
with 5 per cent of the Kibei of both sexes, 8 per cent of the Issei
males, and 11 per cent of the Issei females.

Place of birth was less closely associated with religious preference than was place of education. Not only did the preference-level of the American-born, Japan-educated Kibei bear little resemblance to that of the American-born, American-educated Nisei, but when region, occupation, and sex are held constant, the proportion of Buddhists among Kibei is found to exceed that of Japan-born, predominantly Japan-educated Issei in 10 out of 16 possible comparisons, and the proportion of Christians among them to be appreciably lower in 15 out of 16 comparisons.

Educational Differentials

Sending children to Japan for education and establishing Japanese language schools for Nisei in West Coast communities were only part of the Japanese immigrants' unremitting efforts "to pour formal education into their children."[114] They encouraged the returning Kibei to supplement their Japan-acquired education by attendance at West Coast schools and colleges and pressed the Nisei to utilize to the fullest possible extent all available educational facilities. American schooling thus became an important auxiliary factor in the experience of many Kibei and the primary focus for most Nisei.

Relatively few of the second generation had completed their education at the time of Strong's 1930 survey. The 155 "United States–born" males, aged 21–27, who were included in his sample, had, on the average, reached or finished half a year in college, and the 137 females in this age-nativity group had averaged four years in high school. On the basis of these and other data from his survey, Strong concluded that the children of Japanese immigrants were "taking full advantage of the public schools of California" and were averaging "as well as the whites," and he suggested that fewer of them than "of Americans in general" were dropping out before high school graduation.[115] These conclusions and inferences are confirmed by the following analysis of the more extensive data available in the 1940 census.

---

[114] Miyamoto, op. cit., p. 111.

[115] Strong, Second-Generation Japanese Problem, op. cit., pp. 158, 185–198, passim.

Of 28,000 American-born Japanese, aged 16–24, resident in California and Washington in 1940, more than 46 per cent were attending school, compared with only 33 per cent of the general population. The discrepancy between the Japanese minority and the total population was particularly large at ages 18–19 when high school graduation is normally accomplished. Thus 60 per

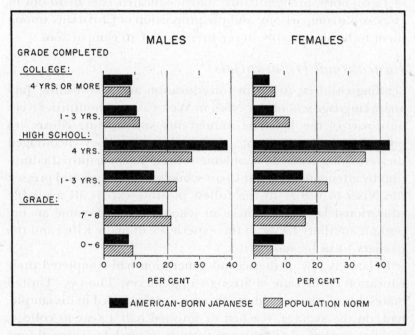

Chart XI. Distribution of American-born Japanese males and females, 25 years of age and older, in California and Washington, 1940, by grade of school completed, compared with age-adjusted, sex-specific norms for the total population of these states. (See Appendix, table 13.)

cent of the American-born Japanese males and 54 per cent of the females, aged 18–19, were attending school, compared with 44 per cent of the general male population and 38 per cent of the general female population. (See Appendix, table 21.)

Of 11,400 American-born Japanese aged 25 years or older in 1940—most of whom had presumably completed their education—the median grade reached or attained equaled or exceeded that of age-adjusted sex-specific population norms in California and Washington. As Chart XI shows, the most pronounced deviation was, again, at the level of high school graduation. The number of American-born Japanese males who had completed the fourth year of high school exceeded the number expected on the basis of age-adjusted norms for the two states by 39 per cent, and the corresponding excess for American-born Japanese females was 21 per cent. The observed total of college-educated males, however, was 1 per cent lower than that expected, on the basis of the population norm, and among females the deficit amounted to 37 per cent. At the lower levels of completed education (less than high school graduation) there were 20 per cent fewer Japanese males than expected, whereas the proportion among American-born females approximated the population norm.

In Chart XII, Nisei, who by our definition are those of the American-born educated wholly in American schools, are compared with two classes of Kibei: those who had completed their schooling in America and those whose last years of formal education were obtained in Japan. The educational level attained by Nisei was very much higher than that of either Kibei group, but the level for Kibei who had completed their schooling in America was appreciably higher than that for Kibei who had last attended school in Japan. Thus, only 3 per cent of the latter category were college-educated, compared with 16 per cent of the former. Whereas the proportion of the college-educated was only 17 per cent for Nisei, an additional 62 per cent of them had graduated from high school, compared with only 33–36 per cent for the two Kibei groups. At the other extreme, almost 40 per cent of the Kibei who had completed their schooling in Japan had had no more than an elementary school education, compared with 17 per cent of those finishing their education in the United States, and only 9 per cent of the Nisei.

Among Nisei, the educational level of Christians and secularists was consistently higher than that of Buddhists, and the level of those with nonagricultural backgrounds or in urban occupations was always appreciably higher than that of the corresponding farming classes. The close association between educational level, religious preference, and occupational class is shown in

Charts XIII and XIV, where Nisei evacuees in the Poston I and
Minidoka camps are divided into age-sex-occupational-religious
groups, and the proportions having had less than 4 years in high
school, having completed high school but gone no further, and

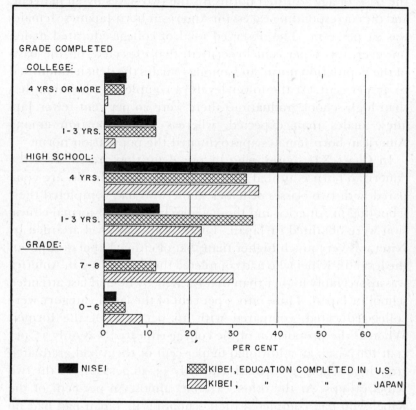

Chart XII. Distributions of Nisei and Kibei evacuees who had completed their edu-
cation before entering WRA camps in 1942 by grade of school completed, and for
Kibei in terms of country where completed. (See Appendix, table 24. Note that
Nisei, by definition, had had all of their education in the United States.)

having had some college education are shown for 30 of these
groups. Among males, there is a clearcut and unvarying progres-
sion in the proportion of college-educated from Buddhists to
Christians and secularists in the agricultural classes to Buddhists
to Christians and secularists in the nonagricultural classes. Within
the older group of males, in the agricultural classes at Poston,

for example, 8 per cent of the Buddhists were college-educated, compared with 21 per cent of the Christians and nonreligious, 31 per cent of the nonagricultural Buddhists, and 44 per cent of the nonagricultural Christians and secularists. Among females of the agricultural classes in both camps there was only a scattering of the college educated, but the educational differential between religious-preference groups in the nonagricultural classes was even more pronounced than among males.

That the educational superiority of second-generation Japanese was qualitative as well as quantitative is suggested by the results of several analyses of the comparative achievement of West Coast school populations. For example, Strong's associate, Reginald Bell, obtained 20,000 scholastic grades ("teachers' marks") for 985 Japanese pupils attending Los Angeles senior and junior high schools in 1930–1931 and compared them with similar scholastic grades for a cross section "descriptive of the entire junior and senior high school population" of the same city in 1927–1928. On a five-point, A to E scale, the Japanese pupils excelled in securing scholastic grades of A in all except the last of eight terms in the senior high school, and in 18 out of 19 divisions of subject matter taught in these schools, being "significantly superior in all subjects with the exception of German." They excelled also in proportions of B's and correspondingly had far lower proportions of D's and E's than did the general school population. Similar patterns and levels of superiority characterized their performance in the Los Angeles junior high schools.[116] In Seattle high schools Japanese pupils were, for many years, selected as "valedictorians and salutatorians"[117] and received other scholastic honors quite out of proportion to their numbers in the schools. As reported by Steiner in 1943:

In one of Seattle's high schools, one-fourth of the twenty class speakers at the graduating exercises during the past ten years have

---

[116] Bell (*op. cit.,* ch. iv) did not fully describe his Los Angeles samples. In his tables "pupils" apparently mean the number of pupils multiplied by the number of scholastic grades they obtained. Strong reproduced Bell's tables in this same form in *The Second-Generation Japanese Problem,* but indicated the number of different pupils involved and the total number of grades. The citations of Bell's work used here are from Strong, *op. cit.,* pp. 189–198, *passim.*

[117] Miyamoto, *op. cit.,* p. 108.

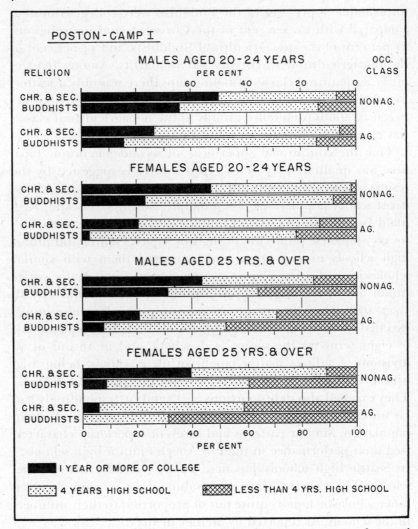

POSTON - CAMP I

MALES AGED 20-24 YEARS

RELIGION   PER CENT   OCC. CLASS

FEMALES AGED 20-24 YEARS

MALES AGED 25 YRS. & OVER

FEMALES AGED 25 YRS. & OVER

I YEAR OR MORE OF COLLEGE

4 YEARS HIGH SCHOOL   LESS THAN 4 YRS. HIGH SCHOOL

Chart XIII. Distribution of Nisei male and female evacuees, 20 years of age and older in 1942, in WRA Camp I at Poston in religious and prewar occupational classes and broad age-groups by grade of school completed. (See Appendix, table 23.)

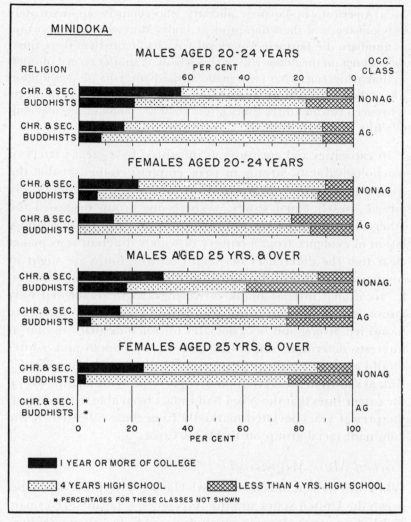

Chart XIV. Distribution of male and female Nisei evacuees, 20 years of age and older in 1942, in WRA camp at Minidoka in religious and prewar occupational classes and broad age-groups by grade of school completed. (See Appendix, table 23.)

been Americans of Japanese ancestry who comprise approximately only one-tenth of the whole student body. Moreover, in proportion to numbers, the Japanese-Americans have had more than three times their quota on the honor roll of this school. A similar record of intellectual achievement has been made at the University of Washington where the Japanese-American honor group in proportion to numbers is between two and three times larger than the honor group made up of white American students."[118]

In capacities and aptitudes as measured by a great variety of psychological tests, Strong, in 1933, emphasized the fact that the second-generation Japanese and the whites had consistently obtained "nearly equal scores." Where one group surpassed the other, the difference was offset in the next measure. "The accumulation of evidence from a battery of widely different tests makes clear that the differences between the two groups are slight in comparison to their remarkable similarity." Scores obtained on a "vocational interest blank" covering 420 items showed only minor group idiosyncrasies. The "slight differences" that were found led Strong and his associates to conclude that "insofar as interests determine one's life career ... Japanese and whites should enter occupations in practically the same proportions."[119] But, as shown in the section on occupatoinal mobility, pp. 36–43, the career lines that the Nisei had in fact been able to develop in the prewar years deviated markedly from those followed by the dominant racial group on the West Coast.

Forced Mass Migration[120]

When the sudden attack on Pearl Harbor precipitated war between the United States and the Axis powers, Japanese, German, and Italian nationals were, alike, declared to be "alien enemies" in Presidential proclamations of December 7 and 8, 1941. Alien

---

[118] J. F. Steiner, *Behind the Japanese Mask*. New York, The Macmillan Company, 1943, p. 61.

[119] Strong, Bell *et al., op. cit.,* pp. 81–113, 174–177, *passim.*

[120] This section is based primarily on D. S. Thomas and R. Nishimoto, *The Spoilage,* University of California Press, 1946. Parts of this summary were published in D. S. Thomas, "Some Social Aspects of Japanese-American Demography," *Proceedings of the American Philosophical Society,* October, 1950, pp. 459–480.

enemies were forbidden to possess contraband, their traveling was restricted, their bank accounts were frozen, and their business enterprises were closed. Some were apprehended on suspicion and held in detention by the FBI. It was announced that all alien enemies might be excluded from military zones.

Because large numbers of German and Italian immigrants had become naturalized, the incidence of the application of these early restrictions was greatest in the Japanese immigrant communities, and, for Issei, the dormant threat to their security of "ineligibility to citizenship" was again revived. Furthermore, there were disturbing indications that the status of Nisei as descendants of the Japanese enemy might take precedence over their status as American citizens. Thus restrictions on travel referred to "Japanese individuals" and were applied indiscriminately to alien enemies and to American citizens of Japanese ancestry. In some instances, similar interpretations were made in respect to assets. Citizens as well as aliens were stopped on the highways, summarily arrested, and held for questioning.

By the end of the second week of the war a number of the restrictions on alien enemies had been relaxed, and many of the misunderstandings regarding Nisei seemed to have been cleared up. In some cases, funds were released, business enterprises were allowed to reopen, and necessary travel was permitted. Federal and local officials, educators, clergymen, other prominent citizens, and most of the West Coast newspapers pleaded for tolerance, for the protection of "loyal Japanese" and of "loyal alien enemies" generally, and they emphasized the citizenship rights of Nisei, their record of service in the armed forces, their participation in civilian defense.

In Japanese American families and communities, there was extensive realignment of leadership and control, since the early FBI arrests had been highly selective of Issei business, religious, and community leaders. Included among those apprehended were officers of the Japanese Association, all Shinto and some Buddhist priests, many newspaper owners and editors, and most Japanese language schoolteachers. Although relatively few families[121] were directly affected by these arrests, the secret nature of the procedures, delay in instituting hearings, local variations in the categories under suspicion, and vagueness about the nature of the categories themselves aroused widespread fear, and stimulated the spread of rumors. In anticipation of further and more severe restrictions on their activities, Issei businessmen and householders made hasty efforts to transfer their remaining liquid assets to citizen-children or friends, and though divisive forces within the Japanese community precluded unanimity, the Japanese American Citizens League assumed the role of spokesman for the whole Japanese minority.

By the end of January, 1942, our serious reverses in the Pacific area made the West Coast seem increasingly vulnerable to attack or possible invasion. Reports (later shown to have no basis in fact) that Japanese American residents had formed a fifth column in Hawaii, given aid and comfort to the enemy, and sabotaged the American defense of Pearl Harbor, were widely circulated[122] and gave rise to fears of similar activities among Japanese Americans on the West Coast. There was a renewed wave of boycotts and discriminatory acts.[123] On January 28, for example, the Cali-

---

[121] *Bulletin 12* of the Western Defense Command and Fourth Army, p. 145, San Francisco, March 15, 1943, gives approximately 30,000 families as the number evacuated from the Pacific Coast, 28 per cent of them being "one-person families," and, according to press releases of the Department of Justice of December 8 and 13, 1941, and February 16, 1942, a total of 2,192 Japanese aliens were placed under arrest in the United States, 1,266 of them from the Pacific Coast. Thus, it would seem likely that not more than 1 in every 15 or 20 families had had some member arrested during this period.

[122] According to Lind, rumors of sabotage were formally denied in the daily newspapers of Hawaii on December 25, January 5, and February 21, and "the state of high excitability and the accompanying susceptibility to rumors soon subsided in the larger Hawaiian community." When the same, and other, rumors of sabotage and fifth-column activities in Hawaii led to official charges and investigations on the mainland, their basis was categorically denied by the Police Chief of Honolulu, by Secretary of War Stimson, and by J. Edgar Hoover of the FBI in March and April, 1942. In May, 1942, Colonel K. J. Fielder, who was in charge of military intelligence in Hawaii, emphasized the repeated denials that had been made "by all authorities" and restated the fact that "there have been no known acts of sabotage, espionage, or fifth-column activities committed by the Japanese in Hawaii either on or subsequent to December 7, 1941." (Quotations and citations from Lind, *op. cit.*, pp. 42–46.)

[123] For a few weeks, Japanese communities were terrorized by Filipinos. Among the incidents attributed to Filipinos by *Nichi-Bei* and other California newspapers

fornia State Personnel Board voted unanimously to bar from future civil service positions all "descendants of nationals with whom the United States [was] at war,"[124] but the restriction was applied only to descendants of the Japanese enemy. Demands for evacuation and internment found increasingly frequent expression. Public fears, organized pressures, and further reverses in the Pacific widened the belief that the West Coast was in imminent danger. And on February 19, the evacuation of the whole of the Japanese American population from the West Coast received national sanction when President Roosevelt signed Executive Order 9066.

Executive Order 9066 authorized delimitation of Military areas "from which any or all persons [might] be excluded." The Commanding General of the Western Defense Command, John L. DeWitt, who was made responsible for implementing the executive order, had already recommended "evacuation of Japanese and other subversive persons from the Pacific Coast," and had specified that "the word 'Japanese' included alien Japanese and American citizens of Japanese ancestry."[125] In later proclamations and directives, General DeWitt referred to American citizens of Japanese ancestry euphemistically, as "American-born persons of Japanese lineage," or as "nonalien persons of Japanese ancestry,"[126] and in the *Final Report of the Western Defense Command* defined "Nisei" as "any person of Japanese ancestry not

---

(cited by Tamotsu Shibutani in an unpublished manuscript prepared for the Evacuation and Resettlement Study) were the following: A 31-year old Nisei was stabbed to death on the sidewalks of Los Angeles on December 23; on Christmas day, in Stockton, gangs broke the windows of numerous business houses, manhandled numerous Japanese, and killed a garage attendant. On December 29, a 57-year old alien was shot in Sacramento. On January 3, fifty shots were fired into a Gilroy home, and two Japanese were seriously wounded. The same night an elderly couple were slain in their bed in El Centro. On January 9, a young San Jose Nisei mother was shot in a night attack; and on January 15, another Japanese was knifed in Stockton. State and local officials responded promptly to this "reign of terror," and set up heavy patrols wherever Japanese were congregated, and picked up and disarmed numbers of Filipinos.

[124] Minutes of the Meeting of the California State Personnel Board, January 27 and 28, 1942.

[125] U.S. Army, Western Defense Command and Fourth Army, *Final Report: Japanese Evacuation from the West Coast, 1942* (Washington, 1943), p. 26 and pp. 33–38.

[126] See, for example, fig. 1, p. 82.

WESTERN DEFENSE COMMAND AND FOURTH ARMY
WARTIME CIVIL CONTROL ADMINISTRATION
Presidio of San Francisco, California
April 1, 1942

INSTRUCTIONS
TO ALL PERSONS OF
JAPANESE
ANCESTRY
Living in the Following Area:

All of San Diego County, California, south of a line extending in an easterly direction from the mouth of the San Dieguito River (northwest of Del Mar), along the north side of the San Dieguito River, Lake Hodges, and the San Pasqual River to the bridge over the San Pasqual River at or near San Pasqual; thence easterly along the southerly line of California State Highway No. 78 through Ramona and Julian to the eastern boundary line of San Diego County.

All Japanese persons, both alien and non-alien, will be evacuated from the above designated area by 12:00 o'clock noon Wednesday, April 8, 1942.

No Japanese person will be permitted to enter or leave the above described area after 8:00 a. m., Thursday, April 2, 1942, without obtaining special permission from the Provost Marshal at the Civil Control Station located at:

1919 India Street
San Diego, California

The Civil Control Station is equipped to assist the Japanese population affected by this evacuation in the following ways:

1. Give advice and instructions on the evacuation.
2. Provide services with respect to the management, leasing, sale, storage or other disposition of most kinds of property including: real estate, business and professional equipment, buildings, household goods, boats, automobiles, livestock, etc.
3. Provide temporary residence elsewhere for all Japanese in family groups.
4. Transport persons and a limited amount of clothing and equipment to their new residence, as specified below.

The Following Instructions Must Be Observed:

1. A responsible member of each family, preferably the head of the family, or the person in whose name most of the property is held, and each individual living alone, will report to the Civil Control Station to receive further instructions. This must be done between 8:00 a. m. and 5:00 p. m., Thursday, April 2, 1942, or between 8:00 a. m. and 5:00 p. m., Friday, April 3, 1942.

2. Evacuees must carry with them on departure for the Reception Center, the following property:
(a) Bedding and linens (no mattress) for each member of the family;
(b) Toilet articles for each member of the family;
(c) Extra clothing for each member of the family;
(d) Sufficient knives, forks, spoons, plates, bowls and cups for each member of the family;
(e) Essential personal effects for each member of the family.

All items carried will be securely packaged, tied and plainly marked with the name of the owner and numbered in accordance with instructions received at the Civil Control Station.

The size and number of packages is limited to that which can be carried by the individual or family group.

No contraband items as described in paragraph 6, Public Proclamation No. 3, Headquarters Western Defense Command and Fourth Army, dated March 24, 1942, will be carried.

3. The United States Government through its agencies will provide for the storage at the sole risk of the owner of the more substantial household items, such as iceboxes, washing machines, pianos and other heavy furniture. Cooking utensils and other small items will be accepted if crated, packed and plainly marked with the name and address of the owner. Only one name and address will be used by a given family.

4. Each family, and individual living alone, will be furnished transportation to the Reception Center. Private means of transportation will not be utilized. All instructions pertaining to the movement will be obtained at the Civil Control Station.

Go to the Civil Control Station at 1919 India Street, San Diego, California, between 8:00 a. m. and 5:00 p. m., Thursday, April 2, 1942, or between 8:00 a. m. and 5:00 p. m., Friday, April 3, 1942, to receive further instructions.

J. L. DeWITT
Lieutenant General, U. S. Army
Commanding

SEE CIVILIAN EXCLUSION ORDER NO. 4

Figure 1. Public notice accompanying Civilian Exclusion Order No. 4

born in Japan," and clarified the meaning of "Japanese ancestry" to cover "any person who has a Japanese ancestor, regardless of degree."[127]

Verbal disregard for and devaluation of the American citizenship of American-born Japanese had its counterpart in the actions initiated and carried through by the Western Defense Command. On March 2 General DeWitt designated the western third of Washington and Oregon, the western half of California, and the southern quarter of Arizona as Military Area No. 1, and on the following day announced that "subversive persons" were being "apprehended daily," and that a gradual program of exclusion from the area would be applied to the following four classes in order: Japanese aliens, American-born persons of Japanese lineage, German aliens, and Italian aliens.[128] No mass action was ever taken against Germans and Italians.

The Western Defense Command planned to clear Military Area No. 1 of all "potential enemies."[129] Deadlines had to be met, but evacuation was to be accomplished voluntarily by the persons or groups covered by successive exclusion orders, with assistance where necessary, from a newly formed operating agency of the Command, the Wartime Civil Control Administration, and with free choice of destination outside the exclusion areas. By the middle of March, however, it became apparent that voluntary evacuation was not workable. Hostility had developed in the eastern counties of California and in the intermountain states, to which some 9,000 evacuees had moved. As explained in the Command's *Final Report,* "This group, considered too dangerous to remain on the West Coast, was similarly regarded by state and local authorities and by the population of the interior. The evacuees were not welcome. Incidents developed with

---

[127] U.S. Army, *op. cit.,* p. 514.

[128] Western Defense Command and Fourth Army, Press Release, March 3, 1942.

[129] In General DeWitt's "Final Recommendation . . . to the Secretary of War" of February 14, 1942, it was stated: "In the war in which we are now engaged racial affinities are not severed by migration. The Japanese race is an enemy race and while many second and third generation Japanese born on United States soil, possessed of United States citizenship, have become 'Americanized,' the racial strains are undiluted. . . . It, therefore, follows that along the vital Pacific Coast over 112,000 potential enemies, of Japanese extraction, are at large today." (U.S. Army, *op. cit.,* p. 34.)

increasing intensity."[130] Plans for voluntary evacuation and free
selection of destinations were scrapped in favor of an *ad hoc*
procedure for controlled mass evacuation and detention. To
implement this procedure, Public Proclamation No. 4, issued
on March 27, forbade change of residence by persons of Japanese ancestry who were living in Military Area No. 1. On June
2 a similar regulation was issued, covering the eastern half of
California—an area which was until then called the Free Zone
and was the officially sanctioned destination of about half of all
those who had been able to accomplish voluntary evacuation.
By August 8 controlled evacuation of the whole of California,
and of those parts of Washington, Oregon, and Arizona that
lay within Military Area No. 1, had been completed in a series
of moves, each move being covered by a specific exclusion order
and announced in posters displayed prominently throughout
the area concerned. (See figure 1 for an example.) Approximately 90,000 persons entered assembly centers[131] which had been

[130] *Ibid.*, p. 43.

[131] The following list of assembly centers indicates location, peak population,
and period of occupancy during 1942:

Center	Location	Date first evacuee arrived	Date last resident departed	Days of operation	Maximum population
Fresno	Calif.	5–6	10–30	178	5,120
Manzanar	Calif.	3–21	5–31	72	9,666
Marysville	Calif.	5–8	6–29	53	2,451
Mayer	Ariz.	5–7	6–2	27	245
Merced	Calif.	5–6	9–15	133	4,508
Pinedale	Calif.	5–7	7–23	78	4,792
Pomona	Calif.	5–7	8–24	110	5,434
Portland	Ore.	5–2	9–10	132	3,676
Puyallup	Wash.	4–28	9–12	137	7,390
Sacramento	Calif.	5–6	6–26	52	4,739
Salinas	Calif.	4–27	7–4	69	3,594
Santa Anita	Calif.	3–27	10–27	215	18,719
Stockton	Calif.	5–10	10–17	161	4,271
Tanforan	Calif.	4–28	10–13	169	7,816
Tulare	Calif.	4–20	9–4	138	4,978
Turlock	Calif.	4–30	8–12	105	3,662

(Adapted from U.S. Army, *op. cit.*, p. 227.)

Manzanar was originally intended for use as a "reception center." It was constructed
on land leased from the City of Los Angeles, which had formerly been occupied
by "ranches and farms [but had] reverted to desert conditions." (*Ibid.*, p. 263.) It
was transformed into a War Relocation Authority project on June 1, 1942. Regarding the other sites, Mayer was "an abandoned Civilian Conservation Corps camp."
Portland utilized "the Pacific International Live Stock Exposition facilities"; Pine-
dale, "the facilities remaining on a former mill site"; and Sacramento, an area
"where a migrant camp had once operated." All of the others utilized "large fair-
grounds or race tracks." (*Ibid.*, p. 151.)

hastily constructed by the Army on near-by race tracks and fair grounds for a "transitory phase" of detention, preliminary to another controlled mass migration and further enforced detention. Surrounded by barbed wire, flanked by watchtowers, and guarded by military police, the 16 assembly centers were in operation from a minimum of 27 to a maximum of 215 days. The largest center, at the Santa Anita race track, had the longest period of occupancy, and its population reached a maximum of more than 18,000, with a daily average of 13,000. Here as in other assembly centers, life in hastily constructed barracks and converted horse stalls presented many difficulties, and as the *Final Report* states: "For extended occupancy by men, women, and children whose movements were necessarily restricted, the use of facilities of this character [was] not highly desirable."[132]

The second controlled migration of the assembly centers' population of 90,000 to more extensive camps, administered by the War Relocation Authority, was completed by November, 1942. There they joined some 20,000 other evacuees who had been moved directly from their homes to these "relocation projects" during the summer.

The swiftness with which evacuation was accomplished rendered plans for the protection of evacuee property ineffective. Governmental responsibility was divided between the Farm Security Administration and the Federal Reserve Bank. The aims of the former were to insure continuation of farm production for the war effort and to protect the evacuated farmer from unfair and inequitable transfer. The two ends were frequently incompatible, and under the circumstances, the former took precedence. According to the Tolan Congressional Committee, "the exhortations of the Wartime Civil Control Administration to the evacuees to continue farming operations up to the time of evacuation as a demonstration of loyalty . . . [has] frequently worked to the economic disadvantage of the evacuees or [has] proved beyond their economic means to carry out,"[133] and the Western Defense Command's *Final Report,* pointed out that

---

[132] *Ibid.,* p. 152.

[133] U.S. Congress, House, *National Defense Migration,* Fourth Interim Report, *op. cit.,* p. 15.

"landlords, creditors, and prospective purchasers were ready to take advantage . . . of the adverse bargaining position of Japanese evacuees, even at the cost of serious loss of agricultural production."[134] The Federal Reserve Bank, which had been given responsibility for safeguarding nonagricultural property, undertook a policy of encouraging liquidation, accepted property for storage only "at the sole risk" of the owner, provided no insurance, and disclaimed liability "for any act or omission in connection with [the property's] disposition."[135] Under these conditions virtually all evacuees suffered heavy losses of tangible assets, and for many engaged in activities and enterprises which could not be transferred or sold, losses incurred through abandonment of intangible assets may have been even greater.[136]

Evacuation was a policy proposed by the Western Defense Command, accepted by the War Department, and sanctioned by the President of the United States. Detention of the whole of the West Coast racial minority in war-duration concentration camps was a policy proposed by no responsible agency, nor was any attempt ever made to justify it officially as a matter of "military necessity"—the basis on which the Command had justified total evacuation.[137] Detention was to be considered "protective custody," which seemed, at the time, the only way out of the dilemma posed by total evacuation, when most of the persons

---

[134] U.S. Army, *op. cit.*, p. 138.

[135] Wartime Civil Control Administration, Personal Property Form FRB-2.

[136] For a retrospective account of losses to evacuees in the Los Angeles area, and for a penetrating analysis of an evacuee claims bill (Public Law 886), passed by the 80th Congress, see L. Bloom and R. Riemer, *Removal and Return*, University of California Press, 1949. In regard to the claims bill, Bloom and Riemer pointed out as of 1949 that "claims are restricted 'to damage to or loss of real or personal property [with an upper limit of $2,500] . . . that is a reasonable and natural consequence of the evacuation . . .' and must be filed within eighteen months of the date of enactment. . . . [Among other exclusions are] damages on account of 'death or personal injury, personal inconvenience, physical hardship, or mental suffering.' . . . The most serious limitation is the exclusion of claims for 'loss of anticipated profits or loss of anticipated earnings.' . . . *If narrowly interpreted,* the law will . . . provide an additional and fatal obstacle to the presentation and processing. A large proportion of the population can do no more than assert that they owned property that was lost, and are in no position to provide legally rigorous documentation." (*Ibid.,* pp. 198–199.)

[137] U.S. Army, *op. cit.*, pp. 7–38. Among the justifications cited by the Command-

ordered to evacuate were physically, emotionally, economically, culturally, and demographically incapable of finding jobs and homes in other areas, and when the few thousand who had managed to accomplish voluntary evacuation were being met by hostility or suspicion in the receiving areas. Detention as a "transitory phase" between evacuation and resettlement was, under these circumstances, recommended or accepted by all agencies concerned,[138] including the socially oriented Federal Security Agency and War Relocation Authority and the ethnocentric Japanese American Citizens League.

Once detention became a reality, however, it ceased to be viewed by the Army as a "transitory phase," and the War Relocation Authority's program was soon perverted from resettling displaced people to planning a way-of-life for them within the confines of barbed wire. Even before most of the relocation projects were ready for occupancy, WRA had formulated tentative plans designed to assure evacuees, "for the duration of the war and as nearly as wartime exigencies permit, an equitable substitute for the life, work, and homes given up."[139] And in June, 1942, the director reported to President Roosevelt that "a genuinely satisfactory relocation of the evacuees into American life" would have to wait until the end of the war "when the prevailing [popular] attitudes of increasing bitterness have been replaced by tolerance and understanding."[140]

ing General in February, 1942, was "the very fact that no sabotage has taken place to date," as being "a disturbing and confirming indication that such action will be taken." (*Ibid.*, p. 34.) But, in Hawaii, although "the top-ranking military authorities were not unaware of the mainland precedent nor insensible to the logical arguments and the pressures in support of wholesale evacuation . . . the policy consistently followed . . . was to assume the essential loyalty of those whose lives had been largely spent under the influence of American institutions and culture." There was no mass evacuation, and "despite the utmost diligence and application to duty by the constituted authorities . . . the total number of Japanese actually held on suspicion during the entire period of the war was only 1,440; and the number actually interned and sent to camps on the mainland was 981, or about 1 per cent of the adult Japanese population of Hawaii." (Lind, *op. cit.*, pp. 72–73.)

[138] See U.S. Army, op. cit., pp. 105–106.
[139] War Relocation Authority, *Tentative Policy Statement* (mimeographed), May 29, 1942.
[140] M. S. Eisenhower to President Roosevelt (letter), June 18, 1942.

During the spring and summer, ten relocation projects[141] had been selected: five in windswept areas on the California-Oregon border and in Idaho, Wyoming, Utah, and Colorado; three surrounded by the deserts of Arizona and southeastern California; two on the swamplands of Arkansas. The California and Arizona projects, which were in Military Area No. 1, were as thoroughly guarded and as tightly enclosed by barbed wire as had been the assembly centers. But at the other projects, though they, too, were designated as military areas from which unauthorized departure could be penalized[142] as prescribed in Public Law 503, the military paraphernalia of barbed wire, watchtowers, and guards were kept at a minimum and soon had only a symbolic significance.

Each project had communal mess halls and utility building, canteens organized as consumers' coöperatives, and schoolrooms. Living quarters were in barracks, arranged in blocks around wide firebreaks. Families or groups of unrelated individuals were assigned apartments, consisting usually of a single room, 20 by 25 or 16 by 20 feet in dimension, "with bare boards, knotholes through the floor and into the next apartment, heaps of dust,

[141] The following list of relocation centers (known also as "camps" or "projects") indicates location, peak population, and period of occupancy from 1942 to 1946:

Center	Location	Date first evacuee arrived	Date last resident departed	Days of operation	Maximum population
Central Utah[a]	Utah	9–11–42	10–31–45	1,147	8,130
Colorado River[b]	Ariz.	5– 8–42	11–28–45	1,301	17,814
Gila River[c]	Ariz.	7–20–42	11–10–45	1,210	13,348
Granada	Colo.	8–27–42	10–15–45	1,146	7,318
Heart Mountain	Wyo.	8–12–42	11–10–45	1,187	10,767
Jerome[d]	Ark.	10–6–42	6–30–44	634	8,497
Manzanar[e]	Calif.	6– 1–42	11–21–45	1,270	10,046
Minidoka	Idaho	8–10–42	10–28–45	1,176	9,397
Rohwer	Ark.	9–18–42	11–30–45	1,170	8.475
Tule Lake[f]	Calif.	5–27–42	3–20–46	1,394	18,789

Adapted from *The Evacuated People*, U.S. Department of the Interior, *op. cit.*, p. 17.
[a] Known also as Topaz.
[b] Known also as Poston; this center comprised three separate units (Camps I, II, and III).
[c] This center comprised two separate units (Canal and Butte camps).
[d] Closed on June 30, 1944; residual population transferred to other centers.
[e] Operated first by WCCA as an assembly center; transferred to WRA on June 1, 1942.
[f] Became a segregation center in September, 1943.

Source: Relocation centers varied in size from 6,000 acres at Manzanar to 72,000 acres at Poston. With the exception of parts of Tule Lake, Gila River, and Granada, they were located on undeveloped lands, where soil or water conditions were deterring factors for agricultural production. (War Relocation Authority, *First Quarterly Report*, pp. 8–12.)

[142] U.S. Army, *op. cit.*, pp. 30–31.

and for each person an army cot, a blanket and a sack which [could be] filled with straw to make a mattress. There [was] nothing else. No shelves, closets, chairs, tables, or screens. In this space, 5 to 7 people, and, in a few cases, 8, men, women, and their children [were] to live indefinitely."[143]

In spite of physical hardships the evacuees were, in the beginning, almost uniformly coöperative and helpful and seemed to share the belief prevalent among WRA officials and employees that a "good life" could be built up in these isolated, war-duration communities. But, before many weeks passed, latent antiadministration and intragroup hostilities flared into the open. Faith in the good intentions of the administration declined when procurement difficulties arose, and shortages of food, of hospital supplies, and of other essentials developed; when promises of producers' coöperatives, under which cash advances on profits were to be distributed to the participating evacuees, were abandoned in favor of "miserably low"[144] remuneration of $12, $16, and $19 per month for jobs ranging from farm labor, cooking, and dishwashing to those of teacher, attorney, and doctor;[145] when payment of even these wages was delayed; when, during the prolonged period of nonpayment, timekeeping systems were introduced by efficiency experts; and when a plan for limited self-government was imposed, which, though enfranchising Issei, made them ineligible for officeholding.

Regional and generational fissures, temporarily closed during the stress of evacuation, were reopened. Rumors of FBI inquiries

---

[143] A. S. Leighton, The Governing of Men, Princeton University Press, 1945, pp. 65–66.

[144] M. S. Eisenhower to Budget Director Smith (letter), May 11, 1942.

[145] As expressed in one of WRA's reports (Impounded People, United States Department of the Interior, War Relocation Authority, Washington, 1946, p. 51): "By June it was clear that so long as one was an evacuee he could get no more than $19 a month, whether he was a doctor in the hospital or a laborer on the farm. At the same time it was clear that white-skinned doctors and laborers beside whom evacuees worked were getting regular wages for what they did. Moreover, in every job an evacuee found himself supervised ultimately by someone not an evacuee. Only the lowest level of supervisory jobs could be occupied by anyone of Japanese ancestry, regardless of competency or experience." The situation was further complicated at Gila when, for some months after its inception, a camouflage-net project was operated at the camp, under Army contract, and evacuee workers in this project were paid "regular wages"; and at both Gila and Poston, when evacuees were permitted to pick cotton on near-by ranches, again at "regular wages."

and arrests aroused suspicions that fellow evacuees were informing the administration about such "harmless" misdemeanors as
listening to shortwave radios, gambling, or promoting "nationalistic" forms of Japanese entertainment. Coöperation with the
administration was soon branded as "collaboration." Every fac-
tion found its convenient scapegoat. In the Tule Lake project
on the California-Oregon border, evacuees from California
blamed the more accommodated evacuees from the Pacific Northwest. In all projects, leaders and active members of the Japanese
American Citizens League, which had been officially accepted
by governmental agencies as a liaison group during evacuation
and assembly-center days, were accused now of having betrayed
the whole Japanese minority. They, in turn, often showed marked
readiness to denounce "hotheaded Kibei" or "Issei agitators"
as the source of all trouble. Mainland Nisei, in some instances,
cast doubt upon the loyalty of Hawaiian Nisei. Christians were
suspicious of Buddhists. Suspected informers called *inu* (literally
"dogs"), were ostracized, threatened, and even beaten by their
fellow evacuees. Revolt against the administration took the form
of major strikes or minor work stoppages during the fall of 1942,
and in two camps, Poston and Manzanar, revolt assumed the
proportions of riots. In the latter, martial law was declared, and
a machine-gunner fired upon the evacuees, killing one and
wounding several others. Alleged agitators were removed to jail
or isolation camps, and a number of JACL leaders and other
"collaborators" were hastily withdrawn from the project and
resettled in the Middle West.

Meantime the War Relocation Authority under a new director
who took office in June, 1942, was pressing the Justice and War
Departments for sanction to reinstitute the program its name
implied. Under existing regulations, relocation—in the sense
of outmigration for permanent resettlement—was almost impossible to achieve. Several nongovernmental organizations, notably
the American Friends Service Committee, were working against
great odds on the problem of student relocation, and under their
auspices "some young people were permitted to leave the coastal
area [assembly centers or relocation projects] for the purpose of

continuing college and university studies." A few other individuals had "under special circumstances" been given permits to join relatives east of the restricted areas. With army approval, about 1,500 workers had been recruited for seasonal labor in the beet fields of the intermountain states under "standard agreements" designed to protect the evacuees. The range of movement of these seasonal workers was, in general, restricted to a single county, and they were required to return to camp at the expiration of their contracts. On July 20 the first general leave regulations for permanent relocation were issued, permitting "American-born evacuees who had never lived or studied in Japan . . . to apply for leave," but such leaves were granted only to applicants who had definite offers of employment outside the area under jurisdiction of the Western Defense Command, and among the other prerequisites to clearance were formal investigations of "loyalty," detailed reports of behavior and attitudes in camp, agreements to provide for the care of dependents remaining in camp, and evidence of acceptability in the proposed community of destination.[146]

By the time the fall semester opened, about 250 students had been granted permits to enter educational institutions, and by the middle of October "approximately 10,000 evacuees were scattered through the Western states helping in the harvest work." But the procedures for obtaining release for resettlement were so unwieldy that not even a moderate number of evacuees were relocated during 1942. (See Chart XIX, p. 114, below.) With the exception of "approximately 750 persons who left assembly and relocation centers on seasonal leave [and] did not return to the center," the movement before October 1 comprised "fewer than 273 evacuees (including students)," and by the end of the year, though "2,200 applications for advance clearance had been filed . . . only 250 applications for indefinite leave had been granted and only 866 evacuees [presumably again including students] had actually left the centers."[147]

[146] United States, Department of the Interior, War Relocation Authority, *The Relocation Program*, Washington, 1946, pp. 10–17, *passim*.

[147] *Ibid.*, pp. 12–18, *passim*.

Hoping to expedite resettlement, WRA officials coöperated with the War Department on a plan for "mass clearance" after Secretary Stimson announced on January 28, 1943, "that the War Department would create an all-Nisei combat team composed of volunteers from relocation centers in the United States and from Hawaii."[148] To implement this plan, representatives of the War Department visited each of the WRA camps during February and early March to "process" all male citizens, while WRA personnel, during the same period, "processed" all other evacuees who were 17 years of age or older. In both cases processing involved registration and the execution of a lengthy questionnaire. Included among some thirty items, questions 27 and 28 were designed to test "loyalty." For male citizens, question 27 read:

Are you willing to serve in the armed forces of the United States on combat duty, wherever ordered?

and question 28:

Will you swear unqualified allegiance to the United States of America and faithfully defend the United States from any or all attack by foreign or domestic forces, and forswear any form of allegiance or obedience to the Japanese emperor, or any other foreign government, power, or organization?

For female citizens, question 27 was modified to ask whether they would be willing to volunteer for the Army Nurse Corps or the Women's Army Corps if found qualified, and question 28 omitted reference to defense against armed attack. The form for female citizens was, however, used initially for aliens of both sexes, without further modification, except that it was headed "Application for Leave Clearance."[149]

---

[148] *Ibid.*, p. 22.

Most of the Nisei and Kibei who had been inducted into the Army before December 7, 1941, had been given honorable discharges after the war began. In March, 1942, potential inductees of Japanese ancestry were arbitrarily assigned to class IV-F, the category reserved for persons ineligible for service because of physical defects. On September 1, 1942, their classification was, in most instances, changed to IV-C, the category ordinarily used for "alien enemies."

[149] War Relocation Authority, *Administrative Instruction No. 22* (Revised), Supplement 3, Jan. 30, 1943. The Selective Service Form was DSS Form 304a; the abbreviated form for leave clearance, WRA Form 126a.

The impropriety of asking aliens who were ineligible to American citizenship to forswear allegiance to the only country in which they could hold citizenship was recognized belatedly. In most projects aliens were permitted to substitute for the second of the above questions an oath that they would "abide by the laws of the United States" and "take no action which would in any way interfere with the war effort of the United States." But American citizens of Japanese ancestry, the bulk of whom were Nisei who had had no direct contact with Japan, were still required to forswear allegiance to the Japanese Emperor.

Registration[150] was postulated on the assumption that evacuees would define eligibility to serve in the armed service or to leave camps for the freedom of the "outside world" as just rewards for loyalty. Contrary to expectation, an appreciable proportion of the evacuees defined these situations as penalties rather than as rewards. A strong protest movement developed among Nisei and Kibei, who, having had many of their rights as citizens abrogated through evacuation and detention, questioned the justice of the restoration of the single right of serving in the armed forces. Numbers of Issei, having lost most of their other possessions, used every means to hold their families intact and to prevent the possible induction of their sons. Others, having acceded to a forced migration from home to camp, were now determined to avoid a further move to an outside world that they had many reasons to believe would continue to regard them with hostility.

Doubt, fear, and anger accompanied registration in all ten projects, and these reactions were aggravated by inadequate preparation of the teams conducting registration; by sudden, unexplained, or incompletely understood changes in administrative procedures and definitions; and in one camp, Tule Lake, by the use of force. In all projects except Tule Lake, the average proportion of the adult population refusing to register or giving negative answers to the "loyalty questions" was 10 per cent, but in Tule Lake the unregistered and the verbally disloyal together

---

[150] The administrative determination of "loyalty" and "disloyalty" by means of the registration questionnaire, and its repercussions, are discussed in detail in chaps. iii and iv of *The Spoilage*, (Thomas and Nishimoto, *op. cit.*)

comprised 42 per cent of all persons 17 years of age or older. The persistence of a collective movement of noncoöperation at Tule Lake was widely publicized, and its residents were stigmatized in the press and on the radio as politically disloyal. In July, 1943, the Senate passed a resolution asking WRA to segregate "persons of Japanese ancestry in relocation centers whose loyalty to the United States is questionable or who are known to be disloyal."[151] Tule Lake was designated as a segregation center in which evacuees whose loyalties were thought to lie with Japan would be confined for the duration of the war.

During the late summer Tule Lake was transformed, physically, from a relocation project to a segregation center. A double "manproof" fence, eight-feet high, was constructed around the whole area; the external guard was increased from a couple of hundred soldiers to full battalion strength; and a half dozen tanks, obsolete but impressive, were lined up in full view of the residents. At the same time, renewed efforts were made to screen the "disloyal" from the "loyal" in all projects. The criteria for segregation, as finally accepted, were the following: applicants for repatriation or expatriation to Japan; persons persisting in the negative answers they had given at time of registration or still refusing to register; persons about whom there was "other information . . . indicating loyalty to Japan";[152] and persons who, falling in none of these categories, wished to be segregated along with a "disloyal" member of the immediate family.

Official pronouncements emphasized that "disloyalty" was not culpable; and that segregation was "not being undertaken in any sense as a measure of punishment or penalty."[153] The privilege of leave-clearance would be denied, but otherwise the center would be run in much the same way as the relocation projects to which the evacuees had become accustomed. However, having indicated their desire to follow the Japanese way of life, evacuees would not be required to send their children to the American

---

[151] 78th Cong., 1st sess., S. Res. 166.
[152] War Relocation Authority, *Administrative Instruction No. 100*, July 15, 1943.
[153] War Relocation Authority, *Segregation of Persons of Japanese Ancestry in Tule Lake Center* (pamphlet), August, 1943.

schools in the center, and they were to be permitted to establish at their own expense Japanese language schools. In other spheres, too, bans on "Japanese" activities were to be removed or restrictions moderated.

Beginning in September trainloads of "disloyal" evacuees were moved from the nine other projects to Tule Lake, and over 6,000 "loyal" Tuleans left for other projects. When the movement was completed in May, 1944, Tule Lake had a population of more than 18,000, of whom 34 per cent were "Old Tuleans." Among these were more than 1,000 persons, themselves "disloyal" by none of the criteria set up by WRA and having no close relative who was "disloyal," but who simply refused to move. Among the transferees were hundreds of the technically "loyal" who had accompanied a "disloyal" relative, and among the Old Tuleans were other hundreds who had remained to avoid family separation, or who were too young to make decisions. Among the "disloyal" in both groups were many individuals who had so declared themselves to achieve war-duration security for their families.

From the short-run standpoint, the 18,000 men, women, and children who were segregated as "disloyal" represent the *spoilage,* as defined and documented in the Thomas-Nishimoto volume, *The Spoilage.*[154]

The extent to which *spoilage* was selective in terms of the evacuees' background and prewar experiences is suggested by the following analysis of the proportions of segregants in March, 1943, among subgroups in the population 17 years of age and older, of Tule Lake (cross-classified by prewar origin in California and the Northwest), of Poston (Camp I), and of Minidoka; with cross-classification for each of the four camp groups by sex, by religion (Buddhists and Christian-secularists), by prewar occupational class (agricultural and nonagricultural), and by generational-educational group (Issei, Kibei, Nisei) and is shown graphically in Charts XV to XVIII.

---

[154] See footnote 120, p. 78 above.

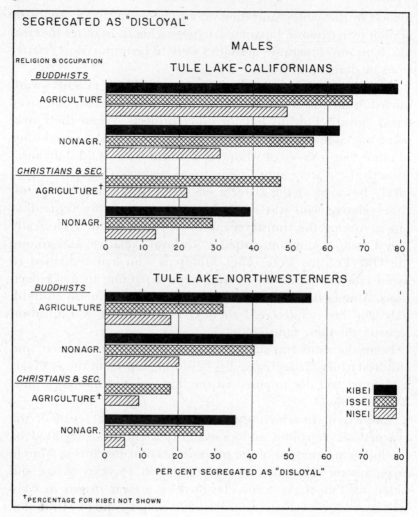

SEGREGATED AS "DISLOYAL"

MALES

RELIGION & OCCUPATION

TULE LAKE-CALIFORNIANS

BUDDHISTS

AGRICULTURE

NONAGR.

CHRISTIANS & SEC.

AGRICULTURE[†]

NONAGR.

TULE LAKE- NORTHWESTERNERS

BUDDHISTS

AGRICULTURE

NONAGR.

CHRISTIANS & SEC.

AGRICULTURE[†]

NONAGR.

PER CENT SEGREGATED AS "DISLOYAL"

KIBEI
ISSEI
NISEI

[†]PERCENTAGE FOR KIBEI NOT SHOWN

Chart XV. *Spoilage:* Percentage segregants among male evacuees, 17 years of age and older and resident in WRA camp at Tule Lake in March, 1943, by prewar origin in California or Northwest, prewar occupational class, religion, and generational-educational class. (See Appendix, table 28A.)

For each of the 4 camp groups there are 12 subgroups for each sex, namely:

(1) Issei
(2) Kibei } Buddhists from agricultural occupations
(3) Nisei

(4) Issei
(5) Kibei } Buddhists from nonagricultural occupations
(6) Nisei

(7) Issei
(8) Kibei } Christian-secularists from agricultural occupations
(9) Nisei

(10) Issei
(11) Kibei } Christian-secularists from nonagricultural occupations
(12) Nisei

These should yield a total of 96 subgroups for analysis of differentials (4 camp groups × 2 sexes × 12 combinations of the generational, religious, and occupational categories). Because of small numbers, however, subgroup (8) had to be omitted for both sexes in all 4 camp groups. The total number of subgroups available for analysis is, therefore, reduced to 88. Exclusion of male and of female "Kibei Christian-secularists from nonagricultural occupations" from the 4 camp groups reduces the number of intergroup comparisons as follows: each camp group can be compared with each of the other 3 in respect to 22 subgroups instead of the hypothetical 24, and the total number of intercamp comparisons is 3 × 22 or 66, instead of 72; each sex can be compared with the other in respect to 44 instead of the hypothetical maximum of 48; each religious group with the other in respect to 40 instead of 48; each occupational group with the other in respect to 40 instead of 48; each generational-educational group with the other 2 in 24 instead of the hypothetical maximum of 32, and the total number of possible generational-educational comparisons becomes 2 × 24 or 48 instead of 64.

If there were perfect consistency in the patterning of inter-

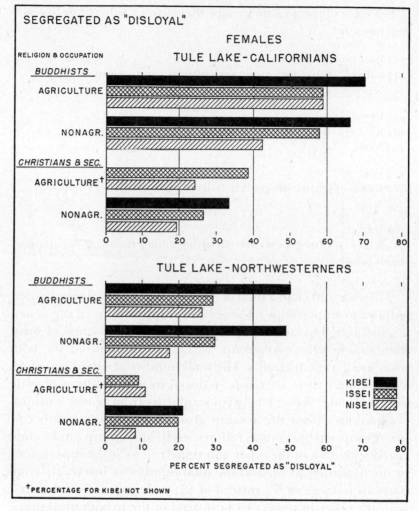

SEGREGATED AS "DISLOYAL"

FEMALES
TULE LAKE-CALIFORNIANS

RELIGION & OCCUPATION

BUDDHISTS

AGRICULTURE

NONAGR.

CHRISTIANS & SEC.

AGRICULTURE[†]

NONAGR.

TULE LAKE-NORTHWESTERNERS

BUDDHISTS

AGRICULTURE

NONAGR.

CHRISTIANS & SEC.

AGRICULTURE[†]

NONAGR.

KIBEI
ISSEI
NISEI

PER CENT SEGREGATED AS "DISLOYAL"

[†]PERCENTAGE FOR KIBEI NOT SHOWN

Chart XVI. *Spoilage:* Percentage of segregants among female evacuees, 17 years of age and older and resident in WRA camp at Tule Lake in March, 1943, by prewar origin in California or Northwest, prewar occupational class, religion, and generational-educational class. (See Appendix, table 28A.)

camp differentials, the camp with the highest over-all proportion in "disloyalty" would have a higher proportion "disloyal" in each of its 22 subgroups than would any of the other 3 camps for corresponding subgroups; the camp ranking second would, similarly, have higher proportions "disloyal" in each of its 22 subgroups than would corresponding subgroups in each of the camps ranking below it in over-all "disloyalty"; the camp ranking third would have higher proportions "disloyal" in each of its 22 subgroups than would the lowest ranking camp have in corresponding subgroups; and the camp ranking fourth would have no single subgroup out of its 22 available for comparison that had a higher proportion "disloyal" than the corresponding subgroup in any of the other three camp groups. If, then, each subgroup in each camp group is assigned a "score" of 3 if it exceeds the corresponding subgroup in 3 other camp groups, 2 if it exceeds that in 2 other camp groups, 1 if it exceeds that in 1 other camp group, and 0 if it exceeds that in no other camp group, "perfect consistency" will be indicated by a total score of 66 for the highest ranking camp group, 44 for the second in order, 22 for the third, and 0 for the lowest ranking camp group. By this criterion, Californians at Tule Lake should score 66, Northwesterners at Tule Lake 44, Postonians 22, and Minidokans 0. The actual scores, obtained as described above, were for the 4 camp groups in the order just specified, 66, 44, 20, and 2, representing a very close approximation indeed to "perfect consistency."

This means that Tule Lake's unfavorable "loyalty" differential persisted for all possible sex-religious-occupational-generational-educational segments of its two prewar regional groups, when compared with either Poston or Minidoka, where decisions had been formed less as a result of administrative factors and collective pressures than on the basis of community and familial influences and individual preferences. The proportions of the "disloyal" were always significantly and appreciably higher for Tuleans, whether they originated in California or in the Pacific Northwest, than for Postonians or Minidokans. In 20 out of 22 possible comparisons, the proportion of segregants among Postonians exceeded that among Minidokans, and since the former were predominantly from California and the latter's prewar residences were overwhelmingly in the Pacific Northwest, the pattern strongly suggests a significant regional differential. But this inference may be questioned because of the possibility of differences in intracamp tensions associated with differences in the administration of the registration program. Within Tule Lake, however, where the administrative factor may be assumed to have been relatively constant, Northwesterners had consistently lower proportions of the "disloyal" than did Californians, and these intracamp, regional differences were not only statisti-

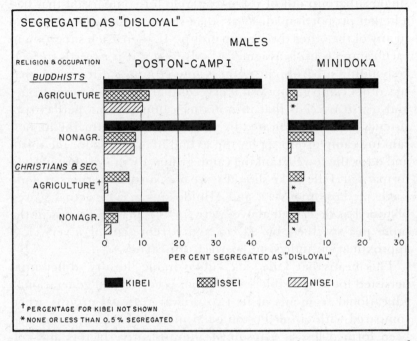

Chart XVII. *Spoilage:* Percentage of segregants among male evacuees, 17 years of age and older and resident in WRA Camp I at Poston and in WRA camp at Minidoka, by prewar occupational class, religion, and generational-educational class. (See Appendix, tables 28B and 28C.)

cally significant but, in most instances, very large. For example, within the most "disloyal" segment (male Kibei Buddhists with agricultural backgrounds), the proportion of segregants among Californians was 79 per cent compared with 56 per cent among the Northwesterners; and within the least "disloyal" segment (male Nisei Christians and secularists with nonagricultural backgrounds), the California proportion was 14 per cent compared with 6 per cent for the Northwesterners.

Patterns of religious, occupational, and sex differentials can be shown by holding occupation and sex constant in the first instance; religion and sex in the second; occupation and religion in the third; and in all three also holding camp group and generational-educational classes constant. The score will then be 40 for one religious or occupational class and 0 for the other, if the pattern of differentials is perfectly consistent; and 44 for one sex versus 0 for the other. The observed scores are 38 for Buddhists and 2 for Christian-secularists, in the religious comparisons; 26 for agriculturalists and 14 for nonagriculturalists in the occupational; 28 for males and 16 for females in the sex comparisons. The two exceptions to the pattern of higher proportions of the "disloyal" among Buddhists than among Christian-secularists were male Nisei agriculturalists in Minidoka, among whom there was no single instance of "disloyalty" for either religious category, and male Issei agriculturalists in the same camp, where segregants among Buddhists represented only 2.6 per cent compared with 4.3 per cent for Christian-secularists.

The exceptions to the pattern of a greater tendency to "disloyalty" among the agricultural than among the corresponding nonagricultural classes were limited to three of the four camp groups (Northwesterners at Tule Lake, Minidokans, and Postonians) and to two of the three generational-educational classes (Issei and Nisei). Thus, there were no exceptions among Kibei in any camp group, or in any subgroup whatsoever among Californians at Tule Lake. Where "disloyalty" in general reached its highest proportions, there was a sharpening of the agricultural-nonagricultural differential.

The three-way generational-educational comparison is made for the 48 subgroups available with camp, religion, occupation, and sex simultaneously held constant. A pattern of perfect consistency would then yield scores of 48, 24, and 0. The observed scores of 48 for Kibei, 21½ for Issei, and 2½ for Nisei therefore indicate an impressively consistent patterning of differentials among the generational-educational classes. If comparison is limited to Issei and Nisei (including agricultural Christian-secularists which had to be omitted from all comparisons involving Kibei), the Issei score is 28 and the Nisei 4, compared with a consistency standard of 32 and 0, and all 4 of the exceptions to the pattern are among female segments of the population.

The sharpness of the contrasts between the American-born, Japan-educated Kibei and the American-born, American-educated Nisei are strikingly demonstrated in the charts. The magnitude of the differences between the two second-generation groups is also demonstrated in the following examples, where Kibei groups having the first, sixth, twelfth, eighteenth, and twenty-fourth intragroup ranks on "disloyalty" are compared with Nisei:

SPOILAGE

PERCENTAGE OF SEGREGANTS AMONG SPECIFIED CLASSES OF EVACUEES

Classes of evacuees	Percentage of segregants (spoilage)	
	Kibei	Nisei
Male, Buddhist, agr., Tule Lake (Calif.)	78.9	49.2
Female, Buddhist, agr., Tule Lake (N.W.)	50.0	26.2
Female, Christian-sec., nonagr., Tule Lake (Calif.)	33.3	19.1
Male, Christian-sec., nonagr., Poston I	17.1	1.5
Female, Christian-sec., nonagr., Poston I	4.4	1.1

The ability of second-generation American-educated Japanese to maintain their orientation as Americans under the extraordinary pressures engendered by evacuation, detention, and registration was a function of many interrelated variables and attributes. In the terms in which we were able to define and measure it, orientation toward America was associated negatively with prewar isolation from the dominant American majority; positively with prewar situations predisposing toward minority acceptance, assimilation, or integration; negatively with residence in California, an occupational background in agriculture, adherence to Buddhism, and schooling in Japan; positively with residence in the Pacific Northwest, a nonagricultural or urban background, acceptance of Christianity or "no religion," and education in American schools.

The conflicts and tensions in Tule Lake after segregation, and the course of interaction between "disloyal" and "loyal," between groups of evacuees and administrative agencies, and among the various agencies themselves, are traced in the Thomas-Nishimoto volume, *The Spoilage:*[155] immediate revolt, led by disaffected transferees; an outbreak of violence following a labor dispute and two serious accidents; the importation by the administration of "loyal" harvesters from other projects as strikebreakers; the institution of martial law for two months; and the establishment of a "stockade" in which alleged agitators were confined for periods up to eight months "without the filing of charges or the granting of a hearing or trial of any kind."[156] During the period of martial law, evacuees maintained a general strike which they called "status quo." Abandonment of status quo was accomplished when a group led by Old Tuleans, prominent in the coöperative enterprises, acted as liaison between evacuees and administration. By the spring of 1944 an underground pressure group, in which Kibei were prominently represented, had come out into the open. Determined to pursue to the limit the Japanese way of life sanctioned in official pronouncements, they accused the administration of failure to "clarify the distinctions between the loyals and the disloyals" and insisted on a resegregation of the "truly disloyal" (namely, themselves), from the "loyal Americans" still in the center, whom they estimated at several thousand. Factionalism bred suspicion, persons thought to be informers were terrorized, there were numerous beatings, and the manager of the coöperative enterprises was murdered during a wave of *inu*-hatred. In July, 1944, the Nationality Act of 1940 was amended to permit the renunciation of citizenship during wartime by American citizens on American soil.[157] Renunciation then became the keynote of the resegregationist campaign, and two administrative decisions announced simultaneously on December 17, 1944, transformed general reluctance to accept the resegregationist program to popular support of its main issue.

[155] *Op. cit.*, chaps. v–xii.

[156] *American Civil Liberties Union-News,* San Francisco, August, 1944.

[157] Public Law 405, as amended, "to provide for loss of United States nationality under certain circumstances."

These were (1) recission of orders by the Western Defense Command excluding Japanese Americans from the West Coast, and (2) announcement by the War Relocation Authority that all projects under their supervision would be liquidated within a year. These decisions, taken together, imperiled the security of

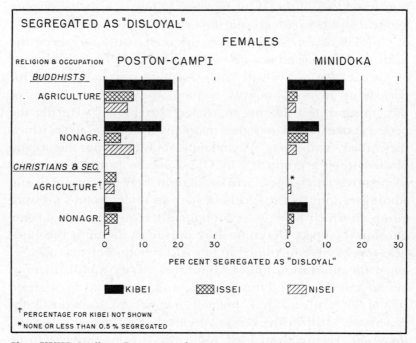

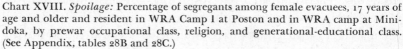

Chart XVIII. *Spoilage:* Percentage of segregants among female evacuees, 17 years of age and older and resident in WRA Camp 1 at Poston and in WRA camp at Minidoka, by prewar occupational class, religion, and generational-educational class. (See Appendix, tables 28B and 28C.)

the "disloyal" who believed that they had attained a war-duration refuge. For all segregants, forced resettlement, and for the young men of draft age, induction into the armed forces loomed as disturbingly high probabilities. By March, 1945, seven out of every ten citizens old enough to be eligible to renounce their American citizenship had done so, and in so doing had, it was believed, afforded "protection" from forced resettlement to more than 3,000 families. One out of five of the male renunciants and one in four of the females were under 21 years of age at the time of renunciation. Family security in 1945 was thus achieved through the medium of children who had been between 14 and 18 years of age when they were removed from the "outside world" in 1942.[158]

Writing in April, 1946, Thomas and Nishimoto emphasized the extent to which American citizenship had been depreciated for the Japanese minority during the cycle that began with evacuation and ended with mass renunciation. At that time a sizable minority of the renunciants had left the United States, voluntarily or with their parents, "to take up life in defeated Japan." The majority who remained in the United States had become not merely "stateless persons" but—ambiguously and without precedent in this country—"aliens ineligible for citizenship in the land of their birth."[159] On August 26, 1949, the legal basis for the restitution of their citizenship was provided through a decision in the United States Court of Appeals for the Ninth Circuit, which confirmed a lower court decision "that the benefits of citizenship can be renounced or waived only as a result of free and intelligent choice," and declared the "purported renunciations" of three Nisei plaintiffs to be, therefore, "void and of no force or effect.[160]

Selective Resettlement

Between registration which ended in March, 1943, and segregation which was virtually completed by October, 15,000 evacuees outmigrated from WRA camps, and 20,000 others left between October, 1943, and the end of December, 1944, when orders excluding the Japanese from the West Coast were rescinded. En-

[158] Thomas and Nishimoto, *op. cit.*, chap. xiii.

[159] *Ibid.*, p. 361.

[160] This opinion was written by Judge William C. Mathes on August 27, 1948, in the United States District Court of Los Angeles. The decision in the Court of Appeals was written by Judge William Denman, and included a scathing denunciation of "General DeWitt's doctrine of enemy racism inherited by blood strains."

In a press release on October 26, 1949, it was announced that the Attorney General of the United States would not ask the Supreme Court to review the order of the Court of Appeals and that this decision would be accepted and applied in all future cases of this kind. It was further reported that some 4,000 Nisei and Kibei renunciants were then seeking restoration of their American citizenship. (*New York Times*, Oct. 27, 1949.)

compassing also a few hundred who had outmigrated before registration, this movement included more than one in three of all the evacuees who had been detained in War Relocation Authority camps. The 36,000 who thus chose the difficult path of resettlement while the war was still in progress were assuming not only "the same hardships . . . being experienced by other American families,"[161] but also the special risks and uncertainties inherent in their close physical resemblance to the Japanese enemy. Their inmigration to communities in the Middle West and East necessarily extended the range of their contacts with many segments of the American population and greatly increased the number and variety of the lines along which they might develop careers. It is by this criterion that they are defined as the *salvage* of the forced mass migration of the Japanese American minority.

The precursors of the *salvage* were the Nisei and Kibei who entered the armed forces. When, on June 17, 1942, the War Department discontinued induction of American-born Japanese and classified them as "not acceptable for service because of ancestry," there were "several thousand citizens of Japanese descent from Hawaii and the mainland . . . already in the Army." In the fall of 1942, Army policy was modified to permit acceptance of a small group qualified "for teaching the fundamentals of the Japanese language to officers of Military Intelligence, and in other capacities as translators and interpreters." About 150 volunteers were immediately recruited from the various WRA camps, and subsequent calls for similar services attracted numbers of others from both the mainland and Hawaii. At the time of the registration program in February and March, 1943, the Army set a quota of 3,500 for American-born Japanese in WRA camps and 1,500 for those resident in Hawaii. In view of the conflicts engendered by evacuation, detention, and registration, it is less surprising that the WRA quota was not filled than that 1,208 Americans of Japanese ancestry volunteered from behind the

---

[161] So described in a skillfully worded document, read to the evacuees in each camp, by a member of the team conducting military registration during 1943. See Thomas and Nishimoto, *op. cit.,* pp. 59–60.

barbed wire of its camps.[162] In unevacuated Hawaii, 9,507 Japanese Americans volunteered, representing six times the quota assigned by the Army and comprising one in three of the citizens aged 18–38 in this ethnic group in the Territory.[163]

The record of mainlanders and Hawaiians in the "all Japanese" 100th Infantry Battalion and the 442d Regimental Combat Team was thoroughly publicized. As described by Lind:

The 100th was subjected to some of the bloodiest and most grueling combat of the arduous Italian campaign and it suffered within ten months over 300 killed and 650 wounded out of a total of 1,300 men, thus winning the name of Purple Heart Battalion. . . . By V. E. Day the 442d Regimental Combat Team, with which the 100th had been incorporated . . . was referred to by military observers as "probably the most decorated unit in United States military history." It had spearheaded four major Allied offensives, three in Italy and one in France, including the rescue of the "Lost Battalion" of Texans which had been cut off by a German advance . . .

The dramatic aspects of "the sons of Japanese parents" fighting against the Germans and Italians were . . . not lost upon the American war correspondents, and members of the combat team were frequently embarrassed by the amount of unsolicited publicity which they obtained. The language used by the official army spokesmen in referring to the fighting qualities of this group were so frequently couched in superlatives as to give the newswriters little choice in the matter. The statement, for example, by the Commander of the 36th Division, whose "Lost Battalion" was rescued by the 442d, leaves little more for the professionals to add. "We have only the utmost admiration for you and what you have accomplished. No finer fighting, no finer soldierly qualities have ever been witnessed by the U. S. Army in its long history."[164]

The remarkable performance of the Japanese Americans who served in the Army, the unabated favorable publicity they received, and the contacts they established in American communities prior to overseas service were undoubtedly primary factors in promoting community acceptance of resettlers in the Middle

---

[162] *The Evacuated People*, U.S. Department of the Interior, *op. cit.*, pp. 125–126, *passim*.

[163] Lind, *op. cit.*, p. 151.

[164] *Ibid.*, pp. 158–159.

West and East from WRA camps. Concomitantly, registration, while immobilizing for the duration of the war the segregants who had been stigmatized as "disloyal," provided the basis for "loyalty" clearance for the 90,000 other evacuees in WRA camps and removed the major obstacle to their outmigration.

In the course of the period, March, 1943 to December, 1944, the War Relocation Authority developed a highly "planned" relocation program and implemented it by deliberate efforts to strengthen the pull, to remove the impediments, to prepare pathways, and to impose pushes as stimulants to outmigration. Nevertheless the population movement that, in fact, took place during this period was, in many important respects, the same sort of migration that had occurred in the overseas movement from European countries and from Japan to the United States, in the westward movement within this country, and in the less spectacular movements from rural areas to cities. It was not a mass migration but a migration of individuals; not forced but voluntary. And, as will be shown later, it was strongly selective, both demographically and culturally.

Once registration was completed and all dockets processed through the intelligence agencies, the War Relocation Authority was in a position to speed up clearance. The project director in each camp could now grant "indefinite leave" summarily to any evacuee who had "answered loyalty questions during registration with an unqualified affirmative," provided the director was satisfied "on the basis of evidence available at the relocation center that the applicant would not endanger national security or interfere with the war effort," and provided, further, that the applicant had not applied for repatriation or expatriation to Japan, had not previously been denied clearance, was not a Shinto priest, was not an alien released on parole from a Department of Justice internment camp, and was not planning to relocate in one of the seaboard states in the Eastern Defense Command.

Seven field offices, which WRA had established in the intermountain states to supervise the seasonal agricultural program, were now directed to promote "permanent resettlement among seasonal workers." Relocation offices were established in Chicago, Cleveland, Minneapolis, Des Moines, Milwaukee, New York, "and numerous other key cities throughout the Middle West and East," and their staffs devoted themselves to "creating favorable community acceptance and . . . finding suitable jobs that evacuees might fill." They "coöperated and collaborated" with resettlement committees which had, in the meantime, been set up by "groups of concerned individuals representing many interests . . . particularly the churches," and they "fostered the establishment of new resettlement committees."[165]

At the end of March, 1943, the War Relocation Authority began to provide some financial aid to "evacuees who were leaving the centers for the purpose of taking a job," except for "those going out on student leave or those with independent means." An eligible evacuee leaving camp without dependents received $50, whereas those leaving with one dependent received $75, and the grant reached its maximum at $100 for "those leaving with two or more dependents." In April and May these provisions were modified to make grants available "to families of men in the armed services, regardless of the purpose for which they were leaving," and to evacuees who were going out to live temporarily in hostels organized by religious groups or resettlement committees, provided they were leaving camp "for the purpose of seeking employment." The grant to an individual leaving camp without dependents was reduced to $25, but the "ceiling" was removed for families which now received $25 per capita. Resettlers were, further, allowed "coach fare and $3 per diem while en route to the destination."

Evacuees wishing to work in war plants or to relocate to the eastern seaboard states had, however, to obtain special clearance through the Japanese American Joint Board, which had been created by the War Department and was composed of "one representative each from the War Relocation Authority, Office of Naval Intelligence, Army Intelligence, and the Provost Marshal General's Office." And early in 1943 the Joint Board undertook

---

[165] War Relocation Authority, *The Relocation Program, op. cit.,* pp. 19, 21, 26 *et passim.*

a complete review of "all evacuee citizens 17 years of age or over." In the course of the next year the Board succeeded in clearing fewer than 500 evacuees for war-plant employment. Although more than 21,000 others were approved for Eastern Defense Command residence, they had not been investigated and therefore not approved for war-plant employment. Some 2,500 approved for Eastern Defense Command residence were, moreover, "referred to Western Defense Command." No action at all was taken in about 500 cases, and almost 12,000 were "disapproved." As expressed in the WRA report, "the Joint Board had functioned more as a deterrent to relocation than as an aid, as had been hoped."

Although Joint Board recommendations were not binding on the War Relocation Authority,[166] evacuees who were "disapproved," or in regard to whom there was other "adverse intelligence information" were summarily placed on a "stop list" and were required to appear before a WRA hearing board which had been set up in each camp. The hearing board's recommendations had, in turn, to be examined by a review committee in Washington, and the latter was empowered "to make independent recommendations for or against leave clearance."[167]

---

[166] After the Joint Board dissolved, early in 1944, clearance for war plants was handled by the Provost Marshal General's Office. "The PMGO procedure called for a system of preclearance before an evacuee could start work in a war plant. It also originally called for the removal from war plants of those who had been hired before it assumed jurisdiction of such hiring. . . . [Because of protests from evacuees and their employers] PMGO removed this requirement and allowed current employees to remain pending clearance. However, many who had rendered months of faithful service were removed."

Among other examples of "Government interference" with the relocation program, cited by WRA, were the following: "[The Navy and State Departments] decided to restrict persons of Japanese ancestry from sailing in the Atlantic without a passport in advance of sailing. . . . An ironic situation arose when Japanese seamen were removed from ships as they returned from war zones, many of them victims of torpedoing and all of them having risked their lives to help deliver goods to our allies. After a great deal of negotiation, the restriction was finally modified. . . .

"On June 23, 1943 . . . the Civil Service Commission issued instructions requiring a special investigation by the Commission prior to appointment of American citizens of Japanese ancestry to positions in Federal agencies. . . . Some of those already on the payroll remained on their jobs pending completion of an investigation and others were immediately removed." (*Ibid.*, pp. 35–37.)

[167] *Ibid.*, pp. 25–28, *passim*.

As early as July, 1943, it became apparent that there were other obstacles in addition to the "stop list"[168] which were deterring relocation. By this time "the large majority of evacuees had been processed and were eligible for indefinite leave." But after due allowance "for the segregation of those ineligible for leave clearance and their dependents, it was apparent that the War Relocation Authority would be left with approximately 85,000 people still in the centers" unless these obstacles were overcome. On the basis of surveys conducted "at several centers" during the late summer, it was concluded that "the principal reason for hesitating was 'uncertainty of public sentiment'; other prevailing reasons were lack of funds against an emergency, lack of information about conditions outside the center, fear of being unable to support dependents, and fear of being unable to find proper living quarters. One principal deterrent which was difficult to classify was that many people had become institutionalized, their wants were taken care of, they knew where the next meal would come from and that they would be looked after in an emergency."[169]

The War Relocation Authority was faced with the necessity of reversing its earlier emphasis on "providing an equitable substitute," in its camps, for "the life, work and homes" which the evacuees had been forced to give up, and providing incentives which would make reëntry "into American life"[170] seem tolerable to these displaced and insecure people. Among the incentives introduced early in 1944 were "trial leaves," under which an evacuee would be permitted "to return to the center at the end of four months or at any time between the beginning of the fifth and the end of the sixth month," thus enabling him "to try out

---

[168] According to the WRA report: "On June 30, 1944, after 10 months of functioning, the project hearing boards had held hearings on 9,177 individual cases, and the review committee had acted upon them in the following ways: 7,187 were approved for the granting of indefinite leave, 1,524 were denied leave clearance and the individuals were listed for transfer to Tule Lake, 50 cases were deferred, and 436 were returned to the project for rehearings.... The extensive and intensive leave-clearance process may in retrospect seem to have been excessive in that aliens of other enemy nations and citizens of other enemy-nation extraction were not generally so carefully checked." (*Ibid.*, p. 29.)

[169] *Ibid.*, pp. 30–31.

[170] See above, p. 87.

relocation before severing all ties with the center." Among the "special efforts . . . to get more families and older people to relocate" were removal of limitations on the weight of personal property that could be shipped at government expense, and provision for shipping limited quantities of work equipment and tools which had, for the most part, been stored in the communities of former residence. Concomitantly, efforts were made to make seasonal leave, under which ties with the camp were not severed, "less attractive," by prohibiting the seasonal worker's return to camp for the duration of his contract and by restricting the annual number of seasonal leave periods to two.[171]

From March to September, 1943, WRA had channeled the attention of its field personnel toward the "loyal" residents of Tule Lake, in an effort to stimulate them to relocate rather than to transfer to other camps. Once segregation was accomplished, the central office released an unceasing stream of propaganda to the other nine camps, emphasizing the advantages of resettlement. "Relocation teams" were sent to each camp, and they took with them "full descriptions of [the] more attractive relocation opportunities," exhibited movies selected from "dozens . . . descriptive of occupations and districts," and prepared "relocation kits . . . bringing together every form of informational printed matter that could be prepared or secured." They addressed large and small meetings and "conducted numerous interviews with individual evacuees."[172]

Separate welfare counseling units were established at each camp "with a view both to breaking down the rationalizations of reluctant families and to gathering information which would enable WRA to plan realistically its future programs."[173] Counselors advised individuals and families about adjustment "on the outside," and in many cases worked out coöperative arrangements with social agencies in communities of destination.

Recruiters from private industry were encouraged to visit the camps, and representatives of the Office of Strategic Services, the

[171] War Relocation Authority, *The Relocation Program, op. cit.,* pp. 34–35, 44–45 *passim.*
[172] *Ibid.,* p. 40.
[173] *Ibid.,* p. 38.

Army Map Service, the Army and Navy intelligence schools, and so on, came in and sought personnel.

Immediately after recission of the exclusion orders, on December 17, 1944, the War Relocation Authority announced plans for its own liquidation. All relocation centers were to be closed "within a period of six months to one year after the revocation of the exclusion order."[174] The following day, "leave clearance" procedures were abandoned.[175] The *residue,* comprising some

---

[174] *Ibid.,* p. 47.

[175] The Western Defense Command's recission of exclusion orders, as well as WRA's abandonment of "leave clearance" were coincident with or followed the decision, *ex parte Mitsuye Endo* of the United States Supreme Court on December 18, 1944 (323 U.S. 283). Mitsuye Endo had applied for leave clearance at Tule Lake on February 19, 1943, and this was granted in Topaz, on August 16, 1943, on the following terms, cited in 323 U.S. 283, p. 294: "You are eligible for indefinite leave for the purpose of employment or residence in the Eastern Defense Command as well as in other areas; provided the conditions of Administrative Instruction No. 22, Rev. are otherwise complied with. [These related to valid employment offer, favorable community sentiment, etc.] The Provost Marshal General's Dept. of the War Department has determined that you, Endo Mitsuye [*sic*] are not at this time eligible for employment in plants and facilities vital to the war effort." Thereupon, Miss Endo refused to apply for "indefinite leave" and her attorney sought a writ of *habeas corpus,* which was denied in the District Court. An appeal to the Ninth Circuit Court of Appeals led to certification of the case to the Supreme Court regarding questions of law. The Supreme Court reversed the judgment of the District Court and returned the case for proceedings in conformity with this opinion.

Mr. Justice Douglas, presenting the opinion of the court, wrote, "We are of the view that Mitsuye Endo should be given her liberty. In reaching that conclusion we do not come to the underlying constitutional issues which have been argued. For we conclude that, whatever power the War Relocation Authority may have to detain other classes of citizens, it has no authority to subject citizens who are concededly loyal to its leave procedure." (*Ibid.,* p. 297). Mr. Justice Murphy, concurring, wrote: "I join in the opinion of the Court, but I am of the view that detention in Relocation Centers of persons of Japanese ancestry regardless of loyalty is not only unauthorized by Congress or the Executive but is another example of the unconstitutional resort to racism inherent in the entire evacuation program. . . . If, as I believe, the military orders excluding her from California were invalid at the time they were issued, they are increasingly objectionable at this late date, when the threat of invasion of the Pacific Coast and the fears of sabotage and espionage have greatly diminished. For the Government to suggest under these circumstances that the presence of Japanese blood in a loyal American citizen might be enough to warrant her exclusion from a place where she would otherwise have a right to go is a position I cannot sanction." (*Ibid.,* pp. 308–309). Mr. Justice Roberts, in a second concurring opinion, wrote: "I conclude . . . that the court is squarely faced with a serious constitutional question—whether the relator's detention violated the guarantees of the Bill of Rights of the federal Constitution and especially the guarantee of due process of law. There can be but one answer to that question. An admittedly loyal citizen has been deprived of her liberty for a period of years. Under the Constitution she should be free to come and go as she pleases. Instead, her liberty of motion and other innocent activities have been prohibited and conditioned. She should be discharged." (*Ibid.,* p. 310.)

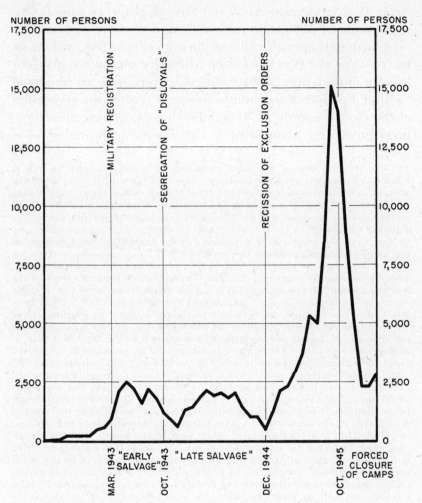

Chart XIX. Outmigration of evacuees from all WRA camps, by months, June, 1942–March, 1946. (See Appendix, table 25.)

62,000 persons remaining in camps other than Tule Lake, had then to be relocated. Among them were babies who had been born in camp, and the aged, the indigent, the sick. In general, they were the core of the evacuee group that in 1942 had been "physically, emotionally, economically, and demographically incapable of finding jobs and homes in other areas" (see pp. 86–87, above). Sitting out the war years as they did, in the isolation of barbed-wire surrounded camps, did not tend to improve their capacities in these respects. With the forced closure of the camps, they faced the necessity of evacuation-in-reverse, and the majority of them returned during the period of liquidation to Pacific Coast communities.

When the war ended, large proportions of the 18,000 persons who were still in Tule Lake "were freed from detention orders," and the War Relocation Authority attempted to develop resettlement plans for the *spoilage*. "However, in view of the fact that the majority of the families in Tule Lake had at least one family member under some type of detention order, it was extremely difficult to carry out a satisfactory relocation plan for most families." Approximately one in three of the Tuleans had been relocated by the end of 1945. In the course of the next three months, most of the others were made "eligible for relocation [by the Department of Justice]. . . . The center was closed on March 20, 1946, when the Department of Justice transferred to internment camps the remaining 447 evacuees."[176] At the date of closing, Tule Lake had been in operation for almost four years.

Demographically, the *salvage* was highly selective. Seven out of ten of the persons involved in the two waves of outmigration between registration and recission (Chart XIX) were young people between the ages 15 and 35 (Chart XX). Their age structure closely resembled that of the immigrant settlers of 1900 (see Chart II, p. 10, above), but the balance of the sexes was quite different. Young men were the pioneers in the migration from Japan to America, but appreciable proportions of young women migrated, alone or with their husbands or their brothers, from camps to the "outside world." Correspondingly, the age-sex struc-

---

[176] War Relocation Authority, *The Relocation Program, op. cit.*, p. 80.

ture of the *salvage* differed radically from that of the *spoilage* and of the *residue*. Although *salvage* comprised, on the average, twice as many persons as did *spoilage*, children under 10 years of age and persons 50 years of age or older were approximately equal in the two groups. And, though the total *residue* was not quite twice as large as the total *salvage*, children under 5 years of age

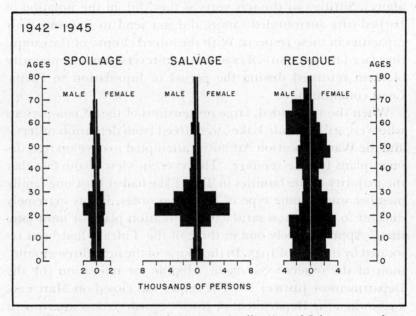

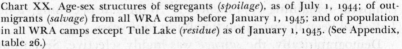

Chart XX. Age-sex structures of segregants (*spoilage*), as of July 1, 1944; of outmigrants (*salvage*) from all WRA camps before January 1, 1945; and of population in all WRA camps except Tule Lake (*residue*) as of January 1, 1945. (See Appendix, table 26.)

were almost four times, and persons 60 years of age and older were more than seven times as numerous.

More significant from the standpoint of assimilation and integration were the incidence, direction, and strength of cultural selection. Charts XXI to XXIV show some of these aspects of *early salvage*, defined as outmigrants 17 years of age and older, leaving specified WRA camps between registration and segregation (March–September 1943), in proportion to the camp population of these ages as of March 1943, when both outmigrants and

population are cross-classified by camp and prewar origin (Northwesterners in Tule Lake; Minidokans, Postonians, and Californians in Tule Lake), by sex, by religion (Christian-secularists
and Buddhists), by prewar occupational class (nonagricultural
and agricultural) and by generational-educational group (Nisei,
Kibei, Issei). As in the analysis of *spoilage* (see pp. 97–98, above),
there are 88 subgroups large enough for comparison. The range
of outmigrant proportions in these subgroups is from a high of
51 per cent for nonagricultural Christian-secularist male Nisei
Minidokans (Chart XXIII) to a low of two-tenths of 1 per cent
for agricultural Buddhist female Issei Californians in Tule Lake
(Chart XXII).

Regional patterns are suggested by camp and origin comparisons, in which (as described on p. 97, above), a consistent pattern
would yield descending scores of 66, 44, 22, and 0. The observed
scores of 55 for Tuleans from the Northwest, 43 for Minidokans,
18 for Postonians, and 16 for Tuleans from California, though
not a camp-by-camp antithesis to *spoilage* (see pp. 98–99, above),
indicate a markedly greater propensity for Northwesterners than
for Californians to reorient themselves toward American life by
outmigrating to the "outside world." The regional differential is
clearcut when comparison is limited to the two Tule Lake
groups. With administration thus held constant, in addition to
the other factors specified above, Northwesterners scored 21 and
Californians only 1, compared with a consistency standard of 22
to 0. When Minidoka and Poston are compared, administration
is an uncontrolled variable, but the score of 18 for Minidokans
versus 4 for Poston probably also reflects a regional differential,
inasmuch as the former originated in the Northwest, and the
latter in California. Tuleans from California had surprisingly
high proportions of outmigrants, in view of the fact that so many
of them had been immobilized by their status as "disloyals." If
comparison is limited to Tuleans from California and Postonians, indeed, the score for the former is 10 and for the latter 12
out of a possible 22.

The high incidence of *early salvage* among Tuleans in general
may be attributed partly to the success of WRA's efforts to stimu-

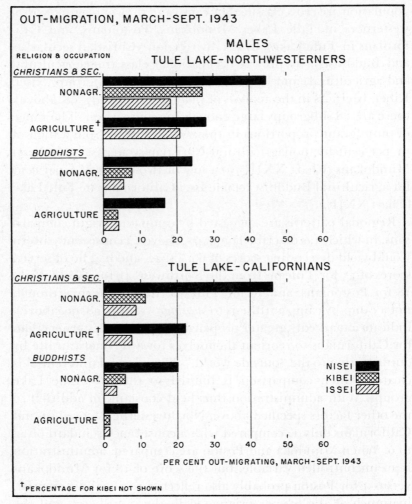

Chart XXI. *Early Salvage:* Percentage of outmigrants, March–September, 1943, among male evacuees, 17 years of age and older and resident in WRA camp at Tule Lake in March, 1943, by prewar origin in Northwest or California, prewar occupational class, religion, and generational-educational class. (See Appendix, table 28A.)

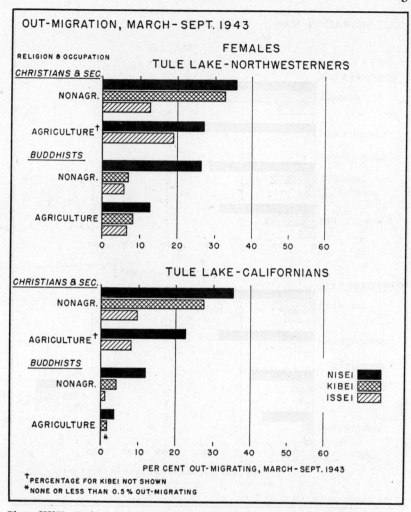

Chart XXII. *Early Salvage:* Percentage of outmigrants, March–September, 1943, among female evacuees, 17 years of age and older and resident in WRA camp at Tule Lake in March, 1943, by prewar origin in Northwest or California, prewar occupational class, religion, and generational-educational class. (See Appendix, table 28A.)

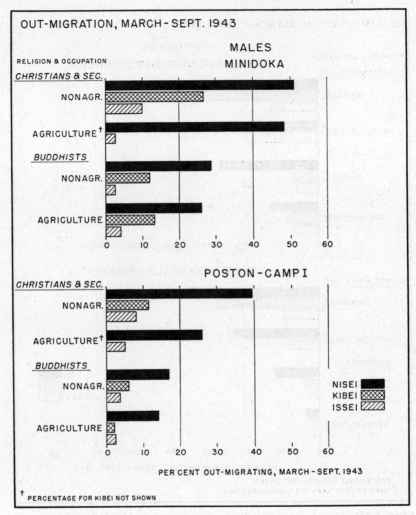

OUT-MIGRATION, MARCH – SEPT. 1943

MALES
MINIDOKA

RELIGION & OCCUPATION

CHRISTIANS & SEC.

NONAGR.

AGRICULTURE†

BUDDHISTS

NONAGR.

AGRICULTURE

POSTON – CAMP I

CHRISTIANS & SEC.

NONAGR.

AGRICULTURE†

BUDDHISTS

NONAGR.

AGRICULTURE

NISEI
KIBEI
ISSEI

PER CENT OUT-MIGRATING, MARCH – SEPT. 1943

† PERCENTAGE FOR KIBEI NOT SHOWN

Chart XXIII. *Early Salvage:* Percentage of outmigrants, March–September, 1943, among male evacuees, 17 years of age and older and resident in WRA camp at Minidoka and in WRA Camp I at Poston in March, 1943, by occupational class, religion, and generational-educational class. (See Appendix, tables 28B and 28C.)

late resettlement of the "loyal" segments of the Tulean population before the camp was transformed into a segregation center,
and partly to the fact that "loyal" Tuleans had either to out-
migrate or to transfer to another camp in order to maintain their
loyalty status, whereas "loyal" Postonians and Minidokans could
still enjoy the security of the home camp without loss of status.
In other words, Tuleans had only two choices—segregation or
outmigration—whereas residents of other camps had three—
segregation, outmigration, or "sedentation." (See pp. 123–124,
below.)

The pattern of religious differentials was highly consistent, the
proportion of outmigrants among Christian-secularists exceeding
that among Buddhists in 39 out of 40 possible comparisons.
Occupational and sex differentials were somewhat less consistent.
Nonagriculturalists scored 32 and agriculturalists 8, compared
with a consistency standard of 40 and 0; whereas males scored 28
and females 16, compared with a standard of 44 and 0.

For the threefold generational-educational comparisons, when
Kibei Christian-secular agriculturalists are again excluded because of small numbers, a perfectly consistent pattern of differentials would yield scores of 48, 24, and 0. Viewed against this
standard, the observed scores of 48 for Nisei, 22 for Kibei, and 2
for Issei form a noteworthy pattern.

Whereas Kibei had consistently higher proportions "disloyal"
than corresponding groups of either Issei or Nisei, the proportions of outmigrants among them were usually intermediate between a high proportion for Nisei and a low proportion for Issei.
Among the factors which may account for the extreme position
of the Kibei in regard to "disloyalty" concomitant with an intermediate position in regard to outmigration are their deviant and
probably bimodal cultural and attitudinal distribution, and
their concentration at ages[177] where the propensity to migrate was
less than among Nisei but far greater than among Issei.

The magnitude of the generational-educational differences is
shown in the following selection of examples, where the propor-

---

[177] Because of the slight age overlapping of the three generational-educational
groups, standardization for age was not considered desirable.

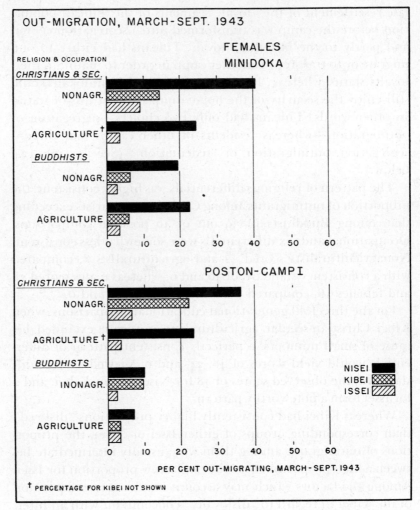

Chart **XXIV.** *Early Salvage:* Percentage of outmigrants, March–September, 1943, among female evacuees, 17 years of age and older and resident in WRA camp at Minidoka and in WRA Camp I at Poston in March, 1943, by occupational class, religion, and generational-educational class. (See Appendix, tables 28B and 28C.)

tions of outmigrants among Nisei groups at the first, sixth, twelfth, eighteenth, and twenty-fourth rank—in a 24-group comparison schedule—are placed in conjunction with those for the same groups of Kibei and Issei:

EARLY SALVAGE

PERCENTAGE OF OUTMIGRANTS, MARCH–SEPTEMBER, 1943, AMONG SPECIFIED CLASSES OF EVACUEES

Classes of evacuees	Percentage of outmigrants (early salvage)		
	Nisei	Kibei	Issei
Male, Christian-sec., nonagr., Minidoka	51.3	26.8	10.0
Female, Christian-sec., nonagr., Poston I	36.2	22.0	6.6
Male, Buddhist, nonagr., Tule Lake (N.W.)	24.3	7.9	5.7
Male, Buddhist, agr., Poston I	14.0	2.0	2.3
Female, Buddhist, agr., Tule Lake (Calif.)	3.6	1.7	0.2

Late salvage is defined as the proportion of the post-segregation population (as of October 1943) outmigrating before recission of the exclusion orders (December 1944). Since there was no longer any population "subject to the risk of outmigration" at the Tule Lake Center, analysis must be confined to the residue, as of this date, of the original Minidoka and Poston (Camp I) populations. Charts XXV and XXVI show the resulting patterns of differentials in *late salvage* for these two camp groups in the same detail as those shown in Charts XXIII and XXIV for *early salvage*. Because of the limitation to two camp groups, there are only 22 subgroups available for intercamp and for sex comparisons, and 20 for religious and occupational comparisons. The standard of consistency for the three-way generational-educational comparisons, correspondingly, becomes 24, 12, and 0. The observed scores for Minidokans and for Postonians were 16 and 6, and for males and females 22 and 0; those for Christian-secularists and Buddhists were 20 and 0, and for nonagriculturalists and agriculturalists 17 and 3. The proportion of outmigrants among Nisei always exceeded that among corresponding classes of Kibei, and these, in turn always exceeded those among corresponding classes of Issei, yielding observed scores of 24 for Nisei, 12 for Kibei, and 0 for Issei. Thus, most of the patterns of differentials were brought into even clearer focus in *late salvage* than in *early salvage,* and the patterns for sex, for religion, and for generational-educational classes achieved "perfect" consistency.

The magnitude of generational-educational differences is again shown by comparing high and low values for Nisei (in this instance classes ranking first, fifth, eighth and twelfth) with those of the same classes for Kibei and Issei:

LATE SALVAGE

PERCENTAGE OF OUTMIGRANTS, OCTOBER, 1943–DECEMBER, 1944, AMONG
SPECIFIED CLASSES OF EVACUEES

Classes of evacuees	Percentage of outmigrants (late salvage)		
	Nisei	Kibei	Issei
Male, Christian-sec., nonagr., Minidoka........................	71.1	50.0	22.8
Male, Buddhist, nonagr., Poston I.....	61.4	30.7	8.8
Female, Christian-sec., nonagr., Poston I...........................	41.2	22.4	16.5
Female, Buddhist, agr., Minidoka.....	22.2	7.7	3.3

As indicated in the section above, on religious differences, Nisei residents of West Coast communities were disproportionately Christians or secularists compared with Issei or Kibei, and their relative level of education was very high. In the camp populations, Nisei density was highest in subgroups composed of Christian-secularists with prewar nonagricultural backgrounds, and it was within this generational-religious-occupational group that the most highly educated segment was to be found. In Poston I, for example, 66 per cent of the college-educated Nisei were "nonagricultural Christians or secularists," compared with 34 per cent of the Nisei, over 20 years of age, who had had no college training. The corresponding proportions at Minidoka were 79 per cent and 53 per cent, respectively.

In general, the college-educated Christian-secular nonagricultural Nisei not only showed the greatest willingness to leave camp and to reënter "American life," but they also, initially, had less difficulty than other classes in obtaining "leave clearance." Moreover, some individuals from this group received special assistance and encouragement from the religiously oriented committees that were promoting resettlement. It is not surprising, therefore, that *early salvage* removed a disproportionately large share of the college-educated, Christian-secular nonagricultural Nisei segment from the camp population, and that *late salvage* practically decimated their ranks. The details of the educational differential *within* the Nisei Christian-secularist nonagricultural group, subclassified by age and sex, shown in Appendix, table 29, may be summarized as follows:

EARLY AND LATE SALVAGE

PERCENTAGE OF OUTMIGRANTS, MARCH–SEPTEMBER, 1943, AND OCTOBER, 1943–
DECEMBER, 1944, AMONG SPECIFIED CLASSES OF NISEI EVACUEES

	Percentage of outmigrants			
Classes of evacuees	March–Sept., 1943 (early salvage)		Oct., 1943–Dec., 1944 (late salvage)	
	High school or less	College	High school or less	College
Poston: Camp I				
Males aged 20–24 years	30.0	49.9	74.5	77.5
Over 25 years	43.1	53.3	70.3	75.6
Females aged 20–24 years	30.7	49.0	47.1	58.0
Over 25 years	37.6	48.5	35.7	47.1
Minidoka				
Males aged 20–24 years	51.3	61.8	73.0	81.0
Over 25 years	45.6	65.5	58.2	79.3
Females aged 20–24 years	39.8	56.3	43.4	76.7
Over 25 years	30.1	59.2	45.9	63.2

The proportions of outmigrants among the college educated always exceeded the corresponding proportions among those who had not attended college and, in general, the magnitude of the differences between educational classes was appreciably greater among the less migratory females than among the more mobile

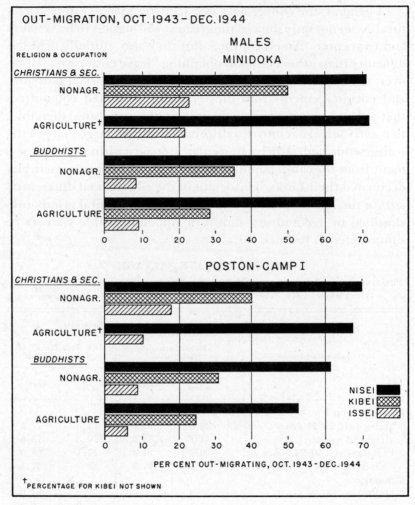

OUT-MIGRATION, OCT. 1943 – DEC. 1944

MALES
MINIDOKA

RELIGION & OCCUPATION

CHRISTIANS & SEC.

NONAGR.

AGRICULTURE†

BUDDHISTS

NONAGR.

AGRICULTURE

0   10   20   30   40   50   60   70

POSTON-CAMP I

CHRISTIANS & SEC.

NONAGR.

AGRICULTURE†

BUDDHISTS

NONAGR.

AGRICULTURE

0   10   20   30   40   50   60   70

PER CENT OUT-MIGRATING, OCT. 1943 – DEC. 1944

NISEI
KIBEI
ISSEI

†PERCENTAGE FOR KIBEI NOT SHOWN

Chart XXV. *Late Salvage:* Percentage of outmigrants, October, 1943–December, 1944, among male evacuees 17 years of age and older and resident in WRA camp at Minidoka and in WRA Camp I at Poston in October, 1943, by occupational class, religion, and generational-educational class. (See Appendix, tables 28B and 28C.)

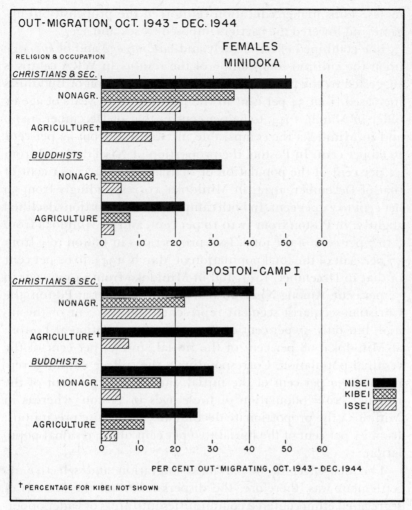

Chart XXVI. *Late Salvage:* Percentage of outmigrants, October, 1943–December, 1944, among female evacuees 17 years of age and older and resident in WRA camp at Minidoka and in WRA Camp I at Poston in October, 1943, by occupational class, religion, and generational-educational class. (See Appendix, tables 28B and 28C.)

males. Thus higher education reinforced the propensity to mi-grate and lowered the barriers imposed by sex and age.

The combined effect of early and late *salvage* and of *spoilage* upon the cultural composition of the *residue* in WRA camps is suggested by the fact that in Poston the proportion of Buddhists increased from 54 per cent in the population 17 years of age or older in March, 1943, to 62 per cent in that of December, 1944, and in Minidoka the comparable increase was from 53 per cent to 66 per cent. In Poston, the proportion of Nisei declined from 42 per cent of the population of March, 1943, to 27 per cent of that of December, 1944; in Minidoka, correspondingly from 39 per cent to 21 per cent. In both camps, Kibei proportions declined slightly: in Poston from 12 to 10 per cent, and in Minidoka from 8 to 7 per cent of the total. Issei proportions in Poston rose from 47 per cent of the total population of March, 1943, to 62 per cent of that in December, 1944, and in Minidoka from 54 per cent to 72 per cent. Among Nisei, 20 years of age or older at Poston, the Christian-secularist segment represented 60 per cent of the in-itial, but only 45 per cent of the residual population at Poston; at Minidoka, 68 per cent of the initial, and 53 per cent of the residual population. Correspondingly the college educated rep-resented 30 per cent of the initial, but only 20 per cent of the residual Nisei population of these ages in Poston, whereas in Minidoka the proportionate decline was even more precipitous; from 21 per cent of the initial to 8 per cent of the residual popu-lation.

The net effect of forced mass migration and selective re-settlement was, therefore, the dispersal beyond the bounds of segregated ethnocentered communities into areas of wider oppor-tunity of the most highly assimilated segments of the Japanese American minority.

Part II

THE COURSE OF INDIVIDUAL EXPERIENCE

The Frame of Reference: Social Demography

Part II of the *The Salvage* is concerned with the train of individual experience, as exemplified by career lines and life histories. It complements the analysis of patterns of change by focusing on the continuity, the range, and the depth of individual experience. Correspondingly, the treatment of mass phenomena in Part I provides context for Part II, with reference especially to the following aspects of sociological history and social demography.

The history of Japanese immigration to and settlement in the United States is viewed as one of accommodation to restrictions and adjustment to the impact of successive crises: labor immigration, relatively unimpeded from 1885 to 1907, brought to an abrupt end with the enforcement of the Gentlemen's Agreement in 1908; family immigration reaching a maximum in 1920 and declining radically in 1921, concomitant with restrictions on passports to picture brides; and after enactment of Oriental exclusion in 1924 return migrants to Japan greatly outnumbering admissions of "nonimmigrant" Japanese to this country.

The racial ineligibility to naturalization of Japanese aliens settling in the United States, and its use by anti-Japanese pressure groups as a means of achieving discriminatory ends were emphasized. It became a serious threat to the economic security of the settlers when the land laws passed in California between 1913 and 1923, and imitated in other states, affirmed rights to ownership and use of land to aliens eligible to citizenship and denied these same rights, by implication, to the ineligible; and it provided the legal basis for Oriental exclusion in the Immigrant Act of 1924. The citizenship issue culminated in abrogation of the birthright of American-born Japanese to American citizenship in 1942, when orders were issued excluding all persons of Japanese ancestry, "both alien and nonalien" from their homes in California, Washington, Oregon, and Arizona. Exclusion was accomplished by controlled evacuation, followed by detention in concentration camps. Accused of no offense, the detained evacuees were subjected to administrative attempts to assess their loyalty by questionnaire, registration, and inquisition during the spring of 1943. The verbally "disloyal," the passively resistant, and the actively hostile—together with dependent members of their families—were segregated in Tule Lake during the fall of 1943 and the early months of 1944, and, concomitantly, programs were developed to stimulate relocation of the "loyal." In December, 1944, orders excluding the Japanese from their West Coast homes were rescinded, and the last concentration camp was closed in March, 1946.

Patterns of social and demographic change were molded by trends toward high survival and low fertility and by the shifting course of migration: the entrance of young male laborers, the influx of picture brides, the return of aging immigrants to the homeland, the sending of young American-born children to Japan for education, and the recall of some of them to the United States. By 1942, the demographic cleavage between the first and second generations, and within the second generation between those who had spent their formative years and received most of their education in Japan and those who had had slight contact with the homeland of their parents was sharply defined. The Japan-born Issei accounted for 35 per cent of the total population, while the proportions represented by the American-born, American-educated Nisei and the marginal, American-born, Japan-educated Kibei were 56 per cent and 9 per cent respectively. The median age of Issei males was 55 years and of Issei females 47 years; of Kibei males and females, 26 years; and of Nisei of both sexes, only 17 years.

The prewar socioeconomic positions of the generations differed significantly. A majority of the Issei had moved up the occupational ladder to become independent businessmen or farmers. Although most of their enterprises were small and depended heavily on the unpaid labor of wives and children, they held virtual monopolies in a few highly specialized and profitable branches of agricultural production and urban trade. The highly educated second generation had been less successful in reaching their occupational goals. A few had attained independence in business or the arts, but many were working as domestic servants or gardeners, and access to white-collar jobs in the larger American community was limited, for the most part, to civil service. By far the largest numbers were still working as heirs presumptive in the family enterprises their fathers had founded, or as employees of other Japanese, on farms, in the produce business, in hotels or restaurants, or in Oriental art goods stores; or they were serving the professional needs of the ethnic community.

The social integration of Issei into the larger American community had been impeded by segregation and discrimination, by the necessity imposed by their enforced alien status of turning toward the mother country rather than toward the country of adoption for aid and comfort, by the paternalistic and protective interest of the consular offices in their welfare, and by the strength and solidarity of their ethnocentered organizations. The extent of return-migration to the homeland suggests that the Japanese, perhaps more than any other immigrant group in America, regarded themselves as sojourners, hoping to make and save money to return and reëstablish themselves favorably in Japan. Although the vast majority of those who obtained footholds in urban business or in agriculture and founded American families had become residents-in-fact, if not settlers-by-intention, their awareness of the implications of West Coast racial prejudice for their children's future, their lack of information about opportunities elsewhere in the United States, their pride in Japan's position as a world power, and their nostalgia, had predisposed them to practices to assure their American-born descendants status as both Japanese and as Americans. On the one hand, they had endowed their children with dual citizenship by registering them as Japanese nationals, sent many of them to Japan for education, and established a network of Japanese language schools for the Nisei in West Coast communities. On the other hand, they had emphasized the privileges and responsibilities inherent in the birth-right of American citizenship and stressed the importance of American schooling.

Parental insistence that American-born Japanese be both "good Japanese" and "good Americans" accentuated the marginal status of the second generation. All of the available evidence suggests, however, that American-born Japanese in general tended to identify themselves politically with America rather than with Japan; that their vocational goals approximated those of the Caucasion majority; and that their cultural orientation was more toward Occidental than toward Oriental norms. There were, however, two sharply defined modal classes along the Japanese American cultural continuum: the Kibei who veered toward the Japanese pole, and the Nisei, whose density was greatest at the American. Within each of these classes there were submodal groups reflecting the extent of isolation from or participation in the larger American community. Among those which could be defined statistically, the following attributes were positively associated with Americanization: a high level of education in American schools, preference for Christianity or secularism, a nonagricultural background or an urban occupation, and residence outside the more segregated California communities.

The strength of prewar Japanese American families derived from their economic unity and from the social control exercised by the family-oriented, ethnocentered community organizations. Their weakness lay in the demographic and concomitant cultural cleavages between the generations and among family members. Age gaps between husbands and wives and between fathers and children were unusually large, and lines of communication were tenuous. Return of the Kibei to their American homes aggravated the cultural diversity within many families, since it was usually only one or two of several siblings who had been sent to Japan for education. Most Issei fathers had grown up in the Japan of the late nineteenth and the very early twentieth century; and the residence of most Issei mothers had terminated before America's entrance into World War I. The Kibei child in most families completed his education in the aggressively nationalistic Japan of the 1930's, while the Nisei children were being indoctrinated in democratic ideologies through the American schools. Bases for conflict, which might have occurred normally between the generations and among siblings were broadened by extreme environmental and temporal contrasts, and after the middle 1930's by divergent national loyalties.

The exclusion orders of 1942 encompassed all persons of Japanese ancestry, however remote or diluted the "racial strain," and the only classes who were not detained in assembly centers and relocation camps were numerically unimportant, including persons who had migrated eastward during the few weeks when evacuation was "voluntary" rather than "controlled," persons who were in institutions for the sick, the insane, and the criminal, and persons who had been interned, on security grounds or on suspicion, by the Department of Justice. In strongest possible contrast with the unselective forced mass migration was the selective intercamp movement, predominantly of family units, during the segregation program of 1943 and the selective outmigration, predominantly of individuals, from camps during 1943 and 1944.

So highly selective of generational-educational classes was the incidence of segregation, of sedentation (sitting out the war years in camp), and of outmigration, that these alternative resolutions of the conflicts engendered within the already culturally divided Japanese minority by the evacuation-detention crisis, may, without undue exaggeration be called the Kibei way, the Issei way, and the Nisei way. Within each generational-educational group, prewar residence, occupational class, and religious preference, to a large extent, determined the course taken. Japanese Americans who had lived in the more tolerant Pacific Northwest were more frequently found in the *salvage,* those from the more prejudiced California in the *spoilage.* Occupation, differentiating as it did the more isolated farming folk from those following urban pursuits where contact with Caucasians was closer or more frequent, stimulated *salvage* among the latter and retarded it among the former. Religious preference was a further index of assimilation, distinguishing the predominantly Japan-polarized Buddhists from the America-oriented who, like the dominant majority in the United States, either professed Christianity or accepted no formal religion. Segregation and sedentation were the ways of the former; outmigration was the path of Christians and the non-religious. Finally, those Nisei who were most highly educated in American colleges and universities were—quite out of proportion to their numbers—the *salvage*.

The Experiential Records: Individual Lives

The train of individual experience,[178] as observed and reconstructed by resettlers in the Chicago area and exemplified in the records which follow, was reported to Charles Kikuchi in the course of numerous informal contacts and semidirected, loosely structured interviews, from April, 1943, to August, 1945. Before the interviews, the subject was usually given a detailed outline to be used at his own discretion in channeling his observations. He was, however, encouraged to talk about any aspect of his life in any order and to any extent that he wished. Kikuchi asked as few direct questions as possible, and tried to limit them to the subject's demographic, educational, and employment history, and, in the last session, to filling gaps remaining in the coverage contemplated in the outline.

The topics under I of this outline, together with those in IX, covered individual and family prewar history.

I. *Brief History of the Individual*

A. Parental Background. (See also IX, which follows.) Individual's account of childhood training, and his own story of relations with parents and siblings.

B. His demographic history: birth date, birthplace, successive places of residence.

C. His educational history: chronological account of schooling received, including schools attended (place and dates), major interest and activities; how long did he attend Japanese language school?

---

[178] W. I. Thomas participated in staff conferences during which procedures for the preparation and utilization of experiential records and life histories were planned and developed. His views greatly influenced our standpoint. See E. H. Volkart, ed., *Social Behavior and Personality. Contributions of W. I. Thomas to Theory and Social Research*. Social Science Research Council, New York, 1951, especially pp. 289–318.

D. His employment and economic history: chronological account of jobs held (type of job, type of industry, rate of pay). Account for all periods of unemployment. Note whether employers and fellow workers were Japanese or Caucasian. What jobs has he tried to get and failed? Circumstances surrounding these failures? Has the income received from his jobs been sufficient to maintain a reasonable standard of living (individual's definition of reasonable standard of living?) Has he been able to save? When and how much? What sources were drawn on in periods of unemployment?

E. His interpersonal relations outside the family. Who were his intimate friends at various times? Note particularly whether they were Caucasian, Nisei, Issei, or Kibei. What instances of prejudice or discrimination were met in interracial friendships?

F. His romantic, sexual, marital history. What were his boy-girl relationships? Were these contacts confined to Nisei and Kibei, or did they extend to other racial groups, particularly Caucasian? Whom did he marry? Was the marriage Japanese or American type?

G. His political activities and shifting interests: voting, party membership, running for office. To what political organizations has he belonged?

H. His associational history. What clubs, organizations and groups has the individual joined? What offices has he held?

I. His recreational history. What have been his dominant leisure activities (sports, reading, hobbies, etc.)? How have these changed? To what extent have these been Japanese or American?

J. His religious history: church membership, attendance at Sunday School. Under what circumstances did the individual join church? Has his religious affiliation been the same as that of his parents?

The second part of the outline, together with VIII were designed to place the individual and his family, demographically, economically, and socially, on the eve of the war.

II. *The Individual on December 1, 1941* (i.e. just before the outbreak of War)

A. His demographic characteristics: age and marital status, household, place of residence.

B. His physical characteristics: size, "looks," disabilities.

C. His educational status: amount of education completed in Japan and in America, his use of the Japanese and English languages.

D. His occupational status: job actually held at that time, pay received for the past month, his usual occupation, for whom he worked—Japanese or Caucasian employer—, nature of industry and job, his fellow workers.

E. His religious connection: Christian, Buddhist, none.

F. His political connections: Japanese Association, JACL, YD, etc.

G. His recreational interests: his voluntary associations and cliques, his hobbies, how he spent his leisure time generally, his friendship groups.

H. His plans for the future: occupational, marital, educational, desired place of residence, desired associations.

Topics under III were intended to revive memories and to stimulate associations concerning December 7, 1941.

III. *The Individual on December 7, 1941*
What was the immediate impact of the Pearl Harbor disaster? The individual should be asked to reconstruct the day, indicating his activities, the contacts he made, the fears he experienced, the rumors he heard, the tentative reorganization of his plans for the future regarding marriage, education, residence, job, etc.

The fourth part was directed toward the reconstruction of behavior and attitudes during a series of "time-identified" crises that culminated in the orders excluding Japanese Americans from the West Coast.

IV. *The Individual between the Day of Pearl Harbor and the Day of Evacuation,* with particular reference to the following time-identified events:
Period of early restrictions on enemy aliens
Period of FBI roundups
Period of Filipino incidents
Period of evacuation of enemy aliens from restricted areas
Announcement of evacuation of American citizens of Japanese ancestry
Where relevant, freezing of the Free Zone

A. Effect upon the individual in his relations with his family. Did he attempt to rejoin other family members, assume added responsibility for relatives, break away from family?

B. Effect upon his schooling and education. Did he stop school, lose interest in studies (did his grade average decline?). What were his relations with teachers and fellow students?

C. Effect upon his personal and marital plans. Did he become engaged or break off an engagement? Did he hurry up a contemplated marriage? Did he separate from his wife? etc.

D. Effect upon his residential status and plans. Did he move? Was the move forced?

E. Effect upon occupational status and plans. Did he lose or give up his job, or change jobs? What were his relations with his employer, with his fellow workers or with his clientele?

F. Effect upon his property interests. Did he sell out his holdings and his personal property, let his insurance lapse? To whom did he sell, and by what mechanism was the sale accomplished (government agencies, friends, relatives, personal initiative)? What losses, if any, were incurred? What measures were taken to safeguard property interests, savings and insurance?

G. Effect upon voluntary associations and friendships. What changes occurred in his relations with his neighbors, with the Japanese community, with Caucasians?

H. Effect upon his identification with America or with Japan (i.e., upon his "patriotism" or his feeling of belonging to or being loyal to the interests of Japan or of America), and upon his identification with a minority group in America (i.e., upon his feelings of sympathy, community of interests, or repugnance toward others of Japanese ancestry), upon his political interests and activities.

I. Effect upon his conduct: drinking, gambling, personal disorganization.

J. Effect in general upon his morale: hopes or fears for the future.

In V and VI the resettler was asked to describe his life during detention in Assembly Center and Relocation Project, with reference to the following categories.

V. *The Individual in the Assembly Center*
A. Preparations for entering center: selection of things to take with him, anticipations of life in the center, official directives from WCCA, etc., rumors.

B. Activities in center:
    1. Making a home in barracks

    2. Job activities

    3. Education

    4. Recreation

    5. Religious activities

    6. Political activities

    7. Making friends; romantic-sexual activities

  C. Attitudes toward:

    1. Administration

    2. Other evacuees

    3. Visitors and other Caucasians

    4. America and Japan

    5. Outside world in general

  D. Changes in plans for future while in center (see listings under II and III).

VI. *The Individual in the Relocation Project*

  A. Preparations for entering the project: efforts made to go to a particular project and why, rumors about the project to which Assembly Center population was to be sent, fears regarding conditions in the project, attitude toward WRA versus WCCA before entering project).

  B. Activities (as in V).

  C. Attitudes (as in V).

  D. Inception and development of plans for resettlement.

Those who evacuated voluntarily to the Free Zone instead of entering an Assembly Center were asked to comment particularly on the economic aspects of "getting a home, setting up a business, or getting a job," and on their "social relations" with other Japanese in this Zone and with Caucasians.

Suggestions for reconstructing the history of resettlement and for discussing the status of the resettler at the time of the interviews were covered in the following topics.

VII. *The Resettled Individual*

  A. Reasons for choosing particular destination.

  B. Mechanism by which resettlement was accomplished.

    1. How was the decision to resettle reached: effect of letters, personal contacts and reports, newspaper accounts, rumors of economic success of others, desire for adventure or to see the world; fear of family being caught "on the reservation" for

the duration unless resettlement was started; fear of being branded an "internee"; dissatisfaction with physical and social conditions of camp; conflicts or fear of consequences if remaining in camp (*inu* situation, beatings, etc.); opportunity to break away from minority group; opportunity to break away from family.

The factors listed above (and others) may be thought of as positive influences "pulling" the individual to his destination, and as negative influences "pushing" him away from the relocation project. Parental or group pressures against resettling, and how they were overcome, should be noted.

2. Sponsorship: religious or welfare group, hostels, WRA, friend on outside, family on outside, associational contact on outside, individual initiative.

3. Extent to which plans that were broken or goals that were temporarily abandoned were resumed; extent to which new goals were established.

C. History of resettling in Chicago (or elsewhere)

1. Initial adjustment to life in Chicago; reconstruction of activities, attitudes, fears in first week. Whom did the individual seek out? Who helped him? What were his relations with and attitudes toward Caucasians? Did first impressions fulfill or fall short of anticipations, and in what respects?

2. Finding a job and making a living. What sort of job was first obtained? By what means was it obtained? Was it obtained before or after arriving at destination? Description of job, wages, hours, employer, fellow workers, work conditions, organization of workers. Relations with employers and fellow workers (particularly interracial contacts). Satisfactions or dissatisfactions in connection with work.

(If several jobs are held successively, detailed record of each to be obtained. Why were jobs given up? Account for all periods of unemployment. Who helped out during periods of unemployment? Patterns and level of consumption in relation to income received. Extent of saving for the future; debts).

3. Getting or completing an education, including night school, vocational school, extension, correspondence school in addition to the regular media of formal education; finding a school; getting credit for past work; problems in regard to residence qualifications; relations with teachers, advisors,

schoolmates; contacts with Student Relocation Committee, with social agencies, with schools, teachers, and so on, in communities of previous residence.

4. Participating in religious activities: attendance at Japanese church or neighborhood church. Why was a particular church selected (any previous connection with minister)? What, specifically, do resettled Buddhists do in connection with their religion?

5. Spending leisure time. How much leisure does the individual have, and what does he do with it: reading (what sort?), visiting Caucasians or Japanese (previous or new contact), writing letters (to whom?), radio, movies or theater, gambling or games, sports, boy-girl relationships or sexual activities (including prostitutes and other extra-marital relations).
   (The important thing in regard to the use of leisure time is not only what the resettler does, but *with whom* he does it, with special reference to interracial contacts or limitation to intraracial contacts.)

6. Finding a mate, establishing a family or continuing family relationships. (See later section for analysis of the family.)

7. Participating in political activities.

8. Participating in other voluntary associations.

9. Changing attitudes toward the war, democracy, American citizenship, Japan, Japanese communities in America, Caucasians (persistence or change of *keto* concept), relief or government subsidization (wards of the government), informers (*inu* concept), education, and the family

10. Establishing status or attaining prestige. What are the resettler's ambitions or aspirations? Does present status satisfy those ambitions? What is the mechanism by which attempts are made to achieve desired status? What, specifically, does the resettler plan to do after the war, for example, return to West Coast or establish himself here? What are his plans for family, education, occupation?

In an effort to build up family histories, the focus was shifted wherever possible by interviewing other members of the family. As a guide to the expansion of observations from the individual to the family, the topics listed below under VIII, IX, and X, and XI were suggested. The resettler almost invariably began his undirected account by covering most of the topics listed under IX and X, in connection with those in I; and incorporated data on his family in discussing topics II to VII.

VIII. *Composition and Characteristics of the Family* (family defined as household, that is, individuals living together at specified time, except in heading A) on approximately December 1, 1941.
   A. Resettler's concept of the family.
   B. Demography of the family: age or birth date, sex, marital status, headship, relationship of other members to head, place of residence, birthplace, indicating *ken* for Issei.
   C. Educational and cultural status of family members.
      1. Grade completed at time of evacuation for American educated. Follow WRA procedure for indicating education in Japan.
      2. Cultural (very briefly): language used by members in addressing each other, etiquette and rituals, celebration of American or Japanese festivals.
   D. Occupation of family members, usual and factual.
   E. Religious connections of family members.
   F. Physical characteristics, notes about general appearance and defects.
   G. Standard of living of family: home ownership, neighborhood characteristics.
IX. *Brief History of the Family*
   A. Immigration: when, how, with whom, from where, to where?
   B. Economic history of family in America: resources when they arrived in America, first job of immigrants, history of rise or fall on occupational scale, periods of depression and prosperity, who helped out in periods of depression, job mobility.
   C. Educational history of family in Japan and America: schools attended, educational goals and achievements.
   D. Interpersonal relationships of family members: headship and authority, roles of each member in family management, conflicts (marital, parent-child, sibling, nature of family solidarity, birth, marriage, death crises). How, in brief, did the family members get along with each other?
   E. Relations of family with Japanese community in America: professional relations, connections with associations, social activities.
   F. Contacts of family with members remaining in Japan.

G. Relations of family with Caucasian community in America. Same headings as for E. In general, as for individual resettlers, evidences of identification with Japan or with America (See IV-H).

X. *The Evacuated Family*

A. Preparations for evacuation: disposal of property, changes in family plans for future, integration or dispersal of family members (supplement to individual record, IV).

B. Experiences in Assembly Center or in the Free Zone (supplement to individual record V).

C. Experiences in Relocation Projects (supplement to individual record VI).

D. Changes in family composition.

E. Changes in interpersonal relationships.

XI. *The Resettled Family* (supplement to individual record VII).

A. Mechanism of resettlement.

B. Initial adjustment.

C. Activities in Chicago, or wherever resettling.

D. Nature of associations.

E. Changes in composition.

F. Changes in interpersonal relationships.

Much of the content of the interviews was recorded verbatim in the presence of the subject, and these verbatim notes were reviewed and amplified after each interview. As soon as possible after the last session with each subject, Kikuchi rearranged his copious notes to conform roughly to the order of the outline, dictated a complete life history, and did not subsequently revise, correct, edit, or style this version. He appended to it excerpts from the daily observational journal and personal diary that he kept in his dual role of research assistant on the Evacuation and Resettlement Study and of evacuee resettler, and, where available, the content of reinterviews with the subject, cross-references to interviews with the subject's relatives and associates, and documentary material (for example, diaries, letters, clippings) furnished by or relating to the subject. In 1946 WRA made available transcripts of the 1942 census record for each subject and for members of his family who were evacuated with him, and these, too, were appended to each life history.

The draft of the fifteen life histories used in *The Salvage* was prepared by the author of this volume, who abridged the Kikuchi version by eliminating many repetitions, abbreviating some of the observations to give better balance, and eliminating some material that might have identified the subjects. In the interest of continuity, a few of the observations were again rearranged. Nothing was added to the main body of the Kikuchi version, and the wording was changed only to correct obvious typing errors or to disguise names of persons and of localities, firms, and institutions. The subjects are identified by numbers indicating the order in which Kikuchi initially interviewed them, for example, CH-1 is the first resettler whose life history Kikuchi undertook to prepare, and CH-64 is the sixty-fourth and the last in his series. The rationale for his selection of the sixty-four subjects, and for the author's further selection of the fifteen used in this volume, is discussed in the following section.

Selected Career Lines and Life Histories

The evacuated people were checked and counterchecked, enumerated and reënumerated, during their period of detention. The resettled people left almost as few statistical traces of their movements and of their changing status as do other segments of the American population in intercensal periods. The record of their dispersal is available only in terms of the destination declared when outmigrating from camp, and their characteristics by area of settlement will be known only in terms of the pattern that has evolved at the time of the 1950 census. Thus, though the static "evacuee universe" of 1942 can be defined, the changing composition of the dynamic "resettler universe" of 1943–1945 cannot be accurately described. The fifteen resettlers whose life histories follow are too few to be an adequate sample of either universe; because of the selective force of outmigration, they are certainly not representative of the former; and it cannot be demonstrated that they are a valid cross section of the latter. Determination of longitudinal validity, that is, the extent to which life histories are "typical" configurations of "career lines" and of "trains of experience" is, moreover, insoluble with available techniques. Under the circumstances, all that can be done to justify the selection of cases is to describe how they were actually selected.

Selection involved many compromises, and depended more on experienced judgment rather than on mechanical procedures. During his thirty months' residence in Chicago, Kikuchi established contacts with several hundred resettlers in many situations: at the WRA field office and at headquarters of the Friends Service Committee; in hostels and boardinghouses; at public dances and in bars; at gatherings sponsored by JACL, by resettler committees, by churches, by welfare agencies; in schools and colleges and at places of employment; and in the rapidly expanding circles of his own friends and of those of his sisters, brothers, in-laws, and professional associates. Through these contacts he hoped to obtain subsamples of the evacuated population, stratified by sex and by generation and by broad groupings of prewar residence and prewar occupational classes.

As of the summer of 1943, Kikuchi planned to obtain life histories representing all of the important strata of the prewar Japanese American population in evacuated areas, in terms of age-sex groupings, educational-generational classes, religious and other cultural criteria, and occupational status. This plan of "total coverage" was overly ambitious at its inception, and became increasingly unrealistic as the nature of the selection involved in resettlement became apparent. After the fall of 1943, no attempt was made to cover the Kibei or Issei categories, and a plan was developed for a series of one hundred life histories of Nisei, to be limited to "involuntary evacuees," who had spent some time in camp prior to inmigration to Chicago, and to include all of the main career lines known to have been developing among second-generation Japanese on the West Coast prior to the outbreak of war. This plan was successful to the extent that a highly diversified series was obtained, but unsuccessful in reaching the numerical goal. Making contacts, establishing rapport, interviewing, recording, and dictating consumed much more time than had been anticipated. When Kikuchi was inducted into the Army in August, 1945, he had prepared sixty complete and four partial histories. Of the sixty complete histories, five had to be excluded from the series: one "old Chicagoan"; two Issei evacuees; one American Indian evacuated as a Japanese from Alaska; and one voluntary Nisei evacuee. Concomitant with his successful application of the criterion of "covering the range," Kikuchi made positive efforts to avoid some of the biases inherent in this sort of sampling. Thus, he did not limit selection of subjects to the accessible or the initially coöperative but included also those who were hostile or indifferent, and those with whom repeated interviews were mutually inconvenient. He did not find it difficult to avoid biasing his selection in terms of the "success" or "failure" of adjustment to resettlement, inasmuch as he interviewed all of the resettlers during the initial stages of resettlement and reinterviewed most of them repeatedly. Thus he was able to record adjustment as an ongoing process. Finally, he was constantly aware of the possible effect both on selection of subjects and on the course of his interviews of his own strong cultural and political orientation toward the Occidental way-of-life and toward the United States.[179]

The author of *The Salvage* chose from Kikuchi's series of life histories the fifteen that seemed, in her judgment, to be the best possible complement to her treatment of mass phenomena. The selections for Part II were not made until the manuscript for Part I was virtually complete. The fifteen life histories, as a unit, did not therefore, directly influence the synthesis out of which the "frame of reference" was developed. Indirectly, however, all of the documentary material available—including not only Kikuchi's series of histories and his diary but also the many case histories, journals, and reports prepared by other members of the staff of the Evacuation and Resettlement Study—influenced the author's organization of Part I and her interpretation of the results of historical and statistical analyses. Parts I and II are, to this extent, interdependent.

[179] Kikuchi's diary (which covers more than 10,000 typed pages) is being condensed and edited for publication, under grants from the American Philosophical Society and the University of Pennsylvania. His autobiography, prepared during the prewar period, was published by Louis Adamic in *From Many Lands* (New York. Harper and Brothers, 1940). Taken together, these represent important substantive additions to *The Salvage.*

The selection of the fifteen histories was influenced most directly by sections on agricultural adjustments, urban enterprise, and occupational mobility, with particular reference to Nisei. Each history includes experiences in one or more of the major and a number of the minor occupations open to second-generation Japanese on the Pacific Coast during the prewar decade. The first three are the life histories of three Nisei from farms in central California: one from the marginal, disadvantaged classes, the other two destined to inherit more prosperous enterprises founded by their fathers; the second accepting his role and actively preparing for scientific farming at an agricultural college, the first and third attempting to escape from farm life through higher education, the former via the distasteful "schoolboy" route, the latter by working for the vernacular press. The other cases illustrate various urban careers, but three of them (the eighth, ninth, and tenth) had also had extensive farming experience: the tenth moved without evident conflict from unpaid labor on his father's farm to become a highly skilled artisan and successful businessman; the eighth started as a wage laborer for Issei farmers and then became a mechanic in a Japanese-operated garage; and the ninth combined paid labor in the fields with unpaid labor in her father's pool hall in the ethnic community. The major outlets for Nisei in the restricted labor market in San Francisco are illustrated by the careers of a newspaper reporter (third); of a Hawaiian-born domestic servant who had planned to become a librarian (sixth); of an errand boy (fifth); and of a white-collar assistant in an Oriental art goods store (fourth). The seventh and fourteenth represent careers of college-educated Nisei in Seattle; the former, frustrated in his journalistic ambitions, worked with his parents and siblings in the family-owned restaurant; the latter, economically and culturally advantaged, utilized his talents successfully as a commercial artist. The twelfth and thirteenth were Los Angeles "career girls," the former just emerging from the family enterprise, the latter still held within the bounds of "Little Tokyo." The eleventh and fifteenth are noteworthy for their abundant and faithful delineation of the tortuous paths of one Nisei in the Issei-dominated fruit and vegetable business in the Los Angeles metropolitan area and of another along the pioneering route of state civil service.

Ecological and demographic range are suggested by a brief inventory of origins and characteristics. All fifteen were children of Japanese immigrants; all but one were American-born; by the criterion of education in American schools, all were Nisei. Two were Northwesterners; two had spent their childhood in the intermountain states and one in Hawaii, before migrating to the West Coast; nine were California born and bred. Only two of the fifteen had visited or sought employment in other parts of the United States before the war; and six had lived all their lives within the boundaries of California. In addition to the one Issei-by-accident-of-birth who was brought to America as an infant, four had visited Japan, but only one of these had a vivid memory of the land of his parents. Fourteen had attended Japanese language schools, and all were bilingual. All had graduated from high schools, and all but four had had some college training. Four were Buddhists, and eleven were Christians or secularists. There were eleven males, and four females. At the time of interview only three were over 30 years of age, and none was less than 20 years old. Six of them were married.

All fifteen had participated in the forced mass migration from the West Coast, had been confined in assembly centers and relocation projects, and had outmigrated from camp to Chicago or other Midwestern cities during 1943 or early 1944. In all cases, evacuation and detention broke career lines, and in all cases the subjects were preoccupied, during the early months of resettlement, in exploring possibilities for developing new careers. Their social and economic adjustment is presented as an ongoing process. Like other resettlers and like other Americans, some of them were awaiting induction into the armed forces; others were working in defense industries and war agencies. Some were entering the ranks of skilled and semiskilled labor; others were moving up the occupational ladder to the clerical and professional rungs. Some were finding difficulties in making vocational, personal, or social adjustments; some were rebellious and disorganized. But whether narrowly defined as "successes" or as "failures," these resettlers represent the wartime *salvage* of the Japanese American minority, inasmuch as outmigration from camps to the "outside world" in all cases broke their isolation, promoted acceptance by the majority group, extended the range of their participation, and integrated many of their activities into those of the larger American community.

Each of the fifteen life histories presented here is preceded by (1) a brief description of the subject, including date and place of birth, marital status at the time of interview, height and weight as recorded by WRA, the dates of the interviews, and excerpts from Kikuchi's impressions of subject and interviews; (2) a chronological summary of career lines, including wherever possible the occupational and educational history of the parents in Japan, the date and circumstances surrounding their immigration to the United States, date and "type" of marriage, prewar residential and occupational mobility and status; and for the subject himself, educational history, prewar occupational history and mobility, postevacuation migration history, educational and occupational history after resettlement. These data were obtained both from Kikuchi's records and from the WRA transcripts. Conflicts between sources as well as other annotations and interpolations are indicated in brackets or in footnotes.

Material from reinterviews, from interviews with other family members, from the subject's diary or letters, and from other documentary sources is presented in footnotes or as an appendix to the life history. Annotation is kept at the minimum considered essential for interpreting the case, and the reader is referred to the section on social demography and to the whole of Part I for the *frame of reference,* and to the index and its accompanying glossary for definitions, for the meanings of abbreviations, and for translations of Japanese words and phrases.

Fifteen Life Histories

CH-27: "SCHOOLBOY"

Male; born in California, 1919; height 67"; weight 130 lbs.; unmarried. Interviewed January–February, 1944. Rapport was established through contacts over several months and interviews, which were "lengthy and intensive in scope" over a period of ten days. CH-27 was described as "thin, with slightly prominent cheek bones." He seemed to the interviewer to be "making an effort to overcome a tendency towards shyness," to be intelligent and sensitive, and to have "considerable insight into his personal problems of adjustment."

CAREER LINES

Parental: Both parents were from the farming classes in Japan. Father (born 1875) emigrated in 1902, returned to Japan to marry in 1914, and brought his wife (born 1895) back to this country the following year. Father had no formal education; mother completed four years of schooling in Japan. Father established himself as an independent farmer in the vicinity of Fresno in 1918, and continued to operate his small vineyard in that area until 1942.

Own: Finished junior year at college in California in 1942. During childhood worked on family farm and by the day for other farmers; farm laborer, 1939–1940; odd jobs, including domestic service, while in college. Inmigrated to Denver in December, 1942, and worked as houseman in a hotel for one month, and as assistant photographer for five months. Moved to Chicago in June, 1943, and obtained work as a technician in a photograph shop. He was still holding this job at the time of the interview, while making plans to complete his education.

LIFE HISTORY

My father came to the United States around 1895. [1902] He was quite young at that time and his aim was to find some work where he could make a fortune very quickly and then return to Japan. He came from a farm family in the Hiroshima province. When he came over to this country he worked in a sawmill up in the northwest for a number of years. Around 1913 my father went back to Japan and a marriage was arranged for him.

When he came back to California with his new bride, he started in to farm [near Fresno]. I don't know how he got hold of his land, but he was able to purchase it with a couple of partners. Eventually his two Japanese partners gypped him out and my father was left holding the mortgage to the farm by himself. He worked hard in order to clear this debt and it meant that he had to pay for his farm twice. My father had saved quite a bit of money before he got married, but he lost most of his money with all of this trouble to get his farm.

Our family was poor from that time on. There were 8 of us children. [CH-27 was the fourth]. Father used to get drunk very often and then he would have a mean streak and insult us children. My mother used to be very upset about this but she couldn't do very much. For some unknown reason my father suddenly stopped drinking, that is, he only drank moderately after that. He began to devote more and more attention to his family which was increasing yearly. As he got older he became much more understanding toward the children. It was my mother who caused most of the trouble after that.

My mother was extremely nervous and always timid about everything. Sometimes my father would want to make some sort of a business venture but my mother would always be skeptical and reprimand him for being rash. This would discourage him so much that we were never able to improve our economic situation. My mother was quite a few years younger than Dad, 21 years to be exact. As my parents got older, my mother began to be more dominating. It got so that she never let my father have his way even in his business life. My father would give in because he wanted to avoid a big argument. I liked my father much better than my mother because he was much more tolerant. I think all of us children felt the same way. Mother was very economical in her ways and this streak became her dominant passion as the family got larger. While we were children, Father used to take us for rides in the car on Sundays because we liked to travel, however, my mother got het up over this because she thought it was a terrible waste of money to be burning up gasoline just to go sight-seeing. As children we were not allowed to go to shows because mother thought this was a waste of money. We were not even allowed to have a little money to buy candy like the other kids. Mother protested quite angrily when father wanted to buy some fertilizer for the farm. She could see no immediate return in that so she thought it was not necessary to spend the money for it. Another time my oldest brother wanted to start a business enterprise so that he could go on his own but my mother was against that, too, and she said that he would not be able to make a success of it. All of this had a tendency of taking away our self-confidence and we became rather timid about everything for fear that we would fail. It was my mother's influence that made us very mercenary and grasping. Even now, I don't like to spend money for clothes, if I think I can get by without it.

My mother would raise holy heck when my oldest brother stayed out until 11 o'clock at night and then slept late in the morning. Finally my brother rebelled completely and he utterly refused to obey my mother. He was 17 years old at the time. He worked at home for 4 years on the farm and he didn't get paid for it at all. He finally decided to go on his own so he suddenly went to Los Angeles.

This revolt process then went on down to my next sister and so on down the line. For example, my older sister wanted to go out on dates when she was in high school and my mother refused to allow her. It was even a struggle for her to be allowed to go to church conferences. She wanted to get a new dress to go to one church conference but my mother did not believe in this. My sister said that she worked in the fields for the family without pay and she felt entitled to a new dress once in a while. My mother refused to give in so that my sister went on a bitter revolt and she wouldn't have a thing to do with my mother for two or three years. This created a very strange feeling in our household and it made things unpleasant for all the rest of us.

My next older brother was rather quiet. He never made any open breaks but there was that current of rebellion running through him also. My revolt was to go up to college and then not want to ever come back home. My next sister revolted after [relocation] in Boston. She seized upon school as the excuse and that was how she was able to leave the family. The rest of the family are young, but I got a letter recently from my family telling me that my younger brother is also getting out of control.

My father was not able to raise our living standards very much because we only had a 20-acre farm and it was pretty difficult for him to feed the whole family. As the children got older we went out and did day work for other farmers in order to supplement the family income. We had to work in the California slave pattern which existed at that time. The hours of work were very long and the pay was very low. We kids were denied all of the things that normal kids had because of our extreme poverty. We never did have good clothes to go to school with. It made us feel inferior. Even when I graduated from high school I had to wear my brother's hand-me-down suit and shoes that were two sizes too large for me. That was a pretty terrible experience for me.

As long as I can remember my family life was very disorganized. We seldom ate together as a family unit because the family was too large and the table could not seat all of us at one time. Our home was quite dirty and that made our poverty look even worse. Originally we had two bedrooms, a living room, kitchen, and a porch in our house. All ten of us had to crowd in there. It was much worse living there than in the camps after we were evacuated. It is a wonder that we did not all get sick because of the unsanitary condition.

Our home was furnished very scantily. There was one large table in the middle of the living room. We had linoleum on the floor but no upholstered furniture. Later we remodeled the house a little bit and two more rooms were added. We got a few more pieces of furniture but it wasn't better than we had before. Most of the Japanese farmers did not believe in putting more improvements into their homes. In our case we just didn't have the money to do it. Because my home was so dirty and poverty stricken, none of us would ever invite our friends over to visit us because we were ashamed. Later we let some Nisei friends drop in occasionally but not very often. I had a very guilty feeling about the untidy squalor of our home and I didn't want anyone to see it. The reaction to this took place when I went off to college and I was finicky about everything being clean and proper. I was perfectly miserable at the thought of ever returning to my home and I hated to go even for visits. I can laugh about it now but it was a very serious thing to me then and I thought that we were about the poorest Japanese family in our area. When I was at the University of California, I went home one summer and I hated my home more than ever. I saw the things all piled up on the table and the house was a mess. A resentful and angry feeling rushed over me and I had an impulse to grab everything and scatter it all over the floor. I don't know why I did this but my mother certainly was angry at me for days.

We had constant squabbles in our family life and I wanted to get away from it. I would get moody and brood for hours. My mother was very frugal even in feeding us and that explains why all of us are so thin. A lot of times one can of sardines would have to go around to the 10 people in the family. We would eat rice with that. Lunch usually consisted of bread with some mayonnaise spread on it. I can't stand the sight of mayonnaise now because of that experience. Once in a while we would pick wild berries to spread on our bread. My mother wouldn't let us use the vegetables grown on the farm because we had to sell them to buy other things. Another frequent meal that we had was four eggs scrambled with milk and this would be cut into 10 pieces and we would eat it with rice. We had hardly any meat at all. It was mostly served Japanese style and rice was the main staple. We never enjoyed any of our family meals. We used to bicker all the time about who should get the biggest piece and that built up my feeling of always grasping things for myself.

My parents were rather Japanesy, but because of our constant rebellion we reacted in the opposite direction. I never did take any of the *kendo* business like so many Nisei fellows did. My parents wanted us to bow to them when we met in the morning but we refused to do this. We did not even bow to other elders until way later and we only did it then to avoid an argument. We all went to Japanese [language] school and I rebelled wholeheartedly against the whole setup. They tried to teach us Japanese reading and writing and I did not take to it very well. I speak Japanese very poorly now and I think that I understand it less than the average Nisei. At times I somewhat regret that because it is good to know another language. Another reason why we did not learn Japanese very well is that we did not have a close relationship [with our parents] so that all of us kids spoke English to each other. We never had any reason to consult our parents for advice very often so that there was no need to know more than a limited broken Japanese.

The only serious conversation I can ever remember having with my parents was when I wanted to go off to college. I didn't have any money of my own since all of my earnings had been contributed to the family pot. I had to ask for $200 and explain why education was so necessary. The most serious conversation my older brother had was when he got married. It was a marriage of his own choice and it was not arranged and he had quite a time getting my folks to accept this fact. I remember how my older sister rebelled when the elders wanted to marry her off to somebody she didn't know. My parents objected to the boy friend she had so she refused to marry anyone and remained stubborn about that.

My parents are not too well educated. My pop can't read or write Japanese. We used to subscribe to the Japanese language paper and my mother would read all of the news to my father. My parents did not think that they would ever go back to Japan because they had such a large family here. They didn't have anything to go back to anyway. Of course, my mother was very strongly pro-Japan. Dad was more passive in his attitude. We would constantly argue with my mother very bitterly when she talked about Japan. After the war began my father said that he did not care which side won, but he wished that it would be over right away. My mother remained pro-Japan and she is still this way. However, political issues never disrupted our family lives because it was not that important to us. The main goal of our family was money. My parents wanted security for all of their children. My mother was always giving us lectures about money. She said that the Nisei were too lazy and she considered them as good-for-nothing spendthrifts. She didn't think that the other parents were training their children right. My mother's idea was that you should buy things as cheaply as possible and not indulge in any luxuries.

I think that our poverty was the reason why we did not have more of the Japanese culture in our home so that it may have been a good thing in that respect. None of us cared for music and we had no fancy for that Japanese art. The walls of our home were quite bare of any Japanese prints. We didn't even have any of those Japanese dolls in the house for the girls or Japanese articles of clothing. My mother wasn't interested in flower arrangement because she was too busy working and raising the family. Most of the Japanese families in our area were interested in Japanese dances for their daughters and at certain religious festivals the Nisei girls would all participate. None of our family took part in this because we did not have any of the Japanese costumes.

Among the children, we had a pretty strong bond. I suppose we were driven into this because of our circumstances. We got along very well and we banded together at every instance where money was concerned. Whenever one of us got a day job on one of the neighboring farms, we always tried to get the other members of the family employed at the same place. For a while my oldest brother was the boss of our group but we became more independent as we got older. I suppose we felt that we should stick together in opposition to our mother although this was never directly mentioned.

I lived in [X], a typical Japanese rural community [near Fresno]. It was composed of about 50 Japanese families, consisting of a little over 200 individuals. The Nisei were pretty young but they were beginning to outnumber the first generation. There were quite a few single Issei men who worked around the neighboring areas during the harvest season and they would rest up in [X] during the slack season. We had a Japanese Association and a Buddhist and a Christian Church. We went to the Buddhist Church regularly and my father belonged to the Japanese Association. The churches were the social centers for all of us. We held all of our meetings there regardless of their nature. The only contacts that the Japanese community had with the larger American society was in economic affairs. Among the Nisei there were a few contacts, largely through casual school association. Each individual of the Japanese community knew everything about each other. That is why my mother was always reminding us not to do this or that because the other Japanese families would notice and then talk about us.

There was quite a great deal of family pride in this community in regards to the family line. However, I think that money was the most important element and the most important people in the community were the richest. Our family accepted its lower position and we didn't try to advance ourselves socially. We felt inferior to some of the other richer families.

It was an agricultural community and the people were very conservative in their ways. During my childhood, the Issei considered that socials and dances among the Nisei was taboo. There was also a general taboo against the Nisei smoking or dating out. The Nisei fellows couldn't date out girls of certain families and we couldn't even go over there for a social visit because of the parents' attitude. These girls were married by arrangement in the Japanese manner and I think that most of the Nisei in our area accepted this practice. Those who rebelled were ostracized for this action.

The only recreational outlet for the Nisei kids was basketball. I started to play this game from an early age. Sometimes the church club would be allowed to hold very stilted socials for the Nisei. The boys and girls did not mix at all because we were all so backward. Very few of the fellows had girl friends that they went around with steady.

There was a great rift between the Buddhists and the Christians. On the whole, the Christian group was more liberal and more aggressive. The Buddhists did not trust the Christians. I know that I was taught that the Christian Japanese were insincere and that they took on false airs and humbled themselves to the Caucasians in order to gain their favor. The Christian Japanese mingled more with the *hakujin*. The Buddhists kept entirely to themselves socially. I think that the children of these Christian Japanese mixed more than we

Buddhist children also. However, the Christian Nisei did not hold any dances either as their parents were also strict. On the whole, the Christian Nisei were not as backward as we were. The Buddhist group outnumbered the Christian group about two to one. The Buddhists were the ones to sponsor most of the Japanese festivals held in our community. *Bon odori* and doll festivals were occasions for quite a bit of celebration and even the Christian Japanese participated in them. *Hanamatsuri,* that is the flower festival to celebrate the birth of Buddha, was the event of the year in our community. This flower festival was climaxed with the *bon odori* dance.

There were quite a few distinct groups in the larger American society and each of them kept to themselves also. We had a colony of Mennonites, a German colony, a Filipino group, and an Okie group. The Okies and the Filipinos were the most despised of all these groups. The Japanese community commanded a certain amount of respect among the rest of the American community because the Issei were good businessmen and not stupid in their business dealings. My father grew grapes and fruits mostly on his farm and he sold them to a local shipping concern. He did not have to know much English because there was a Japanese representative who acted as interpreter and a secretary of the growers' association which they had organized informally.

My older brothers and sisters did not make brilliant records in school. When it came to my record, it was definitely above the average but that was because I studied so hard. That gave me some amount of self-confidence and it accounted for my desire to go on to college. I think that my younger sister is the most brilliant of the family. She was the valedictorian of her graduating class and the first Nisei to achieve this honor.

I was very backward throughout my school life. I thought that the reason for this was because I was so poor. I never let any of the other pupils watch me eat my lunch because I was ashamed. On rainy days I felt so ashamed when my Dad came driving up in a battered Ford car to take us kids home. It seemed to me that all the other kids' fathers had good cars to go home in. It took something out of me when I had to wear a homemade sweater to my classes. I used to think that all the kids laughed at me behind my back because I was dressed so poorly. It was a terrible feeling to have and I felt sad many times because of it.

As I got along in school, some of this attitude broke down a little bit. I got along fairly well with the other pupils. I've only had one fist fight in all of my life. I was very shy in my classes and I hated to recite. I used to try and sit in the back of the class and be as inconspicuous as possible. During recitation I would sweat all over for fear that I would be called upon to recite. As I went on through high school, we did not mix with the Caucasians very much. We didn't speak to Caucasian girls at all. We had a Japanese clique and we all ate lunch together. There were 20 Nisei out of 100 in our graduating class.

The only time I ever expanded out of the Nisei group was when I played on the high school basketball team. I had been playing basketball for years and I became one of the stars. I made a letter every year. I had no other high school activities except I belonged to the California Scholastic Federation. I also worked on the school paper as art editor as I had an interest in art at that time. I used to have to work before and after school on my father's farm so that I couldn't stay to watch the high school football games. This was true for all of the other Nisei kids too.

In 1937 I graduated from high school. I took a Subject A test and I passed it so I thought that I would like to go to [junior] college. I never dared to even dream that I could go because none of the others before me went [from X]. It was the accepted way of life to work on the farm after high school graduation. I was the first Nisei to go on to junior college after graduation. It was not expensive as the fee was only $5 but many Issei parents thought that the children should go on the farm after high school. Later on they began to let them go to junior college and college more because a few Nisei went off. The other families felt that they should keep up and do the same thing for their own children. It wasn't because the Issei objected to education; they believed in it very strongly, but they had an idea that it cost thousands of dollars to send a Nisei to college. It was only after a few of us went and showed that it could be done on a minimum of money that the other Nisei were encouraged to try and work their way through college as we did. The parents did not object to that at all.

I don't think that I would ever have gone on to junior college entirely on my own. My older brothers and sister egged me on as they had been denied the chance themselves. They were working and contributing to the family pot at that time and they thought that I would not be needed so much to help out at home.

In 1939 I graduated from the junior college. I did not know what I was going to do then. I wanted to go on to a college but no other Nisei had ever left our community to go to a college out of town before. It was a remote and fantastic idea to me and I didn't think that I would ever be able to do it. I took a general course at the junior college as I didn't know exactly what I was interested in training for. I knew that I didn't want to settle down to a farm life. I had been pretty good at art but I didn't think it was practical enough for me. I took courses in almost every department of the school in an effort to find out what I was suited for.

I had no money at all so I thought I would stay out of school for a year to save money. I worked on the neighboring farms picking grapes all that year. All of the money I earned I put into the family pot. We had always done that and I didn't even think of keeping a separate account for myself. The family needed the money and that was all there was to it. As the year for a new school term came closer, in 1940, I began to think more and more of going to college. I knew that I just couldn't stand the deadening farm work much longer. My brother, who had rebelled against the family, had gone on to Los Angeles where he was working as a gardener. He wrote and told me to come down there to go to college. That helped me to make my decision. In August my other brother and I took a trip to Los Angeles during the slack season and I suddenly decided to stay on there with my older brother. I enrolled at [a college in Los Angeles] and my parents did not know that I had left the family until my other brother went back and told them.

I had $106 to my name when I started [college]. I had taken this money from the family pot as I felt that I was entitled to it. My parents did not object too much to this as they felt that they could get along without my help. I didn't know what I wanted to take at [college]. After living with my older brother for a short time I went to work in a home as a schoolboy. I had come from a very backward area so that when I first entered my work as a schoolboy, I looked at my employer as being on a superior level to me. I felt like a servant and I used to rebel inwardly to myself when I had to go and scrub the latrine. I thought that I was lowering myself. I knew that no other Japanese would ever scrub a toilet. My boss could never understand me. They treated me as .nice as they could but I was very unhappy. I worked there all semester and after I got used to the place, I had to do more and more work. Soon I was putting in 40 hours of work a week instead of the required 20. Like a fool, I wanted to impress them at first and I did extra things to please them. After that I had to do all of these things as a part of my regular work. I only had one Saturday and two Sundays off during all that semester. I assumed that I would get the Christmas season off so I could go home while my employers assumed that I would stay there. They got extremely angry when I told them that I was going home anyway. They said I was a most ungrateful person for putting them to such an inconvenience. I got fired for the first time in my life.

After New Years I went back to Los Angeles to start another term at [college]. I went to a Japanese employment agency and I found another job as a schoolboy with a Jewish family. They treated me much better than my first boss. However, my year at [this college] was not very successful. I felt all alone during the time I was there. I continued to be shy and I did not make too many attempts to get into even the Nisei society on the campus. I did not know how to dance and that seemed to be about the only thing that the Nisei were interested in.

My idea of what I wanted to do for a career was gradually taking shape. By that time I had started to take some landscape architecture courses. I didn't know what it was all about until near the end of the second semester. I like art and I had come from an agricultural background so that it was natural for me to combine the two things. I knew that I was not good enough to be a straight artist and all the farmer boys wanted to get away from the farm. I thought that if I took landscape architecture there would be a combination of the two things which I had experience and interest in. My brother was a gardener and he interested me in plants and I realized that all farming was not deadening to the mind. Unfortunately [this college] did not offer a full course in landscape architecture and the only place I could get it was [a college in northern California]. At the end of the school term I went home with the vague idea that I would try to get up [there] for the fall semester of 1941.

I worked hard all summer and my mind was set on going to [college] so I would not have to stay home any longer. I was desperately in need of money and I had to contribute to the family fund at the same time. When I left around August I took $125 out of the family fund. By this time, my parents approved of me going to college. They were proud that I was one of the few Nisei from our community to go on to college and that raised our family prestige and social status quite a bit. My parents thought that I might be able to get a good job afterward and make a good salary.

After my experience [in Los Angeles], I didn't want to work as a domestic in a home any more. I found a place to live very cheaply so that I batched with a couple of other Nisei fellows and I got a job working part time. I worked in an ice plant as a maintenance man and I took care of the gardens on the property. In spite of my hopes for a better adjusted life, I was unhappy during my stay [at this college]. I didn't know why I was so depressed exactly. I didn't have much money so that I became very tight with what I did have. I don't think I made a very good impression on my roommates because I rarely smiled and was curt with them. I buried myself in my studies but that did not give me any satisfaction. I was scared of girls and I never had any dates like the other Nisei fellows who were living in the house. I wanted to be an accepted person and I couldn't get in the Nisei circle because they were too cliquish. I began to take an interest in racial relations meetings. I also became more interested in academic discussions of all kinds. Gradually I threw myself heart and soul into the landscape architecture course and I found that I liked this course as it was something concrete.

It was in respect to social activities that I distinctly felt inferior. I could not join in when the fellows began to talk of dances, dates, and girls. I felt very inferior when the fellows all dolled up on Saturday night to go out for a date. I pretended that I had a noble purpose in life and that I did not miss it, when in reality I longed for this sort of thing.

One day I saw a Nisei girl on the campus and she appealed to me a great deal. I was too timid to make her acquaintance so that I had a secret crush on her for months. I got pretty desperate as the evacuation period drew near so that I gained enough courage to go up and make her acquaintance. I almost had a date to go to a flower show with her, but it never materialized because she suddenly left the campus to rejoin her family for evacuation.

I had no political interests at all and I was not aware of the growing war tension which had been developing during the summer and fall. I never read any of the newspapers and I did not belong to any political clubs. My only aim was to get through college as quickly as I could. I thought that I would have to go on to graduate school and know the field twice as well as the Caucasian fellows in order to compete with them for a job. I was aware of the Nisei economic problems and I knew that they had very little chance to start out on their own. I felt that I was in a field where I would have a good chance to get into civil service even though I were a Nisei. I thought that I was equal to a white person and I hoped that I could be eventually accepted on my individual merits.

The beginning of the war caused a great change in my life. I was studying for [exams] that Sunday of December 7, 1941. I happened to be reading a book that morning and I idly turned on the radio to relax for a few minutes. When I first heard the news of the Pearl Harbor bombings, it didn't sink home at all. I thought that the report was false. However, I began to have some disturbing thoughts in my mind so I went outside to ask the other fellows what they thought about it. At that moment another Nisei fellow came dashing down the walk saying that the Japs had attacked America. Suddenly it dawned upon me that it was the real thing and I had a terrific reaction. I felt, "Oh, those damn fools, why are they attacking America?" I didn't conceive of it in terms of right or wrong. I thought that the Japanese Army was doing a hell of a stupid thing and I couldn't see how they had a chance.

A group of us got together to talk about this stunning news. We began to crystallize our thoughts on how it would affect us as individuals. I got in a depressed mood. My whole reaction then was to withdraw into myself as I usually do when confronted with a crisis. I didn't want to talk to the other Nisei fellows any longer. I went out and I became greatly upset. I had immediate fears that I would attract attention as a treacherous Jap. I realized that I would not be able to finish college. The thought occurred to me very selfishly, "Why couldn't they have waited until after the finals before attacking Pearl Harbor?" I knew I wouldn't be drafted immediately as I had been classified 4-F. Everyone in [town] was excited by that time so I thought it was better for me to get off the streets. I went right home and locked myself in my room. I hovered over the radio all the rest of the day and I forgot about my finals. I had a dejected sort of feeling for the rest of the day. We Nisei didn't know whether to go home immediately or not. Toward evening I thought I would go out for a moment but I felt all eyes were staring at me so I didn't go very far. I expected somebody to jump on me and attempt to beat me up at any moment. That evening I was worried sick and I didn't sleep very well.

The following day I had to go to school and I really did hate to go. I had the feeling that everyone would accuse me for the treachery of the Japanese military forces. I knew that I would be immediately tabbed as a Jap. Most of us Nisei had always been led to believe that we were Japs and I knew that most of the Caucasian people would look upon me that way. I was afraid that my classmates would regard me as one of the enemies. When I got on the campus, I was amazed when the fellows spoke to me as an American and we talked about how the war would affect us as Americans. I couldn't get over this reception as I had not been prepared for it. There was only one instructor who spoke of Japan as if it were my fatherland. He spoke to me as if he pitied me because Japan would be whipped in two months. I resented that because I wanted him to understand that Japan was not my homeland.

That afternoon I went to do my work at the ice plant and I had a lot of misgivings. One of the Caucasian fellows that I met by the gate started to talk to me and he was rather apologetic that the United States was going to whip Japan's ass off. He thought that this would hurt my feelings. I tried to explain to him that I did not know a thing about Japan and that I had never been there. I told him that I was a part of this country and I didn't give a damn about Japan. I appeared a little too eager in my efforts to convince him and I was forced to wave the flag. I think that all of the Nisei did the same thing during this period. Our thinking was all confused for weeks and weeks. The rest of the employees at the ice plant and my boss all went out of their way to show that they did not hold anything against me. I was very surprised at this as I had been expecting the worst. I didn't lose my job at all.

My finals suddenly became very insignificant to me. I wasn't in any mood to concentrate entirely upon them but I managed to come out okay in my grades. I stayed around [college] during the Christmas holidays and I only went home for a three-day visit. My parents were quite worried as my father's bank account had been frozen. We had a heck of a problem in trying to figure out how to feed the family when all the money was tied up. My brother S. took charge of family affairs as he was oldest of the children at home and my parents depended upon him for everything as they were frightened. My parents were not concerned about who would win the war as the emphasis was upon our immediate family needs. There were no Issei picked up in our area as far as I know so the community did not have this fear of [the Issei] being suddenly snatched away like in some of the Japanese communities where many fathers had been taken without any notice.

My parents, at first, wanted me to drop out of school but I thought that I should stay on as long as possible. I told them that nothing would happen to me so that they reluctantly gave in. After that I went back and started a new semester. I carried a very heavy load of classwork as I wanted to complete as many courses as possible. Life began to take on a new significance for me. It was at this time that I ceased making myself miserable by worrying excessively over social activities. I realized how insignificant that limited Nisei world was and it had all crashed after December 7. At the same time I got a closer feeling to the other Nisei as we were all in a common predicament. We were simply all Nisei together in a common problem and many of us were stunned for weeks.

Prior to Pearl Harbor, I never gave politics very much thought except where it pertained to race relationships. I began to wake up to the fact that something could be done about race discrimination if the various minority groups could work together. I developed a new sympathy for the Negroes and other minority groups as I began to realize the conflicts that they had to go through before being accepted in any sort of decent way. I had rebelled against Japanese ways all along in my family circle. There was no doubt in my mind as to where I stood. However, since I was a Nisei, I had some sentimental attachments to Japan. I think that this feeling was much stronger among Nisei who came from the rural communities or from a Buddhist background. After the war broke, I could no longer sit on a fence and let my sentiments control my thinking. I wanted to break all ties with Japan as there had to be a choice immediately.

When all of those Army restrictions started to come in I had another terrific reaction. I suffered all sorts of depressions when the evacuation orders were announced. I began to think of how that would affect the Nisei. I still felt a little different from the rest of the Nisei since my home was in the Free Zone and my family was in no danger of being uprooted since General DeWitt had announced in the papers that the people who went into the Free Zone voluntarily would not be moved again. Most of the Nisei students on the campus had homes in the restricted areas along the coast so that they had to quit school and join their families. It was a comfort to me to think that Zone II would never be evacuated so that I had no guilty feeling about remaining in school since my family would not need me. For this reason I was not under such a heavy strain as most of the other Nisei were. I just bored into my studies and I tried to detach myself as much as possible.

In March, 1942, strong rumors began that everyone would be frozen and no more travel permits for getting out of the restricted zones would be allowed. I had another strong conflict at that time and I finally decided to take a chance and stay, as my family ties were not too strong anyway. My school work became neglected and I got to a point where I just didn't care any more. [On] the last day that I could stay [in the college town] without being frozen and evacuated [from there] I went to the WCCA office and I got a travel permit to rejoin my family. Everything now seemed to have ended suddenly and I was in a confused state of mind. I felt that I had nothing left to hang on to. I thought that I could never go to college any more so that I might just as well give up striving for any personal goal. When I got home, I was very unhappy and moody. I worked around the farm areas near town for other ranchers.

During that summer of 1942 many rumors had been making the rounds and we didn't know what to believe. Every day or so some big rumor would start making the rounds and the Issei generally accepted these rumors as the truth. Even the Nisei believed a lot of them because there was no way of checking up. One day our community was greatly upset because of the news that some of the *hakujin* farmers in Tulare County were lynching any Japanese who attempted to voluntarily evacuate to that section. I later found out that this was not true. I also heard that hundreds of Nisei were losing their jobs because of the war. The Issei spread this around. There were a number of Nisei who lost their civil service jobs but the total number was exaggerated.

There were also favorable stories and rumors that went around. I heard that some Caucasians were coming around secretly to [Japanese] homes at night and offering aid. These people would come late at night and offer money so that other Caucasians would not see them. I also heard of other Caucasians who offered to take care of Japanese property. There were a few stories going around that some Caucasian employers would reassure the Nisei employees that they would not suffer any hardships. The reaction to these stories in the Japanese community was that it touched many of the Issei deeply. They felt that there were a few *hakujin* who were not bitter against them. Even some Nisei were moved by these stories and they became less bitter.

Prior to the definite evacuation orders I heard rumors that only Issei would be evacuated. This caused a considerable amount of discussion in our community because many Issei thought they would be separated from their young children. Even my parents believed this rumor and they instructed the older [children] to take care of the youngsters. One of the shocking rumors was that most of the Nisei soldiers were being discharged from the Army and that some of them were being shot by the American soldiers. We heard that there had been a general free-for-all at Camp Hale and 15 Nisei soldiers had been killed. Many Issei used this story to convince their Nisei children that they were not wanted by this country.

A further blow was added when the rumor went around that citizenship would be taken away from the Nisei as an act for this purpose had been passed in Congress. We heard that all of us would be concentrated at certain camps and deported as soon as it was physically possible. This was one of the biggest and most persistent rumors I heard and it certainly hurt our morale.

I also heard that the Nisei who had dual citizenship would be up a tree. I didn't know whether I had dual citizenship or not but I wanted to make sure that I wouldn't get caught in any of this deportation business so I tried to get it eliminated. I went to Fresno to have my dual citizenship dropped because I was so worried but I lost my birth certificate in that deal and nothing was accomplished. I still don't know if I have dual citizenship or not.

One day just before the evacuation of our area, a big rumor went around that California had been invaded and the Japanese Army was running all over the state. Stories went around that submarines were attacking Los Angeles and that Japanese planes were bombing large cities. That certainly created excitement in our community.

Some of the bitterness on the part of the Issei was due to the fact that many rumors had been spread around about the treatment the FBI gave those who had been interned. Stories went around that the FBI had beaten up and almost killed many of the old and innocent Issei who had been picked up after the war started. There were also stories that all men picked up by the FBI were being sent to the coldest part of the United States and many of them froze to death. There were also stories that some Issei had been beaten up with guns and bayonets by the American soldiers who guarded them. It was surprising that so many of the Issei believed these stories. I don't think that any of these stories were true.

There was a great deal of speculation going around about why the FBI had interned so many of the Issei. It was commonly believed that they had been arrested because they belonged to the Black Dragon Society or else they had collected donations for the *Heimushakai*. Many Issei burned their books and Japanese music records, photographs of the Japanese Emperor, Japanese pictures, Japanese directories, and even Japanese clothes because of the fear that these things were contraband and they would be interned if caught with them. I even know of one case where an Issei threw away all his carpentry tools because he heard that any Issei caught with these contraband would be interned. These stories spread around rapidly. One of the amusing stories was that Mr. [T] had been interned in Fresno because he was a secret general in the Japanese Army. Many of the Issei in our community actually said that they knew this all the time. Later it was found out that Mr. [T] was a 77-year-old Issei who had been doing migratory work for 40 years and the only reason why he was arrested was because he had donated some money or something to a Japanese society. There were all sorts of stories of generals being interned. Many Japanese believed that Japan had a secret army in California. That was all silly because such a thing never existed. There might have been some spy work going on but every country does that. I think that I was affected by a lot of these stories myself because I got rid of my knife and all of my photography equipment on account of some of these wild stories.

The people in our community were always suspecting *inus*. They said that these stool pigeons were mostly radicals and they squealed on their parents to the FBI just to save themselves. There were quite a few stories about the JACL selling the Japanese down the river. It was commonly believed that the JACL was in cahoots with the FBI and we heard such stories as "such and such a leader is receiving concessions from the government," and "all Buddhists would be arrested if they held church services as there were JACL spies around to report it to the FBI." The Buddhist Church in our community was actually closed down because of these rumors. There were other stories going around that voluntary evacuees to Texas were being mobbed and many of them were being arrested and beaten up in Arizona.

The rumors about the terrific losses in business also got around quickly. The story was told that the Japanese living in San Pedro had lost everything because they were only given a few hours to dispose of their property. When evacuation was announced for our zone, many people sold their things hastily at a great loss because they felt they would be treated the same way as the San Pedro group. At that time most of the areas in California had been evacuated already and we had heard of the many losses in business during the process. There were stories going around that the government was going to confiscate all property of the Japanese and [it would] never be returned. This rumor was the determining factor in some of the Issei selling their property. Another rumor was that the government would seize any automobiles which were not disposed of and they would not get any pay for them. There were also other stories that the farms would be taken if not sold by a certain date. All of these stories and many others added to the confusion and bewilderment of our Japanese community. Under such a condition it was impossible to have any sort of a stable community life because of the constant fear and worry of what would be happening to us.

When I first heard the news of the coming evacuation of our zone I became very angry and I blew off quite a bit of steam to other Nisei. Many of the Nisei became extremely bitter and they honestly felt that the government had broken its promise and betrayed them. They felt that they were being unduly persecuted and I couldn't exactly blame them for having this attitude. Many of the Japanese in the Free Zone had voluntarily evacuated to our area from the coast area at their own expense in the hopes that they would not be bothered any more. I couldn't blame them for being angry. I was a little bitter because I felt that there was no military necessity involved for Zone II. I felt that it was a definitely discriminatory measure. The evacuation notice had been announced after some very strong agitation by the Caucasian farmers of that district and it looked pretty fishy to me. Most of the town of [X] had been very tolerant toward the Japanese and they did not resent the voluntary evacuees coming in as it created new business. It was the Associated Farmers who were antagonistic because they thought that the Japanese farmers were getting more and more prosperous and they wanted the land to go back to Caucasian hands. They had been agitating for this for a number of years and the war gave them a sudden opportunity to strike their blows at the innocent Japanese farmers. I still believed in the ideals of democracy, but I had a feeling of bitterness against these agitating groups. I was sore at General DeWitt for double-crossing us like that. I did not think that these narrow-minded people were representatives of America as a whole. I figured that it was the dirty work of a prejudiced economic and political interest which used the excuse of military necessity for their own selfish purposes. My morale got very low when I realized that the Nisei were in such a precarious position.

It was about this time that I thought of making an effort to go to school as fast as I could as I didn't want to get caught in a concentration camp. That's why I became very serious about working on the farms and trying to save every cent that I could. I really worked hard for this purpose. I had three jobs in all and I put in 14 hours a day for seven days a week, believe it or not. I hoped to get a permit to leave the Free Zone so I applied to the WCCA office. They were very sympathetic and they worked upon getting me a permit but there was not enough time. They told me that maybe I should wait until I got to camp. It was then that I realized that I really had to go to camp and the future really did look hopeless. There wasn't anything else for me to do, so I began to put all my energies into helping my family. I became lost in handling family affairs and that took my mind off of the disappointment of not being able to escape camp.

My father's farm was leased to a Caucasian farmer. My brothers and I made arrangements with our white neighbor to take the responsibility for our property. It was his job to deposit the rent money in my brother's account at the bank. We disposed of all our farm machinery and the old car that we had. We put the money from the sale of all these things into three separate accounts in the names of the three oldest children in the family. We thought that if it were in my father's name, it might be frozen. There was an understanding among us that all of this money would go back to the family use later on when it was needed. We also made an arrangement about the crops. The lessee gets 60 per cent and we get 40 per cent of the profits after the expenses are taken out. With our 40 per cent, we have to pay the taxes and the water bill. Last year [1943], while we were in camp, our Caucasian neighbor who handles the business for our farm demanded 5 per cent of the total as his share for looking after the farm for us and we had to give that to him as we had to rely upon him to give us any money at all. This Caucasian man is supposed to be a personal friend of my father and Dad feels that he can't say anything to him about it so we have let it go under the present arrangement. This man has us over the barrel since we are not there to check up on him and he could easily cheat us out.

My Dad took quite a loss in the evacuation. He didn't have too much capital but there was quite a bit of money invested on the farm and he was not able to get his money out of it. For example, he purchased a $400 truck about one month before the war and we had to sell it for $100. There were other deals like that and we could not do anything about it because there was not much time. I think my father has an idea of going back to his farm after the war so that he refuses to sell it out entirely. That is also another reason why we have kept a large part of the family bank account in our home town instead of transferring it out here. My father would be too old to resettle now and it would be almost impossible for him to make a new start any other place. Because of the rise in prices of farm products due to the war, the farm now has a value of about four times of what it was before the war. Even with our 35 per cent cut we still get about half the income that we were making before the war, so that it has turned out fairly well for my folks. However, this is still a loss as my father would be making considerably more if he were there on the farm right now. Many Japanese farmers were caught in this fix. They had had a hard time for a few years before the war and prices were just beginning to go up but they were not able to stay and have the benefit of the rise of war prices. Many of the Caucasian farmers who took over these Japanese farms are reaping the benefits of the hard labor of these Japanese farmers who formerly held the land.

By August, 1942, we had quite a bit of information about the camps. That was because most of the other Japanese had already been evacuated and they had written letters to people in the Free Zone. I had an idea that we would have to stay in these camps for at least 6 years. My parents thought that we would not be gone for over one year. Because of this difference in estimate, we had some family arguments about what we should take to camp. We finally arrived at a compromise after many family discussions.

One of the favorite topics during this immediate period before the actual evacuation was speculating about where we would be sent. When we finally learned that it was to be Poston, there was a great deal of objection because the old folks thought that they would quickly die off from the terrific heat there. Everything was exaggerated so that many of the people went there expecting the worst and they were in great fear. When we got on the train for Poston all of the stress and strain of the last minute preparations were suddenly over and there was a terrific mental letdown. I then felt this utter depression again and I thought that I was alone in the world. As we approached Poston, we got more and more into the desert. My morale dropped accordingly and I felt that all hope was gone when I saw the drab desert land which had no break in its monotony. When I saw the camp for the first time, it was worse than what I had even dreamed of. All I saw was row upon row of drab, black barracks. It looked like a dismal cemetery to me. At that moment I saw no chance of ever escaping from camp and I really felt trapped like a rat in a cage.

I arrived in Poston around August 8, 1942. The first day there was the hottest that they had had that year. The nights were just as hot. I really hit rock bottom then and I felt like giving up everything and crawling into a hole to die. But in a few days it got a little cooler; it was only 110 to 120 degrees then. I was only in Poston seven weeks in all. When I first got there, I immediately felt the military hand descending upon me. We had to line up as we arrived and there was no choice in doing anything. It was all regimented. People were yelling orders all over the place.

The second day in camp I went to the employment office to see if I could get some work that I was interested in. I was in the second contingent to arrive at Poston and the camp was entirely new. When I went to the employment interviewer I was elated at all of the job opportunities offered to us. This raised my hopes a little. Before the evacuation, the only jobs the Nisei ever got were in produce stands, farm work, and menial domestic tasks. At Poston I thought there was more of a chance for Nisei in the way of jobs. The first job I had was that of a block custodian. I helped to open the new blocks up as they finished and get the people settled in them. I also helped some of the aliens file their registration cards. I discovered that the Issei suddenly had to depend upon the Nisei entirely and there was a complete transfer of authority. That made me feel good too.

After a few days my hopes for a job climbed upward to a higher level. I saw that other Nisei were getting good jobs so I thought that I should try and do the same. I wanted to get into the landscape designing department, but this department had not been organized yet. I then thought of opening up a sign shop in camp so I put all of my energies into this after the first week there. I was in Camp III and the administrative headquarters were in Camp I so I went over there every day to try and get my sign shop organized. It was so interesting to me to be doing something like this that I became lost in it. It was the first time in my life that I felt complete as a personality and I was proud of the paint shop that I opened up through my own efforts. I recruited all of the staff members and I managed the shop during the time I was there. I had to contact many people during this organization period and I had to rely completely upon myself. It gave me a lot of self-confidence to talk to the Caucasian personnel as equals. I was entirely free of any feeling of racial persecution. The administration coöperated with me as much as they could and we did not have to look up to any Caucasian boss at that time. It was quite a release to me to feel equal to anyone in the camp.

I became enthused with the system of community life that they had there, but I was soon disappointed with the reaction of the people to it. Before the war most of the Japanese had always been very polite. In camp they let down their hair and they fought for lumber very selfishly and they tried to pull all kinds of strings for better jobs. The Nisei were power crazy and they tried to rule with a dictatorial hand. I think they were a little too harsh in thinking that they were superior to the first generation. The Issei were just as bad because they were out for themselves too. All this made me see that Nisei and Issei were not a meek group. I lost the feeling that the Japanese were a sort of romantic people. I had pictured them previously as being a very special minority in this country and on a much higher moral and cultural level than other minorities. In camp I realized that the Japanese did not have a monopoly on human virtues, and that they could be just as greedy, just as selfish, and just as grasping as any other persons put into their position.

In Camp III there was a large group of evacuees from my home town of [X] and we were a very conservative group. There was also a second large group from the coastal areas and they were more aggressive because many of them had come from urban areas. This group had much more money than our group and there was quite a bit of rivalry at first. Because they were more aggressive, they grabbed all of the responsible positions right away. Many of them got into administrative positions and they tried to dictate everything. The people did not like this since many of these individuals were not competent enough so that they were gradually replaced.

I began to go to the Buddhist Church on Sundays. I was on one of the committees that helped to organize the Buddhist Church. We had to have our church in one of the recreation buildings and the members got together to help build the benches and other things. Several of the richer Buddhists donated the shrine and other necessary articles for the religious services.

At the beginning there were no social and recreational activities until things got more organized. Then the socials began to break out into prominence, and the Nisei put these above everything else. All of the Nisei jumped into social activities but I just didn't fit. I didn't think I could bear it much longer.

It was then that the sugar-beet recruiting came along. I told my folks the day before I left. At that time there were wild rumors going around about the hostile feelings toward us on the outside. There were stories of sugar-beet workers being housed in pig pens. We heard that no toilets or bathing facilities were available and that it was a back-breaking job. Nobody actually knew the real condition as we were the first group to leave camp. I went with the attitude that I did not care what happened as long as I got out of camp. This was on September 30, 1942.

There were nine fellows in the group that went sugar beeting with me. The ages ranged from 17 to 26. Most of the fellows just wanted to get out of camp to have fun as they were bored with camp life. After we got to our place of employment [in Colorado] we had to live in very close quarters in an old house. There was no running water in it and not very many facilities. The nine of us were together for the next two and a half months after arriving there on October 1. The farmer who employed us was very nice and he did not take too much advantage of us. We lived 11 miles from [the town of B] so that we were completely isolated. [B] was a small rural town and the townsfolk were mostly tolerant whenever we went there. Quite a few Nisei went to spend their off days there as other gangs of sugar-beet workers were in the surrounding area. One of the things that surprised and angered me in [B] was that the bowling alleys and certain barbershops were closed to us. The first time I went to town I went to the bowling alley just to see what would happen. The man there told me that no Nisei could bowl in that place. I argued with him on general principles and I told him that I was an American even though my skin was colored. This man passed the buck and he said that it was orders from the boss and he couldn't do anything about it. He wouldn't tell me where the boss was and I didn't want to make a scene so I left.

Our sugar-beet contracts ran from October 1 to December 1. We were given 30 days after the expiration of our contracts to find other jobs. Otherwise we had to go back to camp since we were on seasonal leaves. Our transportation back to camp was supposed to be paid by our employers. We were not allowed to leave that county without an official WRA permit. From the beginning I had no idea of going back to Poston.

I made about $75 a month and I had to pay for food out of that. I only broke even during the two and a half months out there in spite of the fact that I did not go on any spending spree. The other fellows with me all griped a lot and they mostly talked about sex. There were no prostitution houses around so that they were very disappointed. My main diversion was writing letters and playing cards. I think the main pleasure for all of us was in eating. We did not skimp on food as the hard work in the field gave us enormous appetites. We worked our pants off 11 hours a day and hardly made expenses. The biggest hitch in the whole contract was that when we topped 100 tons gross one time the boss told us that there was 75 tons of dirt on the beets so that all of this was deducted from the total. That meant that we got gypped out of money for 75 tons and we were pretty sore because it wasn't possible to have that much dirt. We worked three days on that 100 tons and we got $25 to divide among nine fellows for these three days of labor. That really depressed us. Our leader went to talk to the field man and protested. However, [the field man] insisted that we had put 75 tons of dirt in the load. We could not do anything about it as we had no proof otherwise. We were very resentful.

It was near the end of the season. We got even by letting 25 acres remain in the field at the end of this period and we did not feel sorry for the farmer at all because he had played such a dirty trick on us. It was not entirely our fault as the freeze had set in and the farmer had to let us go as there was nothing that could be done to save the 25 acres anyway. My chief desire near the end of the season was to stay out of camp by all means and to seek other work. I wanted to go to school but I had not been able to make any definite contacts so I thought I would work a little longer and save money. Five of our gang were so discouraged about not making anything that they went back to camp. The remaining four decided to stay out. We broke the WRA regulations by going on to Denver in the middle of December without a permit.

When we went into Denver we went to the sugar-beet representative and asked if we could stay there for 30 days and look for a job. We wanted to have our transportation paid back to camp in the event we did not land a job. The sugar-beet representative said that we had to go back to camp that very day or the company would not pay our transportation. That was not fair as the company said in the contract that we would have until the 30th of December and still be eligible for transportation fare back to camp. The sugar-beet representative violated the contract when he tried to get us to go back on the 16th. He said the beet company had responsibility for us in Denver and we had to go back to camp that day unless we got a special permit from the WRA. We finally did get a permit from the WRA to stay in Denver and that was the end of my sugar-beet experience.

After getting our permits the immediate problem for the four of us was in finding housing. We had to stay in a hotel for a couple of days. Housing was a very acute problem in Denver and most of the available places were substandard. Most of the Nisei were living on Larimer Street, [and] crowding the former Mexican and Negro colonies out. This area was also the area for houses of prostitution.

We began our process of job hunting right away. The opportunities were not very good and only menial jobs were offered to the large number of Nisei coming into Denver. About the only choices we had were bus boy, waiter, houseboy, janitor, and domestics. Wages were not so high either, averaging from $18 to $25 a week. I didn't have much money so that I couldn't be too choosey about a job. I finally went to the C. Hotel and took a job as a houseman at $18 a week. I stayed in that job for only two weeks. There were about 20 Nisei employed there and the manager had a fairly good attitude toward us. However, this type of work was not suited to me and I felt that I could get something better. Occasionally customers came in and made protests about the Japs but nothing serious ever happened.

After a period of two weeks I finally landed a job in a photographer's shop. I started in as an apprentice at $15 a week. I got this job on my own and I felt pretty good about that. My boss and the other employees were very nice to me. They were Jewish. It was a small shop and it catered primarily to service men. The boss let me contact the customers and wait on them whenever they came into the shop. There was never any unpleasant incident. Later my pay was raised to $20 a week as I gained more experience. When I took over the responsibilities for all of the printing of photos my salary went up to $22.50 a week. However, my work correspondingly increased. I put in a lot of overtime hours and I did not get paid for that. I did not care at that time as I felt I was learning something useful and I enjoyed my work. It was the first time I held a white-collar job. I looked around and saw that most of the other Nisei were doing menial types of work so that I felt that I had a pretty good job.

In my personal adjustments, I think I also made some progress. I met the secretary of the Fellowship of Reconciliation and she was a good influence upon me. I think that this organization helped me to broaden my outlook quite a bit. It was a pacifist group with mostly Caucasians in it. I went to all of their meetings and other affairs and there were no other Nisei who were interested in it. At this time I tended to avoid the rest of the Nisei as I felt that we did not have common interests. My attitude was that if integration was to be worked out right, we had to lose our group identity even if it were hard for us. [In Poston] I had built up some feeling of racial consciousness and this had been developed further during my period in the sugar-beet fields. For this reason it felt good to get into a Caucasian group where I could lose my racial identity to a certain extent. I was very anxious to impress these people so I went to a free public-speaking class in the Opportunity School and I made speeches on the Nisei cause. I felt that in this small way I was contributing to the Nisei welfare.

Around February the question of volunteering for the Nisei came up. I knew that I wanted to finish college so I had some sleepless nights on whether I should volunteer or not. I did not have any contacts with other Nisei at that time so I could not discuss this problem with any of them. It finally came to a point where I actually went to apply for volunteering. The girl at the volunteering office gave me some forms to take home and fill out. Somehow my mind suddenly changed again. I think that the FOR people influenced me. Anyway I decided not to volunteer for the Army at that time so I did not bring the application papers back to the Army office. One thing that caused me to wonder whether it was worth it all was the attitude of the *Denver Post*. This newspaper was publishing a lot of stories against the Nisei along the lines of "once a Jap always a Jap."

After being in Denver a few months, I wanted to get out of that city because I did not think that it had any opportunities for me. I had not made enough money in the sugar-beet fields to go to school as I had originally planned so that I wanted to save money in Denver for this purpose. But my job in the photo shop did not enable me to save very much. I knew that I could not hope to get a better job there so I thought of coming on out to Chicago. I had no intention of staying in Chicago permanently as the only reason that I wanted to get out here was because I thought I could get into [a Midwestern] university easier if I were closer to it. I wanted to go to that university because it offered my major. Once my mind was made up, I determined to leave Denver so on June 2, 1943, I took the train with $50 to my name.

When I arrived in Chicago, a Nisei friend had reserved a room for me. For the first week I did not know if I would go straight on to [the university town] or not. I still was on a short term leave and I didn't know whether I would be allowed to stay in Chicago or not. I went to the WRA office and the manager told me that I could stay out here if I got a job. I decided that I might as well try to get a job until I was certain I could get into [the Midwestern] university.

During my second week in Chicago I started making the rounds for a job. I wanted to get into photography again since this was the only definite skill that I had. I went to the Eastman Kodak Company and asked for job leads. They didn't have any jobs in their company but they told me of several places where I might apply. I followed the first lead to the [M] Company. To my surprise, they gave me a job right away. The boss was very nice and he did not mention the fact that I was a Nisei at all. He was only interested in my past experience.

Ever since then I have been working at [M's]. My job is a darkroom technician. I work on a bonus system right now. At first I started at $40 a week. Later as the work increased, my boss gave me frequent bonuses because I was putting in a lot of overtime. Every other week he would give me $10 or $20 extra. Around Christmas when the work became swamped, I got myself a Nisei assistant. My roommate helped me for a while and now my sister helps me out as she has come out of camp recently. At the present time I get paid a straight three cents per print with a $40 a week minimum. I'm able to make a very good salary this way. During the Christmas season I was making as much as $102 a week. I've hit $80 a week several times since then. Now I'm averaging $55 or $60 a week which is a larger wage than I've ever dreamed of before in my life.

The staff in our shop consisted of 8 camera men, a head manager, and a secretary. I handle all of the printing with my sister. I pay her by the hour, and she makes enough to pay her incidental expenses while going to [a local college]. My company handles most of the street photographers which you see out on the south side and in the Loop. They stand under a theater marquee and snap pictures of people walking down the street. A little card is then handed to these individuals and if they want this picture they send in 35 cents with it. I print these pictures as they come in. I get along swell with my boss and the rest of the staff. They treat me completely as an equal. I've never gone out socially with any of the staff except to get a coke.

The only thing I hope to get out of my present job is the money in it. I have budgeted my income rather strictly since June of last year when I first came to Chicago. I figured out my total income and expenditures from June to December, 1943, and I am basing my budget for the coming months upon this. For my first half year working in Chicago I was able to put $724.24 in my bank account. Since my income is well over $200 a month now, I'll probably be able to save much more each month than before. I will be quitting my present full-time job by next June if everything turns out as planned. I'm saving primarily for school right now. I also have a sister going to college and I am somewhat responsible for her. She lives with my older brother out on the southside. He and his wife came out here about the same time as I did. I am quite optimistic and I think that I may be accepted for the summer session at [another Midwestern university]. It depends upon whether the Army takes it off the proscribed list. If I can't go to [this latter] university I will try [the first Midwestern choice] or [one of several colleges] in this city.

Sometimes when I am depressed, I wonder why so many colleges are antagonistic toward individual Nisei. For example, [a Midwestern university] wrote me on January 25, 1944, that "it seems inadvisable for students of Japanese descent to come here." That showed that they were still suspicious of us. All I am asking is to be judged as an individual, and it shouldn't matter what color of skin I have to an educational institution.

My present aspiration is to definitely finish college and to get my teeth into something specific. I haven't begun to reach that point yet. After college, the future is still more vague, and I just have hopes of getting established in some way in order to became a definite part of a community. I don't particularly want to go back to the West Coast, and I don't particularly want to stay in Chicago permanently. I'd rather go to some small town as it would be easier to get recognition in that way. I don't know definitely about my family future. My dad is old and my mother is ill now. There are two minors left in camp with them. I haven't decided whether the responsibility lies with my older brother or with me. I think that it lies with all of us, and we have to do our share when the time comes. The ideal situation would be for my parents and the minor children to go back to the farm in California, and we could contribute to their livelihood from out here.

My present life is in a sort of indefinite stage. I realize that I still have many struggles to go through and that things will not be given to me on a silver platter. Sometimes I am quite hopeful about the future for myself and at other times I get depressed. All I can do now is to contribute my share and hope that this will be enough for me to make adequate adjustments to this resettled life.

CH-45: AGRICULTURAL STUDENT

Male; born in California, 1920; height 68½"; weight 140 lbs.; unmarried. Interviewed July–August, 1944. Described as "a tall good-looking Nisei who chases girls all over and the girls chase him"; though superficially "happy-go-lucky" he seemed to the interviewer to be "uneasy and insecure"; to be "in the 'zoot suit' category but not typical of the more rowdy element"; to be "anxious to get things off his chest and more than willing to talk. It seemed that he was just sitting there talking to himself and trying to figure out why he was living in the manner he was."

CAREER LINES

Parental: Paternal grandfather was a grain farmer, maternal grandfather a cabinetmaker, in Japan. Father (born 1884) completed grammar school and worked as a farmer in Japan before emigrating in 1907. He was successively, a farm laborer, share-cropper, and operator-owner in the Sacramento Delta farming area from 1912 to 1942, except for a year's residence in Japan in 1916–1917. Mother (born 1896) was a high-school graduate, was married in 1916, and came to the United States with her husband the following year.

Own: Finished sophomore year at college in California in 1940. Worked on the family farm during childhood, and as laboratory assistant in truck-crops division at college, 1940–1942. Inmigrated to Chicago in March, 1943. Worked as "platform worker" for two months; as garage attendant from May, 1943, to June, 1944; and as machine operator, June, 1944, to time of interview.

LIFE HISTORY

If my old man had not come to this country around 1915 [1907], I probably would have been a soldier in the Jap Army now. Some of his friends who had come out before him told him to come to this country. He was interested in farming and he went out to the islands in the Sacramento Delta with George Shima.[180] Shima later became the "potato king" of this country and he must have made hundreds of thousands of dollars. My father more or less helped him to open the Delta islands to the Japanese farmers. They cleared the land there and planted potatoes, celery, and truck crops. For a while my old man drove tractors in that area. He told me once that he worked with all the old timers there who later became big time boys in farming. Dad was just average in his success.

In 1916, my father returned to Japan in order to find a wife. He spread the word around in his *ken* [Fukuoka] about the Delta farming. He was very excited about the possibilities of farming in [this] area, as he had never seen such rich land in Japan. He brought back my mother and kept working and saving his money. After a time, he decided he would like to stay in this country. That's why he bought about 20 acres of land in the Delta area. He wasn't able to buy it under his own name because of the law so he had it put in a friend's name. At that time most of the Japanese farmers were only planning to make a lot of money here and go back to Japan. When Dad purchased his little farm, it meant that he would be in this country more

---

[180] Shima began his career as a migratory farm laborer and soon became "boss" of a Japanese farm gang. At the time of his death in 1926, he was said to own 6,000 acres and to have an additional 7,000 under lease. Most of his holding consisted of reclaimed swamp land. As described by Pajus:

Shima had had his eye for some time on the barren delta of the San Joaquin river. Situated fifteen miles from Stockton, this expanse of water was studded with small semi-submerged islands covered with tule and other wild growths and entirely inundated during the winter months. Moreover, the whole place was infested with malaria and shunned by American farmers.

Establishing contact with the American firm which owned most of the delta, Shima dyked the islets, dug transverse ditches for drainage, and installed machinery to pump the superfluous water into the river. The virgin soil was then steam-ploughed and permitted to lie fallow for a few years to enable the brush and tule to rot and fertilize the ground. After this preparation, the reclaimed land was tested and found ideal for the cultivation of potatoes.

Yet Shima's great dream did not come true even then. Year after year he lost money through floods and other disasters. To satisfy a mortgage he had given on his steam-ploughs and implements, his creditors at one time deprived him of his entire equipment. It was only after more than a decade of intense labor and financial setbacks that George Shima eventually made good. (Jean Pajus, *The Real Japanese California*. James J. Gillick Co., Berkeley, 1937, p. 85.)

or less permanently. My brother was born in 1918 and I came along two years later.

In the years that followed my father began to branch out and he did some farming on a share basis as he owned a lot of farm equipment. He would lease large tracts of land from Caucasian corporations and they would split the profits 60 per cent for him and 40 per cent for the company. Most of the larger Japanese farmers worked under this sort of an arrangement and very few of them ever owned land in their name. My dad used to hire Japanese, Mexican, and Filipino laborers to harvest all of these crops. Farming was very profitable for him from 1925 on. However, during the depression things slowed down a great deal. Around 1937 my father went a little too far in his farming ventures and he went broke. I don't know exactly how this happened, but I think he borrowed a lot of money from the bank and he could not pay it off because the farm prices were so low that year. On top of that he had a little trouble with one of the Caucasians he did business with and he lost quite a bit of equipment as a result of this disagreement. This slowed him down for a while and he had to go back to small-scale farming on our own property for a couple of years. Just before the war broke out, he started to farm big again and he had about 300 acres of tomatoes ready to harvest when we were sent out [evacuated].

We lived on a little island of our own in the Delta. It was really a backward place and we only had dirt roads. They used a lot of irrigation for farming. It was very rich land but nobody knew how to farm it until the Japanese farmers came around. Our family was the only Japanese one who owned any land around there. Most of the property was owned by huge corporations. A large number of Portuguese owned land around there too and they did their own farming. There were about 12 families living on our island. The Japanese farmers all seemed to get along as they worked hard. They had to in order to support their large families. They didn't have any time for luxuries so that they lived in pretty old houses. Even after they got families some of them still didn't want to invest in homes because they thought they would eventually go back to *Nihon*. My dad was from the Fukuoka *ken* but I don't know exactly where the other farmers came from. We all knew each other, because there weren't too many of us. The Issei had different organizations of their own but I don't know very much about these things as I wasn't interested in their activities. There were about 300 Japanese near by but the numbers were greatly increased during the harvest season when many Japanese gangs migrated in.

Before he went broke, my dad was one of the bigshots among the Japanese there.[181] For a long time, he was the president of the Japanese school and this was an important position which had a lot of prestige. All of the Japanese respected anyone who held this office. My father's main hobby was fishing, and he used to go off a lot with other Japanese farmers during the slack season. He didn't have too much time for other things as most of the year he was busy farming. My father was more or less a happy-go-lucky sort of person. He never smoked but would drink moderately on special occasions.

My mother had a lot to do with keeping the place going, as my old man was not as good a businessman as he was a farmer. We used to have a bunch of bunkhouses on our property and my mother would rent these out to the big companies that hired Japanese crews in their sheds out in the island.

We didn't exactly have a town or anything like that but there was a sort of a central meeting place. There was a community church there and we got a lot of contacts through that. All sorts of people went there so that it became the center for the community social life. The *hakujin* and Japanese mixed fairly well at times although each group tended to have its own activities. On the Japanese side, the Japanese school gave picnics every once in a while and everybody on the island were invited, including the *hakujin*. On these occasions everyone was friendly so that it wasn't a distinct Japanese community that I grew up in.

In our home my folks always used Japanese but as my brother and I grew up we began to speak only English to each other. We used a sort of broken English and Japanese to our folks. Most of my Japanese training was obtained through the Japanese school as my folks were too busy to teach me anything. It was in the Japanese school that I was taught all about manners, respect for elders, and other stuff like that. I used to take *kendo* and the instructors were from Japan. They were very strict about us being courteous to the old folks and we had to make the proper greetings to them. The instructors always reminded us that we should be very proud of our Japanese blood because we came from a great race. But none of this stuff sunk deeply. They couldn't come right out and say for us to be devoted to the

---

[181] CH-45's father reported earnings, as general manager of his own farm, at $15,000 per year.

Emperor, but they used to tell us all the time how great boochie-land was. They told us how the white race would always look down on us and that we should never be ashamed of being Japanese, because our ancestors had a glorious history. Some of those instructors were really batty and it made me laugh when it got so fanatic-like. To tell the truth, I used to take in all this stuff when I was a kid, but as I got older I got peeved at the way the teachers always kept praising Japan. I liked the stuff that I learned in the public schools better. Because of the Japanese school, I began to hate all of the strict things that they had in Japan and I didn't think I would ever like to live there if I had to follow all the things our teachers taught us. We had to bow to the teacher no matter where we met and speak just so. It was embarrassing when I met my Japanese teacher at a time that a *hakujin* playmate was with me. They would razz me about it so that I began to think that this bowing business was a lot of baloney. I didn't like to speak Japanese when I was with my *hakujin* friends either.

At home my parents did not restrain my brother and me very much as they didn't have the time. However, they did insist that we go to the Japanese language school. My old man was quite strong for Japan, I guess. You know how the old Issei men used to brag about Japan's army. They were so proud of the fact that Japan had never been beaten in a war and they thought that she never would taste defeat. My father thought that a war was coming on eventually, as he used to read all of those Japanese books and magazines that were brought from Japan. Right now my folks plan to stay in this country so they can't say very much. But they still have that feeling of being pushed around and that is why they are still sympathetic to Japan. I think that it is a two-faced affair and they want to be for both sides. My folks have a sentiment for Japan because everybody thinks of his homeland, but they also have a sentiment for America because they have lived here for so long. I know that they wouldn't do anything directly against this country. My brother is in the Army now and I will be going in pretty soon.

I went to Japan once with my mother in 1927 [1929?] during the summer and boochie-land didn't agree with me. I got sick a lot and I got boils all over from the lousy food we were fed over there by my mother's relatives. I know that I wouldn't ever want to live there because the standard of living is much poorer. I guess you would like it better if you were rich but we didn't have much money. My mother enjoyed that trip as she got to see all of her relatives. They were all farmers and not too well off. All of my little cousins were so envious of the fact that I came from America. They were always asking me all kinds of questions. At that time the boochies thought very highly of America I guess.

We used to have a lot of fun on the Delta islands when we were kids. All summer long the gang would go swimming or fishing. I knew all of the other Nisei kids around there and I used to go play with them once in a while. But it was much easier for me to play with the *hakujin* and Mexican kids who lived right around me.

All of my education has been in this country. When I went to grammar school, I used to chum around with a gang from our island. There were almost half boochies in our school, but no Japanese families lived right near us so that I began to play with the *hakujin*, Mexican, Filipino, and Hawaiian kids. In our school there was no talk of race as everyone was the same. I was an average student, maybe a little above average because I got pretty good grades.

When I started to go to [a central California] high school, I first discovered that there was a difference in race. I found that the high school had about 350 Japanese students. The Japanese Students Club was one of the largest and most active in the school and they did everything by themselves. It seemed to me that the Nisei were of all different kinds in spite of that. What griped me the most was when a bunch of boochies got together, they spoke right out in Japanese in front of *hakujin* students. They didn't care what the other students thought about them because they were such a large group. They always seemed to stick together and they didn't associate too much with the *hakujin*.

One of the things I looked forward to every year was the conference for all of the Japanese high school students in central California. Our Japanese Students Club usually sponsored these conferences and the boochies all up and down the [San Joaquin] Valley would come and spend the day. These conferences were sponsored for the purpose of getting the Nisei together so we could get acquainted. In 1940 we had a real big conference and I was chosen as the typical Nisei boy.

In those days I never thought of girls much, as most of my time was taken up with sports in our club. A bunch of us boochies organized the Delta Lancers and we played all kinds of sports with other Nisei teams in the area. We had a regular league of our own and it was our ambition to beat the pants off of some of the big city Nisei teams of San Francisco and Sacramento. We also had a football team but we had to play against Caucasians because the Nisei didn't have any league in football.

I didn't know what I wanted to study for, so I took a sort of academic and commercial course. My main pleasure was making the microscope slides, as only selected students were appointed to do this. But my first 3 years in high school were very dull and routine. I only enjoyed my senior year. That was when I started to get around more and I met a lot of the students and made friends, and I entered more school activities. I was among a group of picked students in the agricultural class and we had a lot of social gatherings of our own. In the Ag course we didn't have to study too much as it was more of a practical nature. The teacher used to take us all around for short trips to visit business concerns. It was through taking this class that I was influenced to go to [the agricultural college].

During the summer of my high school years, I worked on a farm and it was a regular routine. Most of the Nisei fellows did it too. I worked on my dad's farm up to 1937 and after that I went to work for my uncle. When I worked for my father, he kept the regular books for me and I was paid the same wages as the other laborers. I was permitted to draw out money whenever I needed it but I never did draw out the full amount for the season. I was more or less on my own after I got to high school and I had to buy all my own clothes and provide my own spending money as my folks didn't give me any.

The Issei around us were mostly Buddhist but the boochie kids became Christian[182] as there was only one church on [our] island. I guess I was sort of influenced by the community and the church although I was not religious. I never did anything bad like drinking or smoking and in our group we didn't even talk about sex in a way that most fellows do. The other parents on the island all thought that I was so good to my folks and they told their sons to be like me. I guess I have changed a little bit since then.

I wasn't sure what I wanted to do after graduation from high school but I didn't want to work on the farm the year around. I decided to go to [a college which had] an agronomy course. A little later on I changed my major to studying truck crops as I figured that I would be doing this kind of work eventually since my dad did it. My mother sent me $30 a month during the first year I was in college but after that I worked my own way. I got a job through the NYA and I was

---

[182] On the WRA schedules, both parents were recorded as Buddhists, both sons as Christians.

placed on the truck-crop project on the campus. I got paid about 35 cents an hour for doing this work.

I think that my college life was the beginning influence in broadening me out. I lived in a home with a Caucasian lady who boarded about seven boys there. I was the only Nisei in the group so that I had to become friendly with the others. It wasn't too hard because I was used to Caucasians back home and on the farm. We all got to be good pals and we got along swell. The lady who was in charge of our house was very good to all of us and she acted like a mother. In many ways I felt much closer to her than I did my own mother because I never had any affection like that shown toward me back home. I guess Caucasian mothers tend to show their feelings toward their children more than the Japanese mothers.

I enjoyed my life at [college] very much and I liked it much better than living at home. I didn't have anyone around to boss me all the time and I was free to do what I wanted. The people all treated me nice on the campus. [It] was a real friendly town and I never had any trouble there. We had a Japanese Students Club as there were about 50 Nisei on the campus. We had our own club basketball team. Most of these Nisei didn't seem to participate in any of the other school activities except sports. I was the only one who went out for the Frosh-Soph brawl. There was a Nisei fellow who was an all-around athlete and he was a star on the football team. He was chosen captain and voted to be the most valuable man after the 1941 season. I got out of the close Nisei circle and I took part in quite a few of the school activities. I served on the Vigilante Committee and things like that. I made quite a few contacts through my roommates and we went to all of the bonfire rallies and games together. I wanted to take in all that college life had to offer because I had looked forward to it. My closest pal was a Russian kid and we did everything together. We lived together, we went out for the football team together, we took the same courses together, and we worked together. The 2 years that I spent in college were the happiest years of my life.

After I went to college [the island] seemed like small-time stuff to me. Our home was not too good either and we didn't have a real close family feeling like many of the *hakujin* families have. I lived in a different house from my folks because our home was so small. I used to live in one of the small houses that my mother rented out to workers during the harvest season. Our regular house was furnished very sparsely and it was all a lot of junk. We had a very dull routine and it was the same the year around. We would just sit and talk in the evenings. We always went to bed early as my folks worked hard on the farm during the day and they had to get up early. My mother used to get quite angry at me as I got in the habit of going out all the time and she didn't think this was right.

Things like being a loyal American and all that stuff never affected me before the war. I just took it for granted that I came from a Japanese home but I thought I was American enough because of my school contacts. I didn't know anything about politics and I was always proud of living in the best country in the world even though my folks stressed Japan once in a while. I just took it for granted that certain parts of me were Japanese and the rest American. In those days it wasn't an important issue anyway. Most of the Nisei kids called themselves Japanese, and they learned a lot of stuff about Japan, but I don't think that they went as far as being loyal to the Emperor like they say.

I was in college at the time the war broke out. I was just 21 years old at that time. The reason I was a little older than the other students was because I had started school when I was 7 years old and I also flunked a grade in grammar school. I lost another year when my mother took me to Japan and I got scarlet fever when I returned after the summer visit. I was 19 when I got out of high school.

I don't know what would have happened to me if the war had not broken out. I probably would have finished school and then gone back to the farm to work. At that time my brother[188] and a Caucasian fellow were close pals and they were making plans to farm together. I was supposed to go in with them eventually. I guess I would have ended up as a farmer. I was supposed to get half of the land that was in my brother's name.

I didn't ever think of marriage before the war. I wanted to fool around for at least 10 years yet. Sports were my primary interest. The real truth is that I didn't actually start dating girls until after I was 21 years old, as we just didn't do those things where I came from. The Nisei girls were all pretty shy and quite reserved in their manners. It was hard to get to know them too well as it just wasn't the practice to take a girl out to a dance and show and the parents didn't welcome the fellows visiting their daughters too much. The Nisei girls didn't encourage fellows either because it wasn't approved. If they did get a little daring, the other people would spread rumors about them.

---

[188] CH-45's brother graduated from an agricultural college in 1938, and took postgraduate courses from 1938 to 1940.

I didn't even suspect that a war was coming along so quick and I couldn't imagine Japan attacking this country. I was sleeping late the morning of December 7th when my roommate came running up to my room to tell me that the Japs had bombed Pearl Harbor. I thought he was kidding at first so I told him to go away. After he went out of the room I got a strange feeling and I suspected that there was something to what he said so I turned my radio on. I was really shocked when I found out that it was true. I was supposed to have a midterm examination the next day but I just couldn't study the rest of that Sunday. All I did was to listen to the radio and talk to the other fellows. They were just as shocked as I was. I didn't know how the public would take it and I was a little worried for myself. It hit me pretty hard and I felt that the *hakujin* were looking at me all the time for about a week afterwards. I realized that this was mostly my imagination but I couldn't prevent myself from feeling self-conscious. The next important thing I thought of was that I should join the Army as soon as possible. I don't know why I got that idea but I suppose it was because I figured that it wouldn't be so bad for me if I were in the Army. I felt that the *hakujin* wouldn't be able to question me at all if I were in a uniform and they certainly couldn't be suspicious. I didn't worry much about what was going to happen to my family until much later.

All of the students were quite sympathetic with the Nisei students. The Dean of the College actually called a mass assembly the next day. He told the student body that the Nisei students on the campus were American citizens and that we were not to be blamed for the war. He warned the students against threatening any of the Nisei or treating them as outcasts. He talked so feelingly that a few of the Nisei in the audience were crying. I had a mixed reaction to this talk because I didn't think he should have called everyone together like that. I felt like a bright spotlight was being placed on me and that everyone was looking at me. I didn't want to be treated with pity because I didn't do anything. It wasn't necessary for the Dean to talk like that because none of the *hakujin* students ever did turn against us.

Most of the Nisei took the war pretty hard and they would stand around in little bunches and talk about it with worried faces. Some of them tried to act like they were not concerned at all but I knew that they were just as worried as any of us. We were all pretty self-conscious during those early days of the war and we did take things pretty hard and worry about how we were going to be treated.

I stayed on the campus doing my work until the semester was over, [but] I worked out in the fields in the truck-garden laboratory on a full-time basis after January. I got to travel around quite a bit during this time because we had to go check on our experiments. The professor and I would go to [a Valley community] about once every week in order to check a lettuce-fertilizing experiment there. While we were there I saw the FBI starting to round up some of the boochie farmers but I never thought that it would ever affect me. The FBI men would take the Issei farmers right off the fields and I watched them go off so scared and I wondered why they were being arrested. I didn't know what was going on at all and I couldn't make heads or tails of this.

When the curfew for the Nisei came into effect, I wasn't able to travel around any more so that I had to work around the campus most of the time. Once I was driving and I got stopped by a soldier on a bridge. He asked me what nationality I was and I told him that I was an American citizen so that he finally let me pass through. I was in a [college] automobile and he was pretty suspicious. After that I didn't get to drive the [college] car any more so he must have reported me.

In May, 1942, I decided to go home as I thought I'd better be with my folks as they needed help. By that time evacuation had already started and it was pretty certain that the valley people would be affected too. At first I thought only the Japanese around the harbors and airports on the coast would be moved but they began to take everybody up to a line in the eastern part of the state, which was still a free zone. My folks lived right in the area which was considered a restricted zone. I couldn't get a permit to travel at all but some of my *hakujin* friends sneaked me into their car and took me home.

When I got home I had to go to work right away to help my folks settle their business. The land was left in the name of an old *hakujin* friend who had known the family for 20 years. He took care of the farm and he still does it. He leases the land out to a farm company on a percentage basis. He puts the money in the bank for us and he pays all of the taxes and other expenses. The money is all in his hands and in his account but we trust him. My father doesn't get a very large income because the expenses are rather heavy. We owe quite a bit of money to the bank. My father borrowed about $2,000 once to do farming and he is paying a small part of it every month now with the money which he gets from our leased property.

My folks were thinking of voluntary evacuation for a while. They were planning to go to Colorado as we had some *hakujin* friends there but we began to hear so many rumors that the plan was dropped. There was one man that Dad owed some money to and this person thought that he wouldn't get paid so he put an attachment on our truck and we had to sell it at a loss in order to pay him. There were other items of farm produce that we never got paid for. Everything was so rushed that we didn't know who was getting the truck-farm products that we were selling at the last moment. My father lost $500 or over in this way and there was no way that we could collect for it. All of these things forced us to stay and be evacuated with the rest of the Japanese.

I figured that evacuation was something that couldn't be helped and it was for our own protection so it wasn't too hard for me to take. At the same time I had a feeling inside of me that the Japanese were pretty industrious and they got ahead in business and farming in spite of being pushed around for so many years and that the *hakujin* didn't like that so much. That is why they wanted to get rid of us as they thought that they could take over all of the property left behind. There was quite a bit of losses, not too much in actual cash as most of them were farming for somebody else on a share-crop basis so that they had no money invested in the land, but it would be awfully hard for them to start out again some other place and they wouldn't be able to get the equipment so that, from this point of view, their loss was great.

I had no bitter feelings against the United States and I still wanted to join the Army. All of my friends at college were going in, but the Army quit taking Nisei shortly after the war broke out. In a way I didn't blame Japan for doing what she did. This is an economic war and the U. S. was looking out for its own business interests in China. It didn't want to lose all of this so it forced Japan into the war by the embargoes and closing of the trade treaties. The American public does not know it, but President Roosevelt gave orders to the U. S. Navy to shoot any Japanese warships in the Pacific if they came near any American island. That's what my father told me anyway. I didn't believe him at first until another Nisei told me that it was in the *Congressional Record*. This news leaked out in the camp later on and everybody found out about it.

I think that the JACL should have fought more for our rights. I heard that they told the Army we would be glad to go and that's why the people waited to get the heads of the JACL in camp. During the time after war was declared and before evacuation, a lot of the Nisei got kicked out of the civil service and I thought that was pretty dirty. I knew some of the girls who were booted out and they cried because they were treated so unjustly.

Another thing that the Nisei were sore about were the FBI round-ups. The newspapers played up these things as sabotage and all that. I suppose that some of these Japanese were guilty but it couldn't have been more than a small number. I know that most of the Issei sympathized with Japan but they certainly wouldn't have done anything against this country. There weren't too many Japanese taken from our area, but there were a lot taken from [near-by towns]. All of the *kendo* big shots were interned. I didn't think that they were guilty as it was only a sport. I took *kendo* myself and it was just physical culture and we weren't being trained for any boochie Army.

I was pretty busy after I got home. I had to do quite a lot of work cleaning up the farm and taking an inventory of our property so that it would be in decent shape when the new tenants moved in. This kept me busy right up to the time of evacuation. We were just finishing the building of our new home through the Federal housing loan so that we had to dig wells, move the furniture, and other things. We didn't get finished until the night before we left. My father was very fussy about leaving everything in good order. We really were disappointed that we couldn't live in our new house after we had built it.

We were sent to the Stockton Assembly Center on May 21st. When I first got into the camp, the place didn't look too bad. Our family had an apartment by ourselves and we didn't have any trouble getting settled down. We set right to work to make furniture and build a gravel walk. We even planted a victory garden in front. My father said that it was best to make the most of everything instead of sitting around and moaning. Our barracks were actually no worse than a lot of bunkhouses I have seen in the country on Japanese farms. The thing that got me down was all that corn-beef hash that they gave us at the beginning.

It wasn't very hard for me to get a job in camp. Like any place else, you can get places if you got pull. I found that there was a lot of red tape until I went to see a friend of mine in the office and he fixed things up. I got a job right away as a relief timekeeper.

I had quite a lot of free time to fool around in and that was to my liking. We usually played cards and sat around and talked. We played baseball together and I went out for all of the sports including *sumo* and *judo* as I never had a chance to do most of these things before. We had track meets and I entered all of these. I really did enter a lot of sports activities and it was all a lot of fun.

I got caught playing poker three times and I was put on probation. I think that camp life was the beginning of the big change in me because I wasn't interested in being a model boy any longer. I wanted to have my fun like I saw the other kids doing. Later on I started to go around with a [central California] gang and there were about eight of us. We used to go around at night to have our bull sessions or else we would go wolfing. I started to dance regularly and I went out on plenty of dates. I sort of felt that "drapes" were the thing to wear and I got myself a sort of zoot suit. It made me feel very self-conscious at first as the other fellows didn't wear them much until they got to Rohwer and saw all of the Santa Anita boys wearing them. I started to go steady with a girl and she was the first one I had ever gone with regularly. Most of the time our gang just sat around and we talked about women and old times. I wasn't bored with the Stockton Assembly Center at all as I was having plenty of fun. Once in a while my mother would give me lectures and tell me to come home earlier but I didn't pay any attention to that.

We had an adult education school in the assembly center and I enrolled to take up trigonometry as I was beginning to get hazy thoughts that I would go to college again eventually. After I got into so much social life, I dropped ideas of further college. There were too many other things going on which interested me more. I even quit going to the adult education school.

I was going to register to vote but I didn't make it. I was actually in a line to register when somebody asked me to get a desk. When I came back there was a long line and I got so disgusted that I couldn't get my place back that I walked out. That was one thing I didn't like about camp life—everything we did, we had to stand in line and I got so impatient with that. I don't think I was too interested in voting anyway because I didn't know what it was all about and my vote didn't mean a thing.

All of the Nisei were out for fun and they got it. They all seemed to be happy and contented with all the social life and they didn't look very bitter to me. I think that they had more fun there than they ever had in their lives. If they had not been evacuated, they never would have been able to have all those dances because the parents would not have approved. They would have had to work on the farms after school and wouldn't have had the opportunities to meet the social groups that existed in camp. I guess they missed their freedom but they didn't get bored until much later on.

The Issei didn't like the Nisei to play so much but they couldn't say much. They didn't like the idea of having dim lights at the dances and the couples getting so close together. I suppose that the parents had a right to do some worrying because there were a lot of affairs going on. All the fellows started to think about sex a lot and that's about all they talked about. I know I got this way and I wasn't like that before. I used to think that Nisei girls were something sacred and never had any dirty thoughts about them. After I got to camp and the fellows started talking about sex, it was natural for me. There were plenty of fellows who took girls out and had affairs. The grandstand was noted for it. There were also a lot of empty stables and we used to walk around at night and see many couples "going to town." That's why the parents kept their daughters in at night and we had a hard time getting them out. I had some idea that I would like to have an affair with a young chick but I was too scared at that time although I did get my share of heavy necking.

I didn't care about the people who ran the camp at all but I did hate the guy who ran the canteen. This *hakujin* thought he was big time and he [was alleged] to charge a big commission to bring things in to the people from the outside. That canteen guy really gypped the people. The rest of the WCCA officials were pretty good.

I was having so much fun in camp that I lost track of the war. I never read the newspapers and I didn't listen to any radio news. Hardly anyone talked about war in camp anyway. I let all these outside things drag and I sort of put them out of my mind.

Finally we learned that we were going to be sent to [WRA camp] Rohwer in Arkansas. We didn't know a thing about Arkansas except that Arkies came from there. I thought that if the Arkies didn't like it there, then it must be a pretty crummy state. I got curious about seeing the place when I knew that we had to go anyway so I volunteered to go on an advance crew. We heard that we had to clear stumps out there but I still didn't care. I wanted to go ahead as I thought it would be exciting.

Our advance crew left the Stockton Assembly Center in September and I didn't have very much of a sensation as I left the state. None of us had ever been that far east before. There was a bunch of seven boys in our car and we really raised hell. They let us off once to get fresh air and some of the fellows brought back some whiskey. I got to feeling very good and I was real drunk for the first time in my life. One of the M.P.'s bawled me out but he could find no evidence and I didn't care anyway. Since that time I have been drinking rather regularly although I'm not a booze hound yet.

We got to the Arkansas center late at night. We were starved as the dining car had been taken off the train at Memphis since it was figured that we would be in camp for the next meal. We were 8 hours overdue and we had nothing to eat all that time and couldn't even get off the train to buy anything. When the train pulled in near camp we didn't know where we were. We were all dumped into some trucks and taken to the block that was ready for us. Right away we took showers but something was wrong with the water as it wouldn't wash the soap or dirt off. We grumbled about that for a while and then we went to eat. Some of the people volunteered to cook. We had to take quinine pills right away as there were a lot of mosquitoes flying around. There were no screens on the windows so that it was pretty tough at first. We would roast if we kept the windows closed and the mosquitoes would bite us to pieces if we opened them. It was so sultry down there that it took all the energy out of us. We all began to grumble and gripe and wrote back letters and told the [Assembly Center] people[184] how bad it was. Some fellows caught big mosquitoes and sent them in envelopes so the people would know what to expect. I heard later that the Stockton [Assembly Center] people bought out all mosquito nets at the last minute when all these rumors about mosquitoes went back. They really didn't need them because screens were put up in the barracks later.

One good thing about going in the advance crew was that we were fed real good food. We all had a friendly spirit and we helped each other in everything. We were all coöperative and we all did our share of the work because we felt like pioneers preparing the way for a bunch of settlers. The WRA people there really made us feel good as they acted like one of us and they didn't get on their high horses like they did later on when the camp was more settled.

We really worked hard to get the camp ready for the people coming in. It looked fairly decent by the time the people came in although they were disappointed with the black tar-paper barracks. There was quite a bit of excitement during the time the new arrivals came in. A

---

[184] The Stockton Assembly Center.

train load would come in every other day and we would all go down to help unload the trunks and baggage and we would show the people to their barrack assignments. This kept up until the camp had about 8,000 people. It wasn't overcrowded like some of the other centers. The people came mostly from Stockton and Santa Anita Assembly Centers.

At first we didn't get along with the Santa Anita bunch at all as they were more rugged. They traveled around in gangs and it seemed that they were looking for fights. They sort of felt superior to the Stockton [Assembly Center] people as they thought we were just hicks. We sort of looked up to them in awe I guess because they were from Los Angeles and they really acted like they had been around. A lot of the Stockton kids would never associate with the Santa Anita bunch but our gang gradually got to know some of them. As the people got to know each other better, cliques developed and then there were some gang fights. The different gangs started to beat up the guys they didn't like. They laid off our gang as we had enough fellows to protect ourselves and we went around every place together. We were called the Esquires and we organized into a club. We would get together every Wednesday and have a feed from all the food we swiped from the warehouses.

When we first went into camp we were too busy to play around very much. I helped my folks fix up the apartment but that didn't take too long. I had no intention of living with them at the beginning as I planned to go live with the gang. My mother started to cry so I finally said I would come back and live with the family instead of living with my friends. My mother was always worried as she thought I was getting to be a little bad. My brother and I had a big argument about the clothes I wore. He thought that I should wear more conservative clothes and I didn't like that.

I had a job as a timekeeper all the way through. I was in the maintenance department and none of the fellows worked very hard. I gave all of them credit for full-time work as they were only getting 16 bucks a month and it was no use working too hard for that measly wage.

My life settled down to the usual routine. We continued our poker sessions and we held bull sessions every night. All we talked about was girls and we got to do more and more of this. Our group got around quite a bit and we considered ourselves sort of experts on girls. We would find out who were the most popular girls in camp and then go after them. We were always competing with one of the Santa Anita groups which was also known as being wolves. I got a new girl friend at Rohwer and she is still supposed to be my steady. In fact, I may even marry her.

It was at Rohwer that the Nisei fellows really changed. The Stockton fellows all went for the Santa Anita girls because they were from the city and this made the Santa Anita fellows sort of sore. That's why there were so many fights at the dances. The Stockton bunch were influenced quite a bit by the Santa Anita fellows, and most of us started to wear drapes and let our hair grow long like the Los Angeles guys. We went to the dances in a gang and we never let anyone cut in on the girls in our group. Once in a while we were able to smuggle in some whisky.

For a while I went to night school as I thought I could get some college credit. I soon lost interest in my classes because I had a lot of fun doing other things. At the same time I still had some hopes of going back to [college] eventually as I knew I could make the football team there.

The people didn't start to gripe at all until the food got bad. We only got rice and tomatoes for about one week straight and everyone was pretty sore about that. We went to the administration and put up a stink. The WRA blamed it on the fact that the shipment of food had not come in. A rumor went around that they were going to starve us out and the old folks got pretty worried. A strike was threatened and after that we got our food okay. From then on the people began to gripe more and more about every little thing and they did not trust the WRA at all. It seemed that they would get all steamed up and a lot of them began to agitate around. Even the young fellows did this.

I wasn't conscious of any of the political things going on in camp until registration. Then everybody got excited and the people said that if we signed up we would have to volunteer for the Army. They told us not to register but I wanted to get out of camp so I voluntarily registered and then forgot about the whole thing. The people started to hold meetings all over the place to discuss this stuff. They thought that the registration questions were unfair and that the Nisei shouldn't be asked to fight for America after being evacuated and kicked around.

I know that there were a lot of agitators among the Issei in camp. The Kibei were pretty bad, too. These people would try to get everyone to write "no" to the registration question. They would stand around the mess hall and call any Nisei who went in to sign up a *bakatare.* Many of them even tried to force the Nisei not to sign. Most of the Issei in camp didn't want their sons to be taken away. My father didn't say too much to me as I was old enough to make up my own mind and I wasn't home often enough to talk to him about these things anyway. My mother was pretty much against my volunteering. She couldn't say anything when I told her that I would go willingly if I was drafted as she said I would not have a choice then and she would not oppose that.

There weren't too many volunteers into the Army from our camp. I thought about volunteering once but I didn't like the idea of going to Camp Shelby when I heard that the Nisei would be put all together. I went to inquire about the language school at Savage but I didn't make the grade. The fellows in my gang weren't too enthusiastic about volunteering anyway so I didn't do anything more about it.

My folks finally decided to sign "yes" to the registration as they planned to stay in this country as they had nothing to go back to in Japan. My brother and I said we would not go there to live and my folks couldn't very well make a living without somebody to help them. I don't think that they will ever regret this choice to stay in this country as they will probably be better off here.

I resettled in March, 1943. I first started to think about it when some talk about resettlement began around November or December. I filed my application for the clearance among the first. My folks were opposed to my leaving camp at first as they thought I would become a bad boy if I started to run around on the outside and they were not around. I told them that I had been on my own at [college] for two years and I could take care of myself. I said that I wanted to go out and make some money so I could buy a lot of clothes. I had plans of saving about $50 a month.

I had a real reason for wanting to get out of camp. I had proposed to my girl friend and we were planning to get married as soon as I could go out and find a good job. I asked her if she would wait for me if I went out to make money and we had more or less of an agreement. But I guess I sort of forgot about her after I started to get around out here and I met so many different girls.

I wasn't afraid of coming out of camp at all as it was an adventure to me and I thought it would be exciting. When it came time to leave my mother finally gave me $30 as she was so worried that I would starve to death. Besides that my uncle gave me $20 and the gang chipped in and gave me $10. Besides that the club also gave me $2 more. My girl friend's mother gave me some money too and that was enough to pay my way out of camp and get started. I guess I had around a hundred dollars to start out life with in Chicago. I only had to use $18 to pay my train fare out of camp.

I left two weeks after my leave clearance came through. A couple of fellows had come back to camp to recruit some people to go to Chicago to work. I was talking to one of these guys and the proposition sounded pretty good so I made up my mind to go at that moment. The job offered was doing platform unloading at the [C] Company and we were to start out at 65 cents an hour. That sounded like pretty big money to me at that time compared to what I had made before the war.

When I got to Chicago it was easy for us as the guy from the [C] Company came to the station and got our luggage for us. He put us in a hotel and he helped us to find a place to live. We even got a car to go look around in. There were seven of us in the group that came out but I didn't know any of them when I was in camp except to say "hello" to. It was easy to find a room out here and three of us got an apartment together.

We started to work at the plant right away. We were on a broken shift so that we began work at 1:00 P.M. and we quit at 2:00 A.M. in the morning. There were about 15 Nisei working at that plant and most of them were getting 65 cents an hour. We were promised a raise of 5 cents after working two weeks but the boss wouldn't give it to us so we started to moan. A lot of trouble began after that. One fellow and I finally got fed up with it and we quit.

The fellow I had quit with was a Santa Anita boy. He and I went around looking for a new job right away. One of the Nisei in the building told us about a free employment agency so we went down to see the manager. He sent us up to the [A] Company and it looked like the salary was pretty good so we took the job and began to work. Right away I found out that it was hard work. My pal wanted to quit after the first day and since there were plenty of jobs around we decided to look for something else and we never did go back to work the second day. I guess that company is still wondering what happened to us because we didn't even go back for our pay.

We couldn't locate anything better and I didn't have too much money so we went to the Nisei foreman at the [C] Company and asked if we could go back to work. He sent us to the boss and the guy bawled the hell out of us for quitting on him without notice. He said that we did not show any appreciation for all the trouble he was going through and that it made it harder for other Nisei in camp. He sort of told us off. I had a guilty conscience so I told him that I would work steady after that so we got our jobs back. We went along on that job for a while but [my pal] got into too many arguments and he just walked out on the job one night. I wanted to quit too as I thought I wasn't making enough money. I was only clearing about $35 a week. I took a day off from my job and went to the American Friends Service and told them I was unemployed. They told me of a pretty good job opening. I went right away and applied. The interviewer said that he would let me know just as soon as possible when the next opening came along. A week later I got a phone call to come to work so I just quit the [C] company there and then.

This new job was in an apartment garage and I was the only Nisei on my shift. I got paid $130 a month plus tips. All I did was wash cars, fill the tanks with gas and oil, and park them as they came in. I would work nights one week and then change to the day shift the next. I stayed at this job over a year. I finally decided to quit as I got tired of seeing the same cars every day. The pay wasn't any too good and all of my friends were telling me that they were making a lot more and I thought that I should be doing the same thing.

[Soon after I] started working at the garage, our apartment house got a new manager and he didn't want any boochies there. He said that we had to get out. We didn't know about OPA or anything so I started to look around for a new apartment since I had the most free time. I walked around for a couple of weeks after work and before and tried to find a place where we could go. Most of the places where I went would refuse me in a nice way. In one place the lady was not so nice. She acted nice until she asked me if I was a Jap. I said "yes" and then she just closed the door in my face and said she didn't want me around. Finally I saw the vacancy sign in the building where we are now living. I didn't think much of the apartment but the landlord was willing to rent and we had to move pretty soon so that we didn't have any choice. I'm pretty sure that we are paying above the ceiling rent but we don't say nothing. We pay $12 a week for the joint.

It was pretty crowded for us but we would take turns sleeping on the couch. We had to get a small reserve room later on in order to put our friends up and one of them sleeps there now as he is the only one of us who is immune to the bedbugs. It's all very complicated because so many fellows have lived here that I don't remember them all. Sometimes I would come home and find a stranger in bed and I would just tell him to move over as I figured that he was my pal's friend and sometimes we'd sit down to eat with strangers. We fed as many as 12 guys here at one time. I think there must have been over 15 guys who have come to stay with us off and on. The landlady used to get real sore at us because we had so many people coming and going.

During the time I was loafing around I spent most of my time taking girls out. When my money began to run a little low, I remembered that the [P] Company said that I could have a job there so I went and applied. That's the job I'm doing right now but I don't care much for it. It's a small shop and it makes automobile parts and repair kits. There are about 5 boochie boys and 3 girls there out of the 20 workers in all. I get paid 75 cents an hour and it is a 9½ hours a day and I could net $48 a week if I worked full time.

The first week at that job, I didn't mind it so much but after that I had trouble. I took 2 days off and it felt good so I began to make a practice of it. At first the boss didn't say nothing. Then I began to go to work late and once I took a whole week off because I felt lazy. I thought that I would be fired so I went to ask for a release but the boss wouldn't give it to me. They still won't give me a release and I have been taking more and more days off. I haven't worked a full week there yet. The best I did was 5 days. Last week I put in 4 days and this week only 3 days. I get put on all of the odd jobs. Some days I am on the milling machine and some days I work the drill press or grinding machines. I don't like the foreman there as he seems to hate to see anybody talking while working. He gripes me the way he gives me orders just to show his authority. The company is too slow in raising the wages above 75 cents an hour. That's why so many Nisei walk out on them even if they can't get releases. The Nisei who are steady are good workers and they give us a good reputation even if some of us play around on the job. The only trouble is that they never get raises even though they work hard. The company gives a bonus every six months but you have to stick around to get it. The last time the bonus was between $100 and $200.

I really don't know what I am going to do with myself or what work I am interested in. I am just hanging on hoping that I will get fired so I can make a fresh start some other place. If I get fired, I'll just look for another job and it won't be hard at all. I think I would like to get a job as a shipping clerk. I'd rather be on a job where I could walk around a bit. But I don't know what my work plans are. I may even loaf around for a while like my roommate but I can't afford it long as I don't have the money. I'll stay there as long as I can go to work any time and take days off when I please. I plan to work full time eventually although I am in a little slump right now. All I make now is my room and board. My plans still are to make enough money to get married on but I don't know. My girl friend keeps asking me all the time and I don't know. She's out here where she can keep an eye on me so I can't play around too much unless I sneak out on her. I'm trying to make enough money at the horse races to get married on.

I'm not saving a thing now. When I was at the garage I worked every day and I was steady for a whole year. I saved my money and I had $450 in the bank when I quit the place but that is all spent now except for $100. I have about $100 worth of war bonds too. It costs quite a bit to live out here. It costs me $25 a month for rent and $30 for food. I spend about $10 a month to send stuff to my folks in camp but that is only when I am flush. I had to repay some debts and it cost around $10 a month for gifts. All the rest of the money goes to recreation and it's not nearly enough for me to do all the things I want to do. I took two trips back to camp already and that cost me quite a bit. I wish I could make about $60 clear a week without working my fool head off.

I don't know what I'll do after the war. Most likely I'll go back to our farm in California. I think I could make a go of that as I have had some experience in farming. I'm not cut out for anything else as I haven't studied for any special field besides farming. Maybe I might go into produce marketing after the war. My brother was working on a quick-freezing project before the war and he knows a little bit about that. But everything is uncertain yet.

I got a notice to report for my preinduction physical last April. I had changed my draft to Chicago so things got mixed up. At present I'm still waiting for the preinduction physical and I am up in the air. I've been under a strain all this time. I want to get it over with so that I will know exactly where I stand. I'm thinking of signing up for immediate induction when I take my physical because it is too much of a strain to loaf and wait around for the call. A lot of the Nisei fellows are loafing around waiting for the draft now and it sort of gets them down.

My folks still don't want me to go into the Army as my brother is already in. They are happy enough now. They are in [a suburb of Chicago], working in a greenhouse and they can support themselves. It's better for them to live out there than to come to Chicago. They have been out there for about 3 months now.

I have an idea that most of the boochies will stick around Chicago after the war as they haven't got anything to go back to in California. It will be hard for me to go back to a secluded farm life after getting used to the gay life of Chicago. A lot of times I think to myself that I should save some money and get ready for the future, but I don't do it as there seems to be too many things for me to spend my money on in having fun right now. I am overdoing it at the present time but that may pass. I should be working more steady and I know that. I guess I will change eventually or else I will get drafted so why should I worry about it.

A lot of my friends out here are loafing right now and a lot of them are steady workers too. The steady ones are more quiet and they are more backward as they don't drink or go to the hot spots. Some of my friends have been loafing around for months and they live off gambling. They only work when they have to. I guess I am slowly getting to be one of these guys, but my conscience does bother me all the time. I hate to have the thought of being without a job for any period of time. If I had a friend living with me who worked steadily, then I would go to work all the time too. But I am living with some fellows who don't care to work right now and I see that they are enjoying themselves so I am beginning to like their easy life more and more. I wasn't always like that.

I led a very quiet life for a couple of months. Then my roommate wanted to get around to meet some people so I started to go around to see some girls with him. We began to visit them more and more often. We met quite a few girls after that and we began to go to the beach and shows together. Then we started to go to dances and night clubs. I started to feel pretty good with this kind of life and I wanted to go out all the more. One thing led to another. We went to all of the Nisei dances held out here last winter and spring. We went in our little group and it seemed to be pretty good to go to these Nisei dances because it was just like camp. A lot of the guys got drunk but I never paid any attention to them as long as they didn't bother me. I only went to those dances drunk once when I didn't have a date. One of my friends had a fight at the [M] dance hall once and he pulled a knife on the guy. Some of the Los Angeles guys carry knives and they are always waiting around to gang up on somebody. One of these days somebody is going to get hurt.

I took some of my dates to the [A] dance hall and other places like that and this cost quite a bit of money. It was at this time that I began to get more and more sexy ideas about girls. I had fooled around with a lot of them but I was always a virgin up to that time as I was always afraid to go all the way. All of the fellows I met out here were experienced and they used to kid me about it. They said I couldn't get to be a man unless I laid a girl. I got more confidence in myself so I began to fool around with the girls seriously but I still was afraid to go all the way with a Nisei girl. It was about this time that we met some Caucasian girls. We got to know them pretty good and we began to take them to the [A] dance hall. We got kicked out of there once because they didn't want any mixed couples. After that we took them to taverns and started to drink with them. One night I was invited to a Caucasian girl's room and I slept with her all night. After that I had ideas about laying any girl whether she was a Nisei or not. I was always on the hunt after that. I never would have gone that far in camp although I had the idea.

One night I went to the [S] Hotel to see a friend. He told me that there was a Nisei girl who was quite free with her body so that I began to date her. After the third date she let me come up to her room. After that I had to have her every night. I began to take her to shows and bars. This girl was the first Nisei girl that I ever had in that way. I began to bring her up to my apartment here a few times and I would sleep with her in the extra room. She used to work overtime at the [S] Hotel on special occasions and they would give her a room for the night if it got too late. She always phoned me and I would go down and sleep with her there. Then one day I found out that she was taking me seriously and she gave me some hints about getting married. I wasn't in love with her or anything like that so I decided not to see her anymore. Since then I have taken a number of other Nisei girls out but only a couple of them would let me lay them. I like to fool around the Caucasian girls better because they don't take you seriously. I have more fun with them because they are a little more experienced.

All this time I was still going to marry my girl friend from Rohwer. I got lonesome here in Chicago so that's why I began to play around with other girls although I was faithful to her the first two months

I was out here. I kept writing her all the time even when I was stepping out. Then our letters began to get less and less so I started to fool around even more. I had an affair with an Hawaiian girl that I met at a dance in July, and I really went for her in a big way. I was so lonesome after she left Chicago that I wrote to my girl friend and told her about the Hawaiian girl. I said that if she came out of camp maybe things would be the same with us. In the meantime I started to go around with another Nisei girl I knew and I got sentimental over her too. We went swimming, picnics, and shows together. I was really serious over her and I didn't try to get funny at all. My girl friend then wrote me that she didn't want to be second fiddle to anyone. Then she came out of camp. She was sore at me so she wouldn't talk to me at all when I went to visit her. Finally I took her to Riverview but she was still cold so I thought it was a break for good. The next night I took the other girl out and told my girl friend it was the end for us and she started to cry and ask me if we couldn't start all over again. I was caught between two girls. Finally I broke with the other girl and haven't seen her since.

My girl friend and I are engaged now and she wants to get married right away. I don't have any money and I didn't want to get married so quick as I think I will be drafted soon and it wouldn't be fair to her. She told me that she would rather have a couple of months of happiness so I guess I will get married if I save enough money.

Right now I don't think we should get married so quick as I have a feeling that I will still play around with other girls as I am not settled in my mind yet. I got a slow start in life and didn't get started with girls until I went to camp so that I am sort of making up for lost time right now. My girl friend is getting disgusted with me for not going to work steadily. She is only 19 years old but she seems to be more mature than I am. The parents of both sides expect us to get married so that is why it is hard to break with her.

My life has spread out quite a bit since I've been out here. I've met a lot of new friends since coming to Chicago. I like to make friends with everyone and I don't care if he's a boochie or *hakujin*. When I first started to work out here, I was uneasy about how the *hakujin* people would take me. The *hakujin* people don't seem to be too prejudiced against the boochies except at certain times. Right now I am more or less in a Nisei group [from central California] but a lot of times I go by myself to go visit some of my other Nisei friends. I am the oldest one of my roommates. At first I used to act as their leader. I sort of got used to being a leader as I was a club president in elementary school and a leader of the scouts. That influenced me to give orders and this used to gripe my roommates no end. I told them to keep the house clean, save money, go to work every day, hang clothes up, help do the cooking and dish washing and everything like that. I thought I was being a good influence on them. But within 3 months I found that I had changed so that now I am more like them. I don't hang up my clothes neatly. I don't care if the dishes are dirty. I go to the horse races, I play poker, and I fool around with women. Before then I used to get after my roommates but now they get after me. I find that I am enjoying this kind of life, only I wish I had a lot of money so that I could play the horses all I wanted to without worrying that it is my last cent.

It seems that most of the Nisei don't feel like working now as it doesn't give them enough time to have fun. They put in about 10 hours a day and they only have time to eat and go to bed. There's no percentage in that and they feel that they might as well go out and enjoy themselves before the Army takes them. They all save their money up at first and then they decide to have fun like me. Some of them just quit their jobs without giving any notice and they loaf around for two months so that they can get an automatic release and then go after another job when their money runs out. I know that this isn't too good for the boochies because it may hurt the future. Sometimes I think of the future but I don't know what to make of it. I'm just waiting around for the draft, as I figure that it will take care of all of my problems for the time being. The sooner the better, as I am getting absolutely no place now. As long as I am not drafted, I will probably continue to play around and it isn't doing me much good. It bothers me a lot and I think of a lot of things I should be doing but I never get ambitious enough to get around to it. The fellows I go around with are my friends and I don't feel like giving them up. There is nothing wrong with them and you can't blame some of them for going wild because this is the first chance they have had to have their fling.

CH-62: JOURNALIST

Male; born in California, 1916; height 65½"; weight 120 lbs.; unmarried. Interviewed May–June, 1945. Described as "a slightly stoop-shouldered, neat, 'intellectual'-looking individual, with a high forehead; wearing thick eye-glasses; soft-spoken and mild-mannered;

rather deliberate in his conversation; using excellent English." He was "most coöperative"[185] with the interviewer who spent three evenings and one entire day with him and allowed him "to go along at his own leisurely pace."

CAREER LINES

Parental: Both parents were from the farming class in Japan. Father

[185] CH-62 kindly made several of his notebooks available to us. The following excerpts are indicative of his aspirations and interests:

December 20, 1938. The problem of self-adjustment looms as a huge problem before me. One always seeks perfect harmony and wonders how in heaven's name he can reconcile some of the confusing paradoxes within his personality. I suppose, however, that complete peace of mind is unattainable and that no matter how carefully and wisely man plans his life, there is no escaping a sense of waste and futility and a desire for what he knows not.

My original plans were to do scientific research in chemistry, devoting my life to it, after temporary employment in some civil service position. However, I no longer feel a deep interest in such work. My interest in literature has grown to replace it.

This afternoon, while reading Bacon's "Organum" and Aristotle's "Organon," I felt a boyish thrill at the thought of delving into the unexplored realms of the mind. This feeling is sincere. Literature is definitely close to my heart, and the life of a man like Thomas Wolfe strikes me as being both exciting and important.

July 28, 1939. I have not yet discovered any philosophy of life which might be satisfying, no way of life upon which to pattern my own, no set of values which I might accept. I find no sustaining values in what Ludwig Lewisohn calls ". . . this impoverished materialistic philosophy, today prevailing."

April 5, 1941. Intellectual curiosity about life is not the only motivating factor behind man's decision to break away from convention and seek out a philosophy of his own. There is a desire to ease the suffering of mankind in general by effecting solutions to civilization's vexing problems. This humanitarian interest is true of all religion, and basic to the philosophy of Asiatics. . . .

The true philosopher is not one who withdraws into an ivory tower to escape the struggle of life. Quite the contrary is true. While the recluse may try to avoid and ignore reality, the philosopher is so deeply interested in the problems of life that he devotes all of his time to a study of it.

May 13, 1941. My ambition is to discover and present new theories about life. In order to do this, I must experience life with the intensity of a Thomas Wolfe, gather all the relevant information possible, and spend a great deal of thought upon the subject. The insight thus gained can be offered in philosophical essays or in stories.

May 30, 1944. LIFE IS A SERIOUS matter for me. It means the complete development of my individuality, and it means the great struggle for enlightenment and progress in an imperfect world. Such an attempt of man to assert his ideals, in spite of both indifference and opposition, must follow a careful plan of action, a strategy so conceived and so executed as to bring about the greatest gains possible at the smallest cost in time and energy expended. In brief, my life must be undertaken with as much imagination, courage, and efficiency as is a well handled military campaign. Moreover, my ultimate goal must be ever fixed before the mind.

(born *ca.* 1876) worked as civil engineer in Japanese Army after completing high school education; mother (born 1876) had no formal education. Married before emigration. Father immigrated to Hawaii *ca.* 1901 and worked on sugar plantation; migrated to San Francisco *ca.* 1903; moved to Sonoma and then to Santa Cruz County where his wife joined him in 1907. In California he pioneered in truck crops and berries and became a successful independent farmer.

Own: Graduated from college in California in 1939, majoring in English. Unpaid family worker on father's farm, 1935; editorial work on vernacular newspaper San Francisco, 1939–1941. Inmigrated to Chicago, June, 1943; worked as "research writer" for a publishing firm for five months; then as typesetter for several printing firms from November, 1943, to date of interview.

LIFE HISTORY

My father originally came from Hiroshima *ken* in Japan. His family had been farmers there for a number of years. They originally migrated from north Japan and they had family records in the temple tracing it back to the 16th century. Dad was always proud of this family line.

After receiving a high school education Dad was employed as a civil engineer for the Japanese Army. Around 1900 he was commissioned to go to Formosa with the Army corps but he heard there was a plague there so he escaped to Hawaii. At that time my father was about 21 years old and he had just gotten married a short time previously. I don't know very much of my mother's background except that she was distantly related to my father's clan.

After going to Hawaii, Dad worked on the sugar plantations for about a year. Many of the Japanese immigrants were talking about California so that he decided he would go and see for himself. Around 1902 or 1903 he landed in San Francisco and he went directly to Sonoma [County] to farm with a few friends. It was not a successful project so that after a year he went to [X, a medium-sized community in Santa Cruz County], where some other friends were just beginning to farm.

Dad was one of the pioneer Japanese farmers in California. For a short time he grew lettuce but he later branched out into strawberries and apples. I believe that he was one of the very first Japanese farmers to grow strawberries in the state. Dad was always talking about returning to Japan but he continued to farm in the [Santa

Cruz] area right up until the present war. He was one of the more successful Japanese farmers and he was satisfied economically.

My father was a very domineering person. He tended to be arrogant and spoiled in his relationships with my mother and he constantly stressed his ruling role in the family circle. That was the general attitude of the Issei men toward their wives. Dad didn't go out for drinking or gambling. He was considered a solid family man and he had a reputation as being a model husband. He never displayed his temper towards my mother in public.

Dad used to say that all of the Japanese had to look after the welfare of our people. He was connected with the Japanese Association and he was the president of the group until about six months before the war. The active members of the Association were composed mostly of the small professional Japanese in town. The relation between the Caucasians and Japanese in [X] was extremely good at the time and we never had any discrimination in business or in school in an open manner. The high school principal was always sympathetic toward the Japanese, and he was regarded quite highly by the Issei. A few of the more successful Issei farmers were recognized in the town. Several of them belonged to the Chamber of Commerce and it was said that if there were no Japanese present at the meetings, it was no use discussing problems of farm shipment because most of the business came from the Japanese farmers.

My dad was a director of the Central California Berry Association for a number of years. Toward the time of the war, he was the vice-president of the board. This Berry Growers Association shipped a lot of produce to the East. The Japanese Association worked quite closely with it in order to adjust certain legal difficulties of the Japanese members. The Berry Growers were able to get a reduction in commission for individual growers and the pool of the reserve fund was used to help the more unfortunate members of this farming group. You know, the war hysteria didn't even affect this good relationship between the two groups very much and we remained friends until the time of evacuation. I would say that the Japanese in my area had economic acceptance but not social. The Nisei group was getting more into the community life on a social basis at the time of the war.

The [X] area was predominantly Buddhist although the Christians did have a growing group, especially among the Nisei. The Christian Japanese had some of the wealthy farmers as members, but the Buddhists were a more solid group. Our community didn't start the practice of *bon odori* festival until the 1930's. This came in through the influence of Japanese movies and through the tours of the Takarazuka Girls (a troupe of Japanese dancers), who used to go to all of the communities up and down the Coast. The *kendo* group also came to our community in the 1930's and the Nisei began to take it up enthusiastically for a while. Certain individuals were interested in getting *kendo* clubs organized for their own financial gains and I don't think it was a Japanese government propaganda effort at all.

The biggest social affair in our community was the annual picnic sponsored by the Japanese Association. The Christian church always had pageants around Christmas time but there was no hesitancy in the whole community to come out and celebrate some of the large Buddhist affairs. The only other occasion for the community to get together was during the monthly Japanese movies and plays.

When Dad first came to the U. S., he was with some Christian friends so that he joined their church since there were few Japanese organizations in existence at that time. He eventually disliked the Christians very much because of the way they preached so that he quit and joined the Buddhist Church. Actually he had a Shinto training but it wasn't strong with him. Religion in itself played only a small part in his life. He was racially proud and he used to lecture to my brother and me endlessly about the importance of the Japanese spirit and how samurais do this and do that according to certain codes of living. We never understood what he was talking about. He preached to us about these things until about the time we got into high school and then we were able to argue back at him.

There were 3 of us kids in the family. My older sister is married now, and there were my brother and I in addition. Girls were not regarded too highly by my father and he was very strict with my sister. She was never allowed to go to any of the social affairs freely like Nisei girls do now. The funny thing was that my father sent her to the Christian Church even though he had become a Buddhist himself.

When my sister was 20 years old, she had to get married by the *baishakunin* system. She was married to an older Nisei man from Los Angeles. The *baishakunin* just brought them together and the parents decided that it was a good match and that was all there was to it. My family was supposed to be a very desirable one to marry into because it was known that we had a good background and our economic position was secure. The Nisei fellow who was matched with my sister wanted to please his own mother and he thought that he could get along in the marriage and that my sister would be compatible with his mother. My sister didn't care very much because by this time she was tired of rebelling against my dad in other things and she wanted to escape his domination. My sister had much more of the Japanese influence than my brother and I did. She put up quite a battle but she was never successful in completely winning her independence.

I think that my father feared that he was going to lose his children to the ways of this country and he tried to hold us down as much as he could. My father was very attached to the family. We just didn't see things in the same way as he did. He never made an attempt to understand us and he discounted the Americanization influences that we were undergoing at school. He was so confident that we would listen to all of his teachings above everything else, but it didn't work out that way.

We always had to speak in Japanese to our parents, but my father would tolerate talking in English among the children unless he was upset about something. Then he would roar to us to speak in Japanese because he was afraid we would be talking about him or laughing behind his back. I never could understand why the Issei were so sensitive and suspicious about the Nisei. Nothing we ever did was right.

In our home, we ate Japanese food all the time and it was a victory for us whenever my sister was allowed to prepare an American meal. She learned to cook in the Home Economics class at high school. Actually my father liked American food but he wouldn't allow it in our home because he thought it was just another evidence of our drifting away from his Japanese teachings.

It was always an ordeal for us to have Issei visitors in our home. My father was always very concerned that we behave correctly. We had to go through a certain form of greeting and follow all the rituals which we didn't even understand. Then we had to sit still in the corner and not dare to speak up in the presence of elders. We didn't have a Buddhist shrine in our home, though, and that was one consolation. In some of the homes the Nisei children had to go through a regular ritual in regard to this Buddhist shrine. We had one of those large pictures of the Emperor and we also had a picture of Admiral Togo. We used to get all kinds of lectures about what a great national hero Admiral Togo was because he saved Japan from Russia and it was through him that Japan became a great naval power in the world.

Our home was not much different from the other Japanese. For quite a period we lived in a rented home because my parents always had an idea in the back of their minds that eventually they would return to Japan. But as the years went by my father began to get resigned to this country and he found many things in it which he liked better than in the old country. That is why he bought a house of his own in my sister's name and that gave us permanency in the community. Up to that time we had lived in a very rudely constructed farmhouse like the other Japanese and it was barren and cold. It wasn't a home at all because we just slept there. But after we bought our own house we had a regular American home and we certainly were glad that Dad decided that he was going to stay in [X] more or less permanently.

My father visited Japan in 1939. After that he never talked so much about going back to Japan because he knew that we would never consent to leaving California. Deep down in his heart he must have been disappointed with Japan. I know he didn't speak so violently in favor of it after his return. My mother said she was miserable the time she went back for a visit [in 1919].

I was sent to the Japanese [language] school from an early age and I attended faithfully for 8 or 9 years. I was the poorest student in the class. I hated the language and I had a terrific time reading it. About half of the class felt like I did. The other half was very studious and they took everything in. My brother was one of those who was good in the language. I just went to the language school to play baseball because we had a teacher who had played on a university team in Japan and he was quite enthusiastic about the game. We were automatically promoted because the parents had to pay a fee to send us to the school and that was mostly used for the teachers' salaries. We got through book 12 in about 10 years, but I can't write a simple *kanji* now. All of the Japanese language books were approved by the State Board of Education so there couldn't have been too much propaganda. The books had a lot of stories of Japanese family life and things like that. We never observed the Japanese festivals in our school as far as I can remember. I don't think we ever observed the Emperor's birthday like in other Japanese communities.

In the American public school I was always a well-behaved student. I was quite shy even though I went to a small elementary school of only 50 pupils. At first my sister, brother, and I were the only Nisei in that school; but after the Japanese got successful in farming in that area, 20 more Japanese families moved into our community and about 12 or 15 of their children started to go to our school. We were all pretty well mixed with Caucasian students so that we never had any trouble about race but peculiarly enough the Nisei still clung together automatically. The Nisei girls were less sociable than the Nisei fellows as they didn't go in for sports so much. My best friends in elementary school were *hakujin* fellows and several of us went all the way through high school together.

From an early age I always respected education. My parents had stressed its importance and my father made a lot of allowances for the American educational system even though he objected to our becoming too Americanized. I always studied hard at school and I was at the top of the class [in elementary school]. The high school was a much larger school and I couldn't adjust myself to a student body of over 1,000 pupils after coming from an elementary school of only 50 students. There were about 10 per cent Nisei in the student body. I did fairly well in my classes so that my grades kept up near the top. My father wouldn't allow me to go out for sports as I had to go home and help on the farm. I didn't belong to any particular group in high school although I chummed around with students who were majoring in agriculture with me. We participated in some of the intercounty high school contests. We used to go to all of the county fairs in our section of the state. I gradually settled into the routine of high school life and I was pretty carefree as far as my general outlook was concerned. I got over a lot of my timidity but I would still freeze up among strangers.

I first became definitely conscious of my Japanese ancestry when I was in high school because I noticed that the Nisei for some intangible reason were more restricted in social activities. I was also conscious that my parents were different from the parents of the Caucasian students and I noticed that my folks didn't mix in with Caucasians socially. I also got conscious of the fact that the boy-girl relationships between the Nisei and Caucasians were not so free. My close friends in high school were mixed because we all went to school on the same bus, and it took us an hour to get to the school from that area. In that hour we were just high school students and there were familiarities. There was little race consciousness on the bus but most of us went our ways once we got on the school grounds.

In my junior year I happened to meet a brilliant Mexican American fellow and it was through him that I got my first awareness of the social problems in this country. I was practically a socialist by the time I got out of high school. This was during the period of the depression and I used to read all the books I could lay my hands on which discussed the subject of planned economy. By the time I got out of high school I was more seriously inclined than most of the students. That was in 1934. I had a vague plan at that time that I wanted to go on to college and learn more. My father didn't see much use in it as a practical thing, as he had a fatalistic attitude that the Nisei would only be able to develop in farming. He considered it a waste of time to learn a lot of cultural things as he said that it would only make me unhappy. I was fed up with the farm and I wanted to escape it desperately but I didn't know how. My father and I had many verbal battles about whether I should continue on with my education. Finally we arrived at a compromise. I was to work for a year on his farm and then he said I could go to the near-by junior college after that.

The year I stayed out of school to work on the farm was most unhappy for me and I led a dull life. My father would make me go around with him to learn the farm business but I didn't care for it. I only worked haphazardly out in the fields and I was trying to escape into my books after work hours. I got interested in reading novels and I ran across some of Thomas Wolfe's books. He inspired me a great deal and I felt that my lot in life was not so bad. Then I began to read some of the Russian novelists. I picked up a vague idea that I would like to become a sort of writer because I had done well in my high-school English classes but I didn't have too much confidence in myself. I did write a couple of poems that were published in the Japanese language papers. During this period my teacher used to encourage me to write all the time and my social visits with her were about the only release I had outside of reading during that year.

In the fall of 1935, I was finally able to start junior college. Most of my courses were in English literature, but in concession to my father I took some chemistry courses as he thought it was practical and I would later be able to apply it in some way in agriculture. The 2 years I spent in junior college were a much freer and happier period in my life and it was worth the monotonous year I had spent out in the fields. I began to come out of my shell a great deal and I got rid of a lot more of my timidity. I discovered to my pleasant surprise that I could hold my ground intellectually with the best students in the school and I had done wider reading than most of them. I made one of the highest grade averages in the graduating class.

In the fall of 1937 I [enrolled in college] with the idea of managing as cheaply as possible so that I wouldn't be a drain on my father's resources. Through a connection of my father I found a Japanese family who were willing to rent out the top floor of their home as a sort of dormitory. Eleven of us Nisei fellows rented it for $55 a month so that our rent only came to $5 a month. We cooked for ourselves in a coöperative sort of way. I managed to get by on a budget of $20 to $25 a month. There never was any money left for recreation and I hated to ask my father for more. There weren't any jobs available outside of housework so that I couldn't earn extra money. Most of the Nisei fellows in the house were from the rural areas [of central California] and they didn't know why they were going to college but they felt that it would miraculously solve their life problems if they obtained a college degree.

By this time I became very conscious of my racial background. I knew that there were certain taboos existing on the campus which governed the Caucasian-Nisei relationship. I knew that I could go no further than a casual friendship with a Caucasian girl, but I just took it for granted that acceptance was not possible, so I just shut myself off without making an attempt. I had an open admiration of American ways and I wanted to get over the border which prevented the Nisei from fully participating in it, but I didn't know how.

When I graduated from college in the spring of 1939, I still had a secret ambition to be some kind of writer. I was clinging to this ambition but I felt that there were not many opportunities to develop in it. I knew that the Nisei were not accepted in very many economic fields outside the Japanese community. A lot of the Nisei students who had graduated from college with me ended up on the farm and very few of them got places. Many of the city Nisei went to work as salesmen [in Oriental art goods stores] on Grant Avenue, or else they became gardeners or laborers. The Nisei used to joke that their only destination after getting their diploma was to work for cheap wages in a small Japanese store. They did not have the optimism of the usual Caucasian graduates because they knew there was no demand for their services. If they even got a half-way decent job they were considered fortunate. Most college graduates did not make more than $70 a month except for a few professional men who had a little better income. Some of them went to work for their parents and they were not even paid. I was aware of all of these things and I became quite worried about my future. When I heard stories about all the Nisei failures, I thought that it was no use to go and bump my head against a stone wall so I accepted farming as inevitable. I didn't even go out and look for a job in the Caucasian community as I admitted failure before I even tried. I just went home and meekly started to work on the farm and I couldn't even answer my father when he asked me what I was going to do next. That was the only time in his life that he was understanding and didn't rub it in. He just mentioned that there were no opportunities for Nisei in this country and I had to learn for myself. Then all of a sudden, I heard that [a] Japanese language paper in San Francisco was looking for a Nisei reporter so I sent in my application immediately. I stressed my background in English literature and I was accepted. I decided to go to San Francisco and take the job even though it paid only $45 a month plus my meals. I managed to make both ends meet on this frugal budget because I had had experience in living cheaply while on the campus. I got a $5 a month room in a Japanese rooming house and I kept my clothing and recreation down to a minimum. Most of the newspaper staff wasn't making much more than I was.

In the Japanese section the newspaper steered a mid-course and it became sort of an apologist for the Japanese government. It took all of the *Domei* dispatches and printed them without editorial comments. The English section of the newspaper more or less reflected the reactionary attitude of the JACL. The English section had a freer hand in its editorial policy, but the owners made sure that the editor was not too liberal minded. I dealt mostly with the Nisei organizations and my chief function was to report the social and sports activities.

I was prone to be sympathetic to Japan myself before the war. I even wrote a few articles defending Japan's aggression. It was a sort of racial defense. We all felt that we were alienated from America in some way and we felt a necessity to defend Japan because our own position was so precarious.

[The newspaper] had its largest circulation in the Japanese communities all over northern California. Our circulation was between 5,000 and 10,000 but I don't recall the exact figure. We also had circulation outside the state in the intermountain district. The newspaper had Japanese correspondents in the principal cities of the coast and they were paid a nominal sum for the dispatches they sent in by letters. At times these agents were also responsible for collecting subscription money. The payment was always bad as half of the subscribers never paid up promptly, much as I hate to dispute the general belief that all Japanese paid their debts promptly. They pay their debts to Caucasians promptly but not to other Japanese.

The Japanese community considered the newspaper as necessary and all of the clubs coöperated with us. The Japanese churches were the most anxious to get publicity because there were so many rival ones.

I knew that there was no future for me on the newspaper. I couldn't think of anything else I could do though I thought of getting into civil service eventually. I did have some ambitious plans for self-education and I followed it to some extent but it only made me more unhappy. I had no intentions of ever going to Japan for a career although some Nisei did do that when they were economically frustrated over here. I wanted to get married just before the war, but I couldn't even think of such a possibility as how could I support a wife on a salary of $50 a month? I got a $5 a month raise after I had worked there for a year!

I didn't do much political thinking before the war. I think that I became less politically conscious after I got out of college and got stuck in a rut of a Japanese community without much contact with the outside world. I thought mistakenly that whatever happened to America politically was outside of the interests of my particular minority group.

That Sunday when the war broke out, I was listening to the radio in my room. The flash of Pearl Harbor came over and the announcer said something about the bombing planes identified as Japanese. My first reaction was of shock and excitement. That afternoon my brother visited me from home and we went for a ride in Golden Gate Park. I don't know if it was my imagination or not, but I thought that people stared at me. We were stopped by a police car along the beach and the officer was pretty sore about the Japs but he let us go. By that time the Army was on alert and when we got back to the Japanese community, the policemen were on all the corners and the whole area was roped off. That made me realize more than ever the ominous consequences of this war.

The next day the newspaper was closed up by the Treasury Department and I never went back to work for it after that. That hit me right off the bat and I was really disturbed then. I thought that the newspaper would be opened up in a few days after the Treasury man had checked up, so I decided to stick around San Francisco and wait.

The Issei were already getting terrified and talk started about *inu* turning them in. Quite a few Japanese lost their jobs right away, so that they were hit immediately like I was. My landlady did some domestic work on the side, and she got fired from her job the third day after the outbreak of the war when her employer was particularly nasty toward her. Many of the Issei stayed indoors because they didn't feel good going out. They were a very worried lot. Some rumors started that Japan might bomb San Francisco at any moment so that it would be hard to get food. My Issei landlady braved the outside to rush out and buy a supply of groceries after taking in this rumor. A lot of the Issei were advising each other to stock up on food.

Everybody began to worry about the Filipinos going on a riot and there was no way of allaying the fears of the people as the newspapers had been stopped. The JACL did put out a few mimeographed bulletins later on. But they carried government instructions chiefly. I heard of two definite stabbings by the Filipinos and I began to get worried. I kept thinking to myself, "This can't be America." My first feelings were bleak but my fears began to subside when the American press took the stand that the Japanese residents of the Pacific Coast should be treated sanely.

After that, talk started about Japanese being caught around strategic areas. Small-time politicians and those motivated by economic greed began screaming louder and louder about sabotage fears. The Issei all began to feel that they would be put into internment camps, and I wasn't too optimistic that the Nisei would be let alone because the trend seemed to be very dangerous. The Tolan [Congressional] Committee came around early in February for its hearings and most organizations were for evacuation. There was talk of protective custody and our whole lives were filled with uncertainty.

I just loafed around and I played cards and talked to my friends. I was just waiting and worrying about something concrete to happen. All of the Nisei had that vague feeling of fear and they didn't know what was going to happen next. They tried to bolster up their courage in different ways but that uncertainty was written all over their faces. Some of the single fellows got pretty disorganized and they went out on big drinking sprees.

We began to hear more and more of incidents of violence. Cars of Caucasian kids used to drive around the Japanese section yelling names at us and we didn't have any comeback. There was always the fear that some mob demonstration would take place. At one time a wild rumor went around that a mob was coming to burn the whole Japanese town down. Other people claimed that they had received threatening notices over the phone. We feared mostly that Japan would bomb the Pacific Coast as we felt that the blame would be attached to us and a mob would seek revenge.

The Japanese who owned businesses were most concerned because they didn't know what to do. They were all hoping that they would not have to sell out all of a sudden. I was indifferent to the war issue because I believed that both sides were wrong. At the outbreak of the war I reacted with a strong feeling of patriotism for the U. S., for my own self-protection, but gradually I began to feel a little bitter about what was happening. After I had thought things out, I concluded that I had to demonstrate outward loyalty to the U. S., and cut all my sentimental ties with Japan, as there was no other choice.

For some reason I began to renew my friendship with my Caucasian friends from high school and college days. I looked up my Mexican American friend because he was a liberal and he kept reassuring me that things would work out eventually.

I was running out of money so I had to come to a decision about what I was going to do. There weren't any jobs available so it wasn't any use to remain in San Francisco. In late February, 1942, I decided to go back to my home as my brother wanted me to come and help on the farm. My father had been picked up by the FBI in late January. It was a rainy day when they came and pulled him out of the house. He was put in the city jail and my mother was pretty sore about that. The constable of the jail was Dad's old friend and he felt very guilty about holding my father. After a day or so, my father was sent to [a detention station] in San Francisco but I was not allowed to see him. A few days later he was sent on to [an inland] internment camp.

I guess my father was interned primarily because of his past activities in the Japanese Association. There were many rumors that the treasurer of the Association was the *inu* who had turned the others in because he was never bothered. Dad wrote to us and told us not to worry about him. After his first hearing he was sent to another internment camp. Our *hakujin* friends sent letters of recommendation for the trial, but it didn't do any good as his appeals for release were denied.

When I first went back home in February, 1942, I had plenty of worries. The first restrictions had already come in and some of the Japanese were being removed from strategic areas. My brother was worried about losing his land along the coast. The Army jeeps used to drive all around our place and large coastal guns were put up on the next hill from our farm. The farm land along the coast was just leased, but the berries were almost ready to harvest and my brother was worried about the possible financial loss.

My Dad and brother had put in a heavy investment on this farm. We had 20 acres and it cost from $700 to $1,000 per acre to bring the berries to harvest in 2 years. We were so afraid that we would lose the entire crop. We hoped that we would be able to remain at least until after our crop was harvested. After weeks of debating, we decided that we had better get what money we could out of the farm by selling immediately because evacuation looked pretty certain. We sold out for about $150 an acre and that's the most we could get. It was a terrific loss for us.

All during this period the Army was announcing that voluntary evacuation was possible and that the people who moved would not be bothered again. Our whole area was interested in voluntary evacuation. The Japanese community held a general meeting to hear a report from the representative who had been sent up to Idaho to look over a run-down apple orchard. The place was for sale at a very reasonable price and the general plan was for all the Japanese [in X] to pool resources and go up there for a new start. We had a plan all drawn up to establish a coöperative community, but the whole project fizzled out due to the fear of the people and the lack of time.

My brother and I then rushed around to see one of our former high school friends. He was a big farmer so that he had big plans for voluntary evacuation. We decided to go in with him, but there were so many delays that nothing ever came of that. Finally, we decided to voluntarily evacuate [to Zone II—the Free Zone] on our own while there was still time. In late March I got in touch with a real-estate agent in central California. He said that he had some places for sale down there [in the Fresno area] so my brother and I went to take a look. He showed us 3 farms and we decided to buy a vineyard which was about 20 acres in size. On that very day, the general evacuation notice for Zone I was announced. We felt that we had to hurry because we were afraid of the freezing order. We rushed right back to close our farm up. My brother had a Caucasian friend who took over our home and the 18 acres there. We sure did a quick job of packing and moving. We were out of that place in exactly one day.

Evacuation was a terrific loss to my family as we only got about 10 per cent out of our berry crop and that represented a loss of around $11,000. Then we only got a small price for the lease of our own home and 18 acres. We took most of our farm equipment with us since we were planning to farm in central California in the new place we had purchased. The farm was in my brother's name and he was much more worried then because he didn't have my father around to give him advice. This was the first time he had all the responsibility of farming on his shoulders as I knew little of such things. My mother and one farm worker who boarded with us went along.

We got down to [the new farm] in early April. We started farming right away so that we could get in a crop for the fall harvest. We were still a little uncertain about our position so my brother decided to put in squash which was a quick crop to grow and harvest. We thought for a while that we were safe, but the Japanese people who lived in central California were all positive that eventually Zone II would be evacuated. They began to put doubts in our minds, and pretty soon we were believing all of the rumors and we could have kicked ourselves for voluntarily evacuating and putting all that money in the farm. All during June, July, and August, 1942, we debated and debated on what we should do next. Finally my brother decided to sell out after evacuation orders came out for our district. We had clung to the hope that we would not be removed again until the very last moment. The squash was quickly harvested and the prices were good so that a small profit was made on that. We took good care of that crop because we wanted to recoup some of our losses from the forced selling out of the berry patch in [X]. The vineyard was also coming along swell but we didn't get to stay to harvest that crop. The tomatoes were not quite ready for picking when Zone II was evacuated. My brother had bought this farm for $2,800 and he sold it for $2,900 but we had put in a lot of crops which we didn't get any benefit out of except the squash, so that it was another loss.

My brother sold all of his farm machinery as he was pretty disgusted and he thought it would be too much bother to store away as it would deteriorate. He lost a thousand dollars on all of his farm equipment. He had 2 tractors and one of them was almost new. He got about $3,000 back for the trucks, plows, tractors and everything so that he got less than 40 per cent back of the total value of this farm equipment. The reason he decided to sell out completely was because we had been fooled about being safe in Zone II and he didn't want to take another chance because he said that the Army was making false promises. He thought that if we moved to Denver or some other farming area, the same thing would happen all over again and it was not worth the effort. We both felt that eventually all the Japanese in the United States were going to be placed in the centers.

During those months in central California, I worked very hard on the farm. My brother and I went around to get different vegetable plants as we wanted to experiment a little bit. My brother had some ideas on farming which my father had never allowed him to practice and this was his chance to do what he wanted. He was enjoying himself so much because he was able to do anything he wanted to on the farm without being bossed by the old man. He had visions of making huge profits but all of this was dashed by the evacuation of the zone.

When the long expected evacuation notice for our zone did come, we got pretty sore. We knew that it was coming but yet we were angry because we felt the sense of injustice and racial discrimination. It was a frustrating sort of anger. We didn't like to get disturbed so many times and it meant moving all over again. I used to write frantic letters to [a central California newspaper], in the hope that I could help swing the public opinion toward a more favorable view toward us. We were absolutely stunned when the order did come through and my brother lost fight completely. He was a raving madman because all of the farm efforts we had put in were lost.

I was in a terrible state of mind during this time. I felt very much like refusing to be evacuated in order to put up a protest. Some of my Nisei friends said that it was senseless to be a martyr because nothing would be gained by it. I was bitter but deep down I knew that my only destiny was America and I couldn't resort to a faith in Japan. However, I had reservations because I believed the whole evacuation movement was a dirty Fascist move. At the same time, I didn't feel a high patriotism for the United States in the war because some of the beliefs I shared seemed to be eliminated. I didn't have any feeling at all when I read of a United States battleship being struck. I was immune to the whole thing because I was so wound up in my personal agony.

My brother was even more bitter than I was. He said that he was going to camp and sit it out for the duration. He had had some hopes of contributing to the war effort by raising his crops but he said that this wasn't wanted anymore so he wasn't going to make a fool out of himself. But my brother had the real farming urge in him and it just about drove him crazy to be idle in camp. Finally he couldn't stand it anymore so he leased some farm land up in [an intermountain state]. He did so well up there last year that he got his picture in [a national] magazine, for having one of the highest yielding crops for the entire state. Now my brother is much more optimistic about the future. He isn't bitter anymore and he feels that in a couple of years he will recoup his past losses. He likes [the intermountain state] so that he may even stay out there to do large scale farming.

When I went to Poston in August, 1942, my morale certainly was low. I was bitter to the day we left and I was trying to convince myself to stay behind but I didn't have the courage. I wasn't sure of myself but I did feel that it was so humiliating to be herded into camp like that. I was opposed to the principle of the thing all the way through. It hurt all the more because I really felt personally betrayed. As we approached the camp, the weather got hotter and hotter. Then when the train got to Parker [an Arizona station near Poston], we had to stay on it for 2 more hours before the busses came. It was almost unbearable and everybody's morale sunk. Some of the older people fainted from all the heat. We got on the trucks and we were taken up the dirty, dusty road and my spirits dropped even more when I saw those black tar-papered barracks. We were depressed by the bareness of the camp and our first gripe was the lack of privacy when we were shoved into those barracks.

When I arrived there, Poston was not very well organized as people were rapidly moving in. Our block needed a lot of mess-hall workers to feed the people so I volunteered for a couple of weeks. My real ambition was to get into teaching or newspaper work. The newspaper group was not organized yet so that I just waited until it was called together. We had difficulties from the beginning to get the newspaper under way. It was mimeographed in Camp I and I lived in Camp III so that I had to commute every day. Each camp would take turns putting out the newspaper so that there were really 3 newspaper staffs in all. We were not supposed to have any censorship, but there were certain things we were not allowed to write about. There were about 15 of us who eventually worked on the newspaper.

[Our] policy was to make a real newspaper which would be a strong constructive force in the community. We took an editorial policy of coöperation with the administration, stopping rumors, and playing up stories which would help strengthen the morale of the people. But we didn't string along with the administration on every issue [and] our newspaper came out with some critical articles. When we started to get a little noisy the administration began to clamp down on us more and more so that we couldn't say anything. They didn't want the people to know that there was a split among themselves and they resented any criticism of their administration by evacuees.

All during this time there was a growing dissatisfaction developing in the center. The people of Camp I had most of the grievances because they had been there for a longer period and they felt that many promises were being broken. They had been there since May and they claimed that their wages had not been paid for months and they didn't get their clothing allowances. A radical group played up the discontent and they did everything possible to weaken the prestige of the WRA. The people became very angry about all the red tape and it wasn't difficult for them to believe that the administration didn't really care for the welfare of the people. That's why the incident of the Poston strike[186] occurred in November, 1942, and the radical pro-Japan minority took over and swayed the people to follow them. People didn't even know what the exact incident was all about that had set off this mass demonstration.

I was in favor of the strike because I felt that the grievances were not unjust but I didn't care for the political element which was injected into it. I certainly didn't condone the beating of Kido and other mob activities of that sort. Our paper was always coming out with editorials supporting loyalty toward this country. This rubbed some Issei the wrong way and every once in a while a delegation would come around to protest so that my position was not so safe either.

After the Poston strike, I became a little discouraged about the role of our newspaper. I suppose that the ineffectiveness of our newspaper was partly our fault because we hesitated about taking a firm stand as we were interested in trying to improve the conditions of camp instead of being troublemakers.

The registration crisis was not as drastic in our camp as in some

[186] For "the story of Poston" and an account of the strike, see Leighton, *op. cit.*, pp. 11–231; also Thomas and Nishimoto, *op. cit.*, pp. 45–49.

of the others because the steam had been blown off at the time of the strike a couple of months before. I don't know everything that went on because I was [visiting my father in a Department of Justice Internment Camp] about this time so I missed out on all the excitement. When I got back I just registered Yes-Yes and most people were resigned to filling out the questionnaire. Our newspaper came out in favor of the registration because we said that this was an opportunity for the Nisei to prove their loyalty and win back their freedom as American citizens if we participated in an American action. The Issei were most pessimistic and they felt that everything was lost as far as this country was concerned so many of them decided to repatriate and they were taken out in the segregation movement which came later. However, I think the Nisei came through this test very well. The majority of them answered Yes-Yes to the loyalty question and there were over a hundred fellows who volunteered [from Poston].

I didn't volunteer for the Army myself as I felt that I would have been rejected anyway. There was a lot of pressure put on me because of my newspaper connection so I felt like taking the token move anyway. But I knew that accusations would later come back that I had just volunteered because I knew that I would be rejected. I also knew that my father would raise a terrific fuss if he heard that I had volunteered. He was still in the internment camp and he would have taken such an action as a betrayal of his family. My father thought that I had lost all my sense when he heard that I was advocating loyalty to this country through the newspaper. When I went to [the internment camp] to see my father, I told him that my position was clear as I saw no future in the Orient. He tried to make me see things his way but I refused to listen.

After the registration issue was over, large numbers of Nisei started to leave the camp because they saw that Poston was only a temporary stop for them and they wanted to return to the more normal American life on the outside. I was getting this resettlement fever myself.

Our newspaper was 100 per cent behind the resettlement move and we coöperated with the administration on this more than we had on any other issue in the past. We felt it was important for the Nisei future for them to get out as soon as possible. We devoted a lot of space to printing all of the notices on relocation job offers. I began to scan each job carefully to find an opportunity for myself because my mind was made up then to leave.

All of the newspaper staff were interested in getting some kind of journalistic work. They were all anxious to leave camp so that they looked for job openings just as much as I did. The American Friends' Service had set up a hostel in Chicago by that time so I put in an application. Then I renewed my efforts to find a suitable job. There was a long waiting list for the hostel so that my departure was delayed. I also had some difficulty about a clearance because my father was in the internment camp.

Finally I found a fairly good job offer. It was to be a writer–research worker for a printing company in Chicago. I sent in a letter of application, and to my great surprise, I was accepted right away. A friend of mine had received a job offer in Cleveland so we left camp on the same day. This was in May, 1943, and the whole block turned out to see us off. My mother had decided to join my father at [another] internment camp in order to repatriate to Japan[187] with him so that I felt that I had to cut all bridges behind me. My mother hated to see my brother and I go but she knew that our wish was to get out and reëstablish ourselves in this country.

I left camp with an attitude of expectancy. It was the best job offer that I had ever received and I thought that $27.50 a week was a huge salary because I had only been making $50 a month before the war for newspaper work. I thought it was a fortune.

On the way out I was very self-conscious about myself and this feeling didn't disappear for several months. I felt like I was coming out of a jail and I thought that people stared at me all the time. It was raining when we got into Chicago, but I was worried mostly about my housing problem. I had heard so many rumors about the difficulties of getting a place to sleep that I thought I couldn't even get into a hotel. There was no place open for me at the hostel and there wasn't anyone I knew out here when I arrived. I certainly did

---

[187] CH-62 translated a letter written from the internment camp by his father, in February, 1944. It says in part: "My son, you were born and raised in California and you have your education in this country, and you believe your future is in this country. However, you are of Japanese ancestry. Even if you were born in this country, like the German and Italian second generation [a section was deleted by the censor]. Since you have never been to Japan, I don't blame you for not liking Japan. But Japan gives all people equal rights.

"I intend to die in this country. I've been here for 38 years and participated in the Community Chest, Red Cross drive, was in the Chamber of Commerce. But here I was confined while Germans and Italians who were in this country for 30 years were not confined. Even the Chinese aliens are receiving citizenship now, however we Japanese are not treated equally. That's why we are having war. Your father."

feel like a stranger. I finally did get a room for the night and the next day I began to attack my chief problem of finding permanent housing. It was purely by chance that I found this place. It was the first house which had a room vacancy sign on it that I went to investigate. The landlady was very nice and she showed me all the vacancies that she had. She is a member of the Jehovah's Witness religious group. She didn't find out that I was of Japanese extraction until I had lived in that house for 2 or 3 months. I never mentioned it to her as I didn't know how she would take it. She treated me even better after that and she was always trying to convert me to be a Jehovah's Witness. My landlady thought that evacuation was an awful thing after I told her a little bit of my experiences in camp. Now she is very sympathetically inclined to the resettlers and she has told a couple of friends who operate rooming houses to give the Nisei a chance to move in. I've lived in this place 2 years now.

I get along well enough with the other people living in this building. There are no other Nisei here. At one time, the people living in the building next door raised quite an objection about Japanese living in this building, but the landlady must have said some nice things because when my brother came here to visit me, the people next door were willing to rent him a room.

I have never had any trouble at the stores in this district and I am on friendly terms with the corner druggist and the barber. There are quite a number of Japanese living in this whole area. At first I was very self-conscious and I didn't want any other Japanese to move to this district, but I don't even notice it anymore.

My job situation has been a little more complicated since coming out here because I haven't been able to get exactly what I wanted. I reported to work the second day I was out here. I was assigned to some simple work at first.

The employees in that first job were all very friendly to me. The whole office staff were liberal in their attitude so they did not hold deep racial prejudices.

I was in that job until November, 1943. Sometimes the work was interesting when we had to proofread a lot of books. Once in a while I was assigned to write a few simple articles. My chief dissatisfaction was with the low salary. All the other office staff had a much higher salary than I did. I found that it was hard to get along on $27.50 a week so I asked for a raise. The office manager said that they couldn't do any better at that time so I started to look around for another job in earnest.

I decided that the time was ripe for me to get a newspaper job so I went to the USES and some of the private employment agencies to place my application. I soon found out that there was nothing available. I wanted to get a job with the *Chicago Sun* because I had heard that it was a liberal newspaper. For a while I thought the *Sun* would employ me but it just dragged along without any definite answer. There were plenty of jobs available but nothing along journalistic lines. I began to give up hopes of getting a newspaper job so I began to look for a job where I could make money. I went to the WRA and Friends offices but they didn't have a thing for me either. The WRA even tried to discourage me from changing my job because they said it was more important to gain a reputation for Nisei workers. But they weren't living on $27.50 a week salary so I thought that they didn't know what they were talking about.

I finally went to a private agency and I paid $20 to get a printing job with a small private company. There were only 3 other workers in the shop. All of them were of German descent and one of these workers used to tell me about how hard it was for him during the first World War. In that job I got paid $1.00 an hour to start, but only 40 hours a week of work was available. It was a better salary than my first job but I still was not satisfied. I knew a little about printing as I had done some of it on the Japanese language paper in San Francisco. All the time I worked there, I was constantly on the lookout for a better job. I contacted a few places all along and I was always looking up new leads. Finally I went to the [A] Company and they offered me more overtime and a higher hourly wage. I was offered $1.25 an hour and a chance to work over 50 hours a week so that I would be getting a salary close to $70. This was much better thany my $40 a week job so I quit after being there seven weeks. It was not a union shop and I didn't make quite as much as I expected. I was still able to clear around $60 a week. I got along well with other workers in my department. After I worked in that shop for six months, I got released because there wasn't enough work during the summer slack. The foreman said that I could come back in the fall but I thought that I could get another job easily as printing jobs were rather abundant. I went through the want ads and I went to a couple of places for interviews. I found that one or two of these places were prejudiced but they would refuse me in a nice way. In some of the places I did not qualify for the more complicated jobs. I didn't get discouraged at all because I felt this was a part of my experiences.

Finally I went to the [T] Company which already had a Nisei printer there. This fellow had worked on the newspaper with me at Poston and he was the one who gave me the job lead. The company didn't hesitate to hire me so I started out at $1.25 an hour and I got 44 hours of work in. The other Nisei fellow got inducted into the Army a short time later so I took over his job. That's why I now get 60 hours of work a week and my salary is pretty large now.

This job utilizes some of my prewar training but it doesn't exactly fit into my plan for a life work. I'd like to be in journalism but I'm just saving money right now. I'm making 5 or 6 times as much money as I ever made before the war. What can a fellow do if he can't get into journalism? That's the only thing I am really interested in for a career.

I don't intend to go back to California at all, but it's not because of fear of public hostility. I can't see an economic future for me there except in farming or domestic work. I'd like to live in San Francisco again, but it's no use going back there without a job. The way things are now, my life is mostly concentrated on saving for the future. It is a temporary state. I make between $80 and $87 a week, but I have to spend quite a bit just to live. My rent is $25 a month and I have to figure on $2 a day at least for food as I eat out. I spend on an average of $10 a month for clothing. The reason for that is that I've had to get everything since I left the center. Before the war I was not able to buy any good suits at all on my limited income. My laundry and cleaning bill runs up to $5 a month. Recreation is a very big item and it costs about $15 a week. It's mostly for dates just to dinner and a theater and $10 a date is about average. I also spend about $15 a month for books, newspapers, and magazines. I send my parents around $10 a month, usually clothes and food items.

Fortunately my doctor bills are low, but I've been going to the dentist for the past year and that averages about $5 a month. My incidental expenses for carfare, etc., runs between $15 and $20 a month. That doesn't leave too much of my salary. I net about $275 a month after my taxes are deducted. That also includes one war bond a month. I've been saving between $40 and $80 a month quite regularly since I've relocated so it isn't too bad. I also have some savings with my brother since I will get a share of my father's farm. I used all of my prewar savings while I was in camp so that I had to start all over again when I came out here.

Some of my friends seem to be able to save even more money than I do, believe it or not, but there are others who do not even save a cent. I frankly admit that I've never had so much money in my life and I never dreamed of getting such a huge check before the war. But it's all relative because my other expenses have gone up and my tastes have improved to a better standard of living.

I don't worry about my draft status anymore. I had a 1-B classification before the war and it was changed to 4-C. I never was notified of the 4-C status though. In April, 1944, I got a 1-A notice. That was when they started to draft the Nisei once more. For a while I thought that I was going in and I made my preparation, but in July when I had my induction physical I was rejected. Now I have a 2-AF rating as my company applied for a deferment so I don't think that I will be taken at all. In a way, I wish that I were in.

My outlook on the war situation has undergone certain changes. Before America entered into the war, I was prone to excuse Japan's aggression on the argument that she had to expand and that it was only an Oriental problem. But when the war broke out between the two countries, it became a question of choice between Japan and America and I took America. From a rational point of view, I knew that I could never tolerate Japanese militarism, not to mention the cultural differences. I felt deep resentment toward Japan at the time of Pearl Harbor, but for a while that feeling lessened when the evacuation took place. I was momentarily bitter. But once I got into the center, I had a renewal of my sense of loyalty to this country and I knew definitely that there was no other choice for me. I realized that all my stakes were in this country and I have nothing to look forward to in Japan. I became more closely identified with the American government than ever through my daily contacts with the WRA. I had a voice in America and this was the real feeling. I felt more patriotically American at that time than ever before or since.

On resettling out here, I had a renewal of my race consciousness and I felt very insecure. I used to go to the interracial meeting and I became more conscious of the liberal movement in America than ever before. For about a year out here, I felt a deep loyalty to the liberal cause which stood up for us but I don't feel quite as intensely about such things now. My present position is still a belief in the democratic ideals, racial harmony, and social legislation, but I am a little cynical as far as my hopes for realizing these ideals throughout the world are concerned.

When I first came out here I believed that the Nisei would scatter all over the country and really get assimilated immediately because so many job opportunities were open to them. Coming into the new areas of the Midwest and East, the Nisei had considerable amount of acceptance into American life and this was extended to the social lines. However, there were certain barriers which stopped at the economic lines. I felt that the Nisei could make social adjustments through church, community, and Caucasian friends if a little more effort was made.

The only group I know of now which is in a real interracial program is a group at the [Z] Institute. Last Sunday we sponsored a dance and it worked out very successfully. There were 35 Nisei, 40 Caucasians, 20 Negroes, 15 Mexicans, and a couple of Chinese present. The Nisei members in this group have become much more racially tolerant in the year I have been associated with the group. They mingle with the Caucasians now without feeling inferior and with the Negroes without feeling superior.

Recently I helped make a brief survey of the Nisei groups out here and we concluded that the total groups only included less than 20 per cent of the total resettler population. I don't know what the other 80 per cent of the resettlers are doing for their social adjustment but it certainly isn't being found through the Japanese organizations out here. The potential for segregation is present, but I'm sure that neither the Buddhist nor the Christian churches have as strong a hold on the Nisei as they did before the war. The appeal just doesn't seem to be present anymore.

My own social adjustment satisfies me. When I first came out here, nothing was going on so I just contacted some friends I knew on the newspaper at Poston. I did practically nothing else except to go to shows. Most of the time I just read or wrote letters at home. Then I began to feel the urge to expand a little more. Through contacts with the workers on my job, I started to go to the Art Institute and Museum. After 6 months of this uncertain type of social adjustment, I got into the [Z] group when I attended an interracial affair. I began to see possibilities of making Caucasian contacts after that. It was something new to me because I had always been afraid to act as an equal and I never made an attempt before evacuation. I started to go to the Fellowship of Reconciliation meetings but I soon dropped out of that activity because I didn't agree completely with its political philosophy. I began to attend some of the Socialist meetings and I made a few friends there. Through this contact I met some union leaders and other interesting people.

My close circle of friends is enough for me now. There are about 7 or 9 of them and one is Caucasian and one colored. There are about 12 more people that I see occasionally and I go to visit them once in a while. I don't feel that I can handle a greater number of friends but I am always interested in meeting people with my same interest. I've been changing friends constantly since coming out here so that my present circle is composed of an entirely different set of people than the ones I knew when I first came to Chicago. It's hard to meet interesting Nisei people with things in common, though.

I always try to move forward though and I think that I have profited by the evacuation experience much more than I realize. It has enriched my experiences and I've become more self-assured. There also has been an economic gain. But my chief gain has been in social adjustment. I feel much more at home among the Caucasians than I ever did before evacuation. And another thing is that I feel the importance of freedom more than I ever did. When I came out of the center, the sense of achieving my freedom was like a load off of my back. I never want to get confined in anything again because that camp life was like a jail to me.

Since coming out here my outlook has broadened and I definitely know where I stand politically. I may be more cynical about politics but I have a strong faith in the democratic method. I haven't lost anything by the evacuation except for some slight fear that evacuation was a large evidence of fascism growing in this country. But I came through it without any bitterness and I think that the future will be partly realized for me if I can get my whole thinking straightened out into a definite line of action.

CH-53: CLERK

Male; born in California, 1918; height 69"; weight 158 lbs.; married, 1944. Interviewed October–November, 1944. Described as "mild-mannered, polite, 'correct'; very level-headed and quite intelligent in trying to figure things out in terms of the future." He was "deliberate in his speech," but "slurred many of his words, and injected Japanese phrases, occasionally, to express his exact meaning."

CAREER LINES

Parental: Paternal grandfather was a farmer; maternal grandfather, a fertilizer dealer, in Japan. Father (born 1876) finished 8th grade as an honor student; emigrated in 1900. Returning to Japan in 1912, he married and reimmigrated to San Francisco two years later. In 1942, was working as general housecleaner and domestic servant for two Caucasian families, one of whom he had served since 1917, the other since 1922; also served various other families as occasional butler from 1905 to 1942. Mother (born 1895) completed 8th grade in Japan; immigrated to San Francisco in 1917. During the 1930's she worked by the day in various types of domestic service.

Own: Finished two years in junior college in California in 1939, majoring in business and insurance; received honor scholarships twice while in high school. Worked as "schoolboy" and at other odd jobs up to 1939; salesman in an Oriental art goods store, 1939–1941; farm laborer, four months, 1941; machine operator (Caucasian firm), 1941–1942. Inmigrated to a Midwestern city in August, 1943; worked as insulator man in a battery company, August, 1943–January, 1944; moved to another Midwestern city and worked as operative in a chemical firm, January–June, 1944; moved to Chicago, July, 1944, and worked as machine operator in a defense plant, July to October, 1944. Was awaiting induction at time of interview.

LIFE HISTORY

I guess my father didn't know what he was getting his family in for when he came to this country as an immigrant around 1900. He came because he didn't want to fight in the Japanese army and also because he heard that there were many more opportunities in America. He didn't have anything to lose by leaving the old country because his family was rather poor. He was one of many sons and he didn't have any direct responsibilities so that he was free to seek his fortunes elsewhere. A lot of his pals had come over and they told him about the money that could be made in America. My father originally came from Wakayama *ken.* Around 1912 he went back to Japan and I think that the marriage [with my mother] was arranged by his family.

At that time my father had made quite a bit of money and he was planning to stay in Japan. He settled down and had a baby girl. He tried to do different kinds of work but he wasn't satisfied. He was there for about 2 years when he finally decided that he would come back to America to make some more money. My mother came along with him but my sister was left with my grandmother. It was arranged that she should follow a little later on, but the years passed.

Around 1924 my father wanted to send for her but the immigration laws went into effect so that he was never able to bring her over. She was a Japanese subject so that it was impossible for her to get into this country after that.

My father's history in this country is all dark to me. He has worked for rich Caucasians in domestic work and as far as I know they all thought highly of him. My mother didn't work at all while she was having us kids [three American-born sons, of whom CH-53 is the oldest] but after we got to grammar school, she started to do domestic work at different places on a day basis. We lived in the Japanese town in San Francisco. We moved about 3 times altogether and all of these places were rented.

Dad was a very quiet person and yet at times his nature was such that he would suddenly explode with a terrible temper. He was 20 years older than my mother so that they never did get along too well because of this difference in age. They never had the kind of love that *hakujin* couples have. They just got used to each other because they lived together for so long. My folks used to have a lot of arguments about money and the proper way to raise kids. My father felt that he should have the last word in this because it was the man's place to be superior. In his younger days he used to gamble a lot and Mother didn't like that. Dad didn't have any other vices as he didn't drink or smoke and he only played with other women on the sly. He was good to us kids but we never got to know him too well.

My father belonged to the *kenjinkai* and he had a lot of old friends there who came to the U. S. with him. They would get together and talk about the old times they had back home. I know that they used to talk about how much they missed Japan but I noticed they never went back there to live because they knew that they couldn't make as much money there.

In 1930, my father started to become a devout Buddhist. His church believed in healing pain through faith and my dad had a strong regard for it. My mother only went to the Buddhist Church occasionally as she was not very religiously inclined. However, she believed that young people should go to church so that she began to send us to the Christian Church [which her best friend attended] from an early age. Then we moved into a house located next to the Japanese Christian Church so we continued to go there. For a while my dad tried to force us to go to his church but we refused so much that he gave up. All of our Nisei friends were in the Christian Church and we didn't know any of the Buddhist kids.

My father believed in a lot of Japanese ideas which he taught us. He always emphasized that it was the best policy to work hard and save money and that the wife should help as much as possible and be quiet about it. He believed also that it was very important for my brothers and I to attend the Japanese language school and he insisted upon this as soon as we were old enough to attend. He told us many times in the years that followed that we should learn everything about Japan because that was the only place where the Nisei would have any future. He said that we could pick up a business or professional field there and have an equal chance for success. He continually emphasized the fact that the Nisei did not have a chance in America no matter how much education we received. Every time he saw or read about some discrimination case in the Japanese language paper, he would gloat over it to us and say, "I told you so." My brothers and I didn't want to believe this because we had been taught differently in the *hakujin* public schools. We didn't believe there was much discrimination because we never felt it while we were growing up. The result of my father's gloating made me more determined than ever to prove that he was wrong about this country. I had early developed a strong pride in America through my school contacts and I believed that San Francisco was the best city in the entire world. I concluded that things couldn't be so good in Japan as so many of the Japanese people were forced to come to America to make a living. I used to ask him when he was going to Japan and he said that he didn't want to go himself exactly because he didn't have any friends over there. Yet, he wanted us to go when it wasn't even our country. My father stressed respecting our elders and he strongly believed in *baishakunin* marriages and the Japanese class system. He believed that there were certain groups in Japan called *etas* who were outcasts and he always stressed that my brothers and I should never associate with any of the *eta* children in San Francisco. I thought it was a lot of baloney because I never noticed any difference in the Nisei from these families. No one would mention these things in public but I know that every Japanese family felt the same way about it.

When we were young my father taught us to respect the Emperor and we used to celebrate his birthday at the Japanese school. I thought I was a Japanese then so I didn't object against it at that time. I did it because all of the rest of the Nisei kids did it. It wasn't until I got older that I became aware of the fact that we really weren't a part of Japan. We learned such things as freedom and equality in the public schools but I couldn't explain these things to my dad although he must have realized that we were Americans too.

My father believed that we should become educated as he felt that we would become famous when we grew up and went to Japan with our American education. During the depression he encouraged doing domestic work as he said that it was the only way the Japanese could make any money in this country and he also said that it wouldn't hurt to do it until we went to Japan. He didn't think we had a chance for any other kind of job in America after we got out of school. He thought we could start out by working for some Japanese company on Grant Avenue but our real future was in the Orient.

My father had quite a few contacts with the American homes where he worked. He learned how to speak English of sorts because it was a necessity in his work. My mother was strictly Japanese in talking although she could speak and understand passable English for an Issei.

Dad used to make $5 or $10 a day all through the depression without too many layoffs so that he had a better income than most of the Issei who were employees. My mother wanted to use this money more for our education and in furnishing up our home. My dad never had a good business head and the money would go right out just as fast as it came in. He didn't even own an automobile. The fight over money got so bad that my mother finally went to work in a domestic job and she started a bank account of her own. Dad didn't like this very much because he thought that it was insulting to have a wife who wouldn't let him control all of the money.

My parents were very strict with my brothers and I when we were young but it got to be a very liberal sort of control after we got to high school. There were some Japanese customs which we maintained in our home right up to the time of evacuation but they were insignificant things. We ate a mixed diet of Japanese and American food. There weren't too many of the Japanese cultural objects about our home, and my folks were too busy to follow many of the traditional Japanese customs.

My mother was more or less the center around which everything revolved. She always had the interest of my brothers and me at heart. She would concentrate upon me because I was the oldest son and I was supposed to set the example for my two brothers. This position in the family for myself had certain compensations because I was treated the best and my mother had the greatest ambitions for me. She wanted me to be a doctor or some kind of professional person.

I don't have a vivid memory of my childhood because nothing exciting happened. I was born in San Francisco in 1918 and my first few years of life were most uneventful. When I was about 4 or 5 years old I began to pal around with a bunch of neighborhood kids my age and we gave our parents a lot of worries as we would steal apples from the fruit and vegetable man and we would also go out and play in the streets with our wagons so that our parents were always worrying about our safety. All of this gang was Nisei kids. After I reached the age of 6, I started the public elementary school. I was one of those quiet Nisei students at first and I was scared to death of attending classes for the first few months. I just sat in my corner being as inconspicuous as possible and I didn't make any trouble at all. I only spoke a little English at that time as my parents were unable to teach it to me. I felt that I was different from the white students because I used to say Japanese words in class and they wouldn't know what I was talking about. After I got adjusted to school I didn't have any trouble at all and I got through in the regular fashion. I got fairly good grades in my class work and I prided myself on that. During recess I played mostly with Nisei children as the school was composed of about half Japanese students. We got along very well with the *hakujin* students, but some of the *hakujin* were from pretty tough neighborhoods so that we had to fight them occasionally. They didn't dare call us names because there were too many Nisei around to object. There were Negro kids in our school also but I didn't fool around with them at that time because I had the impression that they were different from everyone else. At that time I really didn't recognize any difference in race except for the Negroes as [the rest of us] looked upon each other as equals.

The teacher didn't discriminate against the Nisei students at all. In fact, the Nisei were favored for certain honored positions. I was on the traffic-cop patrol of the school and we used to march in front of the City Hall for prizes. We also had field days at Kezar Stadium when all of the San Francisco grammar schools would get together for competition. That was when all of us felt pretty close to our school and we were pretty close to each other too when we competed with the other schools.

I liked singing very much while I was in grade school and I was in the chorus. It was a pretty happy childhood. The only thing that interrupted my playing around was when I started in the Japanese language school. I was about 6 or 7 years old and that experience was a drudgery. I went for almost 10 years. I felt like playing after 6 hours of public school but my father wouldn't let me. It was a very difficult language to learn and the Japanese teachers were not very good. One of them used to hit me on the head with a ruler when I was not quiet in the class. I remember I had a deep hatred of him and that's why I didn't study much. We hated all the Nisei girls too because they all studied their lessons and they were all submissive to the teachers. The teachers were always putting them up for example to us boys. When I got into the 8th year at the language school, we were taught Japanese history and customs and a little about the samurai spirit. The teachers were all from Japan and they considered us as real Japanese. It was in the advanced grades that the teachers stressed the fact that we should be proud of our Japanese blood. After the war with China broke out, the teachers changed their tunes quite a bit and taught us more about being integrated into the American life and they said that we had a certain duty to America. But on the Emperor's birthday we still had to celebrate so I didn't know where I stood. I just took it for granted that I was a Japanese at the language school and an American at the public school.

My American grammar school days were much more pleasant. As usual the Nisei stood out in scholastic standing in that school so that none of us felt any different from the Caucasians as the teachers would compliment us on being smart students. A lot of my playmates went on to this school with me so that it wasn't difficult getting adjusted to it.

I started high school in 1933. I felt awfully small when I first went to high school because for the first time there weren't too many Nisei in my classes as compared to Caucasian students. Right then and there I decided to make some *hakujin* friends. They all were pretty friendly if I didn't act backward and try to hide in the corner. In high school I took a general academic course and I studied fairly hard so that I got good marks. When I got to be a senior, a Nisei girl and myself decided to organize a Nisei students' club. When we approached the school officials about it, the principal wouldn't let us organize because he didn't believe in the segregation of different races. We thought that he was treating us unjustly and we didn't see why we couldn't have our own club. We didn't understand anything about why segregation was not so good. We just thought that we could have more fun if we got together. We went ahead and organized anyway but we held all of our meetings outside of school in the Japanese town.

I also took part in some of the general school activities. In athletics, I went out for baseball and soccer but I didn't make the first team. It was in high school that I learned how to dance. I also took a public-speaking class and that gave me a lot of self-confidence so that I was quite active as a leader. I was very optimistic about the future and I felt that all Nisei should go on to college and enter the professional fields if possible. Quite a few Nisei were already in college and all of us took it for granted that our education would be incomplete if we did not go. I had a number of different plans in mind for myself. I wanted to be a chemical engineer or enter foreign trade or commerce and I also had an ambition to be a bookkeeper.

When I graduated from high school in 1937, my plan was to go on to the University of California, but I did not have enough funds to pay the tuition there so I had to go to junior college instead. I planned to go there for a couple of years at most and then transfer to the university but I never did get around to that.

During most of the time I was in high school, a large share of my social activities were centered around the Japanese community. I went to the Japanese church every Sunday and I looked forward to many of the Nisei events which were held in the community. I was a member of the Japanese YMCA and I took part in the basketball, baseball, and football leagues for the Nisei. I continued to go to the language school. It was during my YMCA days that I first became conscious of being a leader. My aim was to live a Christian life so that I could inspire the respect and confidence of the younger boys. I was even planning to be a minister for a while. It didn't have too much to do with religion except that I believed in living a clean life. My Y activities played an important role in helping me to see a little of what was going on outside of the Japanese community.

I guess I became really aware of racial differences when my high school teacher discouraged me from going into certain fields of employment like banking and insurance. I didn't know what the teacher was getting at at first so I innocently asked why I couldn't enter the same fields that my Caucasian friends were entering. Then the teacher told me outright in a very nice way that there was not much of a chance for an Oriental to get a job in these fields. Then I began to see that they took us a little differently and we were really not quite

American in their eyes in spite of the things they taught us in the classes about equality and so forth. I sensed then that I was from a group set apart from the other groups at school and maybe that's one of the reasons why I went ahead with the plans for organizing the Japanese Students Club. Actually these things didn't strike us very hard in high school and I was only aware of it in a vague way. I intended to be rather optimistic about the future because I wanted to prove my father wrong when he insisted that the Nisei did not have a chance in America. I heard of other Nisei who seemed to be making good so that I thought I could do the same thing. In the normal activities we took part in, we were not barred from the general community. We could attend any of the movie houses in the city and I never heard of any discrimination in eating places or any other public places.

When I started out at junior college in 1937, I began to blossom out into a social butterfly. We had a Japanese students' club there and I was the vice-president of the organization for one semester. My main concern was to have a swell social season for all of the Nisei in school. This was the period which started my many romances and I had a number of girl friends in the years that followed.

I don't know why the Nisei at junior college all congregated in certain spots in the study hall. I know that this didn't make a very good impression on the rest of the students. They had plenty of opportunity to mingle but they were very cliquish and would not spread out even when the Japanese Students Club urged them.

As usual, the Nisei at junior college were the smartest students in the classes and they dominated all of the honor rolls which were published. They had better study habits and it meant a lot to them to have good grades. Many times the list for all A's consisted entirely of Nisei names. I didn't do so well in my studies because I wasn't so conscientious about it. I got lazy about my homework and I began to cut many classes in order to concentrate upon my social life.

My original plan in going to junior college was to train myself so that I could prepare myself to enter business and eventually own my own store. I took up a lot of bookkeeping courses in order to work toward this goal. My main thought was to get away from being just a hired worker.

In my serious moments I became very much aware of the general Nisei plight when it came to job placements. It seemed that our only future was centered around other Japanese in the community and not around the whole community of San Francisco. When I finished a course in insurance, the teacher promised everyone in class a job with [a national] insurance company, so that I studied very hard because I thought it would be a wonderful opportunity for me. I managed to get a B plus average in this course so I was rather elated to think that I would probably be one of the first in the class to get placed. Somehow the teacher never got around to calling me for a job interview. Other students who got lower marks in the course were called ahead of me. The jobs were given to some of those Caucasian students right after I was interviewed so that I knew that it was discrimination. It made me feel rebellious and sort of disgusted with everything. I could not see the fairness in it because it was opposed to all of the principles of America which I had been learning these many years in school.

My parents gave me little comfort when I became so discouraged because they felt that it was a natural thing to happen. It became a sort of struggle between my parents and myself and I didn't want to admit that they were right because I still had some feeling that everything would turn out for the best eventually. I had heard that it took a little time to get success in anything and I didn't want to believe that my Japanese face was a handicap. My father thought I should resign myself to the fact that I would be taken as a Japanese regardless of my American citizenship. All of this made me want to prove my parents wrong instead of resigning myself to a dead-end future.

I wrote to various Japanese and American firms for a job but I couldn't get a thing. Since our family was in need of money, I finally decided to work for a Japanese art goods company on Grant Avenue, to get experience. I told myself that it was only temporary and I would get something better when my family didn't need my help so urgently. It was fairly easy for me to get a job on Grant Avenue through another Nisei friend of mine who worked down there. I started in a Japanese store located in Chinatown at $45 a month, but I didn't think of the wage at all. I was very excited about my first real job and I interpreted it as the first step toward a successful career. The months began to go by and after two years of this slave work with only a $10 raise in that period, I got pretty disgusted at the whole thing. I was employed as a stock boy and the job was very monotonous. I soon found out that the promotions did not come very easily and most of them were based upon favoritism. We couldn't complain about it very much because jobs were too scarce. The firm hired about 12 Nisei and the highest paid in that group only got between $80 and

$100 a month after working for 5 years. All of them put in over 48 hours of work a week. The average pay of the Nisei in that company was around $55 a month. When I finally got up into the sales department actually I didn't get any increase in pay because I put in more hours. The only thing I got was an added prestige and a chance to meet some of the customers. I had to wear clean shirts every day so that my laundry bills went up. I wouldn't have been able to manage by myself but I lived at home and that made my expenses cheaper. Being stuck in a job like that was sure crummy and I don't see how I stood it for those 2 long years. I didn't have the gumption to quit as I was afraid that I could not find another job. I knew that I would get black-listed in all of the other Japanese companies along Grant Avenue if I quit that company because it was one of the more powerful ones. In any of the other stores I knew that I might even get paid less.

My boss used to lecture us about people in Japan who worked for nothing when they started out and gradually ended up being the owner of the business. I never said anything to him but I thought to myself that this was America and we should at least be paid a decent wage. I didn't see how I could save up money to be an owner of those stores on $55 a month. My boss believed that all of his workers should follow the Japanese customs of obedience, kowtowing to the bosses, being prompt on the job, respect for elders, working overtime without complaint for the sake of the business, and fooling the public about the merchandise because lying was excused in that case. He told us to tell the tourists that all of the goods were Chinese goods even though it was plainly stamped on the back "Made in Japan." We were trained to tell the tourist about the valuable Oriental merchandise when actually the stuff was a lot of junk. Many of the tourists were from the Middle West or East and they didn't know the difference. The boss realized anywhere from 200–400 per cent on his sales.

There must have been around 200 or 300 Nisei working along Grant Avenue in the various art goods stores. Maybe there were even more because there were at least 50 of these stores and some of the companies hired quite a few workers.

The China-Japan war began to have effect on our store, especially after the embargo was put into practice. After that my company began to specialize in Chinese and Occidental goods. The Japanese goods were never put on exhibit in the windows because that might have chased the tourists away. The boss always instructed us to sell the

Japanese goods to the customers when they came in, though. Even the things which were imported from Japan began to resemble Chinese goods like the mandarin pajamas and slippers. By the time I pulled out of this kind of work, the company was buying most of its goods from Chinese merchants.

It was a declining business as the tension in the Orient increased and the Americans became more sympathetic to China. Chinese merchants began putting signs in the window saying "This is a Chinese Store." Some of the Japanese stores who had Nisei managers tried to meet this competition by putting out American flags and signs in the window. Some of the Issei owners put the stores in their sons' names so that signs were put up saying "This is an American-owned store."

I knew that some kind of trouble was brewing in the Orient because 9 out of 10 Caucasian customers who came into the store began to ask us if we were Chinese or Japanese. When I was asked this question, that was the time when I felt awfully low. It was a strange feeling I had because I didn't know exactly why I should be asked my nationality. Usually I came right out and said I was a Japanese American. I didn't say it with much confidence in those days though. I think it was during this period that most of the Nisei began to call themselves Japanese Americans. Before all this trouble started we just said that we were Japanese.

Finally in August, 1941, I definitely decided to quit my job in the store as my pay was too low and there wasn't any prospects of a raise. I tried hard to get a job with a Caucasian firm but they all told me that it wasn't the time. I ran into some discrimination too but I was used to it by this time. My mother had backed me up in my decision to quit the Japanese store, but my father thought that I had made a great mistake in quitting a Japanese boss because none of the other merchants would want to give me another job since they would consider me as an unreliable worker.

[The older of my two brothers] also had a hard time finding a job after he left the junior college. He ran around with a rowdy Nisei gang and he learned how to drink and fool around with the prostitutes. He would stay out all night with the gang. He was pretty glad when the draft came around so that he volunteered for the Army in July, 1941. He preferred to be in the Army for a year than wasting his time in Japanese town without a job. Until that time nobody thought very much of my brother.

When my brother first volunteered for the Army, my dad was humiliated and indignant to think that a son of his would volunteer to join the U. S. Army. After my brother went into the Army, all of his Issei friends began to congratulate him for having a healthy enough son who would be accepted by the Army. My dad picked up after that and he was quite proud of my brother going to the Army in the end. Deep down my father believed that loyalty to one's country was the greatest thing a man could do and he recognized that we Nisei had to be loyal to this country of our birth. That's why he didn't discourage us against this country to the point of being disloyal. He just wanted us to get out because there weren't enough economic opportunities here. It was the Japanese way that a person should never be disloyal to his own country and most of them recognized that the Nisei really accepted America first of all.

I thought of volunteering in the Army then but I didn't see any future in it so I went up to Vacaville to work on a fruit farm. I stayed up there for 3 or 4 months and I picked fruit with a Japanese gang. I got promoted to truck driver but I found out that the Japanese farmers tried to gyp their workers just as much as the Japanese merchants. The gang I was working with had been doing farm work for years.

For a while I thought that maybe agriculture was the field for me to go into, but I changed my mind when I saw how some of those Japanese fruit farmers were losing out every year. I had some idea of starting a combination drugstore and fountain in Japanese town but I didn't have the money or the experience to do anything like that immediately.

In October, 1941, I finally came back to San Francisco to start my job hunting all over again as the fruit season was over. I only cleared about $60 a month up there but this was much better than what I had made in the art store work because it was clear profit. My plan was to try to get a higher paying job in a Caucasian store and save up some more money for my future store. As soon as I got back into San Francisco, I heard that a few Nisei fellows were getting jobs in [one of the large steel companies] through the U. S. Employment Service. I thought that this would be just the thing for me and I was quite hopeful of getting in myself. I went down to the USES Oriental department to try and get in to the shipyard work but I was told that the company didn't want to take any more Nisei. I was rather disappointed about the outcome of this prospect but I still tried to get into all kinds of manufacturing companies in the Bay Area. Some days I would walk miles and miles and it was pretty discouraging when the answer was always "No." I knew that I was qualified to do some of the unskilled labor jobs but they just didn't want us. You can imagine what my father's comments were when I told him about the bad reception I had gotten in some of the plants. He didn't rub it in but he just kept quiet. I knew what he was thinking though and I even began to think maybe he might be right.

There were some other Nisei who were breaking into American firms a little bit. The reason for this was that a lot of *hakujin* workers were already going into the shipyard work in the Bay area, so that they left their nondefense jobs open and the Nisei were given a chance in some of them. I kept on trying for several weeks and finally I landed a job at a Caucasian stencil company. I certainly was happy about this. The boss promised to teach me all about that work and he said that he would give me a permanent job with a possible chance at a manager's job in the future if I turned out well. He taught me how to operate all of the machines and how to run the whole plant. We made the stencils and sold them to the wholesale houses. There were only about 10 or 12 Caucasian workers in our plant so that I got along well with all of them. I was quite proud of myself because I was one of the very few Nisei to get a job with a Caucasian company and I had high wages compared to most of them although it was low compared to the older *hakujin* workers. I was glad that I was the only Nisei in the plant.

I stayed on in that job until April, 1942, when the evacuation came. I was working in that plant when the war broke out, but I didn't get fired. My boss was very sympathetic to me. He didn't blame me for the war at all because he accepted me as an American. He knew all about the trouble of the Nisei in getting jobs. He also had a good idea of the problems of Japan because of previous business contacts.

I was able to save most of my salary throughout the time I worked because I didn't have to pay for room and board at home. I contributed to household expenses whenever there was a need. We had a sort of common family bank account. For 2 years I contributed my whole salary into the common pot and I only took out what I needed for my own expenses. The idea was that all of us in the family could share in this money equally no matter what we had contributed as long as it was not spent foolishly. This system worked out pretty well for us.

I was living a very routine life in the period before the war. I was going around quite steady with a girl and I engaged in the usual Nisei activities. Once a week I would attend a Nisei social function at the Y or some other place in the community. I went to almost all of the big Nisei dances. I continued my activity in the YMCA and I was the president of one of the Nisei clubs there. Every Sunday I continued to attend church and there was considerable social activity there. My whole life was in the Japanese community by this time except my work with the Caucasian company.

I began to play the pin-ball machine a lot and all of my spare money went into that. I started to hang around the pool hall with some of my Nisei friends. I hadn't dared to do that when I was working in a Japanese store as my boss had the funny idea that their employees should be perfect in conduct even though the bosses themselves had a lot of vices. They didn't care exactly what we did as long as we were not seen by other Japanese as they thought it would hurt their business reputation if one of their employees was seen around a pool hall all the time. At that time, I used to get shocked when I heard that Nisei fellows went to see the white prostitutes. None of the group I went around with ever did anything like that because it was more of a church and YMCA set.

I never dreamed that I would ever go to another place to live outside the Bay Area. I was used to the life in San Francisco and I felt that I was an established part of the Nisei society in which I traveled.

I first joined the JACL in 1939 because I wanted the social activities which this organization offered to the Nisei. The reason I had joined the JACL besides social affairs, was that I felt that it was my duty to vote and I thought that the JACL could give me some advice on that. Just before the war started, the JACL was engaged in trying to get citizenship for the Issei and they wanted to protect the Japanese fishermen and landowners. They were also telling the Nisei to drop their dual citizenship but none of us paid much attention to that. I only went to the JACL very infrequently and there would only be about 75 Nisei present at these meetings. But when they had a social affair, they would get anywhere from 500 to 800 people out. I was favorably impressed by the JACL and I thought it was a good organization. I didn't hold it against them for having so many socials as I realized that they had to get members somehow and this was the best way to appeal to the Nisei. The JACL began to hold a number of emergency meetings in November, 1941, but nobody in Japanese town got very excited about that. The Japanese newspapers also began to say that no agreement was being reached between America and Japan, so that all the Issei were pretty worried. The majority of the Nisei went on with their regular lives without being aware of the growing tension and I suppose I was included in this group for most of the time.

That Sunday of December 7, 1941, I was in the church service. It ended around 11 o'clock so that my pal and I were en route home when we saw some huge headlines in the newsstand. I almost fell over when I saw that it read "Pearl Harbor Bombed." God, I never had a shock like that in my life. I kept saying to myself that it couldn't be possible that Japan would dare to attack the U. S. I bought the newspaper immediately and read all about it, but the details were very scarce. That made me feel that maybe it wasn't true but somehow I felt that it was. I felt a deep, sinking sensation and a hollow feeling in the pit of my stomach as I read on. I started to be aware immediately of Caucasians looking at me. I didn't know exactly how to react but I thought that things would be pretty tough on the Japanese community.

My parents were all excited about the bombing of Pearl Harbor when I got home, but in a way they were glad that Japan had stood up to America without backing down like a coward nation. But they still thought that peace would come right away because America would realize that Japan meant business. By nightfall we realized how grave the situation was when the Army patrol came to guard the Japanese community against possible riots. The FBI had been busy that afternoon picking up the suspected Issei immediately. That was the time when I was really afraid. I actually thought that all of us would be put into prison or deported right away. I felt insecure because I didn't think that we would be accepted as Americans any more after the way Japan had attacked this country.

In the days that followed, I felt more confident that the Nisei were being taken as American citizens and that we had a place in the war effort. That was because the governor of the state and the mayor of the city and other officials made statements for us to be calm and that we would be treated fairly. I was pretty sure that this country would stand by us and I had a terrific hatred against Japan at that time.

As the days and weeks went by wild rumors began to circulate in Japanese town and my parents made it miserable for me with all of the false rumors which they obtained from the other Issei. They believed all kinds of crazy stories. They tried to tell me that all of the Issei were going to be put into concentration camps behind barbed wire fences and all property and assets would be confiscated. I thought they were crazy because I didn't think that anything like the German system could happen in America. Then my parents told me that people found guilty of owning certain Japanese goods were to be tried for treason. That's why my folks burned everything Japanese that they thought might be used as evidence against them. I helped them burn all of our Japanese books and "Made in Japan" drawings, phonograph records, Japanese pictures, Buddha images, Japanese clothes, and *kendo* outfits. Practically everything Japanese we owned was gotten rid of.

Pretty soon a curfew came into effect and it was applied to all of the Nisei. I had to abide by the curfew because I didn't think of disobeying the law. I was always home by 8 o'clock but many Nisei went to Chinatown just to stay out after the curfew hour because they didn't like the idea of having all suspicions put on them.

I got so I believed some of the rumors which were going around the Japanese community. All of us were convinced that our phones were tapped and that our letters were being censored. The Issei didn't talk over the telephone at all because they thought it was dangerous to use Japanese. My mother hardly wrote to my brother in the Army because she thought it would be held against her if she wrote in Japanese and she couldn't write English. We also had to worry about mobs of Filipinos attacking the Japanese community and my father always insisted upon bolting the door tightly every night so we would not be murdered in bed. There were rumors that Japanese in other towns had been killed in this way.

Pretty soon a lot of travel restrictions and other things began to be applied. The whole Japanese community was upset. Many of the stores had not opened up since December 7, and all of the Issei's money was frozen. For the first time my brother and I were at home with our parents at night as we were unable to go out so much. We would all sit around talking at the dinner table about the latest rumors and I would explain to my parents what was in the newspapers because they could not read English.

Around February some areas in northern California were restricted and the Japanese living there had to move out. I was shocked to think that they had to move out of their homes. The JACL got into swing but they were unable to hold any large mass meeting. I went to a few of the smaller meetings to find out how things were. The JACL tried to get all of the latest news and procedures in order to advise the people and we would take this information home to our parents.

The JACL was the only organization in the Japanese community which was functioning so that everyone depended upon it. We didn't believe all those reports that concealed ammunitions and weapons were found. The JACL advised us to be very careful of our actions because if one person did anything wrong, then it would be bad for everyone.

All of a sudden the news that the Nisei would have to be included in a general evacuation came out like a bombshell. I was stunned. Before that I thought that only the Issei would be taken if anyone had to be moved. I would comfort my parents by telling them that I would come to visit them if they were put into a concentration camp. When it was announced that the Nisei would have to go too the laugh was on us for being cocksure that our American citizenship rights would protect us from anything like an evacuation. I was pretty sore about the increasing restrictions being put on us because I figured that I was a pretty good American. They had no right to take all of our flashlights and radios away during all of the blackouts. I had a very costly camera which I had to turn in. On top of that, I figured that no Japanese in this country would sabotage against America so that they were punishing us too much just out of mere suspicion.

As we waited around for evacuation, it got so that we wanted it to hurry up and take place so that we could get the nightmare over with. The Army wouldn't say exactly when we were going or where. It became sort of a guessing game to figure out the date of evacuation because we had nothing else to do but wait. We had hurried up and stored all of our belongings but we had plenty of time. Some of the other people who had to move first were not that fortunate and they took a big loss in selling out their business interests in a big hurry. God, we never had so many arguments in the family in so short a time before or since then. I guess every one was suffering from evacuation nerves and the people didn't trust one another because of rumors going around about stool pigeons. I wanted to store our belongings with the government but my dad insisted in storing it in the Japanese church because he thought it would be safer there. The arguments over where to store our belongings got so fierce that we finally compromised by storing it with one of Dad's Caucasian employers who opened up his basement to us. My folks wanted me to draw all of the family-fund money out of the bank as they believed that it would be frozen if left there. I convinced them that it would be much safer to leave the money in the bank.

I began to take on more of the responsibilities for the family business during all this crisis. My brother in the Army was rather indignant over all the things that were happening to us. He had plenty of trouble of his own so that he couldn't help us directly. He advised us to sit tight and not worry. He had just gotten married so he was quite worried about what was going to happen to his wife. He threatened that he would even desert the Army if his wife was put into a concentration camp, but he never went that far. He couldn't understand why his folks had to be put into a camp when he was fighting in the U. S. Army. I guess all of the Nisei soldier boys were pretty griped about the whole business. Some of them were discharged after Pearl Harbor.

At the beginning, most of the Nisei were against the evacuation, but the waiting around got us down and the newspapers weren't too friendly. My job had folded up about 10 days before the evacuation and I spent the remainder of the time packing and getting ready to leave. I must have repacked those boxes 25 times just to keep myself occupied. At first my parents wanted us to voluntarily evacuate to the Free Zone but I told them it was no use to do that as we might run into bitter *hakujin* people and I figured that the Free Zone would have to evacuate later on anyway even though the Army said it would not happen. I also thought that it would be much better for my parents to be with friends rather than be in a strange community. We didn't have enough money anyway.

My morale was really low and I wanted to have a last fling at everything. I went out on a lot of dates, and I spent what little money I had quite freely. I didn't drink or go to prostitutes' houses like so many Nisei though. The future looked very hopeless to me and I didn't think there was any use. The thought that the last chance of having a store of my own was gone forever. All of the Nisei were just as confused as I was. I was pretty irritable and moody during that time and sort of mad at everything in general. I sort of lost my religion because it didn't seem to be connected at all with real life.

I was frightened at the outlook and resentful that such a thing could happen to me just because I had Japanese ancestry. I was disillusioned in everything that I had been brought up to regard as the perfect truth. I thought that this was the end of all our hopes and that our lives would end when we went to camp. I was sorry for myself one minute and bitter the next. Once in a while I would see a Caucasian being kind to a Japanese family and that would raise my hopes

a little bit. But there were too many dark clouds in the sky and I
expected a great storm of hate and fury to be lashed down on the
Nisei at any moment if we did not get to camp pretty soon.

That was my frame of mind when I arrived in Tanforan on April
28, 1942. When I saw the place for the first time, I was twice as dejected and the vague spark of hope that I had kept in a secret corner
of my mind died out. What else could I think as I was put into a
musty stable with a fence surrounding the camp? The stables only
had Army cots in them and smelled like manure which the calcimine
was unable to cover. It also smelled like horse's urine. There was mud
all around us and the sanitation was extremely poor. The barracks
in the infield were not even completed yet and the Caucasian work-
men were making $15 or $20 a day so that we could be shoved into
them as fast as they put up the walls. That was the worst feeling to
have that they were in such a hurry to get rid of us.

I gradually got away from my thoughts by occupying myself in
trying to help other people. In this way I forgot my own worries and
I felt less sorry for myself. We were kept busy making make-shift
furniture and things like that so that our homes would be at least
comfortable. The first month passed pretty rapidly in this way and I
gradually got used to the idea of being behind that barbed-wire fence.
But every time a car flashed by the highway right in front of the
grandstand, I would get the feeling that I was a caged animal. Right
across the highway was a farm and I used to see the workers out in
the fields. I longed for the freedom that they had.

I started working in the recreation department after the second or
third week I was in the assembly center. We had very little facilities
but managed to have a very good program and the response was
tremendous. Once we got the whole program going, I felt happy in
a way to find that I was responsible for contributing to something
that was constructive. My job in the recreation department didn't get
monotonous as recreation became the outstanding job and interest
in the center. Those of us who were connected with it on the payroll
felt kind of important because we got a tremendous amount of prestige as leaders. I didn't consider it a slave job at all in spite of the $9
or $12 a month I was making.

I managed to pick up my other former activities and enter into
new ones during this stay in the assembly center. When the churches
were established, I started to go regularly again because I got over the
idea that it was the fault of religion that evacuation had taken place.

The church offered more hope for the future than anything else in camp and I suppose my reaction swung back to an extreme because I became very religious. I took everything in when I heard the sermons as I was seeking some kind of hope for myself. Caucasian guest speakers from the outside would come in to keep up our courage and listening to them would lift up my morale and encourage me to feel that all was not lost.

I made quite a few new friends at Tanforan as all of my former friends went to other camps. It was impossible to remain isolated because we were thrown in so closely together in everything we did. Everyone had to take a part in the life going on there because we ate, played, and worked together and we slept with only a six-foot plyboard between apartments. I saw many Issei growing younger because they were able to take it easy and do most of the things that they always wanted to do.

The only thing that disturbed me was that all of this regimentation was not suited to me and I rebelled against it now and then. It was like living in some sort of a prison. My morale on the whole got higher in spite of this because I plunged so intensely into the general community life. I was less aware of the war going on than before. I liked the WCCA staff as I thought that they tried their best to help the people and they seemed to understand our needs. The Japanese people in camp held a grudge mostly against the Army and the JACL although they didn't like certain members of the WCCA staff either.

Life in camp gradually settled down into a routine and it was only broken occasionally when they had searches for knives, contraband, and things like that. Near the end of my stay in the assembly center I was getting pretty bored with camp. I met a number of Nisei girls there but I didn't go steady with any of them because I hadn't gotten over carrying the torch for a girl who had broken her engagement to me just before evacuation.

Around August rumors began to come out about going to a relocation camp. We would always rush to hear any news from the other WRA centers because we were curious about what they were like. When the notice that we were going to [Topaz camp in] Utah came out I realized that we wouldn't be coming back to California for a very long time. Once again I felt like a prisoner. At the same time I was a little excited about going to Utah as I wanted to see new country. I knew it wouldn't be as good as California, but I was glad to get the chance to travel and see a little of the United States even though we were to be locked up after we reached our Topaz destination.

The trip up there was a disillusionment because we were put into a dirty gas-lighted train, and all my dreams about traveling in class were shattered. I didn't know why the Army had done this to us because they could have gotten comfortable trains for us to travel in since they had the priority on everything. We had gone to Tanforan in nice Greyhound busses so I figured that we would go to Topaz in comfortable style too. As it turned out, it was a very tiresome trip and we were not able to get off the train for 2 days and 3 nights. A lot of the people had diarrhea and that made things pretty bad for all of us because there were only about 2 toilets in each car.

When I got into Topaz it was another terrible disillusionment. All I saw was clouds of fine white dust, and there was no green grass in sight. The camp there was only half completed so that the people had a miserable first two weeks because of the congested conditions. As soon as I arrived I went to the employment office for a job but I couldn't find anything suitable so I spent a couple of days finding lumber to make furniture for our new home. About the fourth day I heard that groups of Nisei were leaving for seasonal farm jobs in Utah and they were telling us that we could make good pay and enjoy the outside life once more if we signed up. I decided to go out in one of these crews as I was so disappointed with Topaz and I didn't see how it could ever be a success.

[The younger of my two brothers, who was with the family] decided to go out with me and he found a good job offer for six fellows so that we got a group together and started out for [a near-by town in] Utah to work on the farm. I was one of the oldest fellows in the group. We went out to the farm on an old truck and we felt wonderful to have our freedom once more. It was such a good sensation to be moving along on those dirt roads away from camp. As we traveled along further, I filled my eyes with the sight of green lawns, individual homes, paved streets, and actually water fountains. I never realized how much I missed those things that I had seen so often in San Francisco. Our first thought when we got to [town] was to eat hamburger and play the juke box machine. There wasn't any feeling against us because we were one of the first to go out on the farm and the Mormons, I heard, tended to be tolerant of us when they heard we were good Americans and helped to harvest the crops. We tried not to be very conspicuous in town because we didn't know what the reaction was going to be at first. At that time the Caucasian people treated us very nice so that we forgot our color for a while.

It's hard to explain that sense of freedom I had. The fact that we were getting paid 50 cents an hour was pleasing to us because that was much better than what we got in a camp job. In fact, it was more than I had made in the same kind of work in California. It really was about the highest paying job that I ever had in my life.

We returned to Topaz after the season was over in November, 1942. After I got back to camp the place looked different because the people had been busy completing it. About the middle of November, 1942, I took a job as a reporter for the center newspaper. I had taken a course in journalism in high school and I liked that sort of thing. The camp newspaper [job] was very interesting as I got to meet all of the intelligent Nisei and many of the Caucasian staff members through the contacts I made in this work. I learned how to interview Caucasian people and I regained my confidence in talking to a Caucasian person without getting all apologetic and having lumps in my throat due to embarrassment. Later on I got [promoted] and I enjoyed seeing my name on the by-line of stories. I did this work straight through until April, 1943.

In the meantime I continued my routine life and I went to church on Sundays and played on the block baseball teams in the evenings. Once a week I went to the movies with a girl, and I was getting very much interested in marriage. I went to all of the dances which were held. My romance didn't turn out, so I began to think of going out of camp again because I was disappointed in love once more and I had some hurt feelings from the previous time I had been jilted.

There was a general change going on in the attitude of the people because they were griping more and more. The Kibei were making it very tough on the Nisei, but we didn't have any outbreak in Topaz. About the beginning of February, 1943, the Army came in to register the Nisei and there was a great deal of excitement for the following few weeks. Every block began to hold mass meetings and the Issei very much objected to the fact that the Nisei were asked to bear arms for the sake of democracy and this country when they didn't get any guarantee that their American citizenship rights would be restored to them. The Issei and Kibei went around and convinced many Nisei that they should not fight after being kicked out of their homes in California. It was mostly the Kibei who were extremely bitter and they did the majority of the agitation which went on. The Nisei were calmer and they figured that the only way was to answer the questionnaire because they still were for this country, even though many of them felt that America didn't want them anymore. It was a hard decision for many of the Nisei to make because the Issei were so opposed to their point of view. At the block meetings the Kibei would jump up and get very hysterical in order to sway the emotions of the gathering. They would even threaten suicide and things like that. The audience would encourage them by giving them a lot of applause.

The night before the general registration was scheduled to begin, a delegation from camp sent a telegram to President Roosevelt and Secretary Stimson to ask if the Nisei could be guaranteed certain rights if they responded to Army service. The Secretary of War answered by saying that it would depend upon how the Nisei responded to the registration, and whether they could prove themselves as loyal American citizens beyond a shadow of a doubt by making a good record in the services. He pointed out how the Nisei combat team could be the symbol for their American rights and that it had to make good if they were to have a future place in this country. He said it was up to the Nisei themselves to do it. This had a tremendous influence among the Nisei in camp although there were many who were cynical about these promises which were being made.

The camp became divided in beliefs between the Yes-Yes and the No-Yes and the No-No. I answered in a qualified way, No-Yes. Not too many of the Nisei answered No-No but later about 1,500 people from our camp went to Tule Lake. These were the more bitter ones and their younger children. Almost all of the agitating Kibei from our camp went to Tule Lake. I don't think the Issei had much respect for these Kibei because they were not consistent in their beliefs. The Kibei just didn't want to fight in any army. They had come back from Japan in order to avoid service there and they were willing to do anything to get out of service in the U. S. Army. If they were so loyal to Japan, then why didn't they go into the Japanese Army instead of running away to America? They were just a bunch of loud-mouthed agitators and I had no respect for them at all.

I didn't want to go to Camp Shelby as I didn't like the idea of Army segregation. But I believed that I should be loyal to the U. S. so I finally changed my answer to Yes-Yes. I had signed "no" to one of the questions on Army service as a protest to segregation but I realized that this was not the time to bring it up.

I almost got into some trouble once I had made up my mind and taken my stand on the registration issue. At my mess hall I gave my viewpoint on why the Nisei should answer Yes-Yes. I was asked to say something because I was the president of the young people's club in my block but they didn't expect me to be so straightforward in my talk. I told the audience that their demands for equality and other American rights were justifiable, but if they answered No-No on the basis of principle, they would be defeating the very purposes they were fighting for. I also told them that the Caucasian people on the outside believed that the Nisei were not loyal to America and a large percentage of No-No answers would only prove it to them. I argued that I agreed with their point of view that we had been kicked around without cause, but I asked them if they had proof that they were worthy of being an American citizen. I told them that they would not be accepted as Americans until they showed their loyalty to this country when the test came. I concluded that as long as they remained American citizens, they could still fight for all the American rights which they had lost at the time of evacuation. But if they answered No-No in the questionnaire, I said, they didn't have any rights left at all because they were giving up citizenship and then it would be a hopeless case for the Nisei. I included the Kibei in my statements because they had citizenship too.

The Kibei were stunned when I had finished my talk. After the meeting they all came around in a big bunch and they argued that I was all wrong. They got a little excited and the Kibei leader of the group started to push me around and threaten me. I told them it didn't make any difference if they beat me up, because my mind was made up and they couldn't change it with threats. They said that I was crazy for believing in this country after the way I had been kicked around. They pointed out that the *ketos* were trying to humiliate me by making me pick up the spit off the floor and beg for citizenship rights which didn't mean a thing. They said I would get better treatment in Japan and I should go along with their way of thinking because the U. S. Government had never done anything for me.

That talk I gave also had some result in flaming the family conflict up. My father didn't want to be the laughing stock of the block by supporting me even though he admired the way I had stood up for the things I believed in. However, he didn't care to lose the family respect in our block so he put up a front that I didn't know what I was saying. In the privacy of our apartment, he tried to persuade me to change my answer but he knew that I would never do this because I had the same ideas as my brother in the Army even though I was not willing to go as far as volunteering at that time. After all of these arguments my dad finally answered Yes-Yes to his own questionnaire even if I didn't fully convince him of the reason why America was best for me.

After the registration was over, everything quieted down and we had about 130 Nisei who volunteered into the Army. Only 50 of these passed the physical examination and were accepted for service. Most of the strong Nisei leaders who were outspoken about the registration volunteered, so I admired them.

Near the end of March everyone started to talk about resettlement all of a sudden. My brother and I were very bored with camp and we were thinking of taking another seasonal leave to go out on a farm job. Just then the NYA training project was announced, so my brother and I rushed to sign up. The idea was that any Nisei between the ages of 18 and 25 would be eligible to take the course. They would be taught machine-shop work, and placement in a vital war industry was promised after the completion of this course. Quite a few Nisei from our camp signed up for it. We went on out to [the school] and there were about 12 of us Nisei and 60 Caucasian kids in the school. The NYA gave us room and board plus $15 a month while we were in training.

I wanted to learn arc welding in the school, as I heard that I could get a defense job in Salt Lake afterwards. The director of the school practically promised us a job in either Philadelphia or Cleveland. I thought that this would be a swell chance to do a little traveling. We were going along well in our training when the school suddenly folded up because of lack of funds. There was nothing alse I could do but go back to Topaz, so I arrived there June 2, 1943.

After I got back to camp, I decided to work on the center newspaper again. I wrote up about the farm program and I tried to encourage the residents to come out and help with the farm work. The administration had quite a big farm program operating there so that it was essential for the people to take part in it because they were the ones who would benefit by getting all the fresh vegetables. It didn't take me long to fall back into the routine of camp life. I played baseball and I went to a lot of small social activities.

I was getting pretty restless as a number of Nisei had already resettled, and I wanted to get out again for good. My folks objected to my resettlement because they didn't want me to leave. They said I would be drafted sooner if I left the camp then. My folks pointed out that I didn't have much chance on account of the war condition and they pointed out the early Nisei failures who had returned to camp because they were unable to make a go of it on the outside.

It took over 2 months before I finally found a job that I got excited about. This job was with a battery company and it called for 4 fellows. The offer sounded quite attractive to me so I decided that I would take it. On top of that, the relocation counsellor told me that he used to live around [X], a Midwestern city, and he said it was a wonderful place for me to resettle into. That just about cinched things so I wrote immediately to the company and asked for details. After a few days I got an answer saying that I would get 5 cents an hour more if I came right away with 3 other fellows. This caused me to make up my mind definitely so I sent a wire accepting the job. I got 2 other Nisei fellows to come along with me but we couldn't find the fourth person until the day before we left camp.

I got an indefinite leave and I left camp about the end of July, 1943. I was a little worried when I got on the train because I had never been that far east before and I didn't know how we would be accepted. There really wasn't anything to worry about because nobody bothered us on the train. We saw a lot of soldiers on the train but they didn't ask any questions. I guess I was rather relieved because I didn't know what to expect. It was just a curious sensation of going into new territory and I looked upon it as quite an adventure.

The battery company worked with the church federation in finding housing for Nisei employees so that we were assisted in finding a permanent place to stay by one of the church officials. The four of us all stayed together. That battery job was dirty work. We worked for 9 hours a day with only a half hour off for lunch. At the time we started there, there were 15 other Nisei in the plant. Most of them were scattered around in the different departments. Some of them put battery cells together while others were on the assembly line. There was only one Negro in our department but there were some departments where all of the workers were Negro. In the beginning I was given the job of filling the battery with acid and it was disagreeable work because the stuff ate right through my shoes and clothing.

The Nisei workers there were from all the different camps and they got along with each other. They also mixed with the Caucasians pretty well. A lot of the Caucasians were from Kentucky and they didn't have any prejudice against us because they had never seen a Nisei before. I didn't get along too well with my foreman because he wanted me to work too many hours without any rest at all. I didn't care particularly for the job because it was monotonous. I tried to get transferred to another department but the foreman wouldn't allow me to make the move. I worked in that battery company for about six months in all. Financially it was a success. I gradually worked up to $60 a week. I managed to live well and saved about $300 during that period.

That first six months of resettlement were not all work because I had a fair social life in my leisure time. We went to the church services quite often, as the Church Federation did its best to get us acquainted with the young people's groups. There were only about 40 Nisei in the city, and I think that the Church Federation did a very good job in getting us adjusted.

The hardest part of getting socially adjusted was that there weren't any Nisei girls around. We heard that there were quite a few at [a nearby coeducational college] so some of us fellows would get together and go visit these girls at the college. We would go out on Sunday and go bike riding, movies, or dancing with them. It was here that I first met [my future wife]. We were supposed to have a blind date and she turned out to be the one selected for me. It was love at first sight I guess, because I really fell for her. Around November 4, 1943, I finally got up the courage to propose to her, as I felt that I had saved up enough money to get married. She accepted me so that we announced our engagement on Thanksgiving Day to our friends.

When [my fiancée] and I decided to get married, I told her to write to her parents for permission. Her folks were very surprised and they refused to give consent because they said she was too young. She was determined to get married, so that we didn't pay any attention to the demands for her to come back to camp. I wrote to her folks in the best Japanese I could and told them that we were engaged and that I planned to be honorable toward their daughter. I had to follow some of the Japanese customs so that they wouldn't get any wrong ideas about me. Then her folks wrote and said that they would have to have full particulars of my family before they would give their consent to marriage. I wrote my folks and asked them to send [my fiancée's] family an account of our family background. A mutual family friend, acted as the middleman. It took about a month and a half to do all of this investigation. The *baishakunin* did most of the checking up on family background, and he corresponded with both sides of the family until they were satisfied and they finally gave us the okay signal. They wanted us to come back to camp for the wedding but we told them that we didn't have that much money to go around and pay respects to all the relatives of both sides of the family. I thought that all of this fuss was a lot of nonsense and a headache. But since I was the oldest son, I didn't want to arouse the anger of [my fiancée's] folks and my parents. It didn't matter if we had a *baisha-kunin* or not because we were going to get married regardless of the findings of the family investigations. We agreed to have as simple a wedding as possible and we didn't get around to sending announcements until after we were married.

When we found out that it was hard to get a suitable apartment in [X], I quit my job in the battery plant. In the meantime my fiancée had left [the college] and she went on to [an institution] in [Y] where she got a job as a [technician]. She started to work a week after our honeymoon was over, but I couldn't get a job [in Y] because I was told that the companies didn't have any jobs for workers who came from another city and they wouldn't recognize my work release. I loafed around until February 1 and then I went to the WRA office to ask them to help me out. On February 6 a chemical company gave me a job after I had an interview with the personnel director. I was glad to get back to work again as I was pretty worried that I was going to be left stuck without anything to do. My job at the chemical plant paid 75 cents an hour and I worked from 7:30 in the morning until 3:30 in the afternoon. I got along swell with both the Caucasian and Negro workers as well as with the Nisei group. I knew practically everyone in my section of the plant and I thought that my job was wonderful. I enjoyed it much better than working in the battery company in [X]. However, I had to eventually give up that job because I found out that I was allergic to the DDT powder which was made for the Army. The plant had about 1,000 workers in all and there were only about 3 Nisei out of this whole bunch. It was pure defense work and I was able to get into that plant because the WRA got a clearance for me. My rash kept on bothering me and I had to take some days off from work, but I didn't want to give up that job because I was making around $250 a month, with overtime, and my wife had a good city job too.

Around April, 1944, my Army physical examination came up and I passed it. My wife and I decided to go to camp in order to visit the folks before I was taken into the Army.

While I was in Topaz I received an Army deferment because of the fact that I was in a vital war plant and the company asked for it.

So I headed back to [Y] immediately to return to that job in spite of
the fact that I was allergic to the powder. We were both glad that I
could be deferred to the end of October, 1944, as we would have that
time together. My rash got worse and worse and I could hardly sleep
at nights. Finally on June 22, 1944, I decided to quit the job. I wanted
to come on to Chicago as I had read that so many Nisei were getting
good jobs there and the wages were high.

I liked living in [Y]. There were only about 500 Nisei there and
the Caucasian public accepted them quite readily. The Nisei could
find apartments there but the jobs were limited. There wasn't any
prejudice at all in the public recreation places and I never heard of
a single case of discrimination. They had a hostel there where the
Nisei could meet without causing any antagonism because the place
was located way out in the suburbs and not too noticeable. A lot of
Nisei received invitations to private homes and they seemed to respond very well to this sort of thing. The Nisei down there were
eager to get accepted into the community life.

I got to Chicago on July 3, 1944. As soon as I landed in the city,
I went to the WRA office and, boy, I was so disgusted. I wasn't welcomed in and everything was so impersonal. I had to find a place to
sleep so that the WRA man sent me out to [D] and that was a lousy
place to live in. None of the Nisei who live there ever acted friendly.
I determined not to depend on the WRA for a job because I didn't
like the cool way they treated me when I got there. I heard of [work
at a defense plant] and I went out there immediately. I got a job [as
a machine operator] and started working from July 6. My wife came
out from [Y] to join me a few days later.

It was quite a problem for my wife to get a job. Our first need was
an apartment, and we quickly found out that housing was very scarce.
She finally decided that she would take a job as a domestic worker if I
were allowed to live with her. She couldn't get a job [as a technician]
because she didn't get a job release when she quit to join me. We felt
that after a wait of 60 days she would be able to go back into her field
of work. We didn't want to depend upon the WRA for a domestic job
for her so we placed an ad in the newspapers. We got an immediate
response for this and we went out to interview one place where she
was accepted.

My wife was supposed to do light housekeeping in that home and
help to cook a bit in exchange for room and board for the both of us.
We stayed in that place for about a month, but the regular cook com-

plained that the food points were too high to feed both of us, so she refused to work there any longer unless we left.

Since my wife saved the list of people who had answered our ad in the paper, she decided to phone some of these to see if jobs were still open. She phoned one place on the North Side and was given another domestic job with the same kind of arrangement after an interview. There were a couple of children in the second place. After a week there we found that the employer was very unreasonable in the amount of work she expected us to do. She would not give us any nutritious food, so that we were too dissatisfied. She tried to make me work over one hour a day in the garden and she wanted me to do a lot of heavy work like cleaning the basement and this wasn't in our agreement at all.

By this time it was September and my induction notice to report came so that we thought of getting our own apartment in the short time we had left to be together. The employer overheard us talking of these plans, so she told us to get out of her place immediately because she was so spiteful. We had a violent quarrel and left. I guess we made an enemy for the Nisei at that place. She was a real Jew and she was certainly stingy in the food she fed us. We were quite glad to get out of there.

Since we didn't have any place to move, we moved into [D] again until we could locate an apartment for ourselves. That was on September 24, 1944. I quit my job the day before as I was ordered to report for induction on September 26. When I got to the Army station to report, I was told that I was put in the reserve. A week later I went back to work at [the defense plant]. I went out there with the idea of getting a job release, but they wouldn't give it to me. I had been working on the night shift, and I didn't like that, so I asked if I could be placed on the day shift and they gave it to me. I worked for 3 days and then I had a fight with the foreman, so I quit. I guess I talked back too much for my own good, but I didn't like the way they tried to take advantage of me.

I liked the job fairly well but I couldn't make enough money. I only averaged $60 gross but taxes took quite a bit of this. This amount was enough to live on, but I wanted to save a lot of money because I was going to get drafted soon and I wanted to have a pretty good bank fund to turn over to my wife. I guess we saved about $600 or $700 before I left that job in September.

I still don't know exactly how I feel about the draft. I guess I will take it when it comes. I want to get it over with either way instead of being so uncertain like this. I can't make any plans for myself at all until I know my exact draft status. This waiting around has made me lazy and I'm not saving any money like I should be doing for my wife. The way things are now, we can't plan to have a family or anything. We will have to wait until after the war when things are a lot calmer.

After the war I plan to start a business of my own but I still won't have enough money to finance it and that's a problem. I'll never be satisfied working for somebody else. I'll open up a drugstore, I think. I would like to open up a business in California.

I am a little uncertain about my own position right now, but I have plenty of hopes for the future when it comes right down to it. I think that I have gained quite a bit by the evacuation experience. I know that I have matured quite a bit in my ways of thinking. I was one of those guys who tried to hang on to the old folks before the war because I knew that I could always go back home if things got a little tough for me. Now I am married and I have to carry my own responsibilities and make my own way. I'd like to see peace forever and I'd like to have my own store and have a little home of my own with all the accessories of a middle-class American family. I don't want to be an underdog all of my life.[188]

---

[188] CH-53's wife (CH-54) was also interviewed. Her father had been in the United States since 1900, and both parents had engaged in general farm work as laborers and as sharecroppers in central California for many years. CH-54 was described as "pleasing in appearance," and as "expressing herself rather easily." Born in 1922, CH-54 worked as a "schoolgirl" prior to the outbreak of war. She had just finished junior college at the time of evacuation. She left camp in September 1943 to work as a technician in a Midwest college.

Expressing a desire to have "a happy married life," she said that her career, as technician, meant less to her than helping her husband to "be satisfied in his work." At the time of the interview, she expected him to be drafted, and discussed her plans and aspirations as follows:

My next problem is to go out and look for a job as a [technician]. I'm hoping that I will get into one of the hospitals around here with my experience, but maybe they will think that I am too young to have such responsible work. If I can't get a [technician's] job then I'll take a typist job for a while and concentrate upon keeping house. If I can't get into an office I'll take a factory job and work for the money. No more domestic job for me, though, because that's too much of a worry. After [my husband] gets drafted, I will take in another girl to live here. I'll have to see what kind of a job I can get first and maybe I'll just keep on with it all the time until I start a family of my own after the war.

I think that we have been doing pretty well in our social adjustments in Chicago even if our economic adjustments are still up in the air. We don't crave a lot of company because we are satisfied with each other. Everything

CH-31: ERRAND BOY

Male; born in California, 1921; height 65"; weight 145 lbs.; unmar-
ried. Interviewed February–March, 1944. Described as "a stockily
built boy, with a smooth-skinned, broad, rather expressionless face.
Not a zoot-suiter." The interviews were "spread out over a period of

that has happened to us is being counted off as a part of our experience and a
prolonged honeymoon. Pretty soon we will have to get down to serious business though and really settle down but that can't be until after [my husband]
comes out of the Army. I'm not worried about myself but I would like to see
him get settled because he has to worry about too many things now.

Maybe things will be even harder for us after the war but I don't care as
long as [my husband] and I are together to make a go of it. We don't have any
roots in Chicago yet as we haven't been here long enough.

I like the idea of dispersal if it isn't done too thinly because I think that the
Nisei would be able to make a happy life by having a wide variety of friends.
In this way the Caucasians would get to know the Nisei in a personal way and
there would be less prejudice. Most of the *hakujin* seem to accept Nisei as
equals after they get to know them. Right now I don't think the Nisei around
here want to mix very much because they are afraid. That's the reason why
they go around looking for Nisei more. I can't blame the single ones too much
as they are thinking of marriage but couples like us should think of getting
acquainted with *hakujin* so that it will become a common practice. The more
we stick to ourselves the less the Caucasians will get to know us and pretty
soon some awful stories about the Nisei will go around. The *hakujins* will
begin to believe all of these stories when they don't know how we live and then
discrimination against us will increase all the more. I think that was what was
wrong when we were living in California.

But it is pretty hard to get to know anyone in such a large city like Chicago.
It's even hard to meet new Nisei out here. That's why I believe the dispersal
process will be very slow and it doesn't look so good right now. I guess all of
us are too backward right now and we don't feel so much like mingling when
we know we should. The life in camp made us more conscious of having
Japanese faces and we are worried that we won't be accepted so much so that
we don't put forth enough effort. The reason I don't feel so strongly about
this is that I had a good start at [the college] and I know there are millions of
Caucasians who will be friendly to us if we make the effort.

I'd like to get assimilated but it's much harder than just wishing that it
would come true. I think that we do it a little bit from month to month and
we don't realize it so much. It's just like I learned to be more of an individual
with self-confidence [outside] after I left my folks in camp. Before I left I tended
to listen to everything they said, but when I got on my own I had to depend
upon myself more.

I think that all Nisei are going through this sort of thing because they are
pretty young. Some of the fellows get pretty wild because people don't talk
about them as they do the girls. They are all hoping that they can live the life
they did before the war when everything seemed so carefree for them. I don't
think that we will ever go back to the way of life before the war as we are
older now and we are going through a lot of new experiences. Getting accepted
into American life is very slow but I think that it's an exciting experience.

about a month as it was quite difficult for him to sit still for an hour. He was quite coöperative and did not seem to be particularly anxious to justify his actions. He talked quite freely and seemed to feel that if he gave a straightforward account, the interviewer could help him to make adjustments in Chicago. He told his story simply, using a good deal of slang, interspersed with profanity. His sex, and poker, and work experiences seemed to be the most easily recalled. He did not object to note-taking in the slightest."
Reinterviewed, March, 1945.

CAREER LINES

Parental: Details of family history unknown. Parents married before emigrating, and had several Japan-born children. Mother, born 1894; completed 8th grade in Japan; immigrated to United States in 1919; returned to Japan for a visit in 1925. Parents opened a drugstore and later became "day workers" (probably farm laborers) in central and southern California until 1928, when they moved to San Francisco and opened a small candy store. Father returned to Japan in 1938. Mother obtained a divorce, and used her "legally restored maiden name." She was proprietor of a Japanese-owned restaurant from 1934 to 1938, and worked as a cook in a private family from 1940 to 1942. Described by interviewer as "a very tiny Japanese woman . . . one of those withdrawing types but a more independent nature than many Issei women, as indicated by the fact that she resettled to Chicago alone. She acted more like a servant than a mother to her son." Inmigrated to Chicago early in January, 1944, after obtaining a job in a sewing factory.
Own: High school graduate, San Francisco, 1940; completed part of a year at junior college; attended NYA trades school, 1941–1942. Did odd jobs until after high school graduation; worked as delivery boy in a drugstore, 1940–1941, then as scaler in a fish market for four months, as janitor in a hotel for one month, as stock boy in an Oriental art goods store for another month. Other odd jobs, such as domestic service, NYA work, and so on, in weeks before evacuation. Inmigrated to Chicago late in January, 1944. Worked as burner at an ironworks from February until April; as a welder in a defense plant until October when the contract was terminated; similar work in another plant during November; and for a few weeks more at still another plant. When the defense contract for this work expired and his wages were reduced, he passed a welder's test for work at another

firm, where he was still employed at the time of the reinterview in March, 1945.

LIFE HISTORY
(as of March, 1944)

I was born in [M], a city in central California, in June, 1921. My folks were running a drugstore in the Japanese section at that time. I don't know how long they were in [M]. My mother never told me when they came to this country. I don't know when they got married or anything at all about them. I never took the trouble to ask them. Holy Christ, I don't know anything. I do know that I have four brothers and sisters. My two older brothers were born back there in Japan and I went to Japan when I was 4 years old with them. My old lady couldn't bring them into this country. The other two were born over there also. I'm the only kid in my family who was born in this country. I don't even remember my brothers or sisters. I was only over there for a year and then I came back with my old man. My old lady stayed over there and my sister was born. Then she came back alone.

We never had very much of a family life. My old man went back to Japan in 1938 to join my brothers and sister over there. I don't know exactly what they are doing. My brothers are in the Japanese Army but I don't talk about that to anyone. My old man probably is retired by now. He was ailing when he went back and he thought he wanted to live on the farm back there. My mother was supposed to go back a little later when she made enough money for the trip, but she never went. I think that my parents are separated. I wasn't old enough to understand all these things and I don't care to ask my mother about it now.

We moved [to southern California] when I was about 6 years old and I started school there. Hell, I can't remember nothing. I know we moved to Los Angeles after that. Then we went on to [a coastal city]. The reason we traveled around like that was that my father and mother were doing day work. Then we came to San Francisco and we stayed there until evacuation. In San Francisco my father owned a small candy shop in the Japanese section. It was sold out after he went to Japan.

I don't care nothing about my old man. He was always drinking and a drunk, and I never liked him very much. He was always arguing with my mother. He would bawl hell out of her and they never got along very well. I guess my old lady was glad when he finally left to go back to Japan. I know she wasn't any too happy living with him. Because we moved around so much, I can't remember ever having a good home life like a lot of guys.

In our home we always talked Japanese and my parents made me go to a Jap school for 10 years in order to learn the language. Goddam, I never learned a damn thing. I was too dumb. It was too much for me anyway. Jesus, I had to go to public school for six hours and then I had to go to the Jap school for two hours. By the time I got to Jap school I was sleepy as hell and I never could stay awake. They tried to make us study like hell in Jap school, but I never paid too much attention. My parents said that I was a Japanese and after all, I had to learn the language in order to get along later on. They thought that I might go back with them to Japan some day but I wasn't interested in it at all. I can talk Japanese with my mother now but I couldn't do it with the other old folks. My mother doesn't understand too much English but she seems to get along okay out here.

When I was a kid, I used to go to the Buddhist Church all the time but I did not believe in it. I just went there because the other guys hung around and it was a good place to meet. The Buddhist Church offered us a gym later on too and that was what brought most of us guys to church.

At home we ate a lot of Japanese food and my mother always wanted us to observe all of the Japanese customs and holidays which were celebrated in Jap town. I never did any of that damn stuff. I always got along with my mother okay. At first she was very strict with me, but when I grew up we came to an agreement, so that she don't bother me anymore. I got too big for my mother; so she couldn't boss me around too much after I got into high school.

I always ran around with a Nisei gang. We lived right in the middle of the Japanese town [in San Francisco]. Jesus, I don't remember much of my school life. I guess I was a pretty sad case. I liked sports the best in school. In high school I played on the high school football team, and that was my greatest achievement. I had more fun playing with the San Francisco Slops. This was a bunch of us Nisei guys and we were sponsored by the Buddhist Church. We used to go down and play in the playground league in the public park and we won a lot of championships. It was a pretty tough bunch and we could take care of ourselves in any scrap. For a little while I went around with some Caucasian kids in high school and I used to cut classes with them. Most of the time I was with Nisei guys and we just spent our time just playing around. Sometimes we would play basketball against the *hakujin* kids and we would always beat them even though they were much taller than we were. We played dirty so that a lot of those guys were afraid to play against us.

I didn't do so hot in my studies. I got poor marks most of the way through high school but I managed to graduate in 1940. Once in a while I used to get called a Jap by the other guys. I had to beat hell out of them so that they would respect me.

I made good friends with the Chinese kids. I used to go to China-town until 8 o'clock at night to hang around with them. Once I even had a date with a Chinese girl at school. I went to her home and her old lady thought I was a Chinese so that she started to talk to me in Chinese. Then I had to tell her that I was Japanese. The lady was nice to me and she even invited me to have supper with them. That was the first time I ever ate with a Chinese family. After that the old lady told her daughter to tell me not to come up there any more because the other Chinese didn't understand.

I was 18 when I finally got out of high school. I had all kinds of ambitions but they were all dreams and not very practical. I guess I didn't know what to do. I wondered how in the hell I could get a job. It got me worried because none of the Nisei guys were able to get good jobs after high school. Most of them worked for their old men any-way. I didn't have anyone like that to work for and I had to go out on my own. A lot of my friends were going to junior college. I guess most of the Nisei kids just went on to junior college after high school be-cause there was nothing else to do. The Nisei had a helluva time get-ting a good job because there was too much discrimination. They didn't get a chance nothing like the *hakujin* kids. The *hakujin* kids were able to get good jobs if they had a high school education, but the Nisei didn't have a chance even with a college education. I started going to junior college in 1940, I can't remember exactly. I just went out there to have fun and I didn't care to study or nothing. I just wanted to take the girls out if I could. I thought I could make the football team out there and that was the main reason why I went.

I got to know some dumb Nisei girl from the country out at junior college. She came from [a rural community] and she was doing a school girl job. She didn't know nobody in Jap town or out at junior college so that she was kind of hot for me. She was just an innocent girl and she thought it was pretty good to be going out with a Nisei who was out for the football team. I took her out to the Golden Gate

Park one night. She told me that I couldn't lay her, because I would not be able to make the football team if I did things like that. I was hot for her, too, but I decided to reform. I thought I would bear down on my studies and quit going around with a gang like before. But my cash began to run low and I got incomplete in my studies. Finally I decided that I would go to work, so I took this girl out to the Golden Gate Park again and this time I laid her. I never saw her again after that because she went home to the country about a week later. And that was the first time I ever had an experience like that. Most of the Nisei girls didn't trust the guys in our gang because they knew that we had a bad reputation. I didn't give a damn anyway.

I got a job at [a drugstore] way out on the Ingleside district, past Twin Peaks. I was a delivery boy there and I held this job for 8 months. The only reason why I liked that job was because I was able to make some side money without the boss knowing anything about it. I only got paid $40 a month and carfare. I thought that I could make some money on carfare so I borrowed a bicycle. We were supposed to get carfare for each delivery but I used the bicycle instead. I was able to make about $30 extra a month that way because I was sent out on a lot of deliveries in that district.

After work I would go down to Jap town where I lived and hang around with the bunch. We would go play pool or go to the show. Sometimes we went to the basketball games. I didn't go in much for sports myself after I quit school. Every night it was that way. I didn't think about nothing and I had a helluva lot of fun with the guys. I liked my job at the drugstore okay and I was making more than a lot of those college graduate Nisei who acted snotty just because they worked out in Chinatown. They were just a bunch of coolies and I had more money to show at the end of the month than they did. They thought they were too high-toned to go out and work with their hands.

After I worked out in that district for a while, I got acquainted with a lot of Nisei girls who were doing domestic work out that way. There were a lot of these girls who came in from the country to earn money in domestic work so they could help out their families. They didn't know nobody in San Francisco and they were pretty lonesome. I got to know them because I had to deliver things to their employers. After I got acquainted, I used to go see them in between deliveries. They were fun for me and it helped pass the time. A couple of them I got to know pretty good and I took them out on dates. I always wanted to go up to their room and lay them but they would never let me. I guess they knew better.

At my job, I used to swipe magazines and cosmetics and other things from the counters to take to these girls when I visited them. I used to cop a lot of junk at the drugstore and bring it home for myself. I bet I had the most tooth brushes, the best toothpaste, and more razors than any other Jap in San Francisco. I got all of it free. Some of this junk I sold to my friends and I was able to make about $20 extra this way. There was a lot of angles to making extra dough and I was pretty well set. I had just as much dough as a lot of those Nisei guys.

After I started working, I used to go to those big Nisei dances but I didn't care for dancing much. I just stood around with a gang. I wanted to dance like the rest of the guys but I guess I was the clumsy type and girls didn't go for me too much. I never drank very much at that time but some of the gang were taking it up, so I learned. I only drink now on special occasions, but I get drunk as hell when I get real griped at something. I don't care too much for it because my old man was a slop and he practically deserted us. I guess it is my mother's influence because she said I would be like my old man if I began to drink.

A lot of times us guys used to hang around the Chinatown night clubs. After we got through fooling around, we would make the rounds of the whore houses. I never paid for one because I was afraid of catching a dose. I wasn't the type to draw girls to me. Once I went to make a delivery at some home and I got acquainted with a colored maid, and I laid her right in the hall while her employer was out. I told my gang about it and they razzed me for weeks because I took on "black meat."

The only reason I stayed on at the [X] drugstore for 8 months was because I was trying to get eligible for unemployment compensation with the social security. I had to work there a certain time before they would start giving me a weekly check. I quit the job after I was eligible and I started to draw 10 bucks a week because that was the minimum they gave. I drew about $150 in all from social security and it was during this time that I started at junior college.

I didn't feel like taking another regular job while I was getting social security because I would not have been able to make much more than the 10 buck check I was drawing from the government. I held a schoolboy job for a while at $20 a month while I was going to junior college but that was okay because they couldn't find out about it. I didn't like the schoolboy job at all. The lady didn't like me either because I was pretty stubborn. A lot of times I felt like kicking her in the ass because she thought she was so superior to me. She thought I was a damn servant. I got even because I never went to work on time. I guess I was pretty sloppy. Finally the lady fired me and I was not unhappy about that.

I went to the Japanese employment agency and they gave me another schoolboy job. I only lasted one day on that job. When I went back to the employment agency, the guy got sore at me for being fired and he said I was lazy. He wouldn't give me another job because he said I would give him a bad reputation. I went to another Japanese employment agency and they sent me out on a different kind of a job. By that time I had quit school. I had a job as a porter at an apartment house. I got $60 a month and I had a small apartment for myself. I never stayed there, because I always went to Jap town after work and then I would go home to sleep. I didn't care much for that job and I tried to do it as fast as I could. I was pretty sloppy in that job too. Then Pearl Harbor came along and I got canned right away.

Hell, I didn't even know where Pearl Harbor was when they started announcing it over the radio. When I first heard that war was declared, I thought we would get pushed around plenty and I was scared and confused. I thought that all Japanese would be fired from their jobs. My main hope was to get into the shipyards. I wanted to get out of Frisco because everybody was scared to hell. There were cops all over the place and the streets were roped off for a couple of weeks. A lot of Issei were getting arrested and most of the big Japanese companies were closed up. Those Nisei working in those stores lost their jobs and they were up a creek. I went to the NYA office. I wanted to get into the NYA training school so I could learn a trade. I was tired of doing those porter jobs and I knew I would not get any place if I had to do it all my life.

I signed up to go to the NYA aeronautic school and they gave me bus fare to go down to [the school]. This was on Dec. 20, 1941. It was the first time I went out of town by myself and I felt lost. There were a lot of other guys in the training school, about 200 of them, and we all lived in the dorm just like the barracks in camp. The guys were all different kinds of nationalities and I was the only Jap in the school. I got to know a P. I. guy good because he was from San Francisco too. He later went to San Quentin for robbing a warehouse or something.

When I knew him in Frisco, he was a good guy and I got along with him best of all during the time I was in the training school. I got along with the rest of guys there too. They were always talking about the war and how they would like to get into the Army. They never bothered me. I wanted to take up radio, but the man in charge told me that it was no use because I could not get a job like that since I was a Nisei. Then I wanted to take up sheet-metal work and I was discouraged in this. They told me that the aircraft companies were closed to me too. Finally there wasn't anything else to take so I took the welding course and I found that I really liked it. Jesus, it's funny how things turn out that way. I wouldn't have picked out welding if I had the choice all by myself.

One night a bunch of us went hiking up a mountain. We wanted to stay overnight and take pictures the next day. I said that I would try to get a camera but I was not able to rent one in town. We went hiking anyway and without knowing it we trespassed on the Army reservation. Suddenly we were stopped by a soldier with a gun. He took us to the main office and all of our names were taken. They looked at me kind of funny when they found out that I was a *Nihonjin,* but they let us go. When I got back to camp, I discovered that the Army officers had come down there immediately in a car and they were waiting for me. They asked me a lot of questions about what I was doing on the Army reservation. They didn't question the other guys at all. I was scared as hell because this was when a lot of stories about Jap spies was going around. They looked up my record and they thought that it was very suspicious that I was interested in cameras. I had put it down as a hobby. Then they found out that I had tried to rent a camera the day before and they got more suspicious than ever. They looked all over my things for a camera but they couldn't find one. Finally the superintendent of the training school squared me off. He said that I was a loyal American like the rest of the guys. I thought sure I was sunk and I didn't know what would happen to me. It was quite a relief when they finally went away after warning me not to go up to that reservation again.

I continued on with my training after that. Guys were being sent out every week to the aircraft company when they passed the test for these companies. They all got pretty good jobs. One of my pals got a job at [a large aircraft company] and he told me to come on down and work with him. But just before I graduated, this pal volunteered for the air corps. I decided that I would not go down there but I would try for another job. I took a test [at one of the shipyards] as a welder. I'm positive I passed, but they canceled all of my tests because I was a Jap. The superintendent said he was sorry but he could not do anything about it. I tried all over to get a job in one of the other big factories, but it was no use. Niseis weren't just getting jobs then because everyone was suspicious of us. Finally I got disgusted so I went back to Frisco in March, 1942. It was a good experience for me because it was the first time I had gotten to know *hakujin* guys real well and they treated me regular. It was just the big companies that were prejudiced and wouldn't give me a chance at a job because they thought I would sabotage or something like that. They were a bunch of damned fools and I was pretty sore about it.

After I got back to Frisco I didn't know whatta hell to do as it looked pretty hopeless to me. I didn't know how I could get a job because the public was getting more against the Japs and they were talking about evacuation. I guess I felt worse then than at the time of Dec. 7th. I tried like hell to get into Mare Island, or one of the big shipyards. I didn't even have a chance because, even before the war, very few Nisei got into these jobs. My instructor at the NYA training school told me that there was no chance for me on the Pacific Coast and he advised me to go to the Midwest. I was afraid to take a chance and go away out to the middle of the country by myself so I didn't do as he advised. After all of these job refusals, I thought sure I'd never have a chance to handle a welding torch again. It looked like a helluva outlook for me.

By that time the Frisco Jap town was in an uproar. A lot of *Nihonjins* were coming in from the areas which were restricted by the Army. There wasn't any work to be had. The cops would not let Japanese get into bunches at all. Almost everyone had lost their jobs and the stores were all closed. The fishermen couldn't go out anymore so they were all hanging around the Japanese cafés. Everyone was worried because they didn't know how they were going to eat after their money ran out. There was a lot of talk about evacuation but I didn't pay any attention to it. I just hung around the pool halls till 2 o'clock every night and passed the time with the gang.

After the curfew came in, we would go to Chinatown after 8 almost every night. One of the guys in the gang had a car and we went with him. We just fooled around and my pals went around to pick up girls. We would park the car and wander around. Once we wandered up toward Van Ness Avenue and got stopped by a cop. He asked us where we were going and we got pretty scared. I thought sure that we were going to get the pinch. We said that we were Chinese so he let us go. He said that it wouldn't be safe for us to go to Jap town. Other times we would go to the Chinese bar and night clubs and drink here and there. All of the whore houses were closed by then so we couldn't pass any time in that way. To round off the evenings, we went to a midnight show if we had money. Then we would go back up to Chinatown and hang around all night bowling alleys or else play pool and the pin-ball machines. We were always trying to pick up whores on the streets and take them to one of the cheap hotels in Chinatown. If we could not pick up a girl, we would sleep in the room or else go some place to play dice. After 6 in the morning, it was safe for us to go back to Jap town again.

It was usually morning before we got home. I used to be all fagged out so I slept all morning. I went to a Japanese employment agency every afternoon after I left my house and I stayed around a few minutes before going to the pool room. My money was practically gone so I finally got desperate and I took a domestic job. I only worked there 2 days because I spilled some soup on the lady's lap and she fired me. She didn't fire me until after I washed the dishes. It sure griped me to hell because I really tried hard in that job and it was only an accident. I went back to the employment agency and I got another schoolboy job for bachelors. I had to quit them after a week because they did not pay enough. I didn't like the way they called me the "Little Spy from Japan" because it didn't sound like kidding to me.

The next job was working in the stockroom for [an Oriental art goods store], I was paid $2 a day. They were selling out the store before the evacuation. This was the last job I had before I went to camp. I forget to mention a couple of other jobs that I held after quitting junior college. I worked for a while in a gardening job and my boss was [a Japanese]. He had his customers over in the East Bay district. I didn't know anything about that work at all but I thought it would be better than domestic work. The boss was a bastard and he never paid me so I finally quit. I was only getting 35 cents an hour, too. Then I worked for another guy who hired about 20 guys. All I did was turn on the water. I would take time out to go bowling or play pool. We used to bowl every time on the working hours because the boss could not check up on all of his crew. After that I remember I got in [an upper class] hotel. I was a janitor there. I tried to get a job [there] as a bar tender but they did not want any Japs to face the public. Every goddam time it was like that, all because I had a Japanese face. It was no use to have any ambition at all. The Nisei just didn't have a chance even before the war. Some of the Chinese kids at the [hotel] got better jobs than we did and these guys went to school with me. I got griped because I did not have a chance there so I quit.

I also worked for a while in [a large] fish market before the war. This was one of the best jobs that I ever had. It was a Caucasian company. We were on piece work and we had to scale the fish. I made about $5 a day. That was damn good dough in those days before the war, especially for a Nisei. Finally the Alaska Cannery Workers wanted to unionize the place so I lost my job after two or three months of working there. I smelled like a fish all the time and the people hated us when we got on the streetcars. There were about four Nisei working with me at that place. After I lost that job, I sold fight programs at the Civic Center and Greenland. I got 2 cents a program and I usually made about a dollar and I got to see the fight free. But all the way through, it was like this. We never got any of the better jobs and it looked pretty hopeless. I can't remember exactly the time I did all of these jobs because there were so many of them. I know it was between the time I graduated [from] high school and the beginning of the war. After the war started it was much worse, like I told you.

Anyway, when they started to talk about evacuation, I wondered what it was all about. I just got ready and went along with the rest of them. It wasn't sad or anything for me to leave Frisco. There wasn't anything for me to stay behind for because I couldn't get a job anyway. We were just a bunch of sad bastards and we were always being pushed around even before evacuation. I got sore a lot of times but I guess I didn't think about it too much and try to figure it out. I only got sore when I was turned down. Then when I did get into camp, I thought I'd never get out and I wanted to be back in Frisco.

I went to Tanforan in April, I guess. I suppose I am a dumb bastard because I didn't have any ideas on anything. I don't even remember all about my life. It gives me a headache when I try to think of it too much. I guess I was griped most about not being able to get a good job and I never thought of anything deep like some of the college Nisei do. I just use my hands and not my head too much. I guess I was too good natured about everything. Inside of me though I got sore plenty of times. Hell, I wish I had more education and then maybe I could figure things out better.

The first thing I thought of when evacuation was announced was to wonder what it was all about. All the guys in my gang were pretty sore about it and we cussed hell out of the government. When I got to camp, my friends told me that all the food was slop. That worried me quite a bit. I thought we would be practically starved. I never saw so many Japs in one place in all my life. I didn't like the horse stall that my mother and I were put into. It smelled just like manure. I griped about that and later we got to move to one of the new barracks in the infield.

I had the most fun in Tanforan. I worked as a server in the mess hall so I would be sure to get plenty to eat. I met all kinds of friends in this job and a lot of the old gang were in camp with me. They started up a baseball league so that our mess hall had a team. This was just an excuse to have big feeds afterwards. We would go to the mess hall and eat cakes and sandwiches after each game. The cooks were okay to us because they liked baseball too, and nothing was too good for us. It was a good thing we had one of the winning teams. Gradually we began to hang around the mess hall all the time and we used to stay until 2 at night having bull sessions or playing poker.

Later on I worked as a coal boy in the mess hall. I had to get the furnaces started in the morning so that I was the first one there. They had to give me a key so I could get started. I had free run of the mess hall. I never started the fire on time, as I couldn't get up in time after staying up so late. One time I didn't get up in time so the people who ate in our mess hall couldn't have breakfast. I was supposed to get up at 5 in the morning and I played poker and then I would go and light the fire and then I'd go home to sleep.

The gang came over all the time and we used to get all kinds of food to take to our barracks to cook. We swiped everything in sight. There were about 8 guys in the gang and I was the only one who worked. My [present] roommate came into the gang then. I knew him before in Frisco but I didn't go around with his gang at all. We had all kinds of guys in our gang.

One night 3 of the guys of our gang were walking by the grandstand and [one of them] made a crack at a Kibei going by and then they laughed. This Kibei didn't say anything but he followed [my friend] home and then jumped him from the rear and kicked him down. [My friend] came running to the dance to tell us about it, so we got about 20 guys together and we started to look for the Kibei. We finally found him with 6 other guys. They had clubs in their hands. Christ, man, we had 20 guys against their 6, so we were pretty confident. The Kibei acted brave too, and they put up a pretty good fight. They swung their clubs first and then the fight started. It was quite a fight and it made it less boring. After that we had to go around in a bunch, or else those Kibei would have brained us from behind. Hell, we had so goddam many fights, I couldn't begin to count them. It was a lot of fun and nobody got really hurt.

I didn't actually dislike the Kibei that much, but I thought they were too damn fresh. I never thought about the war very much so I didn't have too many arguments about this with them. I kept up with Japan's conquests and I thought it wouldn't last long. Hell, I didn't care because we were discriminated against anyway. I couldn't bother about these things as I was having more fun anyway. To tell the real truth, I did not give a damn who won the war, but I hoped that it would be over quick. At times I thought that Japan would win and I thought of going back to the old country. I didn't think I could get a good job here afterwards. I thought we'd all get shoved around and we would never be treated right again. But then, I figured what the hell, I could go back to Japan any time and I wanted to stick around the U. S. for a while to see how things turned out. I felt pretty close to the people in camp, except for the Kibei. They were too much for Japan, and they talked too much against everything American, even though I felt the same way as them at times. Maybe it was the way they said these things that griped me. They didn't even know how to speak English.

I wondered a lot about my draft situation. I didn't want to go into the Army. I thought that the people in camp would not like us to go into the Army after we were stuck in camp. The feeling of everybody was pretty low and the camp people didn't trust nobody. After all, we did get thrown out without any notice and that griped all of us. A lot of the old people lost their shirt. They lost their property and their businesses and they didn't have nothing left. Anybody would get sore if that happened to them. All of us in the gang thought that we shouldn't get drafted on account of all that. I felt the same way as they did. I never did like to get pushed around and all I wanted was a chance to make a living. Hell, it looked like we weren't even going to be given that chance.

All of the fellows in our gang made girls except me. I guess I was more the truck-driver type to them. I think I could have gotten further if I tried. I was too damn sleepy because of my work and I spent most of the time gambling anyway.

In September we went on to Topaz. I was worried about what kind of a place it was. Hell, we were just getting settled down and nobody wanted to move again. It was too damn much trouble. The trip up there to Topaz was not so bad. Jesus, it sure was a long trip. We rode for 12 hours and when we looked out we were only in Marysville. After that the train went faster. We had to wait in Salt Lake City for about 3 hours. The damn soldiers wouldn't even let us get off the train to stretch our legs. It was stuffy as hell and we were tired from the long trip. All the way up the food was the craps. I was curious about Topaz and I thought that maybe I could get a job as a welder if I went up there. I had the NYA training and I wanted to make use of it. They told us before evacuation that we would all have a chance to use our trade.

When I first got to Topaz I saw my pals, [B] and [K]. They were just about ready to leave for the sugar-beet fields. They tried to make me go, but I didn't know whatta hell was going on. They said I could have freedom and I could make a helluva lot of money but I wasn't too sure. I decided to go later on. The first night we were there we had a gang fight and we beat up a guy. He was a big bastard but we made this guy plead for mercy. It was over a girl too. I didn't even know what it was all about, but the other guys had a grudge, so I had to help them out. We were feeling as cocky as hell. The other guys in the gang didn't care what happened as they were leaving camp anyway.

After I was in camp for a week I couldn't take the damn dust storms. The damn food was all dusty as hell. That's all we saw, that dust. I decided to go to the sugar-beet fields to get away from it, so I went up to the employment office to sign up. There was a contractor there signing up sugar-beet workers. I didn't know a damn thing about sugar beets because I had never done it before but I signed up to go to [a town in] Utah. That was the closest I could get to my other pals who were out there already and it was only four miles away from them. I signed up with three other Nisei guys I knew and there was also a Kibei guy with us. We went out there and worked the first day. It was a tough job and my back ached so much that I felt like a goddam fool for ever leaving the camp where I could loaf around. We all got disgusted right away. The company gypped the hell out of us. We got so goddam fed up with it that we didn't feel like working hard. One of the guys in our group even quit and he went back to camp. We all decided to take it easy to get revenge, because we knew that the farmer wanted his sugar beets finished fast. We skipped all over the beets and did a sloppy job. The boss muttered that we were goddam Japs under his breath once but he knew better than to say it out loud because we would have ganged up on him. It was his own fault because if he had treated us right, we would have treated him right.

We didn't have enough facilities. Cripes, even when we took a bath, we had to boil the water in a washtub. We were always glad when it rained as we could run outside naked and take a shower. We had to have a bath every night because it felt lousy to go to sleep all dirty and sweaty after putting in a day's work. Every night we used to visit back and forth with our other pals who were working four miles away. My pals over there were even lazier than we were. They took a lot of smoke time and loafed around, but they were able to make more than us because they had a better beet field. Those guys were just out for fun too. Sometimes we had competition to see which gang could do the most work in the day, but they had the best beets so they always beat us.

The big day came in November [1942], when we finally finished our beet contract. We finally got everything straightened out [and returned to camp]. When I arrived I had less than what I had left with. All I had to show for my work out in the sugar beets for a couple of months was a new jacket. I only had a couple of bucks in my pocket from all that work.

In camp I loafed around for about a month in the barracks where the guys had poker sessions all night long. The block manager always complained about that. Finally, some of us got tired of loafing around, so we decided to go to work. I got on a coal crew, and we led the same life as before. We gambled most of the time. There was all kinds of money running around camp as a lot of guys came back from the sugar-beet fields flush. The guys who stayed behind in the gambling place in camp took it all away from them in a short time. After a while I got tired of the coal crew, so I got in the blacksmith shop for a couple of months. That was a better job.

All of the gang was back in camp from seasonal work so we had a helluva good time once more. We sponsored private dances, and some of the guys smuggled drinks into camp. The same old hags came to these dances and they all had a bad rep. A lot of the guys laid them after the dance.

I kept on with my work in the blacksmith shop. The reason I took that job was because I had a chance to do some welding, at last. After a while I got bored as hell with everything in camp. It was the same old gang all the time. We went all over together and at midnight we would go to the hospital and eat steaks because one of the gang was working in the mess hall over there. I began to run low in cash because of the gambling losses, so I decided to go out again. One of my friends was out at [another Utah town] and he got me a job with him. I owed him 10 bucks from a gambling debt, so he wouldn't let me quit. I didn't like that job at all. After I worked 10 bucks worth, I got into another poker session and lost, so I had to stay another week. It was a hay-pitching job and I got used to it by that time, so I didn't give a damn. [This town] was only 18 miles from camp, so that we commuted every day. We worked from 8 to 5 and we got 60 cents an hour. It was pretty good profit because everything was clear. Finally the WRA began to charge for room and board, so we quit the job then. It was not worth-while after that. I gave the reason for quitting that I was planning to leave camp to go out to school. That's why I decided to go to Salt Lake. A lot of the other guys were going out there too. This was March. 1942.

I didn't give a damn about the war because the guys had to lose property on account of it. People in camp were griped and I thought like them after hearing some of these stories. I didn't think that they should have been given the boot like that. I was thinking about what was going to become of us after the war most. Some of our gang were always arguing about the war. They had the registration about that time and everybody was talking about it. One guy in our gang was for Japan. He was griped as hell because his old man had lost property at evacuation. I wondered what would happen to us if Japan won the war. Then they would bounce us around if America won the war. The Nisei were losers both ways and I thought the only chance was to go to the Philippine Islands or some place and start out where you had some kind of a chance. My plan was to go to the rubber planta-tions in Singapore. Then I would think again and I didn't know what. I thought then that the Nisei who repatriated were crazy because they can always go back to Japan after the war if they want. A couple of the guys in my gang signed up for repatriation because their parents did. They sure regretted it later. One of them writes me from Tule Lake all the time and he is griped as hell that he ever did such a crazy thing. I give him the horse laugh because I am out here having fun and he is locked up with a bunch of Kibei bastards. I really feel sorry for him though.

I thought that the Nisei had no chance anyway they turned. Japan really don't want us and this country don't want us either. I don't give a damn who wins the war just so they don't bother me. But we are getting a raw deal and we are just as low as the Niggers now. As long as I look like a Jap, they make me act like one. Even if I want to be a good American, they think I'm supposed to act like a Jap and they don't want to give me a chance. They think I am inferior. That's why I want Japan to win the war in a way. Then in other ways, I want America to win. I don't know. I just don't give a damn. If I get drafted, I guess I will have to go serve for this country. I hope I won't get drafted as long as possible, because I don't like to kill other guys. Maybe I am timid and chicken, but it is no use going around killing other guys who want to live just like me.

I registered in camp in February, 1943, and I just wrote down what they told me to. Afterwards I wondered whatta hell I was answering Yes-Yes for. The older folks reacted in a different way. They didn't want us Nisei to be in a combat unit. They said we would all get stuck in the front line and get killed off like pigs. I guess a lot of Nisei answered "No" because of that. We used to argue about it in our gang and nobody knew what to believe. I had no intention of volunteering. I felt that they would have had to come and get me if they wanted me for the Army. We forgot about this right away and we went on playing poker. I did not pay any more attention to all the yelling about registration that was going on.

Right after the registration I got my indefinite leave and I went on up to Salt Lake with some of the guys of the gang. The reason I went there was because there was an offer about welding. When I went to find out about the job, the company told me that they had wanted 26 first-class welders and there was no chance for me as I was rated second class and I didn't have enough experience. They told me to wait around and perhaps they could find a job for me later. I sure was griped about that. I went to the WRA office in Salt Lake and told them that I had to go to work soon because my money was starting to run low. We were sore as hell when the WRA said for us to look for another job by ourselves. We blamed everything on them because they had told us to come out in the first place. I didn't think they were treating us right. Some of the guys decided to go back to camp right away. A couple of others went to NYA school to learn a trade.

I didn't want to go back to camp so I started looking around for a job. Another Nisei guy told me that a lot of *Nihonjin* were working at the [C] Packing Company as scalers. I went on out there to apply for a job because I had some experience as a scaler in San Francisco. I got a job right away for 70 cents an hour. At that time there weren't too many Nisei working there but later a lot of them began to come in. They only stayed about a week because they were quitting all the time. They didn't like the smell of the place. The reason I quit after a month was because I got a bone infection in my hand.

After that I couldn't get a release to look for another job for a whole month [May, 1943] so I was unemployed. Jesus, I was flat broke then. I began to lead the easy life again. Jesus Christ, every day we had the intention of going to look for a job but we would always end up by going to a show or a pool hall. I wasn't too interested in getting a job because all that was offered the Nisei was dish-washing jobs and my hand wasn't well yet. I was too proud to do that kind of work anyway.

I had no definite plans of what I wanted to do. After a month I heard that there was some cannery jobs up at [another Utah city] so I went up there with a friend. We found that the canneries were not opening for two weeks yet so it was waste time again. They didn't pay enough anyway. I heard about work in the coal mines, so I had an ambition to go work in a mine for a while. We went up to [another place in] Utah and we got a room there so we could start looking for a coal-mine job the next day. They wanted $6 rent for the room and we griped like hell so they lowered it to $2.50. There was a juke box in the room when we went in and then I knew that it was a whore joint. We stayed there all night anyway. [My friend] had some dough, so that we went to visit the two whores in the next room.

The next day we were all tired out so we did not feel like looking for work. We just stayed around in that whore joint and fooled around with the dames. The third day, a man in the Japanese bait shop downstairs told us how to look for a job in the coal mine. He told us to go ask Pete. We found Pete at a Jap noodle shop so we asked him for a job. All the Japanese in town knew that we were sleeping in a whore joint, so they treated us cool. We thought it wouldn't be so good to stay there and we decided to move on. Pete told us to stay and work in the mines so we stayed there a week. We had to quit the job because [my friend] couldn't take it. It was tough as hell to go into that mine. There were about 6 *Nihonjin* and 6 Caucasians. We worked in a tunnel shoveling coal and the boss said my pal was not working hard enough, so we told him off and quit. The thing that really made us decide to quit was when there was an accident in the mine and one of the guys got killed. We thought the mine was not safe enough for us. The damn rocks dropped on a guy and crushed his face in. It made me sick when I looked at him.

[Three of us] went on up to Idaho and we got a job in a coal mine there. We didn't like that job at all but we stuck around because there was three whore houses in town. We were living in a dump run by a Japanese and we paid him room and board. The three of us stayed in one small room. We had some adventures up there too. The first night up there we met a drunk. He wanted us to take him to a whore house. I saw his wallet, so we took him behind the house and rolled him. I just had to hit him once and he went out like a light. Then we put him on a box-car train going out of town so we felt safe enough. We got the job in the coal mine right away and we went to work for a couple of weeks and made $100 each. Then we decided to go back to Salt Lake as we didn't like that work and there were too many drunks in [this Idaho town].

We got back to Salt Lake some time in July and we just bummed around. I wanted to go back to camp so I could take a real rest. I only stayed in camp two weeks and then I got so damn bored that I decided to go out again. I got a pass to go out to the [G] mines with the rest of the guys. I worked out there for about a month or so. We had planned to stay there until December in remembrance of Pearl Harbor Day, but in August, we decided to quit as we did not have any fun out there.

We went back to Topaz again and they let me in as a visitor. I was supposed to pay 60 cents a day while I was there but I never paid a damn cent. I stayed for a week and then I took a job on a peach ranch. It was piece work and I was able to make about $10 a day. This was in August, 1943. I only worked on the peach farm for one week. Every night we went to town to fool around. We went to shows and got kicked out of beer joints every night. Since it was close to the potato picking season, we decided to go up to Idaho for the next job. We went into Salt Lake City first for a couple of days. Then we went on to Idaho.

When we got up there we found that we were too early for the spud season. We got into contact with a WRA field man and we told him that we couldn't afford to hang around doing nothing. He fixed it up with a fellow from a sugar company to give us jobs as laborers building some spud sheds. They only paid 69 cents an hour and that was cheap. We had to work so we took the job. Over there we slept in a tent and we were the only Japanese in the whole place. There were five of us guys there. All of the rest of the workers were Mexicans. The five of us did odd work like lifting up logs on a roof. Me and a couple of other guys lifted 22-foot logs on a roof while the other two guys went out to chop willow trees.

When the spud season came along we made pretty good money. I guess we made about $56 a week as we worked seven days. To pass the time, we raced each other in competition. I usually was the top man and I always wanted the guys to race because we got the work done that way. The slow guys in our crew didn't make very much money and they got discouraged easy. The guys who loaded the wagons made the best money as they got 85 cents an hour and they worked 12 hours a day.

After we finished three-fourths of the contract, we had a big argument with the boss. It was an American boss and our field boss was a Japanese. One day we were working and it started to snow about noon, so we said we were going to lay off. After we had finished up the row, the *keto* boss said for us to keep working. We told him it was foolish because pretty soon the snow would cover up all the potatoes. He got sore as hell then and said we were not being patriotic. I asked him whatta hell he meant, and he said we should do the work for the country and be patriotic. What the hell, we told him that nobody was a sucker like that, and that even the defense workers were doing it for the dough. We all cussed at him and I was the last one to cuss, so that he heard me mutter that he was a dirty, stinky bastard. Then he turned around and started for me as if he were going to beat me up. Us guys were already for him, so the guy chickened out. He then started to change his tune and he said that we were trying to hit an old man. Then he said that he was going to call the marshal and tell him that we were sabotaging his crop. Pretty soon the marshal came driving up with the Caucasian boss and he wanted to know who the troublemaker was. The guy was a wop, and he had the nerve to say that he would send us back to the old country if we did not get the hell back to work. We didn't like that so much so we said, whatta hell, we were American citizens and we had our rights too. He just took the boss' side and believed everything. He wouldn't even listen to our story. Everything was against us so finally we decided to go back to work. Our Japanese field boss was sore too, so he didn't care when we started to throw the spuds and snowballs at each other. The Caucasian boss made us stay out in the field all afternoon in the snow just for spite. He lost money that way because we threw a helluva lot of his spuds away. Some of the guys went on and crushed them with their heels. We were all sore.

After that the sugar beets started again and we had a contract for a place right near there. We worked like hell at this place but we only made about $5 a day. We worked from 7 in the morning until 7 at night and a lot of times we worked until 11 o'clock loading. The ground got frozen about October so we could not top beets anymore. We had to lay off a lot of times and we lost money every time we did that. Our profits all went just to feed ourselves and we couldn't even go to town anymore. During the evenings we used to talk, and we all had the intention of going east to New York, Chicago, or Cleveland. All the guys said they were going east because jobs paid a lot more than farm work. When it came time to leave, only one guy from our gang went east and he went to Cleveland. The rest of us all went back to camp.

I had about $240 cash when I left that job because the contractor paid us in a lump sum and he wouldn't give us our money before the end of the season because he thought we were going to quit. He wouldn't give us money when we were practically starving. We had to use money we had brought with us and it kept us broke. In the end we felt pretty good to get a lump sum like that, otherwise we would have spent it going to town all the time if we had been given that money before. We went to Salt Lake for a week before going back to camp. I spent the time running around. I bought some clothes too. We went all around to the whore houses about 2 times a day and we drank up and took out dames. It was easy to pick up dames in Salt Lake. When I got back to Topaz I had only $100 left out of my money. I stayed at Topaz from October until December and I didn't work at all. All I did was to play poker and I lost most of my money.

Some of the guys heard of a turkey farm and they said we could make a lot of dough out there by working 11 hours a day. We decided to go out there so we signed up for that job before Christmas. There were 6 guys and 20 dames out there when we arrived. The dames were all rugged, so that we were afraid to try and lay any of them until we got to know them better. At first we played poker all night. We had a session every night. On Sundays we went to the shows. We were there about two weeks before we started to get around with the dames. One night we took a girl out to the apple orchard and six of us made her. She was a Nisei from another camp. [After another affair] I got scared because that was the first time I had ever laid a virgin, so I decided that I had better leave the turkey farm. I had about $25 saved from that job, and during that month I laid the dames there at least 10 times. The fellows in the gang nicknamed me "the sex fiend."

I was back in Topaz right after New Years this year [1944]. After I got back after camp I don't know what happened to me but I was always wanting to lay the girls. I never was that bad before. I guess the success at [the turkey farm] went to my head. I don't know what it was. All I did that month was to fool around the dames, gamble, and sleep. I got pretty scared [about making a girl pregnant] and I decided I had better leave camp before I got roped in.

I was on indefinite leave and I wanted to get my grant money. If I had to pay my way out here I never would have come. My first intention was to go to New York. I didn't have a definite job offer there and the WRA said I could only come to Chicago, as they could not give me any grant money to go further than that. The only reason they let me come out here was because my old lady was out here then, and I told them I was coming to join her. She left in January to work in a sewing factory for 50 cents an hour. I had the intention of going all over the country, but I heard that I could get a job as a welder in Chicago so I got interested. That's what I wanted all the time and I thought this would be my chance to get into a defense plant. I had been sort of trying to get a welding job even when I was out doing farm work.

I left Topaz at the end of January [1944] and I arrived in Chicago on January 30. The first thing I did was to get a room on [the North Side], and then I went to the WRA office right away. They told me that rooms were hard to get in Chicago, so that I had better look for a more permanent place the first thing. [My present roommate] had come out with me and I talked him into staying for a while. We looked around and happened to see a sign and asked for a room and they rented it to us. We were the only Japanese there, but it was a dump.

We then went back to the WRA office and they sent us to the [D] Iron Works. This was on a Monday after I got to Chicago and I went out for the interview. They offered me a job right away but I didn't take it. I figured that it would take over an hour to get out to the factory by streetcar from the place where we lived. I wanted to get a job nearer to our room. [My present roommate] didn't feel like working right away so we just played around for a week. We went to shows and all that. Every once in a while we would drop in [on] the WRA. They didn't like us very much. They made us sit around and wait for hours and we got disgusted. When I saw the interviewer, he wouldn't give me another job. He said I should take the job at the [D] Company because I was interested in welding and it was a good chance for me. I told him of our transportation problem and so he said he would fix it up. He gave me a list of 7 rooming places that I could go down to see on the southside. I agreed to take a job at [D's] if I could find a place on the southside. We went out to look for a house and the first place was no good. We rented the second place, two rooms so that my mother could come out and live with us and cook. We pay $8 a week for the two rooms and that's cheap. My mother was living down in the Loop so I told her to come out here. She has to take an hour to go to work now, but she doesn't mind so much because she only works 5 days a week.

After that I went out to work in the defense plant at [D's]. The plant makes landing barges and bridges which can be thrown together quickly by the army of invasion. When I first went out there, I was hired as a welder's helper. They started me out at 75 cents an hour, but I didn't mind because I thought I would get a lot of promotions and get experienced. After a while they made me a burner. I did this steady for two weeks and then I squawked for a burner's wage. I heard that burners were supposed to start at 85 cents an hour and I didn't see why I shouldn't be paid that too. The boss didn't object too much and he gave me the raise.

When you work at a job like that, you don't have much time to play around. We put in 10 hours a day and we work 6 days a week. We get time and a half after 40 hours. Sometimes we even work on Sundays and we get double time for that. When I first started out there I was tired all the time because I wasn't used to that work. We had to get up at 6 o'clock in the morning so we could be down to the plant by 7. The first week we went to bed every night after we ate; but after we started getting around a bit, we got used to sleeping shorter hours. Now we stay up until all hours of the night and we manage to get to work.

There were only three Nisei when we first went out there, but little by little they started coming in so that there are now about 20 out there. Most of the other workers are colored. I would say that the colored and the Japanese outnumber the white men in that plant. I don't mix too much with the other Nisei except those guys we play poker with. We don't have too much time to talk around anyway.

The wages are too low out there. Even the top Caucasian welders only get $1.10 an hour. Some of those fitters have been working out there for a year and they only get 75 cents yet. They are frozen to their jobs. The work gets pretty monotonous at times, but I think I am learning all about gauges on the burner job so I don't mind. It is still my ambition to be a welder for a while and I would like to do that steady while the war is on.

The other workers in the plant treat me fine and there is no discrimination by them. The Negroes are swell to us and we get along with them the best. [My roommate] is always telling them that we are underdogs just like them. One Negro worker said to me that the Japs had been kicked around as much as them, so that he knew what it was like. It makes you feel good when you know that a bunch of guys like to stick together after going through the same thing as you do. We get along with the *hakujin* too. They are mostly young fellows and they hardly talk about the war. They didn't even know about evacuation. That's why they became interested in where we came from, and they asked us all about California. They tell us that they can't help it if this country is fighting Japan. They say that we are in a tough spot, but they believe we are really for this country like them.

At first I was hoping that there would not be any more Nisei brought in there but I guess the WRA is trying to put them all in. Quite a few come down for jobs. I don't think that it makes it much harder for us, although sometimes it is more noticeable. One good thing though was that the company never gave any raises until the Nisei came in. They gave the excuse that all wages were frozen. [My roommate] and I were the first ones to start asking for a raise and the other Nisei followed. Now a lot of the *kurombo* and *hakujin* workers are getting raises too. I plan to hang on to the job right now because I may get drafted soon. I ran around a lot before and I changed my job quite a bit, but now I have to stick. It isn't because I love that job. I used to change jobs because I wanted to get higher wages. That's natural. If you think the other guy is getting paid more, you want to go over there too. Even now the Nisei guys I know are saying Detroit pays more, and they would like to go there next. I've got intentions of going out there some day unless the draft catches up with me first. In fact, I have plans to go to New York too, but all of these plans don't mean anything because I may not get the chance.

I haven't the least idea of what I will do after the war. I haven't much plans on that because I don't think about it too much. I would like to open up some kind of business afterwards because welders will be a dime a dozen after the war and I will be one of the first fired because I am a Jap. I'll be satisfied if I get to be a welder once because that was my ambition for so long and I didn't have the chance before. Maybe after the war I can open up a grocery or a cleaner's shop. I don't know yet. I have to save some money up to start a business and I haven't been doing that yet.

I just know it's going to be hard for the Nisei after the war no matter who wins. We will all be in the same boat and it doesn't matter if the Nisei has a college education or not. [My roommate] said he would stay in this country no matter what happened, but I'd take a chance and go to another country if I know I'm not wanted here. I just think all this; but when the time comes, I guess I will stick around this country. I know damn well I wouldn't like it if they try to ship us out by force. I would fight like hell against that.

I've been disappointed about the money I could make out here. Hell, I thought it was easy to save a lot of money, but I've had a tough time making a living. I don't know where the money goes. Every time I am flat before the week is over. I get paid about $50 a week and I only have to pay $15 for my room and board. I should have about $35 left for all my other things, but my roommates keep me broke because we have been going to poker sessions and it costs a helluva lot for entertainment. I guess we do spend our money foolishly. We have to have our fun though. We go to shows, night clubs, and pool halls and once in a while we go look up friends. We have a whole list of names and addresses that we got from the WRA office but we have been too lazy to look them all up. I write some letters to the guys I know back in camp and other places. It feels good to get letters from the gang.

I only took out one date since I've been here. I can't even support myself, so I couldn't get married for a long time even if I wanted to. I don't feel like doing nothing and I don't want to get married for a long time anyway. Going to the whore houses don't satisfy me anymore, but that is better than nothing. Since I've been here, I've picked up about three *hakujin* women. I got a white woman upstairs and she isn't bad. She is only about 26 years old and she lets me sleep with her now and then. I won't move out of this place for a while as long as I can see her.

I still don't think much of the war yet. I never read the newspapers and I don't like to listen to the war news over the radio. I worry more about myself and what is going to become of us. I haven't got anything against either country so why should I take sides in the war? All I can do is to sit tight and wait for it to end. If I have to go into the Army, that is a different story.

I want to find out as soon as possible if I am going to get drafted or not. Waiting for it is hell and I can't plan nothing. If I am called, I'll have to go. But I am asking for a deferment on account of my work. I don't think the boss will put it in for me though. A lot of my friends got their reclassification already and I hear they have to report for induction pretty soon. If I am drafted, I would like to go to Camp Shelby with the rest of the Nisei because most of my friends will be there. At other times, I would like to mix with other Americans in the Army as I'm used to it since I mingled with a lot of guys when I was training at NYA after the war started. I got along fine with them and it was just like the Army life. I think I could do the same thing if they mix me up in the Army now. At first I didn't feel so good being the only Japanese at that NYA school, but I found it was better that way and they included me in all their fun. I think that this would be the same way in the Army and maybe it is better if I wasn't sent to Camp Shelby. If there was a lot of discrimination in the Army, then I wouldn't want to be mixed up because it would be hell that way.

I think I have reformed a little out here. [My roommate] is a zoot-suiter and I think he is foolish. Sometimes I hate to walk with him as it is too extreme. People notice it too much. Back in camp, I had a zoot suit but I don't wear it anymore. Our gang wasn't as tough as the reputation we had. We had our fun but we weren't that bad. Every-one was like us anyway. I don't like those lily-white church guys be-cause they are a bunch of hypocrites. At times we got pretty rough but we had to stick up for our rights. All of us will settle down like every-one does after awhile.

If I'm not drafted, I guess I won't want to go back to the coast as it won't be the same as before. I figure I will keep heading east. I guess I would have to leave my mother behind for a while but I wouldn't desert her all the time. She makes enough money to live by herself now so I won't have to worry about that. I feel I will have to take care of her when she gets old. She wants me to stick here, but I want to keep moving, because I don't feel too comfortable staying in one place too long.

Sometimes I feel pretty cocky and other times I feel inferior to guys. A lot of times I'd like to know how to dance like a lot of the Nisei.

I've had a lot of inferiority in my work. I guess that's when I feel it the most, because I couldn't get as good a job as a Caucasian before the war. It used to make me mad as hell before but now it's better for me because there are plenty of jobs.

Additions to life history obtained in reinterview in March, 1945

I think that it was last April, 1944, that I quit working for [D] Iron Works and I started at [N] Company. I got this job through a friend of mine who told me it was a better place to work. I was getting only about a dollar an hour at [D's] and they wouldn't give me a raise because I was a boochie. At [N's] I was given the prevailing wage of $1.20 right from the beginning. The job was okay and I didn't have any complaints about it. We had about 200 workers in the plant and I thought it was pretty interesting even though welding is pretty hard on the eyes. We made prefabricated parts of the Navy ships. I worked there for a while as a welder but my foreman transferred me to do set-up work. I didn't mind this too much because it was a good rest for my eyes. I didn't want to stay out of welding work though because there was more money in it. It wasn't bad working out there at all because everyone treated me swell. There was no discrimination at all in the plant and nobody called us Japs or anything like that. Hell, we were all building parts for Navy ships, weren't we? On October 15 [1944] the contract for the company was terminated. They didn't need so many workers so I was released from the job.

After I got laid off I loafed around for a couple of weeks. All this time I was inquiring around for other jobs as a welder though. Since I was a boochie, I didn't have much of a chance in a lot of places where I went to apply for a welder's job. I figured I might as well stay in my line since I had training in it. A lot of companies that I went to said they were willing to hire me, but they were not so willing to give me white man's pay for the job. That disgusted the hell out of me and I got pretty sore a couple of times. I knew that I was just as good a welder as a lot of those guys who got paid more than I did just because they had a white man's face.

Finally I asked around to find out where the other guys who were released from the [N] Company with me went. I found out that most of them had quit welding to go into some other kind of work because they didn't like to get all burned to hell from that kind of work. I wanted to stay in it because there was more money. There was one colored fellow who was good friends with me out there and he got fired at the same time I did. He told me to come out where he was working because he thought I might have a chance to land a job there. I went right away and I was given the job. It was a small fabricating shop making minesweepers for the Army. My job was to weld the minesweeper parts together. I started working out there in November [1944]. We were working by piece work so that I made damn good wages, the best I ever did. I was averaging almost $2.00 an hour and I thought I would be rolling in dough after a few months. It took me the first month to catch up on all the money I had spent during the [time] between jobs.

I was the only boochie working in that plant and that was okay by me. There were about 8 of us working on the night shift, and 15 guys were on the day shift. There were all white guys except the colored fellow and me. All of us were making pretty good money with the contract we had so we had no kicks coming. Just when I was starting to make real good dough after one month, the boss decided to put on a kind of incentive plan. I found that I wasn't making nearly as much money as before with this kind of a setup. Some of the other guys didn't like the setup at all, so they quit. I decided to quit too. When I went to resign, the boss wouldn't give me a release at all. He said I couldn't get another job unless I got a release. He tried to hold me on that job with this threat but that got me sore so I just walked out.

I went with the colored guy to apply for a job with the [A] Car Company on a piece-work basis. The colored guy couldn't get a job because he didn't have a release. I was put on as a welder because I used my old release from [N] Company and I didn't tell them about the job I had just walked out on. We were making freight cars and I figured that I could earn $12 a day easy as hell. It was my job to weld on the bottoms of the freight cars. Pretty soon I found that I was only making $9.50 a day. I could do the 12 alignments in 5 or 6 hours and after that I would have made a lot of money, but the colored guys didn't feel like doing any more work. They were satisfied with the $9.50 a day and I got pretty disgusted. I could not go ahead and try to work on my own because the other guys wouldn't want me to scab like that and they would have gotten sore. There was another Nisei working there and he tried to put out more but his gang got pretty sore at him and he had to slow down to their pace or they would have beaten him up.

I was netting $50 a week but the contract expired in January [1945] so that I had to go on an hour basis at 80 cents an hour for a while until a new contract was made. I didn't care to stick around there after making good money from before on the contract so I decided to get another job.

It took me 2 weeks before I got my present job. I went to work 6 weeks ago on this job [February 15, 1945]. Most of the time I had gotten my jobs through my friends who worked at other places, but this job I got through the WRA office. The interviewer down there told me to go down to the USES to ask about a job with the [G] Company. When I got down to the USES they told me that they weren't so sure this company would hire a boochie. The USES man told me to stick around while he phoned the company to ask, so I waited there by his desk while he made the phone call. I was surprised as hell when the company told me to come down right away. The interviewer told me to talk on the phone there to give my qualification. I didn't want to make a trip down there for nothing so I told them I was Japanese. They said right away that it didn't matter what ancestry I had just so I didn't try to blow up any of the ships they were building. I said that I was loyal to this country like any of those damn welders so they gave me the okay. The USES man then gave me my release to go out there and take this job right away.

When I got out to the [G] Company they told me I had to take a welder's test and I thought sure I was going to be screwed up again. They said that the A-1 welders started at a wage of $1.20 an hour and I would have to prove that I was fit to work with them by taking this test. I thought it was going to be a hard test but I passed it right away so they started me out at the same wage as the rest of the guys got. I get just as much pay as the white welders so that makes me feel pretty good.

When I first went out there I asked if I could work on the day shift. The personnel man advised me to take the night shift. I found that it was pretty good to work at night. I never saw a job like that before in my life. We worked 11 hours a night for 5 nights a week so we could get in our 55 hours. We had a damn good foreman and he never yelled at us at all.

After I was there for a couple of weeks, the company decided to abolish the night shift as there wasn't enough work going on so I was put on the day shift with the rest of the guys. I didn't like it so much but I find that it isn't so bad now. In fact I like working during the day like most people do. The only thing is that I have to work a lot harder now. I net about 50 bucks a week now but I get $6.22 for war bonds now so that gives me a free war bond every month.

Our big job is to assemble Navy ships. We do the landing crafts and some other small Navy ships which are for the fleet. We put the engine and everything in it so that it is a complete job. Right now I am working on the fo'castle of the ship. I'm learning a helluva lot more about welding. I thought I knew everything about it before but every day I'm learning new things. There's only one other boochie working there now and he came after I did. The rest of the workers are all Caucasians except 6 colored guys who worked there until just the other day.

I don't have a grudge against anyone in the place. Red is the guy that I get along best with because he tries to be friendly. I told Red that I was here in Chicago for a year and I liked the California weather better, but I thought that the Chicago jobs were best for me. I told him that I didn't care to work with Negroes too much as they were lazy. Red said that I shouldn't criticize them too much or look down on them. He's a sort of educated and one of them broad-minded guys. Red told me that he wouldn't like it if a lot of boochies came into the plant and did scab labor either. He said that he looked on me as an individual, and he thought all us guys should do that to one another and there would be less of this racial stuff getting us in trouble. He doesn't believe in discrimination at all. Red would like to get the Negro guys into the union but the rest of the guys won't allow them either. There's one Chinese guy at the plant and I get along with him good. The other guys are always joking because they say they can't tell us apart. Nobody there calls me a Jap though. Most of the guys never saw a boochie before anyway but they trust me good.

I'm working pretty steady out at the plant now and I got a good reputation for myself. The boss gives me a lot of the important jobs to do on welding, even over 'the more experienced guys. They don't get sore at me though because they know I'm trying to learn the job good. I never try to scab on them. The Navy inspector comes to look at my work once in a while because my welding has to be an airtight job and it is pretty important. The inspector never bothers me about anything else though and he never looks suspicious at me. As long as they let me alone, I don't give a damn. Hell, it feels pretty good when I talk to the other welders just like I'm one of them and they take me the same way. They don't believe in discrimination against me and I bet a lot of those guys would be in favor of giving the colored workers an equal chance if they wouldn't be so lazy.

I joined the labor union the first week I was out there. I had to join it or else they would have said I was a scab. I got soaked 58 bucks for membership fees right away. I have to pay 5 bucks a month dues. I don't know if it is worth it to me because it won't help me after the war. I'm a full member of the union (A.F.of L.) and none of those damn associate memberships for me. Some of the boochie guys I know pay union dues but they don't have full membership like I do. That's the craps because it shows that there is that discrimination feeling against them.

I'm planning to stick with this job until the end of the war. I'd like to stay in welding because I like it as much as anything else. I'd hate to work for somebody else all of my life though. It's too risky that way. But I ain't got an education or a business head, so I guess I'll just have to do some kind of work like this all the time.

I've saved some money in the year I've been out here but I don't save too much as I have to spend all of my money between jobs. I've been making damn good wages out here compared to the 40 cents an hour I used to work for before the war. Hell, I don't think that I squander my money. Out of my 50 bucks a week I've been losing around 40 bucks a month just on poker alone. I only play about 3 times a month but I think I'm going to give up pretty soon. I know there ain't much percentage in it, but one of these days I'll get lucky and then I'll really take the boys for a ride. It only costs me about 50 bucks a month for room and board but I eat out a lot of times too. It runs me about 10 bucks a month for my laundry bill and cleaning. I have a dentist bill of 25 bucks to pay up but I'm just about over all of my debts now. I don't have to pay the doctor anything as long as I am protected by the company. It costs me around 60 bucks a month just for entertainment and I don't go out any more hardly at all. I bet that drugstore up the corner makes a helluva lot of money from us guys making milk shakes. I don't even drink any more like the other guys. Hell, they think I'm getting serious and they rib me and call me a square. I don't think I've done too badly because I've saved about 500 bucks in the year I came to Chicago and that didn't take any effort. I saved it during the time I was working on the night shift those long hours and I never had any chance to spend my money. I was getting good pay then too. If I can save up that much this year I'll be satisfied. Hell, before the war, it would have taken 5 or 10 years to save 500 bucks at the wages I was getting paid. The war's not going to last much more than one or 2 years yet, so I have to start thinking of getting a steady postwar job. I'll have to go look for another welding job if I get released. I don't know what my chances will be and I bet I'll get pretty damn disgusted. I'll just keep looking for a welding job until I get so damn disgusted that I'll have to take something else. Hell, I might even have to take a laboring job if there's nothing else. Man, I wouldn't have all that worry if I were in the Army. Those guys will come out and there will be bonuses and everything else. Naturally they will get the best jobs because they fought for the country. They won't give a damn about us guys who work at those plants and make all the bullets and other stuff for them.

I have no intention of going back to California right now as the Negroes have taken over all of the boochie towns and we would not have any place to live. I wouldn't be able to get a very good job out there. I'm still looking for another place to live out here and it's tough as hell. This place is lousy as the landlord is always trying to gyp us by raising the rent. He tried to bully my old lady and I got sore as hell because she can't talk back to him. [My former roommate] now lives with some other guys a couple of blocks over. [Another boy], my old lady, and I are the only ones living here now.

Hell, it hardly seems that a year went by so fast. My mother still works at the same job in the sewing factory. She got a couple of raises since she started but I don't know if she likes the work or not. I never talk to her about it. I never talk to my old lady about nothing. She'd just as soon stick around Chicago as any other place. I don't think she wants to go back to camp or California because she's making more money now than she ever did before. My old lady don't care where she is just as long as I sort of stick around and don't get into any trouble.

I haven't been playing around as much as I used to. I'm not unhappy though. Life out here is not like it was out on the coast but it used to get pretty damn dull out there too. I know quite a few boochies out here but I don't see them all the time except for a few. I see about 10 or 15 guys pretty often but I don't know many dames. I don't go out on too many dates because I'm not the lady killer of the gang. Some of the other guys go visit dames all the time but I only go about once a week, if that much. I have no intention of getting married for quite a while. How in the hell can I support a wife? It takes most of my money just to have a little social life.

One thing that surprises me is that I haven't met any discrimination out here yet. In some of my job hunting they might have discriminated but nobody got nasty yet. I heard a lot about discrimination but I haven't seen it. I'd like to be sociable to more Caucasians as they have a lot of pull and we have to depend on them for many things. After all, if we live here for a long time we have to be friendly to one another. There's no sense hating the Caucasians.

I don't know if I'm better off now than I was before evacuation. I think that maybe I am. A lot of the guys I know are much better off. I guess I would still be doing nothing if I was back in Frisco. I'd probably be an errand boy yet. Now I can say that I am a welder. At least I'm not a bum now and that's some progress I guess. I wouldn't want to live the kind of life I led when I was bumming around out in Utah on the farms and coal mines. That's all right for the experience but not for all the time. I got a trade now so I got some chance for after the war.

CH-12: DOMESTIC SERVANT

Female; born 1912 in Hawaii; inmigrated to San Francisco in 1937; height 60"; weight 110 lbs.; unmarried. Interviewed, September, 1943, during a series of "hurried contacts," while she was awaiting induction into the WACs. Described as "a friendly person," who had "no apparent feelings of racial inferiority," who "used very good English, and spoke very deliberately" and who was "quite frank in expressing her opinions."

CAREER LINES

Parental: CH-12's father (born *ca.* 1873) and her mother (born *ca.* 1883) had been adopted by the same childless couple in Japan. Father, after completing high school in Japan, married his foster sister, worked on a merchant marine ship, and sailed for Hawaii *ca.* 1907. Opened a cooking school to teach western techniques to Hawaiian immigrants, and called his foster mother [and father?], along with his wife, to the islands. *Ca.* 1910, opened a restaurant and bakery of his own, and later operated a small grocery store and a retail produce shop in Honolulu. Died in 1925. CH-12's mother completed the 12th grade in a Christian mission school in Japan, and excelled in her studies. Obtained some training as a nurse, and followed this profession before immigrating to Hawaii. After husband's death, she worked for a time as a manicurist and hairdresser, then resumed nursing career, and became a licensed midwife.

Own: Graduated from college in Hawaii in 1934, majoring in English and journalism. During freshman year, had worked part time as a domestic servant for an Army couple, and after graduation migrated with them to San Francisco, with the expectation of entering one of the larger American universities for training in librarianship. Continued to work for this family as a domestic servant, until their transfer in 1937; then obtained a job as housekeeper and cook in an upper-class suburban household, and held this job until evacuation in 1942. Left camp in January, 1943, for the Middle West and worked again as a domestic servant for a couple who wintered in Florida, until August, when she resigned in order to enlist in the WACs. Inmigrated to Chicago in September, 1943, to await induction.

LIFE HISTORY

Both of my parents are from Yokohama. My dad has been dead for the past 17 years, but my mother is still alive. One of the things about my parents which has always impressed me greatly is that they were both modern in their ideas. They did not rule us with an iron hand but tried to just give us good advice. All of us in the family have gone to church since we were babies so that we have a long background in Christianity.

The way my parents came to Hawaii is a little complicated. My grandparents were childless so they adopted my father in order that he could take the family name, since my grandparents did not want the name to die out. It happened that my mother was also adopted by my grandparents so that my parents grew up together. It was natural for them to get married when they were adults. There was only about ten years difference in their ages and it is not like many of the immigrant Japanese families where the husband is 15 or 20 years older than his wife.

I don't know too much about my parents' life in Japan since they never talked much about it to me. My grandmother used to tell me of some of her former life but I have forgotten most of it. Around 1907 my father decided to leave Japan in order to look for better opportunities. He eventually landed in the islands and he called my mother and grandmother over later.

My father had worked on a merchant marine ship before settling down in Hawaii. He worked on all kinds of boats and he had been all up and down the Pacific Coast from Alaska to South America. He knew quite a good deal about Western cooking, and his travels liberalized him to quite an extent. He decided to open up a cooking school in order to teach the Issei in Hawaii so that they could go work for some of the American families. He did this for two or three years and around 1910 he started a restaurant and a bakery in Honolulu. Later on he opened up a small grocery store but that was not so successful. The last thing I remember him doing was that he owned a produce store and he had a contract with the U.S. Army to supply vegetables to it. He was not in good health during the latter time of his life, so that he got tuberculosis and he died in 1925.

After that my mother had to start to work in order to support the family since most of us were too young to go to work yet. For a while she worked as a manicurist and a hairdresser. She was the chief economic support of the family until about 1933 when some of the other members of the family began to help out.

My mother had quite a career in Japan. I know that she graduated from a Christian mission school and she was a nurse. After she started working again [in Hawaii] she went in for nursing at a Japanese hospital in Honolulu. She also got a midwife's license and she did this work at the same time. Now my mother is more or less retired since my other sisters and brothers all help with the family.

There were seven children in our family altogether but one of them died. I was small and sickly as a child and I could not go to public school for a long time. It was my father who first taught me how to read and write English. I went to elementary school from 1919 to 1926. A junior high school was started in 1927 so that I went there for one year. It was a select school and we had to pass a special English examination in order to get into that school. After that I went to high school in Honolulu, from 1927 to 1930, when I graduated. In high school I took part in quite a few club activities. My special interest was in journalism and literature so that I worked on the school paper and the annual.

After graduating from high school I went to the university from 1930 to 1934 when I got my A.B. degree. In college I took part in about the same activities and I specialized in journalism. During my freshman year I started to work in a home part time in order to help pay my way. In my sophomore and junior year I did not work while attending college since I stayed home and took care of the rest of the family. During this period my mother was working on the night shift at the hospital as a special nurse, so that she had to get her sleep during the day. In my senior year at the university I did not work at all, so that this was the most enjoyable period of my college life.

I did not have too many Japanese friends at any time in my life. All of my close friends in high school and college were of Chinese extraction. Even now I correspond mostly with my Chinese friends. The Japanese college students were studious. Most of them had to work their way through school because they were from the other islands and they did not have parents rich enough to send them, consequently they did not have much time for social activities. The Chinese families were a little richer so that their children at the university did not have to work so that they had a lot more time for the campus activities. I got to know them because I was a native Honolulu girl and I was not working after my freshman year.

I went to Japanese language school from 1918 to 1925. It was quite a large school and there were over 500 students in it. I had to go from the age of six right up through the time I graduated from grammar school. We went from 3 to 4 every afternoon. I don't remember the teachers giving us any special Japanese propaganda as they just taught us to read and write Japanese. Of course, on the Emperor's birthday the school would have a special exercise, but the teachers did not particularly tell us to obey Japan or anything like that. It was a ceremony merely to pay respect to the Emperor. On the Japanese festival days such as Kite Day for the boys and Doll Day for the girls, a special festival would also be held. Most of it was done to cater to the tourist trade because it was a picturesque event. All of these things were a part of the general Hawaiian atmosphere. We did not think of it as fostering the Japanese feeling particularly. We merely took it more or less as a cultural thing.

My home life was never very Japanesy. We learned to be tolerant of the other individuals at an early age because all of us had to give and take. My grandmother more or less brought us up, and although she was a strict disciplinarian, she was also very understanding of children. I suppose that my grandmother has been one of the strongest influences in my life. She was quite tall for a Japanese and she had a face more like an Indian, with a straight nose. I have always thought of her as an Indian. In spite of her age she was quite a liberal person. She was originally a Buddhist, but when she came to Hawaii, she realized that the Buddhists could not get very far, so that she adopted Christianity. Grandmother felt that we children would have more of a chance later on if we adopted more of the Hawaiian ways of living. Mother was also a Christian since she had been educated in a Christian mission school. I don't remember very much about my grandfather, but I do know that the early missionaries to Japan had a great influence on him and he became a Catholic. When he was young, he was in favor of allowing Admiral Perry to open up Japan. He wanted to help overthrow the Shogunate rule as he thought it would be better for the development of Japan to come out of isolation. Since my father and mother were both reared by my grandparents, they got quite a few progressive ideas from them.

I had quite a shock when I was only 13 years old. My grandmother and my father both died in the same year. I was quite bewildered by this because I think that my mother worried quite a bit about how she was going to take care of her large family. After a year or so my older brother quit high school and he went to work in order to make ends meet in the family affairs. Grandmother had taken care of bringing most of the children up but after she died Mother had to do everything and it was too much for her. I became pretty close to my mother then and I tried to help her as much as I could.

My mother was always a thorough person in everything she did. She would always insist upon us children completing everything we did or not tackling it at all. She was modern in most of her ideas, even more than Dad or Grandmother. For example, so many of the first generation parents did not think that their young children should go to dances and associate with the *hakujin* kids, but Mother insisted upon it. She said that as long as we were in Hawaii, we should do as the other people did.

My parents got along very well in their married life. The marriage was not arranged and it was a love match so that they were happy. However, both of my parents were very strong headed so that when they did quarrel, they had violent quarrels. I can well remember some of those house-shaking arguments which they had. However, it did not last very long and they would patch up their differences in a very short time. My father drank a little, but he never did do it to excess. He did not bother us children much as he left most of the necessary disciplining up to Grandmother. Grandmother would spank us on the behind in the good old American way, as she did not approve of the Japanese way of pinching or twisting the arm.

My grandmother never could understand English but my dad and mother were fairly good at it. We children usually spoke in Japanese to Grandmother but in English to our parents. They would answer us in Japanese most of the time but Father did talk quite a bit of English, so did my mother, too, for that fact. My parents encouraged the use of English more and more as they realized that it was an advantage in Hawaii.

My dad never talked sentimentally about Japan much, as he was too busy making a living, but my grandmother did have an attachment to it. She wanted to go back there to die so that she would be buried with the rest of her ancestors. Dad was a sort of a rebel and he did not care for many of the Japanese ways. He did not like Japanese food and that is why he taught American cooking to the Issei. We ate American food mostly and Dad did most of the cooking until his death as Mother did not know how to cook at all. We were drinking milk regularly when most of the other Japanese families did not even know about it as a body builder. The only time that we had pure Japanese food was during the New Year's festival. My mother believed in this very strongly and she said that the Japanese foods eaten at that time stood for certain things. On New Year's morning we had to get up and take a hot bath before breakfast in order to be clean for the New Year. We had one of those wooden Japanese tubs and the water was almost boiling. I never could stand those real hot Japanese baths which the Japanese like. Another custom which my mother followed was to clean up the whole house the last thing she did before the coming of the New Year. At midnight the whole family would get together to eat *osoba,* which is a sort of brown buckwheat noodles. In Japanese *soba* means close, so that all of the family had to be together to show that there was a strong family unity. There was a great stress placed upon family unity and I thought that this was a rather good characteristic, although some Japanese families carried it to extremes. When this happened, the individual did not have much of a place.

My oldest brother was very privileged in our household. It wasn't only because he was the oldest son but more due to the fact that he was the first son that had been in my grandmother's family for four generations, even though this offspring was from her adopted children. My father thought that girls should stay home and not have much of a place in society, which was a carry-over of the Japanese system. However, Grandmother and Mother were more enlightened, because they had a more positive opinion about the place of women. One of the good things about my parents was that they did not believe in arranged marriages. Mother always told us that she did not care whom we married as long as we made the union a success, but I think that she would have been happier to have us all married to *Nihonjin* as she had some racial pride.

We children did not have any sort of racial feelings since Hawaii is cosmopolitan. There were some *hakujin* pupils who tried to act superior, but these were the children of service men stationed at the military post there. But the real old-time residents were very liberal in their race attitudes. In spite of this, however, I do think that the Japanese were more racially conscious than the other groups in the islands. The Chinese were much more assimilated, even the first generation, as they intermarried a lot with the native Hawaiians and other groups. But there has never been too much intermarriage between the Japanese and other island groups. Even the second generation Japanese don't intermarry a lot.[189]

My friends were rather mixed. The group I went around with had a few *hakujin* friends in it but there was only one other Japanese boy. The rest of the group were Chinese. We did not have many Filipinos or Portuguese in our high school and at the university, so that is why I did not know them so well. There were a few Koreans in school but we did not associate much with them. At the university there was only one Negro student and he got along very well as he was a well-known leader in his group.

The first time I was really aware of racial feeling was when I came to San Francisco. I was greatly shocked when I first heard the California Nisei speaking contemptuously of the Chinese and the Filipinos. Then I began to see examples of racial prejudice which were reported in the newspapers. I never heard of the term "kikes" or *kuichis* until I heard some Nisei in San Francisco speak of the Jewish people in this way. I don't think I ever saw a Jewish person before. If there were any that I saw in Hawaii I did not know that they were Jews. So my first impression of California was not so good, as I noticed people talking about the Jews, "P.I.'s," Chinks, and Japs.

I did not come to California until 1935. During my days in college I had worked for a short time for a Captain and Mrs. [S]. Mrs. [S] was an island girl whose family had been there for 50 years, and she had very liberal attitudes. She and her husband were coming to the mainland because her husband had been transferred from his Army

---

[189] Romanzo Adams (*Interracial Marriage in Hawaii*, New York, Macmillan, 1937, p. 193) computed indexes of in-marriage practice for the various "racial" groups in Hawaii, by five-year periods, 1912–1934, "by dividing the number of brides and grooms who marry within their own group by the total number, the quotient showing how many in-married to 1,000." The Japanese had consistently the highest index, varying between 948 and 996 per 1,000, compared with indexes of 721 to 817 for the Chinese, and average indexes for "all races" that varied from 715 to 858.

post to the Presidio in San Francisco. I was getting very restless sitting around the house doing nothing for a year, and I was rather disturbed that an A.B. degree was meaningless. I decided to come with Captain [S] and his wife as a domestic worker as I felt that if I came to the mainland I would be able to save up some money and eventually do some graduate work.

I had great hopes and ambition of becoming a librarian. I was so restless in the islands and I did not see any future there at all. After I got to San Francisco, however, things did not go along according to my hopes. I was only receiving $30 a month in my job to start with. There were so many new things that I could spend money on that I did not even begin to save anything for a whole year. My initial expenses were rather heavy, as I had to get warmer clothes for the San Francisco weather. Then I started to go around and I spent a lot of money seeing plays, operas, and ballets as I never had this opportunity in Hawaii. I was also sending $10 a month home regularly, and even more later when I was getting a larger salary. Because of these things I soon lost my ambition, and I was afraid to get out of domestic work.

I got to know a few of the Nisei girls through the JACL. [I met] two other Hawaiian Nisei girls in San Francisco and after we got well acquainted, they suggested that we should join the JACL in order to meet other people. Around 1936 there was a large JACL get-together so that I went down there for the first time. At that meeting, I met a few interesting Nisei girls and they introduced me around. One of them is still my closest friend. Most of the Nisei girls I got to know were domestic workers and they had come to San Francisco from other parts of California. And most of them were sending money home to help their families also. There were about six girls in our group. After that I got to know some of the other Nisei girls who were working on Grant Avenue. They urged me to get a Grant Avenue job as a clerical worker in one of the Japanese art goods stores. However, the pay was very low and most of these girls were only getting about $50 a month. I decided to stay in domestic work as I felt that I could save more money this way.

In the beginning I was only interested in the JACL because it was a means for finding social companionship. Later on I got more interested in some of the other activities which it was carrying on. It was because of this interest that I became more and more conscious of the Nisei problem in California, and I felt that something had to be done about it. In a short time I began to disagree with some of the ways the leaders of the JACL were handling things. I felt that they were approaching the problem in a wrong way by attempting to work exclusively within the Japanese group instead of trying to draw Caucasians and other minority groups into the organization. I particularly felt that the JACL should have joined with the Chinese Americans since they had common problems.

When the Japan-China war started after 1937, I was disappointed that the JACL would never take a definite stand on the issue. And I thought that this was a big mistake. I met the editor of a small Nisei magazine, and I thought that he had the right view. He was much more positive in his stand and he wanted the JACL to come forth and make a statement against the Japanese imperialistic policy. He felt that this was necessary in order to safeguard the Nisei position. I agreed more with this way of thinking so that I began to help him on his magazine. Another reason why I got in with [this magazine] was because I had had journalistic ambitions at one time. I did most of the copy- and proofreading and I also did some rewrite work. The magazine had only a circulation of about 1,000 so that my work was purely voluntary, but I enjoyed it nevertheless.

After I was in San Francisco a year or so, I found out that most of the Nisei had absolutely no interest in politics. The Nisei were not interested in anything, as far as I could see, except for a few liberal individuals. Most of the Nisei were apathetic anyway and they were too much engrossed in themselves. They were just not educated toward these things. They had gone to college all right, but they never had taken part in any of the campus activities as far as I could see. Since they stuck within themselves, they did not know other nationality groups, so that they had a very narrow attitude towards them.

Another factor was that most of the Nisei only made a bare living, so that they did not have time to think about these other things. They also figured that they were too small a group to do anything anyway. One of the things I noticed about a great number of Nisei was that they seemed to have some sort of inferiority complex. A lot of the Nisei I knew personally did not care to ever go downtown to the nicer places for fear that the people would stare at them. I discovered that there was plenty of prejudice when the Nisei tried to get jobs but as far as I could see the Caucasian people were not openly antagonistic toward the Nisei in other things. In fact, the Nisei could have been very acceptable.

The Issei in San Francisco did not make a very good impression upon me either, as they seemed so Japanesy and yet so Americanized at the same time. They all dressed like Americans while back home in Hawaii many of the Issei were still wearing kimonos. Yet the Issei in California were much more provincial minded than the Hawaiian Issei. They only had limited contacts with the Caucasians and I discovered that most of the Issei women never talked to a Caucasian. The California Issei were very small about things and they did not think of problems in terms of the people as a whole but only in terms of their own limited little community. They acted like small-town hicks in spite of the fact that they were living in a large metropolitan city. This was very surprising to me because I had come over with the impression that the California Issei would be much more modern in their thinking than the Issei in Hawaii.

I have always been interested in my voting privilege. I registered for the first time in 1934 during the Hawaiian general elections. After I was in San Francisco for a couple of years, I became a registered voter and I voted for the first time in California during the primary election in 1938. I never voted a straight ticket although I tended to be Republican in my opinion.

I worked for Captain [S] until 1937. He then was transferred to a military post in Kansas and I did not want to go way out there. I felt that I would like to stay in San Francisco since there were better paying domestic jobs there. I also still had some vague ideas of going to the University of California for the librarian course. I hunted around and got another domestic job with the [W] family and I immediately forgot about my further education. I started out by getting $65 a month at that job which was quite a raise for me, and I also got raises after that so that I was getting $85 by the time of evacuation. This was in addition to room and board.

The [W's] never had employed an Oriental maid before I went there as they had been using Negro servants for years. However, they were quite liberal in their attitudes and they were more than satisfied with me. They also became much more understanding toward the Nisei. I was fairly contented while I was there as they treated me practically like their own child. I was able to save quite a bit of money from this job, and by this time I was getting selfish and I did not want to quit my nice job to go to school. I thought that it would be better for me to save the money as I wanted to have something when I got married.

I met a Chinese American fellow from Los Angeles in 1938 whom I became very much interested in. He was a cadet officer in the United States Merchant Marine. He and I became very friendly in spite of the fact that I did not see him for a long time between trips. He was the first Chinese to ever get the cadet commission in the U.S. Merchant Marine. Later on he had quite a difficult time getting a regular merchant marine commission. I did not get to see him too often after that because he went all over the Pacific but his boat rarely touched San Francisco. However, I did correspond with him a great deal. By the spring of 1941 there was a sort of understanding. A few months before the war started, he wrote me from the Philippines that we would definitely get maried as soon as he could come to San Francisco. I did not hear from him again until December of 1942 when I got a telegram from his brother in Los Angeles saying that the Navy had listed him among the missing. However, on Easter morning (1943) he was heard over the short-wave radio from a prison camp in Java saying that he was a prisoner of war and that he was well. The Federal Communications Authority had informed [his] brother of his broadcast and his brother had written me details of it. This is the main reason why my marriage plans are so indefinite now and it is also one of the main reasons why I volunteered in the WACs recently.

I kept working in San Francisco until the war started. In the beginning, I had frequent spells of homesickness. In 1940 I went home for a vacation and I decided then that I liked it better in San Francisco so back I came. Before the war I had some idea of staying in San Francisco permanently. There were so many things that were better in San Francisco and it seemed much more cultural and sophisticated than the Islands. I knew that I could never get used to the more limited life in Honolulu after that. The friends I had were mostly among the Nisei, but I also had several *hakujin* friends. On the whole, though, my contacts were most with the Nisei. I did not like that so much and I wanted to meet more Caucasians and Chinese but I did not get the chance. I met a few Chinese during the time that I went to the Chinese YWCA for swimming, but I never did get close to them. They were very different from the Chinese in Hawaii and they were even more afraid to mix than the Nisei.

Since I have been on the mainland I stopped going to church completely. The churches in San Francisco seem to be so big and impersonal that I did not enjoy going to them. None of my Nisei friends went to these churches and I did not feel like going all by myself. I didn't go in much for formal religion anyway after I got into college. I think that as long as I don't do anything unconventional and if I live right, I do not necessarily have to go to church.

We had a Hawaiian club in San Francisco and some of the other members played Hawaiian music on their instruments occasionally. In this club we had Chinese Hawaiians also and there [were] no difficulties in mixing. After 1941 I got very interested in knitting as a hobby and I did quite a bit of it for the Red Cross. I also read a great deal since the [W's] had a very good collection of books. I also played badminton and went swimming occasionally. The rest of the time I visited with my friends. Before Japan started the war with China, I had a membership in the Chinese YWCA but the attitude was not so good afterward, so that I decided not to renew it.

I don't think that I was ever very bored before evacuation since my time was pretty well taken up with these things. I had more and more responsibilities in my work because Mrs. [W] died and I had to take care of Mr. [W]. He was quite elderly by then so that I acted as a companion to him. I also did a lot of my corresponding during this period, as I had former Hawaiian friends scattered over a large part of the United States, mostly in southern California however. It was a rather drifting life that I was living before the war and I had no definite plans for anything, except marriage, which was vague also.

How well I remember December 7th because that started a whole lot of changes in my life. Sunday was my usual day off and I was supposed to go see my Nisei girl friend to have lunch with her. She was working in a domestic job also. I was over there about 10:30 in the morning and we were just talking. The radio was not on. About 11 o'clock the nursemaid came dashing downstairs. She was very excited because she said that Pearl Harbor was being bombed. I thought that she was trying to play some kind of joke on us because this woman was in the habit of playing practical jokes. I did not take her seriously as I also felt that it was just some kind of an Orson Welles broadcast. The nursemaid insisted that it was true but I would not believe her. Finally my girl friend turned on the radio in the room and sure enough it was true.

The first thing I thought of during the numbness which came over me was about my family back in Honolulu. I wanted to get word from them or to them immediately. However, the radio said for nobody to use the phone, so that I didn't try to get a radiogram through. I was so excited that I forgot about lunch. My girl friend suggested that we should go to another Nisei girl's home to visit her. After we were there a while we began to wonder what would happen to Japanese town. I phoned down to another friend down there and she said that the police were surrounding Japanese town and keeping all the curious people away. We got curious too, so that her father decided to drive us all down there late that afternoon. When we got there it did not look like Japanese town at all because the streets were all deserted except for about three policemen on every corner and the police car cruising up and down the street. The only thing Japanese we saw was the various Japanese signs.

After dinner I went back to my place of work. Before I went to bed I talked for quite a while with Mr. [W] who was very upset about what had happened. However, he tried to calm me down as he said that nothing would happen to me since I was a loyal American citizen and he also thought that my family were safe also. He said that the radio reports did not say the city of Honolulu was bombed so that I should not feel too anxious about my family or else I would get sick. I was too upset to think clearly on anything and the full impact of the war did not dawn upon me until much later, as I was primarily concerned about my family.

The next day I had a cablegram from my mother in Hawaii so that my mind immediately became more settled. It was such a relief after the tension of the preceding day. I did not give any thought as to what would happen to the Japanese in the United States. I did not conceive of anything like evacuation. My main thought after I got the telegram was to rejoin my family. I had quite a bit of money in the bank by then so that I went to the Matson Lines to see if I could get passage immediately. I was told that all reservations had been canceled and that the Navy had frozen all shipping, so that I could not possibly go. I was feeling rather worried about this and I imagined all sorts of things. I was also getting desperate. Finally I went down to the Pan American Airways office to ask if I could get a Clipper reservation but it was the same thing again. They said that there was no telling when the next boat or plane would go to Hawaii. I had counted on the Clipper as my one chance to get home, and when I found out that this was impossible, I was so disappointed that I broke down and cried and cried right in the office. It was rather embarrassing for the people in the office as there was nothing they could do.

I was very confused during the next week or so and I lost quite a bit of weight from worry. Mr. [W] was very considerate. On December

16, 1941, Mr. [W] moved to [a suburb] and I went along with him, as
I had found out by this time that I could not go home. I did not know
what my plans were going to be as everything was so indefinite. I had
certain fears when the waterfront areas of San Francisco were closed
to enemy aliens and the FBI started to round up Japanese in earnest.
I heard so many rumors but I did not know what to think. However,
I thought that the FBI must have had good reasons for the roundup
because many of the Issei had connections with pro-Japan organizations. This was a justified action because of the war. And the government had to remove the aliens from strategic places right away for
the public safety.

[Soon] the talk started about the general evacuation of the Issei.
More and more reports appeared in the newspapers about this possibility. The papers were generally sympathetic until about February.
The Governor had made favorable statements in regard to the Nisei
loyalty so that it never occurred to me that anything could possibly
affect us. Then around February the sentiment in the newspaper and
radio got more and more anti-Japanese due to the battles that Japan
was winning. Even though I did not think it was fair to evacuate all
of the Issei from strategic areas, I thought it had to be done because
of the danger of invasion. Soon the Japanese started to say that if the
Issei went, the Nisei would also have to go because there were so many
young children involved. I could not believe that all of the Nisei
would ever be moved because I said that we were Americans and that
such actions were against the laws of this country.

I was amazed when all of the restrictions began to be applied to all
of the Nisei. I was a little angry but I felt helpless about it. Then the
news came out saying that we had to register and all go to a camp. By
this time I thought that most of the Nisei would only be gone for a
few weeks at most and then surely we would be cleared by the FBI and
allowed to return to our places of work and to our homes.

I was not very disturbed when I heard rumors that the Filipinos
were killing Japanese along the coast as I thought that such things
were bound to happen during a period of hysteria. It started out after
Manila was taken by the Japanese Army, and I did not blame the
Filipinos for killing the Japanese in what they considered as revenge
since every one is not calm when their blood relatives' homes are being
bombed and parents being killed.

Most of the people in [the suburb] thought I was Chinese and even
when I got on the train to commute to San Francisco for the week end

I never was bothered and people did not even look at me. By that time I had permanently given up any plans for education. Even my work was so indefinite so I just did not make any plans for anything. I still hoped to go to Hawaii.

One day in March, 1942, I went to the Pan American Airways for a final effort but I was told that there was absolutely no chance for my getting passage on the Clipper because the Navy had taken over the company and only the essential people could go to Hawaii. No Japanese were allowed to leave the mainland. After that I began to think of other possibilities in regard to my future plans. I decided that maybe I should go to New York because I had a Chinese friend there who invited me to come.

All of a sudden, bang, everything was frozen and I could not go during the final hours before the restriction set in because I was alone with Mr. [W] who was helpless. His sister was away in [southern California] trying to arrange a place for them to live down there. I could not get in touch with her so that my chance for voluntary evacuation to New York passed. I wrote to the Provost Marshal in San Francisco asking for a permit to allow me to go to New York but this was refused. He said that the only thing that I could do was to register and go to a camp. I was so sure that my plan would be delayed for only a few weeks that I was not too greatly disturbed when the Provost Marshal turned me down.

I only had a few contacts among the Nisei and I was away from Japanese town so that I did not go through a general upset feeling of the Japanese community. I did not feel any bitterness or anything as I realized that evacuation was one of those emergency things that was bound to happen in wartime. I still had faith in the United States but I thought that if the Nisei had taken more part in the community life and if they had gotten to know the Caucasians better, such drastic steps would not have been taken.

I did not have the least idea of where we were going to be sent but I thought that it would be Tanforan. This was okay with me as I felt that I would be able to see my San Francisco friends then. [But for a while] the WCCA would not tell us where we were going. It was finally announced that the [Japanese in our suburb] were going to be sent to Santa Anita and I tried to get to Tanforan but the Army would not let me go. On May 26 I was sent to Santa Anita with the rest of the people [from this suburb]. By that time most of the Japanese in California had already been evacuated. I heard rumors that most of the people going to the camps were caught short without anything. That is why I took along bedding, kitchen utensils, buckets, basins, toilet tissues, towels, all my clothes, and anything else I could think of. I wanted to take as much as I could so that I would be comfortable and I just disregarded the WCCA instructions to take only what I could carry.

We left by bus and it took us to [a city] where a special train for the people was being filled. Mr. [W] was very upset because he felt he had stopped me from going to New York. He gave me $170 as a parting present. This was two months' extra pay. I was lacking those two months to be working a total of five years for him. The uncomfortable part of the trip started when I got on the train. It was so crowded that there were not enough seats to go around so that I had to stand up all night. It was the most uncomfortable trip that I had ever made. It took us 24 hours to get to Santa Anita. We had cold box lunches three times and this upset many of the older people on the train as they were not used to it. A lot of the Issei had brought Japanese food along with them so that they passed it around. That was then I felt that we were all in the same boat together.

Finally after a most miserable trip we got to Santa Anita. I saw the barbed-wire fences immediately and I thought to myself, "This is the end." I realized then and there that it was not going to be a very easy matter to get out. Somebody on the train said that we were going to be in there for the duration and that made me feel almost ill. I think I even got a little panicky. I had some sort of a wild idea to make my escape and lose myself in Los Angeles but this was only a thought as I would never have the courage to do that. I felt that I had been cheated but I did not know why.

After we were registered, I was put into a room with another Nisei single girl. The first few days in camp were very confused for me and I went around in a sort of dream-like daze. It still did not seem true to me. There were quite a few Nisei wandering around who had a bewildered look on their faces. However, people are adjustable and most of the Japanese in camp immediately began to make the best of it and make their homes as comfortable as possible. I had met another girl on the train coming down and she was only half-Japanese. She looked completely Occidental. When I saw her walking around camp bewildered also and when I saw what they were doing to her, I thought that I was not so bad off as she was.

In time I got a little settled and I began to look for friends. There were not very many San Francisco people there that I knew since most of them went to Tanforan. I met a Hawaiian Nisei boy whom I had known in the Islands and I certainly fell upon him as a long lost friend. Later on I did meet a few of the San Francisco people who had been sent there in the first group out of the Bay area. Outside of these very few people that I could count on my fingers, I did not know anybody among the 20,000 people who were there.

When I got a chance to think again, I determined that I wanted to get out as soon as I could. I was willing to take any possibility that would get me out. It did not look as if there would be any sort of a chance. However, in a few weeks after the camp got settled, the Student Relocation people came around and they passed out forms for people who wanted to go out to school. I filled out one of the forms in the hopes that this would be the method for me to get out of camp. I was told that I could get out if I could find a school that would accept me. I had my transcripts from the University of Hawaii so that I started to write the various universities which offered library training. Only the larger schools had this course and they either could not accept Nisei or else they were too expensive for me.

I was in Santa Anita from May, 1942, to September, 1942. During that time I did not work at all as I thought I would be able to get out almost any day. There was not much choice in jobs in Santa Anita anyway and it took a long time to get placed on the payroll. The salary was too small and I did not want to bother with it. As the weeks rolled by I began to take another attitude. I more or less resigned myself and I soon thought that I should make camp a vacation because I had worked for so many years. We had to stand in line for everything and I spent most of my time in Santa Anita this way. I stood in line for meals, for showers, and even for the women's latrine. About the only constructive thing I did was knitting.

I made some acquaintances but they were not very lasting. Being a stranger it was too difficult to break into any of those old-established cliques anyway. There were a number of very worthwhile Nisei in camp but the total was comparatively small. The average Nisei were flighty and they never gave a serious thought to anything. They had no ambition or idea of their future. Most of them were quite bitter, I think, and they did not make a very good impression on me. The majority of the Nisei were too busy trying to get dates to think about anything else.

The Issei took things pretty good. They always are that way and they are able to make adjustments better because of their greater experience. A lot of them went in for handicrafts, making gardens, sewing, and English classes. They did not seem too bitter. I suppose it is a Japanese characteristic to resign oneself easily as they certainly did in Santa Anita.

The Kibei were very unpopular among the Nisei because [they were] outspokenly pro-Japan. Their ideas were so different from that of most Nisei that the two groups just did not get along. I never did like the Kibei and even in Hawaii the second-generation Nisei do not like them. I could not stand their attitude towards girls. The Kibei followed the old Japanese custom and they treated girls as if we were something beneath them. I met a few Kibei in San Francisco and I just did not like any of them because of their attitudes. I tried to be tolerant of them but they rubbed me the wrong way. The Kibei talked Japanese right out in the street in a very loud voice even if they were downtown. I just did not like their looks. There is something different about them.

I liked the Hawaiian group [at Santa Anita] much better. Those that I had known in San Francisco were an older group and they were not like the loud noisy ones in Los Angeles. On the whole, I think that the Hawaiian Nisei are definitely much more Americanized than the California Nisei. That is the main reason why they do not get along so well with the Nisei on the mainland. They don't keep together in restricted communities like in California but they were more adventurous and they had seen quite a bit of America. This country actually meant more to them, even if their English was not so good. The Hawaiian Nisei are much more contemptuous of things Japanese than the Californians. Another thing was that the Hawaiian-Japanese families did not send so many of their sons to Japan for an education because they had been in the islands a long time. These families definitely planned to stay in Hawaii, whereas the mainland Japanese families still thought about going back to Japan more because they were not accepted so much by the people of California. The Nisei in California were much younger as a group and they had not become independent yet.

While in Santa Anita I still managed to keep up my contacts with the outside. I could not get over the feeling that I was in a jail. We had a special visitor's house for our friends to come to. There was a long table running down the center and we had to stay on the other side of the table, five feet across from our friends. We couldn't even reach over to shake hands or pass anything across. There were guards there to enforce the rules. Then another thing, we could only visit with our friends for a half hour even if they had come from a long distance. I resented this more than anything in Santa Anita as I felt that it was an insult. I just did not feel like having any visitor at all to let them go through this awful experience.

However. I did not become bitter against this country but I did blame it on Japan. I hated Japan worse than ever and I blamed it for our predicament in camp. I hated Japan more than Germany and Italy and I even feel the same way now because what Japan has done has touched me more. I realized in camp that the Japanese had brought this upon themselves to a certain degree, and yet I saw that it was something that they had to go through before they are completely integrated. We were born at the wrong time, that's all. The Chinese went through a very difficult stage and I saw the way the Negroes are being treated in the South. Then I realized that things were not half as bad as I thought. But that does not mean that we have to take it and resign ourselves to such a position. One of the main things that we have to keep in mind all the time is that the Nisei have to change their own attitudes first because they are even more intolerant than the Caucasians. I used to get into many arguments with Nisei before the war on these points. I told them that they should not talk so much about racial discrimination when they showed such intolerant attitudes against the Chinese, Filipinos, Jews, and Negroes. I did not think that it was possible for the Nisei to have such intolerant views since they were of a minority group.

When I saw that I would not be released before [the Santa Anita group was] sent to a WRA camp, I began to prepare for moving once again. I did not have very much packing to do. Nobody knew where we were going to be sent next. We were put on the train and it was only then that we found out for sure that we were going to Heart Mountain, the WRA camp in Wyoming.

The barrenness of the place was the first thing that struck me. There was absolutely no green in sight. There was not even a tree except for some small shrubs. The place was covered with rocks. In the camp itself it was even more barren. I felt like I was in the middle of nowheres. That determined me more than ever to devote my full time to getting out of camp. One of the most depressing things about Heart Mountain was the guard towers which were placed around the camp. At night we would see the search lights going back and forth. In addition there was a barbed-wire fence around us and these things made me feel more than ever that I was in prison. We could not even step out of the camp at all. When I got there, the first thing which greeted us was a dust storm. In the days that followed we found that nothing could keep this dust out as it would sift through the tiniest cracks in our barracks. Everything appeared so dirty about the camp. The barracks were very discouraging. They were made out of wide planks with dreary, black tar paper on the outside. Later on, we had some white plaster boards put on the inside. They also put celotex in the barracks to keep the cold out.

When I first got there, I was moved in with my girl friend's family. However, it was too crowded there with seven people in one room so that I went to the women's dormitory. There were four single girls there with me.

I did not work at all during the time I was in Heart Mountain because I was so determined to get out. It was not until January 15 of this year that I succeeded. I had written various letters in order to get out of camp. I did not care where I went or what sort of job I was offered just so I could leave. Finally a girl friend in [a Midwestern city] told me of a job up there. I went immediately to see the leave officer in camp, so that I could fill out my application for a clearance and an indefinite leave. The leave officer thought I was applying for a job through the WRA, therefore, he sent my application to the Washington office and said that I was available for a domestic job. It just happened that a Mr. [K] was looking for a Nisei girl to go with his family to Florida. He had written to the WRA and asked for a person immediately. The WRA employment section gave him my name. Right after New Years I got a telegram from him asking for my qualifications. It specified that I had to be a Protestant Christian. I sent him a special delivery letter telling him of my work experience and also referred him to my former employer for a character reference. A day or so after that Mr. [K] sent another telegram and he said that he wanted me to come right away. The WRA quickened my release so that it was the fastest that any evacuee had ever gotten out of Heart Mountain. I packed my things in great haste and on January 14 I left camp forever. I doubt if anyone missed me because I did not know many people there. I got to [the Midwestern city] on January 15 after traveling all day and night on the train. On the following day I came to Chicago and I met Mr. [K] and his family here. We left for [a resort city in] Florida on the 17th according to the schedule.

It is really hard to describe the elation I felt as I walked around [these cities]. I felt like a released jail-bird and I was very happy to leave the drab camp life behind me forever. Nothing could have ever gotten me back to camp again. I would have gone to any length to stay out of camp after I got out.

I got $60 a month when I first started to work for Mr. [K]. After loafing around for eight months the work seemed extremely hard. It was a very large house so that I had plenty to do. For some reason I did not get along as well with Mrs. [K] because she always seemed to strike me in the wrong way.

Florida is a beautiful place in the winter time and it reminded me very strongly of Waikiki Beach. The only difference was that the homes in Florida were much more elegant and occupied by wealthier people. [The resort] was just full of soldiers who were in various training camps in the area. Most of the soldiers thought that I was a Chinese so that I got along extremely well with them. There were quite a few Chinese fellows attached to the air corps there and I got to meet most of them through a Chinese friend that I had formerly known in Hawaii. I went out on a few dates but I didn't go out too much. I met quite a few of the *hakujin* boys who were in the air corps. They were mostly from the New England states so that they thought I was quite a novelty. They had never seen an Oriental before. They were even more interested when I told them I was from Hawaii and most of them were very much surprised when they found out that I spoke fluent English.

There were two Japanese families living in [the city]. They had been there for many years and both of them had operated nurseries for over 30 years. I met one of the couples and they were quite elderly. They did not seem Japanese at all and they spoke much better English than most of the Nisei I had seen in California. The Japanese [there] did not know much about the evacuation because they had not been affected at all. They were doing business as usual with the same old customers. About the only time they were ever questioned was at the outbreak of the war and when those German saboteurs who landed in Florida from a submarine were caught. The Japanese families there had been accepted by the community, so that there was little suspicion placed upon them.

One of the things that I noticed in Florida which bothered me was that there was quite a bit of prejudice against the Negroes. I felt very sorry for them because of the hard time they had. Most of the *hakujin* people I met in Florida took it for granted that I was Chinese so that sometimes we would stop to talk about Madame Chiang Kai-shek. I think that she is a remarkable woman, so I did not mind talking about her. I did not tell these people that I was Japanese. It was not because I was ashamed or anything like that but it was more convenient to let them continue to think that I was Chinese, and then they would not bother me with so many questions.

In the middle of May we went back to [the Middle West]. For the first couple of weeks I was busy getting used to the work so that I did not see anybody. The work was not so bad but I was just not satisfied for some reason. The restless feeling began to increase more and more. I had done domestic work for years and I never was this restless before.

I met quite a few Japanese [who came to the city from a near-by Army Camp]. They were lonesome too, I suppose. so that they would call on me and I went out on quite a few dates. I had much more of a social life than in camp but I still could not get away from the feeling of being unsettled. I went to almost all of the dances at the YMCA, [Army Camp], and the USO. I went chiefly with the Hawaiian Nisei soldiers that I met from [the Army Camp]. The USO and [Army Camp] dances were not limited to Nisei alone. The "Y" dances, however, were for just the Nisei and every Saturday night about 150 of them would come.

The Nisei soldiers mixed with the Caucasians quite a bit and quite a few of them were taking out Caucasian girls. I never noticed any antagonistic feeling up there because the people seemed very tolerant toward the Nisei. There are a number of German-descent Americans in that area, so that they were inclined to be more sympathetic toward the evacuees. Because they are put together [in the Army], the Nisei soldiers do not feel the need of spreading out so much. It is rather funny that the government puts all of the Nisei together in the Army but tells them to spread out when they are resettling. You can't expect the Nisei in the Army to spread out when they are treated in this way.

I had no strings attached to me and I was getting more and more restless all the time, so that I began to think of joining the WACs. I knew that I could fulfill all of the requirements and this seemed to be a good opportunity for me. I was getting sick and tired of doing domestic work all the time and I wanted a change. I wanted to do something more directely related with the war effort. I felt that I would not feel so restless if I got into the WACs. Then I would have the satisfaction of knowing that I was doing something directly to help [my fiance] out instead of waiting around in a rut. Then I also felt that the Japanese were going to have a harder time than anybody else after the war. I thought that if I joined the WACs, I would be better fitted to get a job afterward. The prospects of doing only domestic work all the time was not very pleasing to me and I knew that I would not do anything about further education.

I also had other reasons. I felt that the Nisei had to do more than give lip service to the United States and by joining the WACs I could prove my sincerity. Some of the Nisei girls I knew said that I would be sent overseas and would get killed. But this is the chance everybody has to take. After all, this is everybody's war and we all have to put an equal share into it. I don't know why the Nisei objected so much to my joining the WACs. They said that I was crazy because the WACs had a bad reputation and only the cheap girls went into it. A lot of the Nisei thought that I was joining because I was "a sad case" and going to be an old maid. The Nisei boys thought it was unwise for me to join the WACs also. Some of them told me that a whole boat load of WACs had been sent back from Africa with venereal diseases but they could not prove it. One Nisei girl told me that the other Japanese would look down on her family in camp if she joined up so that was the reason she was against it. Most of the Nisei girls said that they would not join because they would never be able to get married then.

I refused to listen to all of their arguments as I was determined to join anyway. I did not think that the other Nisei were being patriotic enough when they gave me all of these selfish reasons for not joining but I could not condemn them for it. You know how the Nisei are. They are very much on the defensive and when a good opportunity is opened up they are opposed to it. I went to the WAC recruiting station late in July with my mind made up. However, I did not apply for enlistment on that visit, as I only wanted to get the full information. I wrote to my mother and explained that I wanted to join the WACs and I asked her to give her consent. In August my mother sent me a letter and she said that she approved of the idea very much because I had made up my mind by myself. She told me that perhaps it was best for me to do it, as there was not much future in my remaining in domestic work. As soon as I got this letter I went to the WAC recruiting station and volunteered. I filled out all of the papers and in August I took my physical and mental examination. The WAC officer told me that I could expect to be called early in October but she was not sure.

I am disappointed that the Nisei are not volunteering into the Army or the WACs as much as they should. They are not even joining the U. S. Cadet Nursing Corps as much as they could. They make me sick when they give me some of the silly excuses for not joining. I have an idea that most of the Nisei girls are afraid to take the first step. They are waiting for a few guinea pigs to go in and send back a report. This seems to be typical of the Nisei. They don't want to do anything on their own. I feel that I want to be one of the first as there will be more chances for advancement than if I went in with a mob. The only thing I worry about is that they may put all of the Nisei girls in a segregated unit like the Nisei combat team. That would be unfortunate as it is better if we can spread out.

After I get into the WACs, I think that I will get the chance to learn some sort of a profession or a trade. I will be able to use this after the war in the event that I have to work after I get married. Now that I feel that I am doing something constructive, I feel like a useful individual. It will be very good for my morale. I have never been satisfied doing domestic work as there is always that slight feeling of being in an inferior position. Now I can go into the WACs and be on an equal footing with everybody else and this has given me quite a mental lift. I also feel that I am contributing something toward the real achievement of democracy. If we just look at it from the Nisei point of view, it will do more to get them better known among the Caucasians with a greater resulting tolerance. Not enough *hakujin* have known the Nisei up to now and this is our great chance.

CH-21: RESTAURANT KEEPER

Male; born in Washington, 1916; height 64"; weight 118 lbs.; unmarried. Interviewed "intensively, over a period of two weeks" in November, 1943. Described as "a rather slender person, who does not smile too freely." He was "most coöperative throughout the interviews, and talked easily and at great length."

CAREER LINES

Parental: Both parents came from farming classes in Japan. Father (born 1881) completed five years' elementary school and two years in a middle school in Japan, "specializing in Chinese classics." Emigrated in 1902. Worked as schoolboy in Tacoma, then operated a general merchandise store in Seattle from 1909 to 1923. Lost the store during depression and worked as dishwasher at a lunch counter from

1923 to 1925. Proprietor, manager, and cook in his own family restaurant from 1925 to 1942. Mother (born 1889) finished grammar
school in Japan; immigrated to Seattle as picture bride in 1914.
Own: Completed sophomore year at college in Washington in 1942.
After high school graduation in 1935, worked for a few months in a
Japanese-owned produce house. Started to work in his father's restaurant at the age of 15, and continued, intermittently, as "unpaid
family worker" and as managing partner until 1942. Inmigrated to
Chicago in May, 1943. Worked as laborer in a printing firm until
September, 1943, then as clerk in an advertising agency. He was hold-
ing this job at the time of the interviews.

LIFE HISTORY

I don't know much about my parents' background. I don't think there
was anything to be proud about. My father came from a farm family
in the Kumamoto *ken.* He was the fourth of five sons and he was not
in line to inherit a thing. Two of his older brothers came over before
he did for the same reason. That makes my father the third of his
family to come to America. My mother was also from a farm family.
However, her father was also a merchant at times. Dad first heard of
her through some relatives or friends. My father came to America in
1902 and he has never gone back.

I only have a vague picture of what my father did before he got
married. I know that he first came to Tacoma, Washington, and he
worked as a houseboy. His older brother was in Seattle then and this
brother was in the hotel business for the other immigrant Japanese.
It was quite a boom time in Seattle so that this uncle of mine became
rather wealthy. When my father was working as a houseboy, his employer promised to help him get an education, but Dad heard about
how rich his older brother was getting and he decided that he wanted
quick money himself, so he went to Seattle in 1910. After he saved up
a little money he opened up a combination variety and fruit store in
the Japanese section which was developing around [X] Street. Several
years later his marriage was arranged. He called my mother over and
the family was started. In 1915, my brother was born, and I followed
a year later. There were three boys and two girls in all.

During the First World War there was also a boom in Seattle and
my father was doing quite well. However, the downfall was just as
rapid and in 1919 my father's store went broke. From then on the
family had a pretty tough time of it. My mother suffered extreme

ill-health and she was bedridden for quite a while around 1923. My father opened up a fruit stand and a soft-drink parlor on [X] Street, right in the center of the Japanese town.

It was quite hard on my father after all our troubles began. Mother was bedridden because I think that five kids in six years was quite a strain on her. My father would work 14 or 15 hours a day at the store and then come home to take care of all the little kids. This did not do his disposition any good. When my brother was 7, some more trouble came upon the family. He fractured his leg and it got infected so that he had to be sent to a hospital. It was a huge expense and my father's second store went broke on account of all the money that had to be spent. Dad did not have any capital to start another store, so he worked a while as a porter and dishwasher in a hotel. I think it might have been in my rich uncle's hotel but I am not sure. Anyway, I know that my father held three jobs all at one time and he almost wore himself out in trying to keep the family going. After that, mother got better so that the family strain was relieved a little.

About 1927 my father had saved enough money to buy a restaurant. This time it was not in the Japanese section, but on the skidrow a little distance from the Japanese community. It was a cheap slop house which catered to the unemployed and the bums. We had this restaurant until the evacuation.

There were very many good qualities about my father, but I did not appreciate them fully until after I was out of his control. Dad was very immaculate in his home life. He was highly principled and he demanded it of others. He was inclined to be quite severe in judging other people's characters, especially his own kids. I would say that he was of average intelligence although at times he appeared to be a little smarter than that.

Dad was always very careful of his money because of the hard time he had. He frowned very much upon one of my uncles who went out on frequent splurges. My father said to us that we had to go through life on our own strength and not depend upon others. He has always followed this rule himself and he never asked his richer brother for money. I suppose that was due to his stubborn pride and he did not want to admit to anyone that he was a failure. He just considered things as temporary setbacks and he always believed that his boat would come home some day. [But] during the depression, my father was extremely despondent and he was ready to throw up the sponge. There did not seem to be any way at all by which we could save the business. The business was only saved when mother secretly borrowed some money from my uncle in order to carry on. My father got extremely angry at this, but he used the money and that was what set him back on his feet.

My father was always puritanical in his attitudes and he never talked about sex to his children. Sex was always around in a very ugly form in the neighborhood we lived in, but Dad never mentioned it to us. I did not learn about what the prostitutes did when they walked around skidrow until I was almost through high school.

Dad was quite a stickler for things Japanese. He was sympathetic to Japan and that increased with the passage of years. He had that "naturally-Japan-will-win" attitude by the time the war broke out. We got this sort of thing constantly when we were kids and I adhered to it until I was in high school, because I was naïve. I did not have any strong conflicts on this point up to then. After that, I began to have my own opinions and naturally there were clashes with the old man. I couldn't stand his longing for Japan because I didn't think that he really believed it or else he would have gone back. When I was home I was quite severe in criticizing him, and this used to burn him up no end. I couldn't stand the way he tried to pound his ideas into me. I used to feel quite bitter toward him.

When Dad was younger he used to be active in the various Japanese clubs and particularly in the Kumamoto *kenjinkai,* which consisted of the people from his province. They used to get together a lot and chew the rag about the old country. Dad was also in the Japanese Chamber of Commerce for a while. His religious history is peculiar. When he was in Japan he became a Christian and attended the Japanese Congregational Church, and when he came over to this country he continued to be a Christian. My mother was a member of the *Konkokyokai* sect. They had a funny ceremony and they would clap wood together. Dad would snicker a lot about this and he finally was able to convert my mother to the Congregational Church. But during the last 15 years my father became very antichristian because of his political sympathies, while my mother became more and more of a devout Christian. It used to be quite a point of argument in our household because my mother wanted to send the children to the Congregational Church also. The conflict influenced my older brother and me the most and that is why we have never cared too much about religion.

My father would never give in during an argument. He was very dominant and he demanded absolute obedience by mother and the kids. He would even call my mother down if she slipped and used some form of speech to him which he considered an improper way of addressing the head of the household. He always assumed his place as the head of the family and he expected to be served first during meal times by my mother. However, Dad did have his lighter moments and he was quite proud of his family. But he was always conscious that the Nisei would not listen to their parents' advice. He thought that all Nisei became communists after they went to high school and he did not like this at all because he was quite opposed to this doctrine. He had an implict trust in the Japanese section of the language paper. A lot of the news releases in that paper came from Japan and naturally it was very anticommunist.

I think that Dad was never satisfied with his lot, but as we grew up he accepted his position more. He then put all of his hopes and ambition into his children. My mother was much more easy going. She was less strict upon us. The only trouble was that she was under Dad's thumb and he would not let her be too easy on us. After she recovered her health she worked hard. She worked in the restaurant for 15 hours a day in order to help out.

There was no love in my parents' marriage. They never had a freedom in showing affection for each other or even us. This was completely absent like in many of the Japanese families. The Japanese don't believe in kissing, you know. My parents' marriage was not too happy because of the hard struggles to make a living. There were periods of crisis as far back as I can remember.

Dad did not have much ease in his social relationships but mother got on well with other people. Dad's circle of friends talked mostly about politics and Japan's great future. He did not drink, however, like the other old Issei men in his circle.

When Dad was young, he had great ambitions because he came from a poor family and he thought that he would become very wealthy in America. It was a bitter disappointment for him to have to go through the poverty we went through and to have an ill wife and five young children to worry about besides. My uncle had a much easier time of it because he was a great success from the beginning. He owned one of the biggest hotels in Japanese town of Seattle. He was a big shot in the Japanese Hotel Association for a number of years and also prominent in some of the other Japanese organizations. He was a *baishakunin* on his own and he was always meddling around with other people's business. Whenever there was a death in some family in the Japanese section, he would go over to the house on his own and comfort them. He was a great Christian of the fanatic type and he loved to get up in front of the church audience and give an emotional, tear-jerking testimony. He was a sort of Seventh Day Adventist screwball. He had eight kids in his family.

I had quite a few relatives in Seattle. On Japanese and other holidays, it was mandatory for all of us to eat together at a big feast. It was one big family of over 25 members.

At home we ate Japanese food exclusively and we always spoke Japanese. We lived in the heart of Japanese town until my dad later moved us outside where the restaurant was located. Everybody spoke Japanese in the Japanese section and I did not pick up English rapidly until I went to the public schools. I can't speak Japanese very well now as I never used it with my Nisei friends.

While I was young we lived in a flat but later on we bought a house. I went to a public school where 1,000 other Nisei went. The school was 95 per cent Japanese. I also went to a Japanese language school for seven years but it was unprofitable. I can only write the simple stuff. I don't remember much of the propaganda although some of the teachers I've had were politically minded and they tried to make us kids take their point of view. Most of the time the teachers just taught us about the Japanese culture. It didn't go over very well because the majority of the Nisei students were antagonistic to the Japanese language school. They had to go to it after the regular school hours and that meant that all of their leisure time was tied up. It was felt to be a sort of honor among the boys to be less conscientious in Japanese classes. We were expected to go in late and make noise in class. The Nisei boys would never think of doing things like that in public schools.

As a youngster I was sort of timid. I had cross-eyes for a while and that made me draw back too. I felt sort of persecuted and I didn't think that any of the other children liked me very much. I did not mix much with them and I never was completely in any of the gangs although I palled around with some of the gang members. For a long time I was undersized and underage in school. I was behind the others until the fourth grade. My older brother was in the same class. He was a little smarter than I was, so that I got an inferiority complex about that.

By the time I was in the eighth grade I got in more with the fellows and led a more normal life. I went to another school, and there were more white students there. My first year in high school was in a class which was predominantly Caucasian students. It was a new experience to go to school with a lot of white children. But my adjustment to high school was not very good because I was working in my dad's restaurant as a kitchen helper after school and I could not fully concentrate upon a school life. As soon as my classes were over, I would have to rush down to the restaurant and start work right away. I did not get to play around like the other students did. That sort of spoiled my high school days and I regretted it very much, though I accepted the fact that I had to help in my dad's restaurant too.

In my junior year in high school, my dad pulled me out of school for a year because it was the worst part of the depression and the family was having a hard struggle to make both ends meet. My Dad could not afford to hire another worker so I had to step in and work. I went back to high school the next year and after that I wised up and I took a more mature attitude towards my studies and I did my homework regularly. School meant much more to me after working that year in the restaurant. It was a fad for all of the Nisei to try and make the Honor Society. I tried to make it also but it was a little beyond me.

I did not have any definite ambitions but I had secret desires to become a good writer. My greatest success in school was in the composition classes. I was taking a college preparatory course because I had vague ambitions to go to college. I did not take any extra curricular activities at all. My closest friend in school was a white kid. I just saw him around the class and we rarely had contacts after school because I still had to rush home to the restaurant.

In my senior year I started to go around with Japanese kids a lot. But I sort of sneered at the Japs and I felt superior to them because I felt that most of the Nisei had undeveloped [personalities] and that was why they were afraid to mix in more with the other students. It was during my senior year that I began to go in for a preponderance of heavy reading. All of the literature during that time emphasized the proletarian stuff and so I wrote themes about it for my high school classes. I could write about some of these things with feeling and that was another reason why I wanted to be a writer. I felt that I could champion the underdog as the skidrow side of life was open to me and I saw a lot of it.

It happened that when I was working in the restaurant, I was by myself mostly and I read a great deal. I felt sort of tied down by the restaurant work all the time. I did not have any social life at all. I used to argue a great deal with my dad over this but he did not seem to think that I was missing anything. He put it up as a sort of obligation for me to help out the family, and I could not very well argue too much against that. That is why I had my biggest arguments with him over our differences in political ideas.

It was during my last year in high school that the big longshoremen's strike broke out all over the coast. There were many street meetings held around our neighborhood and down by the waterfront and I would go to hear the speeches. Dad was very disapproving of this and he said that the longshoremen were all Communists. The more he argued, the more I became aware of the opposite point of view and I began to stick up for it. It seemed to me that the laboring groups had a great deal of justification for going on strikes. That strike during 1934 had a great influence on me. I could see the battered workers who had been tossed aside after years of work by their employers, and I did not think that it was right that they should be thrown out upon the streets without any protection at all. I began to give free meals to some of the strikers who came into the restaurant. I had to do it on the sly because my dad would have raised the roof if he ever found out. Most of the Nisei have not gone through experiences like this and they have never seen life face to face until the evacuation.

I did not have any girl friends at all during my high school days and dancing was a thing of another world. The only high school club I ever joined was the German club and that was because my Caucasian friend was in it.

I graduated from high school in 1935. I did not know what I was going to do but I felt that I would like to take a job working for somebody else besides my father. For three short months, I worked on the Japanese produce row in Seattle. I was legally underpaid. I worked from 4:30 in the morning until 1 or 2 in the afternoon and I got $25 a month for this. Can you imagine anyone but a Nisei working for wages like this? My boss did not have to pay union wages to me as I was only a part-time worker. Actually I worked a full day because I was always being imposed on and asked to put in an hour or so overtime without pay. The Nisei had to put up with this sort of thing because jobs were scarce and there were family obligations. I could not take it so I went back to work for my father, much as I disliked that work.

I worked in my father's restaurant for the next five years until 1940. I had the night shift and I usually worked until 4 in the morning. I did not start getting a day off until 1938 when the Japanese restaurants were unionized. Instead of hiring the extra help for the day off, the Japanese restaurants rotated and they closed on the seventh day. I was not paid a regular wage or allowance. I had to ask my dad for the money. He was pretty liberal and I just took it out of the cash till whenever I needed it and then made a small notation of it. Dad wanted me to take an active interest in the restaurant and eventually take over the management of it. I did not particularly care for this work but I figured that I would be doing the restaurant work for a long time so I resigned myself to it. More and more of the restaurant responsibility was upon me and I was doing all of the buying and other business for my dad. My two sisters worked in the restaurant also. After they got out of high school, they did full time. They just took it for granted, because girls don't have such great ambitions as fellows.

I had wanted to go to college in 1935 but the restaurant work prevented me. Finally in 1940 I got my chance but I was a little reluctant about going because I was older by then. My dad told me to go because he said that I had earned it by working in the restaurant and he would pay my way. It happened that my kid brother was slated to go, but he ran around too much in high school and he did not care for college. My dad thought that this was wasting his money so he took him out of school and put him in the restaurant. He then decided to concentrate on me. It was a good thing that I did go to college for two years. I regret very much that I did not get to finish up and I don't see how I'll ever do it now.

I did not get into the college activities too much because I worked about six hours a night in the restaurant. I was not a member of the Japanese Students Club although I went there a lot and hung around. I did not know what my ambitions were but I took a journalism major. Dad did not think this was very practical as he said that I could not get a job on Caucasian newspapers very easily and that working with Japanese papers did not pay very much. I knew that, but that was the closest I could get to my desire for writing.

We were not living in the Japanese community any more but I went around there a lot during my spare time. I started to drink when I worked in the restaurant. I used to drink sake on the sly and I wondered what they could like about it. Some college Nisei gave me my first drink of whisky and it made me feel good. It helped in the social intercourse and it made me feel more at ease.

I was always conscious of the fact that I was Japanese [but] I just took it for granted. Because of my background, I had a certain pride in the Japanese fleet as a kid, but I was pro-America in my attitudes for as long as I can remember. The fact that I was not closely identified with the Japanese community or with Japanese gangs made me lose contact more easily with this feeling for Japan and I had lost it completely by the time the war broke out. I had broken away from the Japanese influence but I had no experience of knowing whether I could get into American society completely or not although I felt that I could. I lived in my own little world at that time. Most of my white friends were students or of the working class and there was little distinction among us. I knew that there was racial discrimination in existence and that is why I subscribed to the progressive and radical ideology in my political thinking. However, I did not go around with a chip on my shoulder. I enjoyed both Japanese and Caucasian company and there were members of both groups that I disliked.

When I went to college I found that the ROTC was closed to the Nisei. Military training did not appeal to me anyway, but the idea that we were barred made me sore. It was little incidents like this which made me aware of the fact that I was Japanese and I felt a little helpless about overcoming the blind prejudices of many people. One thing I can't stand is when I hear those Nisei who are discriminated against and yet who say derogatory things about "niggers," Filipinos, and other groups. It is things like that which prevent the Nisei from becoming united with these other racial groups and recognizing the common problems of all of them. The Nisei live in a glass house and yet they throw rocks.

The Nisei opinions in many ways are Japanesy. They did not worry about dual citizenship or their uncertain status in this country. Many of the Nisei went to Japan after they got out of college because of the possible economic opportunities. Many Nisei still think that they may have to go back to Japan after the war because things will be too tough for them. I had dual citizenship myself but I told my dad to cut it off as I never intended to go to Japan. The reason I didn't want to ever go to Japan was because I heard of the poverty and the low standards of living over there. I never considered myself a Japanese subject because my sentiments were far away from the Japanese ideas.

I figured I was a helluva lot better American than a lot of the

Americans. I felt that I was living up to more of my responsibilities of an American than many of the Caucasians. I was aware of the Spanish Civil War and I thought that the Franco supporters in this country were traitors to democracy. I was writing small articles in the Japanese language papers at that time, so I wrote some articles against Franco. I was also against this country sending any scrap iron to Japan and I stood in the picket line down by the waterfront to signify my beliefs. I also attended a few mass meetings on these questions but the general American public was too apathetic to take much of an interest. There was even a smaller percentage of Nisei interested in these things. My father did not know about my activities. He thought that all Nisei were turning communists. The truth was that the Nisei at that time were very conservative.

The Issei were much more politically minded. The Nisei were apathetic and all of their opinions were decided for them by their parents. The Issei parents read reactionary Japanese papers and magazines and they even told their sons how to vote in the elections. The Nisei had no opinions at all and they all stayed Republicans. Even the cannery union was controlled by the Japanese Association and only a few members of it were progressive. The Nisei were interested only in small things and the camp life was the peak of what they wanted— dances and sports. Most of the Nisei students were children of small Issei businessmen and a very few of them were proletarian. That is why the bulk of the Nisei were so conservative. Before the war, the JACL was a very innocuous group and not socially conscious at all. It played the middle of the line on all the political issues. I felt it was no good so I made no attempt to join it. I started to vote when I was 21 and I usually voted the Democratic ticket. The state of Washington was Democratic and it was liberal in many ways. It got most of its reactionary ideas through California.

I had been out late on Saturday night, December 6, on a sort of a bender so I was in bed until 2 the next afternoon. My sister came in and told me about the war. It was quite a surprise as I didn't expect it because Nomura and Kurusu were here on a peace mission. Pearl Harbor seemed to be a figment out of my dad's imaginative mind.

Regardless of the political convictions of the Nisei, we all went through a shock phase. Some busybody old bastard stopped me on the street that evening to ask me what I thought about it. My reaction was utter indignation but I did not act upon it. It was essentially true that I was completely identified with the United States more than ever before, but when the superpatriots stuck their noses in and tried to bring the blame of the war on to me, that sort of thing angered me. I did not see why they should try to blame me for Pearl Harbor just because I had a Japanese face.

I went to work as usual that night but I was a little apprehensive. In the back of my mind there was a thought that guys would throw rocks at our restaurant window and cause other destruction. However, nothing of that nature did happen. A bunch of young guys did come in late that night and I sensed their ugly tone of voices. I started to explain the Nisei situation and it didn't take too long to convince them that I was an American because I said the superficial things like "We've got to beat the hell out of the Japs for this treacherous attack." Naturally I was sort of on edge all evening and I was in a raw state of feeling and a little jumpy. I tried to keep control as much as possible but it was impossible to be perfectly calm. The Caucasian friends in my group went out of the way to be unusually considerate of my feelings. They even came over to the restaurant that very night to tell me how they felt about my position.

That night I was going home very late and the bus happened to be crowded a little bit. A drunk guy got on the bus after me so I moved over a little to make room for him. He interpreted this as being due to my fear of him so he started calling me a spy and mumbling something about Japs should be thrown out and drowned in Lake Washington. I did not make an issue of it at all. The attitude of the people in the bus showed that they disapproved of the drunk, so I felt better and more confident that the fair-minded opinion would prevail in spite of what happened in the Pacific warfare.

The very next night I decided to walk home. A couple of cheap-looking women were standing out on the streets and when they noticed me, they started to follow and yell "Jap" at me. I was burnt up inside, but I did not say anything to them. After that there were no more incidents and life quickly went back to a more normal routine.

It is difficult to say exactly what the general feeling among the Nisei was during the month or so after the outbreak of the war. Many of the Nisei went around in a daze and they expected almost anything. The thing that seemed peculiar to me was that some Nisei actually felt guilty about the war just because they were of Japanese ancestry. On the other hand, there were many of the JACL type who had formerly been in the middle, and who now suddenly began to say superpatriotic things in order to emphasize the fact that they were Americans too. I suppose most of the Nisei were a little confused like I was. I think that they were loyal enough in their way, and I think that if they had been called by the Army then they would have responded even more favorably than the people of Hawaii did. The longer they had to wait around, the more confusing things got for them and they were not so sure by that time that this country had a place for them. They were aware of the fact that the American public as a whole identified them first as Japanese, and secondly as citizens, if they went that far.

My life was affected, but not too drastically. After the quarter ended at [college], I dropped out of school. The last thing I did on the campus was to write an editorial for the school paper. The student body received it very favorably. In my editorial I tried to stress the point that the evacuees were not too extremely bitter about the sudden uprooting from their homes. I attempted to point out that the evacuees had certain rights as American citizens, although I recognized that special interests were the motivating forces for the evacuation. Therefore the chief point I made was that the purpose of it was an all-out defense effort and the evacuees were leaving with this in their minds as their contribution to the national security. I have changed my mind a little bit since then. I now feel that the selfish interests within this country were much stronger than what I had figured and it was through their emotional clamoring that the Army arrived at the decision that evacuation was a military necessity.

Throughout this period there were not too many changes in the family relationship although I had to assume more and more of the responsibilities and to take care of the final business settlements and property disposition. Our house was in my name and we were still making payments on it. I had to go to the property agents to get the management fixed up. We still had the feeling that we would return soon and therefore it was best to hang on to our house. I arranged to rent it out to a shipyard worker and now he has moved out. The first tenant walked off with our radio and much of the furniture is now missing. The place is going to the dogs and it is a helluva mess. We are still making payments on the place but it comes out of the rent.

We did not finish settling the restaurant business so that we left it. We sold some of the fixtures but most of it was a loss. My old man felt pretty badly about this loss but we could not do anything about it. On top of that we had a new 1942 car and we had to sell it at a price cheaper than the prevailing market price because of the haste of departure.

With all of these worries facing me, education was not important to me any longer and things were too uncertain at that time for me to sit back and mull over the loss of my education. I felt more and more that we would be gone for the duration because the public attacks through the press and radio were getting more and more emotional. Therefore I was evacuated with the thought that I would be in the camp for the duration. I didn't want to [go to camp] but it was impractical for me to leave voluntarily for the East. One of my sisters left before the restrictions set in, but she went with the intention of marrying somebody in Chicago. I had to stick around the house and take care of the family business.

We continued to work in the restaurant almost up to the day of evacuation and we did not have any incidents at all. Our regular customers who had come for years continued to patronize us because they were well acquainted with us and they knew that a great wrong was being done.

I got drunk more often after March because I was out of school and I did not have to get up early any more to rush to classes. Thinking back on it now, I suppose my life was more disorganized than I realized at that time. Even the younger Nisei started to drink because they had nothing to do but sit around and wait for the day of evacuation. I realized that my old routine and a certain amount of security was all shot, but I still was sure the government would dispose of the problem fairly and honestly. I did not think the government would leave the Japanese completely destitute as their businesses had been shot after the war broke out. I felt that the conscience of the American public would prevent such a deplorable situation from coming about. I did not particularly feel more closely identified with the Japanese minority. I later got closer to them by the mere fact that I was associated in camp with so many Japanese. I was willing to accept what the Western Defense Command said about military necessity, although I felt it might have been only a political necessity. I realized it was impossible to weed out the disloyal from the loyal Japanese, but I did feel that the Nisei should have been kept out of the camp. I also felt that the Army should have been consistent about the Nisei in the draft. They took the Nisei for a few days after Pearl Harbor and then closed the draft to them. The Army also kept some of the Nisei, while others were released. This sort of thing created a great deal of confusion in the Nisei mind. It's like being kicked out of the house and not knowing whether you would be welcomed back after the initial emotional excitement of the old man passes.

It was a muddy day when we [were evacuated] to Puyallup. I thought that the lack of privacy in camp would really cramp my style and I did not think I would ever get used to it. The public latrines really disgusted me. They should have at least put up sideboards between seats. The food was awful too. It made me feel physically and psychologically rotten. I griped just as much as any of my friends.

The very first day I was in camp, they needed aides for the medical examination during the reception of the people. A guy asked me to be a clerk so I just went and did the work. It was quite a job to speak Japanese to the Issei but I managed to make myself understood.

After a couple of days, some of us began to make attempts to get a camp paper started. It was very slow work because of all the red tape. After a few weeks we finally put out a mimeographed sheet. The paper was a nonpaying job and the advisory council also volunteered its services. This was mostly the JACL group. They seemed to have run the camp as a great deal of power was given to them by the WCCA. The newspaper was not too happy a job because there was a great deal of censorship.

I did not take part in any educational activities in camp and I did not even finish reading a book at Puyallup although I did read the newspapers. I did have more recreation than I had in Seattle. I lost all my desire to drink while I was in camp. I played tennis and volleyball. Occasionally I went to the dances and I met quite a few girls. This phase of my camp life gave me a less restricted life than before, but in the bigger things I definitely was restricted. Emotionally, I became closer to the Japanese than ever before in my life. The full realization of what had happened to the Nisei did not dawn upon me until later when I gave it more serious thought. I didn't go to church in camp except when they had some forums on worldly matters. I did not take any interest at all in camp politics. I associated mostly with a nonintellectual type so I did not have to think too much. My group were of the average run of card-playing Nisei. I just gambled moderately because I was not so good at cards, but the others went in for it more steeply until their money ran out. We had bull sessions at night once in a while but not of a very high order.

My general impression was that the assembly center in spite of the restrictions, gossiping, and other handicaps was more or less a holiday for everyone. The people as a whole did not have to work their heads off any more in order to make a living since the food and shelter was provided by the government. All in all, the evacuees felt that they were part of a community more than ever before because of the fact that they were all in the same boat facing an unknown future.

The summer passed quickly enough. I didn't leave Puyallup [for Minidoka] with any regrets because I thought that the WRA camp would have less congestion and better sanitary facilities. The size of the camp had been publicized as 68,000 acres and that meant more freedom for the people. I was also aware of the fact that its basis would be a farm program and I did not object to that because that could be very constructive. I determined to get down to something more serious instead of the aimless life I led at Puyallup. I intended to work on the newspaper at Minidoka if I could get on the staff and not to fool around so much.

When I got to Minidoka, a blanket of dust blew in our faces and we got the cheering report that this was only a mild day. I could not help but feel the excitement of the place. There was a big job to be done about making the camp more livable. This feeling was in the atmosphere, and it was reflected in the very way the people fought for the jobs. All in all, it seemed less of a picnic than the assembly center.

I had worked with most of the staff members of the newspaper before so I immediately went down and asked for a job as reporter, which I got without any difficulty. I wrote mostly columns and covered beats around camp. It was the most enjoyable work that I had done even though my experience and the subject matter were limited. The incentive for the kind of writing I wanted to do was not there, but at least it gave me some opportunity to see what I could do. I still did not know if I could make the grade as a professional journalist since the camp paper did not give me much training for this.

In October, 1942, I took time out for one month from the camp and the newspaper work in order to go to work in the sugar beets. It was the first opportunity to go on the outside and this appealed to me. The outside meant that I could get away from the restriction of camp life for a while. Some of the Nisei really felt that in answering the call for farm work, they would help the war effort. But the fact that we wanted to get out was probably one of the most important factors. The seemingly high wages in sugar beets as compared to the camp salary was also one of the attractions. I did not have illusions that I would make a fortune as I knew that my farming ability was not good. As it turned out, I did not come back with a cent ahead although I grossed about $250 for the period of almost two months I was gone.

We stayed in a camp which had several hundred Nisei. [A small city] was only two miles away from our work camp and my money was quickly spent on clothes, food, and entertainment. We did not have any unpleasant incidents. All of my bosses were understanding and I had long talks about the Japanese problem with them. The work itself was tough as hell and most of the fellows wanted to go home. I stuck it out until the end of the contract. The other young Nisei workers in my gang were afraid to tell the boss they wanted to quit and I wouldn't do it so they had to stay on with me.

After the sugar-beet work was done in late November, I went back to camp and started working on the newspaper again. I began to fit in once more with the camp life and it was not hard to do as my taste of freedom was not financially successful. Farm work was not my idea of permanent work. I could not see any resettlement possibility in doing that kind of work.

The recreational facilities were extremely limited in Minidoka for a long time. The inevitable dances were the only things held consistently. I soon found a girl friend and went sort of steady with her. It was only a casual friendship and I did not have any plans of matrimony. There wasn't anything of intellectual interest about the goddam camp. Minidoka was one camp where the primary emphasis was on resettlement and there was not too much stress put upon the internal development. I was very restless during the winter because it was windy and cold and there was nothing to do to keep me very busy. I had to stay indoors most of the time and I got bored and in a depression. When spring came and the tempo of resettlement speeded up, my one idea was to get out of camp.

Minidoka was a definite improvement over Puyallup, but that did not solve the big problem which was in the minds of all the Japanese. The quality of the WRA administration was much better than the WCCA. They had a definite interest in the people's welfare, and the project director had a lot of dreams of making Minidoka a community to be proud of. He was even respected by many of the Issei.

Generally the registration was successful at Minidoka. The WRA there handled it extremely well. The response was slow at first but the people came around as it was explained to them more clearly. The project director showed up at all of the meetings. He was a very eloquent speaker and this appealed especially to the Issei. He did not threaten the people at all. He explained the idea of the combat unit and he said that it was needed to be the torch bearers for the Nisei. He said that the record of the combat unit would help all of the Japanese in camp as well as being an achievement for the Nisei soldiers. There was quite a bit of resistance at first but it ended up with over 300 volunteers and the majority of the Issei answering "yes" to the Army questionnaire.

My dad could not see any of us volunteering but he became resigned. He answered "yes" to the questionnaire like most of the Issei. I think he was influenced by the decisions of his sons and my parents realized that they were more tied up with this country than ever before. My two brothers volunteered. I had a lot of mental conflict about volunteering. Our family felt that one of the boys should stay with the family. I was the one selected because I had been given a 4-F classification before and likely to be rejected even if I did volunteer. I felt that a general draft was coming soon anyway, so it didn't make much difference. My older brother also had a physical disability but he was in a prominent position in camp and he volunteered to show that he was sincere. I felt that my younger brother was much more physically fit than any of us and I was pretty sure that he would be taken. That would leave me with the family. I had one sister left in camp. The other one had married before evacuation, and it was a certainty that my dad could not support my mother if he ever got out of camp. It was pretty much of a rationalization on my part when compared to the fact that four brothers from another family in our camp had volunteered. Now my conscience does infringe upon me occasionally and I have a feeling of guilt. I hold certain convictions and I think I am willing to fight for them. That is why I have wondered about volunteering from out here. I am beginning to think seriously of it but I haven't decided what to do. All the young fellows are in uniform now and it makes me feel sort of conspicuous not to be in the service. I don't know what I will do about it, though I probably will wait for the draft now.

The whole tempo of resettlement speeded up right after registration and I got the fever. I looked around for any sort of job as an excuse to get out. I wasn't getting any younger in camp and I knew that I had to act soon. I knew that if I remained in camp I would not get the opportunity to find out exactly what I could do because camp life impressed me as a temporary phase in my life. I knew that I would have to make a fresh start on the outside. I was full of anticipations and expectations but at the same time I tried to be practical about it and realize that there were certain obstacles which would not make it too easy.

In early May I finally got a chance for a job that would get me out of camp. I signed up for unskilled labor at the [C] Press in Chicago through the WRA representative in camp. The Press offered us 62½ cents an hour and a promise of a later raise to 67½ cents. They also said that there was a nickel bonus if we wanted to work on a night shift, plus time and a half for any overtime work. This sounded like pretty good wages to me for unskilled work and I thought I would do it until I found something better.

There were three of us who came out together on this job. We stopped at the YMCA for a week or so. Then we started to look for an apartment of our own. One evening we went to visit a Nisei friend and he suggested [M] House. We went down there and inquired for rooms right away and the landlady accepted us. For a while most of the occupants were Japanese but now it is about 50-50. I don't know the exact number of Japanese in the house now but there are about 40 or 50. I don't have too many contacts with most of them.

There was nothing exciting about my unskilled job at the Press. At first I started as a piler for a machine which sewed the books together. Then I helped out on some other machine like feeding the smashers and doing a little layout work.

I was looking for another job all the time and once I took a day off to go see about a job. When I came back to the Press, the floorlady was angry, so she said that I would have to go on a night shift. I averaged around 50 hours per week on the night shift. There was an important reason why I did not object to going on the night shift. The three of us lived together, ate together, slept together, and worked together so I figured that I should see less of them or else they would get on my nerves. I worked on the folding machine and it was a little harder. I did this for two months. The night shift was from 7 in the evening until 5 A.M. the next morning, and this ruled out my social life entirely. The day shift had more openings after the summer vacation since the students were going back to school so I finally went back on the day shift.

There must have been about 200 Nisei in all of the shifts at the Press. They were on all three floors. Many of them were girls. The Nisei were mixed in with the other workers, but there were predominantly Japanese on some floors. The Caucasian workers seemed to be pretty tolerant of the Nisei and did not treat them as inferiors. There were some Nisei zoot suiters working at the plant and they made fools out of themselves by acting in a boisterous way and trying to draw attention to themselves, which was not very favorably received by either the Caucasian workers or the other Nisei there.

I didn't mix too much with the other Nisei workers except for the ones I had come out with as most of them were young squirts. I did not like the idea of working among so many Nisei and this urged me on to find another job. I had been contacting various newspapers in this area for possible employment since journalism had been my major in college and I thought I'd like to give it a trial. I only had one job offer as a proofreader and nothing else. I didn't hit the big newspapers in Chicago as I knew I would not have a chance with them. I hit the newspapers in the suburbs but they said they had no opening although they were nice about it. I then began to answer several job calls for rewrite man and advertising apprentice for magazines. I said I was a Japanese American in my letters and I got no answers at all.

In the middle of September I answered an advertisement for a job as office clerk, mailing, filing, and errand boy, and I was successful in getting it. I also do proofreading in this job. It is in an advertising agency. I get less pay than at the [C] Press, where I was making between $35 and $45 a week. Now I only get $100 a month. However, I made the change for the opportunity it will eventually offer. The job I am doing now is routine, but it requires a little more headwork and there is more variety to it. I don't like the mass production stuff in a book factory. I wouldn't have taken my present job but the vice-president said that he would give me training in advertising copy writing. I am not getting that training yet but I will pretty soon. There is a guy there who is willing to break me in. It is only a medium-sized advertising agency with a total of about 24 people in the staff. I get along excellently with the office staff and it is very informal during the office hours.

My present ambition is to learn advertising copy writing as soon as I can so I can make a living at it. But personally, I believe that advertising is a parasite business. My literary and journalistic ambitions have been put to bed. I feel that there is less of a future for me in journalism than in advertising copy writing.

I now feel that it is doubtful whether I will go back to Seattle after the war. It will depend upon my chances of making a living and whether there will be any opportunities for me. There is no restaurant for me to go back to, but we are still making payments on our house yet. That is our only root left in Seattle. The house is deteriorating because the present tenants are ruining it. I don't rule out any part of the country for living [in] if there is a chance for economic security there. I follow the economic security reasons more than the geographical or sentimental choice of places. In my line of work I hope to end up eventually in New York City because the most chances for advertising work are there.

On the whole, the way most Nisei are existing now is not satisfactory to them. They are restless and they have no definite place to go for recreational activities. I make the same complaints myself. But all of the small Nisei groups seem to have reasonably enough to do even if they don't get together with each other. A part of the Nisei tendency to be restless and to run around a lot now is the sowing of wild oats. A lot of my friends are content to spend their pay checks on clothes and dancing at the [A]. They don't save anything and it doesn't even worry them. They don't think much of the postwar period because they don't know what is going to happen. That's why they're more interested in getting larger pay checks and spending the money. They felt that they had been deprived of a lot of things during the time they were in camp and this is a relief to them. It looks pretty good to many of the Nisei to get a two hundred dollar a month pay check because such things were undreamed of before the war. When I get in groups for bull sessions, all they talk about is about having a social good time and about money they can make. Actually most of the Nisei are making more money now than they could have ever hoped to make on the coast.

I most emphatically do not want to see a Japanese colony started here. That would ruin the whole resettlement program. I don't know how this spreading out of the Nisei will work out but I hope that the Nisei can do it individually and not organize into groups. It looks like it is leading into segregation right now and there is nothing that can prevent it. It is an extremely difficult problem for the younger Nisei because they miss the social life. It may be that a good adjustment will not come in their lifetime, but it is worth the try and better than to fall back on the old ways. If the Nisei can establish themselves and lose themselves, they may be taken as individuals. In this case, they will be able to find a place in American society. If it comes to the point where there is no concerted effort against the Nisei as a group then you can expect the Nisei to achieve the full use of their education. They do have talents and they are pluggers.

CH-35: MECHANIC

Male; born in California, 1915; height 64"; weight 130 lbs.; married, 1942; one child; husband of CH-36; brother-in-law of CH-37.
Interviewed March–April, 1944, after contacts extending throughout "several months." Described as "a slim person, with a rather expressionless face." Gaps in his life history were attributed more to "basic inhibitions than to unwillingness to tell his story." He impressed the interviewer as "tending to give subjective and personal opinions," as "exhibiting quite a degree of bitterness," but as having made "a fairly satisfactory social adjustment, with an increasing extent of stability" during the resettlement period—marred only by "feelings of uncertainty about his draft status." CH-35's wife's life history follows his— as CH-36.

CAREER LINES

Parental: CH-35 was orphaned at 4 years of age. His grandfather, who assumed responsibility for him, came from a farming family in Japan; immigrated to Hawaii near the turn of the century, and worked on a sugar plantation. He brought his family, including CH-35's father, to California *ca.* 1906; farmed independently but unsuccessfully for a few years, and was forced back into agricultural labor in southern and central California. Continued in this work until his death in 1927.
Own: Graduated from high school in the Santa Maria Valley in 1935; attended a trade school in Chicago for a few months in 1939. As a child, worked on farms, with his grandfather. After the grandfather's death in 1927, he became a "schoolboy" and a helper in a Japanese-operated store. In 1935, worked as a packer, and from 1936 to 1942 as a mechanic in a Japanese-owned garage. Inmigrated to Chicago in June, 1943, after obtaining a job as mechanic in an automobile sales firm. When interviewed was still working for this firm, while awaiting induction.

LIFE HISTORY

I was born in 1915. I lost my parents during the influenza epidemic of 1919 so I don't remember them. They died one day apart and we were living in Los Angeles at that time. My grandfather took care of me after that and he raised me up to the age of 12 years.

As far as I know, my parents were farmers in Japan before they came over here. My dad was a bootlegger during the prohibition days, I've heard. My uncle was born in Hawaii during the time that my grandparents were there. They brought the family over to this country in about 1906. They passed through San Francisco one week before the earthquake. My grandfather took his family down to southern California to enter farming work. My parents were later married by the picture-bride method and I was the only child. My dad had two brothers and one sister and one of these uncles is living with me now.

Although I was born in Los Angeles, I don't remember much of my early childhood. My grandfather took me back to Japan with him once[190] and he tried to leave me with my mother's folks. They wanted him to pay so much a month for my support because they thought he was rich. My grandfather got sore at this so that he got married again so that he would be able to take care of me. He brought his wife back from Japan and I came along with him. I sure owe him a lot because he was like a father to me.

My grandfather was a typical old fellow. He left Japan many years ago and he was one of the pioneers. He always longed to go back, and he used to tell me a lot of stories about the old country when I was young. He used to drink a lot with other Issei and many times he got drunk. He didn't like his new wife very much because he only married her in order to have a mother for me. He treated me just like his own son. I never paid much attention to my grandfather's second wife and she didn't bother with me much either, because she was an old maid and not interested in me. My grandfather was quite old at the time I was living with him. He had come to Hawaii at first to work on the sugar plantations over 50 years ago. I know it was that long ago because my uncle was born there 48 years ago.

My grandfather had made money in farm work at times and he specialized in raising tomatoes. I think that he was one of the first Japanese farmers here to specialize in tomatoes, and in the years that followed a lot of other Japanese farmers took it up and they raised most of the tomatoes in California. Grandfather lost his farm about the time that I went to live with him, so that I moved around the state with him quite a bit when he worked on different farms [in southern California].

Grandfather was pretty strict with his discipline. He made me go to the Buddhist Church all the time whenever we were near a Japa-

---

[190] According to WRA records, CH-35 was in Japan in 1925.

nese community. He died in 1927 when I was 12. At that time he was working on a Japanese ranch so I stayed on there. They had a store also and I had to work after school as a schoolboy. I didn't like it at all because I didn't have any time for sports like the other kids. The old lady was mean to me and a lot of times she hit me for no reason at all. The old man wasn't so bad but he rarely spoke to me kindly. I stayed with this Japanese couple for three years until 1930. It was a typical Japanese home. Both of them had worked as domestics in Caucasian homes, so that they had some American ideas. They ate American food quite a bit, but we always spoke Japanese in that home. I had to follow most of the Japanese customs which they had and I never thought of turning against them.

During the time I was with them, I gradually made a lot of Japanese friends at school since the old folks I worked for got less strict the longer I worked there. I remember a lot of the kids I played around with. I ran around with these Japanese kids all the time I was growing up. There was one boy I went around with for quite a while and he was a close friend of mine. When he got out of high school his parents sent him to Japan to finish his education. When this boy came back to this country, I saw that he was so different and I didn't agree with him any more. He was studying for a diplomatic career and when he came back in 1940, I found him so greatly changed that we just didn't think the same way anymore. We used to have a lot of arguments and finally I didn't pal around with him anymore. He was on a speaking tour to raise some money for some Japanese organization. Later on I heard he was interned but I don't know if that is true or not.

In grammar school I didn't make many *hakujin* friends as there were so many *Nihonjin* kids around the school and we all stayed together. A lot of these Nisei kids were sent back to Japan for an education after they finished high school. Most of the Nisei I knew came from small town merchant families or from farm families.

As soon as I graduated from the elementary school I went to [U, in the Santa Maria Valley] and left the old folks I was working for. My uncle was working in a garage there and he found a place for me to stay and go to school. He paid my way. The house was a part of the Buddhist Church and a number of kids lived there. There were only about 5 fellows staying there during the time I was there. The reason for this home was that many of the Japanese families lived way out in the sticks, so that the parents sent them down to the Buddhist Church to live so that they could go to the public schools and also attend the Japanese school run by the church. I went to that Japanese school during the time I was there.

I really liked living in [U] and that was when my real fun began. I had a chance to do everything that the other *Nihonjin* kids were doing. I took part in all sorts of sports activities and also social programs. During the time I was in high school I went out for the football team and I was elected captain of the lightweight team in my last year there. Most of my social activities were centered around the YBA which was sponsored by the Buddhist Church. During the next 10 years I held all kinds of offices in the YBA. I was president and all sorts of other types of office holder. We held many different kinds of socials among the Buddhist Nisei in town.

I was also a member of the *judo* team and we made a lot of trips to the various tournaments in the other Japanese towns on the coast. Around 1940 the YBA organized a bowling team and we entered the Caucasian major league in town. This was the first time that any Nisei group had entered a league which was not composed entirely of Nisei teams. We made quite a few Caucasian friends in this way and we also traveled all over California playing other Nisei teams.

I look back on my high school life as a lot of fun. I got along with everybody but I didn't have much use for the girls. There were about 40 Nisei out of 1,000 students in the student body. There were about 10 Nisei in my class. The Nisei in our district mixed pretty good in sports, but they were clannish in social affairs, and they didn't take part too much at dances and school plays. The YBA didn't mix much with the Christian Nisei either, so I guess we were rather clannish. In our town the YBA was the biggest Nisei club and the Buddhists were in greatest number.

At school the Nisei did well in their studies. During the four years I was in high school, a Nisei was the valedictorian three times. I majored in math when I was in high school but my plans for the future were very indefinite. I took all of the shopwork courses that I could because I thought I would be able to use [the training] some day. I got a B average in high school because I took all of these mechanical courses.

In 1935 I graduated from high school. I had to start earning my own living after that. I worked for a while at [a Japanese] packing house as a packer and I made pretty good wages. I made about $170 a month during the season but there was no future in it so that I quit. After I started to work regularly, my club activities gradually dropped down. I wasn't able to travel around California so much any more, so I took up bowling. I won a cup in one of the bowling tournaments held in town. Every Saturday the fellows would play poker and on Sundays we went to a show. Around 1936 I got a job in a Japanese garage as my uncle was there. The boss knew I was interested in cars so that he let my uncle break me in. I got $20 a week when I first started. I used to work from 8 to 6 but I put in plenty of overtime after I learned how to be an auto mechanic. I kept that job right up to the time of evacuation. A lot of times I threatened to quit as I had better offers from other Japanese garages in Los Angeles but I didn't care to leave [U]. I really worked hard in that garage and I was greatly underpaid. However, I couldn't complain about it too much because jobs were pretty scarce in those days and it was almost impossible to get a job in a *hakujin* garage. Most of the Japanese employers expected us to put in overtime without pay and it was no use to complain about it because they would think we were lazy if we made a fuss.

Most of the other Nisei in the valley went to work in the Japanese packing houses after they finished school, but a lot of them went to work on their dad's farm. There was quite a future in farming work in Santa Maria Valley as the Japanese farmers were quite successful there. They owned or leased quite a bit of land and every year they shipped out many carloads of vegetables. The farmers there were about the richest of any along the coast, but there were also a lot of poor Japanese farmers around too.

The Japanese community in [U] was pretty small. [However] about 30 per cent of the population of the town was Japanese and they got along pretty well with the *hakujin* people. There were quite a few Mexicans and Filipinos living there too and they did agricultural work. Many of the landowners were Portugese and they leased land to the Japanese farmers. There were three big Japanese companies in the Santa Maria Valley and it seemed that all the rest of the Japanese worked for them. They also hired many hundreds of Filipinos, Mexicans, and *hakujins*. It was a large scale type of farming that they did. A lot of outsiders came in after 1938 when the Okies started to come into California. A lot of these people later agitated the most about the evacuation because they were jealous of the Japanese since they had nothing themselves. I suppose a lot of the old time *hakujin* residents were jealous too but they never said too much against us and the Japanese managed to keep on friendly terms with them.

Their real feelings came out after the war started and I know a lot of these *hakujin* wanted to get us out of the valley. They were just two-faced about it.

In town the Japanese had a very few stores which were mostly for the Japanese people although other races also patronized them occasionally. The Filipinos went to some of the Japanese restaurants and pool halls. The town was pretty quiet during the week but it went full blast on week ends when all of the farm workers came to town to spend their money.

There wasn't much for me to do except go to the movies or bowling. Sports took a lot of time of most of the Nisei who were working. Once in a while they held Nisei dances but I wasn't too interested in them. I used to hang around the pool hall quite a bit and I occasionally played poker to fill in the time. I went around in a group of about 5 fellows. Two of them were real close friends and we went around every place together. I had a car so that we would go visiting around to some of the other Japanese communities in the valley. Once in a while we would take a trip down to Little Tokyo in Los Angeles and look around.

[U] was primarily a Buddhist community and most of the social life was around the church. All of the young Nisei went to Sunday school to learn of Lord Buddha. Buddhists claim you live the Buddha life every day. I don't see much difference between Christianity and Buddhism but I had to go pretty regularly to the Buddhist Church.

The Buddhist Church used to sponsor most of the Japanese festivals in town but the Nisei put most of the effort into the YBA. Our purpose was to promote better citizenship and understanding. We tried to get into contact with some of the Caucasian organizations in order to exchange ideas but it was only successful to a very small degree. The Nisei did not care too much about mixing with the *hakujin* people and the *hakujin* did not care about mixing with the *Nihonjin* except in business.

There were several other important Japanese organizations in the community. The JACL, the Japanese Association, and the Japanese Farmers Association were the biggest ones. The Issei influenced us pretty strongly in [U] and in the Santa Maria Valley. There were a number of older Nisei there and they were established in the big Japanese companies. It was these guys who were behind the JACL. The Issei donated money to it and the Nisei couldn't do as they pleased. I guess this wasn't such a good connection because 90 per cent of the Issei fathers were interned after the war started because of some connection with Japanese organizations. Most of them were later paroled.

The Issei in our valley pretty well dominated everything and I suppose they had a lot of Japanese ways and many of them must have donated to Japan or else they would not have been interned. The Nisei did not know what was going on or they did not care, because most of us were not interested in politics anyway. We had to depend upon the Issei quite a bit because the best jobs for the Nisei were in the big Japanese-produce companies or with the rich Japanese farmers. After the older Nisei got into these companies, a lot of land was leased in their names because the Issei were not allowed to do it. The older Nisei therefore all held pretty responsible positions because they represented the rich Japanese farmer and heads of the produce companies.

My interest in politics can be put onto a pinhead. I took some interest in the local elections and I did vote in the state elections after I got to be of age because the JACL head said it was our duty. I was a member of the JACL but I just joined it because the other fellows did. The JACL got the Nisei in the valley to support certain candidates and they told us about the candidates who were anti-Japanese.

In my social life I never went around with girls very much. I started to go around with my wife from about 1937. It was nothing serious until after the war. She had six sisters and only one brother so that she had a lot of obligations for her family and we could not talk about marriage. Her parents were both barbers in [a coastal town], and they came to [U] with the family around 1935 or 1936 and opened a pool hall. Later on they were working as farm laborers. The older girls were helping out with the family until they got married. The oldest one [CH-49] married [CH-37] down in [Y] and the next oldest was in a sanatorium, so that my wife had to take most of the responsibility for her family. The others were in school yet. We just went around occasionally and we couldn't think of marriage for the longest time.

I was still working in the Japanese garage as an auto mechanic just before the war and at the same place. We used to have all sorts of mixed customers as we were the biggest garage in town. The war did not make much difference in our work because they all continued to come there.

I was living a pretty good life before the war and I was fairly happy and satisfied with my position. The only thing I missed was that I didn't have any folks or family. I think that I would have gone on to college if I had parents. That's how most of the Nisei got on to college because they couldn't have done it without their folks sending them. I was lucky about one thing though, and that was traveling all around by myself. That was more than the other Nisei kids could do because their parents would not let them go off on their own whenever they got a notion to do so. I even made trips up to Seattle by myself when I got the urge and I often went to Los Angeles by myself to have some fun. Many of the other Nisei never got out of Santa Maria Valley until they were evacuated.

My best trip was in 1939 when I first came out here to Chicago to go to a refrigeration school. I went to this school as I thought I would get a chance to get a job with a big *hakujin* company. I wanted to see the country so I pulled up stakes and left [U]. I went to New York and to Washington when the King and Queen of England were there. I was flat broke after that because the refrigeration school took most of my savings. I just went to the refrigeration school for two months, but I had taken two years of correspondence work with them. I wouldn't have spent all my money traveling if I had known that I wouldn't get a job. The refrigeration school guaranteed us a job but when it came to my turn, I was out of luck. They just kept me waiting around. Finally I got homesick so I went back to California to see if I could get that kind of a job out there. I looked all over southern California for a refrigeration job but there was no opening for a Nisei, so I had to finally go back to my old job in the garage. I got stuck there and I thought I would never be able to practice refrigeration work because there was discrimination against Japanese.

When those sort of things happen to you, it makes you feel pretty good to be accepted in the Japanese community. Otherwise I didn't care too much. I knew most of the Nisei in the valley and I never ran up against any discrimination in anything except when I went job hunting that time.

December 7th was a Sunday and I was sleeping till noon that day. About one o'clock I went to see my girl friend and her family told me that Japan had bombed Pearl Harbor. I thought it was all baloney and I did not believe it. A lot of the Filipinos were gathering around in groups and the *hakujins* and *Nihonjins* also gathered around but nothing much happened in our town. After I learned the whole thing was true, I wondered what was going to happen next. I didn't have any particular worries and fears although I was pretty shocked. The other Japanese were quite excited and they were running back and forth to each other's homes to discuss the war. I stuck around at my girl friend's house and for the rest of the day we talked about what was going to happen.

I thought that I would be taken into the Army along with the rest of the Nisei fellows right away and I never figured on such a thing as evacuation. I didn't even know the meaning of the word. I'm the type who takes things as they come, so I didn't worry too much about what was going to happen although I do admit that I was disturbed more than I let on. Everybody in town was talking about the war and it was quite a surprise to all of us. The Caucasians did not have anything against the Japanese living in town and it did not make any difference. They did not start to intern the Issei until later on.

I went back to work the next day and I kept working in that job until two days before the evacuation. The Caucasian workers in the garage didn't talk very much about the war at all. The Japanese owner didn't get interned because he had a good clearance. We never had any trouble in our work at all, from the day of the war to the time we moved out of town to the camp. In fact, the *hakujin* workers were quite sympathetic to us.

In the meantime I got engaged at the end of January and in March we were married. We had a very simple wedding with only a few close friends in attendance. Right after that we had to get ready for the evacuation. I didn't like the idea of moving, but we had to. I had only a few things of my own, so that most of my time was spent in helping my wife's family get ready for the evacuation. I helped them pack and take care of their belongings. The JACL got busy and it helped make a lot of arrangements such as selling property and helping to store things in the government warehouse. It also passed all the information around about when we were going to be evacuated.

It's hard to say exactly how I felt when I had to leave. I felt pretty sad inside. I thought that the United States was meddling too much in other people's affairs. I didn't think that there was a thing as a war to end all wars. I believed that the United States should not have meddled in other country's businesses. Japan was the aggressor but that was because she was overpopulated. I personally thought the United States Monroe Doctrine was a similar thing that Japan was trying to set up in Asia. I didn't see why the United States should get so excited about it when this country had grabbed a lot of land itself in the past when it was expanding. The white countries were trying to push Japan around because they wanted to keep her in a small position on the islands. They were afraid that Japan would get too powerful. At the same time they wouldn't give Japan a fair chance in the world trade. They had set up all kinds of discriminations against the country. They weren't allowed to migrate into the United States any more because of the 1924 laws. The United States considered Japanese as inferior people and this was a great insult. I saw the effects of some of these things myself and I could not understand it. I couldn't believe that this country was all right in everything and that Japan was all wrong. I felt sorry for Japan because I knew how hard it was to be discriminated against because I had tried to get a job in refrigeration and I had been pushed around too. But when Japan attacked the United States, I thought sure that I would be in the U. S. Army and I wouldn't have fought against that. I didn't know what country I wanted to win the war but I knew I didn't want United States to be defeated because I was born here and I had American citizenship. It made me a little bitter when the *hakujin* started to push us around as if we were to blame for the whole war. They should have trusted us and given us more of a chance so that we could have proved our loyalty. They weren't willing to give us a chance and that didn't make us feel too good. I still believed in this country and I never thought of repatriating to Japan or anything like that. I just felt that it was a dirty deal and it was all a mistake. That's how I felt when I went to Tulare. I guess it wasn't a very good mood.

When I first got to Tulare I thought that it was one of the worst places I've had to live in. There wasn't any system to anything and it was all crowded. Everyone was rushing around trying to get things done for themselves and nobody knew what was what. So many people were coming in that we didn't have any privacy at all. The conveniences were not very well established either and the hot weather made it most uncomfortable. However, I had friends there so I soon got used to the place. For the first few days I just took it easy and fixed our place up a little bit. Everybody was rushing around for jobs, so I finally got a job repairing the trucks in camp and I got $12 a month for that. Naturally I didn't work too hard for this kind of a wage, but I did get a chance to ride a car around camp.

The whole thing was a new set of experiences for me and I met a lot of people in the mess halls and I made friends that way. We didn't fix our barracks up too much since I knew we were going to move again soon. We never thought too much of it but just lived our lives

and tried to be as comfortable as possible during the hot summer. I
didn't think that the U. S. would keep us in a camp all the time. Gradually I began to feel my style cramped and I wanted to get out. I
applied for a leave clearance while I was in Tulare because I heard
that a few people had gotten out. I had no destination in mind but I
just thought that I would like to get out of that place. It was just a
feeling that I wouldn't know how to describe. It wasn't that I disliked
the people in camp and I did have a lot of friends there. I guess it was
just the idea of being pushed into a camp without any say about how
innocent you were. That didn't seem right to me and I missed my
freedom.

The one thing that really got me down was the strict military guards
around the camp and the watch towers. We were being evacuated but
I didn't think that we should be treated as prisoners of war. I didn't
think that evacuation was justified at all. They gave us the reason
that the American people couldn't tell us apart if the Japanese Army
landed. If that were true, then the Army would have to evacuate the
whole eastern coast of this country in case the German Army landed.
On top of that, the Hawaiian Islands were much closer to Japan and
they did not move the Japanese from there. I think it was all politics.
Some of the California politicians wanted to use the Japanese people
as a stepping stone for themselves and they did not care how they discriminated against us. There were also some agricultural interests
which wanted us out for their own gain. They couldn't make so much
money in farming and they were jealous when the Japanese farmers
came and made the land pay off. Even though they have the land now,
I don't think they are doing as well as the Japanese farmers could do.
There were other people in California who were always against the
Japanese and they were talking about overpopulation of the state and
things like that. It was a hell of a deal all around and it did look like
all of our rights were lost forever. The Constitution and democracy
didn't mean a damn thing when it came down to the pinch. Naturally
that made me pretty disgusted because I didn't think that such a thing
would ever happen. I just wasn't enthusiastic about serving in the
Army at all when such things as evacuation were allowed to happen.
They just assumed that we were all guilty and they didn't even give
us a fair trial. When we were evacuated, I felt that we were definitely
cut off from our American rights for a long time to come. It didn't
give us much hope. I didn't like the idea at all and I wanted my freedom back, but I had no idea of where I wanted to go.

In early September [1942] we were sent to [the WRA camp at] Gila, Arizona. It was right in the middle of the desert. They sure did want to put us away from everything. They didn't want us in California anymore and they put us where nobody else wanted to live. A lot of rumors went around that they put us in the desert to kill us off but I don't think that that was true.

I felt that Gila would have been much more livable if it had been completed when we arrived. There were open ditches all over the place and the pipes were not even laid yet so that we didn't get running water for a couple of weeks. There was dust all over the place and the heat was terrific. It made my spirits go way down to think that I would have to live in a place like that. I was quite discouraged when I started my life there.

I don't have much of a memory of my Gila life as it wasn't important to me. I just existed. The only important event in my mind was when my baby was born. I spent most of my time worrying about that and I didn't have time for any of the other camp activities. I was worried that the hospital would not be able to give proper care. They didn't open the hospital up until about three months after we were there. By the time my baby was born, the hospital was running pretty well, but a lot of the doctors and nurses were leaving.

I took it easy when I first got there as I wanted to relax. I worked for a while in the community activities service division, in the athletic department. I was interested in getting the sports organized and I had had previous experience in being the athletic manager of the YBA back home. However, I didn't see any future in doing that kind of work. One day I heard that they needed men to do some refrigeration work. I thought that this was a good opportunity for me to put what I had learned into practice so I applied for the job and I was given a placement. We went around from mess hall to mess hall and maintained all of the ice boxes and refrigerators. It was during the hot weather so that a lot of the mess halls were having frigidaire trouble. A lot of the Japanese cooks were not used to electric refrigeration and they did not know how to take care of it. Our hours were easy and we knocked off whenever we felt like it. It was quite enjoyable work and I didn't mind it because it was the first real chance that I had to put into practice what I had learned. We got in good with all the cooks and they gave us plenty of extra food to take home or to eat. When I first started working, I was under another Nisei but I later took charge of the crew when he quit. I had the most experience then so that the responsibility fell to me.

I was only getting $19 a month and I needed more money because I knew that we were going to have a baby. I didn't have much money saved up so that when the camouflage work came around I saw a chance to make more money. I went into the net work in January, and I never did like it. It was too hard for me and the working conditions bothered me. I didn't like all of that lint floating around but I kept on because I was making pretty good money. After the hot weather started, the work got too uncomfortable for me and I didn't like the rashes I was getting from the lint so that I decided to quit in March. I made about $200 in all and I felt that this would take care of buying the things we needed for the expected baby. I wanted to be closer to home anyway so I could look after my wife. I was hoping that we would get a boy and I even had a name picked out for him. Our baby was born in May and that was quite a worry off my mind. It was a boy. That made me pretty happy and my wife liked it too because she had so many sisters.

After I quit the net factory, I went back into the refrigeration work. I continued that until the time I relocated out here. It was the only job in camp that I felt contributed to my skills and that is why I kept it up. I think I did learn quite a bit from the practical experience and I will always have that. Some day I may be able to go into that kind of work again out here.

The Gila life was pretty monotonous and boring at times and it didn't seem to lead anywhere. I had to think of a future beyond that because I had a baby and a wife for which I was responsible. I knew that I could not provide any sort of a future for them in camp. I felt I was just wasting my time there if I stayed too long. It seemed that the war was going to last for quite a while and I didn't want to stay in camp for three or four years. I had nothing against the WRA. They did as well as they could considering all of the problems that they had. Naturally the Japanese people in camp were resentful about a lot of things and many of them were looking around for gripes. They just didn't care for the *hakujins* and they wanted to blame them for everything. There were all sorts of gripes about the food, barracks, dust, linoleum, clothing, and everything else. I don't know what all of the bickering was about because I wasn't in contact with any of it. I know they used to have a lot of block meetings to talk over these gripes but I never attended.

When the registration came, that is what touched everything off. The Army did not handle it in the right way. They had a Nisei sergeant trying to explain and justify the evacuation to the Issei and it was all wrong. Any simpleton could have seen through that. The Japanese people felt that they had been pushed around and evacuated and it was silly to ask the Nisei to go volunteer after all that. I couldn't blame them for feeling that way because I felt the same way. I didn't see why they wanted the Nisei in the Army at that time. It wasn't to give them a chance but it was because of the manpower shortage and because they needed guys in the translation work. The Nisei sergeant gave talks about how everything would be made smooth if the Nisei volunteered and naturally this made all of the Issei sore. If they had just asked the Japanese people to take a vote for this country without the evacuation and all those things coming afterwards, I think that 90 per cent of them would have said "yes." It was too late to ask them about loyalty to this country when they had already said that they did not want the Japanese in California because they distrusted them. When the people in camp asked the sergeant about returning to California, he didn't have an answer for it. He tried to tell the people that it was better to stay in camp than go back to California because it was dangerous. The Issei just couldn't swallow this and they said that if their sons were good enough to go into the Army, then the parents should be good enough to be allowed to go back to their homes in California. The Army wouldn't even think of this at all and yet they expected the Nisei to rush into volunteering. Another thing was that it was a segregated unit and the Nisei in camp couldn't see anything democratic about that. It seems that the Army wanted to keep them together because the Nisei were not trusted in the regular Army. They weren't even given a consideration to serve in the air force or other branches of the service. I don't blame the Nisei for not being enthusiastic about that. That is why only about 100 of them volunteered. Most of the others were worried about what was going to happen to their folks and about getting established once more. They felt that it was up to them to get their family started once more but they didn't know how to go about it.

There was quite a bit of excitement during registration and the FBI officers finally had to come in and round up some of the agitators. I felt that the agitators had gone too far when they put forth all of those pro-Japan ideas instead of sticking to the issue. They had no business trying to sway the other people into thinking their way. I felt that if they were for Japan and if they wanted to repatriate, that was their own business. But they should not have tried to get everybody, including the Nisei, to answer "no" to the registration form.

Most of my friends answered Yes-Yes. We didn't discuss the thing too much as we were old enough to know what was the only course for us to take. There was no use in trying to show our discouraged feelings by answering "no" because that would not have gotten us any place. We wanted to be loyal to this country, but it often looked like the odds were against us and we were distrusted too much. I answered "double yes" myself as I felt that if I didn't I would be shipped out to Japan. I knew that I had nothing to do with the old country and I had no business there. There wasn't anything else for me [to do].

If it were not for the evacuation, every one of the guys would have been willing to go into the Army, even those who later went to Tule Lake. I know that for a fact because a lot of Kibei were drafted into the Army before the war and they didn't protest against it at all. Some of my best friends went to Tule Lake and I don't hold it against them at all. They had a right to answer whatever way they wanted to. I didn't care what they did as long as they did not try to convince me into their way of thinking. However, I thought that they were running into trouble by agitating against the registration and I didn't approve of that. I didn't argue with any of them and lose my friends. I felt that this was supposed to be a free country and they could do what they pleased. I think a lot of those Kibei would have been happier in Japan so it was no use trying to force them to answer "yes" when they disliked America so much. The Kibei had a pretty tough time because they couldn't speak English so well and even the Nisei tended to blame them for everything.

A lot of the parents influenced the young kids into signing the way they did. Maybe that was too bad as these Nisei would never be accepted in Japan. But what could they do about it? They either had to answer "no" and stick with their parents or else answer "yes" and be split from their family, perhaps forever. A lot of these kids were young and they wouldn't have been able to make a go of it on their own. They didn't see any future ahead of them by staying in camp and at that time resettlement possibilities had not opened up like they did later on. Naturally these kids wanted to be with their families so that they could stick together whatever happened. I can't blame them for that.

After the registration I really began to get down to definite plans for resettlement. I planned to go as soon as my baby was born. I often took time out to think of the postwar period and that was another reason why I felt I should get out soon. I didn't want to get into a rut because I had more than myself to think of. I thought of all different ways of how I could get established so that my family would have a chance. I wanted to resettle when the chances were still good.

I began to go to the employment office every day to look over the job offers on the outside. One day I happened to see a job offer for an auto mechanic in Chicago. Up to that time I still didn't have an exact idea of where I would be going to resettle. I didn't particularly care as long as I got a good job. I had heard that a lot of people were going to Chicago but I wasn't too anxious to go there. I would have gone to Detroit, Cleveland, or New York just as easily if I had a job offer from these places. The auto mechanic job offer looked good to me so I wrote to the boss of the garage and asked him for the job. He sent a telegram back right away saying that he was willing to accept me for a trial and he asked me to come out as soon as possible.

I came right on out here as soon as my baby was born and I arrived in Chicago in June [1943]. Housing was my biggest problem since I already had the job before I left camp. I had to stay in a hotel at first. After work I would look around most of the evening for a suitable apartment. I tramped around all Saturday afternoon and Sundays. I never walked so much in all my life. Lucky for me, my boss got a good impression of me in my work so that he was kind enough to loan me a car while I was looking around.

That was when I ran into my first discrimination in housing. There were some flats open but the landlords just didn't want me in there. A few places told me that they could not take in any Japanese. It was no use arguing with them, so I just left. It made me feel pretty funny and I didn't like it at all but you can't force them to take us in and they don't understand us. Other landlords told me that the vacant flats were already taken, but I noticed that the signs were still up when I passed by a few days later. Other landlords told us that there were no openings in a very awkward way and we just felt that they didn't want us around. I was pretty discouraged about the whole thing and I didn't feel good when I saw this discrimination, but I had to keep on trying.[191]

One day in November my boss said that there was a vacant flat about a half block from the garage. I thought that it was going to be

---

[191] CH-36 kept the letters written her by CH-35 during June and July, 1943, and she kindly permitted us to make copies of them. Excerpts from these letters, which are an important supplement to CH-35's own account, follow his life history.

another refusal but there was no harm in trying. I went over right away and talked to the landlady. I told her that I was in the garage and the boss would give me a reference. I looked the flat over and it was just what I wanted. The landlady seemed agreeable and she let me rent the flat right away. The flat rented for only $25 a month unfurnished. I spent about $400–$500 in furnishing it up and in buying all the other things to get started. I paid $30 for our large refrigerator and fixed it up myself so it was quite a bargain. We had to buy a new stove and a lot of coal since it was winter time. We had to buy beds and even blankets because we didn't have any. It took us quite a while to furnish the place because we went around to second-hand dealers.

This is the first real home that I have ever had in my life, and I certainly feel proud of it. I like it swell and I think that we are located in a good neighborhood. The neighbors are not too friendly yet but they seem to mind their own business and we mind ours. We get along fairly well with the [landlady]. She understands our position. Her husband is a German and during the last war he lost his job on account of all the prejudice so that they had a hard time to make ends meet. That is way our [landlady] sympathizes with us. If I am drafted I plan to come back here and live here after the war. I have all that money invested in the furniture so I might as well hang on to it.

I've been getting along very well in my job. Before I arrived here, my boss got all of the other employees together and asked them how they felt about having a Japanese American coming in with them as a mechanic. They said that as long as I was an American citizen they did not care. After I was in the garage for two weeks the boss told me that all of the workers liked me and that made me feel pretty good. I felt that I was accepted just like them. After I was there a week or so a group of the other mechanics took me out and bought me beer. That really relieved me because I knew that things would be okay and they would not resent me after that.

My wages are paid on a percentage basis so that the more work I do the more I will make. I usually work from 8 to 5:30 and half day on Saturdays. I make around $250 a month now. That is enough to meet all of my present living costs. We don't live by any definite budget at all as long as the money keeps coming in. I think that I am making more money now than most Nisei for the amount of hours I put in.

The one experience that I feel resentful about is the union business. The A.F.L. union will not accept Orientals as full-fledged members. They charged me $25 initiation fee and gave me a duration-working permit. I had to pay the regular $3 monthly dues like the members. I wasn't going to join it at all as I said I would only join if they gave me equal membership. Then the union representative went to the boss and told him that I would have to be fired or else become a member on their terms. If I refused to join, the union said there might be a strike against the shop. There wasn't anything I could do about it, so I reluctantly joined up. The boss felt just as bad as I did about it and he paid half of the initiation fee. I can't even attend any of the regular union meetings and I have no voice in any of the voting. That's not very democratic. It sure burns me up. Even the boss was griped and he said that it was a helluva deal. The other workers are all union men and they thought it was unfair too, but they can't do anything about it because it is a union rule. There are a few colored men in our garage but they only wash cars and run the elevator. They aren't in the union either. There are about 20 workers in the garage and only three of us are Nisei. I got my uncle and the other Nisei into the job after I was accepted.

I think that my boss is one swell guy. The rest of the guys in the garage are okay too. My boss thinks that I am American and just as good as the next guy. The only thing that he is concerned about is whether I can do the work or not. I've got quite a few friends in the garage now and some of us go out bowling, playing pool, or drinking together. I wouldn't care if a lot more Nisei mechanics were hired now, as I don't think it would hurt my job any since I am pretty well established in the place.

Although I don't have a wide contact with other Nisei workers, I get the impression that a lot of them are not steady enough in their jobs. I've heard of many cases of Nisei changing their jobs around quite a bit. As a whole, the Nisei do not have any special trade so that they just jump around from job to job trying to get the best wages they can. I don't quite blame them because many of them are dissatisfied with what they are doing and they don't feel that they are making enough progress. A lot of the younger kids jump around from job to job unnecessarily because they do not know what they want. I think that it hurts the chances of the other Nisei because it does create a bad impression. On the other hand, it is a good sign as these Nisei are not satisfied with any old job tossed to them. The Nisei haven't had experience enough so that many of them are not steady workers yet. I think that this sort of thing is true for the *hakujin* too but they don't get blamed for it like we do.

I plan to stay in my present job as long as I can and do it after the war if I can come back to it. The big question mark is what the union would do about it. I only have a working permit for the duration and the union may not want to renew it after the war. However, I don't think they can do much if I serve in the Army. If they do, then I don't think that it would be worth fighting for democracy when these discriminations are still practiced right along. I think that my present job is better than the one I had before the war. I know that I am more satisfied with it. I never was entirely satisfied with the cheap pay I got at the Japanese garage before the war.[192] In my present job the amount of my pay is up to me and if I want to make more money, I have to produce more. In my job before the war I just got a certain weekly wage and I had to put in plenty of overtime without getting paid for it. I figure that I have more of a chance to hang on to my job than the other Nisei who are doing more unskilled work out here.

I manage to save a little money each month, but the expenses are pretty great for keeping up a home. My garage takes out $7.50 every week out of my paycheck for the purchase of war bonds so that we will always have that as a minimum savings. I manage to save a little cash besides that though. I gamble for small stakes but I only do it for the thrill. I took quite a beating betting on the football games last season. I can't bet on the horses any more since I got married since I can't afford that.

I get enough leisure time now as I have most of the week ends and the evenings for my social and recreational pleasure. I have much more time for myself than I had in my old job before the war. I visit friends about once or twice a week out here and we go to shows once a week too. Other times we go to the various sports events. Once or twice a week friends may drop in on us for a visit. We went to a couple of the Nisei dances. Whenever we feel like it we go bowling. Occasionally I go play pool with some of the fellows in the shop or with Nisei friends. I only drink occasionally and I haven't really gotten drunk out here.

We have a Nisei circle of friends of about 10 or 15 people and we visit with them the most. We usually get together with friends at their home or our home. You know how the circle grows and grows. It seems that other people are added to the group all the time. Most of the time we talk about the old days or about camp life but we don't

---

[192] CH-35 was earning about $160 per month at the outbreak of war.

go into anything too serious. We sit around and play cards too or the girls talk about their babies.

We have very limited contacts with the Caucasians although we have visited the homes of some of my co-workers. They are always inviting us over. We just talk shop with them and we don't go out on parties with them since most of our social activities are among our Nisei friends. My wife is making a few friends among the neighbors and I think they will understand us better after we get more acquainted. They are too suspicious now but that is because they don't know us. We are really trying to get to know the neighborhood because that is a good policy. After it gets a little warmer my wife will be able to talk over the back fence with some of the mothers.

I don't think it would be a good idea to have a Japanese community out here right now. It is not such a good thing to have segregation like that I guess. It should be all Americans mixing and everybody accepted like Mrs. Roosevelt says, but that isn't possible now. I think that it is possible to have Nisei social groups, along with mixing in with Caucasian groups at the same time. Gradually the Nisei will become accepted more and it would break down a lot of the prejudices.

I think that the Issei would be happier in a Japanese town, but they are getting old and the main thing to worry about now is the future of the Nisei and Sansei. All I ask for is that my son is given an equal chance like the Constitution says. I wouldn't want more segregation and prejudice to spring up now as we have gone through enough of that.

My real ambition is to go to a small town and have my own shop. In any event, things just won't be like before the war. I don't think that too many Japanese will go back to California because there aren't any opportunities for them. There are too many Okies going out there and California is overcrowded now.

I've got my 1-A now and I am officially in the Army. The war is something that has to be finished up and the sooner the better. As it stands now, I don't think my American citizenship is worth fighting for. It doesn't mean anything the ways things are. Maybe we can have a democracy. It certainly is not in practice now. It seems that you can have just as much of a dictatorship in a democracy as in a fascist country. The only good thing is that there is some hope, although slim, for the future and I guess we have to fight for that slim chance now. I am quite disillusioned and I don't mind admitting it.

APPENDIX TO CH-35
Letters from CH-35 to CH-36

June 11. Darling: Reached here 9:30 last nite safe and sound. Had no trouble at any time of the trip. . . . I'd say better than two-thirds of the passengers are soldiers. . . . [Two Nisei], a *hakujin,* and I got a seat together on a pullman used as a chair car. We played cards quite a bit. [After making contacts with a number of Nisei friends in Chicago] I went to see my new employer and he seemed like a pretty nice egg. He suggested that I start work from Monday when my tools come. . . . I can't say I like this place yet but I'll give it a try. . . . [A Nisei] and I went to eat at the YMCA tonight and I'm telling you I saw at least 15 *yogore* like us . . . mostly all in sport clothes and look like hicks. . . . How is Johnny [their baby]? Does he cry more now that I'm not there? Ha, ha. . . .

June 13. Darling: I certainly miss you and Johnny. I wish you both were here and then maybe I won't feel so bad about the place. I certainly can't say I like the dump. [Describes difficulties of finding housing.] There's any amount of work here. . . . Most of the places will hire us *yabo* but like I said [a] place to stay is hard to find, unless there single so they can stay at a hotel and eat out. It sure cost though."

June 17. Darling: How are you and Johnny? I hope everything is okay at camp. I'm sure glad about them giving the double "no" guys a chance to change. I hope lots of people take advantage of it. Some I know won't change. . . .

Here it is one week since I came here and I still am not settled. [X] and I been looking all over the section of town where we work and we can't even get a decent hotel room let alone an apartment. The north side sure is crowded. We're staying in a cheap small smelly old place where we can't even take a bath because its so dirty. Keep your chine up—I find a place yet. . . .

The boss and all the boys we work with are sure swell bunch. Few even go out of their way to be nice to me. They're all keeping their eyes open for an apartment for me. One of the boys even spent all evening taking me around in his car looking for apartment, no soap though.

The smallest mechanic's check last week was $66 and $81 was the top for mechanic at our garage so I have hopes of making at least the bottom pay when my tools come. [A fellow worker] was good enough to let me share his tools untill mine comes. I hope it's pretty dam quick. [More details about wages and living expenses.]

That's enough of all that lets talk about Johnny. How much did he weigh last Tuesday? I'll bet he's taken on lots of fat, eh? ... I'd send him lots of toys and things but it'll be lots more excess baggage when you come so I'll buy then when he comes here. Okay. Gosh, I like to see and hold him. Has he changed any more since I left. Is he catching up to [a friend's baby]? I don't expect him to pass him but—. Take good care of him, darling, I'll be seeing youse soon. ... I hope to be settled by the time I wrote again. I hope. Kiss Johnny for me. I love you darling.

June 21. Darling: [Details about Nisei friends.] I'm still struggling along on borrowed tools and last week five days, I have a check of $39 coming which I'll send to you. This week if my tools come early enough I hope to do better than $50.

Everybody sure is nice to us. Tomorrow night the boss is going to loan us a car so we can find a decent place to stay. A furnished apartment is almost impossible to find but there are quite a few unfurnished places so I *might* buy some furniture. They tell me its cheaper that way anyway. ...

I wonder what Mom has to say about that bad son-in-law that left her darling daughter in camp. Is she very angry with me? ... I'm glad mom know where dad is at least and I think he'll be released. They really haven't anything on him. I'll bet mom looks lot different with her teeth in. Give her my best regards. I love you darling. Tell Johnny I'll be seeing him real soon. Love.

June 23. Darling: ... Enclosed you will find my first pay check. It's smaller than I thought. ... Last night our boss loaned us a 1941 Pontiac eight with ten gallons of gas to look for a place to stay. We bought a paper and went to all the place advertised but no soap for an apartement but we got a pretty good room with bath and we are paying $10 a week. ...

Today a mechanic union guy came around and said that I'd have to get a working permit for $25 initiation fee and $3 a month thereafter, and he tells me I can't be a regular member because I'm a Japanese. I got mad and I told him I'm not a Japanese, I'm an American and he had nothing to say. The boss told me later when I told him about it, that he's look into it for me. ...

How's Johnny. Take care of him. I'll be seeing you soon. Love.

Saturday, 3:15 p.m. Darling: [Details about visiting Nisei. Instructions about fixing up fan for the cooler in camp.]

I went to see about the apartment I had picked out but just my luck or call it dumbness, someone else already moved in that place so I'll have to look around again. Don't worry I'll have a place when you come. But don't expect anything fancy. Like [R] says—he lost fight in a kinda place people live in Chicago. He certainly was disgusted. Anyway after you come we'll look for a place with everything the way you like (within our reach of course). . . .

I'm kinda broke and don't feel so good. I hope you bring some cash out too[?]. Good thing I haven't got the bonds. I'd be cashing them now. . . .

About that date—try and make it as soon as possible. Not later than Aug. 15th. Okay. I really miss you darling. After all [R] tells me about Johnny I miss him too. Don't forget now, August 15th.

Oh yes, I was thinking if we save enough by the time Dad comes back, released I mean. We could take a trip to Gila to see him. Don't worry you see him again aright.

I'll close for now. Kiss Johnny for me darling. I love you. P.S. . . . Don't forget our date.

June 30. Darling: [Details about Nisei friends. Relays advice from them about how to pack, arrangements to make with WRA, etc.]

Yesterday my boss and I went way up town to see a landlord about a 4 room flat that's open right near the garage but she tell me a Filippino and a white girl that stayed there caused some complaint so she didn't rent it to us. My boss went as far as to offer her a hole year rent in advance. He sure thinks lots of me. He sure is swell guy. Coming back to the garage he told me he's got a 200 acre ranch in Wisconsin and he told me I can work there if I liked after about 18 months from now.

I've got a few apartments lined up so I think I can take a pick. They're all pretty dingy but for time being untill we find better ones it'll have to do. . . .

Last week I only made 37 dollars but this week I think I'll get over 60 bucks. There's a tecnique in the way you arrange your time and you get more done with less effort. I'm catching on. . . .

So Johnny is getting to be a big boy now. I think you better come while you still able to carry him. I sure wish I was there to help you with all the packing and things. . . .

I'll write in a few days. Until then take care of yourself and Johnny. Love.

July 5. Darling: Since the fourth came on Sunday, we get a day off today. [Describes activities with Nisei friends. Explains why he is not sending motor for cooler to camp.]

By the way, did you get Johnny's birth certificate? Be sure to get it before you leave. As soon as you settle the cash grant business I want you here as soon as possible. I certainly miss you and Johnny. I don't know what Mom will say to your traveling yet but I saw lots of babies on train and they didn't look very old to me. . . .

How's the situation there in camp. Is everybody OK? How's the chance of Dad's release? If he's going to be released soon I might take a trip into camp because I haven't got my cash grant so it won't cost me anything if I collect it there. It's just a thought, don't take it seriously.

[More about housing.] I'll close now darling. I love you.

July 11. Darling: Today being Sunday, I sure feel lazy. . . . Last nite we were invited to [a Nisei couple's] place for dinner and their relatives living around here. [The husband] came back from Detroit saying the housing situation is worse there then here. As bad as it is here, you don't have to share your room with swing shift worker. . . . [The husband] suggested we get a big house and live together. I don't think it's so good unless it's a duplex apartment. [He] hasn't got a job yet but I guess they're staying here. That's certain and [N] sure want you to come out quick. She thinks you'll be here before the end of the week. I sure wish you could. . . .

Last week was financially bad. Monday we didn't work and Tuesday I was busy and earned about $13 but the rest of the week was good for nothing. I'll be lucky if I get a $30 check after taking out for employment ins. (social sec.) 20% income tax and $3 war bond saving. On top of that I'm thinking of buying a car. It's a 1939 chevy coupe for $425. The boss is giving it to me wholesale and I figure I can get that much back out of the car 2 years from now because they aren't making any more and the use car price is going up all the time. The boss will give me over six months to pay for it I think. What do you think of the whole thing? We'll sure be short of cash because when you come out we'll need lots of things but think it over eh? But quick.

Are you sure they sent out my cash grant? Did [X] sound like I was going to get it? If not I'm going to write to [the project director] personal and see if he can't do something about it. Let me know eh. I told you to get your cash grant & things ready but I guess it was too late eh? When do they think they'll be able to make grants again?

You don't seem to realize it but it means $216 and boy that no hay. Keep after them and let me know. I should have gotten mine by now if they really sent it. Check up on it. Go to the head guy whoever it is if you can't get information from [X].

I saw [N's] baby and she sure has grown. I can just about imagine how big Johnny is. [N] tells me Johnny's feet is just as big as her. Boy she kicks and smiles just like [friend's baby] use to when I was there. I'll close now and hit the hay.... Love.

July 18. Darling: Here I am five almost 6 weeks since I left camp and am still not settled. I sure miss you & Johnny. Sure wish you were here now. I know I can get a place to stay but I'm still undecited weather to rent a large place or a small two room just for us. Anyway I wish you'd bring Johnny out as soon as things are settled there in camp. If I can get my cash grant you can forget about yours but try hard to get one or the other. I sure miss you & want you out here as soon as possible.... [Describes poker session.]

I was pretty lucky. Last week was pretty busy and I earned close to sixty dollars. I'm only subscribing three dollars a week for war bond and I am exempt $12 for myself, $12 for you & $6 for Johnny or $30 a week so on $60 check I pay 20% of $30. So on the $60 base check I get is only about $49 with $3 for war bond to my credit. It's not too bad but rest of the boys are kicking and we are asking for [a raise]. I think it will take couple of months before it comes into effect....

The way I write I'll bet you think I've gone money crazy. Well it's not that but in this town money sure talks and makes you money conscious. I really don't like talking money.... I don't like it that's all but I can't help it right now.

I'm sure glad [friend's baby] took the baby contest. I always told you he would. Give my congratulation to [his mother] and I guess Johnny was too young to be entered eh? He wouldn't have taken anything anyway. He looks too much like me. Ha ha. How is he doing these hot days?

As for the cooler I'm sending bunch of motor and fan to [a friend] so if they come after the motor in our cooler ask [him] to install a motor for you. Be sure to pack my fan away when you ask him. I want that fan here. I can't get a good fan like that here....

[Describes a Nisei friend.] I guess it pays to be good looking. The other nite on our way to [X's] some colored girls made a play for him and we sure kid him about it.

I got a job for [a Nisei] at the garage but he only lasted one week. I guess he doesn't care for car-washing jobs. To tell the truth, it sure is tough on these guys here without traid. The attractive pay here attract lots of the guys who left camp on domestic jobs quit and they're sure sad. They were lots better of getting $75 a month room and board because they never have that much left over working at 75¢ an hour on other jobs.

I wrote [CH-37] but haven't got any answer yet but ask him if he wants me to I'll go see the jobs he picks out. Defense jobs are sure hard to crash. Even *hakujin* have lots of red tape. The kid who was working at the garage took 2 months to get in. The pay there isn't so good either unless your a specialist in some thing. I'm trying to line up a job for [some other Nisei. Gives details]. . . . I guess I didn't tell you but I bought a 1935 chevy for $60. It's pretty much of a junk but I know with little fixing it'll be worth $150 and I have something to ride around on too. It's an investment and I'll get my money back out of it.

I sure hope [Ch-37] comes out here. The place isn't too bad when you get use to it. The only thing I'm worried about now is the draft. After buying furniture & things and get settled, I'd sure hate to give it up if I'm drafted. Let's not worry about that now yet eh? I'm sorry I ever brought it up. I know how you feel about it. . . . I'll close now. By darling. By Johnny. I hope to see you real soon. Love. Daddy.

July 19. Darling: I just received your letter of 15th, this afternoon and I'm sure glad you decided to leave. I guess it's going to be hard but heck it has to happen soon or later eh? I'll bet Mom didn't like the idea at all. No, I haven't wrote to Mom or Dad but I shall right away. I was thinking of writing to Dad but I didn't know his knew address.

I'm enclosing my check that I got from the bank. I know it's hard to cash it but I think if you *tanomu* the canteen manager I'm sure he will cash it for you or at least have it cashed at the bank for you. I could cash it here but they charge 1% and that's one dollar and then I have to pay money order beside so I'm sending the check. . . . [Nisei friends], my boss and all the guys I know ask me when your coming and I didn't have any answer for them but I have now. . . . Tell Johnny Daddy's going to spoil him when he gets here. Good night darling. Love.

July 24. Darling: Here are some more *otsukai* that you don't like. I'm sorry but it has to be done. First I've sent you some money and I hope you have enough for all nessecery obligation. I could get some things here but you know how long it takes me to get anything. . . . I'll also send a fan & motor to put in our cooler and give it to Mom. Don't you think she can use it?

As for the apartment there are quite a few open now and . . . we are going apartment hunting tomorrow. . . . I'm enclosing a map of Chicago so you can get some idea as to where the streets are. The map is put out by the street-car line and only shows the street that cars run on but it gives you an idea anyway.

In packing if it makes it any easier, leave the bowling ball and crib, you can give it to somebody that needs it. I don't feel like bowling like I used to and there are lots of used cribs that can be bought cheap. [More instructions about leaving camp.] . . . I'll close now and write on Monday or Tuesday. I hope to have an apt. by then. Love.

August 2. Darling: You should have seen me when I got your telegram. Boy was I one happy guy. [A fellow worker] said he hasn't seen me in that condition for a long time. Really I was getting pretty darn disgusted with the whole darn things here. I'm really counting the days now that I know when you'll be here. . . .

Try and travel as lite as you can but since you have a pullman I don't think it will be too bad. Be sure to have some quarter & half dollar piece for tipping. 25¢ for lite service & 50¢ when they do lots for you. Take it easy tho. It'll really run up befor your through. A good place to send a telegram is Kansas City because you stop there over half hour. You just tell the porter and he'll take care of it for you. You're traveling first class. You can have your breakfast in bed and everything. Be sure to enjoy it. I don't think it'll happen again. Not for a long time anyway. When we're old and gray. . . .

I've been making about $60 for the last few week but I'll be darn if I can tell where it all go. I hope you will be able to see it when you get here. I don't expect to save any right now but I haven't anything to show either. Anyway we'll make out and have fun eh?

I'll have everything ready for you darling. Don't worry. I can't hardly wait to see you & Johnny. Oh yes, when you reach Chicago, don't try & jump out of train like the rest of the passengers. The train don't go any further than Chicago so there's no hurry in getting off. If you don't have any help—just sit there & I'll come get the bags and things. I'll be there with bells on. Love.

CH-36: COUNTER GIRL

Female; born in California, 1918; height 62"; weight 104 lbs.; married, 1942; one child; wife of CH-35; sister-in-law of CH-37. Interviewed

April, 1944. Described as a "fairly tall and slender Nisei girl," who was "timid with strangers" but "very adjustable" and "quite interesting once one is able to penetrate beneath the surface shell of coldness." Although "it took a considerable time for her to open up and tell her story, once she started there wasn't any difficulty at all." In the interviewer's opinion, she was "well-suited to her husband" and the marriage had "turned out very well." Her greatest worry seemed to be "what to do when her husband is drafted."

CAREER LINES

Parental: Father (born *ca.* 1875) from farming class in Japan; immigrated to Hawaii *ca.* 1899. Worked on sugar plantations for "about six years," then moved to Los Angeles where he did farm work before becoming a gardener in southern California. Opened a barbershop *ca.* 1912 in a coastal town and later added a bathhouse; continued in this work until 1935, when he moved to a smaller town in the Santa Maria Valley and opened a pool hall, which he operated as a family enterprise until evacuation. Mother (born *ca.* 1890) immigrated to southern California as a picture bride in 1912. Assisted her husband in his business and, during the late 1930's, worked as a farm laborer. *Own:* Graduated from high school in southern California, 1935. Worked as counter girl in father's pool hall, 1935–1937; as clerk in brother-in-law's (CH-37's) grocery store, 1937; as picker on a seed farm, 1938; and as vegetable buncher on truck farm, 1940 to 1942. Inmigrated to Chicago in August, 1943; housewife.

LIFE HISTORY

I am the third oldest of eight children. My parents both came from the Kumamoto *ken,* but they did not know each other over there. About forty-five years ago, my dad went to Hawaii. He was then in his middle twenties. After working on the sugar plantations for six years, he decided to go to Los Angeles. After working around Los Angeles for a while he moved up to [M, a coastal city] to work as a gardener on some rich peoples' estates. It was about this time that he got married under the *shashin kekkon* system. When Mother came [in 1912], he started to work in town as a barber and he also ran a bathhouse behind the shop.

My father never made too much money and since we were a large family it was hard for him to support us. During the depression my mother had to go out and do day work so that us 8 kids could get enough to eat. We were really poor then and this worried my father quite a bit. My mother was the real boss of the family. However she was smart enough to let Dad think that he was the real head. She was much younger than my father, 15 years, so that she tended to be more active. She taught us children most of the things we know and she gave us more good advice than Dad ever did. One of the things that my parents taught us was duty to the family. And they emphasized it a great deal. We were given the impression that our parents had done so much for us that we felt obligated to them. That is why I later worked in the pool hall and went out on the farms without thinking any more about it. I just did it for the family.

My parents were Buddhist but they were not religious. When I was small, I was sent to the Christian Church as there was not a Buddhist Church in town at that time. When the Buddhist Church did get established, we just had to go along with the other kids and attend it because the parents sent us. My parents did not feel it was wrong to send us to a Christian church before then because they thought it was better for us to go to any church than none at all.

We had quite a bit of Japanese traditions in our home. I remember in my grammar school days we ate mostly Japanese food. If we had an American dinner of bread, potatoes and meat, this was considered quite a treat and a special Sunday meal. We had to take part in all of the Japanese church and school festivals whenever these things came up. I rather enjoyed these things and I didn't resent it at all until I was much older.

Our family was always poor. We had a miserable home in [M]. The barbershop was located in front and behind that was the four public bathrooms. It was behind the bathrooms that we lived. We had two bedrooms and a kitchen and the 10 of us lived there. All of the beds were crowded together, much more than in camp, and we didn't have hardly room to move around. The roof always leaked in the winter time, so we had to move the beds around to the driest spots. One of the things that scared me most was to hear those rats running all over the place. Occasionally I would see a rat run right out of the toilet and that really frightened me. My mother always wanted to move the family out of that place but we were too poor. Finally when the family got too big, my sister and I were allowed to take a room in a Japanese boardinghouse next door. We just slept there and we continued to eat at home and do our usual chores. I had to look after the younger kids a lot of time because my mother helped Dad run the barbershop and bathhouse out in front.

Most of the people living in the Japanese community in town came from the same *ken* in Japan and we were all practically relatives. I used to call all of them *obasan* and *ojisan* from the earliest age and I never called them *Tadasan* or anything like that. There were about 500 Japanese living in or near the Japanese community. A lot of them were domestic workers in the rich American homes but they always came to *Nihonmachi* on their days off. The rest of them worked out on the truck farms and they would always come to town for the church festivals or other events. Those who had their own businesses were located in the Japanese town and they catered mostly to the Japanese and Mexicans. A few of them had businesses among the *hakujin* but these were mostly older Nisei. The leaders in the Japanese community were the old pioneers and everyone looked up to them. They really decided everything which affected the Japanese community. These pioneers were all types of workers and only a few of them were really in the money. None of them were really able to hit it rich in their work so that not too many of the Japanese families were able to send their children to college for an education.

There was nothing outstanding about my grammar school experience. I did well in all of my subjects like all the other Nisei, except in arithmetic. I had always been shy and I had the hardest time mixing in with other people. I felt inferior to the *hakujin* kids as it seemed that they were not afraid to go talk to the teacher. They always dressed better than I did and I thought they were so rich. I was ashamed of living behind the bathhouse with all of those rats running around. I never brought any of my friends home because I didn't want them to see where I lived. It seemed that all of the *hakujin* kids had nice homes to live in and they didn't have to live behind barbershops. The *hakujin* kids didn't notice the Nisei very much but they didn't have any attitudes against us because we were all kids together.

After I got into junior high school, I went around only with *Nihonjin* girls and we ate all our lunches together and we took the same locker. We always consulted each other so that we could take the same classes together. We were very clannish and we didn't realize that we stuck out by staying together so much. I felt much more comfortable among these Nisei girls and I didn't want it any different. After school I would play only with Nisei kids and my whole life outside of school was in the Japanese community.

I just went on to high school and nothing eventful happened there either. I just stuck with my Nisei friends and took the same courses and did the same thing as they did. We all studied hard and we never entered into any of the other school activities. The higher up in school we went, the more clannish we got. I didn't have any idea of what I would do after high school although I thought I wanted to take up nursing. But I knew that my father was too hard up to send me on after high school so I just had to drop all of my plans. I graduated in 1935 when I was 17.

Our family still was not able to make a good living and Dad finally decided to move all of us to [U, in the Santa Maria Valley] and start a pool hall. It was a shock to us to leave [M] where we lived all our lives. I knew that [U] was a dirty old town and I didn't think that I would ever like it there and it was the last straw when my dad said that we were going to have a pool hall. I had always crossed the streets in order to avoid pool halls because I thought they were evil places. Imagine what a shock it was when we learned we were going to live in one. We could not say anything as we felt that Dad knew the best. After we got to [U] in the summer of 1935, I used to work behind the counter in the pool hall with my sister in order to help out.

The Japanese town was only about four blocks long and most of the Japanese stores were in this district. It was mostly grocery stores, barbershops, saloons and pool halls, and a few restaurants. Our pool hall was right in the middle of this Japanese town. Our family lived in the rooms behind the pool hall and it wasn't much of an improvement over the rooms we had lived in behind the barbershop in [M].

I never got along with the Filipino customers in the pool hall from the beginning. They made wisecracks at me and tried to get fresh. I didn't like it at all, but Dad asked me to be patient as he said it would only be for a year or so until he could get on his feet. I thought I could stick it out this long for the family's sake. At first the business was very good as all of the Filipinos were curious about the girls in the pool hall. But after 2 or 3 months business fell off because we didn't act very friendly. My parents always stayed around in the pool hall as they wanted to protect us in case anything happened. My mother said we should act more friendly just for business reasons, but I just couldn't get around to doing it. It was mostly Filipinos and Mexicans who came there and only one bunch of Nisei fellows came around.

In the pool hall, I did get used to talking to Nisei fellows more and I wasn't so reserved as before. This was where I first met my future husband [CH-35] as he used to drop over occasionally to play pool with another Nisei fellow. I didn't have time to go out on social dates because of my work. The Nisei in town sort of avoided me because I worked in a pool hall and they had the same attitude about pool halls as I had before. They thought there was something wrong in my family to go into that kind of work.

I continued to work in the pool hall for two years until my brother-in-law [CH-37] wrote and said that he needed a helper in his grocery store in [Y]. I decided to go up there as this was a chance to get away from the pool hall. He gave me room and board and 10 per cent of the gross sales as my wages. I generally made about $30 a month as my brother-in-law was making most of his money in his radio section. I couldn't save anything on this salary, so I was not able to send anything back home to help out the family. By this time I had been taking over a lot of the family responsibility. I sort of resented it very much because I felt I was restricted and I couldn't lead my own life like the other girls. The work in the grocery store helped me out a little as it gave me a chance to get away from my former drab life. The work was very easy even though I did put in about 12 hours a day. I would help out at my sister's home after work and I enjoyed this life very much because we had mostly *hakujin* customers in the store. However, I got sort of homesick after several months so I decided to go back to my family. My older sister and her husband got along well in their marriage and I enjoyed living with them. I sort of regretted leaving them to go home. After I got home I started to work in the same old routine at the pool hall.

My next older sister got tuberculosis and she became an invalid so I had to do most of the work myself. The Japanese have a funny attitude about tuberculosis and they always try to hide it from the other people because they are ashamed. My mother was worried that it would affect our chances of getting married, but I thought that was silly. I had a few arguments with her about this before she was convinced. By that time I was beginning to say more of the things I felt.

I continued to work in the pool hall until about June, 1938. The business kept getting worse and worse and my mother finally had to go out and work on a farm. She took Dad along and soon I started to go with them during the day. In the evening we opened up the pool hall and by that time my next sister was old enough to help out and she took my invalid sister's place. I worked on this farm most of the summer of 1938 and I made about $50 a month. The workers were mostly Filipinos, Mexicans, and Japanese. After the season we went back to the pool hall again. I felt much more responsibility for the family as there were a lot of younger kids and we did not have a steady income to feed them. On top of that we had a sick sister to pay doctor bills for. It wasn't so easy for us, but we managed to barely scrape by. My original idea in going out to do farm work during the day was to save up money for the future education of the younger kids, but we had to dip into this fund all the time to keep going from day to day.

In the summer of 1940 I went out with my parents to bunch vegetables. It was necessary for us to do that because we were getting poorer all the time. Soon I was doing the work regularly. We bunched carrots, broccoli, and other vegetables. We did this work all the year around. If it rained, we put on our raincoats and rain pants and we sat right out in the mud and bunched the vegetables. The wages were not too good as we only made about $8 a day among the three of us. However, this was enough to keep the family going. At night, we still ran the pool hall and that gave us a little additional income. We did that farm work right up to the time of my marriage in March, 1942. Even after that I continued to do the work until almost the day of evacuation since our family did not have a lot of money saved up and we did have to keep eating.

I never did understand the position of the Japanese on the coast before the war. The Issei talked the most about discrimination and things like that because they had faced it more in their business relations. I knew that a lot of Nisei kids who got out of school had a hard time getting jobs but there was always a place at one of the larger Japanese produce companies and it seemed as if things were going along pretty smoothly. A lot of those Japanese farmers were really making good money. Workers like my parents and I had the hardest time. There wasn't anything I could do about it since the only outlook was to do the field work. I wanted to help my younger sister through school so that she would be in a better position to take her turn and help the family out later on. Since my older sister was an invalid, I felt I had to do double share. Sometimes I resented this quite a bit, and I felt sorry for myself. But I just had to get used to it so I just accepted the fact and settled down to the routine. I couldn't even think of marriage. It bothered me at times about not getting married and I had a lot of mental conflicts about that. I didn't want to be an old maid but I felt that I had to make the sacrifice because I had certain family responsibilities, which I considered as my first duty. Our family life was not unhappy in spite of our poorness. In fact, I think that it brought us together.

On December 7 we were listening to the radio when the news of Pearl Harbor came along. I believed it right away because I always believe what the radio says. I ran to tell my mother and she would not believe it. She thought it was all some kind of a joke. My boy friend came over right away and we started to talk about whether war would come now. I guess we were all pretty excited. I wasn't afraid of the Caucasians at all but I didn't know what the Filipinos would do because they were sort of savage. The thing that scared me the most was that I thought they would come breaking in as a mob and tear up our place. Dad was stunned too. We all stayed together in our room in back for protection. Gee, that was some day for us.

The next day we went to work out on the farm and we certainly didn't want to go. The crew cutting the broccoli were all Filipinos. Before the war they used to come and help us pack the crates. The day after the war they just parked their cars near us and they looked ugly. We thought sure that the Filipinos would go berserk.

The second day after Pearl Harbor I didn't want to go back to work because I was still scared. But my parents felt that we had an obligation to our work, so they said that we had better go. When we got to the fields, we still felt that there was an air of resentment among the Filipino workers but they didn't come after us. They just ignored us and they didn't help us load the crates anymore. My parents were even more scared than I was. They sort of leaned on me to get them out of any trouble in case the Filipinos did come after us with their vegetable knives. As if I could have done anything against a Filipino mob! I had all sorts of wild ideas in my mind that I was going to get stabbed by the Filipinos or something like that and I did not relax from my tension for a couple of weeks.

In the meantime we decided that it was better to open the pool hall as usual. However, it was very quiet and not many people came around so we closed early for about a week. The Filipino customers did not come in at all and the Nisei fellows stuck close to home as their parents did not want them to get into any street fights with the Filipinos. We still were quite worried that the Filipinos from the barbershop would come and tear the place down anytime.

The FBI men came into town the night the war broke out and they picked up 6 or 7 of the wealthy Japanese. For a while the whole Japanese community felt that they would come again at any moment. As the weeks went by the people began to breathe a little easier. The FBI did not come into town again until February [1942] and this time they took after every male Japanese alien in town. They came in very suddenly and many of the Japanese men were taken right off of the fields so that they had no chance to go say good-bye to their families. The FBI men even tore up the floors in some of the Japanese homes to look for evidence.

It was at this time that my own dad was picked up too, but the FBI men were kind to our family. My family still doesn't have any idea why Dad was interned even to this day. None of the family saw him again until March of this year [1944] and I haven't seen him since he was taken by the FBI men two years ago. I felt quite bitter and resentful at this whole procedure because I didn't think my father was guilty of anything. Our family was too poor to give much money to Japan anyway. All of the families were forced to make donations to Japanese organizations and we didn't know what it was all about.

Dad's internment made our whole family come closer together as we knew we had to look after Mother and try not to worry her in anything. Our big worry was how we were going to get enough money to live and that worried us plenty. It was up to my mother and me to keep on working in the field.

My boy friend and I had been going around together more and more after the war and we decided to get engaged at the end of January just before Dad was picked up. The Buddhist Church woman who represented him discussed the marriage plans with my mom and dad. My father was quite pleased and he said that it was okay. When rumors of evacuation started, the *baishakunin* wanted to rush the marriage as she said that the men and women would be split up and put into separate camps. We believed her, so for that reason we got married as quick as we could. We couldn't even get a minister for the ceremony as all of the Buddhist ministers had been interned. We had a simple service by the Justice of Peace in town. Our marriage took place on March 15, 1942.

Right after that I kept on working in order to support the family and my husband was also willing to take care of them as my dad was gone and he didn't have a family of his own. My mother didn't want this as she thought it would make hard feelings later on. However, I decided that I could keep on doing my work and contributing any money I earned towards the family.

Then the curfew came into effect so that my husband and I just moved in with my family. It was about this time that evacuation was definitely announced and that was another shock. I didn't think that evacuation was fair as we were American citizens. All of the Nisei felt that it was prejudice. I didn't understand the order at first and I didn't realize that they were moving us because they suspected us of sabotage. I thought that the government should find out all of the facts before they started to kick any of us around. I was pretty sore at the high-handed way in which we were evacuated. I had gone to school and learned all about the Bill of Rights and all those things and I had always believed that these things were a part of this country. Then it was suddenly thrown right back into our faces. I don't think that evacuation was necessary at all.

It was after camp that I became less bitter against this country and I think that the *hakujin* will finally realize that it was all a mistake. I sure wish America would hurry up and clean the thing up and get it over with. I would like to see the war end in a negotiated peace because I guess I do have some feeling for the Japanese people. I really do feel that I have some relationship to them and that they are not completely wrong. If this country can make a mistake against the Japanese in California and evacuate us, then couldn't it also make a mistake and be the cause for the war? My folks are Japanese and that is the real reason why I don't like to go against all of the Japanese people, even those who are living in Japan. I don't know anything about the political part of it but I do think that democracy is better. I'm telling you what is really in my heart right now. In camp I really wanted Japan to win the war but I don't feel so much like that now. For the *hakujin* I have to make my stand for America much stronger, but they just don't understand that I do have a feeling for the Japanese people and I'd want them to be treated fairly.

My mother was very bitter and resentful that Dad had been interned and she just wouldn't coöperate with us for the evacuation. She said the government had to supply us with everything and we shouldn't spend any of our own money as we would need it later on.

There was quite a bit of family tension during this time. I got together with my older sister for family conferences on everything and we had to persuade Mom before any final decision could be arrived at on anything.

I felt much closer to the Japanese in [U] at the time of evacuation than ever before. I appreciated all of my neighbors who tried to help us out. Our family had been pretty well cut off from the Japanese community before then even though we were living right in the middle of Japanese town. I remember the night after my dad was taken, all of the Japanese families came and offered us help when they couldn't even afford it themselves. I forgot all about the past talk against us and when they did not care to associate with us too much because we were in the pool hall business. When we left for the Tulare Assembly Center, I thought that I would never see that valley of ours again. I saw some of the early groups leave and when my husband and I walked back to the Japanese community afterwards, we saw all of the empty Japanese homes and it looked so lonesome. The Filipinos stared at us as we passed by and it seemed that every one got hostile all of a sudden. I had a funny feeling going down my back and I felt quite lost. When it came our turn to go, I was sick. On top of that it was hard to say all the good-byes and look at the town for the last time. I didn't know hardly any Caucasians, but I still felt that I was leaving something behind. It wasn't even my hometown either. I was bewildered and I couldn't understand why it had to be this way.

When I first glimpsed Tulare Assembly Center, I thought that the barracks were like sheds and that we weren't really going to live in them. I kept looking around for the houses but I could not find any. When the truth dawned on me, it was quite a shock and then I got angry for being treated like this. However, all the other people seemed to be taking it pretty well, so I couldn't say too much. We had to walk through an alfalfa patch to reach our stables. Our apartment was located on the other side of camp from my parents. A couple of weeks later, my husband and I managed to move into the same section as my family and things were better after that.

The best thing I remember about Tulare was meeting all my old friends and making new ones. I got a job in the hospital and I really thought I was somebody, so I enjoyed the work immensely. It was much better than working in a pool hall or out in the fields.

I thought that the administration treated us well and I had no gripes against it. The only contacts I had with the war was listening to the radio news commentators. After I got used to camp, I even lost interest in this, and I didn't mind living in Tulare as there was always enough going on to keep me busy. The fact that this was my honeymoon in a way also took a lot of my time and I had to get used to it.

My husband and I had a lot of private discussions about whether to have a baby or not. We really decided to have a child just after my husband received a draft notice. My husband was against having a baby until after we got to camp. He thought we should wait until after the war, but I didn't want to wait that long because I thought we would be too old by then. We had many long discussions on this at night in our apartment and my husband finally agreed that we should have a baby because my family was near by and they could help us in an emergency.

My husband and I went with one of the last groups to Gila. It was terrifically hot when the bus finally got us into the camp and I was almost ready to faint. We wanted to stay near my mother's apartment but the camp was so crowded that we had to stay for a while with another couple. I thought that Gila wasn't too bad after all of the conveniences were put in. I didn't work at all during the time I was there as I was pregnant.

During all this time my family and I kept writing all sorts of letters in order to get Dad back with us. We were disappointed many times because the promises were always broken. Finally my mother got a little desperate and she made plans to join Dad in [a Department of Justice internment camp]. The WRA said that interned families could be rejoined there. A lot of the mothers in our camp were signing up for this because there was no other way to get the family together. My mother wasn't thinking of repatriation at all. My sisters and I did not think much of this plan and we kept talking to her in an effort to get her to change her mind. Finally Mom did withdraw her application as I kept telling her not to be so hasty, for the sake of her children. I knew that my younger sisters and brothers would not get an education at all if they went to [the internment camp]. It was a lucky thing that we did convince Mom because my dad was finally given a rehearing and paroled in March of this year [1944]. It was exactly two years after he was taken. It was just like serving two years in prison for being innocent.

At the time of registration I answered Yes-Yes the first thing. There was no question as to my own answer and most of my friends answered the way I did. My mother did not understand the issue and she tried to get my younger sister not to answer "yes." My sister had her own mind so that there was ill-feeling for a few days. My mother was afraid that if she answered "yes" she would never see Dad again and that is what caused her to hesitate. Later I explained the whole thing to her and she answered "yes" when her turn came around.

In the meantime my husband and I had started to seriously discuss resettlement plans. It was in the back of our mind all the time and we had applied for leave clearance back in January. We had many long discussions as to where we could go and what we could do. I didn't want to go out too far from the camp as I felt that if we got a chance to go back to California, I didn't want to be left stranded way out in the East. My husband had been out to Chicago before and he thought that the Midwest was the only place which offered much opportunities in the way of work. He was much more enthusiastic about resettlement than I was.

I knew that eventually we would have to leave camp, but I didn't want to leave my mother alone, and that made it a conflict. When I thought it over many many times, I thought that I had better go out as I didn't want to raise my baby in a place like camp. My baby was born in May.

My husband and I believed that there would be a grand rush to leave the camp after the war and we wouldn't have so much chance if we did not go earlier. We wanted to get out and save a little money before the war ended because we felt that times would be harder afterwards. We finally decided to definitely make our plans to leave after the period of the registration was over.

In talking it over, my husband decided to go out first and he wanted to leave immediately even before the baby was born. I didn't want him to do that as I felt I would need him when the baby arrived. The baby didn't come until May and my husband was very impatient. He wanted to get out and start our future as soon as possible. He was even thinking of calling my mother and the rest of the family out if he got a good start on the outside.

I agreed with him completely by this time, as I wanted my baby to know what the outside world was like and I wanted him to know what a bathtub and streetcar looked like. Another reason was I thought my baby would get bad habits if I had to bring him up in the camp. I wanted to bring my own baby up in a real home and under my own care. I was anxious to keep a real home for my husband for the first time. I wanted to be free to go where I pleased without any restrictions. I also knew that all of my friends were leaving camp and I didn't want to be the only one left behind.

At the same time the thing I was afraid of most was discrimination against us like before. I was afraid that the people out here would resent us and not rent us a place to live. We heard that Nisei were being treated well out here, but we didn't know exactly what to expect because there were rumors going around about the bad parts of resettlement. Another thing was that I was afraid of being so far away from my family in case something did happen to them. Then I was also afraid of the cold winter as I had never seen snow before and I heard that Chicago winters were quite severe.

My mother didn't help things out at all because she was against my resettlement. The things she said really made me the most afraid and undecided at times, even though I really wanted to come out deep down in my heart. My mother said I was a fool to come out with a baby as it was too dangerous. She said that we wouldn't be able to get enough vegetables in Chicago because the prices were so high. When she tried to force me to stay, it only made me want to go out all the more and prove to her that we could be successful. Then my mother said that I wouldn't be able to get any seats on the train and I would have to stand up in the aisle with my baby in my arms all the way to Chicago. My God, she heard so many crazy rumors and I didn't know what to believe.

My husband had come out in June and I was supposed to join him by August [1943]. My mother then said that the change of climate would be too hard for my baby and I should wait for six months because the baby would get sick from the change of heat and die. That scared me quite a bit and I almost postponed leaving. My mother really was concerned about the baby, and she believed all the rumors she heard, and she was thinking of me when she said those things. She did not realize that it made me more afraid, and it made it harder because I was determined to go. Finally she realized that she couldn't hang on to me forever as I had my own family to raise so she didn't say so much after that.

I really was quite impatient all summer as I had to wait for the baby to get a little older. I didn't know if it was safe to take the baby while it was too young. I decided to ask the doctor about it and

I was so sure that he would okay everything that I started to pack. The doctor strongly advised me to wait until the baby was at least 3 months old so that he could get his strength. Things weren't too hard for me after that as I knew for sure that I would leave in August.

In the meantime my husband had been encouraging me right along and that gave me arguments to break down my mother and get her to accepting the fact that I was leaving. My husband had quite a few housing problems and that caused me some worries. Every time I got a letter I didn't know what to expect but I knew that things would turn out eventually. His letters really kept my morale up during the summer.[193] He kept writing me letters to tell me of the exact steps I should take when I left.

I had quite a bit of trouble getting my release but my husband kept me posted on everything and that gave me more confidence. As the day for my departure came closer, I got more and more excited about the prospects of the trip and I thought less of the dangers that I might face on the outside. There was a lot of red tape in getting my indefinite leave and I had to go back and forth to the administration building so many times before they could get anything straight. This was hard on me, as I had to leave my baby at home while I waited around the administration building. I had to go through a board of examiners for screening to get my release and they gave me a cross-examination to check my loyalty. They were a little doubtful of me just because my dad was interned. That really burned me up and I really felt like telling those dumb fools off. Then they wanted to be sure that my husband could support me out here. They asked me questions of this sort and I became quite impatient at them. After this was all finished, I was granted my indefinite leave just like a prisoner given a pardon.

Parting was very hard, and our family never felt so close as that before. We all cried, and we didn't think we would see each other again for the longest time. I felt so sad and forlorn as I got on the train, but everybody was kind to me, so I soon relaxed and enjoyed the scenery.

As I drew near Chicago my interest picked up and I began anticipating the new life right away. It wasn't bad at all after I got settled down here. I wrote back enthusiastic letters to my sisters in camp and urged them to come out if Mom would let them. It was easier for them to convince Mom after I had gone through with the whole

---

[193] See pp. 361–367, above, for excerpts from these letters.

thing with her first. My younger sister did come out the early part of this year [1944]. My brother-in-law [CH-37] also came out here and his family will soon come out to join him if he is not drafted.

Housing was my biggest problem when I got out here. I was really disappointed to see all those dark and dirty buildings when I first came in on the train through the dirty part of Chicago. I had expected to see all skycrapers like in a big city but that is only in the Loop. At first we lived out on the northside. I was so disappointed with the apartment as I expected something much better. I almost passed out when we had to pay $40 a month rent for that place. We had bedbugs galore and it got so bad that I thought I had scabies. The landlord was nice but I couldn't stand that tiny apartment and it wasn't good for the baby.

We began to look around for another apartment and we followed the want ads in the newspapers every day. The landlord had a cleaner and bigger building in the same block and we moved over there as soon as he had a vacancy. We had to pay $52 a month for three small rooms. The only consolation was that it had fewer bedbugs. Another Japanese family lived in that building and the woman helped me quite a bit with my baby. I still wasn't satisfied living there and when I found the bottom of a drawer where my baby slept filled with bedbugs, I determined then and there to get out of the place.

We began to think of finding an unfurnished place so that we could have more space. After much hunting my husband finally located this present flat. I feel like we have our own home now and it is much better than what we had to put up with before. It was fun getting our flat all furnished even though we had to spend two or three hundred dollars for second-hand furniture. It certainly is a lot better than living behind the barbershop and pool hall like we did before. Our kitchen now is much bigger than anything we have ever had before. We never had a refrigerator before either. It's not nearly as crowded as my home before the war and in camp and we never even had a living room before. That really is quite an improvement. I think I'll stay here as long as I remain in Chicago. We get along very well with our present landlady and she is wonderful toward us. She doesn't discriminate at all and she is so pleased with us because we keep our floors clean, pay our rent on time, don't ask her for impossible things, and we don't make a lot of noise at night.

At first our neighbors resented us very much and they tried to cut us off, but they were just scared and lately I have been meeting them out on the streets when we all air our babies on warm spring days. They were just scared of us at first and now I think they are getting used to us, so they are not suspicious.

We live quite comfortably out here and it isn't as bad as my mother thought it would be. Vegetables are reasonable, though I did think the prices were outrageous compared to what we paid in California before the war. We make our expenses easy enough since my husband earns around $250 a month and that covers all of our needs.

My baby gets very good care out here. A Mexican fellow's wife that my husband met told me about the baby clinic and I go there twice a month. The clinic checks the baby's diet and weight and answers any problems that I may have. They will also sell medicine to me cheaply. I really appreciate this service.

When the draft was announced, I didn't think it was fair for the Nisei to be put into the combat unit altogether like that. I think the Nisei should be allowed to go into all of the services and the Army should not put reservations to their loyalty. By putting them altogether like that it looks like they are still suspicious. I worry quite a bit about my husband being drafted, but it's no use. If he has to go, there is nothing we can do about it. I won't be the only wife left in a spot like this and I suppose I'll be able to manage somehow.

When it comes right down to it, after the war is really the biggest worry. I'd like to go back to the coast, but it may not be such a good idea. We don't exactly want to go back to our old home town as it has no opportunity for my husband. I'd like to get back to California chiefly because of the climate and because I'm used to that state.

I really do feel inferior and self-conscious when I'm with the *hakujin*. I think I feel less that way now than before the war. We are among the *hakujin* a lot now, so I've learned to feel freer. Before the war I rarely went to a Caucasian store. I think I have made more Caucasian contacts out here than I have done before in my life and it has done me a lot of good. When I go to the stores out here, the storekeepers are friendly. A lot of people I meet in the store are curious and they wonder if I speak English. Having a baby really helps to break the ice for me. I still don't feel perfectly at ease among the Caucasians but the longer I stay out here the better and easier it will be for me. I guess that's something like what they call assimilation, isn't it?

CH-37: BUSINESSMAN

Male; born in California, 1910; height 70"; weight 170 lbs.; married, 1932; three children; brother-in-law of CH-35 and CH-36. Interviewed April, 1944. Described as "rather reserved and conservative"; and as not having "the usual Japanese characteristics."

CAREER LINES

Parental: Both parents from farming class in Japan. Married in Japan "before 1900," emigrated to Hawaii and worked on sugar cane plantations and came to California *ca.* 1900. Grower of strawberries, of seeds, and of truck crops in central California. Operated two farms, owned in his sons' names, until 1942.

Own: Graduated from a central California high school in 1930; attended a watchmaking school in San Francisco, 1930–1931. Worked on father's farm during summer vacations, as a child; did odd watch-repair jobs while at high school. Operated own jewelry store in a town in central California, 1931–1936, and own grocery store, with a radio shop on the side, from 1936 to 1942. Inmigrated to Chicago, August, 1943 ("unemployed for three days"); worked as radio repair man in one shop from September to November, 1943, and in another from December, 1943, to date of interview.

LIFE HISTORY[194]

I don't know very much about my parents and what they did before they got married, because they never told me much about these things. I do know that they got married in Japan and they went to Hawaii and worked in the sugar-cane plantations for two years. They had a close relative in Hawaii and that's why they went there. They also had another close relative in America and that's why they later came to California. Originally they left Japan in order to make money, because all of the people in Kumamoto *ken* were rather poor. They couldn't make a living in agriculture so that whole villages left for work in Hawaii. It was mostly men because the women followed later on.

They arrived here in California around 1900. My dad started farming on his own [in the Santa Maria Valley] after he got here. After

---

[194] W. I. Thomas wrote the following marginal comment, in 1945, on CH-37's biography: "Most interesting case; man of extraordinary genius and energy; deserves to be considered for incorporation [in *The Salvage*]; nothing like it in the records."

a few years my parents moved to [X, a small valley community], which is only a few miles from [Y], where they lived right until the time of evacuation. All of us were born in [X]. I am the oldest in the family. I have two younger brothers. I think I had two sisters who were born before me but they both passed away.

After my parents came to California, they made a good living. They had quite a tough time during the period they were working in Hawaii. Being so poor, it was natural for them to be careful of the money they earned so that they were able to save quite a sum in the following years. My father built a nice home near [Y] around 1922. He raised strawberries and vegetables for a couple of years. He had another small farm [near by] where they went into truck gardening there and this was quite profitable too. This was a 22-acre farm and it was put into my name. The other farm is in my brother's name. In comparison with other Japanese, my dad was a very successful farmer and he didn't have a hard time at all after he got started. Such things as the depression didn't bother him very much. He was a natural born farmer and all of his hard times had been passed through when they first came to America. I think that one of the reasons why my dad was successful as a farmer was that he had a good business head and he knew what crops paid the most dividends.

The reason I don't know anything about my family background is because my parents came over so many years ago and they never returned to the old country. When they first left their *ken,* they told everybody that they would be back in a year or so after they got rich. They never made any money during the first few years over here, and even after they started to make money, they didn't feel like giving it up to go live in their poor village in Japan. My mother always wanted to go back for a visit but Dad kept postponing the trip because he always got so seasick whenever he got on a boat. My parents only had a few relatives back in Japan anyway.

My father was only of average size and my mother was quite small so I can't understand where I get my height. It must be in the family line some place because my brothers are also quite tall for Nisei. Both of my parents were always hard-working people and they earned their money the hard way with their hands. My mother got right out there and worked along with my father. Maybe that is why she lost her health after raising us kids.

Most of the time my father was easy going and a sort of a good-natured type. On the whole my parents got along very well and they never had any real serious arguments. My mother always knew when it was best to give in. Dad was not a drinking or smoking man and he was extremely fond of the home life. He never went out too much for social affairs because he was too busy working on the farm. He didn't take an active part in many of the Japanese clubs in the area, but he was a member of the Japanese Association and the Kumamoto *kenjinkai*. He hardly ever went to the meetings though.

My folks spoke very little English but this didn't seem to be any handicap for dad. He understood enough English to get by in his farm dealings. Neither one of my parents ever read the Japanese newspapers or magazines regularly, as far as I know.

When I was a child, I had a life just like any other farmer boy. I had to help out before and after school on the farm. In a farm family all of the members work long hours so that my brothers and I didn't see much of our parents. They always got up real early in the mornings to go work in the fields and they had to go to bed early to get their full rest.

We always ate Japanese food at home and we spoke Japanese to our parents. Later on as we went to school we began to use more English but not too much. We just used it among ourselves and we talked Japanese to our parents. I didn't go to a Japanese language school until I went to high school so I can't carry on a Japanese conversation now. I don't understand it very well either. My parents were too busy to teach me the language and I didn't have very many occasions to use it after I started my own business.

I started school in the [X] grammar school but I don't remember much of those days since it was many years ago. I do remember that there were a few other Nisei going to that school. At that time there weren't as many Nisei children as there are now. I suppose I am one of the older group and we are rather scarce. I never cared much for school studies as all I wanted to do was to play with the other kids. I flunked the third grade, I know, and there were a couple of other times that I failed also. Our school was located about one mile from my home and I used to walk every day. All of my playmates were Caucasians and I don't believe I ever talked to the other Nisei in that school. I wasn't conscious that I was any different from the rest of the kids and I was inclined to chum around with the less studious pupils. The other Nisei all studied hard, so I didn't have any occasion to want to know them.

After I was in the sixth grade in 1922 my father built a home near [Y], and I started to attend school in that town. When I was in the eighth grade I got interested in mechanical things. I started to monkey around with watches about that time and by the time I got out of the eighth grade, I was able to take a watch apart and put it together again. It was also about then that radio started to appear on the market. I was interested in it right from the beginning and so I began to dabble with it. I bought a small home-made radio and I started to experiment and build little radios from then on.

In high school I took up the usual courses. Science and math were my major courses. I was earning my own spending money by then by repairing the watches of my friends. In my classwork I was best in math and I used to beat everyone in that. I also took some commercial courses and this came natural for me too. I didn't care very much for English and history.

In high school I never was much of an athlete. The only [extra-curricular] thing that I ever got recognition from was in the annual typewriting contest. All of the schools sent the best typists to this contest and I represented my high school. I took third place for accuracy. I still had to help out the folks on the farm so I didn't have too much time to play. I didn't pal around with any special person. It wasn't that I was shy but I was more interested in mechanical things which I could do by myself. A lot of the other fellows weren't interested in the same thing as I was, so I didn't join them too much. I had a regular work shop of my own at home, and I spent a great deal of my free time there tinkering with watches and radios.

When I graduated from high school in 1930, I was already 20 years old because I had been kept behind a couple of times. I wanted to go into the watch business right away and start a shop of my own, since I already had a long list of customers who were used to coming to me. My parents insisted that I attend watch-making school in San Francisco for a year, so I went there. I didn't have any trouble at all in the watch-making school and I learned everything in six months instead of a year as the other fellows required. I had my own car at that time, so I enjoyed my experiences in San Francisco greatly. I was boarding with a married Caucasian couple during this time.

While I was in San Francisco, I went to visit the Japanese section a great deal and I made some friends there. I took an interest in tennis and I used to play a lot after school with some Nisei fellows I got to know. I went to many movies during the time I was there because this was the first chance I had to do that. I was always a movie fan. I didn't have any girl friend at that time and I didn't know any of the Nisei girls in San Francisco.

After I finished the watch-making school, I went back to my home town to start out on my own. I started to look around for a good location for a jewelry shop. In the meantime I helped out the folks on the farm. After about a month, I bought out the home-town jeweler who was a Caucasian, and my folks gave me the money to make the payments. It was just a small shop located in a drugstore but it was good enough for me. I had no trouble at all getting business as I had fixed a lot of watches for my friends for many years, and they brought me all the trade that I could handle.

After I got a little experienced I found that watch sales were a little limited because the town people went to the two larger cities nearby to buy a greater variety of watches. I found that I was limited in buying my merchandise and through inexperience I often got stuck with a lot of stock which I couldn't dispose of very easily. I made plenty of mistakes during this time. However, I was making good money in comparison to other Nisei fellows in the valley. About 95 per cent of my customers were Caucasians and I never had any trouble with them. In spite of the fact that I worked up to a net income of around $3,500 a year in a period of 3 or 4 years, I was not entirely satisfied. This was during the depression time, too. However, my expenses were rather large as I got married during this time.

I first met my wife in 1932. It was love at first sight, so we decided to get married. Jesus, what a wedding we had. We had to go through all of the Japanese forms for the sake of our parents. The older Nisei didn't think so much of rebelling like the young kids do nowadays. We thought we had to go through all of these forms because everyone else had done it. Our wedding was held in a Buddhist Church in [one of the larger towns in the area] because my wife was a Buddhist.[195] We had to go through all of that formal *baishakunin* stuff as that was about the only way Nisei could get married at that time. It was a pretty expensive thing and my folks had to help me out on some of the bills. The Japanese had the idea that you had to spend a lot of money at your wedding to show that you were successful in business. We had to invite all of our Japanese friends to the wedding and I also invited all of my Caucasian friends. After the wedding we gave

---

[195] CH-37 had a Christian background. His children were given Buddhist training in camp, but, along with his wife, attended Methodist Sunday school and church after resettlement.

them all a big dinner. I think we had to spend over $3,000 just for this wedding. This is where all of my profits went, but we also received a lot of gifts from friends because that was Japanese style too.

After our honeymoon we rented a home in [Y]. From then on it was more and more expense for me, as I soon had three children. At first we lived near my shop. We both liked shows a great deal so we went quite often. We also entertained a lot of friends and they were mostly Caucasians. It was a little hard for my wife at first because she didn't have so many Caucasian contacts in her home town and she wasn't used to it. I had gotten to know most of my Caucasian friends through my school and business contacts. Fortunately my wife had a very friendly personality, so that she soon got to know all of my friends and she enjoyed it quite a bit. She had an open personality while I was more reserved in disposition.[196]

[196] Our files include a complete biography of CH-37's wife (CH-49). Details regarding her family background will be found in her younger sister's biography: CH-36, pp. 367–383, above. She was described, by the interviewer, as having "quite a personality," as being "rather talkative," in contrast to CH-36, and as looking "surprisingly young" to be the 31-year-old mother of three daughters, then aged 11, 7, and 6. She was "pleasant, hospitable and coöperative" but "primarily interested in talking about her children." Excerpts from her biography will be used to supplement her husband's account in this and following footnotes:

When I got married it was the first time I ever went away from home. We went to [Y] to live and that was where my life changed completely. I was awfully lonesome for a long time as I was 100 miles away from my family [who lived in a coastal city] and I didn't have any friends at all down there. Gradually I began to meet my husband's friends and I was amazed to find that they were all *hakujin*. I couldn't get over it when they went out of their way to be good to me. They were also nice to us in town and most of the *hakujins* were quite friendly. The *hakujins* in [the coastal city] had just ignored all of the Japanese so that this was quite surprising. I couldn't get over my timidity for a long time as I felt hesitant and I didn't really know if we were going to be accepted as equals all the time. The way I overcame my timidness was to meet these friends socially and go to their homes for card parties. I had never played cards in my life before as my folks were so terribly against card playing as they considered it a great sin.

After I moved to [Y] I felt that I was in America for the first time in my life as all the people there took me in. That was when I knew that I was for America 100 per cent and I knew definitely that this was the only country for me. That is also the reason why I do not object to my husband's being drafted as it is his duty to serve his country even though it may become hard for me to take care of my children.

When I was a child I didn't have too many Nisei playmates and I played with all of the kids of the neighborhood. As we got older we didn't play with the other children anymore as we went around in our own groups. The reason for that was the city was quite prejudiced against the Japanese and the Caucasian kids soon learned it from their parents and the other older people. We felt more comfortable going around in our own group. My social life became

After I got married, I had to work harder than ever in order to increase my business. Year by year it did improve. My family and I lived a very good standard of living and we never had to skimp on anything. We just spent what I earned and I didn't want my wife and children to lack for anything that they needed. After the children started to come, we moved to a much larger house. Then as my income grew, we moved a couple of times more and each time it was a better place. In 1935 we moved into a large place and we stayed there until the evacuation. It was a brand new stucco house with 5 rooms. We only paid $22 a month rent, believe it or not. I certainly wish I had that place right now. We put in over $2,000 worth of furniture in that

---

centered around the Japanese church and the Japanese school. I was very conscious of a difference in race as I soon saw that the Japanese were looked down upon. My worst ordeal was to get up in front of a classroom to recite. I dreaded that so much that I used to break out in a cold sweat when I thought the teacher might call on me. I still have this inhibition as I could not even talk in front of a dinner group now if there were over six people present. I don't know how my three daughters got so extrovert as they don't have any of these inhibitions as far as I can determine. Maybe I made them that way because I didn't want them to be timid as I was.

The Issei parents made us so dependent upon them that we were backward. We didn't get out of the home enough to mix with other people. Our parents never taught us to rely upon ourselves so much so we didn't know what to do when we got into a strange group. We were raised to hang on to our mother's apron strings. I'm certainly seeing to it now that my children do not develop that way and I want them to have individuality and initiative in doing things on their own.

I tried to raise my children strictly American style right from the beginning because I was sure I would live in [Y] for the rest of our lives. We just seemed to fit into the life there and we were accepted as equals in everything. I gradually overcame my sense of inferiority as my husband began to make good in his business and we were considered one of the better-off families in town.

I made my children learn to do things for themselves but I never was too strict with them in the way my mother was with me. My husband didn't know hardly any of the Japanese language so I developed the use of my English since I had to use it with all of his friends. I did send my oldest daughter to a Japanese language school because some of the other Japanese children in the farming area were sent. I thought that it would be good for my daughter to learn Japanese so she could talk with her grandparents when she went to visit them. She didn't like Japanese school and she couldn't grasp the language at all as we didn't use it very much at home. From the time my oldest daughter was old enough to walk, she had Caucasian playmates. She did make a few Nisei friends when she went to the Japanese language school, but they lived too far away from her so that she rarely had contact with them outside of school. My husband's mother thought that it was terrible because I didn't teach the children more of the Japanese language and customs and my children never understood Grandma when she talked to them. I didn't want to force my children to learn these things as I didn't think that it was that important.

new house to begin with and everything was quite modern. I was also able to buy a new car and we felt that we were living in class.

About 1936 the drugstore where my jewelry shop was located moved to a new location. It was about then that I started to sell and repair radios. When I did this, my income went even higher. I had been keeping up my interest in radio all along and I read all of the latest radio magazines in order to keep up with the newest developments. I found radio work much more intriguing than watch repairing, so I began to spend more and more time with it. The radio business kept increasing all the time as more and more people were buying radios during this time.

I decided that I needed a larger shop of my own, so I finally bought a grocery store. It was the oldest established Caucasian grocery store in town and I thought I could handle it on the side because I had been good at the commercial courses in high school. I thought I could run it along with my radio and watch work. I was the only Nisei or Japanese businessman in town during all of these years.

When I took the grocery store over, I expanded my radio section much more and I gradually began to drop the watch repairing work. There was no other watchmaker in town so that my former customers kept on bringing their watches to me. I took them home and fixed them at night. From then on, my annual income went on up to $5,000 net a year and my family was well off. By the time of the war I felt quite prosperous and established for life.

I didn't know a thing about the grocery business when I started, but I soon learned. It turned out to be a successful venture too. The grocery store had been quite shaky when I first took it over, but when I finally had to close it, it was one of the busiest establishments in town. I made a pretty good margin of profit because I bought my vegetables from my father and a few other Japanese, so that I didn't have to deal with the middle man. However, as business increased, I gradually bought most of my produce from the wholesale Caucasian firms. I did quite a business with one of the large Caucasian produce companies in Los Angeles. After I got established in the grocery business, I bought a lot of new equipment for the store in order to modernize it. I had my sister and wife help out and I hired one other Nisei in the store. I spent most of my time on the radio work and I let the others take care of the grocery section.

By the time the war broke out, I was ready to be on easy street. My radio business had boomed way up all during this time. I guess

I was making anywhere from $5,000–$6,000 clear a year and I was able to save quite a bit. During this time it was my ambition to get the exclusive rights to [a national radio] agency but I was not successful in this for a long time because another man in town had it. Finally in 1940 the [radio] people asked me to take over their agency in town, so this ambition was realized. After that I had tremendous radio sales, and my radio business more than tripled.

After the war started, all of the short-wave radio parts had to be removed from the enemy aliens' sets. They had to turn in the radios to the police station and the police sent them up to my place to get the short wave removed. The first thing I knew I had a whole store full of radios. I took out all of the short wave and then returned them to the Japanese customers. This was actually the first time in my life that I had any amount of business dealings with the Japanese people. I found out then that I couldn't get along too well with them in business because they were too critical, and I also learned that I couldn't speak to them in Japanese too well, since my language had gotten rather rusty from not using it for many years.

Yes, life really did change for me when the war broke out. I never figured that anything like this would happen. I was planning to become a permanent part of that town and devote my time to bringing up my kids in the right way. I figured on sending them all through college and to give them the best of everything I possibly could. I had a life insurance policy for all of my kids which would mature in time for them to go through college with. I had been paying ahead on the premiums and that was taken care of for five or six years ahead. I also was putting quite a bit of money into the bank so that I had a fairly comfortable reserve fund for my family. We were planning to buy our own home.

I was a member of the town's businessmen's club and I was the only Nisei in it. I never had any discriminations in business against me and I got along well with most of the businessmen. The reason for that was I had grown up with a lot of them, and these fellows had taken over their father's business after finishing school. I felt I was quite accepted there and everyone knew me. The town only had a population of around 1,200, and the people were all friendly. It never occurred to me to think of the situation of the other Japanese because I wasn't particularly aware that they had any special problems. I thought that the Japanese in Santa Maria Valley especially were doing quite well in farming and a lot of families were pretty rich. I knew that the Nisei in Los Angeles were having a little harder time, but I thought it was because of the depression. I didn't understand that the Nisei had limitations in looking for a job.

I didn't have the occasion to have too many contacts with other Nisei because I didn't deal in business with them. However, my wife and I were charter members of the [local] chapter of the JACL. We entertained Caucasian friends mostly at our dinner and card parties. I was a member of a card club in town and we used to get together about 2 or 3 times a week. We would take turns being the hosts. Later on it got to be more of a poker club. My wife belonged to a couple of clubs in town because she was the mother of several children. Once in a while we made trips to Los Angeles and occasionally we would visit my wife's folks in [U]. That was our only real connection with the Japanese community and even then my wife's folks didn't mix too much in the Japanese society. Often in the summer time we went out on picnics with our Caucasian friends. I was quite happy in that life and I didn't have any worries at all, except business worries. We had a nice home, we ate good food, we attended a lot of parties, we had an opportunity to travel, our social relationships with the Caucasians were good, our children were starting to get a good education, and I had a very good business. We didn't lack a thing in the way of comfort.

All of my peaceful life was suddenly disrupted by the war and it only took overnight to do it. I was in Los Angeles on Pearl Harbor day with my dad and brother. We were sitting in a Japanese record store, getting some Japanese records for my dad when the news of the Pearl Harbor attack blast over the radio. I only heard a part of it and it just didn't register in the minds of any of us. I wasn't sure of what it was all about and I didn't believe that it was true. We had the impression that it was only a radio play when we started home in our car. I turned the car radio on and it was then that we really realized that Pearl Harbor had been attacked and that it was not a play. The whole thing took me completely by surprise and I just couldn't believe a thing like that was possible. I didn't know what to think or say.

I had no immediate fears at that time as I couldn't imagine that it would affect me very much. My dad was just as surprised as I was and he just wouldn't believe it. When he finally realized that it was true, he thought that if the United States declared war that Japan would not be able to last very long. When he left Japan, it had been a backward country and he didn't think that Japan was strong enough to ever battle such a powerful country as America. He thought that Pearl Harbor had been bombed by some madman in the Japanese Army and that the Japanese government really knew nothing about it. Dad had a strong sentimental attachment for Japan, but he didn't know anything about the politics. He was quite worried because he didn't like the idea of Japan fighting the United States. He always tried to think of America as his home, but he knew that he would be in for a hard time. We talked about it all the way home but we didn't get stopped once.

I thought that it would only be a very short war and Japan would be licked in short notice. I had no sympathy for Japan as I had never seen it. I didn't even think of the possibility that the Nisei would fall under suspicion at all. At that time it didn't occur to me that my business would be affected because I knew all of my Caucasian friends were life-long friends and that they would not turn against me in spite of any war. I was justified in this opinion as they did stick by me later on. It was only the out-of-town *hakujin* who aroused all of that anti-Japanese feeling in California. I didn't lose any of my old customers after the war started, but a few of the newcomers in town got distinctly cooler towards me.

My immediate reaction that day was more for personal things and I thought I would be drafted very quickly. I was rather bewildered by the suddenness of the whole thing. When I got home my wife was very excited because she had heard over the radio that some Jap had been killed on the highway and she thought that it might have been me. It was a great relief for her to see me all in one piece and we immediately started to talk about the war and how it would affect us. I was a little worried that my business relationships might be affected, but in the days that followed nothing happened. Business kept on as usual and the war did not seem to affect it at all. I was more worried about the draft, but I thought I would get an exemption for a while as I had 3 kids, and the Army was not figuring on taking pre-Pearl Harbor fathers at that time. I did have to give up any ideas of expanding my business because I wasn't sure about anything.

My father had all of his money deposited in a Japanese bank and it was all frozen. My brother had two farms of his own and he took over most of the responsibility of looking after dad. The property had been put in his name many years before. Dad was pretty well established after all of those years of work on the farm, so that I did not have to support him at all. He had done very well on his farm and he had a number of successful crops so that he had plenty to retire on. For a while we thought that he would never get any of his frozen money back but the greater part of it has been released to him now. Fortunately my dad did not have any Japanese bonds.[197]

Even when the first Japanese were evacuated from around Seattle and some of the defense zones in southern California, I wasn't worried about being removed myself. I kept right on with my business, but some of my creditors began to demand cash, as they thought that even the Nisei would eventually be evacuated. Around March the rumors of complete evacuation got pretty strong. By the time the official notices came, I was convinced that evacuation would hit me, so I started to dispose of my business. I guess I was pretty disappointed by the whole thing and I didn't see how it could possibly happen. It was more like a dream than anything else.

I couldn't find a buyer to take over my store, so I started to sell everything at a discount. All of my competitors and the grocery mer-

---

[197] CH-37's father-in-law was arrested by the FBI, and interned. The incident is described by his wife:

After the war started the FBI just picked up the Issei in wholesale lots in [Santa Maria Valley]. The reason for that was that everyone was donating to the *Heimushakai,* but I don't know what it was. They said later that this organization was to collect benefits for the Japanese soldiers in China. It was compulsory to contribute to it. I don't think very many Issei really knew what it was all about. They were always donating to the Community Chest and other things like that.

My father was sympathetic to Japan because he was born there. He also had a feeling for America for he lived here for 45 years but he couldn't get citizenship papers. He wasn't so violently pro-Japan as many of the other Issei in the valley. I never dreamed that he would be taken as he had done nothing except contribute money to many organizations, including the Japanese ones. But on February 18 I received a frantic phone call from my younger sister to tell me that the FBI agents had been to the house to take my father away. I was so shocked that I didn't know what to say. I wondered what it was all about and I thought it was all a big mistake. I gathered all my children and I drove to my parents' home immediately. Everybody was so nervous and upset when I got there. All of the Japanese families in [their town] were going through a similar experience as the FBI loaded up truck-loads of Issei from that vicinity.

I drove down to where the trucks were parked immediately and I asked the M.P. if I could speak to my father. The M.P. was rather sympathetic and he said that he didn't mind although very few people were given that permission. My father was very upset when I saw him and he couldn't figure the reason why he was being interned. Rumors had spread around that they were going to be locked up in a jail but nobody knew where they were going to be taken. It was such a pitiful sight that my emotions began to overcome me and I couldn't stand the sad scene any longer. I told my father that my husband and I would look after the family so he didn't have to worry about that.

chants in town bought me out at wholesale prices, so I didn't lose anything. In fact, I had bought a great deal of my stock on a rising market, so when I sold it to the other merchants, the wholesale prices had gone way up and I actually made a little profit. I didn't have any trouble disposing of the lease on my grocery store as the owner was a life-time friend of mine. I wanted to sell all of the equipment so I closed the store on March 31. After selling the grocery mechandise out at a big discount, I sold the store fixtures. This was my greatest loss, as I had to sell it at a fraction of the original cost to the next door butcher. I figured that I had lost about $1,000 on my store fixtures even with the depreciation values deducted.

As for my radio-testing equipment, I stored it in the basement of the town bakery as the owner was a friend of mine. I didn't want to sell my watch-repairing tools either, so I stored them with some of my Caucasian friends. I stored all of my best furniture with my friends and I just left the rest of it right in my home. The only thing we sold of our household goods was the piano. I signed my car over to one of my life-time friends.

By the greatest stretch of my imagination, I only anticipated being gone from town for a year at the most before I could go back and start over. I didn't think I would have any difficulty in doing that because I knew my former customers would come back. Business must certainly be good back there now, and I suppose that my greatest loss was in the fact that I wasn't there to enjoy it. There is no way of figuring out my loss in good-will and business possibilities. That's where the evacuation hit me the hardest. I was making a net income of over $5,000 a year before I left and the loss of that was quite a blow to me.

For that reason I didn't like the idea of evacuation at all. I didn't see how the Army could evacuate a mass of people like that, especially when it included Nisei who were American citizens. I didn't think there was any danger of sabotage from any of the Japanese in California and this was only an excuse. I think that the whole evacuation was really unnecessary. It was caused by a bunch of politicians in California and I didn't think it was a military necessity at all. It was just a group of selfish people who were after our money and businesses and they were the ones who wanted to get us out the most because they didn't like our competition. I couldn't imagine the Issei as being dangerous to this country as they had always been law abiding and very few Japanese had ever been sent to prison for committing crimes. I felt that the Army could take care of any dangerous ones, and a lot of the Issei had already been interned.

Although I felt badly about the loss of my business, I did not turn against America at all. I blamed Japan for the war, but I was also bitter because the government treated us so unjustly and it cost me my lifework which had taken 12 years to build up. It completely disrupted my life and even now the pieces are not altogether yet. But as far as loyalty and patriotism was concerned, it didn't change at all, as this was the only country that I knew. I realized that the President and a lot of government officials had been fooled by the pressure groups in California to remove us and that made me sore. Some of those California groups were taking advantage of the war to persecute us because they never did like the Japanese in California. This was particularly true of the Hearst papers and the American Legion. They were always talking about America for the white people only and I thought they were crazy, because I believed that true Americanism was in the heart and not in the color of the skin. I just took most of these things for granted and I figured that everyone else thought pretty much the same way. I didn't think that the pressure groups would ever completely fool the American public that easily.

I began to feel a lot closer to the other Japanese people in the valley about the time of evacuation, as I had to make more contacts with them. I felt that we were all in the same boat together since we were all being evacuated and we had all of the same problems. For that reason, I began to see much more of them than ever before. When I saw so many of the Japanese people suffering like that and losing everything that it had taken a lifetime to build up, it made me angry to think that such a thing could happen in this country. I really was disappointed in America. I didn't think that there was much use in making personal protests because the odds were too great and the feeling was rising against us on account of the war. Any voice of protest would be like a voice in the wilderness and the public temper was not favorable to listening.

My wife's folks evacuated with my family, but I had to stay behind for 10 days. I was coming down with German measles so that the WCCA office slapped me in quarantine at the town hospital. When I was well, I was given a ticket on the Greyhound bus and told to report to the Tulare Assembly Center. I evacuated myself without any escort. Nobody paid any attention to me on the trip out to camp. I just said good-bye to a few of my life-long friends and they assured me that I would be back very soon. Nobody was curious about me on the bus and I wasn't asked any questions.

I had been feeling fine, but as I went through the camp gates I suddenly got a very depressed feeling and I felt like a prisoner. There were guards at the gate and it was all fenced in. The barracks all looked dirty and I hated to think of having to live there for any length of time. This was the start of my life in a concentration camp. I could have escaped so easily if I didn't have a family that was waiting for me. There was nothing to prevent me from buying a train ticket out of town to the unrestricted zones. I didn't even think of it though, as I didn't want to break any laws. But when I saw camp for the first time, it was depressing and my morale sunk way down. I wanted to see my family right away in order to find how they were making out. My family had done very well without me and my wife had the barrack fairly well arranged. We didn't have any furniture at all so I ordered a clothes closet and some other things.

After a short time I decided to go to work in radio if I could but I didn't know if there were any possibilities for it in camp. It was hard to get work in camp at Tulare as a certain group had control over everything and they gave the good jobs to their friends. They told me if I wanted to work right away, I would have to start in the mess hall or as a common laborer on construction crew. I took the job on the construction crew and I handled a pick and shovel for the first time in years. It was very hot during those days but I didn't mind it at first as I had not done hard work like that for years and I thought it would be good for me. I wasn't able to do this too long because it was too tough. I got a job in the recreation department next. I took care of the public address system for the talent shows and thinks like that. The highest job I could get in that department was to operate the moving picture projector.

A friend of mine was taking care of electrical appliances and he wanted me to open up a radio repair shop in camp. I applied for this job and on the basis of my experience I got it. For the next few months I did this work for $12 a month. We repaired all of the radios free of charge and we also took care of the sound system in camp. There was nothing exciting about this work, though once a rumor went around that we were putting in short-wave systems for the people. I never saw any short waves in camp while I was there.

I didn't take too much part in the other activities of the camp. I went to some of the dances and a number of private parties. I had my own public address system and I loaned it out to mess hall dances free of charge, so that I got free admission to a lot of private affairs in this way. Other times I played cards quite a bit with the fellows I knew. Sometimes we had poker sessions which lasted half the night. I never did do much reading, as my wife took care of most of this. For a while I did fix a few watches for my friends in camp. Most of my watch repair tools were in storage back home but I sent for some of them. I didn't charge the government for the use of my radio repair tools either. I really thought it was amusing that I would be working for $12 a month after all those years in business of my own.

I made a lot of new friends while I was in camp. I didn't have any particular trouble in mixing with them although the Nisei tended to stick to their own group. I didn't associate with the Issei at all as I couldn't speak their language. I certainly did miss my friends from back home though. Quite a few came to visit us on week-ends and this was usually the high point of the week's activities.

My children had never played with Nisei children before, but they soon got in with their own little groups and after that they began to stay out all hours just to play. My wife and I knew that this camp life would be harmful for the children if we completely neglected them, so we made them eat with us at the mess hall in order to teach them the proper table etiquette. We didn't want them to learn a lot of bad habits by going all around without any parental supervision.[198]

---

[198] As related by his wife:

My children had an awful time in making their adjustments to camp. They couldn't get used to the food and the washroom. However, they soon found some playmates and they forgot our past life after a couple of months. It was the first time my children had seen so many Nisei children, and most of the little Nisei children around camp spoke Japanese and my daughters didn't understand. They were like foreign children for a while but they gradually began to pick up what the other Nisei playmates said. It was this influence which taught my daughters some undesirable things. They learned such bad table manners. I tried to keep my daughters' table manners closer to what is acceptable in polite society, but most of the other Nisei children didn't have any training at all as their Issei parents did not know of American table habits. Many of the Japanese families in camp had never eaten food American style and the Issei had a difficult time trying to use knives and forks. My daughters also learned a lot of bad words as everyone seemed to swear, and I had a hard time trying to teach them not to use these words because they didn't know the difference.

I was quite worried about their further education so I sent them to summer school which was opened up in camp. I didn't have too much confidence in that school as I was afraid the Nisei teachers didn't know how to teach very well because most of them did not have any training to teach. One of the things that I was so afraid of was that my daughters would get an inferiority about race if they lived among Japanese entirely. That was the thing I worried about throughout our stay in the centers as I thought that my children would get the same kind of race consciousness I had before moving to [Y].

I thought that the food in camp was pretty terrible and I could not blame my three children for complaining. The longer I stayed there, the more unjust I thought the whole thing was. But I tried to fit in as best as I could since there was no other choice. There was no political activity at all in our assembly center since the Army controlled everything and the people did not have any voice. For this reason there was not any use to have a Nisei organization to discuss our problems. The Nisei were not interested in such problems anyway.

It was my impression that the administration was very good. We heard a lot of rumors about the bad administration and graft in the other camps but we didn't have anything like this, so we had no cause for complaint. The administration sympathized with the people and they went out of their way to make us as comfortable as possible. I made a number of friends among the appointed personnel but we did not mix too much socially. I still did not hold anything against this country for moving us all out like that and I became more resigned to the situation. I realized that California was the only state with attitudes like that.

The rumors started to go around that we were going to be sent to Arizona next. Nobody knew for certain and the rumors went around for a couple of weeks and it was on everyone's tongue. I was hoping that we would be sent to Tule Lake as I figured that it would not be too far away and we would still be in California. I didn't like the idea of going out of the state as this would make things kind of definite, and we would feel that we really had been kicked out. However, there wasn't any choice for us about what WRA camp we wanted to go. When it was announced that we were going to be sent to Gila, I didn't have any great reaction one way or the other. There wasn't any way out of the situation, since we were not given any alternatives. The Japanese people began to pass around all sorts of rumors about the snakes, scorpions, and heat in Arizona, and a lot of people in my block made a petition to ask the Army if they could not remain at Tulare. All of us wanted to stay in Tulare and we dreaded the idea of going to Gila. But when the first group started to leave, the people all wanted to go there so that they could stick together as one group.

I was really disgusted when I got to Gila. It was nothing but a desert and everything was so dusty. The camp looked so primitive and we felt pretty well cut off from everything. Everything was confusion when we arrived. The baggage lot was an empty block which was covered with dust so that all of our clothes in the bags were practically ruined. This dust was so soft that we would sink in with every step. We had no choice in housing, as other Japanese were coming in every day. It got so crowded that a lot of families had to double up. Fortunately my wife and family got a separate apartment but it was located in one of the hottest spots in camp. We figured that we would be in Gila permanently for the duration, so we began to fix our apartment up much better than we had at Tulare. I stole lumber along with other people so that I could build the benches and table. My wife ordered material for curtains, awning for the windows, and other things like that, in order to make living more comfortable for us. I purchased a cooler from Sears Roebuck, so that we would not roast to death. I was fortunate in being able to buy a new one for less than $30. After Sears Roebuck ran out of the coolers, the people in camp were paying $70 and $80 for a fan. I found out that some Caucasians in Arizona had bought the supply of coolers out. A man came to camp in a truck loaded with these coolers and he sold the identical fan that I had for $30 to other people for $70 and $80. Later on the administration found out about this and they made the man give a refund of $30 to $40 for each fan, according to the ceiling price. The only trouble was that a lot of the families did not save their receipts, so that they were out of luck.

We didn't have any privacy at all in our apartment, and I did not think this was so good for our children. I bought some sheeting material and I was able to partition our room up into 2 small bedrooms and a living room. We ordered quite a few things from the mail order company in order to complete our household. We also sent for some more of our clothing and other necessities from back home. I was expecting to get a whole box of canned goods from my former grocery store but somebody switched the boxes and we were sent a case of noodles instead. That was the last thing we wanted because we were getting plenty of noodles in camp. I also sent for my electric hot-plate so that we could cook little snacks at home for the children and also for company.

With the left-over lumber I built a nice big porch in the front of our apartment so that we could sit out there during the hot evenings. Later on we put in a lawn. We had some trouble with our next door neighbor because he infringed upon our property and this burnt my wife up, because she wanted the space for a garden. Some people in camp were certainly greedy and they wanted everything for themselves.

After everything was fixed up at home, I went to look for a job. Again, I had some difficulty in finding work as the good jobs were monopolized by the first-comers. The employment officer finally told me that there was an opening for a typewriter repair man. There weren't too many typewriters in camp so I wasn't very busy.

A little later the adult education department started to look for a radio instructor. I coöperated with them, so I began to teach radio about three evenings a week besides fixing the typewriters. I had a nice crowd of enthusiastic boys who were interested in learning about radios, so that I enjoyed this experience. I did this combination of work until the end of the semester in January, 1943.

After that I had an opportunity to become the manager of the repair department for the Community Enterprises. I had quite a difficult time getting it organized. My first job was to get the watch-repair shop started. It took me a long time to find the right man to do this work. We had to build all of the benches and fix up the shop ourselves. I could only find one man in camp with his watch-repairing tools, so I had to give him the job. Later I sent back home for some of my watch-repairing tools and I loaned this equipment to Community Enterprises. The dust and heat in camp had ruined many a watch so that we got more work than we could handle in the watch shop. After this shop became successful, I began to fix up a radio repair shop in the same room. Business was very brisk and we really earned our $19 a month.

There were many evacuees who brought their radios to my apartment to get fixed. I never charged them anything for this work but sometimes they insisted on giving me small tips. It would have taken them 3 times as long to get their radio fixed through the radio shop, so I felt justified in taking these tips. I usually gave it all to my three children. Before the war I used to make more in one day than I did in the whole month in camp for doing the same work.

About this time I got an idea that I wanted to make a little quick money, so I thought I would go to the camouflage net factory for a while. I made quite a bit of money compared to the WRA wages, but a lot of it was deducted for the net trust fund and taxes. I made about $212 in all for the 15 days of work. Then they started to close up the factory because the net contract with the Army was ended. After this job, I got a job as an electrician for the camp. I had to take care of the electrical troubles for the whole center. We even had to repair the power line occasionally. It was something a little different for me and

I learned quite a bit. Some of the Issei wanted me to put in short-wave systems for them but I refused to do this. I know that there were a few short waves in camp, but I never located them myself.

My social life in Gila was not quite as interesting or as varied as my work. I made some new friends and we spent most of our evenings playing cards. I also went to a number of dances and private parties with my wife. The social life in Gila was about the same as it was in Tulare.

Life at Gila became pretty routine after being there for some months. I had to go to church a few times as I took care of the sound system for the Christian Church. My wife sent the children to the Buddhist Church because she had been brought up as a Buddhist. I didn't mind it at all because I didn't particularly believe in any religion. Back home we didn't have a Buddhist Church in town. My wife wanted her children to know a little bit about her religion so I couldn't object about that. I didn't think it would influence my children's thinking to more Japanese ways anyway. I really didn't know what they taught in the Buddhist Church, but I did not think it was harmful to my children while in camp as long as the religion taught them to be good and honest.

Two of my older girls were going to school in camp and the youngest was in kindergarten. I realized that my children wouldn't get as good an education as on the outside and that bothered my wife and myself at times. We tried to train our children to behave properly in all aspects of living because there was so much of a tendency for young children in camp to go unsupervised. I also thought at times that it was too bad that my children did not have the Caucasian contacts in the regular school, but I knew that it would not be for all the time. I didn't want my children to grow up with the feeling of inferiority to the white people.

My youngest girl always used to ask us to go back to our white house in our home town and it was difficult to answer her. We just had to tell her that some day we would go back. It was hard when they asked questions like this. Sometimes the children asked my wife why we were moved from California and it was hard to explain to them. Once my oldest daughter wanted to know if we were going to be sent to Japan. These were the most difficult times for me and I couldn't answer them definitely except to say that some day we would all go back to California to the life we had before. I never liked it when these "why" questions were asked as I didn't know what to say. We would just tell the children the news of our home town when we got letters from friends.

I think my wife had a great deal of difficulty in adjusting herself to the condition of camp life for a long time as the housekeeping facilities were not what she had been used to. But she did manage to mix with the people much easier than I did since her mother was there and she knew more of the people from before.

The registration for the Army in February, 1943, was about the only thing which broke the routine of life in camp. It was too easy to slip into the routine life there and forget about the outside. The registration didn't affect me very much although a lot of people were greatly disturbed about it. I didn't go to any of those public meetings as there was no question about how I would register. I answered "yes" to both 27 and 28 and my wife did the same thing.

The registration did make me stop to think that there was a great deal of resentment against the government by the people in camp. There were a few pro-Japan people there and they influenced a lot of the people who would have answered "yes" if they had not been so aroused by these agitators. I didn't know who all the pro-Japan individuals were, but I was acquainted with a couple of them. I talked to them a few times, but I found that it was no use arguing with them, as they were stubborn and set in their ways of thinking. I tried to keep away from them as much as possible after I found out their type of thinking. A lot of the Kibei signed up for a segregation camp because they felt they had been kicked out of the United States Army after the war started, and they said they were not wanted here anymore.

Many of the Issei who went to Tule Lake were rather bitter against the United States because they had lost their life earnings and they did not see a chance for themselves in this country any more. They thought that their children would have more of a chance to be accepted as equals in Japan. They thought that Japan wanted them to go back there. My opinion was that they were doing wrong and they were being misled. I thought that they would have even less of a chance to get back on their feet in Japan. I felt sorry for the Nisei children whose parents signed up for repatriation, as I knew that they would have a difficult time ever getting adjusted to life in Japan, when and if they are ever sent back.

It looked to me like the draft was getting near but I was willing to take my chances. I didn't even consider volunteering as I had 3 children that I was responsible for. I was already very tired of camp life but I had no definite plans for resettlement then.

As the summer of 1943 went on, it got to a point where my few friends were resettling quite rapidly. I felt that if I did not hurry up and leave, I would not have any friends left in camp. I was very anxious to get back to a more normal life so I thought I had better come out and look the situation over to see what the possibilities for me were.

I was thinking that I could get my family out so that the children could get started in a regular public school some place. I wanted to do it before I was drafted as I knew it would come eventually. Registration in February had made me aware that the camp influences would not be too good if my children were there for the duration. I knew which side of the line I stood on, and it was expected that we would eventually find our way back to the normal life. I thought I was wasting time in camp and I wasn't making any money to set my family up on its feet. I knew that I could better myself by getting out as soon as possible. I also realized that if I came out, I could be helping the war effort in some way.

I heard rumors that wages on the outside were much higher than before the war. I also heard that living costs were higher too and that made me hesitate. But the prospects of getting out of a barbed-wire type of life was more appealing and I wanted my freedom. I got letters from my brother-in-law [CH-35] and he encouraged me to come out. He said that there was plenty of work out here and he offered to let me stay with him until I got settled on my own.

I first started to make definite plans to resettle about in June after the net factory was closed. I watched the job offers listed in the camp papers very closely and I made personal contacts with the outside employment office. I discussed the whole thing over with my wife many times. Since I had a wife and 3 children, I couldn't afford to take any old job as I had to make enough to support them decently on the outside. I didn't want to dig into my bank account any more than I had to because this was our reserve. At first my wife was a little hesitant about coming out because she heard a lot more rumors from the old folks than I did. She didn't want to jump into anything hastily and regret it later. I didn't bother too much about all these rumors regarding the hostility on the outside as they were all amplified too much anyway.

I had a friend who went from Poston to Salt Lake to resettle so I wrote him a letter to ask him about the possibility for a radio repair job there. I wanted to settle as near as I could to the West Coast as I figured that afterwards I might be able to go back to California. My friend from Salt Lake wrote and told me that he had contacted several radio shops in Salt Lake and there were some good openings with pay up to $65 a week. I made up my plans to go to Salt Lake on a short term leave and look the situation over myself. I even went so far as to get my permit from the WRA. Then just before I was scheduled to leave, I found out that Salt Lake was still within the Western Defense Zone. I heard a persistent rumor that there was a possibility that it [might be] evacuated in the future and I didn't want to go up there and be forced to move again. This made me give up the idea of going to resettle in Salt Lake.

I kept on watching the list of job offers in the outside employment office. My brother-in-law wrote more and more letters urging me to come. Finally a job offer came through from Chicago for a radio technician that would pay $100 a week. I immediately applied for this job because this was what I had been hoping for. I was disappointed in my application as I discovered that somebody else had beaten me to the job. I decided to try out Chicago anyway, so I began to communicate with another radio shop in Chicago from a contact I had made through the WRA. The radio shop wired back an offer of a job at $45 a week to start. I didn't think that the offer was good enough so I wrote back and said I would have to have more pay to come out all the way out there. I wanted a guarantee of a raise within a definite period of time if I took the job. I became impatient for an answer because either the mail was slow or the employer was cold to my reply. Before I got final word from him, I decided to come out any way, job or no job.

I took the indefinite leave and left Gila on August 13, 1943. I landed in Chicago 3 days later. I came out here alone as it was arranged for my wife to come out a little later after I got established. I started in at the WRA office on my job hunting after resting for a day or so. The WRA interviewer told me that an offer had just come in a few moments before. I went to see this place in the Loop. I had quite a long chat with the manager and he made me an offer of $50 a week to start. But I didn't want to take the first job that came along, as I felt that I would be able to get a larger salary if I looked around some more. I went down to the southside to see the employer I had been communicating with from camp and he was just going to mail a letter to me in camp saying that I could start out at $50 a week, and if I proved to be good he would give me a $5 raise in two weeks, then another $5 after a month. I was still undecided about what to do exactly so I told him that I would have to think it over and let him know for sure the next day. I debated with myself on the two job offers I had received that day. I was living with my brother-in-law way up on the northside and I decided that it was too far to go all the way to the southside for work. I didn't care for the job offer of the Loop radio store either, as the hours were not favorable. I also thought that the place of work on the southside was not up to standard. Therefore I decided to look for another job so I glanced through the classified ads that evening. A radio shop made me an offer that if I could get the radio department going again, that I would be paid $25 a week plus 40 per cent of all labor charges I made. I thought this was a good setup, so I accepted the job. I worked there until December, 1943.

I worked steadily for two months and then I started to catch too many colds. I had to get up at 6 in the morning in order to get to work on time and I wasn't used to the weather out here at all. The radio shop was very drafty and that wasn't good for me. I had to lay off from work for two days at a time on several occasions on account of these colds. It was breaking my health down so I finally quit the job even though I was averaging around $60 a week in pay.

I took a few days off to recuperate and then I started to look in the want ads again. I went to 2 or 3 places but I wasn't satisfied with any of the offers. Finally I found my present job. It is strictly radio repair work and I have to manage the place and do all of the buying for the boss. I have complete freedom in my work and it is quite convenient for me. I only work 42 hours a week and I make around $260 a month. I am the only worker in the shop and I deal with most of the customers myself as the boss is in and out. The real boss is in the Army and his dad is running the place for him, so that he doesn't know as much about radio work as I do.

My present job is very much to my liking. I get along fine with the boss and he never bothers me. The business has actually increased since I went there because I think I do the repair work much better than the boss was doing and the customers are satisfied. I wouldn't care if the boss gave another job to a Nisei radio man because I have too much to handle now. I don't think he could get a Caucasian radio man now.

I think that I will be holding this job for the duration and possibly even after that. There is no doubt that I could get a little better job if I were not an evacuee, as I could get into a defense plant then and make higher wages. But it would be a factory job and I would rather stay with my radio work. A Caucasian repair man would not be getting any more wages than I am getting now for this type of work.

I am saving plenty so that I can get a good start for my family. I'm buying about $150 a month of war bonds right now. I only pay $30 a month for room and board so that my living expenses are cheap. I bought my own bed and linen and I eat my lunches out. My only other big expense is this noon-hour lunch. I buy clothing every so often but not too much because I have plenty of clothing from before. Recreation is quite an item and this runs to about $25 a month. I send quite a few things to camp, about $20 worth. The rest of my expenses are incidental.

I asked my wife to come out as early as last December as I found out that the winter was not as severe here as the rumors said, although this may have been a mild winter. My wife did not want to come out, so I did not send an ultimatum. One of the reasons for this was that she was expecting her dad back any time from the internment camp and she said she would like to spend a couple of months with him before coming out here as she may not see him again.[199]

I got my draft reclassification on Feb. 15. I felt very low as I was desperately trying to get my family resettled. I didn't see how this was possible as I thought my time had come to serve my country. I knew that being married didn't make any difference at that time, especially since my wife and children were still in camp. I was sure that I would have to go right away so I wrote back to camp immediately to let my

---

[199] His wife's account:

 We waited and waited for Dad to get his final release but it was held up for some reason. I had promised my husband that I would come for sure in April [1944], however Dad came late in March so I canceled my leave to spend some time with him. My family was thrilled to finally get him back. Dad was so happy to be back that he was raring to go see his old friends to see what they had been doing during the year and a half he had not seen them in. I thought that my father would come back in a very bitter mood from the internment camp, but it wasn't that way at all. He saw everything from a completely different viewpoint. He said that he had heard many rumors about people getting into trouble on the outside. In the internment camp he had heard over the short-wave that Japan had advised the people to stay in camp. When he came to Gila and saw that the people were leaving anyway, he knew that he couldn't hold the family there permanently so he became adjusted to the idea.

 I stayed on in camp until June. I finally decided that I had better leave pretty soon as I knew that camp life was not good for the children and I felt that things on the outside couldn't be as bad as I feared. I was convinced that I could rear my children better if I had a more normal household.

wife know of this new development. But radio was considered essential on the home front and at the end of February I received a notice saying that I was deferred for six months.

In a way I don't think that the Nisei should exactly be drafted because of all the evacuation. It sort of stops resettlement plans. At the same time, the draft will put us in the same category as the rest of the Americans. If I do get drafted, I don't think that I could make the grade to go to Camp Savage for the intelligence work. I'm not in favor of a segregated combat team, but if they make a good showing, it will help all of us. If the Nisei were allowed to go out into a mixed group in the Army, there would be no direct showing so that the combat team does have its point. But there are also disadvantages to it too. If I am called, I would like to get into the signal corps since my training would become of value there. We Nisei have to respond wholeheartedly when the time does come as it will help our future if we each do our part. We will get credit for everything we do, and that certainly will be needed after the war.

The present plan is for my family to come out permanently, but in case I get drafted, we have temporarily agreed that it is best for her and the children to go back to camp. We may change that plan when the time comes. Right now we figure that my income from the Army allotment would not be sufficient for her to make a go of it with the three kids. She would be in better hands in camp since her parents are there and I wouldn't worry so much.

After the war I plan to stay in radio work. I may stay in Chicago for a while if the wage level stays up. However, I think that it will be due for a decline. In any event, I will either go back to California and start out a radio shop of my own in my home town all over again, or else I may try to get started in a small city some place in the Midwest as I don't like the big city. I plan to put my daughters through college and I want to give them the best opportunity I can.

At present, I suppose the Nisei are a little young and they haven't had time to develop the sense of responsibility yet. They like to play around too much and they don't realize that this is war time and things can't be like before. However, I do feel that the married Nisei couples are really trying to make good and they are more conscientious. I have a feeling that a lot of the Nisei will leave Chicago, but I don't think that they will ever go back to California as they have nothing to go back for. Those with property will go back, but I don't know what is going to happen to all the people in camp. I'm afraid that the government will have to keep a camp for a long time as the old people don't have any chance at all to resettle and they have no choice unless their children make a go of it and bring them out.

The war hasn't made me more conscious of my race, although I realize that the Nisei do have a tough time. I'm not bitter about it at all, although it has worried me because things were so unexpected. I've always told people that I was an American and it takes a long time to get this point over. I feel that I should do it every chance I get for the sake of my children as I don't ever want them to be misunderstood like we were. I suppose I tend to be easy going, but I always like to be doing something constructive. I know I am a little reserved and I don't talk freely with strangers because I have a difficulty of expressing myself. I tend to be on the conservative side in everything, but that doesn't make me any less an American. At times I have gotten an inferiority complex in regard to my race, but I think I was more conscious of it in camp than on the outside. It has not affected my life too much as I had made the break in the past and I think that I will do it again after the war in spite of the fact that the future does look dark. I try to be self-confident most of the time and the fact that I had a lot of experience in radio and watch making helps out. This can't ever be taken away from me and I am a little better off than those Nisei who have no skill at all. I'm not any less of an American just because the Dies Committee and other groups like that in California made those statements doubting my loyalty. I know that this is my country and I have a certain feeling for it and that is all that matters. The big thing for me now is the work for my own future and also for my children. I just hope that the war doesn't last too long because I do want to get that settled feeling again and I haven't had it ever since that day we were evacuated from [Y]. It's been one uncertainty after another and one can't help wondering about the future when life is like that.[200]

---

[200] In an interview in September, 1944, his wife remarked:

I'm now gradually beginning to feel more at home out here and who knows I may even stay in Chicago. I hope that the war hurries up and ends as I will be able to breathe easier. I think that it may be hard for us for a while after Japan is beaten because a *hakujin* will still look on us as Japanese. There is still a lot of work needed to explain our position here. I know that I'll never go to Japan to live and my children's place is in this country. I feel that they are very much Americanized now. I think that the only way to look at resettlement is in terms of the future of the family and coming generation of children who will be more Americanized than the Nisei. It will be too bad if they are still discriminated against.

CH-34: FRUIT STAND WORKER

Male; born in Montana, 1916; inmigrated to California, 1935; height 68"; weight 165 lbs.; married, 1942; one child.

Interviewed, February–March, 1944. The interviewer was himself a member of a "secondary and peripheral circle" of Nisei resettlers, which involved "a surprising number of relatives or related inlaws" of CH-35 and was estimated, as of January, 1944, to comprise "over a hundred and fifty people in all." He had known CH-34 for several months prior to the interview and described him as having a "rather pleasant personality"; as being devoid of "peculiarly Japanese" characteristics; as a "serious type"; and as "very much a family man."

CAREER LINES

Parental: Father (born *ca.* 1888), immigrated to Seattle *ca.* 1903; attended high school and business college in Seattle, while working as a "schoolboy." Subsequently became a court interpreter for a short period; then obtained a job as paymaster for a company furnishing Japanese workers for the railroads. Married in Seattle in 1914. Migrated with his wife to Montana, and remained there until 1935, working successively as part owner and operator of combined restaurant, pool hall, and barbershop; owner of a photography studio; boiler washer in a railroad roundhouse. Inmigrated to southern California in 1935 and became a clerk in an Oriental art goods store. Inmigrated to Chicago in June, 1943, after obtaining a job as caretaker. Mother (born *ca.* 1892), graduated from a woman's college in Tokyo; immigrated as a picture bride to Seattle in 1914. Worked as self-employed laundress in Montana for some years after 1925. Taught in Japanese language school in both Montana and California, and was interned shortly after outbreak of war.

Own: Graduated from high school in Montana in 1934; completed one year of junior college in California during 1935; majored in electrical engineering and was member of honor society in high school; recipient of an athletic scholarship. Did odd jobs throughout high school period, and worked as "schoolboy" while at junior college. Driver for a Japanese citrus-fruit firm, in the Los Angeles area, 1935–1936; clerk in retail fruit stand, 1937–1940; manager of a fruit stand for two months during 1940; worked in wholesale division of produce firm, 1940–1941 and as packer and buyer for several firms from December, 1941, to April, 1942. Inmigrated to Midwest, June, 1943, and moved after a few days to Chicago. Attended a defense trade school during evenings and worked as checker in a merchandising house from August to October, 1943. Obtained work in a "semidefense" factory as an operative, October, 1943, and was working there at time of interviews.

LIFE HISTORY

I only have a vague idea of my own family background as it was never discussed very much in our family circle. I have an idea that my dad came over here when he was about 8 years old, or it might have been when he was 16. He worked as a houseboy and then he went to school in Seattle and learned English. I know that he graduated from a business college in Seattle because he has a certificate showing this. He told me once that he worked as an interpreter in the Immigration Bureau for a while. During the last war he enlisted but he never went overseas.

My father got married about 30 years ago. My uncle talked to him or something like that and things were arranged. Anyway my mother came over by herself a short time afterward. I never did ask them how they got married because it never occurred to me. All I know is that the kids started to be born after that. There were 8 of us in all. I am next to the oldest. After the kids started to come along, my dad worked as a paymaster for an employment agency for the Great Northern Railway, Northern Pacific, and Union Pacific. They hired all of the Japanese workers to build the railroads and they were paid through this company. My dad knew English fairly well so he was given the job as paymaster. He went into the railroad work too late because after the war Japanese workers were not hired so much. He took the whole family to [A, a small town in] Montana because he thought he had some good connections there. Things did not turn out as he planned, so he went into the photography business. He also had some sort of an interest in a pool hall and restaurant. It catered mostly to the Japanese railroad workers. In his photography business he catered mostly to Caucasians. After a short time he lost everything but I don't know exactly how it came about. He moved on to [B, another Montana town] and the family followed him. Dad got a job in a roundhouse and he did this for many years although he never did like that work.

When I was about 11 years old my parents started a home laundry on the side. Then after I was in high school, my dad went to California for a short time and he was unemployed. He later went back to California when my sister and I went [there] in order to go to college. My dad worked for an oriental fish shop in the Los Angeles area, and in a flower shop for a while after that. After that he opened up a fruit stand but it was no good, so that it failed. Then he went to work in a gift shop during the holiday season. Since then he only worked part time.

Dad was always a wanderlust and he was always dissatisfied with every job he's ever held. I guess that is the reason why none of us are close to him because he has never assumed the full responsibility for the family. When he was successful with a good job, he would quit it all of a sudden for no reason at all and go off on a vacation without telling any of us at home. I never had any deep talks with my father, so I don't know why he was so restless. I know that he was never happy at any of the jobs he held. Mom used to make him take a steady job because she did not like the way we were living. We would be rich at one time and then poor at another. During the time my father was a photographer, we had everything and we were quite well off. Then when he went off to [B], we were pretty poor for a while, and we had to live in a box car.

My dad was always too easy going and good natured. He did things for everybody on his own time and at his own expense. He would even take days off from his work to go running around on some problem of a Japanese. The only pay he would take afterwards would be some beer.

I never saw my father very much at home when I was a youngster. He went to work real early in the morning and he would go to bed about 6:30, during the time he did not go out to visit other people. Usually he would go off right after dinner to do business things for other people. He went to the Japanese café a lot to hang around and talk with other Issei.

My mother was the driving factor in our family. She was the brains and she ran all of the important things that had to be done. It was her idea to start the home laundry and she ran it by herself. My sister, younger brother, and I did all of the delivering after school. At times my dad would go off for days on some business deal but he was not very successful. The laundry business would keep the family going during these frequent trips of my father. I know that my parents had many differences of opinion but they only talked about it behind closed doors late at night.

I remember in [A] there were only three of us kids. My dad used to take us every place then and we got a lot of things. I was only about 3 years old and I think I remember being carried by my grandmother when my mother took me to Japan with her. This was after the war and my father was making lots of money then. I was only in Japan for about six months and then we came back. It wasn't long after that that my dad lost everything and we all moved to [B] where we had a much tougher time.[201]

As long as I can remember we always ate American breakfast and lunch at home and we would have Japanese food at night. We never used chopsticks except for my parents. Mother and Dad both knew English and Japanese but they tended to use more Japanese at home when we were young. Later on they began to use a little more English because that is about all we knew. English was the dominating language in our home.

Whenever other Japanese came to visit us, we never understood them. We didn't have a Japanese language school in [B] until after

---

[201] The following excerpts from the life history of CH-34's oldest sister (CH-25 in our files) add further details re family background:

Dad never talked very much about himself. He came to this country when he was 15 years old and he worked as a schoolboy for a number of years in Seattle, Washington. Dad came from the Ei-mae *ken* in south Japan. He told us children once that the reason he came to this country was that his father died and his mother married her husband's brother. Dad had heard quite a bit about the United States from the missionaries who came into his *ken* so that he was filled with an adventurous spirit and he thought that he could come out here and make his fortune. There really wasn't anything for him to stay in Japan for. He came to this country all alone, but there was another relative living around Seattle at first and he sort of looked after Dad until he got used to this country. I don't know very much about what he did during the time he was working as a schoolboy. He managed to go all the way through school and he did tell us once that he went to high school in Seattle and he was one of the few Japanese to go there. Later on he went to business college in Seattle and he got a credential from that place. After that he worked off and on as a court interpreter for a while.

His first real job was working on the payroll car for a company which was hired by the Great Northern Railway to take care of all the Japanese laborers. Since my dad knew English fairly well, he was able to get this fairly good job. He did this for a number of years. Around 1913 my dad decided to get married. He was about 24 years old then. He contacted his relatives in Japan and one of his uncles arranged the marriage with mother. She arrived in Seattle in 1914 and they were married.

Dad then decided to start a business of his own so that he went to Montana and he became a part owner of the [B] Café which was a combination of a restaurant, pool hall, and barber shop. I was born in 1915, and there were eight children in all altogether. The youngest is now 17.

My father was always a very gentle person. He never did express himself

I went to high school because there were few Nisei kids in town. My parents never did stress the fact that we had to learn the Japanese language as they never expected us to go back to Japan. I never heard my parents discussing about ever going back to Japan to die.

I suppose we had a few Japanese customs in our home, but I don't know if they were Japanese customs or American because I always felt that I lived just like the other Caucasian kids in our town. On the whole, we did not follow the Japanese customs, limited as they were, very rigidly.

My parents used to keep up with the news of the other Japanese communities on the coast by subscribing to the *North American Times*. It was a Japanese language paper which was sent to us from Seattle. My parents used to trade Japanese magazines with the few other Japanese in our area. These Japanese magazines used to pass all over the state of Montana because some of the railroad workers would carry them around with them and they would leave them with Japanese families who felt isolated in some sections of Montana. This was the way they carried news around about all the Japanese families in the state, so that all of the families were greatly concerned that they

---

to his children very much. I suspect that he has had a lot of disappointments during his lifetime, but he never let it twist his personality at all. He was happy having such a large family. There were times when he was quite depressed because he did not have the success in this country that he thought he was capable of, but he never got bitter about it or tried to take it out on the family.

My mother was much more of a definite personality. At times she revealed quite a violent temper. Mother was quite broadminded for an Issei. She came from a Tokyo *ken* and had a very good education. Maybe she was disappointed with the life she led over here because she always longed to go back to Japan to live. In 1918 she did go back for one year and I went along with her. Naturally I was too young to remember the trip at all. My mother intended to leave my brothers and myself with some of her relatives in Japan so that we could have the advantages of a good Japanese education. However, she was disappointed with Japan when she got there and she didn't like it at all, so she lugged us right back again. That finished her longing to go back to Japan and she has been fairly contented living in this country ever since then.

My parents were fairly coöperative with each other. Dad was automatically the boss in business matters but he let Mother run the rest of the household. My parents got along well enough on most occasions although they did have a number of financial differences. That was because the family was getting larger every year and it was difficult for my father to take care of all of us in the manner Mother expected. Things got tough in 1925 and Mother had to take in laundry for a while to supplement the family earnings. By that time our family was fairly big. As I recall it now, I would say that most of the time our standard of living was above average. We never lived in deep poverty although we came pretty close to the edge of it.

had a good reputation. I guess that is why my father tried so hard to gain prestige among them. My mother also received a school paper from the Women's College of Tokyo where she had graduated.

Occasionally big shots from Japan would come through on their way east. They would usually stop by our house and stay overnight. My parents often entertained officials from Japan. I remember meeting Prince Konoye once. He was well guarded. It was always a great event when the Japanese delegations passed through. In those days even the Caucasians in town were impressed by these delegations from Japan. All of the Japanese in the area would bring gifts. My father had a pretty high standing among the Japanese because of all of the legal help he had given them. We had a new house so that visitors from Japan usually picked our home to be guests in. I guess we had the best looking house of all the Japanese families in town.

My older sister and I had to take most of the responsibility among the kids. Each of us had different friends as we grew up, but we stuck together as a unit if anything threatened us. My next younger brother and I had a lot of fights. When I was in the fourth grade, there were kids 18 years old in the class and my brother and I had to stick together when we had a fight. They were a lot of immigrant kids and that is why they were so old. My brother and I had to make the way and fight for our position and after that the rest of the kids in the family lived on our reputation and they never had any trouble at all. It wasn't anything racial about it at all. The kids always picked upon the newcomers into town.

It was easy for me to make friends at school. I was always accepted as far as I knew. I would often gang up with some of the Caucasian kids in my class and we would go pick on some immigrant kid until he could prove he could take it. Then he was accepted into the gang just like I was. There was never any other Japanese kids to play with in town, so I wasn't conscious of the fact that I was of Japanese ancestry. I just thought I was one of the crowd and I played in all the games with them. I was pretty good in baseball and that made my acceptance easier.

Other times I would go hiking with the gang. Often we went out on fishing trips overnight too. The river ran right through town and we would sell all of the fish we caught to the Chinaman. He ran a small hand laundry and this ancient man was always a great mystery to us kids. I never connected the fact that I was an Oriental too, and the other kids never thought of it either because we would all joke against the Chinaman as a group.

From the fourth grade on, my older sister and I were in the same grade together. I wasn't interested in my studies and I never tried to compete with my sister. I just accepted the fact that she would get the better grade. After I got to high school I studied a little more. There were a lot of kids I helped through the examination period at high school. I let them all copy my papers because they were my friends. I was getting pretty good grades then because I was in a different class from my sister and I felt more free. I was just average in grade school, but in high school my grades climbed way up and I graduated 15th in my class. My sister graduated among the first 10 in the class. I tried for grades when I was a junior because my studies were interesting. I got a scholastic pin and that made me feel pretty confident. When I graduated I was given the chance to go to any college in the state on an athletic scholarship but I didn't take advantage of it because I went to California.

I played three years on the high school varsity football team and I was considered one of the backfield stars. I was also the stage manager for the school play for two years. In my senior year I was elected to a lot of prom committees and I felt I was a pretty big shot in high school. I didn't dance at all, but I was asked by a lot of people to go to dances. I didn't go out on a single date in high school. It wasn't because I was racially conscious since I knew a lot of Caucasian girls at school and they always made a big fuss over the athletic stars. It was just that us fellows usually went out in groups.

It was in high school that I first became a little conscious of the fact that I was a little different in race but it did not cause me any worries or mental torments because I was treated like anyone else and I had a great deal of prestige in the school through my athletic activities. I used to go visit some of the Caucasian girls at their homes and the parents didn't say anything about it.

I graduated from high school in 1934. I had an ambition to become an electrical engineer. The government was just starting to build a large dam in Montana and I had an idea that I would study to be an engineer and then go back and get a job there.

I wasn't really the one who decided to go to California. My uncle asked us to come and he said that we could go to college down there. My sister wanted to go to school down there very much and she could not go alone. Therefore she kept persuading me to go along. I didn't have any money to go to a college in Montana, so I gave in. I was curious to go myself anyway. I felt it was a good chance to get away from home and travel. We went on down to [R, a Los Angeles satellite] from there with the understanding that we would both go to college. I didn't think I would like California very much because I heard there were a lot of Japanese there. I thought I was superior to them and didn't think I would be able to get along.

When we got to California, I found I liked it very much. There were a lot of Nisei athletic clubs down there and they all seemed to be interested in sports. I was amazed when they said that only Nisei played on their teams and they only played other Nisei teams. I couldn't figure out why they didn't have more American friends when they went to school with them. Another thing was I couldn't understand why they tended to look so scornfully on the *hakujin*. On the other hand, I could not understand why the Nisei were referred to as Japs. It made me so angry whenever I heard it. I stayed at Reverend [X's] house when we first arrived. The oldest son of that family belonged to a Nisei athletic club and he started to take me around.

The Nisei fellows accepted me right away because of my athletic ability. I began to play football and basketball for them right away as they were looking for new stars. I don't think I would have gotten in with the Nisei group otherwise as they were inclined to be pretty cliquish. I never could understand them when they talked Japanese. They always laughed at me when I asked them to translate the Japanese. I didn't think very much of the Nisei girls I first saw as they did not compare with the Caucasian girls I knew back home. They were built differently and they didn't act like the Caucasian girls. They were not too friendly either. The cuter ones had a high opinion of themselves and they tried to act like movie stars. They didn't seem normal to me.

Living with Reverend [X]'s family was quite an experience for me. They made me go to church every Sunday and we had to say grace before every meal. We had never observed any of those things at home. I had a hard time talking to Mrs. [X], as she only talked Japanese. I felt very lost with the Issei because I never could answer them. I thought it was very funny that they did not learn English and I often wanted to ask why. Mrs. [X] had to tell me a lot of times that the other Issei friends of theirs thought I was rude and that I had no family upbringing because I didn't observe the proper Japanese manner. I lived with the [X's] for one month during the summer of 1934 and I wasn't too crazy about it.

My uncle did not like the idea of my sister and I living in a church. He was a self-made man and he didn't want me to get any of the church people's ideas. He finally got us to move in with the [M's]. Mr. [M] was an ex-world war veteran but I thought that he was pretty Japanesy in a lot of ways too. His wife was just like the other Issei women and she was nowhere near being as Americanized as my mother. The [M's] had the idea that I should go to bed at 8:30 and I was 18 already. I couldn't understand why they sat up and waited for me when I stayed out late. I stayed there for two or three months. The family liked to eat Japanese food all the time and there was a funny musty Japanese odor around the house because they made a lot of Japanese pickles downstairs. They had a lot of Japanese customs and they were pretty sloppy. Mrs. [M] spoke nothing but Japanese all the time and I had to use her son for an interpreter. Mr. [M] was always bragging about himself and I resented that. It made me feel pretty miserable for a while and I got homesick for my own family. In spite of all that, I did not want to go back to Montana. [R] was much larger and the city was quite a novelty for me. My uncle gave me all the spending money I needed and the other Nisei fellows accepted me.

As my first summer out in California went by, I began to fit into the life in a Japanese community. I went out of my way to make friends and I found that the ice would be broken if I took the first step. I also found out that the Nisei were okay after I got to know them so that I gradually did not miss my *hakujin* friends back home so much.

When the fall of 1934 came along, I enrolled at junior college. I wanted to go out on my own so I went to try out a schoolboy job. I wanted to get away from the [M's], as I did not like their way of living.

My uncle had told my father that it would be better to come to California because there were more jobs for Japanese in California. I was disappointed when my family came because I knew it would interrupt my own plans. We couldn't make a go of it at first as Dad did not find the job that he wanted. I didn't feel like being a schoolboy any longer so I decided to quit school and go to work in order to support the family. I had in the back of my mind that I would plan to go back to school in a couple of years after the family got settled but I never got to go.

This uncle helped us out quite a bit. He was my mother's brother and he had never married. He had worked in a Caucasian home for a number of years and he was making around $120 a month, board and room, so that he was able to save up quite a bit of money. He was very liberal with his money for our family and that helped us through the hard times we had at first.

I quit school in 1935 and went to work for Mr. [Z]. He was a wholesaler in citrus fruits and I got my first experience in that kind of work and I had to continue in it until evacuation although I worked for different employers. My first boss was from the same *ken* as my dad and he thought he was giving me a break by letting me work for him at $22 a week. I usually worked about 60 hours a week. Mr. [Z] usually hired Mexican boys because he paid them very cheap wages and that made his profits bigger. The other Japanese thought he should hire more Nisei boys in order to help the families out. My boss thought I should speak Japanese because I was a *Nihonjin*. He got too embarrassed by my mistakes in Japanese in the store, so he started to let me drive his truck and sort the fruit in the back room with him. Gradually I learned to buy the fruit myself at the wholesalers. Later on when he got sick, I ran the business for him for a while. I quit that job after a year and a half because I didn't like the idea of being tied down, and there was not too much chance for any future advancement.

After I went to California, my social life changed quite a deal and I became more involved in the social activities of the Nisei. Back in Montana I had been a member of the DeMolays. I would have had an opportunity to work up to be a Shriner if I continued it. After coming to California I didn't renew my membership in the DeMolays because I didn't have the time. Another thing I dropped was the Boy Scouts. I had been in the Scouts for a number of years and worked up to a life member.

When I got to [R], the only Caucasian social group I joined was the YMCA. I played basketball with them when I first went down there and we won second place in the league. I was the only Nisei in that group. After that I began to play more and more with the Nisei clubs and I dropped my Y activities. During the time I was at the Y I got along swell with the Caucasian fellows and they all called me Ike. Never once was I called a Jap. I think I could have gotten in pretty well with them if it were not for my work which made it impossible to be with them.

I started to attend some of the JACL meetings from 1935 on but I never was too active a member after a year or so. I voted as soon as I was of age and I have attempted to vote in every election since then on a nonpartisan ticket. At that time, the Nisei in the JACL were not too interested in politics. The boys and girls just used the meeting as an excuse to get off the farms and come to town to meet social friends.

After I quit working for Mr. [Z] in December, 1936, I got a job with the [C] Produce Company. It had a branch office in [R] and the whole company was Japanese owned. I worked there for four years in all. The [C] store catered to the rich people, because it was located in a pretty high-toned district. It was one of the best Japanese fruit stands down south and it was glassed in and quite modernistic in design. A lot of the other Japanese fruit stands were just sheds or open air places. [C] Company had nine stores in all throughout the Los Angeles area and they made very good profits. It was one of the richer companies, although there were others which had a much greater chain of stores. [C's] usually worked it in a regular system so that they took full advantage of Nisei employees. They would train a Nisei from a greenhorn position and work him right up. But many of the Japanese workers stayed with a company for years and years and they never got promoted. [C's] employed many kinds of Japanese including Issei, Kibei, Nisei, Hawaiian-Nisei, Seattle-Nisei, and young kids from the farms. The original group which stuck with the company from the beginning in 1929 eventually were made managers of one of the stores and they got a salary of $45 a week plus $50 to $100 bonus for Christmas.

I held the sales record for our store. I sold $120 worth of produce in one day and I got a bonus for that. We used to race to see who could sell the most produce during the day and the competition was pretty keen. You had to have a good personality in order to please the customers. I used to make a lot of tips too and that is unusual. In most of the other fruit stands the customers never gave any tips. I started out working for $21 a week and after three or four years worked up to $27.50.

I used to start work at 7:30 in the morning. The minute I got there I started to trim all the vegetables and fix the displays for the day. The fresh produce arrived from the wholesalers in Los Angeles as soon as we got to work so that we usually had to help unload the truck. The door would open around 9 and we would start waiting on the customers. Most of the customers came between 9 and 12. During noon we had to keep busy too as the working girls came in then to buy their vegetables. We took shifts for lunch. In the afternoon we would work on the displays again until about 3:30. Between

3:30 and 6 we would usually have another rush of customers. After this rush was over we would take down all of the perishable vegetables and put them in the refrigeration room. Around 7 or 7:30 we would be through for the day. It was a pretty long working day and we earned our money. In some other stands the hours were even longer than that.

The life of the fruit stand workers began to improve after the union got organized. We were in the Japanese fruit stand union at first. At that time our boss paid us a little better than the union scale. The Japanese controlled about 90 per cent of the fruit stands in Southern California so that the owners and even the workers didn't want to join the A.F.L. because we feared that it would pass rules saying that the ratio would have to be four Caucasian employees to one Nisei and that would throw a lot of *Nihonjin* out of work. We were told that the Nisei would not be allowed to have any votes in the A.F.L., so that we feared that a lot of rules would be railroaded through and it would be harmful to the Japanese workers. We were all told that the Issei and Kibei would be ruled out of fruit stand work if the A.F.L. ever got into control. That is why we stuck with the Japanese fruit stand workers union for a long time.

The fruit stand began to be strongly unionized about 1938. At first some of the employers violated the union contract because they thought they could get away with it. The Japanese union was still not strong enough. The funny thing was that when the union sent an agent to investigate these contract violations, the workers refused to testify because they were afraid they would lose their jobs. They did not have any faith in the Japanese union. It was hard for the union to improve conditions for the fruit stand workers when the union members were like that. The union finally had to guarantee the worker that it would pay their wages if they were fired in the event they testified. It also guaranteed the workers another fruit stand job.

The Japanese union got much stronger after that and it began to offer more to the members. It offered the workers an opportunity to take out accident and sickness insurance on very liberal terms. This insurance was optional and it was much better than any of the insurance which the owners of the company offered to the worker. This Japanese fruit stand union lasted until 1940 when the president resigned to go to Japan to sell some rubber patents. His departure left the union without any strong leadership so that the A.F.L. began to renew its efforts to get the Japanese workers to affiliate. The Japanese union finally voted to go into the A.F.L. and it got its own charter. The A.F.L. immediately got higher wages for the employees but the dues were doubled. The Japanese employers saw that they could not do any more underhand stuff, so they had to stop making the workers put in long hours on the sly.

The fellows I worked with were mostly from Seattle. They were honest and hard working and different from most of the other L. A. workers. They were an older group and they had come down to Los Angeles because they couldn't find any economic opportunities in Seattle. Almost all of them had gone to college. Some of these fellows were pretty bitter about being pushed down in work like that but they couldn't do anything about it, so that they gradually began to accept their position.

The Los Angeles fruit stands also had a lot of Hawaiian boys to work there. These Hawaiian Nisei were noted for their quick temper, laziness, slipshod methods in their work, working irregularly, and pocketing a lot of the sale money. Most of them needed watching all the time. They were mostly single fellows and they went around in gangs. They weren't educated too much either. The majority of them had worked on ships, and they were left stranded in Los Angeles. Some of the better Hawaiian Nisei made advancements in the fruit stand work, but the bulk remained at the clerk level. They were smart alecs and quite rowdy. They didn't like to take orders at all. They were strongest for the A.F.L. union idea because the employers did not want them so much. They would put the Hawaiian fruit stand worker on the split shifts.

More and more of the Los Angeles Nisei started to go into fruit stand work by 1940 after they got out of high school and college. At first they were too proud to do this kind of work, but they had to take the fruit stand jobs because they could not get any other type of employment. A lot of the Nisei college graduates started to work on the fruit stands on a temporary basis during the depression. The longer they stayed, the more they lost their own ambitions and they got into a rut. It seemed that the best jobs in the Japanese community could only be obtained through pull of relatives. All of the Nisei working in the fruit stands knew that this sort of work could only end in a manager of a Japanese chain store or else opening their own fruit stand. It only took a capital of between $1,000 and $2,000 to open up one's own fruit stand, but it was a pretty risky business and quite a few folded up every year. It was run on credit mostly and everything was sold for cash, so that the margin of profit was pretty big if the store was located in a good spot. If the store turned out good, other Nisei would be hired as clerks and the owner would begin to think of branching out with a chain of his own. Then the process would start all over again. The only future for the workers beyond that was to have their own store and start their own chain, but there was a · lot of competition and the number of failures each year was much greater than the successes. The successful stores usually hit the jackpot.

I began to have ambitions of my own after I learned all about fruit stand work. Around the beginning of 1940 I decided that I would take a chance so I quit the [C] Company in order to take a manager's job in a fruit stand in [another suburb]. I was offered a salary of $35 a week and this was an improvement. I had the idea that if I were successful as a manager, then I would think about becoming an owner and starting my own store. The owner of this chain had 22 shops scattered over southern California, and he thought that [this suburb] was a good spot to open a new stand. The store he gave me to manage was rather modest. I had 5 workers under me. It was an open-air market and we had to put in long hours as the union had not gotten around to it yet. I only stayed in that job for two months because I soon found out that the employer tried to take advantage of his workers. The store catered more to the poorer people and business was not so good as in the [R] store I had worked in before. I soon found out that I couldn't get along with the boss at all. We could not agree on wages and hours of work for the other employees. He only wanted to give them $15 a week and he felt that they should work 12 hours a day for six days a week. The boss wanted me to work the other employees too hard and he was always yelling about profits. Finally I got sick and tired of this and I quit.

I went back to [C] in March, 1940, and this time I got into the wholesale division. My job was to help buy and deliver fruits and vegetables to the various fruit stands owned by [C] Co. I was getting $35 a week so I felt that it was an advancement in pay for me. One good thing about that job was that I only had to work 8 hours a day instead of the usual 10 hours I had been used to for years.

I still wanted to start a fruit stand of my own, but I didn't have the capital. It would have been a good proposition for me because I could employ about six or seven members of my immediate families to start out with and that would have kept the expenses down and it would have been a family affair where we would all share in the profits. I never got to realize this ambition because one thing after another happened to postpone it, the greatest thing being the outbreak of war.

It may be strange, but my real ambition was not in fruit stand work. I didn't want to be doing it all of my life, but I was sort of forced into it and I couldn't find any way out. I really wanted to get into some kind of profession and live comfortably. I always wanted to be an electrical engineer. That was my ambition in high school, and I started out in college with this in mind. When my dad came to California with the rest of the family, I had to quit school as it was my duty to help the family out. Nobody told me to do this but I couldn't exactly sit around and watch the family have a hard time without doing something about it. My younger brother had received better grades in high school and he wanted to go on to college as he had a strong ambition to be a chemist. He later went on to [a college in California] and now he has his M.A. degree from [a Midwestern university]. During all this time he was going to school, I just kept quiet and let him go on because I wanted him to have his chance. I kept working in the fruit stand instead of taking my turn to go to school.

I got older every year so that the dream faded. On top of that, I saw so many Nisei college graduates in fruit stand work, and it did look a little hopeless to have a college education and then drop back into the same level of work as I was doing with only a high school education. I thought I would be quite bitter if that ever happened to me.

The only other large field of work for the Nisei in Southern California, outside of farming, was gardening. They worked for the Caucasian families, and a lot of Nisei were taking up gardening after getting out of college. They had competition because the Caucasians saw how profitable it was, so they started to come in and displace the Nisei. This happened until some of the defense plants opened up in the Los Angeles area, and then even the Okies were able to get good jobs and the pressure was lifted off the Nisei for a while. In [R] most of the Nisei girls went in for domestic work.

There was a little more opportunity for Nisei girls in the Los Angeles' Little Tokyo but wages were extremely low. The average wage for girls was about $12 a week. The Nisei girls in the fruit stands worked split shifts and they got short hours (8 per day) with a wage of $2 a day.

The whole economic condition of Little Tokyo was tottering before the war. The Jews were getting to take over the fruit stand work and they cut-rated on the Japanese in order to force them out of business. The Japanese community could not have lasted much longer or else they would have had to go more into domestic work. Everybody just couldn't get a job in the Japanese community. It just couldn't be self-sufficient the way it was. It turned out that in the Japanese community the people with the money from before kept on top and the average Japanese worker got poorer and poorer because more Nisei were coming of age to work. This meant that there was more competition for jobs and the wage level went down accordingly. The fruit stands were the main economy of Little Tokyo and that really was shaking. There was plenty of unemployment among the Nisei before the war.

If you look at things from this point of view, then I think that the Nisei made a definite advancement as a result of the evacuation. The way it was going, more and more of the family members had to work to keep the income of the family up to the former level. The economic basis of all the Japanese towns up and down the coast was pretty shaky and the Nisei had not been able to burst through these limitations before the war started.

At the time just before the war, I gave political matters little thought and I did not read the newspapers too carefully. The longer I remained in fruit stand work, the more I lost interest in other things.

I never was too interested in the JACL movement although I had more interest in it after I got into the union. I was nonpartisan in the elections as I was undecided about what party to vote for. I thought that I should be more interested in politics so that the Nisei would be able to gain a place for themselves. I knew that the Nisei had to take the first step to break the ice. But most of us were too busy earning our bread and butter and the majority of the Nisei were still too young to take politics seriously.

I was working nights in the period before the war so that I didn't see so many of my old friends. I didn't have too much time for leisure activities then except to go to occasional movies. Making fishing poles was my favorite hobby and I also spent a lot of time fixing up my own car. I didn't go to church at all. Up to then I had never been serious about any girl but I started to go steady with my present wife about 4 or 5 months before the war.

When I first came to [R], I started to go around with a few Chinese, Korean, and *hakujin* girls because I didn't care for Nisei girls at all. For a while I was going around with a *hakujin* girl who came from a rich family. I got to know her pretty well because she used to shop at the store where I was working. After a while I started to take her out on dates. I didn't want to get involved so I finally called it quits. Later I began to go around more with Nisei girls and the longer I was in [R] the more contacts I made among Nisei, only I thought that Nisei girls were too cold so I wasn't particularly interested in getting too serious with any of them. They didn't know how to be casual and friendly.

My first serious date was on July 4, 1941. That was when I first met [my future wife]. It was a beach party and she had just returned from New York where she had been working at the Fair. I was attracted to her right away and somebody introduced us. I found out that she was going around with a friend of mine who was working in a fruit stand, so I decided not to cut his throat. However, I had nothing to do during the day so I used to drop over to her place in Los Angeles just to talk to her. I didn't have to go to the wholesale market until the evening. Gradually I got more interested in her because she had traveled a lot and she seemed so different from most Nisei girls I had known before.

We began to go ice skating together and other places. I never took her to a Nisei dance as I was still the third party in this triangle. About August I got much better acquainted and I began to go to Nisei parties with her. About September I began to win over first place, so I went to visit her more and more. By October I was in first place and just before the war, we were thinking of getting married eventually.[202] I wasn't sure of how the family would take it, as my brother had

---

[202] CH-34's wife (CH-4 in our files) was described by the interviewer as "a wholesome, friendly, and very interesting young matron, with a great deal of ambition and initiative and a very pleasing personality. Prior to her marriage she was much sought out socially by the eligible Nisei boys in Los Angeles." Like CH-34, she had spent her childhood in one of the interior states. Her father—an inventor and businessman—had achieved more than ordinary success, and CH-4 felt that she had had a "wonderful childhood," and that "the world was pretty grand to me." She said she was "never conscious" of racial differences although she could not understand why she "had black hair and all the other children were blond." She remembers that the white children seemed envious of her because her mother "had come from such a far away and strange country." Her family migrated to Los Angeles when CH-4 was 13, and although "she wanted to be accepted by the Nisei," she never did "get over the feeling of always being on the fringe." She spent three years in Japan where she worked, for a time, at the American con-

eloped and more of the family burden fell on me. We had a sort of an arrangement where I had to take care of the family for three years, then a younger brother for the next three years and still a younger brother for three years and right down the line. However, this plan was disrupted because one of my brothers got drafted and another got married, so my period turned into eight years. I wanted all the rest of my brothers to go to college as I felt that a Nisei had to have at least two years of college training as a minimum. For these reasons I really couldn't think seriously of marriage. I had a 3-A rating in my draft status because I had five dependents and I was the only one who was in a position to support them then.

I had become more or less the head of the family in economic affairs after I started working regularly, but my mother still held most of the authority in the family affairs. She never told me what to do although she tried to advise me at times. My father had no position at all in the family. He just loafed around and took it easy. My younger brothers all respected me but I never bossed them around or gave them lectures. I was just a working man, and I didn't take too much of an interest in the close family problems at that time since my mother could handle most of it herself.

We were solid as a family. We had our arguments, but they never assumed major proportions. Whenever any of us worked, all of the money was turned over to my mother and she did all of the planning with it. It didn't matter how much any of us earned because we were all sharing in the responsibilities. I was working full time, so naturally I contributed the most, but this did not give me any special privileges. If I did get any special privilege, it was because I was older.

---

sulate, and took a "short course on silk culture." She was sent as a lecturer to the New York world's fair by a Tokyo company that was putting on an exhibit.

CH-4 describes her meeting with her future husband as follows:

I met [Ch-34] in the late spring of 1941. We were attracted immediately to each other. He was born in Montana and he had similar views as I did. His father was a World War [I] veteran and very Americanized.

[CH-34] was an ambitious Nisei and he was helping his family out a lot even before the war [World War II]. He did not run around like a lot of the other Nisei. He was a buyer for a Japanese wholesale company. We started to go all over together. He would take me to dances, shows, golfing, and the beach. We went mostly to public dances and we did not associate too much with the bulk of the Nisei, although we had our circle of friends. I used to visit my Caucasian friends that I had first met in New York and sometimes [CH-34] and I would go out with them. By early winter we were sort of engaged although we had not made any announcements.

We bought our house in 1935 and we were still making payments on it when the war came. We had about $1,000 more before the house would be cleared. Each month we would take out the payments from our family fund. Everyone [else] in our family worked part time. My sister and mother held half time jobs and my other brothers worked part time also. When we bought the house, the property was put in my name.

I think I was disturbed about the future. I often felt that I was wasting years in the fruit stand work like all of the other Nisei. All of the Nisei hated to be forced into the fruit stand racket but they could not help themselves. They couldn't do anything about it even if they were ambitious because the job openings for them were so limited. Great numbers of the Nisei had been going into college all along in order to postpone the time when they would finally have to go to work, but they didn't know what they would do when they did get out of school. The testing period was still ahead when the war broke out and changed everything.

On Pearl Harbor Sunday I was working in a fruit stand job which I held during the day in addition to my regular job. I was informed about 2 o'clock in the afternoon that Pearl Harbor had been bombed by the Japanese. I didn't believe it at first as I thought it might have been an Orson Welles radio play. I began to feel uneasy when various people came by the fruit stand and they all told me the same thing. They said that the radio had been announcing this event since 10 that morning. I couldn't hold my curiosity any longer, so I went to a radio and turned it on. I heard the news immediately, so I just closed up the fruit stand and went home. I was shocked and I didn't have full control over my actions. I guess it was like being sort of punch drunk. I still continued to think that it was impossible for such a thing to happen. The thought occurred to me that the U. S. Navy must have really been asleep to be caught like that.

When I got home, everyone was pretty excited. None of us could believe that it was really true. I called my girl friend right away and I told her to be as calm as possible because the news had disturbed her just as much as it had shocked me. I told her that I would come over to Los Angeles right away in order to see her. My dad wanted all of us to stay away from the Japanese community in Los Angeles, as he said that there might be some riots there. I told my younger brothers to stick close to home and look after things while I went to see my girl friend. Just before I left somebody from the JACL office phoned and advised us to avoid crowds for the next few days and not to discuss the war with anyone. They said that we should show our feelings for this country if we were forced into a discussion. After that I left the house for Los Angeles.

I couldn't resist taking a look at Little Tokyo so I drove by there on the way out to see [my girl friend]. The whole community was in an uproar and there were people running all over the streets in great excitement. There were police cars around also so I decided not to stop at all. [My girl friend] was curious about what was happening downtown so we went out to a Japanese place for dinner and we did not see anything out of the ordinary as it was located in the better part of Los Angeles. People did not stare at us or anything.

The next morning, all of the bosses at the company looked exhausted as they had been up all night. They were really concerned and worried about what was going to happen. The public was not against the Japanese business at all because all of the customers came to the market, and they expressed their sympathies for us and said that they believed we were loyal and they would stand by us in the event of any difficulties. They were just as curious as we were about what was going to happen, and the only thing I could say was that I thought I would be in the Army soon like the rest of the fellows. They said that they would give us any recommendations or help if we ever needed it.

Just before I went out on the truck to deliver the day's supplies of vegetables and fruit, the boss came up to me and told me to tell all of the store managers to be extremely courteous to the customers and not to discuss the war as they might be mobbed and the store wrecked. As I drove out that morning, it was still all a dream for me. I had gone to the market about 3 that morning and nothing out of the ordinary happened and I delivered all of the things as usual that morning of December 8.

The workers at the various fruit stands had a shock reaction like I did. There was one Kibei store manager and he said that at least the Japanese people had the guts to do something and they had been forced into it because they had been squeezed so much. He thought that it was too bad that Japan attacked at that time as all of us in this country would suffer for it. Another Issei store manager told me that Kurusu had not been given a fair chance by the American government, so that he was helpless to smooth out the relations between the two countries. I suppose that most of the Issei felt this same way, although they were not talking about it too much because they were so frightened. They did not blame the Japanese people at all as they said that the military power got mad and they started the war. They thought that Japan's hands were forced and it was a face-saving move that they had to take. They felt that the United States gave Japan no other choice but to attack.

After delivering all of the vegetables to the various stores I went back to the warehouse. When I arrived I discovered that the FBI agents were already there. They were ready to take over the entire management of the store. They said that they would have to question all of us before we could leave so I called up my mother and told her that I would be delayed in coming home because I misunderstood the FBI man and I thought that I would be put in a jail. The FBI would not let anything in the warehouse be moved. Even my own personal car was searched thoroughly and all of the road maps were taken out and kept as evidence. I had to stay there until 11 that night before I was finally released.

I was dumbfounded by it all because it happened so fast. I was out of a job, as this job was closed for good and I didn't know what I would do. The boss told me to call up [the Caucasian general manager who leased the concessions] and ask him for a job. The boss was only operating on a special foreign license. I suppose that is why the FBI closed him out of business so fast.

The following day I went back to work again as a clerk in the [R] store. The customers were very nice to me, and they were all sorry and they all offered help. Many of them had been my old customers when I had worked in that store before. I was only getting $27.50 and this was quite a reduction from my previous wage, but I didn't have any choice. The company had to take all of [C's] fruit and vegetables off the table as it was being held by the FBI. It took two days just to put the new stock in. A Caucasian manager was put in the store but he did not know anything and he had to depend upon the Nisei employed there. All of our old customers came back to us and they did not go to the Caucasian clerks who had also been put in the store by the company.

I worked in that store until January and then the warehouse was opened, so I asked to be transferred there. I was supposed to start working on January 2. When I went there to inquire, the warehouse supervisor said that they didn't know anything about a job as a driver for me. I got the run around so that I was out of a job again. One of the fellows told me that [a banana firm] needed packers, so I went over there and applied and I was given a job because I had had some previous experience. I worked there January and February, 1942, but business was falling off steeply since there were no boats coming in from Central America. Finally business got so bad that the company discontinued bananas because it was losing $1,000 a month on account of the poor business. They began to put us on an every other day shift about February, and pretty soon it got to be only two days a week, so I finally decided to quit in March. It didn't pay me to go all the way to Los Angeles from [R] and only work a couple of hours.

I got a temporary side job and our family was living on my $20 a week social security money. I had enough money saved up for the immediate needs of the family and my social security was coming in so that I finally quit the job. I knew that we were going to get evacuated soon anyway.

After the war started [my girl friend] and I talked of marriage more seriously. When the evacuation was started, we thought that Los Angeles would go to one camp and [R] to another. We knew that Manzanar would be a permanent camp so we thought that we should get married so that we wouldn't be split up. We wanted to take her family along with ours as her parents were pretty old and she did not want to leave them alone to take their own chances.

At that time my dad was already in Manzanar as he had volunteered for an advance crew. He sent back favorable reports of the camp so we thought we would like to go there. Dad had tried to run all of the preparations for evacuation but he couldn't do this because we did not listen to him since he hadn't taken the authority before which he should have done. My mother had been interned and none of us children would take any advice or orders from Dad. He got sore at this and he always wanted to argue. Finally he gave up, so he decided to go off alone to Manzanar. I didn't think he should have left just then and I told him that this was his opportunity to win the family back. My dad felt that he would make $50 a month at Manzanar because that was what the pay was supposed to be at that time. The advance workers later got fooled and they didn't get paid that much. Dad thought that if he made this much money he would be recognized as the real head of the family and the little kids would respect him as they should a father.

My mother had been interned[203] as she had been teaching in a Japanese school in [R]. She was taken at the end of February. Her going was quite a blow to our family and it disorganized us completely at a time when we needed her around. I didn't feel this so much myself, but the rest of the family did because they were so used to having her handle important affairs. My sisters managed to take over most of Mom's functions. The younger three kids went to school as usual since we did not see any reason for pulling them out. My oldest sister was planning to voluntarily evacuate, so that she didn't say much in the family affairs since she was going her own way. A brother was married, so that he was considered more or less as an outsider. This left most of the important decisions in the family up to my other sister and myself.

I wasn't in a very good position to take over all these functions as I was all excited, since my marriage was set for April 2. The curfew and all those things had come in March and [my girl friend and I] couldn't go to see each other so often because of the 5-mile limit rule [and R was more than five miles from Los Angeles]. I continued to see her on the sly but I was taking a lot of chances. I had a phony Japanese address for every 5-mile distance all the way [from R] to Los Angeles, but it was getting pretty risky.

Since it was evacuation time, a lot of the Nisei were getting married on the spur of the moment because they thought they would be parted forever if they didn't get married. [We] felt that it was foolish to have a large banquet when we were about to be thrown out of our homes. We dropped some hints to [my fiancée's] mother about elopement but her mother was very disappointed as she said that my mother and dad were both away and at least one of the parents should see us get married. We decided that we could have a very small wedding and only relatives would attend.

---

[203] Another of CH-34's sisters (CH-39 in our files) commented as follows on their mother's internment:

In March my mother was interned so I had to quit school to go help out with the family. There still was no talk of a general evacuation of [R], although a number of Issei had been interned in other areas. Very few were taken from our town.

I was very, very bitter when my mother was interned as they had no right to take her. I knew that her ideal of America was high and she had always told us that we should pledge allegiance to the United States. She said that she never wanted to go back to *Nihon* because she didn't like it when she went for a visit some years before. My mother was interned just for being a Japanese schoolteacher. She only taught the language and nothing else.

Finally [my fiancée] quit her job and came to stay with my other sister in our home so that we could get married, just in case a blockade between Los Angeles and [R] was thrown up, and since most of [her] relatives were in Los Angeles, we went there to get married. The following Sunday we went over again and had a wedding dinner in a Chinese restaurant so that we could meet all of her relatives.

Los Angeles was already being evacuated in some sections so after a family conference it was decided that [my wife's] family should all come over and join us so that we could all go to Manzanar together.

During all of this time I had been busy in some of my other activities. When the talk of evacuation first came up, the [R] JACL chapter offered to assist the WCCA. I donated my services since I had a lot of free time and I had some connections in renting or borrowing trucks. I wasn't a member of the JACL but I felt it was my duty to help out the people as much as possible. The WCCA rented an office for the JACL to help the people with their problems. I did this work since it gave me a chance to go to Los Angeles too after the curfew came in. We got all sorts of things donated to help each other out and a lot of the Caucasian friends also kept their word that they would help us if the time ever came. The churches were particularly helpful. Because of all of this assistance, very few of the Japanese families had to ask for regular relief. There was a choice of storing household goods in the [R] Union Church or in the WCCA warehouse. Very little of the goods were stored with the government as most of the people felt that they would not be gone too long. They stored their belongings in the church or else sold out what they did not want to keep.

Through the JACL, we were able to make special provisions for the home owners. I don't think any other Japanese community used a system like we had. There were about 40 Japanese home owners and we all banded together and formed a trust company with a Caucasian [who was] given the power of attorney to look after our interests. Not one Japanese had to sell out his home outright in great haste and it is all being leased or rented out now so that they get an income from it. We had to pay 1 per cent a year of the value of the property for the Caucasian's services. It was his job to collect the rents or sell the home later if the owner decided while in camp. The whole payment for a year only came to about one month's rent and we got the rest for income so that it was quite a good arrangement. Our home is under this arrangement now. All of the tax bills, mortgages, insurance payments, and upkeep costs are being taken care of in a satisfactory way. Our home was mortgaged so that we borrowed some money from my sister-in-law's father, and he is getting the rent of the house until it is all paid back. It is one of those family deals, so that we don't have to pay any interest on that loan. In this way, we are able to keep our home and not worry about the mortgage. We thought it was the best plan because we didn't know when we would be able to have a regular income again.

Through the coöperative organization set up by the JACL, we helped people sell their cars. We sent the owners to reliable dealers so that they would get a fair bargain. Sometimes we even went out in order to do some price listing for some Issei. I sold my own car in this way. We also kept up with all the news of changing government rules and regulations and we helped Issei get into their safety deposit boxes at the banks. We took all of the complaints to the WCCA.

The Japanese in [R] took quite a loss because of the rush of things. They would have taken even more of a loss if the JACL had not helped them out. Up to the time of evacuation the people were so bewildered that they had turned to the JACL and depended upon it for everything. I think the JACL did do a lot of good in helping the people out and it could not prevent all of those losses as we could not do everything for the people.

I didn't take a loss on anything that I had except the sale of my car. I had paid $1,250 for it about six months before the war and I had to sell it for $750. In camp there were a lot of rumors that the JACL members did not take a loss on anything because they looked after themselves first of all. I don't think that is true, because a lot of members were sacrificing the personal disposition of their property in order to help out the other people. I say this even though I was not a member of the JACL. I didn't agree with some of its policies, but I certainly don't think that any criticism directed against their activities in helping the people evacuate is justified.

I thought that evacuation was very unfair since the government didn't say that German or Italian aliens had to go before the American citizens. If I had the money, I would have liked to stay behind and let them force me out just to see what the outcome would have been. Most of us were too bewildered to think of it then so we didn't protest much.

I really did not have too much time to think of all the complications of evacuation or whether it was right or wrong because of my personal activities. My dad was in Manzanar and my mother [was interned] and my older sister was getting ready to [evacuate eastward, voluntarily], so that I had to assume more and more family responsibilities. I was running all over the place and sending on things that had been left behind by my sister. I also had to send things to my mother and do many other necessary functions like that.

I think that most of the Nisei in [R] were busy like that and they were very coöperative. It was at this time that I felt closer to the Japanese community than ever before in my life, especially to the families which had young children. Many of the parents could not go out and sell their household goods because they did not speak much English. They could not even keep up with the changing rules and regulations unless we helped them out. I felt sorry for them and I thought that it was such a great tragedy for them to be booted out like that. I felt sorrier for their predicament than for my own situation, because I did not feel that everything was entirely hopeless for me, whereas I didn't see how some of those Issei parents with small children would be able to get on if they had to shift for themselves.

My loyalties were still with America as it had always been. I did not blame evacuation on the American people as I thought that it was more due to politics. Persons like Mayor Bowron of Los Angeles turned against us, and all of the Los Angeles newspapers agitated against Manzanar. They wanted all of the Japanese sent out of the state altogether. They said Manzanar was city property and they thought the Japanese would poison the water if sent out there. The American Legion and Native Sons started to make public statements and that griped me, as I could see it was for selfish profits. It was these small groups who were really behind evacuation and they had the whole country fooled.

In a way I blamed a lot of things on the Japanese government too. It was trying to take too big a step and I didn't agree with their methods. I felt that America would eventually make Japan pay for Pearl Harbor and everything after a lot of suffering of people in both countries. The fact that we were being evacuated made me feel a little bitter too. I was more conscious of the fact that I was a member of a minority group and that people would not accept us as Americans. There were still a lot of Caucasians in [R] who tried to help us all along and they did a lot of things in helping to prepare for evacuation day. They were willing to go way out of their way to look after our property and I couldn't understand where all the hatred against the Japanese came from. When I realized how the people in [R] were really reacting and how helpful they were, I didn't feel so bitter about being pushed into a camp, as it was my firm belief that some day all of the people in the country would be more sane and that organizations like the American Legion and Native Sons would not always have the loudest voice in the press. I knew that most of the people were decent at heart and this drew me closer to the fact that I too was an American. I felt that I could sacrifice this little and not turn my self against the country that I felt I belonged to and which was a part of me. I also had a faith that if the public had been allowed to vote on whether evacuation should be accomplished or not, they would have voted against it because most people are decent and they don't like to persecute another group which happens to be on the spot.

There was some talk that the camps would only be temporary, but I could not see how there was a future beyond it for me when everything was so disrupted. There was some talk that we would be allowed to go to the Midwest or East eventually. I thought that I would like to go east and be free if we had a chance, but I couldn't see how we could make a living. I had the mistaken idea that the whole country was turned against us like the newspapers in California made out. My sister was in [the Southwest] living a free life and she was being treated okay, although she did have some trouble being accepted.

My family was scheduled to go to the Pomona Assembly Center. Then it was announced that the [R] group would have to go to the Tulare Assembly Center since too many were going into Santa Anita at one time. We tried to shift to Manzanar right away but we were unsuccessful, and the WCCA told us that we had to go to Tulare first. The reason for all of these last minute changes was due to the Japanese themselves. The Army was trying to evacuate a group of 1,000 people at a time from each section [of a city or area]. However, a lot of Japanese families wanted to go with their friends, so they would all move into the district at the last minute and register with that group. The Army calculations were thrown way off when all of these extra people moved into the districts scheduled to go at a certain time. Sometimes as many as 2,000 people would register from a certain district when the Army only figured on 1,000. Quite a bit of this shifting around at the last minute was going on, and that is why we didn't get to any of the camps of our preference and we didn't know until the last minute that Manzanar, Pomona, and Santa Anita were closed to us.

We left [R] about the end of April [1942] for Tulare Assembly center. The Japanese people were quite relieved to know that they were actually getting started after waiting around so long in suspense. I tried to kid myself into feeling that it was the first real vacation of my life and I would have no more responsibility for the family for the time we were in camp as the government was providing everything. At the same time I knew that my freedom would be limited and this bothered me quite a bit. This fact was emphasized to me when the M.P.'s refused to let us get off the train at all during our trip to camp. I talked to one of the M.P.'s and he was quite sympathetic. He said that he had been placed on the train to protect us in case people threw rocks at us and not because he was afraid anyone was going to try and escape.

We arrived in Tulare at 7 o'clock in the evening since the train went on a round-about way through the Mojave Desert. It was a very tiring trip and we were exhausted after going in such a big semicircle. As we approached camp, a lot of young fellows inside the gate started to boo us and they told us to go back from where we came from. The reason for this was that they thought we were from Boyle Heights [a section of Los Angeles] which was quite a notorious place and they didn't want us there. It was all young Nisei and they kept yelling, "We don't want you. Go back to Los Angeles." A lot of us felt that this was a disappointing reception. Ordinarily we would have laughed it off but we were so tired that it hurt us.

After I got into the gates of the camp I recognized a few friends and that lifted my morale a little. I also knew a lot of the [R] people, so that I knew that we would be among old friends. I guess I started my life in camp with mixed feelings, and I didn't know exactly what to expect. I was disillusioned on one hand, and full of curiosity on the other. We had to go through a lot of registration and then I became quite depressed as I realized that I was going to be cooped up with a lot of other Japanese.

On the whole, life in Tulare was pretty sad. I was tired out when I got there, so I decided to take a vacation for a while. I figured that food and housing were provided by the government, and it was supposed to be no more worries for anybody. I enjoyed it for the first few days but after that I found unlimited time on my hands and

I got bored. There was no place to go for amusement and we were confined into a small space by a high wire fence. The fact that the fence had barbed wire on top of it made it much worse and I resented it.

We were living in the stables when we first arrived there. However, it was too smelly so we went to the housing department and got changed to one of the new barracks in the infield, since my wife's father was not in such good health. These barracks had been reserved for two more trainloads of people coming in but we got the special permit. The floors of the barracks were right on the ground and weeds were coming through the asphalt. However, it had plenty of windows and it was light and airy so we liked it better. The walls were that black tar paper and when it got hot, it became almost unbearable inside. There were nine of us living in that one room so that we had to put up sheets for curtain. I put up some bedspreads in one corner of our room for our "honeymoon cottage." What privacy! We soon got used to living all crowded together like that and we started to fix it up some more.

There was no lumber to be found in camp, so we had quite a hard time getting wood. Fortunately I had on my old clothes one day and I saw a loaded wheelbarrow with all kinds of lumber on it. I just made off with it and I acted like I was a carpenter. I took it home and I made a closet out of the wood. We also went to the mess hall and got a lot of orange crates to make our shelves with. To put the finishing touches on, we ordered a rug from Montgomery Ward in order to put over the grass that was coming through the floor. We also ordered a card table, four chairs, and some other things. Then I bought some magazines and settled down to relax. I wrote letters, visited my friends, and read a little, but the day was still too long and I got tired of doing the same thing every day. I decided to look for a job then.

There weren't many jobs available in camp but I found that the recreation department had some openings. Since I had previously been active in sports, I decided to get into this work. The Caucasian head of the recreation department said that he had an empty recreation hall which he wanted to turn into a library and play room. He asked me to organize that for him.

When I went to this recreation hall I found that it was very disorganized and the children had no supervision at all. Some churches had donated toys and books and these little children were throwing them all around the room and tearing them up. There were some Issei there who wanted a section of the room so they could play *goh* and *shogi*. I was very disgusted at this setup but I decided to give it a trial. I got a lock to put on the building and I divided the recreation hall into two sections so the old men could have half of it for their games. Another corner was reserved for a library. The old men really appreciated it having their own section and we never had any trouble with them. We had the most trouble with the young kids and we had to discipline them by not allowing them to come into the rec hall for one day until they learned to take care of the various games. Later on we organized ping pong and checker tournaments and we had a well-functioning recreational program in about two weeks.

School had just started in the center and since I knew all of the younger kids, I decided to teach physical education in the school system instead. It was pretty hard at first to get the children to attend these classes. Finally we had to make it compulsory up to the age of 16. We even had to threaten to send truant officers after the delinquent students. The children steadied down after that and it turned out to be a very successful program. All of the parents in camp were in favor of the P. E. program in school as it kept the children away from the barracks a little longer. This gave the old folks more time to themselves. I continued this work until it was time for us to leave in September, 1942.

During the time I was at Tulare I also took part in other affairs. For my own recreation I played volleyball in the court in front of my apartment. We also had a basketball team in the recreation department and we played against some of the other departments in camp. Since we had most of the good athletes in our recreation department, we won most of the games we played. My wife and I went to quite a few of the crummy camp dances and watched the young kids jitter-bugging. We also went to the talent shows after they were started and once in a while we went to the camp movie. On some of the warm evenings we took long hikes around and around the race tracks without getting anywhere. Sometimes at night we would go to the fence and look across the highway at the grocery store, and our mouths would water for cokes but we could not go through the fence. I even went to church to fill in the time. It was the only chance for me to put on my good clothes. Every month we got two and a half dollars in scrip so we would spend it at the canteen.

I was recently married so I devoted most of my time to my wife. She was already pregnant before we left Tulare, so she required more of my attention. We had quite a few discussions on whether we should start a family or not. At the beginning we did not like the idea of having a child in camp without any future for it. We felt that if we had a child it would be a shame that it was born in a camp. There were also rumors going around that any baby born in camp would not be able to have citizenship since there was no place to register the birth. After a great many deliberations like this, my wife and I decided to have a baby anyway. We figured that there would be good hospital care and the doctors were adequate. I knew that the baby would have citizenship, so we disregarded that rumor. We felt that we wanted a child while we were still young. We didn't know how long we would be in camp, and it was no use waiting indefinitely to see how things turned out. I knew that I wouldn't be able to make any money in camp, but I was still willing to take a chance and have a family anyway.

I looked back on my Tulare life as an interesting set of experiences on how one can get along on nothing and use one's time for the good of the community developments. I got over my restless feelings the longer I stayed in Tulare and I guess I was sort of resigned to the routine I had worked into. There was the future to think about and that was the biggest problem, but it seemed to be generally over-looked in the daily routine of living from day to day, except on those occasions when the subject was directly face to face to us.

The administration at Tulare fortunately was very good and the officials tried to help the people out in every way they could. I made several attempts to get our family transferred down to Manzanar to join our father but we were unsuccessful in this because of all the red tape. Mother was released [from internment] in July and she later took the rest of the family to Manzanar in August when the camp was being broken up. My wife and her family decided to take their chances and go wherever we were sent. Various Caucasian friends on the outside kept visiting us, so we weren't entirely cut off from the outside world.

My wife and I were among the last to leave for [the WRA camp at] Gila River since we had volunteered to stay behind and help clean up the place. The administration promised that we would get good jobs in the WRA centers and they said that housing would be saved for us.

By the time we hit the town of Casa Grande [near Gila] my heart had sunk into my shoes as I felt that we were being left out in the middle of nowhere and it was so isolated. The train line was the only sign of civilization and we even had to move away from that. At Casa Grande we changed to the busses and we had to ride 17 dusty miles to camp. I was immediately disgusted with Gila as a whole because of all that powdered dust and heat. The camp wasn't even finished and there was no running water in the washrooms. The Army never should have pushed all the people into there when it was uncompleted like that. My wife and I were fortunate since my mother-in-law had saved a large room for us to join them in. The other people who came with us had to sleep on the floor for the first few nights without any mattresses or cots. The first night I slept soundly because I was all tired out and the camp looked so immense. I was grateful for that in a way because it meant more freedom.

The next day we immediately set to work to collect lumber and fix up our place. There were only five of us in the one room there so it was much roomier for us than at Tulare. My brother-in-law got a truck to haul lumber with and I set to work building furniture. I made tables, closets, chairs, shelves, dressers, and many other things. My wife ordered some more things from Sears and Roebuck to complete the furnishings. I built a large cooler so that we did not suffer from the heat so much.

It took me about a month to build all of the furniture. In late September I decided to go out cotton picking since there was a great call for volunteers. I figured that I would be able to make some good money and it was better than the camp wages. We had to get up at 4 in the morning and go out 25 miles to the cotton fields. I would have taken a camp job but there weren't any decent jobs at that time. I figured that if I worked in cotton picking for one day a week, I could still make as much money as doing a camp job.

The school was just opening up, so I got a job in the physical education department as an instructor in the elementary school system. At the beginning we didn't have any texts, tables, or seats in the school, but the principal was a very energetic fellow and he pushed the WRA into supplying things. The high school was much worse off than we were and it never was completed during the time I was there. It was always a fight for equipment and there was a lot of red tape to go through all the time. All of these things made it difficult to get the school system properly organized. In spite of that, the morale of the children was good and they had an interest in their classes.

At first the Caucasian teachers did not know the Nisei students and some of them had prejudices. These teachers had come from Arizona and some of the other Midwest states and they never had contact with Nisei before. However, they had an interest in teaching and they worked hard to put the program across. Those who were in teaching just for the money did not last very long. Only the broad-minded teachers stayed on.

My wife and I continued our social and recreational activities: visiting, bridge games, movies, going to church, and other things like that. I made some new friends from the other centers through the contacts I had in my school work. I wasn't bored at all because the whole setup was a definite improvement over Tulare and there was constructive work to be done. I felt that the WRA had a much more liberal policy than the WCCA.

At this time I became more and more aware of the real attitudes of the Issei. They griped about everything. The block meetings were all held in Japanese so that I had a hard time understanding what they were saying. The thing the Issei wanted most was the voting power in the governing body in the camp. They wanted the WRA to provide them with more food to be put into storage also. This whole thing was a result of the fear of starvation they had and it was one of the biggest camp issues before the registration. The reason for this was that the progress of the war was getting in Japan's favor and the Issei felt that great hatred would be turned against the people in camp as the time went on. They felt that Japan would eventually bomb some of the cities of the West Coast and then the Caucasians would shut off the food supply for the camp in revenge. They said that the single railroad going through would be taken over by the military and the camp food supply would be forgotten about. They pointed out that Phoenix was 50 miles away and Gila could never feed all of the people by itself since it was the fourth largest city in Arizona. The people were really afraid of starvation and they knew the people could not march all the way to Phoenix for food; besides they figured the Caucasians would shoot them down if they left the camp. All this resulted in debates and one cook even hid food in the block manager's office and this created quite a scandal.

There were many other gripes at the block meetings but most of them were over petty things. They would spend hours arguing whether the guys should flush the toilets with the hands or feet. Many of the Issei had never used flush toilets before since they came from rural areas and they didn't know the right etiquette. There were also gripes about women washing bedpans in the washrooms and others griped about wasting toilet paper and things like that. The Issei had to have long winded discussions about every little thing and they didn't know how to reach a conclusion. When a camouflage net project was started in December, 1942, our block council griped against that. The Issei didn't want the Nisei to help the war effort at all.

The biggest issue in the camp, however, was the registration which started in February, 1943. The biggest questions in controversy were No. 27 and 28. Some of the Issei said they would answer "yes" if question 28 were interpreted to mean that they would only have to defend their homes if invaded by any country. Their opposition died right down when this question was changed into asking them merely to abide by the United States laws. I was helping with the registration, and I didn't sign up any "no" among the Issei at all in the section I helped to register. The Japanese are pretty law abiding and I don't think they wanted to cause any trouble. Most of the "noes" among the Issei came from the blocks where there were a lot of farming people. The Kibei group was the strongest in opposition to registration. They were supported by the radical Issei and they made it a hot question all over the camp. Everyone was confused and the majority of the people didn't really know what it was all about. The Army unit that came in to explain only added to the confusion.

I was sort of disgusted at the Nisei reaction to the registration. Some of the fellows were puzzled about how to answer it and it seemed very obvious to me that there was only one answer to make. In any other country, they wouldn't even be given a chance to answer against the government. I think that many of the Nisei really didn't understand the question because of all the agitation going on. They didn't want to volunteer into the Army but they all said they would go if drafted. There were some of them who didn't want to fight against Japan and kill some of their own blood. I know this is one of the arguments the agitators passed around and it did affect the Nisei.

I gave some serious thought about volunteering myself. I felt that it was one means of getting out of camp. I felt that if I volunteered myself, I would be able to obtain a rating by the time all the Nisei were drafted in one or two years at the most. I understood that we would be sent to [Camp] Shelby and there would be cottages set up there so that the soldiers' wives could come and stay. I figured that I would be able to get my wife out of camp in this way. I also thought that if a lot of Nisei volunteered, it would help the rest of the United States to get to know more what the Nisei were really like.

I hadn't volunteered for [Camp] Savage in December as I learned that the Nisei who did would be called in January and I didn't want to go then as I expected my baby in February. When registration started and the time came nearer for my baby's arrival, I didn't feel like volunteering so much because I had more family responsibilities. Then I discovered that I had stomach ulcers. All of these things caused me to change my mind about volunteering and I decided to wait until I was drafted.

Around March I started to work in the [camouflage] net factory. I had wanted to go into it in January when it first started, but I had my school duties and I didn't want to let the community down, as it was too hard to get teachers. The baby was born on February 28 and the mounting expenses forced me to go into net work immediately. I then felt that it was foolish to stay in the school work for $19 a month when I needed more money for the needs of the baby, so I quit my school job a few weeks after the new semester had started. I worked in the net factory until it was closed down at the end of May. I was on a slow crew but I made a fairly good salary. The only trouble was that it was easy to get the rash from all that lint and dust flying around. My highest pay check out there was $79 for 10 days of work. I made about $310 during the two months I was out there, and that wasn't bad considering that I had been making only $19 a month before.

I had made preliminary investigation about leaving camp, but the employment office was so vague and I didn't push the thing until the net factory closed down. I took most of the month of June to rest up and work on my resettlement plans. The prospects of high wages on the outside sounded very good and I wanted to honestly earn my own living and have our own home without other family influences butting in. There were good jobs on the outside and I figured that the possibility of going to some trade school would be good. I knew that I would have to start working for a postwar job soon. I figured that if I got a good job on the outside, I would be able to have seniority rights and a good working record by the time the war ended. The prospect of having our freedom once more was one of the greatest inducements. I didn't think in terms of going back to California but I thought in terms of going to movies, plays, out to eat at restaurants, and things like that without restriction.

It was the coming of my baby that forced me to make definite plans about leaving soon. We actually did not get off until June 26 [1943]. When the stories of the Tokyo executions broke out that made me hesitate for a little while. I never thought of postponing my resettlement indefinitely or to leave my wife behind. We wanted to start out together right from the beginning so that we could share our experiences.

I was writing to a lot of companies for jobs but they didn't answer. I wrote to a fish company on the Great Lakes to see if I could get a job as a truck driver. I thought I could take that job and go to trade school at night so I would be able to get into Ford Company later on. I also wrote to a foundry company in Cleveland. They offered me a job but they could not provide housing and provisions so I gave that up. I was also thinking of taking a physical education director job in Minneapolis but I figured that this would require too many extra hours, and I wanted to devote more time to my family. My wife's brother [in another Midwestern city] sponsored us, and we left camp without a definite job offer. I decided to go on by myself to [this city] and leave my wife and baby with my sister in Chicago. [But] my brother-in-law had not been able to arrange an apartment for us because of the housing shortage. After walking my feet off for two days, I got quite discouraged when I realized that it was impossible to find living quarters. I then decided that it would be better to go back to Chicago and find a job there.

When I got back to Chicago, my wife wasn't too displeased about remaining here, because a lot of her in-laws and friends were here. We stayed with my sister for about a week. It was quite crowded. She gave us the use of the front room and sometimes I had to sleep on the floor. Other times I went over to stay at my other sister's place. We started to look around for our own apartment right away. We found several places open on the near north side but the better places were unfurnished, or else they didn't want to take in children. A friend who was leaving for another job had a flat on the north side and he asked me if I wanted to take it over. My wife and I jumped at this chance as we had not been successful in finding anything else. The unfurnished flat had 5 rooms. My wife and I went to all the second-hand furniture shops and we bought about $200 worth of furniture. Later on we got some of our household goods from [California], so we were quite comfortable.

When my baby is ready to go to school I would like to move out to one of the suburbs where there is not all this factory smoke. However, I can't complain too much about our flat. Our landlady is good to us and she is sympathetic towards us since she is of German descent herself. I wouldn't want other Nisei to move into this building though because that would be too conspicuous. I wouldn't even want them to move into this neighborhood. There are only 5 Japanese families within a 5-mile radius and that is plenty.

At first I wasn't able to rent and furnish this place up on what I was making. A friend came out from camp about then and we decided to go together to share the rent expenses. He came on up to this flat with us alone and he agreed to pay $40 a month for room and board and to share some of the household duties. After living with him for a while, he began to irritate us as his habits and characteristics weren't the same as ours. This caused quite a bit of conflict and it got on my wife's nerves. He finally went back to camp in January. In the meantime my younger brother had come to live with us and my father came in November [1943] for a month before going back to camp. Then my wife's younger brother came in from Denver so we had 7 boarders in our apartment at the peak.

I didn't have nearly as much headaches with my job problems. All this time I had been working on my plans for a job. When I first arrived in Chicago to stay, I planned to attend a defense trading school day and night and use up the money that I had saved from the net factory and the WRA cash grant. But when I went to the USES, I found that the government was sponsoring a defense trade school which had free tuition. I enrolled in that defense trade school immediately and I found that the day courses had been discontinued. I would have had to attend for at least 4 months in the night classes so I decided to take a temporary job during the day to meet current living expenses. I heard from a friend that it was easy to get a job at the [M] Company and since it was only two blocks away from where I first lived, I went over and applied for a position. I got a job as checker and found the job very easy. I got $40 a week to start and this was raised later to $45. I made more than that with the overtime. The firm was the wholesale house for all types of merchandise which was sold to small retail stores in the city. It carried a similar line of goods like the mail-order houses.

The Nisei were being hired in large numbers in all types of jobs at [M's], including office work. They were treated very well and the company was fair to them. Nobody was fired from there as far as I know. The Nisei turnover was very quick, but the company rehired them if they wanted to come back. I got in good with the boss and he told me the company was only planning to keep 10 Nisei in the key positions after the war and he promised me one of these jobs since I worked pretty hard. That job is still open to me if I wish to go back. There were over 100 Nisei out of 800 workers when I was there and it stood to reason that they could not all hope to remain permanently.

I was going to the defense trade school two or three times a week in the evenings all this time. I was taking a tool and die course since I planned to take a defense job after I completed the course. I figured that I could move into one of the defense housing projects if I did this. I had an idea that I could serve my apprenticeship in a defense plant and work up to a big salary quick. After I was working for 3 months at the [M] Co., one of my Nisei friends quit to go to the [T] factory. He was there for only one month and he did so well in piece work that he encouraged me to come. He said it was a semi-defense plant so I decided to investigate it. I found that the company was willing to accept me so I decided to quit and go out there. It was much closer to my new flat anyway.

There were already 10 Nisei working there when I first arrived, but now there are about 35 *Nihonjin* out of 300 workers. Some of them are Kibei and Issei. At first I was a layer off. This work consisted of pressing [materials over forms]. It was quite new to me and very hard since it required a great deal of technique. The forms were steam-heated and I often burned myself. I was only getting 60 cents an hour for a three weeks' trial. Then I got into piece work and I found that I could make money. The first week I averaged 68 cents an hour for this piece work, but by the end of the month I was making $1.05 an hour. In two months I was making $1.25 an hour. I could have made much more, but last Christmas the union was anxious to raise the price for this piece work so they asked all the workers to slow down to $1.20 an hour. This helped some of the slower ones get a more uniform wage. Recently I got my draft reclassification, so I raised my rates above the union level so I could save up some money. I put in about 52 hours a week right now. I average around $73 a week gross but the company takes out 10 per cent for war bonds for me. I buy these bonds in my baby's name.

I don't have any direct contacts with the boss of the factory since the union runs the shop. Everybody is left alone as it is piece work and we can loaf if we want to. Since everyone wants to make money, there is little loafing around during the working hours. We get two rest periods and a lunch hour during the day but I don't visit around much during this time.

We are able to live fairly comfortably on my salary. After bonds and taxes are deducted I still net over $55 a week. I figure that my [gross] income roughly runs to about $328.50 a month. Out of this I am able to save $80 in cash and $30 in war bonds. On top of that my younger brother contributes $5 a week for his room and board since he works after school and that goes into my wife's miscellaneous fund.

When I was reclassified to 1-A from my prewar 3-A status, 2 or 3 months ago, I wasn't prepared to go. We had just completed all of the payments for the furniture and we had no savings whatever, except a hundred dollars or so in war bonds. Since I was reclassified we have budgeted, and that is why we are saving about $100 a month now. I wasn't too anxious to be drafted and there was a chance for deferment so I asked about it. At first my company was reluctant to ask for it but after advertising for replacements, the company found it too hard to get new workers, for they have applied for deferment for all Nisei in the plant. I haven't heard yet whether I have been given the deferment, so that is why I started to work hard to save what money I could before being taken. I wanted to make all preparations I could for my wife so she would not be left in a hole. I have also inquired about the various means of hospitalization and Red Cross help available to service men's wife in case of illness. I don't want my wife to ever go back to camp to live except for the very last emergency.

I've been wondering whether I should apply to go to [Camp] Savage, but I don't think I can make the [Japanese language] requirements. If I went to Camp Shelby a lot of my Nisei friends will be there. I would rather be in an unsegregated unit in the air corps or ordinance service, but I don't know if I will have the chance. If I go into the Army, I would want to learn something in the mechanical line which I could use when I got back.

A Nisei combat team has some good points. It may be able to prove that the Nisei are loyal like other Americans if their achievements are given the proper limelight. From this point of view it is a good thing. The bad things about it is that it is a Jim Crow unit, and segregated. I think that 90 per cent of the Nisei resent the segregated unit and they would all like to be spread out into all branches of the service and be given a choice about what line they want to serve in like other Americans.

Regardless of what type of service the Nisei do, the draft will definitely help their future. After the war, they can hold their heads up and say that they have served this country and there will be no question of what side of the fence they were on. I already have a brother in the service down in an Army camp in Texas. The rest of my brothers and myself will go soon. I wouldn't want a postponement altogether as I feel I should go eventually. I have to do my part along with the rest of the guys. I wouldn't feel right after all this is over if I was not in. Even my dad was in during the last war. I don't think I could very well look all those Nisei in the face if I did not go in eventually. I don't worry too much about not coming back from the war as I will have to take the same risk as anybody else.

The Nisei do have a future in America. I doubt if they would ever be accepted in Japan, as the people of Japan would belittle them just like they do the Koreans. A few Nisei may be able to go to Japan after the war and get good paying jobs but I bet they won't be happy there. It would be just like a Jew going to Germany; he wouldn't be happy either.

After the war, I hope to get into one of the big manufacturing industries like automobile or aircraft as a skilled laborer. I doubt if I ever return to California even though I do have a home out there in my name. I won't remain in Chicago either, but I wouldn't mind moving to one of the suburbs. City life is too hard on children and they don't get the chance to make the best associations. City life moves too fast to suit me and I want to have more home life.

I hope to have three more children yet. If I have the means, I want to have them during the war. But I don't think I could do it on a soldier's pay. It may be a long war, though, and I would like to be a father again. I'm thinking about it right now. I want my children to go through college and give them all the advantages. I can't predict how I will do after the war and it may all be a pipe dream.

I don't see all of my former friends out here, especially since the baby takes so much of our time. In spite of that, we get enough leisure. For example, last week was a pretty average week. Last Friday a Nisei married couple came over to play bridge with us, and they brought a soldier friend with them. Afterwards the wives stayed and talked and us fellows went to a night club for a while to show the Nisei soldier boy around. When we came back we had waffles and it was way past midnight before we got to bed. Saturday I took my wife shopping and that night five of us fellows had a poker party until about 4 in the morning while the wives had a party at my place. On Sunday we slept until noon. Then another friend and his wife picked us up in their car and we went out to Jackson Park for the afternoon. In the evening we played bridge with some other friends at my friends'. On Monday I was rather tired, so I only did some light reading and then I went to bed early. On Tuesday another friend visited us. Wednesday two of my wife's friends came to visit and we had to put them up and entertain them. One was from New York and the other from Minneapolis. Thursday evening I canceled a bridge party so I could be interviewed by you. On Friday some of my friends [from R, in California] that I hadn't seen since the war came over for dinner and we entertained them. We just sat around and talked. Saturday we went out to a show and Sunday we went visiting. Some weeks we are not so active during the week days. I would rather not have so many people to entertain and I would like to get another half day off in order to go shopping. We usually go to movies about 3 times a month. Right now we like to see only the light pictures. I don't like all those war pictures as I get too much propaganda in my everyday life. Sometimes I like to see heavy drama if Bette Davis is playing in them. I like musical comedy with Deanna Durbin and Jeanette MacDonald.

I keep up with the news by buying three newspapers, *Chicago Tribune, Chicago Sun,* and the *Daily Times.* I just go through them lightly. I usually read the news section and the editorials the most. I like to look into the "Voice of the People" section to see if there are any reactions about Nisei in Chicago or on the various soldiers' issues. Lately I have been reading all the news about soldiers' benefits. I don't keep up with the sport section much any more since those days are gone forever. I also look at the stock section but I don't do any investments. I like to get some idea of how business is doing. I also read the classified ads to see what type of jobs are open and what the wages are. I don't have any particular favorites among the newspapers. The *Chicago Tribune* seems to treat the Nisei pretty good. It usually has articles about the Nisei and it writes the truth and it doesn't take sides. The *Herald American* [Hearst] always scandalizes the Nisei and the good points about them are buried. I take this paper instead of the *Daily Times* a lot of times. I try to keep on the look out for any newspaper articles on the Nisei because I am interested in seeing what is happening to them. It makes me sore when I see false stories in the *Herald American*. But then, it represents people who think like that. In that way I am able to keep on the alert. I think that these newspaper stories make the Nisei act cautious so that they will be able to take any slams and be in a good position to protect themselves. I don't read many magazines unless they are brought to my attention. A friend of mine said that the April *Fortune* has an article on evacuation and he is going to lend it to me next. I usually get any article about the evacuees because some of my friends bring it around eventually. I'm not a regular subscriber to any magazine. I don't subscribe to the *Pacific Citizen,* [the JACL organ], but I go to a friend's house to see his copy to see what is happening to the Nisei. I'm lucky to read one book a month these days, but my wife reads a lot more and she tries to read up on all the best sellers.

The only free time I really have is when the baby is asleep. There are always things to be fixed around the house and this keeps me busy. I only listen to the radio for about 20 minutes in the morning during my breakfast. I get the news summary and the weather reports for the day. In the evening I don't listen to the radio at all. Since we have been out here we haven't been able to see a single play or go to one concert. I've gone to some ice hockey games, Ice Follies, bowling, and one baseball game. We've been to only 3 of the Nisei dances and they were awful flops. The first time we went out of curiosity and the next two times were obligations to a friend who sponsored the Nisei orchestra playing for these dances. I should think these dances should be discontinued as they are all unsuccessful and very poorly organized. Very few of those Nisei who go are actually having a good time. Those who aren't having a good time try to drown their unhappiness by drinking at the bar below the dance hall and loitering around the hall. This makes them very conspicuous to the public eye. There seems to be even more of this rowdyism than before the war since there is no one here to tell them different. A couple of times we have gone to the [A, a popular dance hall]. Those were a lot better dances. I think that more Nisei should spread out to these public affairs because no one ever looks at them. We were used to going to public affairs in the past and we never felt uncomfortable once like some Nisei say they do. We have never faced any discrimination in our public recreation yet.

Including relatives and friends, I would say that we have been seeing 20 or 30 people quite frequently. There are only about 5 couples that we see fairly steadily and we don't have so many contacts with our relatives and their friends because I've made such a fuss about it. Before, we used to have relatives and their friends up here almost every night. My wife naturally likes to see a lot of people as she is home a lot. She also wants to take in plays and operas, eat out, visit historical places of Chicago and things like that, but we haven't had the time. I'd like to do a lot of these things too but I'm too tired from my work and I can't be running around every evening.

I'd like to meet more interesting people. I wouldn't care if they were Nisei or Caucasians as long as they were interesting. The trouble with Nisei is that when they get together, all they talk about is the draft, how much they're making, their life in the centers, and their former life back home, and what fun they used to have. If their experiences were unusual, I wouldn't mind listening, but it seems to be the same old stuff all the time. Most of the Nisei follow a routine of living like ours and it is boring to hear of it all the time.

My wife and I had many quarrels over these Nisei parties and through experiences and process of elimination it is finally peaceful around here now. This last month is the first time since we were married that we have been able to live as a normal married couple. Ever since evacuation we had to live with one relative or another and be responsible for them.

When we first came out here, we used to get invited to a number of Caucasian homes. I'd like to keep up these contacts because it will be of advantage. The Nisei should take advantage of all these contacts that they can. They don't have to pick up any old bum but should be friends with people from whom they can learn something useful. I haven't developed near enough Caucasian friends that I should have. My wife wants to do this too but she got caught in the Nisei circle and it took all this time to get unwound. The only Caucasian contacts we have now are a doctor, lawyer, gateman at Chicago stadium, and an Army sergeant who invited me up to his home. I met this sergeant at the induction station when I got reclassified. From now on we will get plenty of Caucasian contacts and we will have time to follow some of them up. I don't mean that I am going to cultivate any old Caucasian just for the sake of doing that, but only those on my same level or above.

If I come back from the Army and I see a big Japanese town here, I certainly will leave here in a hurry because my own chance for a job would be that much less. I honestly was happy in Montana without the Japanese contacts and I know I can do it again. There are too many headaches with all that segregation. I think that after a Nisei is married he should move out because there is no future in a Japanese town and very little opportunity for expansion. There was too much of squeezing of each other in Little Tokyo before the war and I don't ever want to go through that fruit stand business again.

Even if the Nisei out here have a hard time integrating, it will be better for them because if they are segregated now, they will be just like the Issei before. I think if the Nisei expand now it will be a lot easier for the third generation to get the place that they deserve. I have an idea that there will be a lot of intermarriage by the next generation. We should make it as easy as possible for them by doing the right thing now. The fourth generation will really intermarry. We want to give the third generation all the advantages like college but we don't know what things will be like after the war and we don't know if we'll be able to do the things we want to for them because there may be things we haven't control over. But the Nisei have had an easier time than the Issei in spite of the evacuation and I think the Sansei will be that much better off than the Nisei. A lot of the Nisei will be frustrated but that can't be helped. Besides thinking of the Sansei, the Nisei have to let the Issei lean on them right now.

Looking at it from this angle, the Nisei are getting a break with evacuation since the old folks are being taken care of in camp while they get a good start on the outside. It will be up to the Nisei now to stand on their own feet and this pioneering work is no picnic. It's no use for the Nisei to keep dreaming about their before-the-war social life any more as they have to get down to business and earn a living. The Issei came over here with nothing and that's why they left Japan. Yet a lot of them made out pretty good before evacuation. I think the Nisei are starting off with about 10 times more than the Issei did. Most of those Issei pioneers didn't even have a fourth grade education when they arrived in this country while the Nisei are at least starting off with high school and college education. They also can use good English and they have American citizenship. It makes me disgusted to see a lot of those Nisei out here crying and running back to camp just because they can't have all their dances and sports leagues like before. They have to expect a few hard knocks and nobody is going to hand their future to them on a silver platter, not by a long shot.

CH-26: BOOKKEEPER

Female; born in Japan, 1921; immigrated to California at age of 4 mos.; height 60"; weight 106 lbs.; unmarried. Interviewed November, 1943–February, 1944. Described as "a little plump but extremely attractive," as having an "exceptional personality," and as making "satisfactory adjustments to resettlement with a minimum of effort." Life history was obtained in a series of "brief interviews extending over two and a half months. It was difficult to schedule definite hours for interviews because of her intense social activity. For a while she was going out on dates seven nights a week."

CAREER LINES

Parental: Father from farming class in Japan; born *ca.* 1885; high school in Japan, before emigrating to Hawaii *ca.* 1901; worked on sugar plantations, then came to southern California *ca.* 1903. Worked as farm laborer, hotel manager, and so on before opening his own retail fruit stand in Los Angeles in 1921. Mother, born 1891, finished grammar school in Japan, before emigrating in 1913; helped husband in fruit stand, 1921–1925; and worked as caretaker in a Los Angeles hotel, 1926–1929.
Own: Partly completed junior year in a Los Angeles college in 1940, majoring in shorthand. Helped father as bookkeeper, 1939–1942; worked for few weeks as salesgirl in florist shop, 1940, and as typist in steamship ticket office, 1941. Inmigrated to Chicago, May, 1943; worked as secretary in a local college from May, 1943, to date of interview.

LIFE HISTORY

Like many of the Japanese immigrants, my dad first left Japan for Hawaii in order to make some money. He was only 16 years old at that time. His parents had died when he was quite young, so he did not have much of a reason for remaining in Japan. He was rather adventurous and he wanted to see a little bit of the world. Maybe he also didn't want to serve in the Japanese army. He mentioned this to us at one time. After working for a few years among the gangs in the sugar plantations, he decided to come to the United States.

My dad did not intend to stay permanently but as the years passed, the less sure he became about whether he wanted to go back. He found that the standards of living were much better in this country. He has been here for forty years. Even my mother has been here for over thirty years.

As far as I can remember, my dad has always been fairly broad-minded in rearing the family. Of course, he has old Japanese ideas too. My mother is more Japanese and conventional than my father. I suppose that is because she only had contacts in the Japanese community during all the time that she lived here. These old people coming over from Japan could not change over entirely to American ways because they did have a lot of Japanese culture in them. It wasn't all bad like you hear nowadays. People only pick out the worst parts of it and they think that the whole Japanese culture is that way.

My dad did all sorts of work during the time he was here. He never spoke too much of it so that I do not know the details. I know that he did work on a farm as a laborer for quite a while [and that] at one time he had a hotel and all of the people coming from Japan used to stay there. We [children] have lived in Los Angeles all our lives and I only remember my father as operating a retail market.

I was born in Japan in 1921 because my mother went there to visit my granddad who was ill. She wanted to see him for the last time. This was unfortunate for me because I did not get American citizenship, and I don't know if I'll ever be able to get it now. I've often wondered if I can become a citizen by marrying a Nisei but nobody knows for sure whether this is possible. I really am not an Issei at all because my mother brought me back to California when I was only 4 months old and I have never been back there since. If my parents knew that it would have caused me such difficulty I am sure they would have seen to it that I was born in good old Los Angeles. I never realized the importance of the place of my birth until I got a lot older. Because of the fact that I was born in Japan, it has done certain things to me, although there is no question that my loyalty is with America. I would like to see what Japan is like just out of curiosity, but I certainly would not want to ever live there permanently. I would be too different from the other people and they would laugh at me for not having the same ways of acting as they do. My environment has been completely American and I would be a big misfit over in Japan.

I've had a very happy childhood and I never did have any big conflicts. My dad was always full of fun and he enjoyed life. He was optimistic about the future and I think that he made a fair success out of himself although he may not have reached all of his ambitions that he had. Even though he has been here over 40 years, Dad does not speak very good English. It is a broken English like most of the Issei although I would say that he has a much better vocabulary than they have. Dad felt that he had to bring up his children properly so that he was quite strict on certain things. When I was in junior high school, my parents would not let me date fellows like so many of the other girls did. Dad never lost his temper but he would try to explain the reasons for his discipline in a very calm way. I've had most of my conflicts with my mother because she just didn't understand us as well as Father did. She was very conservative in her ways and she was always afraid of what people would say about our family if we were bad. Most of the time she was a lot stricter than Dad and when she made a ruling she didn't want it questioned.

When it came to the more important family decisions, my dad had the upper hand. He was the one to have the final say but he was not a dictator about it. He always used to talk it over with my mother first. My parents got along well and they never did have serious arguments. I was the one who argued with my mother most of all. Later on, my big sister did stick up for me quite a bit even though she was much more Japanesy than the rest of the kids. That was because she had a college education in Japan. It is a funny thing because my older sister was born in America and she has citizenship, while I was born in Japan and I don't have citizenship. Yet, because of her education, she is more Japanesy than I am. In fact, I consider myself twice as Americanized as she is. It wasn't her fault that she had to go to college in Japan. My parents had the idea that it would be better for my sister to go there for her education so that she could learn some of the Japanese culture which they had not been able to teach her. A lot of the Japanese parents did this to their children and that is the reason why there are so many Kibei. My parents asked me once if I wanted to go back to Japan to go to school, but I definitely rebelled against that. My mother talked to me for quite a while on this but I would not give in. Finally my parents saw that I could be pretty stubborn so that they did not force the issue any more.

As long as I could remember, our family has always had what we wanted and we lived fairly comfortably. I never knew what it was to be in poverty although my dad told me that at first he had to struggle quite a bit to make a go of it. He did rather well for himself and he had some prestige in the Japanese community. He was on the Board of Directors of the Japanese language school and that was why he was interned when the war broke out. He didn't belong to any other Japanese organization as far as I know.

In spite of my father's many liberal attitudes, we did follow quite a lot of the Japanese customs. Some of the things we stuck to quite religiously although I never did understand why. My parents were always careful to see that we observed all of the Japanese holidays. I think that the reason for this was their close connection with the Japanese language school. Before the war many Caucasians thought that these Japanese festivals were quite colorful and they used to come down and see them themselves. Right up to evacuation, we had the Doll Day festival every year and that was one of the big events in our family. We always spoke Japanese at home and there was quite a Japanesy atmosphere in our household.

I know that I began to rebel more and more against my parents on little things and I got so that I would not heed their words of advice too often as I thought I knew more than they did. I had to go to the Japanese language school for 12 years. I can read and write Japanese now because I did have to study, and in a way it has been most helpful to me because I am able to correspond with my parents quite frequently.

When I went to the public school I didn't stay much around the other Japanese kids so that I did not develop that timidness that they had. I was much more aggressive in everything I did and I found that the Caucasian kids had quite a big influence over me in this respect. I was just trying to act natural but it looked like extreme action to the Japanese parents because most of their Nisei children were quiet and hesitant all the time.

It was when I was in high school that I first found out that I was different from the other Nisei kids. A lot of the girls were taking civil service examinations because they wanted to get a job after graduation. I found I was not allowed to take any of these tests because I did not have citizenship. It was quite a blow to me when I fully realized what it meant. I knew that I wasn't any different than the other Nisei because they had grown up in a similar environment as I have. The only difference was that I had accidentally been born in Japan while my mother was on a visit. Another time I felt the difference keenly was when I first enrolled at UCLA. I had to pay a $75 non-residence fee and that really made me angry because here I had lived in Los Angeles all my life and they considered me a foreigner just because I couldn't get American citizenship. I didn't think that was fair at all. Later on I had to register during the alien registration and after the evacuation started I found that not having American citizenship was very inconvenient. Even now I have to report to the Department of Justice office if I want to travel to another state. It's all so silly but that's the rules and I can't do anything about it. That is why I've always wanted to become a naturalized citizen because I think that I am American just like the Nisei. My parents were very sorry about my not having an American birth certificate when all of these inconveniences began to come up.

I never did get along too well with my big sister. Maybe that was because we were such different types. She went to Japan and got an education and she was much older than I so that she seemed to be too conventional for me. She tried to boss me around a lot and I never would listen to her. She always said that I was too noisy and Japanese girls should be quiet and nice. My mother always took her part when she said that, so I rebelled against a lot of the Japanese customs in revenge. Once in a while I did go to the Japanese movies and I didn't like them nearly as well as the movies made in Hollywood. I thought they were too sentimental and artificial. They were always pictures with a moral theme and I don't remember them having very much of the militarism stuff although these Japanese pictures did tend to glorify the samurai spirit. It used to make me laugh when I saw how timid and submissive the Japanese women were in these pictures. My big sister told me that it was like that in Japan and she just accepted it. I couldn't understand that and I knew that I would never be happy living where I had to suppress myself continually. There were other Japanese movies which were educational in nature and they taught me a little about Japan and I liked these pictures. Maybe they only presented the best part of the Japanese life but I found that I had a certain attachment for Japan and I never have been able to get rid of it.

I had a lot of fun during the time I went to high school in Los Angeles. I used to go to all of the school functions and take as active part as possible in the general school life. I had quite a few dates with Nisei boys. However, I did not belong to an exclusive Nisei group. I was in a sort of a melting-pot group because there were all kinds of racial backgrounds among us. All of these kids were born in Los Angeles even though their parents had come from the old country.

There was also a Jewish kid in our group. We all got along swell and racial differences didn't make any difference at all. I often used to go to their homes and they would come to mine. I think that a lot of the Nisei were hesitant about inviting Caucasian kids to their homes because they were ashamed of the place where they lived. We had our own home and we had it furnished well so that I was never ashamed of it.

I also belonged to the Girl Reserves when I was in high school and I took part in a lot of its activities. I was very much interested in sports so I went in for that too and I also went to see all of the varsity games just like any high school kid would do. I even went to a lot of the school dances. Not very many of the Nisei went to these affairs because they felt conspicuous. I didn't feel that different at all. At first my mother objected to my going to these dances as she felt that the *hakujin* kids were all wild and that they all got drunk at these school dances. When she saw that nothing happened to me, she gradually gave in. I also went to a lot of the Nisei dances in the community. Dancing was my main pastime and I enjoyed it immensely. Most of my out-of-school social life was exclusively with Nisei groups. In school my social activities tended to be mostly with *hakujin*. It's funny that these two things never did cross and mix in with each other. I was even a class officer several times. Most of my friends in high school were most surprised when they found out I was a noncitizen and they often remarked that I was more Americanized than most Nisei in school who had been born in this country.

I suppose that my social life was the main enjoyment of my high school days. I can look back upon it as a happy period of my life. I took a business administration course and because of this I got to be a cashier in the faculty cafeteria at school. I did not neglect my studies at all because I did my homework faithfully. I used to study a lot with the *hakujin* fellows and they would help me out on subjects that I did not know so well. I got good grades in high school and I did not have to be a bookworm either.

My parents wanted all of the kids in the family to go to college and they worked very hard to make this possible. I didn't want to let them down so that's why I went. I enrolled at UCLA after paying nonresidence fee and I started out as a freshman, not knowing what major to take. Finally I decided to take a liberal arts course. A lot of the Nisei girls were majoring in business administration so I decided to change to a secretarial course before I finished my first year there. I later changed to [another college] in order to complete this major. I had definite plans to go on to USC but the evacuation came along and spoiled this ambition.

I never did like UCLA. I didn't care for all of those Nisei there and I wasn't able to have as many *hakujin* friends as before. The college was too large so that it was hard to get to know the other kids. Another reason was that I did not like the school for charging me a nonresidence fee. That is why I transferred over to [another college] in 1940 and I graduated in 1942 just before evacuation.

I used to hear stories about discrimination against the Japanese but it never occurred to me that some day it might also affect me. Before the war, I did not care to think about anything serious. Some of the Nisei used to tell me that there were certain places in Los Angeles closed to the Japanese but I never did go to find out if it were true. On some of my dates I used to go to many of the first class entertainment places and I was never discriminated against.

I was taking part in a lot of activities of the Inter-Y Club during the time I was in school just before the war. We had quite a few social activities and our minds were always on these things. The club was composed entirely of Nisei girls and we sponsored a lot of discussion meetings and dances. I learned to jitterbug and that craze was the chief topic of life among the young Nisei then. I was going steady with a fellow but he suddenly left me and got married to another girl. That deflated me quite a bit but I soon got another boy friend and things went along as normal. I never did have any difficulty in getting dates to go to dances. I also went to church every Sunday but I am not a religious sort of person. My mother made me go to church when I was a young girl and I just kept it up. I quit going for a while before the war, but after Pearl Harbor I started to go again every Sunday. It was a Japanese [Christian] church and a lot of Nisei used to go there.

I was living [in a part of Los Angeles] where there was a big community of Japanese. There were quite a few Japanese living around our home. However, there were also scattered groups of other nationalities around us. My mother used to be quite close friends with a Caucasian woman who lived next door. Usually my parents' social activities were confined to other Japanese affairs. Once in a while the whole family clan would come together in our home and there were about 20 in all. My dad was the oldest of the group and they always came to him for advice. He was a sort of a head for the whole clan and he felt that he was responsible for them in time of trouble or sorrow.

My dad allowed me to drive the car to school and that was another advantage I had over the Nisei kids. After school I would drive him home. My dad was doing well in his business which had suddenly improved, although I didn't know the reason for that. He owned 4 stores at one time but just before the war he only operated one large store and he had about 6 Japanese working for him. My dad was a very sympathetic sort of person and he liked to help people out. He got into more complications because members of the family clan and others borrowed so much money from him and most of them never repaid. It was a good thing that most of his business was with the *hakujin* people or else he might have gone broke giving credit to a lot of Japanese. The last store Dad owned was in [a suburb] so that I drove 20 miles after him every day after school. My father had quite a bit of money saved up from his life work and he really did want to give us all the advantages that were possible. My only real plan for the future before the war was to get through school. I wanted to get training for some kind of professional work but I was not sure of what I wanted. I wanted to be independent and on my own so that I would be in a position to be able to help out my parents in case they ever needed it. I thought that I would be able to determine exactly what I wanted after I got enrolled in USC. I was looking forward to that quite a bit when the war came around and ruined this dream.

During all of my life up to the war I was not interested in politics at all but I often did secretly hope that I could become a citizen so that I could vote like the rest of my Caucasian friends. I guess it would really be something to be able to vote. During the fall of 1941 I did become more and more aware that there was trouble brewing in the Orient because my parents and a lot of the other Japanese were talking about it. At times I didn't blame Japan for taking things into her own hands because since the Exclusion Act, she was not able to expand at all and the only place where she could go was to China. I wished that Japan could have gotten along better with America and it disturbed me when I saw that the tension was increasing.

On Pearl Harbor day our whole family was home taking it easy. My brother was listening to some popular recording music and my sisters and I were sitting around and listening to it also. Then my sister turned the radio on and all of a sudden a news flash came over the air which shocked us. I didn't get the significance of it at all when my brother said that the Japanese had bombed Pearl Harbor. I just couldn't think straight. We thought that maybe it might be a mistake or some kind of a play. A few minutes later the announcement came over the radio again and I realized that it was true. We were scared stiff so that we stayed home all day and listened to the radio. My dad was also quite scared because he didn't know what would happen to his business. He didn't want any of us to go out into the streets that day and my mother backed him up on this because she thought it would be too dangerous. After the first shock my dad thought that the war would be over very quickly. He didn't say very much except, "So, at last, Japan has declared war." My mother was the one who was scared most of all. She imagined all sorts of things and she frightened me quite a bit when she said something drastic would happen to all of us. I tried to calm her down by telling her that nothing would happen to us but she wouldn't believe me.

When I began to calm down a bit, I began to wish that it did not happen. I suppose I was selfish because I immediately thought my school life would be interrupted and all Nisei fellows would be drafted. I knew that my life would be disrupted but I didn't know exactly how. I was too confused about things to be able to think straight. I wondered what would happen to our store. I had visions of mobs going down there and tearing it apart just because there was a Japanese owner.

The fact that I did not have American citizenship did not enter my mind until later. Mother had the idea that all of the Japanese aliens would be put into prison and I would have to go along with the Issei. I thought that this was a fantastic idea because I couldn't imagine myself being stranded with a lot of the old Japanese people. I had nothing in common with them and I knew that I would not be able to agree with their way of life at all. I had been trying to get away from it as much as possible for years.

The war also affected our financial status. On Saturday, December 6, my mother had gone to the Sumitomo Bank to get $500 out. She was given a check for it and she decided to wait until Monday before cashing it. By that time the war had broken out and the bank funds were frozen. It was a lucky thing that Dad kept most of his money in the *hakujin* banks. I think that he had some Japanese stocks which were frozen and he also had stock in the Manchuria Railroad. I don't know exactly how much money was frozen or lost and it may have been a large sum. We owned our own home and my father also had some [suburban] property. He was worried because he thought that this property might be taken away from him even though it was in the name of my older sister who was a citizen.

When I went to school the day after Pearl Harbor, I felt very uncomfortable riding in a streetcar. My dad thought it was better that I did not take the car since he needed it to do some of his business. I was conscious of the glaring headlines in the newspapers and I felt that the people were glaring at me just as hard. I thought that they all knew that I had been born in Japan and that made a difference. I was even called a Jap by some fellow who looked like he was drunk and I felt quite hurt at that.

All of these things gradually wore off and I settled down to a more routine life as the days went on. For the longest time I did not go to a movie because I was afraid that people would notice me and call me a Jap. I guess I was scared for quite a while after the Pearl Harbor shock. For the first week or so after the attack, a Nisei friend of mine started to take me to school in his car so that I would not have to ride the streetcar [where] people could stare at me. I was grateful to him for that.

I did not have any unpleasant experiences at college. I heard Roosevelt declare war and all the teachers told the Nisei that we had nothing to worry about. I thought I had an extra-special worry because I wasn't even a citizen. I was so numb that I didn't realize the full effect of the war for several days. Nothing unusual happened after the first week except for the FBI raids. I didn't go into Lil' Tokyo at all as I felt it would be better for me to stay out of that district.

After a few weeks a lot of restrictions were put on the aliens and all I could do was to go to school. I wasn't able to travel out of a certain area and a curfew was applied to me. That scared me again, but after a while I went places on the sly as I figured that I would be taken for a Nisei anyway. My mother got worried about this as she was afraid I'd be arrested at any time. We read the Japanese language papers every day to follow the new developments. It seemed that the *hakujin* people did not even notice me after the [first] few weeks of the war.

One of our constant worries was that Dad would eventually be interned and we expected it at any time. My girl friend's dad was taken after the first day and we felt sure that Dad would be taken before Christmas. Nothing happened in January and February so we figured that the FBI was not going to bother Dad as they had probably cleared him. In February I graduated from [business college] but I did not enroll in USC because I could not travel that far. I reënrolled at [another college] for the new semester to take a few more courses until I could learn exactly what my status would be.

My dad worried a lot about his financial affairs since some of his money was frozen, and he did not know if the rest would be taken away. He worried mostly about what would happen at his store. It was located in a wealthy Jewish district and you know how they discriminate against another minority race. Some of the customers tried to take advantage of my father and get things cheaper just because he was on the spot. That made me pretty sore. I suppose that was the beginning of my racial consciousness and I tended to blame the Jews for a lot of things and I had some very prejudiced ideas about them. I think that I am prejudiced against the Negroes also. There is no reason for that at all as they never treated me badly. I just wouldn't care to get too chummy with them. At times I have a strong hatred against the Jews. In school I had quite a few Jewish pals and I accepted them as individuals. The thing that got me sore was that the Jews had been kicked around themselves and suddenly they went against the Japanese when the war came, just for spite.

I continued to keep up my friendships with the *hakujin* I knew although I did lose a few friends. Most of my real friends, however, did not feel different toward me. In fact, they were sympathetic and they said I was just as good an American as they were since I was in Japan only for four months. All of these things helped me to regain my self-confidence. Our Caucasian neighbors remained just as nice as they had ever been before. They made a special point of coming to us to tell how they felt about it so that we would not think they were against us. It was at this time that my big sister got more sympathetic toward the United States even though she did have a lot of Japanesy ideas. Our parents worried about the facts that the Issei and Nisei would be separated. It was quite a strong rumor that the Issei would all be interned and we didn't know what we would do if that ever happened. My dad gave a lot of instructions telling us to sell the store and dispose of everything if we were ever separated.

I was at school when my father was interned. When I came home I had a funny feeling because I heard my mother crying. I realized immediately that Dad had been taken at last. He was put into a jail two blocks away and we were allowed to go visit him. Dad put up a cheerful front and he told us not to worry at all as he would be out in no time as he had not done anything wrong. Instead of us cheering him up it turned out that he had to cheer all of us up because we were so depressed. The FBI officers went through all of our things at home but they did not find anything that showed evidence that my father had done any sabotage work or anything like that. The only reason why they did take him was that he was on the Board of Directors of a Japanese language school.

Dad was suddenly transferred to [a near-by internment] center and we went to visit him about 3 times a week. My sister had worked as an interpreter for the FBI office, so that they gave us some special passes. Every time we went up there Dad was worried mostly about what would happen to his store. A close Caucasian friend of Dad's was a sort of silent partner in the business and Dad told us to rely upon him a lot in disposing of the store. He helped Sister and me make arrangements to sell out. Dad told us to sell everything so that we got rid of all the stock in the store.

The next thing we knew Dad was suddenly shifted to [a distant] internment camp. He was not able to join the family until July, 1943. I missed my father a great deal since I was pretty close to him. I kept hoping that he would be returned soon but I was doomed to disappointment. I was convinced that he had not done anything bad. I did not see why he should be arrested for being a member of the Board of Directors of the language school because he had not tried to give the children a lot of military propaganda about Japan. All he was interested in was to give the Nisei children a chance to read and write Japanese fluently. A lot of the Issei had been interned for this reason and some of them were released fairly quickly, so that I felt sure that Dad would come back to us soon. However, Mother was in the habit of worrying a lot and she thought she would never see him again. She even believed the rumor that the American soldiers were killing the men in internment camp and beating and starving them all the time. She even thought that all of us would be locked up and deported to Japan immediately.

After my father's internment I quit school entirely as I felt that I would be more needed at home to help out. Father believed that we would be interned also, so that he had one of his nephews and his family of four come and stay in the same house with us. My father felt that he would rest easier if he knew that there would be a man around to protect us. Another couple from the same part of Japan as my father also came to live with us in our home. [In all] we had 13 people living in our home until the evacuation day. It was quite crowded but we managed to get along somehow.

There were all sorts of rumors going around about who would be evacuated and when. When evacuation was finally announced, I was relieved and glad as we had no means of supporting ourselves anyway. We did not wish to use the family [savings] because we didn't know what was going to happen in the future.

Our district was not scheduled to go until June but after long family discussions we finally decided to volunteer to go to Manzanar on the first of May. We felt that this would hurry up Dad's return. I didn't know what to anticipate in camp. I thought that we would not be left there for the duration. I figured that eventually they would let us out, and I was quite curious about a camp. My mother and most of the Issei felt that they would be there forever.

We were among the first group to go to camp. There were rumors that it would be a rough life, so I prepared myself accordingly. I felt that we would be in a place without any modern conveniences at all. We took only our essential things as they had told us that we could take one bag apiece. They told us that our stay at Manzanar was temporary and later we could send for our things after we went to a more permanent camp. Consequently we stored most of our belongings in the basement of the house and then rented our home out to a Caucasian family. We left our house the night before evacuation and we went to Maryknoll Church so that we could evacuate with the group that was leaving from there.

It was a little sad leaving Los Angeles even though it seemed like we were only going on a trip. My emotions were sort of tangled up. I was glad that Dad was going to rejoin us soon and I was sad that we were leaving our home. It was such a strange feeling to leave Los Angeles in those busses. As soon as we got out of the city I began to look forward to what was coming. We had a lovely trip down there and we all enjoyed the scenery. As we turned the bend approaching camp I saw Manzanar for the first time and it looked beautiful with the mountains in the background. I guess I had the impression at that moment that I would be living in a sort of paradise, but I was doomed to disappointment. As we got closer, we saw the dirty tar-paper shacks and the crowds of people, and it really was depressing. Everybody was nice to us though, and they tried to make us feel at home. My first impression of Manzanar was that it was so dark and dirty. There was sand blowing all over the place and the barracks were just filthy. My morale was at a low point until I met my best girl friend and then I was suddenly glad. I knew that all of us were evacuated, so that the best thing to do was to make the most out of our situation. I didn't like the idea of lining up for everything and it took me quite a while to get used to the straw ticks we had to use for mattresses. I didn't like the way they allotted clothes later because it made me feel like poor people taking charity.

Since my father wasn't there to fix up our barracks, a couple of cousins came over and they helped us clean up the place. We never did have much furniture since none of us were good carpenters. Later we sent for some of our stored stuff and our barracks became more homelike. We were quite disappointed as the weeks went by and Dad was not allowed to rejoin us.

After we got our place fixed up, I began to look for a job and I managed to get one in June. I was assigned to the maintenance office as a secretary. This job got pretty dull, so that I transferred over to the census office to file forms and interview people. I liked this job a lot better because it was more interesting work and we were able to find out the background of all the other people in camp, since they had to put their personal history down in the form which they filled out. We had a very large staff of about 40 people, so that I made friends with a lot of them in a very short time. They were all Nisei, so that we had a lot in common.

It wasn't long before I started to go out on social activities quite a bit. I had a lot of fun as soon as I got to know a lot of people. That census office where I was employed was sort of a social center, and I worked there until September. The job began to get routine after I got used to it, so I got a little restless. The school system was beginning to start up and I thought I would like to get into that. I tried to get in as a teacher but I did not have enough credentials to qualify. After making a large number of applications I finally got into the adult education division as a secretary. It was quite an exciting job as we set up a junior college, night classes, and vocational training courses. The head of the department, Mr. [X], was very friendly to the Nisei and he was the one who helped me get my present job in Chicago. I was his personal secretary and it was through him that I was encouraged to resettle.

Besides my secretarial work, I used to teach shorthand in the adult education division once in a while. I attended a couple of classes also for a short time but I lost interest in that. The start of the junior college was the most fun that I had. It was really thrilling to see a junior college organized in such a place as camp. In this work I was with Mr. [X] constantly as his secretary so that I got to know quite a few of the Caucasian teachers, which was very worth-while to me. I began to go to some of the open forums to listen to the discussions and I also joined several clubs.

It was about this time that my interest in completing my education was revived. I had dropped all plans to go to USC when the war came along and I didn't give it much thought until I got involved in the adult education department in camp, as I could not see any prospects.

In camp I did not think too deeply about more serious things as it was mostly fun for me. I was in a girls' club and we put on a lot of socials. At other times I attended the symphony concert under the stars, and I also went to all of the basketball games and other recreational programs. I went to the Christian church quite regularly but I was not particularly religious. Everybody went to church on Sundays as there was nothing else to do. I wasn't interested in politics at all. I suppose my life was centralized mostly around the adult education department, my family, and my social life.

Manzanar was a very backward camp because most of the people there were farmers. There were a lot of pro-Japan individuals in there. That's why we had so many disturbances. The December riot[201] was caused by these people. In this December incident everybody was afraid to speak up and tell what was on their mind. The Nisei did not have any power at all since the Issei took all the control. The Kibei sided with these Issei so they became a pretty strong group. Many of the parents made the Nisei obey everything they said. At the time of the riot I was not able to go to work at all because I got condemned as an *inu* for working in the administration building. I went to work anyway but Mr. [X] advised me to stay home as he thought I would get beaten up. I didn't sympathize with these people who were so fanatic at all. I didn't wear a black ribbon on my sleeve like all of the old people were doing. I suppose that most of the Nisei were afraid to go out for fear of being called an *inu*.

Around February the Army registration came in and I helped to interview one of the worst blocks. It was composed mostly of Kibei

---

[201] Cf. Togo Tanaka's account of the Manzanar riot in Thomas and Nishimoto, *op. cit.*, pp. 49–52. Military police fired into a crowd of evacuees, killing two and wounding a number of others.

On the next day, block managers distributed black arm bands, instructing residents to wear them until the funeral of [one of the slain evacuees]. It was estimated that between two-thirds and three-quarters of the residents wore some symbol of mourning for several days. Many Nisei voluntarily wore their mourning stripes; others were openly coerced, mothers being told that their children would be treated as *inu* unless they conformed. (*Ibid.*, pp. 51–52)

and Issei bachelors. All of the police in the internal security department were Kibei and they were very strong for the Japanese government. I was scared all the time I was doing these interviews because
the Kibei were pretty nasty toward me. They thought that just because I was a girl, they could treat me with contempt. I suppose they
thought that this was the Japanese style. I was disgusted with the
whole lot of them but at the same time I feared them. They all came
out quite openly and said that they were for Japan and that they
wanted to go back there as fast as they could. The Issei bachelors were
just as nasty. They were crude and uncouth and they made fun of me
when I tried to reason with them. It was no use at all. There were a
few families in that block and the Nisei all signed No-No in the registration because of the family and block influence. There was one 18
year old boy who came in to register and I asked him why he was
answering "no." He said to me, "You are a Japanese, what do you
think I should do?" I told him that he should follow his own convictions and realize what he was doing. I told him that he should value
his American citizenship because he didn't even know what Japan
was like.

I answered Yes-Yes immediately and my mother agreed with me.
The reason for that was my mother thought that if she answered "yes,"
then Dad would be returned more quickly to the family. A lot of the
wives who had an interned husband answered "yes" for this reason.
The interned husbands also answered in the affirmative so that they
could rejoin their families. I know that my dad did that.

The biggest issue was whether the Nisei should volunteer for the
Army or not. This was where most of the bitter arguments in the
family circle took place. The Kibei always stood around and mocked
everybody. The Issei were not favorable to volunteering and I don't
suppose the Nisei were too keen about it either. We only had about
a hundred volunteers from our camp. Frankly, I don't think I would
have volunteered either if I were a boy, because I didn't approve of the
segregation idea in the Army at all. You would just see Japanese guys
all the time and you wouldn't have a chance to assimilate and meet the
hakujin soldiers. They gave a lot of ballyhoo about the Nisei combat
team, but I thought that it was the same thing as a colored segregated
division.

In spite of the crude life at Manzanar, I did enjoy the experience
and I don't regret it one bit. I think I grew up a little in camp and I
did meet a lot of college kids. I also made a number of Caucasian

friends and I had always wanted to do that. I never did get such a good chance to meet Caucasians until I started working in the adult education department. I enjoyed the Nisei I worked with also because the ones in the adult education department were more educated than those I had known formerly. I never had an opportunity to meet any Nisei with M.A. degrees in Los Angeles since we were in different crowds. I learned a lot through contacts with them also.

It was after the riot that I started to think seriously about resettlement. The talk of resettlement started to get strong among the Nisei and I was influenced by that. Many of the friends I had were among the first to leave camp. I heard a lot of stories about Nisei going out and getting good jobs with terrific high pay. I thought that I would be able to do the same thing if I took the chance. Those $60 a week jobs really looked big to me when I compared it to the $16 a month I was making as a secretary in camp. I started to discuss relocation with some of my other friends and they all gave me favorable reports. After the registration, I was sure that I wanted to go out definitely. By March [1943] my whole group was all beginning to go out. I would have come out a lot sooner but my mother would not let me. She kept stressing the point that my dad would be returned to us at any time, and I wanted to see him before I left because I didn't know when I would have another chance. I had my application in at the employment office but I had to turn down job offers because of this reason. In April I was offered a job in the WRA office in Cleveland but I had to turn this down also. I began to talk to Mr. [X] about what I should do. He influenced me a great deal. He said that I should take the chance and get out of camp as soon as possible in spite of everything else. He wanted all of his office staff to go out and get jobs. I had quite a time trying to make up my mind but I finally decided that I should get out before it was too late.

In the meantime, my older sister went out to get married, so that my mother got used to the idea of part of her family being away from her. After that she began to break down a little. She finally said that she did not care but she thought that Dad would be very disappointed when he came back and found me gone. I wrote to my father in the internment camp and I told him that I just had to get out of camp because I couldn't stand it much longer. He wrote back and said that my mother would be very lonesome if I left but I could do what I thought best. I talked to my cousins and they all agreed that I should leave. We had many family discussions on this and the older persons in the clan were against resettlement for girls. They thought that it was too dangerous. My mother was very hesitant in her approval but she finally did give in.

I got a job offer at a [Protestant] college in Chicago and I decided to accept it. I was quite depressed when I left camp because the train was so dirty. There were so many soldiers and sailors on the train and I didn't know how they would react to me. I soon found that they were the most understanding people of all. I was feeling a little ill from the train ride and one sailor went to all the trouble to bring me my dinner. I had to laugh then at my fears because I really was frightened and I had built up my imagination to the point where I thought I would be the victim of some kind of incident.

After a few days of grimy travel I finally arrived in Chicago exhausted. This was around the first of May, 1943. The first thing that impressed me was the dirty tenements that I saw as the train pulled into the city. I thought that I would never like Chicago because it was so old and dirty. When I first arrived in Chicago I had to go to the FBI office and fill out some special forms and get an okay. The people from the school met me at the station and they were very kind. They arranged everything for me so I had no difficulty at all in getting settled. I stayed in the dormitory right on the campus until the Navy took it over. Now I am at another college dormitory and I have been here since September [1943].

During the summer I was out of town at the college summer camp. When I left for the college summer camp last June, I had to get another special permit to travel out of the state. My life really began when I went to the college camp. I met all sorts of people and they were all interested in the resettlers. Many of them had known the Japanese people through missionary work, so they all came and talked to me. There were a large number of Y people and they were all friendly and coöperative. The summer camp reminded me a lot of Manzanar as it was rugged living. However, the atmosphere was much better so that I enjoyed it immensely. It was such a free and easy life and it seemed so far away from the turmoil of the world. We all got very close to each other living coöperatively like that and I certainly enjoyed the experience. The Japanese in camp were never coöperative like that.

This experience ended in September and I came back down to Chicago and I moved into this girls' college dormitory. I get along swell with them and we do everything together. They are a lot of fun and I am always being invited out by them. During Christmas I went to [a contiguous state] with one of the girls in the house and I got along wonderfully with her parents and friends. I bunked with my girl friend and we used to talk practically all night. Her parents even conserved gas coupons so they could ride me around to visit all of their relatives. They just accepted me as their daughter's college girl friend.

It didn't take me very long to get used to my work. At the college, I am a private secretary. I like the work very much because the people really try to help me out. They encourage me to go to school, so I take an hour off each day for a class. They don't deduct the wages for this either. My boss always includes me in the college activities as he just takes me as a student. I go to all of the rallies and other school functions. Maybe it is because I live in such a nice environment that I just take things for granted now, and I don't realize how lucky I am.

I will get married eventually but I don't feel like it now as I am having a good time. I just hate to give it up now when I have so much. If I felt lost and helpless, then I probably would have considered immediate marriage. As it is now, I think I am assimilated quite a bit and I am enjoying the process. Maybe I will even be a career woman, but I don't think so. For the next few years I think that I can get married any time, so I don't worry about it at all.

I know that a lot of Nisei think that I am fast, and they don't agree with the things that I do. They think that I am bad just because I smoke and go out on a lot of dates. I think they are hurting themselves by being narrow minded and clinging to their own group. I think that the Nisei should go out into Caucasian society more and they should be willing to go more than half way. They don't have to like every Caucasian they meet but I think that it is very important that we should let the public know that we are individuals. I don't like to see the congregation of Nisei at all. It is in little ways that integration is accomplished and I don't think the Nisei will get any place by crying about all their troubles.

I have not consciously been trying to break away from the Japanese group. We just seem to be leading a different kind of life out here. It is mostly my present environment that makes the difference. I go out with Nisei when they come over and ask me and I don't try to avoid them at all. However, I do feel embarrassed when I see them on the streets in a group. I don't know why I feel that way because I know that I am no better than they are. At the same time they try to avoid me too. So I guess all of the Nisei do that. They just get together behind locked doors where the Caucasian eyes can't see them. I don't know why they feel so afraid.

I think that the future will be up to the Nisei alone. They have to get established now and try their best at their jobs so that they will not lose them after the war. The Nisei may complain about not getting the best jobs out here but I think they are better off than in California. I certainly don't want to go back to California, that's a cinch. I know that in Los Angeles the Japanese only got to be domestic workers, fruit stand workers, and the rest were students. The college graduates didn't even have a chance. Now most of the Nisei are getting all kinds of chances of different types of work and I can't believe that all of this is going to be wiped out just as soon as the war is over.

CH-59: MUSIC TEACHER

Female; born in Wyoming, 1915; inmigrated to California from Utah, 1934; height 60"; weight 110 lbs.; unmarried.
Interviewed, November–December, 1944. Described as "very intelligent," as having "an unusually good vocabulary," as speaking in "a timid and faltering voice, barely above a whisper," and as seeming, at first, reluctant to tell her story. Because there was no privacy in her own home, she agreed to come to the interviewer's apartment, but when she arrived "she was afraid to ring the front door bell, and waited around until somebody came outside and opened the door." Although she subsequently broke several appointments, without notifying the interviewer, she kept others "at a very considerable sacrifice of her own time." She continued to be "timid, hesitant, and easily frightened" during the later interviews, and had to be "handled cautiously" and not "questioned too directly," but she "spoke much more freely and revealed quite a bit of feeling, and voluntarily explored personal problems which many Nisei are too sensitive to discuss."

CAREER LINES

Parental: Father (born *ca.* 1870) came from "a long line of scholars"; mother (born 1884), from the merchant class. Said to have been frustrated in his ambition to become a dramatist, father opened a small factory in Yokohama but lost it during an economic crisis of the early 1900's. Worked as a labor contractor in Hawaii and on the mainland until about 1910, when he returned to Japan, and married. Remigrated to the United States in 1911, and brought CH-59's mother with him. For some years, the family operated a restaurant and hotel for Japanese railroad workers in a Wyoming town, but this business failed after World War I. Attempts to establish similar enterprises in several other communities uniformly unsuccessful until, during the early 1920's, family gained a foothold in a medium-sized town in Utah, where they operated a retail produce market for about 10 years. Between 1932 and 1936 all members of the family moved to Los Angeles. Father was in ill health and unable to work, and died in Los Angeles *ca.* 1936.

Own: Finished high school in Utah, in 1932, majoring in languages; received private instruction for 14 years and took some extension courses in music in Los Angeles. After inmigration to Los Angeles (*ca.* 1934), worked as a salesgirl in a retail fruit stand for about two years, and as a domestic servant for a year and a half. Music teacher in a kindergarten, 1938–1940; self-employed music teacher, 1940–1942. Inmigrated to Chicago, April, 1943. Clerk in a book firm, April, 1943–March, 1944; unemployed for two months due to illness; took business course and became comptometer operator, June, 1944–October, 1944; from October, 1944, to date of interview she worked as "dice measurer" in a factory.

LIFE HISTORY

My father's family has a fairly good background and a long history in Japan, but I only know it sketchily. Father's dad died when my father was still a young child. His mother was some sort of a schoolteacher in Japan. Dad's family belonged to some sort of a lesser nobility class. They were known as a line of scholars for hundreds of years, and that represented one of the most respected social classes in Japan right up to modern times when the westernization of Japan began to stress the merchant and military groups more.

After my dad's father died, he went to live with an uncle in order to complete his education as a scholar. This uncle was one of the first Japanese to go abroad to study. My father was a rather brilliant individual but he did not especially care to be a scholar according to the family pattern. He had a liking for drama and his uncle considered this a disgrace to the family name, so he disowned my father completely. In those days drama was looked down upon as some kind of low profession.

After my father went on his own, he began to do all sorts of jobs. He tended to go more and more into business activities because the merchants were beginning to be the most respected class in Japan at that time. There were plenty of opportunities because Japan was just coming out of isolation and there was a great haste to modernize the country overnight. Somehow or other my father learned American business methods and he started to manufacture monuments in Yokohama. He was very successful at this so that he became rather prosperous. A panic started, and my father lost his business completely. He even owed money after it was all over.

Dad was afraid to take another business risk. He began to hear and read about the golden opportunities in America. Many impoverished Japanese had migrated into America and they sent back glowing accounts about what great fortunes could be made there. My father didn't have any particular attachments to Japan, so he decided to come to America in order to pay back his debts and build up another fund for himself. He thought that after he made his money in America, he could return to Japan.

My father was not the first member of his family to come to America. His younger sister was here already. Dad was quite close to this sister because they had lost their parents quite early. This younger sister had married a very adventurous person who had a keen business sense. She urged my father to come to America in order to share in the great profits which her husband was making. Her husband was the first one to bring Japanese laborers to the mainland and he was making thousands of dollars profit each year as the result of this.

Dad came to America to join him in this enterprise. There was an office in [S, a town in Wyoming]. The big railroads paid my uncle and father large sums of money in order to bring over Japanese workers. Dad traveled back and forth to Japan several times to recruit workers. He went to the poorer farming districts and told magnificent stories about the riches which could be made in the United States. Dad also helped to recruit workers from Hawaii. After a few years of this work, Dad went back to Japan to live. He thought that he had enough money to start a business, but he was used to a higher scale of living by this time so that his money soon ran out. He had to spend money freely because all of the people in Japan believed that he was such a successful business man that he had to uphold his prestige. An arranged marriage was made for him and then my father decided to come back to America to make more money. He was not satisfied to settle down in Japan and make smaller profits.

My mother was from a very prosperous and well-to-do family from Tokyo. She had never worked in her life. Her father owned a large rice mill. Her side of the family was considered the new rich and they didn't have the status of a scholar family. All of her side of the family were merchants.

My mother expected a life of leisure and riches in America. The possibility that she would have to work when she came to this country never entered her head. My father described America to her in golden terms, so she really expected something wonderful. She arrived in this country by way of Vancouver and she was amazed at the modernness of the city. She only saw the best side of it. Then they continued on down to Seattle and she thought that America was such a wonderful country. She began to have a letdown when she saw the dirtier part of Seattle where the Japanese lived. She didn't like it at all because she had always lived in such a clean and fastidious atmosphere in Japan. My father was planning to take her to [Wyoming] with him. There were some other Japanese ladies who came over on the boat with my parents and they advised her to go to California instead of the wild territories inland. They told her that California was the golden state of her dreams and the best opportunities would be there.

My father didn't want to go to California. He wanted to go join his younger sister and her husband in [S]. I think that my parents made their big mistake when they went inland to Wyoming.

My uncle became quite wealthy, as he got a commission for every worker he recruited and he also managed the affairs for the gang since he was their spokesman. He got a commission for almost every deal in which he engaged. All of the railroads wanted Japanese laborers because they worked so hard. Uncle branched out and he opened offices in Denver, Omaha, and other railroad centers. By the time he was finished he had made his fortune and then he pulled out and went back to Japan to retire in about 1920. My father had an excellent opportunity to become my uncle's partner in this contract labor work but he missed out on this due to his personality difference. My dad didn't like to approach people directly and he couldn't understand their point of view. He tended to look down on the Japanese workers, so that he was never able to develop a close feeling for them and be recognized as a leader. My uncle was successful in this kind of work because he had a warm personality and the men used to come to him all the time for advice. He was just like a father to them, because he told them just how much money to save, how to send for picture brides, how to send letters, who to work for, and he even settled arguments and difficulties among the men. My dad wasn't able to do this because of his aloof disposition.

During the period when the Japanese were in Wyoming in large numbers, they were not allowed to live in many of the residential areas in [S]. My aunt saw a need for housing, so one day she went out and bought a lot of shacks on the edge of town. She rented these shacks out to the Japanese workers and eventually all of the Japanese colony was housed there. My aunt made quite a profit out of this business venture.

When my father got to [S], my uncle helped to finance him so that he could build a hotel and grocery store there. There were many Japanese workers in the state at that time. It was the period just before World War I, and the city was quite prosperous because of the war boom. Then all of the soldiers started to be sent away to war and [S] became a deserted city because there were no war industries there. Many of the Japanese laborers were moving to California, so Dad had to give up his hotel. He was rather disappointed by this failure. He couldn't go back to Japan because several children had already arrived in the family. Finally he decided to move to [a small intermountain town] in order to start all over again. He opened a grocery store and a restaurant there. It served Japanese food to railroad workers in that district. He also sold sake on the side. It was a booming mining town and a lot of Japanese laborers were constructing a railroad through there at that time. The Japanese went there in droves and my mother often told me that they all made money, even the common workers. She said that she knew of many of these workers who sent anywheres from $1,000–$5,000 back to Japan. The early Japanese workers on the railroad tended strictly to business and they did not begin to gamble and drink excessively until later on when their hopes of returning to Japan as big successes vanished. After the main line of the railroad was constructed, many workers returned to Japan but a lot of them went to California to work on the farms and orchards throughout the state.

When the Japanese railroad workers left [this town], my father went bankrupt again because it became more of a deserted town. My parents decided to return to Japan even though they did not have a large fortune built up as they had expected. My mother was very disappointed with this country as she had not expected to have such a hard life here. Her parents in Japan had asked them to return. The plans for going back were just about completed when a family friend arrived from Japan and told them that prices were sky-high there as Japan was going through another inflation period on account of the war. My dad then thought it would be foolish to take his wife and four children to Japan under such conditions as he did not have enough money to get us started there. He decided that he would try again in some other Japanese community.

My family then began to travel around to different Japanese communities where the laborers gathered but none of my father's business ventures turned out successfully. We came right down through the Rocky Mountain states and went through Denver and a few other cities. We finally landed in [M], Utah, when I was about 8 years old, and my father opened up a produce market.

After we started to live in Utah, 4 more children were born to the family and it became almost impossible to move around to other localities after that because it was too expensive. By that time my mother had given up hopes of ever returning to Japan. My father was used to America and he no longer had dreams of returning to Japan because he knew he couldn't take a family of 8 children along with him.

My dad, as I remember him, was a very moody and a disappointed man. He always had the love of drama in his blood but he was never able to do anything with it in America. He was really a misfit in this country. Dad was always very impractical in business and he had wild dreams of sudden success. He wanted to make his money all at one time like my uncle did. He was totally unfit to struggle along in business because of his sensitive personality. For that reason my mother gradually became the dominating force in the family. She had to do it in order to provide sufficient food for the growing children. That's why my mother was always the family head as far as any of us children can remember. Dad lived in a sort of dream world. He was kindly enough to the children but we always looked upon him more as a stranger. We did not feel very close to him because there was the absence of a real family warmth. He was the only member of the family who was excluded like this, but that was because none of us could understand him. My mother did nag him at times because Dad's impractical business methods put the burden of support on her. Dad really meant well but he could never make a go of it. He died a very disappointed man. He never did make the money that he wanted to.

My father was educated far above the standards of the Japanese immigrant workers, but his education was in impractical lines, so that he didn't know how to apply it. I guess I sort of inherit that trait from him because I am very impractical too, and I tend to be more of the dreamer type. Because he couldn't get along with other men, my father turned more and more to reading. He read all about Japanese art, singing, and dances. He knew a great deal about Japanese culture, but it was of absolutely no use to him in the rugged Wyoming of his days.

Eventually mother got much better at the business at the hotel than my father because she was willing to make adjustments to the new life. I think she managed to make a pretty good go of it, considering that she was the chief breadwinner for many years and she brought up 8 children besides. She did all of the family business ever since I can remember as my dad was in very poor health for 10 years of his life prior to his death. Mother worked and slaved away for the large family and she had to learn to speak English a little in order to carry on certain business contacts. That is why she speaks better than the average Japanese women who have been buried in the home and occupied themselves with raising children only. My father knew English quite well.

Although I don't know too many Issei intimately, I think that my mother was very broad minded in comparison to those I know. In her youth she was a little too impatient and disgusted with my father, but she became resigned to her lot in life. Near the time of his death, my mother became very sorry for my father, and I think for the first time in her life she began to understand why he was a failure. My parents used to have such violent arguments on just how the children should be brought up. My father had more of the strict Japanese ideas because he had a greater knowledge of Japanese culture and he believed that it was much superior to the American culture. The unfortunate part of it was that he never came into contact with the better aspects of American culture due to his work in making a living in the lower level. He compared this to the upper level that he was used to and naturally the American culture suffered in comparison. Dad would never recognize this point but my mother was more understanding. She knew that there was a better part of American culture to which we were not exposed, as she had seen the large cities on the coast.

Dad was not much of a social mixer himself, so that he wanted me to stay home all the time. He was strict to the point of tyranny. He wanted to shut me away by myself and not have any contacts with any children my age because he was very ambitious for me, and he thought that this was the best way in order to give me the training for my future. He wanted me to take dancing and music lessons while the other children got to go out and play. He spent his last cent to buy all the books that I wanted. But he would never allow me to go out to even church parties because he had some sort of an idea that I was a little better than the other children who came from the Japanese peasant families. Dad tried to maintain the difference in social status in Wyoming and Utah, and it just didn't work out because we were all from workers' families regardless of what our families had been in Japan.

My mother opposed my father on my training because she thought that I should be allowed to mix more with other children. My mother's argument was that we catered to all of the people in town, so that we shouldn't feel above them and snub the children of our customers. She also felt that this kind of a secluded life for me would ruin my future personality.

Dad maintained his point of view because he said that if I did not get the strict training, I would run around with the children of the cheap Japanese families. He was stubborn on this point and insisted upon it. That's why I became so timid and shy. There was another reason why my father tended to seclude me. In Utah, the Mormons were very nice to the Japanese people, but [in our town] the better families among them wouldn't allow their children to play with the Japanese children. Dad felt that it wouldn't be such a good influence on me if I were allowed to play with the wilder American children of the lower class families. My parents argued endlessly about this point but my father seemed to have the upper hand in this, even though my mother made most of the other important decisions for the family. My brothers and sisters were treated more or less in the same way. As a result, we children were very strictly brought up according to my father's plan.

The Nisei in the small western towns in the interior United States grew up in a different way than the Pacific Coast Nisei. There was a [Japanese from the coast] who came to our Japanese church once and he told us that we were nineteen years behind the times when compared to the Pacific Coast. I hate to admit that the interior states

Nisei are more backward and conservative than the Pacific Coast ones but it seems to be true. On the Pacific Coast the Japanese colony had a higher economic standard, especially in the Los Angeles district. In the interior states like Utah, the Japanese didn't have real poverty, but they were not so well off. Therefore, they didn't have the spaciousness of the coast Nisei in character development because they were more restricted in their outlook. There was a certain harshness reflected in the inland Nisei personality due to circumstances. In a small inland town, the Caucasian atmosphere was very prejudiced and strict. However, the Japanese felt a greater warmth toward other Japanese and we trusted the new Kibei and Issei who came into our group. We didn't develop any of the strict classification like Issei, Nisei, and Kibei as they did on the coast. We were all one and we didn't fight among ourselves like they did on the coast.

We had a better command of the English language than the majority of the coast Nisei, I think. The inland Nisei didn't speak English with a Japanese accent or mix up half-Japanese, half-English in their speech. On the other hand, I think that the inland Japanese families were much stricter on the Nisei on social relationships. They never allowed the boys and girls to come together. All of the marriages had to be arranged by the parents according to the traditional practices. There was quite a bit of rebellion against this but the majority seemed to accept it as a part of their lives. There were quite a few who came after me and they were much more rebellious. That's why many of the Nisei eloped in order to marry the person that they loved. Some of them became intimate before they got married because their parents objected so much, and then they had to get married, shot-gun style. This was always a great blow to the family name.

While I was growing up, all of my friends were Nisei students. There were 8 or 9 girls of my age that I palled around with mostly. I didn't have very much to do with the Nisei boys. When I was in grammar school I didn't make many close friends because my folks were traveling around to different places. We never stayed long enough for me to get real acquainted with the other pupils. During this time I had mostly *hakujin* friends at school but my dad didn't want me to play with them too much.

I became shy and I often had my moody spells. I was afraid to mix in too much with other children of my age and I always felt a little reserved while around them. I was also influenced by the belief that I was a little superior to them. Because of my father's training,

I was a little too mature for my age. That's why I never craved dolls or went around with other little girls, doing the things they were interested in. It got so that I didn't enjoy being with them at all and I guess I became sort of queer. I shut myself up in a shell and I sort of withdrew into my other activities. I took my dancing and music lessons and concentrated on that.

The thing which changed me even more was when I discovered the public library at the age of 9. From that time on, reading has been a passion with me. Since I was very impractical from an early age, I developed a day-dreaming life. I imagined myself as all different kinds of heroines and I put myself into a life of leisure like I read about in the book. It became my desire to live a different kind of life from what I had been used to when I grew up. I never did gain the courage to take a definite step until quite recently though. I just continued to day-dream all the way through. I read about adventure and far away places, so that I became dissatisfied with my existing life. I began to hate the small town in which I lived. I only found my release when I took piano lessons. This made me further withdraw from other people.

Since I was the oldest girl in the family, I more or less became the head of the family after my older brothers got married. As much as I love my family, I never did well by them, as I didn't have a knack of understanding people. As I got older I even tended to withdraw from them. In spite of these feelings we had a close family unity, largely because of economic necessity. I think that we were more eccentric than the average Japanese family. We all seem to differ greatly individually. We were drifting a little apart and going our own way just before the war but we have come together since then. The camp experiences might have done that. Now our family relationship is quite close. In many other cases, I definitely know that the evacuation broke families up completely and they will never come together again.

My brothers and sisters all went to the Japanese language school with me. All of the girls in my family studied music because my father thought it was a good cultural polish for us to have. One thing was that we didn't speak Japanese in our home as we grew up and we never speak it now. Mother never stressed the Japanese holidays to us though we observed them occasionally. None of us like Japanese food as we got an inferior quality in the inland states. We were brought up more on the bread and milk diet rather than the rice and tea.

At the public schools, I always spoke in a timid voice and I never overcame this deficiency. I got very good grades as my parents insisted upon us studying all our lessons. I didn't have to be coaxed in this but my parents went to the extreme. That is why I developed the practice of going to the public library on the pretext of studying and then I would spend my time reading novels.

I went all the way through high school in [M]. This was really the first time that I became acutely conscious of my race. I tended to be a little proud of my race at first, but certain things happened which made me a little ashamed. I became all mixed up because I didn't know what was wrong. The Japanese students were really the ones who forced me to become conscious of my race. At first I had a few Caucasian friends in high school and I became friendly with them, but the Japanese kids all stuck together and pretty soon the *hakujin* students left us alone. Pretty soon, then, we became accustomed to be doing things only among ourselves. We all lived in the same neighborhood and we went to school together. It was natural for us to form a separate group at lunch time.

There was another reason why most of us felt self-conscious. The Japanese were all poor in that area and the Caucasians were in much more comfortable circumstances. We couldn't go around with the richer Caucasian kids even if we wanted to because we didn't have the money to enter into their activities. They weren't as restricted as us either, so we had to consider that. Very few of us came from the merchant class in town and we didn't have a lot of money to buy clothes and other things. Most of the families were barely scraping along because they never had a real prosperous time in that area even before the depression came along. There was a wide barrier between us and it was difficult to scale it. I entered a few of the general high school activities in spite of this fact. I played the piano for the glee club and I actually belonged to the debating society, believe it or not.

I did meet a few nice *hakujin* who came from cultured homes. I never did like that school very much though. My main ambition at that time was to do something special in life, but I didn't know exactly what it would be. It was the first faint stirring of ambition that I had. I knew that I would never be contented to remain in that small town all my life. I became much more aware of my race and I recognized that the Caucasians on the whole were really superior to the Japanese culturally. The Caucasian students came from good stock and they had a poise which we Nisei lack. I really admired the characteristics

of the Caucasian students and I often wished that I was one of them.
I was imagining all sorts of things like this in my daydreams. I began
to believe that I would be much happier if I could acquire some of
their better characteristics. They seemed much more wordly than us
and they were not so tied down with rigid conventions as we were.
I knew that I could never hope to master the English language as
they did as my parents hardly knew English at all. I started out with
a great language handicap. The Caucasian kids acted so normal and
at ease and they were able to mix into social gatherings so easily. I
often wished that I could do the same things that they did. I tried to
emulate their social graces but they were years ahead of me, and I had
nobody at home to advise me on these things. That's why I have not
been able to acquire some of the better characteristics of the *hakujin*
to this day. It's really a part of American culture that I am seeking
and I want to fit into the general pattern instead of being one of the
discarded pieces.

One of the great joys of my life during high school days was having
a woman Sunday-school teacher who became a good friend of mine.
Through her I met a judge and some other influential Caucasians. My
admiration, my respect, and my liking for Caucasian ways of living
increased even more after I got these contacts. I regretted bitterly
that I could never be like them.

Up to this time my mother had entertained some ideas through my
father's influence that I would go to Japan after high school in order
to finish my education. But I was definitely opposed to such a plan
after I made my contacts with these *hakujin* people. I knew then that
I wanted to learn the American ways more than anything else. I did
keep up with my Japanese language lessons, but I never entertained
the idea of going to Japan to be a citizen there. That was a prepos-
terous idea.

I graduated from high school in 1932. Right after that I went to
Los Angeles to join my brother as I thought I could work there for a
while. It was my big chance to get into a large city and I had always
dreamed of that. Los Angeles wasn't my first choice. I really wanted
to go east to Chicago but my family had no Japanese friends out here
and they thought it was too risky for me to come out alone. On the
coast my brother could help me in case I got into any difficulties, so
I was talked into going out there. I thought that possibly I would be
able to mix in well with the Nisei there but I was sadly disappointed.
I will always regret the decision of going to Los Angeles instead of

coming east because it set me behind ten years and I am just getting started to do what I wanted to do now.

We made some family plans for all of us to gradually get to the coast because there was nothing holding the family in [M]. All of the Japanese talked in glowing terms about how rich the Japanese in California were. They emphasized the fact that the Japanese in California got on well with the *hakujin* and that there were plenty of opportunities there. My main desire was to study music right along, and that's why I wanted to go east. I knew that the eastern schools were much better for this but I had an accident which threatened to end all of my musical ambitions. My arm was injured quite severely so that my fingers have never been as flexible since then. However, I was able to gradually get back to piano playing.

When I first got to California I found that it was totally different from what I had hoped it would be. Right from the beginning I noticed that there was a certain barrier. The Nisei in Los Angeles struck me as being very poised. I immediately ran into the Nisei social class friction. I never did seem to fit into any special Nisei group during the next ten years. The out-of-towners among the Nisei tended to form a separate group of our own because we couldn't penetrate any of the local Nisei circles. We were worse than strangers in their midst. We were looked upon as some kind of untouchable outcasts. I longed to go east all along but by that time the depression had hit every place. My family came on out to Los Angeles to settle and I had to find work in order to help them out. I just couldn't stand by and watch them starve, since my father was so ill that he was unable to work. I had to help them get adjusted to a new kind of life. My dad had been suffering a great deal from asthma and his condition was aggravated by old age and a general physical crack-up. I finally quit my work and I stayed at home in order to take care of him until his death. My brothers supported the family during this period. I went to school part time and I kept on with my music. I also did a lot of reading since I was alone around the house a great deal. I didn't meet very many new friends and I never did join any sort of a group as groups frightened me.

After my father passed away, we had to learn how to live all over again without a father bringing in any income. It was a new sort of life to us in California. My oldest brother had some experience in the produce business, so he went into it at Los Angeles. All of us older children who were out of school worked and somehow managed to support the family. It was a pretty difficult struggle though, but it was true for everyone.

My family was never happy while living in Los Angeles. My brothers struggled 12 to 14 hours a day in the fruit stands and they only had a half hour off for lunch. They only received a pay check of $18 or $20 a week because they didn't have any unions in those days. We were certainly disillusioned because we had hoped that California would offer us a brighter future. We had a harder time economically than in [M, Utah]. My brothers were worn down with this gruelling work in the fruit stands and it was a heart-breaking experience for them. I began to see the life of the Japanese in California through my brothers' eyes and it was the worst side of it, so I found it even more undesirable than ever.

Our family made many attempts to fit into the community social life there but it was a very slow and painful process. It was much easier for an established family to make these adjustments. If we had been a local family, we would have had our own church and cliques developed over the years. But the outsider coming into this community had no place to go. The Japanese church failed miserably in getting us into the community and the working Nisei could never get any comfort or sense of satisfaction out of the church. All my brothers did was work and sleep. They went to the movies on their days off. After several years of this dull and monotonous experience, my oldest brother went back to school to finish up his last two years in art school. By this time the younger boys were working so there was no longer a strong need of my [oldest] brother's help in the family.

I spent 3 or 4 years doing all sorts of jobs in the Japanese community. I worked in those fruit stands too for a miserable $15 a week. The Los Angeles Japanese community seemed to be stable and well-organized on the surface and it had a certain prosperous appearance due to the fruit stand and other business activities. But underneath this surface, it was a place of many frustrations. The Japanese there didn't concern themselves about trampling over others just so that they could get a little ahead. But even those who made a better go of it were blocked from going too far because the limitations of the Japanese community had a strangle hold on them. The Nisei group was too young to cope with this problem by themselves and I don't know what would have happened to them if the evacuation had not come along.

I spent a miserable few years in seeking my outlet and I'd rather not discuss how I felt at that time. I found the fruit stand work most distasteful. It was hard work and the hours were long. The wage standards were horrible. Girls had to work 10 and 11 hours a day for about $15 a week and we didn't get paid for overtime. After the unions came in, it was a little better for the Nisei produce workers because they didn't have to put in such long hours. I think the Japanese market owners took advantage of the Nisei workers during the depression and they bled us for everything they could.

I couldn't stand the frustrating fruit market work, so I quit and got into a domestic job. I've never regretted doing that kind of work for a year and a half. I had very good relationships with my employer and I was treated almost as one of the family. This work gave me an opportunity to enjoy the sort of American culture I had always longed for. It opened up a lot of new possibilities for me. My employers were musically and artistically inclined and they had traveled widely over the world, so that I benefited from listening to them. They encouraged me to continue with my music lessons and I was able to practice on their piano in the afternoons.

My music teacher who had formerly been a music examiner in the civil service for the state of Illinois recommended that I work in with her. This was in 1938. She wanted me to learn her methods in teaching young children. She used her school as a sort of a laboratory to give her own music pupils experience in teaching young children. I thought I would like to specialize in that sort of thing and some day have a school like that of my own. I spent two years there and they were rich and satisfying years to me. I was getting paid $50 a month for this work. I got along with the children very well and I thoroughly enjoyed the experience. It was much more enjoyable than working in the fruit stand or domestic work.

My own piano-teaching school came about in a rather accidental way. Some of our Japanese neighbors asked me to help teach their children piano, and I got started in that way. I eventually had about 23 pupils in all. I taught them at my home and I was able to get a fairly good income from doing this. For the first time I was able to help support my family. My wage was very high compared to what the Nisei were making in the fruit stand, but it was never quite enough for me as there were so many things I wanted. I was doing this work at the time of evacuation and my income averaged around $100 a month.

During the few months before the outbreak of the war I again started thinking about going east and I made some tentative plans. The idea was dormant and it was the one longing that I had carried in my mind ever since my arrival in California. Now I began to think of it more seriously and the possibilities interested me very much. I wanted to broaden my scope and become an individual. I had always lived with my family and I wanted to go on my own for a while and see what I could do. My family relationships were close but I longed to go off and be by myself, because I thought I could create a better social condition if I got out of Los Angeles. I wanted to emphasize studying a little more. It was my plan to go to a small college town in the east and get away from a Japanese community. I had a deep desire to become an educated and cultured person. I always had in my mind that I would like to go to Boston to live. I knew that it was the seat of American culture because I had read a great deal about the old Boston tradition. I wanted to get there and take part in this way of living as it held a fascination for me. I dreamed of it all the time.

By this time I was beginning to feel that I would never get married. It was a cause of great concern to my mother because she thought that I should get married before it was too late. Once I almost did get married but somehow the whole affair ended disastrously. The fault was all mine as I couldn't go through with it. It was sort of an arranged affair and a lot of pressure was put upon me, so I consented. I really didn't love the person and I was going through with it because the family kept stressing the point that it was much more terrible to be an old maid. At the last moment I balked and I wouldn't go through with it. I didn't think I could make a success of [this sort of] marriage. That was because I was neither a Nisei, Kibei, nor Issei. I just didn't fit into any of these groups. Eventually I hope to fall in love deeply and get married.

My routine of life was fairly established by the time of the war. I went to church from the age of eight, but religion never gave me very much spiritual satisfaction. In Los Angeles I was playing the piano for the Japanese church every Sunday, but it was just a routine thing and it had no meaning to me. It got so that I began to hate that church, but I continued to go to it out of habit. The religion in itself as preached by the Japanese minister was boring and even more of an escape from real life than what I had been longing for in my wildest moments of daydreaming. The Japanese community was bled by the Japanese church. It was a small, petty, and clannish organization which belonged to the Japanese cliques in the community. The minister was always trying to make peace among all the conflicting cliques in his church but he never succeeded in gaining full harmony. He had to play politics in the church and cater to all of the different groups, as the church had to have their financial support in order to keep in existence. That income meant the livelihood for the minister and I am afraid that he became a little swayed in the pursuit of worldly gains, so that it became the most important thing in the church and the spiritual element became secondary. The Japanese community supported that Christian church because it was a good social gathering place. I doubt if many of those Issei or Nisei who attended that church had a real understanding of the Christian doctrine because the minister was a little behind the times too. My experience in that church did not help my adjustments at all.

I wasn't interested in politics at all, but I had always believed that war was inevitable. I vaguely knew that Japan was getting very ambitious in the Orient and I also knew that America couldn't afford to tolerate this ambition in order to maintain its predominating economic position in the world, so that a clash was bound to happen sooner or later. When Japan deliberately invaded China in order to grab up territory, I felt that she was acting much too aggressively. But being a Japanese, I felt sorry for Japan as I believed that inevitably this course of action would be her ruin and that she would lose everything that she had so painstakingly acquired during the previous 75 years in which she had become so hastily westernized.

The fact of whether I was a Japanese or an American never bothered me since I tended to be more internationally minded. I took certain American rights as a matter of fact and I never, for a moment, thought that these things would be annulled in a time of crisis because we were also Japanese. I suppose I felt more internationally minded because I was a member of a minority and this made me feel sympathetic for all the other minorities in the world, regardless of what country they lived in. That was why I didn't hate the Negroes or the Jews, even though there was a great deal of public feeling against them in this country. I felt that it was the individual which counted the most and I accepted them on this basis, even though I did not have much of an opportunity to meet them. I knew that America had adopted an attitude that the white races were superior and they were condescending to the minorities in this country without ever fully accepting on an equal basis. This never bothered me very much because I just accepted that idea. It was true that I was attempting to break into the more acceptable levels by imitating the American culture, so I suppose I did feel inferior unconsciously.

The day the war broke out, I was at a party given for one of my Caucasian friends. I was the only Japanese present at the gathering. It was a sort of luncheon. The radio was turned on and that was the first time I heard of Pearl Harbor and it was such a shock. Everything in the room went blank for me. It's a day I hate to think about now and I hope I never have to live through another day like that. I felt fear, horror, and every other emotion. I felt like I wanted the floor to open up and swallow me. I felt like I was sitting on the edge of an abyss. I was scared to death. I dreaded the thought of war and the hatred which it would arouse. I felt everybody's eyes on me and I desperately wished that I was in a dark cave alone. The people at the luncheon were very understanding and they immediately comforted me. I felt a sense of guilt for what Japan had done. I was too stunned to even think straight.

I went home immediately and three of the other girls escorted me. My mother could hardly believe the news when I told her. She got very excited and she thought immediately of the safety of her children. She sensed that because we were of Japanese blood, it would become increasingly difficult for us. I shared these opinions with her although I did not anticipate any mass riots immediately. My brothers were quite stunned too but they were more philosophical about it than I was. They didn't think they could do anything about it but to continue work and carry on. They felt they would be drafted into the Army in a short time. It didn't enter their heads so clearly that we would be placed on the other side of the fence.

I didn't dare step out of the house to see what was going on the first day. We were even scared to go out to the store; we just isolated ourselves in the house and hoped that nothing would happen. We didn't know which way to turn because we didn't have anyone to lean upon for support. We felt alone.

In the days which followed, our home ties became even closer than before. We tried to comfort one another as best as possible in order to maintain our morale. Even though the shadow of war and fear loomed large in our lives, we tried to forget it as much as possible. I really felt like I wanted to run away from the thought of war but I couldn't get away from it. We had to talk about other things in our home so we wouldn't go to pieces. My brothers worked in a Japanese produce market located in a Caucasian community, so that they were under constant suspicion. They were quite worried about what might happen in case the public got aroused against them. There was some ill-feeling directed toward them, but no incidents occurred as a result of it. The American people were orderly and well-behaved, even though many of them blamed us for the war. We were much more worried about what the Filipinos would do in the event they had an uprising because we had heard rumors that they were getting into gangs to beat up any Japanese they saw in the streets. I never witnessed one incident of this nature although other Nisei told me that it was true that the Filipinos were going around.

My imagination ran wild during this period but I had so many confused thoughts in my head that I didn't know what to make out of the whole mess. Pretty soon restrictions began to come in and we just accepted all of them. Things did become more frightening each day that Japan made progress in the war. Japan seemed to be marching right through the islands in the Pacific and I thought there might be an actual invasion of California. I had a lot of fears like that. The whole American public was jittery. It didn't affect our economic position too much. My brother's business in his store continued to be fairly good in spite of these developments, but that did not lift the morale too much because I was always afraid that something drastic would happen the next day. My family lived with these fears for the next two months although we settled down a bit after the first month. Everything was so uncertain that we didn't know what was what.

When the rumors of evacuation started, my reaction was that I had lost my last chance to escape from the Japanese community. I was still numb with fear, although not as intensely as previously. At first I was not sure whether evacuation would be a reality or not. There was talk going on that only the Issei would be taken. Then we heard rumors that it was to be a complete evacuation. Then we were assured that evacuation would not take place. This went on and on and fresh rumors piled on top of one another continuously. I kept the hope alive in my mind that evacuation just couldn't happen to us as we were American citizens. I was very concerned for my mother as she was subjected to almost anything due to her noncitizen status.

I just had to stop thinking about my own personal plans as we had to live from day to day in a state of great anxiety. My piano classes were cut down drastically as the lack of finances prevented many

Japanese families from sending their children any more. I got so that I tried to dismiss everything from my mind and nothing important disturbed me so drastically after that as I was waiting for the war to settle down into more of a routine. A lot of agitation started against the Nisei about February, 1942, but I thought this was only a natural reaction to the war. I expected much worse to happen and I was surprised that it wasn't as bad as I thought it was going to be. I was amazed that the American public was so decent toward us.

When the voluntary evacuation came along, my sister-in-law's sister decided to come out to Chicago as her husband was in school out here. This was my last opportunity of escaping with her but I decided that it was impossible for me to run out on the family by then. Our whole family just decided to stick it out and see what would happen. When evacuation became more definite, some of my in-laws moved into the house with us, as we were not taking any chances of getting all separated.

When the total evacuation was publicly announced by the Army in the early months of 1942, it was one time in my life that I really got angry to the point of bubbling over. I knew that evacuation was morally necessary if one looked at it wholly and objectively. The Japanese in California were everywhere and the United States government at this time was attempting to stress hate in order to win the war—hate against Japan, I mean. If the Japanese in California had continued to run around loose within the state, it was only natural that the white people of California wouldn't hate Japan so intensely. The Caucasian people would have had to continue business dealings with the Japanese in the state and they would naturally arrive at the conclusion that all Japanese people were not so bad because they would judge on the basis of the actions of the Japanese who had lived there a long time. On the other hand, there was the possibility that so much hate would be engendered towards Japan, that there would be mob violences directed toward the Japanese residents in the state. It was a rather inconsistent policy in which the government found itself caught. If the populace was to "remember Pearl Harbor" and "hate the Japs," it was necessary to get the resident Japanese out of the state as they wouldn't hate Japan so much if they kept up business with the Japanese within the state. The Caucasian people were human and they would see this basic contradiction. It was easier to get the populace to hate Japan if all the Japanese in the state were removed because the stereotyped pictures of the sneaky Jap could then be more effectively spread. The average American by nature was good and the continued presence of the Japanese in the state would have been a contradiction to the government appeal. I was angry because the Nisei were placed in such a ridiculous position and we didn't have a voice in the matter at all because we were all assumed to be guilty while the government was removing us under the heading of "military necessity."

I was angry, also, because everything we had so painstakingly acquired had to be thrown away in one grand rush. How could we dispose of these things in the three days we had? We were among the very first group of families to evacuate. We didn't have time to go about preparing for the evacuation like some of the later evacuees. We threw everything into boxes and I don't know whatever became of our belongings. We sold some of our things in the time we had but we didn't get very good prices because it was all too rushed. We owned three automobiles and we left them with friends who promised to sell them for us and send us the money later. We never did get the money for one of the cars. We had a lot of things scattered around the house and the people in the neighborhood went right through our house like vultures after we left. They took all of the small items like lamps and furniture so that our friend who was supposed to gather up all of these loose ends found nothing there when he arrived. My brother disposed of his produce market at quite a loss. I had two pianos of my own which cost me $1,200. I only got $30 for one of them. We had paid $300 for a phonograph about a year before the war and we had to sell it for $50. My car had cost me $900 the year before and I only got $250 for the sale of it. If we added up all of our losses for our family, it would run up into a few thousand dollars at least, maybe as much as $5,000. The WCCA would only allow us to carry one suit case and bedding to camp so we had to practically throw away all of our chinaware and kitchen utensils.

I was extremely angry about all these things at first, but I thought afterwards that it was an act of God just like a fire burning our home down or an earthquake destroying all of our possessions. I also thought that I was lucky being able to evacuate in a fairly orderly way when I compared myself to the people of China who had to flee time and time again in the middle of the night. Or I thought of the Nazi refugee who left everything behind in order to save his life. When I made these comparisons, it consoled me since I got to take along at least two suitcases of my belongings. I didn't let it bother me after that. I felt at that time that I just didn't belong to any country so I could sit on the fence and be a spectator at last. I thought that if countries were foolish enough to go to war and destroy everything, they could do it until they got sick and tired of it but I didn't want any part of it.

My family and I evacuated early in the morning and we rushed around getting the last things together. I had a mixed feeling of sorrow and anguish as I left. I had a deep stabbing pain in my heart. I sat on the train for about an hour before the actual departure and I had an unbearable feeling that I would like to fly off and go back to my home because that was the last peg of security I had left in California. But I tried to perk up after we got on our way. My family used to go camping every summer when I was a little girl and I had an idea that Manzanar would be something like the camping ground that I had known in the past.

When we got there I found that it wasn't even ready. I thought that Manzanar was located in a very beautiful setting but the camp itself was a horrible place. I didn't have the strength to feel too much of these things as we were herded through the station and tagged like cattle. The dust was two inches thick on the ledges and floor and we discovered that the glass had not even been put in the windows yet. The outside grounds stunk to high heaven because of the buried manure from the past. It was supposed to be a new camp but the place was filthy. That was our official reception to camp. It was amazing that the Army officials could have found such a dump. They must have searched high and low for the dirtiest places they could find for us.

I thought that since all of the Japanese were in the same predicament, they would understand one another and be more tolerant. I idealized camp life as becoming something like a Utopia, but I was sadly disappointed. It soon became a small community full of rivalry and pettiness. Manzanar was a very sad Utopia. The only good thing about camp was that it gave the elders a chance to rest for the first time in their lives. It also broadened certain of the Nisei who were able to do a little thinking, but it ruined most of the group as they learned to grab, grab, grab—whether it was getting into the mess halls or showers first or getting a clothing allotment or lumber. They didn't learn how to share things because their selfish natures really came out in camp. They stuck to their same clannishness. Life went on as usual and they tried to make everything as it was before. They may have been capable of deeper thinking due to the crisis, but I saw little evidence of it. They stressed sports and dances most of all and they were not too concerned about the issues of evacuation and what they were going to do next. Perhaps it was just as well that they didn't think too deeply as they would have gotten even more frustrated. Most of them lost their idealistic belief in America and a lot of them lost ambition. Many of those who had been in school on the coast were not able to continue, so that they became discouraged and they sought outlet in social affairs.

I didn't witness so much conflict between generations because the Nisei seemed to have taken over most of the control. There must have been an undercurrent there because it ended up with the December 5, 1942, riot. I've always sympathized with the Issei and Kibei as the accusation that they were extreme pro-Japanese political individuals was unjust. Culturally the Kibei is broader than the Nisei. He has seen and lived in two different worlds. The Kibei were in a difficult spot after they went to camp. They were very much disliked because of their crudeness in dress as they didn't have the polish of the Nisei. Some really tried to become Americanized but the Nisei refused to give them a chance. The Kibei had gone through some rough times before. Most of them had come back from Japan after completing their education and they had to struggle for existence in the produce markets. They were very isolated in that work so that they were not able to get adjusted into American life so readily. Because of the great cleavages in camp, the Kibei became even more Japanesy. It was more or less in self-defense that they became pro-Japan because nobody liked them and would give them a chance. The really intelligent Kibei were in a hard position, but they really thought that there was a great advantage in being an American citizen and they appreciated it. From this viewpoint they were even more loyal than the Nisei as they had to make a definite choice when they were scorned. The Manzanar flare-up of December, 1942, could have been prevented if the Kibei had been allowed to live in a more balanced society on the coast and in the camp.

Camp life was characterized by going to excess in everything. It seemed that the whole camp had suddenly lost their values and ideals, although most of the families tended to cling together. However, there were many families which were torn apart because of the stresses and strain of evacuation and camp life. Whole families were living in one room and the family control slipped because of the methods of living there. There was no privacy at all. Everything was done community style, so that the parents lost their hold over the children. Fortunately, in our family the youngest child was 14, so that camp didn't deteriorate my family so much. We didn't have any serious problems and the family relationship went along fairly smoothly in spite of crowded living.

I knew that I just could not sit around camp and do nothing for an indefinite period of time. So I got a job in the recreational program for the younger children. At first I was quite happy in camp doing my work with the children, but living close to people gradually got on my nerves. I decided that I could not sit around camp forever, so I began to think of the possibilities of getting out.

Camp life was a waste of time and I'm sorry I ever went to it. There was a little compensation in that I observed and learned a few things. I would have come out of camp with pleasant memories if I had only stayed there for a few months. I was there almost a year and it became very monotonous and boring after the first three months.

In early 1943 there was quite a rumpus over the registration for the Army. I've never been to Japan so I answered Yes-Yes. It didn't disturb me in the least. It disturbed some people who had been to Japan and they didn't hate their relatives. Some of the Nisei were really bitter and they didn't trust this country any more. Many of them were torn two ways between their parents and their ideal of the United States. I could appreciate their problems but my way was clear and I had no mental conflicts about giving my answer. My mother just registered in the same way as her children did and we didn't pay any attention to what was going on after that.

I had decided to leave camp at the first opportunity by the time the registration came around. We talked about relocation among our friends. My mother was opposed to my leaving camp. She felt that she wouldn't ever see me again if I left at that time, but she didn't argue with me on the resettlement issue as she knew that I wanted to get out very badly. What held me up was that I became quite ill during my first few months of camp as the diet was wrong for me and I had diarrhea. I also had a severe case of sinus.

I registered in the employment office to let them know that I was interested in resettlement. The camp authorities were vigorously pushing resettlement by then and they practically chased people out of camp by telling us that we could get good jobs and wages on the outside. They emphasized how friendly the people in the Midwest were and what an advantage it would be to resume the old way of life. I was the first one of my family to resettle, and I left camp in the latter part of March, 1943.

I had read in books what an exciting place Chicago was back in my high school days. There was supposed to be a sort of electrical energy in the atmosphere there. I understood that it was a great big, bustling metropolis composed of people from the four corners of the earth. It was America in the raw. I had read Sandburg's poems about Chicago while in camp and this impressed me so much that I decided that I would like to live in a city which possessed such vitality.

There were about 15 of us who were leaving in the group but not all of them had Chicago as a destination. They were scattering all over the Midwest. My trip out here was a strange experience. The train was my first touch with the outside world and the passengers on it didn't seem to be any different from before. I do admit that I had a marked feeling of self-consciousness and I thought everybody was looking at me. I was expecting some sort of unpleasantness and I was surprised to find that there was none. There were a lot of soldiers on the train and I was frightened of them. However, they treated us very nicely. A few of the soldiers even went out of their way to talk with us. They guessed that we were just coming out of camp but they didn't take it as anything out of the ordinary. In fact, they condemned the California people for treating us so unjustly. They were nice college fellows who had only been in the Army for a short time.

When I arrived in Chicago, I was very disappointed because the city was nothing like Carl Sandburg's poems. The dirtiness of this city sounded exciting in poems but it was a big disillusionment in real life. Everything seemed so grim and cheerless. It made my morale go way down and I felt low, strange, and alone. It was cold that day and the March winds were blowing. I was pretty confused because I didn't know my way around. I didn't want to step out of the station for fear of getting lost so I phoned [one of the church-sponsored hostels] and they sent somebody to get me.

I must confess that I was in very low spirits after the first week in Chicago. I had started out so bravely, but I was really frightened to death after the reality of being here dawned upon me. There was nothing else I could do but make a strong attempt to overcome my natural timidity and strike out on my own because I knew that there was no turning back to camp for me. Those first few nights I almost felt that I had made a mistake in leaving camp, as I realized that things were not going to be so easy for me. I was in a sort of daze but I knew that going back to camp would be cowardly and much less desirable than taking advantage of the new experience facing me. I had left camp with the idea that I would be glad to leave that distorted atmosphere. I admit that I was badly maladjusted in camp, because there was no place that I could really fit into in such a limited community. I was one of the group and yet I felt I was apart from them. I was still able to escape into my books and sort of dreams, but I couldn't do that when I came here because life was real and it went at a much more rapid pace and I had to look after myself or else go under. I went out job hunting after the third day because I had to rest up first. I got my first job through a couple of girls I had known slightly in camp. They suggested that I go along with them to a wholesale book store in order to apply for a position. I was hired but I didn't like it very well. I was very disappointed in that job as I barely made enough to keep going.

My main concern was to get away from the hostel, so I proceeded to look for housing as soon as I got my job. I managed to move in with a girl friend for a month. My sister and brother decided to come out of camp, so I had to start apartment hunting. It was the hardest thing I ever did in my life. After I had been refused a few times, I began to think that it might be racial discrimination, but I wasn't sure. There were some places where I didn't go and ask because I was sure they would discriminate. After a hard time of hunting, I found a place.

Life was much more enjoyable after my brother and sister came out. We had a flat so that we fixed it up. Later on other members of the family came out to join us. The building where we lived was very run down. The landlord had promised to get us a stove, refrigerator, gas heat, and other things but he forgot about these things so we had to use a two-burner stove for some weeks. It was during the summer and it got so hot in the ramshackle building. We didn't have a refrigerator at all. I never saw such poor housing in Utah or California. All that summer we suffered grave inconveniences. Living in such a small place was rather disappointing. We missed our ten-room house on the coast. We came out here expecting better housing conditions but our return to normal life was in cramped quarters and it was hard. We were so dissatisfied with our place that we began to think of moving out. But after we found out how our friends were living, we concluded that we were rather fortunate in having as large a place as we did.

All of my relatives live in 3 of the 14 apartments in the building now. It's a sort of international house. We have Chinese, Filipinos, whites, and other nationalities living there. We get along well with all of them.

The landlord is very nice to us now and most sympathetic toward the evacuees. He is very broadminded in his way of thinking. I think he is a German but I'm not sure. The biggest fault is that he is slow in getting things for us. We don't have much contact with other Japanese in the building as we all go to work. We act cordial to them when we run into them in the hallways. There are no other Japanese living in the block. I like it better that way as I want to get away from that sort of life. In a way, I really was trying to escape the sight of any Japanese faces when I first came out here because they were symbolical of all my shattered life hope and I knew that it would be impossible to ever pick up the pieces again so I didn't want to be reminded about it in any way. I know I am a *Nihonjin* myself but I don't like to be constantly reminded about the fact.

The people out here are more kindly toward us than in California. For instance, every morning there are two American girls who always wait for me to walk to the streetcar. I didn't know them at all until we met on the street. It shows that the Caucasians would be willing to get acquainted with us and progress can be made little by little if we take the time. None of the people in the block seem to resent us since we are so few in number here. I have made a few casual acquaintances in the block and I find these contacts pleasant. It makes the day brighter to start out and nod to the neighbors. It gives me a sort of lift to think that in America it can be done in such times as this. I feel glad that those two American girls would go out of their way to be kind to a stranger.

My first job was very different from anything I had ever done before, so I didn't have the energy to keep up with it. I had nothing definite in mind as far as work was concerned so that was part of the reason for my dissatisfaction. I just wanted to get experience in all sorts of things. My job was in a publishing company where I filled orders. I worked there about 8 months before I quit. I guess I averaged about $30 a week income during this time. The job had started at $22 a week and I was receiving $32 when I left. There was a whole slew of Nisei working out there. I just didn't like the job at all. I knew that I had to work in order to earn my bread and butter but I didn't have any other incentive. I left the job in February.

I got my next job through friends. I had been going to business college after work and I took a concentrated course in comptometry. I got a job in a wholesale dress company as a comptometer [operator]. I was a little ill during that period and unemployed for a few weeks but I began to work regularly again around May or June. This new job was more down my alley and I found it rather satisfying. After a while my eyes began to give out. I went to an optometrist and he urged me to change to a job which would be less of a strain on my eyes. There wasn't anything else I could do so I finally quit in November, 1944. I was making about $35 a week and I thought it was a very good position. I regretted leaving that job very much. I was the only Nisei in the plant and I was getting along well with all of the employees. The more mature workers were very sympathetic and I found them educated and cultured. I found these contacts socially satisfying. I got to know a couple of the workers very well and I went to concerts, symphonies, theaters, and walks with them. I still see them occasionally and they call me up when there's an interesting event in town.

My present job is in a dice factory. I heard about this job and I didn't know whether to take it or not. I didn't think that nice girls should be doing such work but I thought it would be a good experience. I flipped a quarter and I finally decided to take a job there. I had to take some kind of a job as my health was breaking down in the comptometer job and it was necessary to make a change. At the dice company we manufacture straight and crooked dice and cards. About three-fourths of the workers on the manufacturing floor are Nisei. The salaries are very good at that place. I make over $35 a week myself now. I measure the dice and it's rather easy so that I am not exhausted in the evenings.

It worried me quite a bit to be working there at first and I kept it a secret. It seemed to be rather contrary to the Christian principles that I learned in church. I used to think that cards and dice were an awful vice but I don't let it bother me any more. The other workers there are good people and they are honest people. It's sort of fascinating to be among them. Doing this type of work is giving expression to something I always wanted to do. Before I am through, I want to try all kinds of different jobs and I know now that I can do it. I may even work in a tavern eventually just to try it, because that's the real life. It won't corrupt me at all and I think I will be better for the experience. I've lived in a secluded atmosphere most of my life and I have been overprotected. I want to live more of the real life now. My curiosity has been aroused and I would really like to experience some of the things I've read about in novels. It wouldn't even hurt me to work as a cigarette girl. A lot of European refugees who held good positions in Europe are now waiting on tables and doing janitor work and they manage to keep their self-respect so I can do it too. I think that we Nisei are confined in a limited circle of work. We should branch out more and really live like other people.

It doesn't bother me if a lot of Nisei work [at the factory] as I never go out of my way to approach them. They have just as much right to work there as I do. I do notice that the Nisei workers cluster around in groups and that is rather conspicuous. Most of the Nisei at the plant seem to be nice but there are a couple of pretty rough ones working there. These are the fellows who steal marked cards and loaded dice. One of the Nisei girls there told me that these fellows have poker sessions that last for two days at a time, so that's why they don't show up regularly. All of the Nisei are there for the money and none of them expect to be making dice and cards after the war. A lot of the Nisei fellows are getting drafted and some of the others have gone into defense factories since the opportunities are open.

I make enough on this job to live fairly comfortably but I suppose that I am too much of a spendthrift so that my money just slips through my fingers. I make roughly $150 a month, but I only save about $18.25 each month. I pay close to $20 a month taxes. My living expenses come to about $40 a month. On top of that, eating out costs me about $15 or $20 a month as I don't like to eat at home all the time. Entertainment is a big item for me as it runs around $25 a month. Carfare costs an additional $5 or $10. I haven't been spending too much for clothes but it still runs around $20 or $25 a month as I have to get outfitted for Chicago living yet.

It bothers me not to be saving more money. I should have something for the future since my present job means nothing for me. This is the best chance for the Nisei to save for the future but living costs are high too. The Nisei have restricted themselves for so long that they suddenly have found it pleasurable to enjoy their money for the first time in their lives. Before the war money among the Japanese was used for bare living purposes and the Nisei never did get enough of an income to taste the cultural things which are obtainable to most middle-class Americans. The Nisei really want to improve their standards of living and it is ridiculous when stories are passed around that we lower the standards of living when we go into a new area.

I'll probably drift along for a while. I haven't even thought of what I would be doing after the war is over. Of course we can go back to the Pacific Coast now, but I don't think we could resume our former way of living. I just don't care to go back to a Japanese community anymore. My plan now is to get back to my comptometry work eventually as I could earn a reasonably good living in this way and it is a little better than plain unskilled work. I would like to stick to the music field and I just hope that there will be a chance some day to use it.

I would like to see my family get together out here and start some sort of a business so that we can be self-sufficient. It's too risky to depend upon others for employment. Our family group has talked this thing over now and then but no definite action has been taken because we all want to wait a little longer to see how things turn out. We have even considered the suggestion that we go to live in a suburb of Chicago and start a nursery business. My brothers have had a little experience in this type of work and there should be quite a market for it, since the Japanese used to ship a lot of flowers back east. We have also thought of opening up a restaurant some place in Chicago, but we wouldn't restrict it to just the Japanese trade as we could get further if we catered to the general public as a whole. We have thought of this in terms of a large restaurant and not one of those hole-in-the-wall places that the Japanese have.

It is a great problem to work out the economic future for a family as a whole during such a time as this. We just haven't been able to make any definite arrangements other than thinking in terms of possibilities, because my brothers and brother-in-law are being called into the Army one by one. We can't do anything definite without the assistance of the boys in the family. Everything will depend on whether my two oldest brothers will be taken into the Army or not. Naturally my brothers will have to go sooner or later as the war gets more bitter. It's only natural that the Nisei be called upon to do their part. The Nisei would just be fighting as plain Americans and it might help all of our future because they are making a good reputation now.

It is difficult for Nisei to realize how much we have advanced because we are fearful of so many things. We are afraid that we will get our fingers burnt if we get too venturesome. A lot of this feeling of fear is groundless. I think that the Nisei encounter some prejudice out here, but on the whole we Japanese are treated quite well by the Caucasians and it doesn't begin to compare to the Negro problem.

I still don't feel that I have any definite roots in Chicago. I still feel quite unsettled in many ways in spite of the fact that so many of my family members are living here. It's a good feeling to be able to talk over some of our problems with other members of the family and we don't have to make all of the decisions by ourselves. We get a great measure of individual independence so that the family life does not impose upon our individual careers. We all feel that we have something definite to work towards. But it is hard to try out an exact path to follow, not knowing what is going to happen next in things which we have no control over. That is why I just live from day to day.

I've noticed that there are considerable numbers of Nisei out here who are still bitter about the evacuation. I can't understand that because they had been able to get many new opportunities as a result of it. I've always thought that evacuation was a necessity and it will actually turn out to be a blessing in disguise for the Nisei. The future is fraught with grave uncertainties, though, and we can only hope that some of our ideals will be realized. But the great majority of the Nisei seem to be incapable of becoming completely integrated now, so that the process may have to carry on into the next generation. It seems that the Nisei find it impossible to live without their own group now and they insist upon having their segregated dances and affairs regardless of the future consequences. But I still think that it has been a very good experience for the Nisei to come East and they can't help but become broadened a little because of this.

It's no use trying to hide and get lost in a crowd. That is what I have tried to do ever since I came out here. That is the reason why I left camp. I still will continue to do it. But there is no denying the fact that I am *Nihonjin*. I might as well accept the fact because I will never be accepted in Caucasian society on an equal basis no matter how hard I try. Very few Nisei will ever be able to do that. We just have to go along and make the best of things. I don't think that life has cheated me and I long ago gave up wishing I had been born with a white face. I just try to make my life as full as possible and I think that I am making some progress in this. There is no use dreaming that all of the prejudices and discriminations are going to suddenly vanish.

CH-11: COMMERCIAL ARTIST

Male; born in Washington, 1915; height 66"; weight 125 lbs.; unmarried. Interviewed September, 1943. "Purposeful interviews were conducted almost every evening during one week" after "casual contacts" for several months. CH-11 described as "intelligent-looking; sharp-featured; nonaggressive; speaks in a moderate tone of voice; dresses meticulously, and has a wardrobe of very expensive clothes." Although he "may have idealized his former life a little because of his obvious lonesomeness," interviewer felt that there was no reason to doubt that he had experienced most of the things he related." Interviewer refrained from taking many notes in his presence "in order to encourage the free flow of words without any distraction, [but made] extensive notes immediately after the interview."

CAREER LINES

Parental: Both parents from farming class in Japan. Father (born *ca.* 1876) had "several years" of college and mother (born 1886) completed 5-year high school course there. Married before emigration. Father immigrated to Vancouver, B.C., in 1905, thence to Seattle, where his wife joined him in 1913. Father worked for the same Seattle import-export firm (a branch office of a company with headquarters in Japan) continuously from *ca.* 1905 to December, 1941.

Own: Graduated from college in Washington in 1941; summer sessions at various West Coast colleges. Worked as free-lance commercial artist 1936–1941; as packer in Alaska canneries during summers; for a short time as curator at an art museum. Inmigrated to Chicago, March, 1943; and immediately obtained work as commercial artist in an advertising agency. Still held this job at time of interview.

LIFE HISTORY

I don't know much about my family background except for what I picked up casually. I do know that my mother's family held huge tracts of land in Yamanashi *ken.* There were many peasants working the land for her family. My mother lived more or less within her family and her own class of people as that was the thing for her to do when she was young. After the Shogunates were abolished in Japan, the nobility had to enter business life and much of the personal property was taken away from them. My mother's family were of this class, so that throughout the years more and more of the property has slipped from the family hands.

I know less about my father's family. His father was a great man in his community. He was living in the Goshu *ken* in northern Japan, in a rather mountainous country. When I visited there one of the peasants took me on top of the hill and I could see only hills and valleys for miles around. The peasant said that all of this land as far as I could see had belonged to my father's family at one time. I thought it was a lot of land for anybody to own for such a crowded place as Japan. While I was there I looked up some of my father's friends who knew of him, and it made me feel funny because they cried all over the place when they found out that my father was still alive. Evidently he had never kept up his contact with his home village. The family was a sort of seminobility, I think. Father never spoke much of his background because he had more of the western idea that the individual should be judged only according to what he had accomplished by himself.

Dad was going to a college in Tokyo when he was young and my mother's brother was one of his close friends and classmates. One year he brought Dad to his home and he met my mother for the first time. The feeling was apparently mutual so that the brother suggested why not get married? The marriage was soon arranged between the two families.

Dad was in the Russo-Japanese war at the beginning of this century. He was married just before he went off to war. When he came back, he felt very restless and confined in such a small place as Japan. He decided that he would seek adventure in America. At that time the Japanese looked up to America as the most civilized country in the world. My grandfather had an admiration for western civilization and he wanted to make Japan like America in many ways. He was the first one to import Holstein cows for milk into Japan. He also introduced horses into the community and, believe it or not, I saw descendants of these cows and horses when I was in Japan. My grandfather also introduced the first Christian church to his community and that church was still standing when I went there. I don't say that grandfather was an "American" but he did have a very liberal and western outlook on things.

After the Russo-Japanese war Dad was on his own. He had left home when he was 24. Since he was one of the younger brothers, he did not get to inherit any of the family estate but his name was very influential in certain sections of Japan. Dad had not graduated from college in Japan but he had gone several years. He has kept intellectually alive, so that through his own efforts he is one of the better educated Japanese in this country now.

Dad came to Vancouver, B.C., by himself in 1905. He left my

mother with her family and he said that he would send for her as soon as he was established. He did not send for her until 1913, and my mother continued living according to the old Japanese traditional ways of a wealthier family. I think this is one of the main reasons why my mother is more conservative and Japanesy than my father. Dad went down to Seattle and he got a job with the [Z] Company through some family contacts. He soon became a friend of the owner and he has worked in this company ever since his arrival in America. The company was a branch office of an importing and exporting company with the main office in Japan. For quite a while, Dad was living in the home of Mr. [Z] and even after he brought Mother over, they were living there until he could get a home of his own. After that my sister and I were born. My sister is four years younger than I am.[205]

Dad worked himself right up to becoming the president of the company. He sensed that the war was coming on as early as 1939 so that at that time he severed all connections with the foreign branches. He also shifted the personnel around so that there would not be direct contacts with Japan. He retired more or less into the background of the company, so that at the time the war broke out the president of the company was an American. Dad was still the chairman of the board and he continued to manage most of the business. I think that this was probably the reason why he was interned after Pearl Harbor. Dad was released from the [intermountain] internment camp after a short time because his record was as clean as a whistle. It happened that one of my close friends was the chief of investigations of alien properties. This man went [to the internment camp] to see Dad and he checked up with the FBI. There were many other innocent Japanese who were held in internment for months before their hearings came up.

Dad had ups and downs in his business and it was a little tough for him during the early part of the depression. The greatest profit that he made was during the 1920's but he sunk a lot of this back into the business. For a brief time during 1935–1937 or 1938 business was very good but, as war got closer and closer, Dad had to make many readjustments in his business because it was harder to import the goods. The embargoes prevented him from bringing in the usual thing. The firm was closed on December 8, 1941, by the government and reopened for a short while before evacuation in order to clean out the stocks on hand.

[205] According to WRA records, CH-11's sister was born in 1917.

It was too bad that my father had to see all of his life work go to nothing. He had worked hard to build himself up. Dad was probably the most liked person in the whole firm. The Nisei working for him liked him very much because of his liberal attitude. He knew many people in Seattle, both Japanese and Caucasian. Everybody seemed to like him as a friend. In his youth Dad had a reputation of being a very handsome fellow. That's what my mother tells me anyway. He was unusual looking and I don't think he looked like the average Issei. He was striking in appearance, with deep-set eyes and high nose, and he was always well groomed. He spoke English passably well. He had very Americanized ideas and he was definitely not Issei in his thinking. He always told the Nisei that America was their country, and he encouraged them to live the typical American way and not follow the Japanese customs too closely. He said that Japan was changing into a westernized nation anyway and he said that if we followed the Japanese customs like the Issei brought over we'd be way behind the times.

Dad was a very even-tempered person and he rarely exploded. He was never strict with me. He let me do almost what I pleased if I used my judgment wisely. He never insisted that I go into the firm with him like many of the parents did. He said that it would be up to me to decide my own career. He was a little stricter with my sister and he used to set a curfew for her to be in the house at a reasonable hour.

We lived in a fairly large house. It was rented because a Japanese could not own land there and it was hard to get property in their name. Dad never did like to do anything shady like taking out things in another person's name. He was very honest not only in his business life but also in his personal life. A good example of his honesty in business was during the time many companies were sending scrap iron to the Orient. Dad could have made a tremendous fortune after 1937 by exporting scrap iron to Japan but he did not believe in it. He was that much of an American. He said that he could not do it and have a free conscience.

My mother was a different type of personality from my father. She was small and frail and almost physically weak. She is not so broad minded as my dad. She thought too much of her former family status and I don't think she could have made her own life over here as she was too dependent. Mother is much more sensitive to the old Victorian ideas than my father. Dad felt that a man should be judged only on what he had accomplished himself, [but] Mother felt more cultured. That is why she sometimes criticized Dad's Japanese friends who were just ordinary working people. She went to church and she had some Christian friends but on the whole, she held herself a little aloof from the other Japanese. Besides her few church friends most of her friends were from my dad's firm or occasional representatives from Japan. Mother seemed to live in the past. All her happy days were the ones she spent in Japan in her upper-class life.

My parents got along all right but I do not know whether they were ever really happy together. At first I suppose they were in love but they had gone such different paths that their outlook on life was entirely different. It was not a typical Issei marriage in the beginning but the way they lived it soon became like one. They were just used to each other and I never did see much emotion between them, although I am sure that under the surface they do have a deep regard for each other.

I do not mean to say that my father was completely Americanized like a Caucasian American. One of the strong Japanese characteristics that he had was that he definitely made all of the important decisions in the family. Mother never did try to put her foot down on anything but she accepted his decisions. Aside from this Dad was much more democratic than mother, in fact more than most Issei. He adjusted himself very well to any group, especially the working group. He had worked his way up in the business so that he did not hold himself above other workers once he had established himself. He knew almost all the farmers in the communities surrounding Seattle and they all seemed to like him, for they always made a call upon him when they came to town. It is hard to describe Dad's personality. I would say that it was scintillating and he has a sort of contagious smile and a very keen sense of humor. He made friends very easily and he had few enemies.

Dad was not an original pioneer to Seattle, but he was one of the first Japanese to move into the district north of Jackson Street into a residential area. The main Japanese section in Seattle was around Jackson Street but they had been expanding out too, and Filipinos, Negroes, and Chinese were all mixed up in that area. We lived north of Jackson Street because Dad had moved out there in the early days. We only moved about two or three times during all the years Dad was in Seattle.

When I was a child we lived in an average American community composed of all nationality groups. There were only a few Japanese families in our area at that time, so that I never did have many close contacts with the other Nisei in the Japanese sections of town. In our neighborhood there were two gangs of boys and we stuck together in our respective gangs from grammar school right on through high school, college, and up to evacuation. All the fellows of our gang got through high school and about half went on through college to get their A.B.'s. One or two even went beyond that. Everyone of us has traveled around extensively on our own hook and we have seen quite a bit of the country. I do not know exactly what nationality these fellows were because they were a mixture of many European races. We never noticed any difference. We were pals from the same neighborhood and that was all there was to that.

The first time I experienced racial discrimination I was greatly hurt. I was only a young boy at the time and I wondered how come anything like that had happened to me. Our gang was going to go swimming in one of the public pools and when I got to the window they said that I could not go in. My gang came up and asked why. Then the man came out and he said that no Japs were allowed in the pool. I never felt so hurt in my life and all of the color drained from my face. One of my American friends began to cry because he was just as much hurt as I was over the incident. He said that he would never go to that pool again and in all the years that I knew him he kept his word. I have gone to many public places in Seattle and elsewhere, and I've never run up against this sort of discrimination since then. I think that most of the first class places didn't discriminate like this.

We did not pay attention to girls until after we went to high school. After we got to high school, we became girl conscious and we necked around a little bit but nothing serious ever came out of it. About the only girl friend I had then was a full-blooded Hawaiian. I was not especially interested in the Nisei girls, since I would have had to go out of my way to see them, because they lived in a different section of town.

Even in high school, we were more interested in sports and activities like that. We had our own neighborhood team also and I can tell you of one case where we got discriminated against by the Japanese, strange as it seems. It happened that we had a pretty good basketball team and the Seattle *Courier,* a Japanese-owned paper, organized a basketball league. We went to make an application to join the league but they would not let us in because the team was not Nisei. I was the only Nisei on the team and the rest were Caucasian. We were just young boys, so that we got very mad when the *Courier* refused to let us in, so that we free lanced and we made a special effort to play all of the Nisei teams in the *Courier* league. We skunked every one of the teams.

There is not too much to say about my home life. It was not spectacular and we were just brought up like any other children in the United States. Of course we did have some Japanese culture and habits. This was chiefly my mother's idea. Five out of six of our meals were Japanese food and we ate much more rice than bread. I used chopsticks for quite a while but gradually shifted over to knives and forks. In our home we used a mixture of English and Japanese because I did not know Japanese very well. My mother got to understand English a little so we spoke more and more of it to her. Usually she talked to us in Japanese though. The standard of living of our family was probably much higher than that of the average Japanese family on the coast. We lived comfortably and we spent money very easily.

Our home had a fairly good intellectual atmosphere about it. My father was very fond of books and he probably is the widest read Issei in the Japanese language in the United States. He told me once that if circumstances had been different, he would have been a writer. Business was only a second choice but a necessity. Dad was the leader in the writer's group among the Issei in Seattle. He had also many well-known Japanese writers as friends in Japan. He could understand the old literature better than anyone on the coast, so that he was often consulted by professors in the university who were interested in Oriental culture.

I did not have much of a religious life. Both of my parents are Christians but I have never been very devout. I went to church for a while with my gang because the church had a league in sports and we wanted to play in it.

My school experiences were fairly average. In grade school I cut up a great deal with the gang in the classes but I made good grades. A Danish friend who lived next door was the valedictorian of the 8th grade and I was the class president. We had an 8th grade club and our gang held all of the offices. At the same time we monopolized all of the good grades and we were also the outstanding players on the school team. I was the captain of the baseball team. The only way I differed from the rest of the gang was that I learned more toward the arts. The teachers recognized that I was artistically inclined because I was usually outstanding in the art and music classes.

The first day that I was in high school the school paper interviewed me because I was a grade school leader, and I had a record of never cutting a class except for illness. I was interested in going to school and I enjoyed it very much and I did not have any reason to cut. It was always a lot of fun for us.

I went to the [Y] high school from 1929 to 1934. There were only 30 Nisei there, but eventually the school had over 500 Nisei students. I think in 1940 there were even more than that and half of the student body were Nisei. I am glad that I did not have to go to high school with so many Nisei. I concentrated more and more on art and I entered the national high school contests for art students. There was a Chinese student in our class also, and he and another Nisei and I won the first, second, and third places for four straight years. We also won prizes in many other types of contests. I belonged to the art club, German club, and drama. About the time I was ready to graduate from high school, the Nisei there organized a Japanese students club. I did not even know about it until after I graduated. I had a pretty good scholastic standing at the time I graduated, in fact, most of the members of my gang were in the Honor Society with me.

In 1934 I graduated from high school. My father expected me to go to college and he was willing to send me to [an outstanding one]. I wanted to go on my own and work my way through like the rest of my gang was doing. I had saved some money by working during summer vacations and after school by driving a truck for a grocery store. I also had a part-time job for Saturdays managing a district for paper deliveries. I kept this up and did other work all the way through college.

The first year in college I made the best contacts that I have ever made in my life. Two Caucasian boys that I met became what you might call my life-long friends, and I also made other friends who have stuck by me all the way through. When I first got on the campus I was surprised to see an invitation from the Japanese Students' Club but I did not care to join, since I did not know any Nisei in spite of the fact that I had lived in Seattle all of my life. Later on I made attempts to get to know the other Nisei better but I was considered an outsider by them. The other Nisei would all stick in their little cliques and they would not make any attempts to invite an outsider into their group. I never did attend one single Nisei affair the whole time I was in college, not even one of their dances. I got into [a national fraternity and a campus social club] my first year. One of the other Nisei told me that it was impossible to get into that fraternity because they did not want any Orientals; however, I investigated their regulations and it did not say anything about a Nisei and the fellows in the frat welcomed me in. There was one other fraternity that I was rushed for, but the alumni members would not vote me in because I was a Nisei. I felt bad about this for a while but it did not matter much because I was getting into many other campus activities. There were a few other Nisei who were even more Americanized than I was and a couple of them got into frats, but on the whole most of the Nisei stayed at the Japanese Students' Club. They were really not considered a part of the campus life by the Caucasian students, as the Japanese Students' Club was looked upon as a sort of a foreign element on the campus. It was largely the Nisei's fault because they refused to get into the wider campus activities. I quit bothering with them and I stuck with my own gang.

I majored in art right away. After my first year at [college], a well-known artist from Japan came to the United States to lecture at all of the big colleges and universities. He was lecturing on Oriental art. My father knew him fairly well, so that this man asked me if I wanted to go around the United States with him as his assistant. I thought that this would be a wonderful opportunity to see the country so I dropped out of school in order to make this trip. I drove him all over America and I helped him prepare the lectures. I got my expenses and $50 a month. We spent the first six months on the West Coast lecturing at all of the large colleges before we started our loop around the country. I enjoyed the traveling very much but the personality of the Japanese man sort of dampened things. He had funny Issei ideas and he thought I was a child that he could boss around without any consideration for my own individuality. I wanted it to be a purely business proposition but he expected me to be sort of a valet to him. I finally quit on him. He was very much put out at this because I was supposed to go to the Orient with him to conduct an art tour. I gave the job to one of the Caucasian teachers in the art department at [college].

I went back to school in the spring of 1936. Being on the go continuously for one year sort of disrupted my study habits and I got the poorest grades of my life. I almost flunked out. I was restless and I just could not settle down. I also got interested in the women and I horsed around a lot with my pals. The girls that I was going around with were all college girls and there was not one Nisei among them. I had a helluva good time and I went to proms and on hayrides, parties, and cruises.

When I took the Caucasian girls out the only time I felt different was when people would stare at us when we were off of the campus. It was okay on the campus though. The Nisei were the only ones who stared then but I did not mind that. I was infatuated with several of the Caucasian coeds and a couple of them were the same way with me. But nothing serious ever came out of it.

From 1936 until the spring of 1941 I continued at college. I took my time getting through since there was no rush and I enjoyed the college atmosphere. I went to different colleges because of scholarships and then I was invited to special sessions because of my art work. I got one of my scholarships because of the fact that I was a Nisei. It was [at a small liberal arts college], and the emphasis was on International Relations for that session. Then I was [in a college town in California] once and there was a big conference at [the college] during the summer, so I enrolled since I had money to spare. I also enrolled at [another California college] for a summer session.

It was a happy-go-lucky period of my life and I had no responsibilities at all so that I would take my time and take all sorts of trips. I would get an idea that I wanted to spend a winter in California, so off I would go with one of the members of my gang or a college friend.

We never had to worry about money and we stayed in the first-class hotels and ate expensive meals. I was beginning to sell more and more of my paintings. If I was broke while out on the road, I would go to a small restaurant on the highway and offer to paint a picture on the wall or else some signs, and I would get from $5 to $15 for that; then we would go live in style. In Hollywood I would go to [night clubs] and sell a painting to some of the rich patrons who went out to dine. Sometimes I got as much as $100 for a painting and we lived on that.

I heard that a lot of the Nisei were going up to Alaska for the salmon fishing during the time I was in college. I wanted to go to Alaska just to see what it was like so I decided to sign up also. The first time I went was around 1936 or 1937. It was up there that I made the few Nisei friends that I knew prior to evacuation. It was a relief for me to get away from things and live crudely. I made over $200 a month during the short season up there, and I went up five or six summers in all. The salmon canning work was very hard but it was good for me. Another Nisei and I sort of ran the union for the workers there and we made most of the deals for them. The average Issei and even the Nisei were so damned dumb that a few of the more intelligent Nisei had to take over to make the deals for them in order to see that they did not get a lower than standard wage. I was not a union delegate, but we were the ones who worked behind the scenes.

About the time that I was going to graduate I got a job. One day the dean of men phoned me and I thought sure that I was going to get the ax because I was not doing so well with my studies, except in art work. Instead of dropping me the dean told me that he would recommend me to do a special job for the [S] Advertising Agency. It turned out that Mr. [S] was greatly interested in the Nisei so that he gave me the job. He gave me a lot of pointers in commercial art that served me in good stead later. I settled down quite a bit after that though I still liked to have a good time. I used to handle his art work exclusively and after I got out of college in the spring of '41 I made as much as $85 a week during the rush season. We illustrated ads for newspapers, magazines, and pamphlets. I kept on working with the Ad agency from the spring of '41 on.

During the summer of 1941 I also had an extra job. I was the curator of [an] art gallery. All I had to do was to check in paintings, write correspondence, and hang up some of the paintings. I had one assistant to help me. For this work I received $125 a month, besides my regular job in the advertising agency from which I was making anywhere from $200 to $400 a month.

I never saved any money and it just went when I got it. I do not regret it because I had a very good time. The most I ever made in one month before the war was $1,000 but the next two months I did not work much and I made practically nothing so that it averaged about only $330 a month. I worked at home and the only overhead I had was income tax, which was quite a bit. I lived at home but my parents did not need any money at that time, so that I did not contribute regularly to the family expenses. Once in a while I would buy my mother a rug or my dad a collection of pipes or something like that. Occasionally I would bring groceries home. I did not especially have to give my family any money since they did not need anything. My sister was also self-supporting at that time.

I spent most of my money taking the dollies out and living high. I imagine I lived a much more carefree life than most of the Nisei. I often flew to California for a quick trip when I got the urge. I didn't have anything in particular to go for but I just wanted to go and my money went for things like this. Then we would have a big party and I would spend at least $100 on it. Even for hayrides it was expensive, as I would have to charter trucks. We would go to our summer club for a party. I also had a sailboat that I spent a lot of money on. Collecting popular records as a hobby was also another investment. I bought quite a bit of clothes and this also ran into money.

I was not going steady with any girl before the war, but I was infatuated with a Caucasian girl, and I made a painting of her which I still have in my room. She was a wholesome girl and we had lots of fun together but there was nothing serious. Once in a while my dad would mention that I should be getting married one of these days but I never thought about it seriously. I was still at loose ends and I wanted to be a professional bum and go around the world sketching my way.

I had my share of travels I guess. I had even been to Japan once in 1925, only two years after the big earthquake there. Tokyo was still largely in ruins and the reconstruction was going on, so that I did not get a very good impression of Japan. My mother took me and my sister so that we could go to see what her life was like in Japan. I was just old enough to appreciate the visit. I think that mother was the happiest I have ever seen her in that trip. It was not such a happy experience for me. I remember I got into a lot of fights over differences in opinion with the other Japanese kids. I was different from them, and that is why I never made even one friend during the time I was over there. Usually I can make friends easily, but those Japanese kids made fun of me. I was in Japan almost a year but I could hardly wait to get back to Seattle to play baseball with my gang once again. It irritated me the way that the Japanese police officers ordered us around and expected us to jump in a military fashion. I did not understand what they were saying, but I cussed a blue streak in English to them when they shoved me. They thought I was too sassy.

One of the things that depressed me was the poverty in Japan. I was not too young to notice some of that. Even my mother's home was not as much as she had built it up in our minds. To me it just looked like an average American home, even though her family was of the upper middle crust. The girls there were shy and retiring and they did not seem to be natural in their actions. I could not joke with them like I did with the girls in Seattle. Hell, I wouldn't ever think of going there to live permanently.

Just before the war, in November, 1941, I was taking a vacation in San Francisco and all over California and even down to Mexico because I had quite a bit of money on hand from my summer's work and I wanted to enjoy it. I got back to Seattle on December 5. I did not think that a war was going to break out two days after I returned.

December 7, 1941, was a day that changed everything, not only for me but for everybody in this country. I had gone out the night before and it was late when I came home so that I slept most of Sunday. By the time I got up, everybody was running around like mad. I was angry that Japan could do such a thing. It did not seem very sporting to me to make such a sneak attack and I reacted as violently as anybody else. I did not see hardly any of my friends that day since it was so late when I got up. I listened to the radio most of the evening and I did not speak to anyone. I did not know what I was going to do. I thought that it was time for me to go to the Army and fight like anybody else, and I thought about that quite a great deal that night.

The next morning I went to my club on the campus and everybody was running around and talking about the war, so that the atmosphere became infectious with this feeling of tension, suspense, and general excitement. Some of my friends were saying that they were going down to enlist right away. They were Caucasians. I thought about my own position and I wondered what I should do. The more I thought about it, the more I became convinced that I should join the Army too and there was no reason for me to hold back because I was of Japanese extraction. I walked around for about an hour by myself to think it over and then I made my decision. I thought that it was my duty to go and enlist right away. I don't think that it was any high motive that compelled me but it was the general sentiment and the thing to do.

I went downtown to the Army recruiting office right after lunch and there was a long line of fellows standing there waiting to enlist. There was some questions that I had in my mind which I wanted answered before I enlisted. When I got to the sergeant who was filling out the enlistment blanks, he was feeling sort of gruff and irritated because he had worked so hard that day. I asked him what were the possibilities for me in the Army as I told him that I did not want to enlist blindly, as I felt that I had certain qualifications which would fit me to other types of service in the Army. The sergeant suddenly noticed that I was Japanese and he said that I should just sign up now and stop bothering him with all of these questions. He did not say anything about the fact that I was Japanese but I could see that he noticed it. I told him that I could not enlist without having my questions answered and he said that he was too busy and there was a long line waiting, so I stepped out of place to make further investigations before signing up.

The next day I went to see the commandant of the military post that I was once a member of. I had had ROTC training in college and had been stationed at that post for a short time. The commandant was very friendly and he told me all about the details of the routine for enlistment. He suggested that I should sign up for the Army engineers but I felt that there would be little chance for me to get into that. I tried to get into the Army Air Corps the next day but that was out. They said that the quota was filled. The officer said that no Nisei was to be taken in but he could not find any written statement to that effect. I did not press the matter. I ran around for the first few days after the war started without any satisfaction at all. I was a little discouraged, so that I decided to wait a few weeks to think it over. By that time the enlistments into the Army were closed to the Nisei. I tried to get into the Navy and even the Marines, but that was out. They didn't take the Nisei. I soon began to hear rumors that Nisei and Kibei were being mustered out of the service because of the suspicion that they might sabotage the United States because the war was against their parents' homeland. I knew one boy, who was in the Air Corps. But, Washington, D.C., where the brass hats run things, kicked this Nisei out of the Air Corps. When I heard this it hurt me a great deal. There was no reason to it at all because he was just as much a loyal American as any other fellow in that air corps post. These things began to stir up some sort of an insecure feeling in me and I wondered if the Nisei were going to be treated roughly as the war went on. I began to hear rumors that all of the Kibei were being released and I wondered why the Army was doing this, since it would only make them very resentful. Then some Nisei who had gone into the Army before Pearl Harbor as draftees were transferred to different outfits.

Even the Issei, before the war, felt that the Nisei should go into the Army and fight for America and they were quite proud of the fact. It is too bad that things turned out as they did and disillusioned them. My father was fairly agreeable to my idea of trying to get into the Army but I never did tell him that I had gone to about every enlistment station in Seattle and had been turned down at all of them.

The boss at my advertising agency had died while I was on [that vacation trip] so that my job was defunct. I went down [to the agency] about Christmas time to give presents to the girls at the office, and I met Mr. [N], the new boss. He had heard about how I was trying to get into the Army, so that he was very much in favor of me. He said that he had seen some of my art work and he liked it. He told me to come down and he would give me work on a free lance basis. It was during the Christmas season, and I got so busy that I had to hire two assistants. Around New Year's is the biggest season in the advertising business because there is a lot of work getting ready for the new spring season. When Dad was interned in March, 1942, I had to give up this work as I felt that I should devote my attention to his business.

It dawned upon me about that time that the Nisei were going to be included in the evacuation. We had never thought much about it and when restrictions came in, we did not think they were legal. The Nisei in our neighborhood got hold of "China buttons" and we went around just as much as before. I did not feel so good about wearing a China button but I felt that it was justified because curfew was just unfair. The Chinese in Seattle were pretty sympathetic to Nisei. The thing that got me the most was that the Italians and Germans did not have such restrictions.

In the meantime my father lost heavily in his business. It had fallen off sharply even before the war. Dad knew that the export and import business was shot, so that he opened up a small department store just before the war. It was the best equipped Japanese store in Seattle with all modern fixtures in it. Everything was on the cash basis because no Caucasian companies would extend credit. He sunk a lot of money into it and there was a grand opening for the store. All of the big shots in the Japanese community came and the big Caucasian companies gave away favors to the new customers as advertisements. This was on December 2, 1941. The store was open for only five days when the war came. It was a total financial loss. That store was closed four months before the Treasury Department let us open it up in order to sell the fixtures and stock.

Mother was very bitter about this huge loss. She said such things as, "Why should everything happen to us and why should all of these restrictions be put against the Japanese?" Dad was philosophical about the whole thing, and after the store had closed, he said it was the first vacation he had in 25 years. Deep inside though I think he was hurt and depressed to think that his business which he had built up had smashed about him.

One by one his business associates were being rounded up by the FBI. Dad was amazed that he was not taken sooner, even though he knew he had not done anything wrong. Everybody thought that they would get to him soon because of the business he had been in. It was

March when Dad was finally taken. One morning three FBI agents came to our house and they proceeded to tear the house upside down in the search for incriminating evidence. We did not have anything of contraband nature in the house. I had the only thing which the FBI took. It was a hunting knife that I had used as a Boy Scout in my younger days and I had not even given it a thought. They also took my movie camera but it was no damn good since it was so antiquated and I was just keeping it as a souvenir. The FBI man was a decent fellow and while he was searching my room he told me that he was sorry that such a thing was happening and that I should ease my mother's worry as much as possible. He said that if my father was innocent, he would be released soon. I admired the way he did his duty. After that they took my father off to jail. My mother was frantic about what had happened for she did not understand it too well and she insisted that I go visit my father that evening at the immigration station. I took his pajamas and other things to him. My father was there for two months, so that I visited him every day. My mother took him Japanese food. Finally my father was shipped to the Montana internment camp. We communicated with him a lot but all of the letters were strictly censored.

We were the only Japanese store in Seattle that had Federal agents there around all the time to protect us in the business deals. I did not know a thing about my dad's business so that I don't think that I was very useful around there. However, I did work hard—harder than I had ever worked since going to the Alaska cannery. The Jews used to come down and they offered us very cheap prices for things. I had to bargain with some of them and all I could get for a $100 cash register was $10. When they would not even try to give us some sort of fair deal, I would send these Jews to the Treasury Department man in our store and he would try to get a fair price for us. A lot of people came into the store and they admitted that they wanted to buy big cases of stuff cheap so that they could resell it. Dad only managed to salvage about $4,000 out of his total investment. I can't tell you the exact size of my father's business but I do know that it was quite a large concern.

I had to assume more responsibilities for the family after Dad was interned, but my sister paid all of the living costs as she was working. We became closer as a family unit than ever before. Dad had an insurance policy and we kept the payments up on it. I did not have any savings at all so that most of this burden was placed upon my sister. I did not feel so good about this and I realized rather late that I should have taken more responsibility before the war and should have at least built up some sort of reserve.

As the evacuation day drew closer, a lot of the Nisei took up drinking and gambling because they had time on their hands. This was a foolish thing to do and I did not think that they were being very wise in going to such excesses like that. I took a drink now and then but never to excess. I continued to see my close Caucasian friends and they were exceptionally good to us and they helped out a great deal. They did everything in their power to help out with our storage. At the present time all the things we have are stored in their homes. There is no doubt that our morale was dampened considerably with such uncertainty all about us. I had no fears of the future but I did not have any hopes either. We just lived from day to day and wondered what was going to happen next.

When we left for the Puyallup Assembly Center we thought that we were going to be taken there for the duration. That did not raise our spirits any. It was raining the day that we left Seattle so that this made me feel worse. Just before I had to evacuate I looked around for the last time in Seattle and I felt like I was leaving something that was very dear to me. Beyond this sentimental feeling I was rather anticipating what was going to happen in camp. It was an adventure to look forward to and something that we could develop although I did not know what. I felt to myself "Gee whiz, I'll probably meet a lot of pretty Nisei girls there for the first time in my life and then I can have a lot of fun." I knew what Puyallup was like as I had been there to the fair grounds many times before.

When I got to the camp I was astounded at the flimsy buildings that the people were expected to live in. There was nothing in the room except a stove. Immediately upon arrival I got busy building furniture like everybody else. I did this for the first two weeks there as I wanted to make our shack more livable and artistic. I did not even think of getting a job like most of the Nisei. I knew that I could get an art job easily after a while.

Finally the five commercial artists in camp got together, and got a space for an art department. After much finagling around, the WCCA put us on the payroll as senior recreational leaders. We were listed as professional workers for $16 a month. We started poster work right away and in a short time all of the social activities in the camp became dependent upon us for art work. We put all our efforts into decorating the recreation halls for dances and also made artistic signs for people and departments. We became well known in the camp among the Nisei because we also did war work for which we received publicity. We did some posters for the War Bond drives in Seattle. We also made the signs for the town of Puyallup for its Fourth of July parade. We got big write-ups in the [West] Coast papers because there was a human interest angle to the story that interned Nisei had such a loyal interest in the United States war effort. Besides this, we carried on some of the cultural aspects of art and we even sponsored art exhibits which were a big success in camp. There were a number of fine artists in camp and they contributed their work.

I met a lot of Nisei girls for the first time in my life and they were not bad. They were more sociable in camp than on the outside. I think that they made more of an effort to be friendly with other Nisei and they tried not to have such small close cliques. Everybody in camp was in the same boat and former social standing did not count anymore. I still did not feel completely at ease among the Nisei girls because there seemed to be something different about them. Fortunately I got to know a Eurasian girl and I ran around with her most of the time.

I did not enter any of the political activities in Puyallup. I thought that the WCCA men in camp were the dumbest saps I ever ran across. Some of the personnel was not so bad but the rest were WPA workers and they certainly were ignorant. I don't know how they got their jobs. They must have been either bums or political grafters before. They guy at the head of the art department and the newspaper was the most hated man in camp because he was so dumb that he censored everything and he was always suspecting the Japanese of being up to some subversive activities. He would even spy on us when we had our bull sessions at night in the art department in order to get some evidence, but all he ever heard was talk about girls or something like that.

I have to admit that I had a helluva lot of fun in the assembly center and it was a relief from the strain of evacuation when we had to sell out everything and uproot ourselves. My Caucasian friends [brought] me gifts at the gate but I did not see them as much as before. I missed them but I merely attempted to adjust myself to the people in camp. Japan still remained a foreign country to me and I did not give a God damn what happened to it. In a way I think that my feelings tended to become even more Americanized after I went to camp because I missed the freedom I had before.

I suppose that I did not give a damn about the outside world after the first week I was in camp. I thought that I would not see it again for a very long time. I don't think I even paid much attention to the progress of the war although I did read the headlines of the paper occasionally. I felt that I did not have much of a future anyway. Some of the fellows I knew were thinking of getting out but I did not give it a thought. I was having too good of a time running around and I did not get over this until my Eurasian girl friend left camp. She got to go back to Seattle. When she left, I really felt the injustice of the whole thing and I wished that I could go back to Seattle too. I did not think that it was fair that they would allow one person to go back to Seattle just because that individual had 50 per cent less Japanese blood in her. I thought that the Nisei should be judged according to their mental attitudes and loyalty toward this country.

I did not prepare much for leaving Puyallup. One day I just packed up and off we went to Minidoka. My mother and father worried and fussed around a great deal and it took them about two weeks to get ready. We were herded like cattle into an antiquated train. It was hot and dirty that day and we had a miserable trip.

The first thing that impressed me [at Minidoka] was the bareness of the land. I never saw anything like it. There wasn't a tree in sight, not even a blade of green grass. Coming from the northwest where there were a lot of green fields and forests, the sight staggered most of us. On top of that we had huge dust storms which made life miserable. There were no toilets or showers in operation, so that the sanitary conditions were very bad. The barracks were unfinished. There is no need for me to mention the food; it was fit for a pig and that's all.

There was a sign shop already established there when we arrived. We signed up also, and after a time we got one of our gang in as foreman. I would say that we made over 100,000 signs during the time we worked. We did this for $16 a month too. We tried to get a professional rating of $19 a month but this was not successful at that time. We found out that the WRA officials were of a much higher caliber than WCCA.

Soon after we got into Minidoka many of the Nisei started to go out to do farm work in Idaho. Many of the Issei also went. I think that the fact that many of the evacuees both Nisei and Issei were able to make money on the outside had something to do with the more patriotic response of Minidoka during the registration for the Army.[206] There were hundreds of people who went out to do farm work in September. About the latter part of that month our whole sign shop decided that maybe we should go out too. It was the thing to do and we got the fever.

One day a man came around with an offer that he would pay 12 cents a sack for picking potatoes. This was two cents a sack more than the price offered at any other place so that our art department figured we could make money at it and have a lot of fun even if we did not have any farm experience previously. The farm was owned by two young brothers. They seemed to be swell fellows, so that we decided to sign up with them. We told the WRA that we were going and they gave us the permit. There was one fellow in our art department who did not want to go, so we left him to carry on the work in the sign shop. I packed everything to take along as I did not know how long I would be working. Besides my personal belongings I even took the cots, mattresses, and blankets. Besides that we raided the sign shop and took whitewash, brushes, tools, nails, and anything else that we thought might be needed. We loaded all this on the truck and hid it under our baggage. It was a 200-mile drive to the farm.

When we got there we were amazed at the tumble-down house that the farmer lived in. We whitewashed the walls, cleaned off all of the rough spots, drove in the nails, hung up a few pictures, and brightened up the place considerably. After it was finished our attic dormitory looked better than the home downstairs. The brothers were amazed at the change which we had made. We worked a total of 10 days for them and I got a check of $90. Besides picking potatoes I also drove a truck. I could have made much more if I worked harder. It was backbreaking work and I was soft. One thing that I didn't like about the place was that it didn't even have a bathtub or a shower. Another thing that really got me down was that the flies were so thick that they got in our food. It was nothing to find flies in our soup. We paid 50 cents a day for our food. After the second day of working we were pretty demoralized and one day we decided that we were going to quit. There was no potato picking that day, so that

---

[206] Minidoka had a very low proportion of "disloyals" at the time of registration. Only 4 per cent of its adults were transferred to the segregation center, and over 300 young men (21 per cent of those eligible) volunteered for induction in the weeks following registration. "With less than 7 per cent of the total male citizen population in [WRA camps], Minidoka accounted for 25 per cent of all Army volunteers." Thomas and Nishimoto, op. cit., p. 66.

we had a big bull session and I was appointed to inform the farmer that we were going to leave. I told him that we were not fitted for farm work as we were artists. He wanted us to stay until the end of the crop as he said that he would not be able to get other workers and he would lose everything if we left. He said that he would even give us our meals free or a raise of one cent per sack at the end of the season, whichever was the best deal for us. We went upstairs again and talked about it long into the night. Finally we decided that we would stick it out. I was glad that we did because it gave us a certain satisfaction to realize that we had accomplished something and also helped the farmer to save his crop.

One Saturday we decided that we were not going to work, so we hitch-hiked a ride to [a near-by town]. It was the first town that I roamed around in freely since May [1942], and there is something about it that I can't describe. We ate the most expensive meal we could buy at the restaurant. While we were there we had a rather unpleasant incident. An Indian came in and he started to call us filthy Japs and every other name he could think of. We did not want to get into any kind of brawl because we knew it would create bad publicity for the Nisei and we would always be blamed. The Indian got pretty nasty, so that the manager finally kicked him out. This was the first taste I had that the town was hostile. I was angry that I was being treated differently, as I had never experienced this hostile feeling before. When we went outside the restaurant and stood on the corner an old man came up and he spat at us and called us dirty Japs. Then a car came by and a person yelled "Japs." We went to a show and the manager wanted us to sit in a separate place apart from the other people but we would not do this. These experiences dampened my spirits, and I did not quite know what to make of it, though I did manage to dismiss the whole thing later as an example of how provincial some Americans were. We did not go to any bars for a drink in town as we felt that it might create more trouble. We bought a lot of cans of beer which we took back to drink in the seclusion of our room on the potato farm. One of the fellows wanted to go look for a "cat-house" but we talked him out of it because we did not think that it was the thing for him to be going to prostitutes when the town was so hostile.

We were certainly glad to get back to camp. I had $60 in hard cash burning a hole in my pocket but no place to spend it. We decided that we would never again go out to do farm work because it was too hard and dull work. The very day we got back a Nisei came up to me and he said that he had gone to [a larger town]. He told me that the best sugar-beet contract could be obtained there. We started to figure it out and it looked like we could make about $10 a day. There was also a fairly large town near by and we were dying to have fun and spend some of our money. So in spite of our resolution not to do farm work again, we were off two days later for [this town].

The contract for topping sugar beets called for $30 an acre and there were 10 men on our crew. None of us had ever done the work before but the first day we made $9 a piece. We thought that this was pretty good and it wasn't as hard as potato picking, but I suppose we weren't serious enough about our work and so we broke the contract. One by one the fellows in our crew went off to pick carrots because that work was even easier and it paid by the hour. In a short time there were only four members of our original crew left so that the farmer got angry and he fired us for breaking our contract. It was our own fault because we were trying to get too much and we did not care about the work. It was Thanksgiving Day when we arrived and there was a big dance that evening, so I took a girl who had cooked for us in the FSA camp to this affair. The girls our gang took all had corsages and we were dressed to kill, so that it looked very conspicuous at the dance since most of the Nisei were more casually dressed. That dance was a fitting climax to the fun we had at [this town].

By the time we got back the Nisei were beginning to resettle in larger and larger numbers. It was around Christmas time and I began to get the itch to leave also. I wrote to a couple of advertising firms in Chicago. Two offers were sent to me but I could not even consider them because I had no transportation money. My mind was not fully made up to leave anyway, as I was having a lot of fun with a girl friend. The bug to leave finally got into me after more and more of our art staff left, and my girl friend said that she was leaving soon also. I wrote back to Chicago about the job offers but they were filled by this time so I was out of luck. One day, around February, I decided definitely to leave, so I borrowed some money from my parents in order to pay my transportation and have a little to live on while I went job hunting. I didn't even have a permit to leave camp indefinitely but I used a short-term leave that had been granted me to go to Spokane for a job interview. I just got on a train and came to Chicago as it was the easiest way to get around the red tape.

I had talked to a representative from the American Friends' Service committee before leaving camp and he told me that I could go to the hostel which was getting under way. I was the first one from Minidoka to be assigned to go to the hostel. When I got to Chicago I was asked if I would mind turning my space over to a Nisei family. I agreed since I figured I could get a room easily. I moved to a YMCA hotel and got a room there.

The first two days in Chicago I made a few preliminary investigations of art possibilities and also looked around the town. I went to see the art director of the *Chicago Tribune* the third day I was here to ask him if there was a chance for a job but he did not have an opening. I put in an application at various agencies but I did not get any response right away. After the first week here, the art director of the *Chicago Tribune* phoned me and he said that there was an opening with the [T] corporation. The company had an advertising department and there was a job for an artist there. I talked to the manager and he offered me a job at $140 a month after seeing some of my work. I did not think that this was much of a salary but I decided to take it temporarily since my money was running low. While I was looking for a job, there was nothing in sight but as soon as I landed a position, all sorts of job openings developed. Some of the offers were very good, so I told my boss that I could not turn them all down since the salary was much better. After the first week of work he raised me to $175 a month and at the end of March I was raised again to $200 a month. I thought this wasn't so bad since it was better than what most Nisei were making. I figured that it was pleasant work and there were excellent chances for further raises, so I decided to stick it out. In April I got another raise to $225 a month and in May this was raised to $300 and now I get $87.50 a week. This amounts to around $368 a month roughly. It is the ceiling wage that I can get.

My title now is the art director of the advertising department and there is a manager above me. The only way I can get another raise is to get five more artists under me and this may happen by November or December when the Christmas season gets into full swing. I do quite a bit of the art layout for our department. Recently we put out a line of [products], so I had to design the containers. All of us plan the campaign together as there are about five workers in our department now. During the business part of the rush season we will hire a maximum of 50 workers. When it reaches that figure I'll have a good job. The postwar work prospects are fairly good but there is an indefiniteness about it. My biggest and only fear that I have is that I may possibly get squeezed out of a job. You know how it is when there is one Nisei fighting for a job against 10 Caucasians, there is going to be a tough time for him to keep that job. I'll have to be a lot better than the rest of the skilled commercial artists coming back from the Army.

The working hours that I have in my job are very pleasant. I only work seven hours a day and I have a five-day week. Sometimes I work late in the evenings depending upon the particular job I am doing. We get a generous salary and at the end of the year there is quite a large bonus.

I like the other workers and I get along pretty good with them. They never notice that I am of Japanese ancestry and they are friendly. Some of them are helping me to look for an apartment now. The only thing is that they have expensive tastes. Some of our office workers live in penthouses and belong to country clubs. They must have money of their own because even with their large salaries they could not live in such style. I go to lunch every day with one of the woman advertising managers who is about 35 years old. My secretary also goes to lunch with us. I've also had some social contacts with the other workers at the firm. I have been invited occasionally to their homes. The company has a pretty fair opinion of me and through them I have run into a lot of good job offers. The firm asked me if I knew of any Nisei who can fill them, but I really don't know any competent Nisei since my contacts among them have been limited.

I don't stay in the office all the time as I travel considerably for the company throughout the Middle West, down to Kentucky and east to New York. I go to Iowa and Kentucky quite often. The company sends me to make certain business contacts with our printers. We do a lot of catalog work on the side and recently the company published a catalog of its own. We have also done some work for some of the big mail-order companies on the side.

I am not thinking of changing my own job in the immediate future since I think that there are quite a few possibilities in the work I am doing at the present time. The way I look at it is I am doing the type of work I want to do and I don't like to look to the future too much, as there is no use of building up hopes too high. I do some art work on the side and I suppose I could sell some of the paintings anywhere from $7.50 up to $25 but I don't try very hard, as I do it chiefly for my own satisfaction.

I think I know a few more Caucasians in Chicago than Nisei. I only know about 20 Nisei here. Maybe not even that many. Most of those I know, I met in camp. I've been around with one or two Nisei girls since coming here.

There is nothing much I can say about my sex life. Like many fellows who went to Alaska, I went around with a gang upon our return to civilization, and we made the rounds of the prostitutes. I don't particularly care for prostitutes as this sort of relationship is not very artistic. I am able to sublimate my sexual desires into other more wholesome channels, chiefly my art work and other interests. I think that I am eventually going to get married, so this sort of thing does not worry me too much. Since I have been in Chicago I have not visited any prostitutes although I do know that the district is on [X] Avenue. I also knew of several places in camp but I never visited them. I've had my share of girl friends but most of it was nice and clean.

I had been thinking about going to some kind of night school soon in order to occupy myself more constructively during the evenings. I only need a few more hours of credit for my master's degree and I feel that I might as well finish it up. I don't go to church. I don't belong to any clubs and I have no interest in politics. Most of my leisure time is spent in visiting or reading.

I've been trying to find a suitable apartment here for my family. As soon as I can do this I will wire them and they will come right out. I would like to get my family out as soon as possible because I really do miss the family life. I want a home to come back to at night and not just to a room. I know that my parents would like to be independent once again and not have to be supported by the government although they may be lonesome for a while. They realize this but I think that my father will be able to make sufficient contacts among the Issei who are already in Chicago. It will be a little harder for my mother but as long as we are all together as a family we could get along and it certainly will be a happy reunion.

For a while I even thought of buying a home out here, perhaps in one of the suburbs in Chicago. But this is a little too expensive. I don't know how long I'll be in Chicago. On that basis, it is too temporary a thing to sink a lot of money into a house. I will have to have an initial outlay of $2500. However, I don't have that much money, so it would be out. But I will have to consider something like this if I can't find an apartment.

I should be saving some money but I just don't seem to be able to. I've thought of budgeting my money but this is too much trouble. Usually at the end of the month if I have any money left I send my folks something that they may want in camp. I just don't seem to be able to save although I know I could do it if I made an effort, but my money comes to me pretty easily so it goes the same way. For example, I made over $350 last month but my living expenses are pretty high and I don't think that I squander my money. Last month I was paying $20 a week for a small suite of rooms, however, I moved to a cheaper room at the beginning of this month. So last month rent alone cost me about $90. Then my food bill is pretty high as I eat out and I like steaks. As a conservative estimate let's say that I spend about $2 a day or $60 a month for food, then you have to add $25 extra because I take people at the firm out for lunch pretty often. That alone amounts to $175 a month and that only takes care of the barest necessities of living. On top of that I spend quite a bit on dates and things and the rest of my money goes. For example it costs me from $5 to $10 a date and I go out on about one or two dates a week, so that's about $40 more. Then I buy cookies to put into the cookie jar at the office and this runs about $10 a month. Everybody in the office takes turns in doing this. Then I borrowed quite a bit of money from my parents, so I send them about $25 a month and about $25 worth of stuff that they need. On top of that there are other expenses like clothes, and I have been thinking about buying a $105 suit at a reduced price. Then I buy some books every month and also some art equipment so that after I get through doing this my money is gone. I even get broke sometimes before pay day which is twice a month.

My attitude toward this country has never changed and I am still a staunch American citizen. I don't know where I stand in the draft right now. I really don't care. Once I get my family established I won't mind going into the Army. However, I do not feel like volunteering right now as I did try at one time. Maybe this is a selfish attitude but I can't help that. Even among the Caucasians, patriotism only comes after you get what you want yourself first. Not many men really want to go into the Army and that is why they have a draft system. I would say that most of the men only go in because they have to and I certainly am not different from them. I felt differently before evacuation but I did not have family responsibility then. Things have been pretty well shaken up since then and there is a lot of resettlement work that I want to get finished first. I don't consider myself any more patriotic than the average American. Right now there is not much of a democracy here in this country, but I like the American way of living. Everything else is foreign to me and I wouldn't give up my American citizenship for anything.

I don't know much about my own future but I am not confused by it. I want to have some position in the American society. By that, I don't mean some height that is too high for me, but I would like to become fairly well established as an artist. I am not satisfied with the progress I have made [but] I think that I am making pretty good adjustments now and I won't have a single problem after I get my family resettled out here.

CH-64: CIVIL SERVANT

Male; born 1914; height 64"; weight 129 lbs.; married, 1942. Interviewed August, 1945. Described as a "well-proportioned and neatly dressed, rather quiet, very friendly" young man, who was "very cooperative" with the interviewer, and who showed "keen insight" into his own problems and an understanding "of the purpose of these case documents."

CAREER LINES

Parental: Father (born *ca.* 1878) and mother (born *ca.* 1888) were from the farming classes in Japan; neither had had more than 4 years' formal education. Father emigrated to Hawaii "in late 1890's" as a contract laborer; inmigrated to San Francisco in 1906; worked for a few years with Japanese labor gangs; then opened his own barbershop in Sacramento. Mother immigrated from Japan as picture bride in 1913. Both parents died from tuberculosis in 1931.

Own: Graduated from junior college in Sacramento in 1935, and attended business school during this same year. Worked as farm laborer during the summers of 1930–1932; as part-time and for a short period full-time, sales clerk in a Japanese-owned shoe store, 1930–1934. Clerk under NYA while in junior college; clerk for Japanese lawyer, 1936. Entered California state civil service in 1937, starting as a junior account clerk at $80 a month, and after passing several promotional tests, worked in a supervisory capacity for three and one-half years, until suspended by the State Personnel Board in April, 1942. Inmigrated to a Midwestern town to attend a liberal arts college in October, 1942, and received his A.B. in 1944. At the time of the interview, he was making plans for graduate study.

My parents were originally from the Hiroshima *ken* in Japan. My father was not a very educated man. He only attended 4 years of formal school and that was the same level which my mother achieved. I know that his family did have some property in Japan because I was supposed to have inherited some of it. I think I still am the heir to it.

My father came to the United States by way of Hawaii. He went to Hawaii late in the 1890's as a contract laborer. I know that he traveled around with Japanese labor gangs. He picked up some extra money by cutting the hair of his friends and in this way he acquired barber training. In 1906, my father arrived in San Francisco just after the earthquake. He must have accumulated a little savings because he started to write letters back to his relatives in Japan to arrange for a *baishakunin* as he wanted to get a wife.

My mother came to America in 1913 as a picture bride and it did not take her long to get disillusioned with her position in life in this country. She later said that Dad had exaggerated his economic position. There were five boys in all born to my mother at intervals of two years. One of the Issei women later told me that my mother had drunk something in order to become sterile after the arrival of the fifth son.

An old man who came from another province in Japan became a sort of godfather to our family. He took a great interest in our welfare, and later he took over the responsibility for the children. He was the owner of a small store, and I was born next door to it in 1914. He adopted me sort of and he became important in my family life later on.

My father's barbershop was located in the center of the Sacramento Japanese community. Surrounding us were Japanese bathhouses, boardinghouses, and restaurants. Near by were the so-called slums of the city, and it was a usual sight to see the inmates of the brothels soliciting on the streets or from the windows. There were third-grade saloons and pool rooms all around the edge of the district which catered to transient Caucasians, Mexicans, Filipinos, and Negroes. Some of the small Japanese businessmen catered to these groups but most of their businesses were for the Japanese residents. All of Dad's trade was from Japanese, but he had a few transient Caucasian customers because his prices were a bit lower than the Caucasian barbershop. He only had two chairs. For a time we had one pool table in the rear room, but this was eliminated when we had to use it for living space as the boys came along.

We just had two rooms in the back of the barbershop and seven of us lived there. There was only two large double beds and we were quite cramped. We had practically no ventilation or light. I never knew what it was to have a real bathroom. There was a little corridor leading from our dark kitchen to the Japanese boardinghouse which had a bath house behind it. The whole family used to take a bath there every night. Us kids used to have a very good time. All of us would go sit in the large community tub and talk to each other for hours. It was the regular custom of all the Japanese families in the block to come here for baths.

Up to my thirteenth year, Dad was a heavy drinker. There were many nights in which he would stagger home so drunk that my mother would have to put him to bed. This was always distressing to me. He used to go drink with his old Japanese cronies at one of those Japanese beer parlors, and there were quite a few who had come from his province to America with him, so they got together to discuss the homeland among other things.

My father was a very dominant person. He never wanted to be crossed in anything. He would fly into a terrible rage if his absolute authority was questioned. There were many quarrels between my parents whenever my mother said anything contrary to my father's wishes. There were numerous occasions when he beat her with a broomstick. When I was a child, I used to sleep between my parents, and these quarrels which took place between them were very unpleasant to me. Not all picture-bride marriages turned out badly, but in my parents' case it just did not click.

Dad was never mean to me. I don't recall ever being beaten by him, although my younger brothers did get beaten, but not very often. I just could not do any wrong in his eyes because I was the oldest son and destined to carry on the family name! He tried to give me the best that he could afford. He never bought my mother anything except a diamond engagement ring eleven years after their marriage. My mother was quite proud of this ring and she gave it to me shortly before her death. When I was ten years old, my father bought me a $15 professional catcher's mitt when that money should have been used to purchase food for the family. I was considered a coming ball player by the Issei sport fans, and my first ambition was to get into the Pacific Coast league. Dad was proud of my ability in baseball so he encouraged me in every way. I was never bitter toward my father because he treated me so well.

I accepted my superior position in the family without questioning. I used to get very angry when any of my brothers interfered with me. I never spoke gently to them but I always used a dominating tone in the attempt to enforce my will. I was just following the pattern of my father and my brothers seemed to accept it until they got a little older.

My mother had to work in the barbershop in her spare time and she must have worked twelve or fourteen hours a day in order to accomplish all of her duties. My mother had a lot of common sense and she always had a great interest in me. She tried to impress me with a sense of responsibility toward my younger brothers and to lead an exemplary life. One thing which was hammered into me was that I should never do anything which would bring discredit to the family name. Mother always said that I should consider other people's rights and that selfishness was a poor trait. She also emphasized that I should always try to become expert in whatever I set out to do. One thing I regretted was that none of us helped her around the house very much after she became ill.

At home we generally ate Japanese food and we had rice twice a day. For breakfast we ate the regular American dishes, but in the afternoon we had our *ochazuke* and *tsukemono*. In the evenings we usually ate raw fish, fried fish, and other Japanese delicacies. One of the things that my brothers and I refused to eat was green vegetables and my father backed us up whenever my mother scolded us for that. However, we did drink a lot of milk.

My parents used Japanese in conversation to each other and to us since they didn't know any English at all. My father subscribed to two Japanese language newspapers and they were able to read the *kana* part of it. Our Japanese was the rough Hiroshima dialect and we distorted it by mixing in the English words we had picked up in the public schools. [During our childhood], my brothers and I could not speak either Japanese or English proficiently but we gradually began to stress English more and more. My father was able to understand a little of this because of his limited contacts with Caucasian customers in the barbershop. When my brothers and I spoke to each other and to other Nisei, we used this hybrid language of mixing Japanese words and phrases with our atrocious English. We would use a lot of expressions like you-*ra* and me-*ra*. Our parents were shocked with our poor Japanese, but we thought that it was sissified to speak in pretty

Japanese, so we picked up a lot of the vulgar dialect from the Issei bachelor men.

My parents contributed to the Buddhist Church, but they were not religious themselves. They didn't care what religion I believed in and they said that I could go to any church of my selection. I started to attend the Japanese Christian Church.

One Japanese custom which was stressed in our home was the New Year's feast. We always looked forward to this annual event as New Year's was the day when we had the best food of the entire year. My father would always place two large *mochi* with a tangerine on top on the barbershop table. Japanese characters would be pasted on the mirror. On our front door, we would have pine boughs hanging. Many years later I found out that this was done in order to offer gifts of thanks to the local patron gods. This tradition had been followed in the *kens* in Japan and all of the homes in Sacramento followed this practice, especially in the Buddhist homes. There were not many Christian Issei in our block. It was the New Year custom for the head of the families to go around and visit all of his friends during the first week of New Year's. My dad always closed his shop for three days and he would be drunk day and night. My brothers and I were inclined to be shy and we preferred to remain at home and eat instead of visiting our friends' families. All we did that day was to get up and eat the first thing in the morning, go to movies, come back to eat, go out and play, and then come back to eat some more. We had about ten times as much food in the house as we needed and we always hated to see that day end. We even had three or four cases of soda pop for the day.

Twice a month the Japanese community had Japanese movies. They would show us the movies of brave samurai killing off a hundred enemies and that really fascinated us. But we were always disappointed because only half of the picture was shown one night and the other half would be devoted in presenting a sentimental and weepy style of Japanese movie. We had to go two nights in a row to see a complete samurai picture. One thing I distinctly disliked was when they showed the Japanese flag over the battleships and the Nisei boys would yell and cheer. I never did do this but I don't know why. As we got older we went more and more to the American movies. We learned more about Japanese national and local heroes in our home life. My dad used to tell me stories of old Japan samurai heroes during the feudal days and I used to enjoy listening to stories about the battles and the rescue of the downtrodden.

Dad never mentioned his own background or the reasons why he migrated to this country. Whenever I became curious and directed some queries about his past life, he would become reluctant and suddenly break off the discussion. Once in a while my mother let slip that my brothers and I should feel very lucky to be living in this U. S. as we would have led a very difficult life back in Hiroshima *ken*. She said we would have had to go out and work in the farms instead of having the opportunity to go to school like in this country.

I can always remember that there was a strong sense of family responsibility with us and we accepted the fact that it was our duty to look after each other. This was rather inconsistent because my dad was a drunkard and he apparently had little regard for my mother. He had continual financial difficulties and it seemed to me that they were not bringing any credit to the family name. The thing which impressed me was that drinking was a terrible thing, and to this day, I don't voluntarily take a drink. This attitude was reinforced in the Christian church.

I went to a Japanese Catholic kindergarten but I hated it very much. My parents felt that they owed it to the Japanese nun to send me there as she had done some kindness for our family. I went to the kindergarten for one term and I got so fed up with it, so I jumped over the fence one day and came home. My parents were indifferent about this and they accepted it as a matter of fact.

When I started Japanese language school at the age of six, I already knew the alphabet so I got ahead rapidly. I was able to memorize all of the vocabulary easily and I was considered a very good student. For the first few years I enjoyed this prestige because all of the kids in my neighborhood were going to the same school. Most of my Nisei friends were a little older than I, and I was anxious to catch up to their class. I was accepted by this older group because I was proficient in marbles and in baseball playing. I enjoyed this companionship more than the Japanese language school as time went on. I became quite bored with the Japanese language school as my public school became more advanced and I preferred to play rather than learn Japanese after the American classes.

The Japanese language teacher patronized my dad's barbershop and he complained that I should study more. I guess I managed to do fairly well despite my attitude because I skipped the seventh grade and I finished the Japanese elementary classes a year early. Most of the kids were like me as they hardly studied at all. We all went to

Japanese school because we wanted to play there and the parents forced us to go because they were paying for lessons. My parents were quite anxious for me to learn Japanese well. My mother said that our dealings would have to be with the Japanese people and that we could never escape our racial background. Some of the JACL leaders and our language teachers emphasized that we young Nisei constituted the bridge which would have to be built between Japan and the U. S. in order to overcome the gap of misunderstanding. They emphasized the fact that we held a unique and favorable position to do a great service to both countries and that it would help to create international friendships. We were somewhat impressed by these stories; but I soon learned that my Japanese could never be proficient enough to help build any bridges. I identified myself as an American, but I also felt that I had to have some loyalty to my racial background. I used to get angry at some of the unfavorable newspaper articles appearing in the Sacramento press as I thought they didn't understand us at all. In the early days Sacramento was the hotbed of anti-Japanese agitation.

The Japanese language school was operated and financed by the community, but it was located right next to the Buddhist Church. After I finished the fifth grade there, a couple of Buddhist priests from Japan came to instruct us. All this talk about being taught loyalty to the Emperor was not true, because these Buddhist priests never told us that we had to swear allegiance to the Emperor. As a matter of fact, most of the teachers emphasized that we were American citizens and that it was our duty to teach Caucasian Americans the better part of Japanese culture.

Once when a Nisei friend came back from a trip to Japan, he told me that the Japanese nation all believed that the Emperor was the son of God and everyone had to obey him. I was very bothered by this news because I had learned in the Christian Sunday school that God did not have any earthly descendants, so I asked my mother about it. She neither denied nor confirmed the Emperor myth, even though her sympathies were for Japan. My mother was usually too busy with the household tasks to be bothered with any political issues and her attachment to Japan was purely sentimental.

We had to learn and sing the Japanese national anthem on occasions. Once a Japanese naval training crew came to Sacramento and they sang a stirring Japanese naval song in the school yard. That song became very popular and all of us kids sang it and played it on our harmonicas for a long time. But that soon died away.

When I first started at [F] grammar school two-fifths of the pupils were Nisei. I knew a number of the Nisei in my class, so I didn't mind public school at all. My favorite subjects were spelling, penmanship, reading, and arithmetic. The school entered the city-wide spelling bees and I generally was up in the top rank. It was during this period that I increased my English vocabulary immensely.

Reading was the subject which fascinated me the most and I became an avid reader. I went to the public library all the time. I hated drawing in grade school and it used to mortify me when I fell behind my classmates in this subject. I didn't like manual training either.

In school, we assembled in the yard the first thing in the morning to salute the flag and sing the "Star Spangled Banner." I didn't learn the words to this anthem until I was in the sixth grade. But it was a stirring sight to see the American flag and hear the song. I never showed my feeling overtly but I was stirred.

I liked most of my teachers in grade school and they were kind to me. They tried to help me as I was such a quiet student. I got my best grades in conduct as I never made any noise. I was very shy and I was always nervous whenever I recited a poem. I disliked giving talks before the class and I would stumble over my words constantly. I feared people looking at me and my knees shook. I still haven't entirely overcome this handicap. All of us students were always wishing that the school would burn down and this is what happened when I was in the seventh grade. I had to transfer to the junior high school, and it was a very trying time as few of my friends went with me. I had the worst time speaking before strange classes and I practically trembled for fear that I would be called upon. I really suffered inward torture and I used to sweat all over.

In school I became involved with a tough mixed Caucasian and Nisei gang. We used to go around at night to beat up on kids that we didn't like. Sometimes we would go to a store and snitch candy and food. But when this gang began to carry knives and guns later on, I dropped out. They would take a strange boy out on an outing and make him jump by shooting a gun at his feet. My mother warned me to get out of the gang when she heard that it was bad. We didn't have any racial feelings among ourselves, but we wouldn't allow any Chinese kids to join. The gang used to egg me into fights as they were training me to become a professional boxer. I didn't want to hit other fellows but I had to in order to maintain the gang's respect. During this same period, I also associated with the Sunday School group and the baseball playing group, which were all Japanese. My activities were spread out and no one group held my entire allegiance until the church group eventually won out.

When I got into high school, I envied a couple of Nisei fellows who had been reared in Caucasian districts as they were more American-ized, and they had more self-assurance about them. These fellows had more friends among the Caucasians and they acted more normal. I was never very happy in high school as I did not get the feeling that I fitted in. I went out for the baseball team and made the second string catcher position on the varsity, and I did feel more comfortable with them. Aside from that I didn't engage in extracurricular activities. I had to work after school and I even gave up baseball after my junior year in order to work. There was one teacher whom I disliked in-tensely—the English teacher. In one of our oral classes, I gave a poor speech and she insisted that I go to a speech correction class. This was quite a blow to my pride. But I did get some pointers on public speak-ing in that correction class, and I got rid of a couple of nervous mannerisms. Most of my other classes were more agreeable to me. I was taking a semicommercial course though I had enough college credits. I wanted to become a banker during the first year in high school. I knew that bankers were usually college graduates, so I took some college [preparatory] courses.

My group associations in high school were primarily with a few of my old Nisei friends. There was a Japanese Students Club and all of the Nisei students were members. I didn't particularly care for the group and I found it difficult to spare any time to participate in any of their activities. They emphasized things like dancing and I wasn't very much interested in that.

I felt a little bit ashamed of our home conditions, my parents' lack of education, the financial insecurity of the family, and the barber-shop status of my father. I compared all of this with other families and I thought that we were not doing as well. When I associated with Caucasians, the fact that I was uncomfortable in their presence and sensitive about my racial background made it difficult for me to act natural among them and to develop good friendships. I did have a few Caucasian friends, but none of these were very lasting and we soon drifted apart. I've never completely got over this sensitivity. I still have some feeling that people are watching me and interpreting my actions.

My father gave up his heavy drinking when I was a freshman in high school because he was suffering from a recurrence of a frequent illness. We didn't know the nature of his illness, but he gave up everything which he thought might be harmful to his health. He even gave up smoking. We later found out that he was suffering from active tuberculosis for three years before he was finally hospitalized. The doctor told him to remove himself from the rest of the family so that he would not give us the disease, but he was rather stubborn about it. That's why my mother and brother contracted tuberculosis. At that time, and even now, the Japanese people had a great dread of t.b. and they said that it was inherited in the family. They pointed out that whole families had this disease and they gave it to others when they married. This was a source of great concern to me as I was fearful of what the community said of my parents. I also feared for my future hope of ever getting married if such attitudes persisted.

My father finally went to the County Hospital because our family couldn't afford to send him to a private sanatorium. I was working on a celery farm fifteen miles from Sacramento. I was only fourteen years old at that time. This job had been given to me through friends of the family who were also working there. They washed my clothes and took care of me. For the first two weeks I wanted to go home every night, but because my mother had bought me a complete work outfit, I felt that I had to stick it out in order to pay her back. I stayed on that farm for the whole summer and one of the happiest moments in my life was to give my mother my first complete summer check for $125.

The next summer I went again, but I only worked two weeks before the pastor of our church wrote and told me to come home immediately because of illness in the family. My mother had been working so hard and her resistance was so low that she had contracted an active case of tuberculosis. It was a terrific blow to me and my brothers and I didn't know what we could do to support ourselves. Fortunately my father and mother had kept up on their insurance policies and we existed on the $70 income. We gave up the barbershop and sold out to another man. We moved into an upper-story flat on the outskirts of the Japanese community.

I was a junior in high school then, and I was anxious to complete my education. Some of the family friends suggested that I learn barbering and go to work immediately, but my mother backed me up in refusing to allow me to quit my education. Some of the family friends in the Japanese community donated money to pay for my father's debts while others canceled old debts. I was very grateful to Mr. [K], proprietor of a Japanese shoe store, as he offered me a job for after-school hours and on Saturdays. With the $32 salary and the monthly insurance payments, we were able to get along on a very narrow margin, but it was not easy.

At this period, my godfather appointed himself to look after our family interest. He had a family of his own back in Japan but he had lost contact with them after living forty years in this country. He had lost his business by then and he was an agricultural worker. He helped us at home and did our housekeeping. We didn't have to pay him anything except his upkeep. We received much better care from him than we had ever had. He did all of the washing, ironing, and cooking for us.

My parents were both at the county sanatorium and our godfather bought a second hand model-T Ford and taught me how to drive so that I could take out a license and take my brothers to go visit my parents every Sunday. Most of our old family friends no longer came to see us because they were afraid of the disease. But people were kind to us during this period. One of Dad's barbershop friends cut our hair free and he wouldn't take any payments. The family doctor and dentist reduced their charges for us. I was impressed that people could be kind and I determined that I would help others who were in a difficult position like I was. I felt a keen sense of responsibility in looking after my four brothers and I tried very hard to impress upon them that we had to stick together.

This was about the time that my religious life became very earnest. I became active in the young people's group. At the same time, a Caucasian woman missionary came to our church. She was a very dominating individual and very fundamentalist in her theology. I was persuaded to become a Christian and I accepted Christ as my savior and I attempted to live a life like his. At that time I was playing baseball for a team made up of Buddhist Nisei. They became associated with the Young Men's Buddhist Association and one of the members said that it was now necessary that I either become a member of the Buddhist church or give up the team. It was a difficult decision for me to make as baseball was my love. But I felt a deep conviction to the Christian church so I finally gave up the baseball team. This was a great surprise to my teammates as none of them felt a similar loyalty to Buddhism. From that time on, I became closely connected to the

Christian church. I quit playing cards and I never went to movies on Sundays. I maintained my temperance pledge. I was sincere in what I believed. It was a difficult time in my life and religion gave me comfort and security. I could understand how God tried people by fire and suffering in order to mold their character. I was very intolerant toward those who did not follow what I believed in. I didn't think that they should dance and enjoy themselves in such an earthly way. My friends thought that I was getting too prudish and narrow in my views. However, I did hold a very respected position among the young people's group of our city and I was highly regarded by the Christian Issei. I was appointed Sunday School teacher at the age of seventeen and appointed junior deacon when I was eighteen. My brothers came to church largely through my influence, but they never believed in it as strongly as I did.

We became worried because we could see that our parents were steadily getting worse and in September, 1931, my father finally died. I saw my mother immediately after his death and she told me that she was not particularly grief stricken. I gathered from her remark that her love life had never been happy. The funeral was held in Sacramento but my mother did not attend because she was confined to the hospital. There were enough contributions at the funeral to take care of the expenses for burial and my father's insurance gave us a lump sum to use as a fund for family care. My mother's condition got worse and three months later she also died. I went to see her almost every day during this period. My mother's funeral was quite an ordeal. The Buddhist wake and funeral lasted for hours and hours and after that the family's friends came to our house in order to count the donation money and to reminisce about experiences which they had gone through with my parents. My brother and I didn't want so many people around the house but we had to submit because these people had been so friendly to us. The members of the Christian young people's group came over and held a prayer meeting and I was quite touched.

Soon afterwards, my brothers and I got a few thousand dollars of the insurance money, so for a time we were able to breathe easier and I was able to continue school. That's why I decided to go on to junior college for the next year and a half. I was now determined to become a minister, largely at the suggestion of the Caucasian missionary lady. She helped me meet new people and develop self-assurance. I felt that it was my chosen mission in life to follow the church.

However, there were certain seeds of doubt creeping in. One of the things which disgusted me about church life was to discover that the members were very unchristian in their relationship with one another. These Issei deacons were very jealous of their authority and they didn't want the *hakujin* board to tell them how to run the church. They were anxious that no Caucasian leader get the dominance over them. They had little enough prestige as it was and they didn't want their positions undermined in the least. I was a sort of inbetween person in all of the debates which went on as I had to draft all of the complaints for the Issei deacons as I was the only one who could handle English well enough. Some of the complaints were justified, as the Baptist Home Missions board did act in a highhanded manner at times.

The thing which came the closest to making me resign was the Issei pastor who was jealous that the Caucasian missionary lady was drawing all of the young people to her. He spread the story, consciously or not, that there was something going on between the young lady and me. He hinted that all of our relationships were not strictly confined to religious activities. This was not true at all because this young lady's mother was always with her during the time I visited her home. As a result of the spread of this vicious gossip, the lady was forced to resign. When I found out what it was all about, I threatened to quit the church. She wrote to me and advised that I should be Christian enough to forgive personal insults and to work that much harder for the development of the church.

I was appointed as the superintendent of the Sunday School as a sort of an appeasement reward and I became a regular deacon, so I just continued, but I drifted away from the fundamental theology. I don't know how long I would have continued taking an active part in the church if it were not for the war. It was only through the general evacuation that I was able to emancipate myself completely from formal church connections. I did take part in some church activities in camp but since resettlement I have severed all church contacts except for a brief period when I sang in a choir at [a Midwestern college].

In 1933 my godfather died of cancer of the throat. He had refused to go to a hospital so that we took care of him at home. During his last weeks, he suffered a great deal and we had to stay up all night with him. His old Issei doctor refused to give him morphine in order to alleviate his pains as he said that the shock would be too great. He made my godfather suffer to the very end.

About this time I noticed that after playing basketball in the church gym my heart would palpitate hard for a couple of hours after I went to bed. The Issei doctor told me that there was nothing wrong with me but I became worried so I went to see the junior college doctor. He told me that I had a murmur from a leaking heart valve and he advised me to lay off of all strenuous activity. I didn't feel ill at all while I was playing sports so I continued with my activities. Several months later I had to go to bed with severe joint pains and palpitation of the heart. The doctor said that I had a valvular disease and he advised hospitalization. I didn't want to go to the county hospital because it was considered a kind of disgrace for a Japanese to take charity from public funds. However, there was no other alternative so I reconciled myself. I was released with the doctor's warning that I could never again do any work involving physical exertion and that I had to give up all athletics. This was a blow to me and I found it difficult to conceive of a life in which I could not do the things I wanted to. I didn't obey the doctor's orders strictly.

In 1935 I graduated from junior college "with great distinction." My brothers and I then went through the severest financial crisis we ever had to face. Our money ran out and we had absolutely no income at all because I had given up my part-time job on account of my health. I did all of the washing, cooking, and cleaning for my younger brothers. My third brother got a job in a Japanese drugstore at $5 a week. My old employer Mr. [K] again came to the rescue and he offered my second brother my old job at $25 a month. The wages had to be cut because of the depression. This income from my two brothers was still not enough to meet the expenses for the five of us, so much as I hated to do it, I applied for orphans' relief from the County Welfare Department. There was no other way for us to get by, and I was terribly conscious of what the people thought, so that it was doubly difficult to make the application. We got $20 each for my two youngest brothers. Even this was not enough to provide our living expenses so every week I had to go to the welfare commissary department and bring home food. It was embarrassing for me to carry this bundle home through the Japanese community, as I would run into people whom I knew. They knew that we were on relief and our problems were common knowledge to the community. I felt that it was a stigma on our name.

We had some difficulty with the County Welfare Department as we had no guardians and I wasn't yet twenty-one. We wanted to stick together so that we refused adoption of the two youngest boys by an Issei couple. We also refused to be placed in an orphanage. A Caucasian lady was sent by the State relief administration to be our housekeeper and she did our housework. Two out of three of these housekeepers were nice and we got to like them. We didn't have any money to buy wood for heat, so that these ladies were always complaining about the cold. The county department sent some wood to us and we didn't like it very much because everyone in the Japanese community could see that truck coming to our house and they could see that it was for more relief. The State Board of Rehabilitation heard of our case and it offered to put me through commercial school so that I could get a desk job.

[All this time] I was so afraid of getting tuberculosis but my second brother got it and he had to stay at the sanatorium for the next five years.

It was still my ambition to become a minister, but I realized that I had to give it up in order to support my brothers. My original Caucasian lady friend got a rich sponsor to guarantee putting me through college and the theological school, but I refused to take it as I thought I would be a bad risk. I went through business school in 1935, and a Nisei friend opened up a law office, so I got a job as his secretary. There wasn't much to do so I just read books and held bull sessions with the doctor and dentist in the same building. It was in this job I got to know most of the Sacramento professional Japanese.

While I was doing this job, I decided to take the State civil service examination for junior account clerk. I got sixteenth on the list and I was appointed in 1937. I was quite happy to get a state job because the $80 a month was a higher salary than I had been receiving. I was certified to a department which was just being set up and I was the first Nisei to be hired there. When I first went into that office, my Caucasian co-workers were very curious about my nationality and my classification. I didn't know if I could do the work until they put me to filing and checking figures. I was able to do this well so that my supervisor took me out of the clerical unit into the accounting unit.

After seven months, I took a promotional test and I passed first so I became an intermediate clerk at $110. This was still a busy time in our department, so I actually worked two shifts for a period of three months as I had charge of as many as sixty state employees at the peak. I was the only Nisei in the large office and I had a lot of responsibility, but I didn't find any resentment towards me. I tried not to be bossy in any way and I usually sent mild memos in order to get coöperation.

After three months new machines were installed, so I went back to the supervisor's office where I continued to write letters for him. He asked me to make organizational charts and write up procedures also. When another promotional test came, I passed among the first three and I went to work in another section of [this] department. Later on I was put in charge of a small unit at $150 and was later raised to $180.

About a year after I started, a large number of Nisei began to come into civil service. Every time a Nisei came into our department, he was put into my unit, so I had four or five of them. I felt that the supervisor should have scattered them around in the department more. Eventually there were so many Nisei in our department that they were readily noticeable. By the time I became a senior account clerk, there were twenty-five Nisei in our department. By the time of evacuation there were close to sixty of us. I had been promised a supervisor's job, but my unit was disbanded at the outbreak of the war.

My second brother came back from the sanatorium after five years as an arrested case of tuberculosis. Through my suggestion he passed a test as a junior account clerk in civil service. He was quite happy at his prospect and he was seriously thinking of marriage, but his fiancée's parents objected to him because of the presence of tuberculosis in our family. I felt terrible about this as I was thinking of marriage myself with a girl I had known for some time. My brother suddenly became ill again and a month after Pearl Harbor he died at the County Hospital even though we could have afforded a private hospital by then.

My other brothers all finished high school. My third brother went to work in a vegetable and fruit market in North Sacramento. It was a Japanese store but it had mostly Caucasian trade. He became a hard worker but I thought he would turn out to be a black sheep when I found out that he had taken up smoking. I reconciled myself and I think it was so silly to make such a fuss at that time. I certainly did disapprove though. My fourth brother finished up one and a half years of junior college before the evacuation and the fifth brother finished one year. The fifth brother was the only brother to be interested in college and he finished a year and a half at [an eastern college] after his resettlement and before he was drafted into the Army.

In the period before the war I didn't have much interest in politics. I was against radicals like Harry Bridges and I voted Republican. I was pretty naïve in my political thinking. I resented Hearst's attacks on Japan and the Sacramento *Bee*'s attacks on Japanese in California.

My identification was with the U. S., but I hoped that our feeling for things Japanese was not inconsistent. I had become a member of the JACL at one time through the appeal of a personal friend, but I only paid my dues and I rarely attended any of the meetings. I was not too sympathetic to the Sacramento JACL chapter because of its domination by the Nisei professional group. I felt that many of these professional Nisei were in the organization for personal glory and for economic gain.

All throughout this period, I went to Caucasian churches to speak and I got to know them better. We held interracial meetings and I used to attend some of the church conventions in order to talk about the problems of a Nisei church. After I got into civil service, I joined the State Employees Association. It was a conservative group and I wasn't active in it. I played on the departmental softball team and this increased my reputation as a regular fellow. This was against my doctor's orders. I was invited to the parties of my Caucasian co-workers, but I still had certain religious scruples and I didn't dance or drink beer. I joined [a choral club] in the city through one of the contacts of a fellow worker. I was the only Nisei in this group and I filled the tenor needs. I took part in some of their concerts. That was about the full extent of my Caucasian contacts before the war.

In the Japanese community I was a bit more active. I was a dues paying member of the junior Hiroshima *kenjinkai* but I gave that up when the tension between Japan and the United States started to get strong. There was a bit of pressure to contribute to the *Heimushakai* as its sponsor said that the money would be used for the Japanese Red Cross. I donated a dollar a month for a few months and then I dropped out. Later there were many Issei said to be interned for making this donation. I was also active in a community dramatic group within the Japanese section. We also had a book club in our church.

At that time I thought that my prospect for advancing in civil service was good, so I started to go to night school to learn more accounting. I thought that I could work up to a salary of $300 a month and I could get married and then send my kids to college.

Three of my brothers were working full time by 1941. In all the time we worked, my brothers and I pooled our salaries and after the expenses were paid, I allocated the savings on a 2–1–1–1 ratio, in favor of myself. I felt that the division was fair since I made twice as much and I had been supporting my brothers for so long. I intended to separate from my brothers after my marriage. I wanted to move to another district to build a home as I had no economic stake in the Japanese community any more. My second brother wanted to get married and he wanted a larger share of our savings. I didn't want him to get married ahead of me since there were two young brothers to look after and I had taken on this responsibility for a long time.

The general run of the Nisei were not as economically secure as I was before the war. I had a permanent government job and a high salary compared to what the rest of the Nisei were making. Even in civil service, I had one of the best jobs of any Nisei employee because I had gotten in early. There were only three hundred Nisei in civil service throughout California, and most of them were girls in clerical jobs. The only other Nisei group which enjoyed any degree of financial security were the professional men and those in a few businesses. Many of my high school and junior college Nisei friends were just doing odd jobs. Quite a number of them had gone to the University of California in order to get engineering degrees, but they worked for their fathers afterwards. Many of those who could not get regular jobs went to farm work. Among my classmates, most of them eventually took over their father's businesses, but the younger brothers had a tougher time as there wasn't much left for them to do. The only ones to work for Caucasians outside of civil service workers were those who worked in domestic jobs. The economic prospects for the Nisei were very dim before the war. All of the Nisei had to depend on the Japanese community but I was a little smug as I thought that I was set for life. But we were among the first to get kicked out.

The day of Pearl Harbor I was in church. After the Japanese language service I went home and then I found that I had to go to the Japanese ten cent store in order to buy some small article. I drove down there in my car and the Nisei proprietor had the radio on. He said to me in a strange voice that Japan had attacked Pearl Harbor. I thought that he was just kidding and I thought it was incredible that anything like that could happen. I turned my car radio on the way home but I couldn't get any spot news. When I got home, my brothers confirmed the news. I had a feeling of dismay as I knew that it would be tough for the Nisei because of the natural suspicion aroused by Caucasians toward us. I went to see my fiancée and we expressed our mutual feeling of concern and anxiety as to what would happen to us. We were particularly afraid for her alien mother but we didn't think at that time that the Nisei would be touched, as we had done nothing disloyal toward this country.

That night at the church meeting the atmosphere was rather tense and strained because the congregation was still stunned by the day's news. The Caucasian secretary of the city church council came and he asked permission to speak. He told of the gravity of the situation and he offered any help that his organization could give to us in order to face this crisis. It was a rather sleepless night for me and I dreaded going to work the next day as I didn't know what to expect from my fellow Caucasian co-workers. I tried to act as if Monday was just another day and I tried not to bring up the subject of the attack. I was hypersensitive and I thought that people looked in my direction much more than usual when I went to the office. I couldn't help but see the headlines of the newspaper that they were all reading.

We suspended work in order to listen to President Roosevelt and he branded the attack as dastardly and treacherous. I was very conscious of my racial origin at that moment and I had a sort of a sinking feeling. I tried to look and convince myself that my allegiance was to the United States and I shouldn't act self-conscious but I couldn't help it. I got through the morning by keeping busy and avoiding any informal conversation with the Caucasian workers. At lunch time I sat next to two Caucasian women from our department. One said, "I bet the Japs will feel sorry for this." The other lady noticing me said, "You mean those Japs over there." The first lady looked at me and said, "Why, of course." That didn't make me feel too good but I got through the rest of the day.

The next day I thought that the best thing to do was to reaffirm our loyalty to the United States, so I wrote and took around a petition which I had the Nisei in my unit sign. The director was pleased with the statement and he wanted to post it on the bulletin board, but he wanted all the Nisei in the department to sign. I spent the rest of the day going around to get the other Nisei to sign it. Photostatic copies were then made and it was posted on various bulletin boards. I'm not sure if I did the right thing by calling attention to the fact that we were of Japanese ancestry, but we felt that our statement would clear the atmosphere.

Most of the Caucasian employees in my department went out of their way to express sympathy. But a few did come up to me and say, "You fellows here may be O.K., but what about the rest? How do we find out whether to trust them or not?" Then they would begin to cite stories about University of California class rings being found on a Japanese aviator who had been shot down over Pearl Harbor and stories about the fifth-column Japanese driving trucks on the high-ways in order to block the defense of Hickam Field. They also brought out some stories headlined by Hearst regarding Japanese naval reserve officers on the Terminal Island fishing boats. I said that I couldn't either confirm or deny all of these stories, but there was no question of the loyalty of the Nisei group and that some had already gone into the Army before Pearl Harbor and the rest were expected to do so now that this country was at war. They were still not convinced that the disloyal ones could be picked out and this was a dilemma for us. I tried to argue logically that people should be judged individually and not condemned as a group because of racial origin.

But mostly, my relations with the department were good. The Nisei there never organized any kind of a formal group, but every once in a while something would come up and we would have to answer charges. One man said that two Japanese girls whispered in Japanese in the office and the director warned me that we should be extremely careful not to get together and act like we were saying things that should not be heard because it could be misinterpreted by the public too easily. It was later found that it was a Chinese girl who had whispered.

I was suspended from my job with the state despite the sympathy of my co-workers. The state senators demanded that we should be removed because of our racial origins, and we didn't know how to defend ourselves. I went to see one of the lawyers in my department and asked if the State Personnel Board could discharge us on the grounds which the state senators gave. He assured me that the State and Federal constitution protected the Nisei employees. However, he qualified himself by saying that there was a fly in the ointment. He said that they could suspend us in a wartime situation if the charges warranted. Our department head was quite sincere in his expression that he was not going to dismiss any Nisei workers until there was definite proof that we had performed some disloyal act as individuals.

When the charges against us became more severe and things looked darker, we called a meeting of all the state Nisei employees. About 100 of them turned up and this represented about 90 per cent of the Nisei civil service workers in the Sacramento area. Since I was one of the oldest state employees, I was appointed co-chairman of the meeting with Mr. [Y] who was an income tax examiner. We organized this group on an informal basis in order to study action which might be taken to safeguard our jobs and rights.

We went to Senator [S's] home because he had been the original one to demand our discharge and we wanted to know why he did this. We took along our Issei minister and a JACL representative. Before the war Senator [S] had claimed to be a great friend of the Nisei but after Pearl Harbor he began to attack us rather viciously. When we talked to him, he answered that every individual would be given a hearing to determine his loyalty before dismissal. We went away with our hopes on a higher level than what they had been for a long time.

A few days later all of us were amazed to be handed blanket charges[207] and a notice that we were suspended from civil service. The temporary Nisei employees and those on probation were discharged outright. Those of us with permanent civil service status couldn't be discharged without the consent of the department head. Our department and [one other] refused to give this consent, so the State Personnel Board just suspended us. We were given a questionnaire[208] which asked us about everything as if we were aliens. The two things that they harped on the most was our attendance at Japanese language school where we were supposed to have been inculcated with Emperor worship, and our dual citizenship status which they said made us subject to the dictates of Japan.

In order to forestall action on the second charge, we all filed affidavits renouncing our Japanese citizenship and reaffirming our loyalty to the United States. A Caucasian lawyer helped us draw the form and the National Secretary of JACL also had a hand in it. What got me mad was that the JACL leaders in the national office began to berate us for not being JACL members. They said they would help us anyway even if we were ungrateful. We felt that it was a common problem, so we allowed the JACL to come into the case. The JACL president recommended a lawyer for us after we decided that the Civil Liberties Union was tinged too much with leftist leanings and it would hurt our cause. I regret very much that we didn't get the

[207] On January 28, 1942, the State Personnel Board voted unanimously to bar from future civil service positions all "descendants of nationals with whom the United States is at war." (See p. 81, above) In the case of Japanese, the Board voted—again unanimously—on April 2, 1942, "that all state civil service employees of Japanese ancestry employed by any department, agency, board or commission be suspended, effective immediately" and instructed the Secretary "to file charges within the statutory time limit." An exact copy of these blanket charges follows CH-64's life history.

[208] The questionnaire was distributed in February, 1942, to all persons having "Japanese names" who were then employed by the State or who were on civil

Civil Liberties group to represent us at that time, but our conservative attitudes were strong and we listened to the JACL leaders. We were politically naïve.

I was on a committee of five to go confer with the JACL president about the next step to take. We got a Caucasian law firm to represent the case.

We duly filled out the questionnaire which the Personnel Board gave us and we got supporting statements from our friends. But indi-

---

service rolls. It included 75 questions concerning the respondent and 13 questions to be filled in about his father, his mother, and each of his siblings. The respondent was warned that "every question ... must be completely answered," that "all answers were "being given under oath," and that an affidavit attesting that all answers were "true and complete," and that "no facts pertinent to the questions or answers [had] been withheld or omitted" must be executed. The questionnaire ended with a statement concerning the "penalty for perjury" and a further warning that "any false statement" would be "grounds for dismissal from the California civil service or removal of [respondent's] name from state employment lists." The following selection of questions indicates the coverage of such matters as dual citizenship, attendance at Japanese language schools, subscription to Japanese or vernacular newspapers, conforming to the requirements of the anti-alien land laws, contributions to ethnic or Japanese organization, family connections in Japan, etc. It would have been difficult to find a respondent who would not have one or more of his answers defined as "derogatory" according to the Personnel Board's criteria. Moreover, the actual charges were of a "blanket" nature and were not based on the specific answers of a specified respondent. They were uniformly and indiscriminately applied to all persons suspected of having Japanese ancestors, in accordance with the unanimous resolution cited in footnote 207. The following items indicate the types of questions included:

Selected Items from Questionnaire:

14. What is the nearest large city to your place of birth?...
    How many miles from your birthplace?................ In what direction does it lie?.....................

15. Give name of physician or midwife attending your birth..................................
    Give names and addresses of at least two witnesses who attended your birth:

    ....
    Name   Address   Name   Address

16. Give names and addresses of persons who can testify to the time and place of your birth:

17. When and where was your birth recorded?

    ....
    City   State   Country   Date

32. Name all countries of which you have been a subject or citizen:

33. Was your birth registered with any foreign government, organization, association, or other foreign representative whatsoever? If so, give the following information:

    ....
    Name of officer or organization   Country Represented

    ....
    Place of Registration   Date

vidual charges became hopeless when they handed us blanket charges. The charges against the Nisei civil service workers were so unexpected and ridiculous that we didn't know what to make of it. At first we were both amused and fighting mad. Apparently the very fact that we were born of Japanese parentage made us disloyal according to these charges, and therefore we were considered a bad influence on the morale of Caucasian fellow workers in civil service. I don't know how they arrived at such a conclusion as this, but it was tinged with

---

34. Have you ever taken an oath of allegiance to any country other than the United States?

....

yes–no   Name of Country   Date of taking oath

35. Do you now hold, or have you ever held, dual citizenship?.....................If so,
yes–no

name other country...

36. Have you ever formally renounced citizenship or allegiance to any country including the U.S.?.............If so, give the following information:
yes–no

....

Name of Country   Place of Renunciation   How Accomplished   Date

39. Name foreign languages you speak................................or read................................

40. To what foreign (or foreign language) newspapers and periodicals do you or your family subscribe?

53. Have you attended any schools not conducted in the English language?
yes–no

	Language	Location of	Conducted by	Dates of
Name of School	Used	School	Whom	Attendance

56. Give names of all clubs, organizations, societies, or fraternal orders of which you have been a member or with which you have been affiliated at any time:

Name of Organization	Place	Dates of Affiliation

64. Have you ever sent money out of continental United States?...........................
If so, give following:

In Whose Name Sent	To Whom Sent	Relationship to You	Address	Amts.	Date Sent	Name of Agency By Which Sent

66. List all your contributions to any associations or organizations whatsoever within the last five years: (Use reverse side if necessary)

Name of Association or Organization	Address	Amount	Date of Contribution

68. List all real property presently or formerly owned by you, showing location, date and from whom acquired, and indicating whether it is business, residential, or agricultural property.

69. Is any of the property described under question #68 held in your name for the benefit and use of others?................ If so, give location of property, for whom held and his relationship to you, and whether business, residential, or agricultural property.

74. Do you have grandparents, uncles, aunts or first cousins living now in any foreign country................ If so, list below:

Name	Relationship	Country of Residence

the Hitler doctrine of race superiority. The charges said that we went to the Buddhist language schools which were controlled by the Emperor of Japan, and its sole purpose was to inculcate us with Japanese doctrines, and therefore we were dangerous to this country. It said that we were a part of the fifth column movement controlled by the Emperor. After we received these charges, we were determined to take the matter to the Supreme Court if necessary in order to clear our names.

At this time the FBI were rounding up Issei leaders and we thought that it was unfair in some instances. A few were taken on the flimsy excuse that they possessed knives more than eight inches long. Actually, these knives were used to cut fish. One ridiculous case was about a Boy Scout who had made a Morse code set, and the newspapers played it up and said that he had a sending and receiving wireless set to communicate with the Japanese invaders. There were all sorts of newspaper accounts of caches, ammunition, and guns being found on aliens. We felt very helpless in the face of these newspaper articles and radio reports because we just didn't know what we could do to disprove these false stories. Most of us were afraid that the FBI agents would start picking up the Nisei next, so we all destroyed every evidence of Japanese articles in our homes. We destroyed books and flushed the Emperor's picture down the toilet. Our fears were sort of silly but quite real to us then. Everybody was busy destroying any Japanese article. I was particularly afraid for my fiancée's mother since she was a language school teacher. We had heard that all language school teachers would be interned, so we expected the worst. We knew that many Issei had their bags already packed so that when the FBI agent came they would be ready to go. It was the uncertainty of not knowing what to expect which made our lives miserable.

In my circle, we believed that the government wouldn't do anything to Nisei although we expected some action to be taken against the Kibei. We felt almost sure that the Issei might be placed in concentration camps. But some of us argued that this would bring hardships on the family with young children. We used to discuss these things by the hour and day after day.

In rapid succession, contraband restrictions, zoning, and curfew came through military orders. When we heard that all of us had to be evacuated, we were relieved that some definite action was going to be taken. This didn't mean that we did not think that the principle of evacuation was all wrong. When we became reconciled to mass evacuation, we kidded each other that the government would have to support us and we would live the life of ease. Some of the more idealistic Nisei thought that this was a great opportunity to build Utopian communities and demonstrate to suspicious Caucasians that we were still for this country in spite of what happened.

During all of this period, I took the chief responsibility for my family. Since I was engaged, I was worried about the rumor that Sacramento would be divided into two parts and people in the two areas would be sent to different camps. I told my brothers that I preferred to go with my fiancée and her family and they agreed to that. I had no other relatives to worry about so that we didn't have the special problem that many Nisei families had. Both of my brothers decided to quit junior college even though I insisted that they attend classes as long as possible. They didn't feel like studying any more and they said it was senseless in view of the evacuation so I gave in. My third brother kept on working until his boss sold out the produce store to a Chinese fellow.

My chief problem during all this period was to hasten our marriage. I had been going around with my fiancée for seven years before the war but we were both the oldest in our respective families and we had responsibilities so that it was difficult for us to get married and start our own lives. She insisted that she didn't want in-laws living with us, particularly her mother. My fiancée was inclined to be quiet and reserved in her ways. I was interested at first in trying to bring her out of her shell. During the first few years we went around together, it was difficult to do this. She wasn't interested in boys and she thought I was too conceited. Her father had spent all of his savings to take his church out of debt and he neglected his family, so she resented [my church activities]. Her mother was intelligent and forward. My fiancée was afraid that I would also come under her mother's domination and [that] our married life wouldn't be very happy. She had reasons to expect this as I would always do errands for her mother, like cutting the lawn and driving her places. I was a very practical person as far as her mother was concerned. I did all these things to further my cause and she formed a great deal of liking for me.

We had seriously considered getting married before Pearl Harbor but we decided to wait until her sister could graduate from [a state college] in the summer of 1942. We felt that then her sister could take over the family support. When the war broke out, we had a long discussion and we decided that we couldn't wait any longer because there was a great danger of getting separated. We were married in May, 1942, just one week before our area was evacuated. Our honeymoon was spent in a local hotel for two nights as we couldn't go out of the county on account of the travel restrictions imposed by the Army.

After the honeymoon we went back to my wife's home as I felt responsible for her family. The next five days were spent in feverish packing, storing, and buying things. The furniture in my house was all sold at a slight loss. I sold my car to a fellow employee and he paid me two-thirds cash. He gave me a promissory note for the other one-third of the balance, but it took me three years to collect that. All of my wife's family's things were stored away. They owned their own home and it was rented out. They sold their car and they ended up by not losing so much.

Actually I was in pretty good spirits during those last couple of weeks before evacuation. I was happy that I had finally materialized my hopes of marriage at the last minute even though it was at a pretty big price. My wife and I had talked over our future plans with a Caucasian woman who was a close friend. She suggested that I should make every attempt to finish up my education since I had been wanting to do that before. She thought that the break from the past would be the opportunity for me to realize my hopes in getting an education. She suggested that I finish up at [a liberal arts college in the Middle West] where she had graduated some thirty or forty years before. But at that time I wasn't thinking too much about my personal future because things were so uncertain and we didn't know how long we would have to remain in the center. At first I had hopes of doing something real constructive in the camps in order to help make something beneficial out of it and try to achieve coöperative living.

But even before evacuation there were some things which made me doubt that the Japanese could live together coöperatively. We had a great deal of difficulty in the Japanese community because of the selfish nature of some people. Some of these incidents which I knew and heard of made me pretty disgusted. One of these incidents developed as a result of the plan to inoculate the whole Japanese community against typhoid. A group of the Japanese doctors announced that they would do it free of charge. Our church was used for this purpose and hundreds of people came the first day. On the second day the City Board of Health representative came and said that the procedure was not correct, so it had to be stopped. This action was instigated by Dr. [X], an Issei who had resided in this country for many years. He claimed that it was fine for the doctors to give their service gratis, but it was unfair to ask only them when the Japanese lawyers and other professionals were literally cleaning up on the evacuees. As a result, he got the Board of Health to stop the inoculation on the technicality that the church was not a certified health clinic.

The feeling against Dr. [X] ran high and what made it worse was that he was appointed a Japanese administrator of the Walerga Assembly Center by WCCA officials. Dr. [X] was scheduled to go there a week in advance of the general evacuation of our area, and he was placed in charge of all evacuee job appointments there. The Japanese community couldn't understand why Dr. [X] was appointed to head all of this and there were rumors circulating that he was an *inu*. It was later said that he got a big cut out of the clothing and scrip allowance in the assembly center, and that he was tied in with JACL leaders who were also getting cuts. This might have been all a rumor but some of my Nisei friends claim that they had conclusive evidence to prove it. This was all tied in with the resentment against the JACL for "asking" for the evacuation, and the JACL clique did rule with strict control at the assembly center. The community also resented the Japanese lawyers who were charging exorbitant fees to fill out even the simplest federal forms, and it just happened that these lawyers were connected with the JACL. Many Nisei were bitter in denouncing these individuals for taking advantage of their own people in such an unfortunate situation. Not only that, but many rumors were going around that the JACL leaders were *inu*, reporting to the FBI. Another Japanese doctor was threatened with beatings several times because of these suspicions. It was a fact that the FBI agents were visiting JACL headquarters frequently. I attended one of these meetings and the FBI man complained that none of the Nisei were turning in names of disloyal Japanese.

Throughout this period, my identification was with the United States unequivocally. I resented the Issei who were pressing their pro-Japan sentiments on the younger Nisei, although I could understand the logic behind some of the things they said. Yet, when some individuals like a Chinese on the radio gloated over the fact that Japan would be cleaned up in three months, I felt resentful. At that time I inwardly wanted Japan to make a good showing in the war, but not win. This was an inconsistency on my part; but with all the confusion of this period, I couldn't think too clearly.

In the preëvacuation period, I continued my association in the Caucasian organizations to which I belonged. I had to resign from the State Employees Association when I was suspended from civil service. Just before evacuation, my [departmental] supervisor gave me a farewell gift of a fountain pen which I am still using.

I kept up my church attendance in the Japanese community. On the day of evacuation, the church council furnished cars to help us take our belongings up to the embarkation point and we were very grateful for all the help we received. I'll never forget the real Christian spirit which they performed for us at that time, and I'm sure that the majority of the people in California did not hold ill-feeling toward us. They just didn't speak up because of the hysteria going on at that time.

When we actually got to the Walerga Assembly Center, in May, 1942, we were superficially examined for weapons and liquor before we were permitted to enter the camp. We didn't like the living arrangements at all, as my mother-in-law and sister-in-law were in the same room and we didn't have much privacy. Blankets suspended by ropes were the only partitions we had. One of the things which irritated me about the assembly center was the disgusting way in which people ate at the mess hall. Some of those older Issei had crude manners and they thought nothing of reaching across our plates. I felt that it wasn't a very nice place for me to take my wife on her honeymoon! We had to wait in long lines before we were served any meals. Some of the food was fairly substantial but nothing fancy. We got spam regularly during the time that we were there.

I was asked to teach a business-correspondence class twice a week in the evenings for interested adults and my wife was asked to teach a shorthand class. These classes were not set up until the third week that we were there. There were not many educational activities going on because of the persistent rumors that we were going to be removed to another center shortly. The church held its regular meetings near the oak grove and I conducted a young people's class. The most enjoyable feature of camp life was the recreational program. Huge crowds would attend the softball games, and the most popular meeting place for the young Nisei was the canteen.

The camp administration was in the hands of the WCCA, but the director of the center appointed an evacuee council of five to help.

This council was composed of JACL officials and Dr. [X], and it practically ran the camp. The residents resented this tight-knit control. The thing which almost resulted in an open conflict was the news that the residents of the other assembly centers were getting clothing allowances and $2.50 individual scrip each month. Our camp never did receive these benefits. An ugly rumor circulated that Dr. [X] and his clique were getting a cut from the administration, and the people were getting gypped. A large part of these suspicions toward Dr. [X] was due to resentment of his preëvacuation activities. In the case of a prominent Nisei lawyer [also] the people were willing to make him the scapegoat because he had certain disagreeable personality traits. He also catered to the Caucasians before the war, and the Japanese people said he came from a not-so-desirable social class in Japan [eta]. He was a politician and he was always ready to further his own ends. He was particularly dogmatic in some of his viewpoints and at times I thought he was too hasty in condemning the Nisei for their lack of patriotism. [There were many other incidents, conflicts, and rumors involving these two persons.] All of these intense feelings were taken along to Tule Lake and they contributed to the conflict which broke out there later on.

On June 23, 1942, my wife and I left for Tule Lake. On the way up there we had a tough sergeant who ordered us around on the train and we didn't like that at all because we didn't consider ourselves prisoners. The first sight of Tule was very impressive because it was surrounded by snow-capped mountains. However, as we came closer, we were dismayed at the barrenness and the size of the camp. I had a sinking feeling of being lost. We were put through the intake process and my wife tried to get a separate apartment for us, but there were none available because of the housing shortage. We were very much surprised at the cool climate there, and it was paradise to have flush toilets after five weeks of the outhouse system at Walerga. At first the meals at Tule were very good, but we began to get more and more "slop-suey."

I didn't have any job difficulties. I was placed in the procurement section when I applied for a position. My supervisor was a very inept individual so that another evacuee and I had most of the responsibility. I helped to get supplies for the various departments of the project. We got into a lot of hot water with the project hospital as we didn't have any medical priority and the Army was slow in bringing in supplies. The doctors were very unreasonable about things and they got into all sorts of squabbles between themselves and with other departments in the camp.

I definitely realized that all of this talk about coöperative camp living was an utter failure as there were too many factions and jealousies. There were Issei-Nisei conflicts, conflicts between northwesterners and Californians, JACL vs. non-JACLers, fights between church groups, fights between Nisei cliques, etc., etc. Some of these small cliques formed coalitions with each other and Tule was a hotbed of group struggles. I was also pretty disgusted with the constant complaints of the Issei. The Issei tended to be antiadministration on every issue, even those which would have been beneficial to them. They led a strike on the project farm because they didn't get enough lunch. They were opposed to the establishment of the canteen and movies as they said that the people would spend too much money foolishly and the families couldn't afford it. I thought that they were justified in trying to achieve a higher wage scale as promised before we went to camp, but some of the methods they used alienated a number of their Nisei supporters. This was because a nationalistic issue was injected, and the issues did not involve political beliefs at all.

My own reaction to all of these conflicts and confusion was to withdraw into my private life and do as little as possible for the community. I lost all of my idealistic aims and I kicked along with the rest of the people when the administration asked us to work 48 hours a week for the $12, $16, and $19 a month wages. I began to count the time that it took me to walk to the office as part of my work because it took us a half hour to walk that mile and they would not provide any busses. I was rather active in social affairs. I was on the forum, recreation, music, and church committees and I spent more time on these affairs than I did at work. I got to meet a lot of Nisei leaders during this period. But my heart wasn't really in the development of Tule life.

I continued my efforts to get into [the Midwestern] college. My wife and I asked for our military clearance to leave the center and we became rather impatient as we had to wait day after day for it. It was very discouraging. We were anxious to get out as soon as possible because I wanted to register for the fall term.

Our clearance finally came late in September. We immediately arranged for sleeper accommodations from Reno and we had to pay our own transportation as the WRA was not providing it at that time. Two days later we left Tule and we were glad to get out of there at last. I think it was around October 4, 1942.

On our way out to [the Midwestern college], we didn't know what to expect. In our correspondence with the school, our hopes were lifted a great deal because of the friendly tone of the letters we got back and because of housing and employment arrangements which had been made for my wife and I. When we arrived in the town late on a Saturday night, we phoned the Dean and he came over for us immediately and he drove us around the town and campus in order to get us acquainted. We were very impressed with this reception, and we were further pleased that our future landlady was just as friendly and cordial to us as the Dean. We later learned from her that when the Dean first approached her about housing accommodations for us, she wasn't quite sure whether she wanted to rent an apartment to anyone of Japanese ancestry. The Dean persuaded her and my letters of recommendation also helped.

It was surprising to find that most of the Caucasian students there were quite ignorant of the events leading up to the evacuation. To us Nisei, it was one of the most important things that had ever happened in this country. However, these students were very sympathetic in their attitudes toward us and they suggested that we continue to tell the story of evacuation to organized groups other than the students. Some of the Caucasian students even served on our panels to give these talks to off-campus groups. We formed about three panels in all, and we appeared before all of the organized groups in the town, such as churches, service clubs, and women's organizations.

The townspeople weren't as willing to come to our support, however, as the students and faculty of the college. There were some influential individuals in town who were most suspicious of anybody with Japanese faces in their midst. Fortunately, the leading newspaper in town came out strongly for us, and with our presentation of the evacuation story, we found that the great majority of the Caucasians there were tolerant of our presence and even cordial.

It was difficult for me to get started on my studies after a seven-year lapse from college work. There were some required courses I had to take and I suffered a great deal in the math class. The teacher was sympathetic to my position and I managed to come through with a higher than average grade. My ambition was to continue in school as long as I was able in order to fit myself for a teaching job on the college level afterwards. My finances were limited so I didn't know just how far I could progress in these plans. Fortunately, the college gave me aid, and I got [a scholarship] after the first semester there by keeping up my scholastic grades.

I realized that keeping up with my scholastic work was important as it would be taken into account if I were ever considered for jobs later on. My primary interest was to learn as much as possible so I studied with purpose. I found that after the first two months, I could easily get into the swing of college work and I did get a lot of knowledge from each course. Perhaps my greater maturity helped me out, and I found that I didn't have to exert undue efforts to stay along with the class. I was elected to Phi Beta Kappa in my next to last semester there and I also signed up to read for honors, which was a customary practice for the top ranking students. At the commencement, to my great surprise, I was graduated *summa cum laude*.

I hope to receive my M.A. by the end of this year and I am working on my thesis now. After that, I'll continue [graduate work] as long as I am able. My hope is to secure an academic position in a small college after I get my degree. I don't have to worry about my education being interrupted by the draft. My draft status has been 4-F ever since the selective service came into effect because of my heart condition. I suppose that many of the Nisei who were drafted [might be] envious of my position since I could plan my life without interruption by the Army. On occasions I have thought that it would be much better to be physically sound as a 4-F is not worth that much.

When the draft was reinstituted for the Nisei as a whole, I thought that it was a very good thing. Despite the feeling on the part of some Nisei that it was an injustice to be asked to serve this country when their families were confined in camp and when they were evacuated, I think that the very fact that they were asked to serve will place the whole group in a better position in the eyes of the American public during the postwar period. It is a source of great pride for the Nisei to have the Nisei combat unit with the record it has made to back them up. I think that all of us owe a great debt to the Nisei troops for improving the position of the Nisei in this country and for providing a potent argument against those anti-Japanese groups which are still trying to deprive the Nisei of civil rights.

I hope for a complete military defeat of Japan, not so much because of the ideology about which we are being propagandized today; but because I do believe that a democratic form of government is much more desirable than a ruling military clique in any country. With all of the imperfections of the American democratic form of government, I still think that the possibilities it offers for all of us are much more attractive and conducive to the welfare and happiness of the general mass of people than any other system.

It is difficult to predict how things will be in the future, but I can pause and appreciate all of the benefits achieved as a result of the war. The evacuation did disrupt my life plans on the Coast, but it has given me the opportunity to work for something that I had given up as impossible. So in that sense, I am glad that we were forcibly removed from our old restricted Japanese community life. The re- settlement process has given me a wider perspective on life and it has helped me to emancipate myself from the close knit ties of the Japa- nese community, and to consider our particular problems in the light of the greater economic and racial problems of this nation.

In a certain measure, I've lost some of the security in the way of jobs and roots established in a community, but it has been more than compensated for by the realization of my ambitions and the increased opportunities to make friends. I'm fairly optimistic about my future in America although I'm not quite certain as to what it will be like for all the Nisei. The fact that they have been dispersed rather widely will give them a better chance to make their way and become accepted as individuals.

My first reaction to the announcement that the camps were closing up by the end of 1945 was one of resentment as I didn't know how the WRA expected the aged and disabled to make a living by being forced out. But when I heard about the reasons why the WRA wanted to close these camps, namely, to enable these people to resume a more normal type of community life and to get them started in this direc- tion before the war was over, I could see the logic of the WRA argu- ments for its announced closure policy. The Issei life span in any case is nearly completed and the problems may be solved in the next 10 or 15 years as they pass on. Some of the Nisei may seek their final adjustments by going to Japan to aid in the reconstruction work, but 95 per cent or more of them will just stay on in the United States to make their adjustments here eventually because they feel that they are part of this country.

Appendix to CH-64's Life History

The following is a copy of the "blanket charges" filed indiscrim- inately against all California State civil service employees of Japanese ancestry—including Ch-64—in April, 1942:

BEFORE THE STATE PERSONNEL BOARD OF THE STATE OF CALIFORNIA

In the Matter of Charges Against

      : Charges, Information
      : of Time and Manner
      : of Answer

      : Case No.

Defendant. :

. . . .

Comes now E. Vayne Miller, the duly and regularly appointed and acting Secretary for the State Personnel Board of the State of California, and files charges against the defendant, ..., pursuant to order of the State Personnel Board made at a meeting of the State Personnel Board held April 2, 1942, in the City of Los Angeles, State of California, for dismissal or other punitive action for failure of good behavior, fraud in securing appointment, incompetency, inefficiency, and acts incompatible with and inimical to the public service and violation of the provisions of the State Civil Service Act, and alleges:

I.

That at all times herein mentioned the said defendant was and now is an employee of the State of California, and did hold and occupy the position of ...., and is assigned to the ...., with permanent civil service status in that position.

II.

That particular and specific instances of many acts and specific examples of acts showing a course of conduct on the part of defendant constituting failure of good behavior, fraud in securing appointment, incompetency, inefficiency, violations of the provisions of this Act, or the Rules of the Board, and acts incompatible with or inimical to the public service, and violation of the provisions of the State Civil Service Act, are as follows:

A.

That during the time afore-mentioned the defendant was a citizen of the Empire of Japan, and a subject of the Emperor of Japan.

B.

That the defendant does read and write the Japanese language, and that the defendant and/or defendant's family, during the time afore-mentioned have subscribed to a Japanese newspaper, printed in the Japanese language and that defendant has read said newspaper, and that during defendant's tenure as a State employee of California has been exposed to the propaganda printed and disseminated by said Japanese newspapers, which propaganda has been detrimental and inimical to the United States, State of California, public service, and the Civil Service of California, and that defendant has been influenced by the insidious, inimical and incompatible propaganda and doctrines advocated by said Japanese newspapers, which constitutes the ideology of the Rulers and Emperors of Japan who are now viciously and ruthlessly attempting to impose that ideology and sociological doctrine upon the people of the United States of America by force and violence, and that the reading of said propaganda has been an act inimical to civil service.

C.

That during the time afore-mentioned and while an employee of the State of California, the defendant did attend a Japanese school conducted by the officials of the Buddhist Church, an organization controlled by the Rulers and Emperor of Japan, and that in said school the defendant was taught to read and speak the Japanese language, thereby enabling the subversive and fifth column agents of the Empire of Japan, by direction and indirection, to obtain valuable information for transmittal to the Empire of Japan for use to conquer the United States and that the doctrines taught defendant in said Japanese school have served to strengthen the ties between defendant and the country of defendant's ancestry, Japan, and that the teachings of said school were in conflict with the political and social doctrines of the United States, which did adversely influence the loyalty and fidelity of defendant to the United States of America.

D.

That the defendant is a member and officer of certain Japanese organizations whose membership consists entirely of persons of Japanese ancestry, and which are controlled and which advocate the same deceitful and treacherous influences which have been afore-alleged in subdivisions B and C of this Paragraph, and which seek to attain their secretive objectives against the United States of America by a unified system which is more craftily directed than that which exists in Japanese schools, and all of which is violently opposed to the Democratic form of Government of the United States of America and to its principles.

E.

That defendant is a person of Japanese ancestry and descendant of enemy Japanese aliens and at all times has been under the influence thereof; and that in the course of the performance of defendant's duties as an employee of the State of California, defendant must of necessity come into direct contact during business hours with employees and people of the State of California who are not of Japanese ancestry. That a state of war does exist between the United States of America and the Empire of Japan and that since the unwarranted attack by the Empire of Japan upon Pearl Harbor on December 7, 1941, that all loyal employees of the State of California, and people of the State of California, have become justifiably suspicious and distrustful of the defendant and of persons of Japanese ancestry and do resent contact, association, and have antipathy for defendant and persons of Japanese extraction, whether the same be in the scope of State employment of defendant, or otherwise, and that this situation has seriously impaired the morale of those employees and people of the State of California who have and will be associated with defendant in State employment, and has mutually impaired their morale, reduced their efficiency, lowered their performance of public service, created discord, hostility, unfriendliness, opposition, antagonism, disharmony, truculency, and made it impossible for said employees and people of the State of California to associate tranquilly and that the acts of defendant as afore-alleged and as an employee, of Japanese ancestry, of the State of California in the State service have become acts incompatible with and inimical to the public service and do now and in the future will interfere with the orderly, proper and efficient conduct of the State's business and have and will destroy the efficacy of the provisions of the State Civil Service Act.

F.

That the defendant did file an application for employment with the State Personnel Board wherein defendant did apply for employment with the State of California and did request to take a civil service examination and that in said application the State of California, acting by and through the State Personnel Board, did request that defendant furnish information and list the names of all schools that defendant. had attended, and that defendant did fill out said application for employment and did not in said application or otherwise indicate that [he] had attended Japanese schools wherein [he] did receive instruction on how to read and write the Japanese language and instruction on the history and political doctrines of the Empire of Japan, and that defendant did deliberately and without cause withhold said information from the said State Personnel Board, which is an act in violation of the State Civil Service Act, and did constitute fraud in securing appointment.

G.

Because of the increasing danger attendant upon the ruthless prosecution by the Japanese Government of its evil intentions designed to crush the democratic peoples of the world, public opinion has brought about a change in the social status of the defendant, and other persons in the United States, particularly in the State of California, of Japanese ancestry, and because of the urgent necessity of protecting ourselves against attack by the enemy, which attack may be facilitated by the children of the enemy within our borders, the military authorities of the United States of America have created numerous restricted areas and prohibited zones within various States on the Pacific Coast, notably the State of California. The order increasing and extending such restricted areas and prohibited zones provides in effect that such persons or classes of persons as the situation may require will by subsequent proclamation be excluded, and the defendant is now subject to the provisions of that order. The change in social status plus the military restrictions which are ever increasing in their scope and severity are concurrent circumstances which render the defendant incapable of, and indisposed to, effectively perform necessary duties as an employee of the State of California, totally unsuitable for relief duty which would be required in other parts of the State to prevent a breakdown of the provisions of the State Civil Service Act, unfit to cope with war exigencies, and completely out of accord with demands which would be made upon defendant in times of grave crises precipitated by the aggressive military, naval, and air forces of the defendant's own people, and unable, due to these circumstances, to have full and free unrestricted access to all of the territory within the exterior boundaries of the State of California, and which will preclude defendant from fully, adequately, competently, and efficiently performing necessary duties as a civil servant in California, and in violation of the provisions of the State Civil Service Act, which acts of defendant were and are incompatible with and inimical to the public service.

WHEREFORE said E. Vayne Miller as the duly and regularly appointed and acting Secretary for the State Personnel Board of the State of California, prays that the said defendant be dismissed from the State of California as a civil service employee of said State, or that such other punitive action be taken as may be meet and proper in the premises.

AND AS AND FOR THE PURPOSE OF INFORMING THE SAID DEFENDANT OF THE TIME AND MANNER IN WHICH, UNDER THE RULES AND REGULATIONS OF THE STATE PERSONNEL BOARD AND THE STATE CIVIL SERVICE ACT, DEFENDANT MAY ANSWER TO THE CHARGES HEREIN-ABOVE SET FORTH AND ASK FOR A HEARING THEREON, THE SAID E. VAYNE MILLER GIVES TO THE SAID DEFENDANT THE FOLLOWING NOTICE:

YOU, THE SAID .... ARE HEREBY NOTIFIED that Section 1 of Rule Nineteen of the Rules and Regulations of the State Personnel Board provides as follows:

"Time to answer charges. Within ten days after service upon the employee of the charges referred to in section 173(a) of the State Civil Service Act, the employee must file his answer to or explanation of the charges."

YOU ARE FURTHER NOTIFIED that section 173 of the State Civil Service Act provides, in part, as follows:

" *** The employee may within ten days after service file with the board a written answer to or explanation of the charges, and request a hearing, and a copy of such answer, or explanation, and request shall at once be mailed by the board to the appointing power or other person who has made the charges. ********** Failure on the part of the employee to request a hearing and to give such written answer or explanation to the board within ten days of the service upon him of the charges, or to appear at the hearing, shall be deemed an admission of the truth of such charges without further hearing upon the part of the board unless further time should be granted by the board.**"

You are hereby referred to Statutes of California, 1937, Chapter 753, as amended, for a full text of the State Civil Service Act.

Dated April 13, 1942.

Secretary, State Personnel Board
of the State of California.

STATISTICAL
APPENDIX

The tables which follow include all of the statistical data which were utilized in the descriptions and analyses of Part I, except those which were adequately represented in footnotes or in text tables. Their order is approximately that of the sections in Part I. Thus, tables 1–11 cover prewar demography in terms of immigration and settlement, nativity and age-sex structures, mortality, fertility, and the migration balance; tables 12–18 bear on prewar agricultural adjustments, urban enterprise, and occupational differentials; tables 19–24 include data on prewar religious, educational, and generational-educational differentials; and tables 25–29 are basic to the analyses of sociodemographic selection in postevacuation segregation (*spoilage*) and outmigration from War Relocation camps (*salvage*).

TABLE 1

JAPANESE IMMIGRATION TO, AND EMIGRATION FROM, THE CONTINENTAL
UNITED STATES: 1891–1942

Fiscal year ending	Immigration (aliens admitted)	Emigration (aliens departed)	Fiscal year ending	Immigration (aliens admitted)	Emigration (aliens departed)	Fiscal year ending	Immigration (aliens admitted)	Emigration (aliens departed)
1891	1,136		1908	9,544	4,796	1925	3,222	7,265
1892	1,498	No	1909	2,432	5,004	1926	4,652	7,751
1893	1,380	data	1910	2,598	5,024	1927	5,477	8,192
1894	1,931	from	1911	4,282	5,869	1928	5,935	8,016
1895	1,150	1891	1912	5,358	5,437	1929	6,293	7,281
1896	1,110	to	1913	6,771	5,647	1930	6,274	7,490
1897	1,526	1907	1914	8,462	6,300	1931	5,810	7,124
1898	2,230		1915	9,029	5,967	1932	4,137	6,138
1899	3,395		1916	9,100	6,922	1933	3,065	6,225
1900	12,628		1917	9,159	6,581	1934	2,927	5,368
1901	4,911		1918	11,143	7,691	1935	3,483	5,333
1902	5,330		1919	11,404	8,328	1936	3,719	4,855
1903	6,996		1920	12,868	11,662	1937	4,254	5,140
1904	7,792		1921	10,675	11,638	1938	3,908	4,610
1905	4,329		1922	8,981	11,173	1939	3,200	4,265
1906	5,192		1923	8,055	8,393	1940	2,942	4,206
1907	9,959		1924	11,526	9,248	1941	2,642	4,974
						1942	480	1,600

NOTES TO TABLE 1

Data for 1891 to 1930 from *Annual Reports of Commissioner General of Immigration* as cited by E. K. Strong, Jr., *The Second-Generation Japanese Problem* (Stanford University Press, 1934), tables 37–40, pp. 275–279. Data for 1931–1942, manuscript tables, furnished by U. S. Department of Justice, Bureau of Immigration.

Until 1898–1899, data on immigrants refer to country of origin (Japan) rather than persons of Japanese "race," which is the classification made in subsequent years. From 1900–1901 to 1906–1907, the official classification is merely in terms of "immigrant aliens" and "emigrant aliens," whereas for subsequent years the classes are subdivided as "immigrants" and "nonimmigrants," "emigrants" and "nonemigrants." Since there was little consistency in these definitions, we have, following Strong, combined the two immigrant and the two emigrant classes in the above table.

TABLE 2

INDEX OF UNITED STATES BUSINESS CYCLES: 1890–1920

Calendar year	Index	Calendar year	Index	Calendar year	Index
1890	0.96	1900	0.21	1910	0.46
1891	0.70	1901	0.19	1911	−0.17
1892	0.93	1902	0.60	1912	0.26
1893	0.02	1903	0.26	1913	0.34
1894	−1.37	1904	−0.37	1914	−0.66
1895	−0.52	1905	0.00	1915	−0.70
1896	−1.23	1906	0.52	1916	0.62
1897	−1.15	1907	0.90	1917	1.08
1898	−0.73	1908	−0.97	1918	1.25
1899	0.12	1909	0.08	1919	0.35
				1920	0.81

NOTES TO TABLE 2

The index is a composite of 9 economic series (prices, employment, imports, and so on) for which annual data were available for varying geographical coverage for the period 1870 to 1920. It is an unweighted average of the percentage deviations of each series from its trend in terms of their respective standard deviations. See W. F. Ogburn and D. S. Thomas, "The Influence of the Business Cycle on Certain Social Conditions," *Quarterly Publication of the American Statistical Association* (Sept., 1922), p. 327.

TABLE 3

Japanese American Population in Selected States, Regions, and Continental United States, 1880–1940, and by Nativity and Sex, 1900–1940

Census year	Sex	California	Washington	Oregon	Arizona	Calif., Wash., Oregon, Ariz.	Intermountain states	All other states	Total continental U.S.
				Total					
1880	*Total*...........	86	1	2	2	91	3	54	148
1890	*Total*...........	1,147	360	25	1	......	26	480	2,039
1900	Male........	9,598	5,432	2,405	264	17,699	4,790	852	23,341
	Female........	553	185	96	17	851	36	98	985
	Total........	10,151	5,617	2,501	281	18,550	4,826	950	24,326
1910	Male........	35,116	11,241	3,124	351	49,832	8,383	4,855	63,070
	Female........	6,240	1,688	294	20	8,242	343	502	9,087
	Total........	41,356	12,929	3,418	371	58,074	8,726	5,357	72,157
1920	Male........	45,414	11,322	2,802	383	59,921	6,736	6,050	72,707
	Female........	26,538	6,065	1,349	167	34,119	2,564	1,620	38,303
	Total........	71,952	17,387	4,151	550	94,040	9,300	7,670	111,010
1930	Male........	56,440	10,200	2,919	532	70,091	5,972	5,708	81,771
	Female........	41,016	7,637	2,039	347	51,039	3,671	2,353	57,063
	Total........	97,456	17,837	4,958	879	121,130	9,643	8,061	138,834
1940	Male........	52,550	8,033	2,271	354	63,208	4,332	4,427	71,967
	Female........	41,167	6,532	1,800	278	49,777	3,069	2,134	54,980
	Total........	93,717	14,565	4,071	632	112,985	7,401	6,561	126,947

(Continued on next page)

TABLE 3—*Continued*

Census year	Sex	California	Washington	Oregon	Arizona	Calif., Wash., Oregon, Ariz.	Intermountain states	All other states	Total continental U.S.
					Foreign born				
1900	Male...........	9,511	5,402	2,399	264	17,576	4,789	820	23,185
	Female..........	497	164	92	17	770	36	66	872
	Total..........	10,008	5,566	2,491	281	18,346	4,825	886	24,057
1910	Male...........	33,497	10,833	3,043	346	47,719	8,279	4,732	60,730
	Female..........	4,687	1,341	237	19	6,284	259	382	6,925
	Total..........	38,184	12,174	3,280	365	54,003	8,538	5,114	67,655
1920	Male...........	34,550	9,018	2,312	319	46,199	5,602	5,412	57,213
	Female..........	16,588	3,948	845	110	21,491	1,618	1,016	24,125
	Total..........	51,138	12,966	3,157	429	67,690	7,220	6,428	81,338
1930	Male...........	30,751	5,590	1,685	288	38,314	3,420	4,163	45,897
	Female..........	17,726	3,329	912	127	22,094	1,412	1,074	24,580
	Total..........	48,477	8,919	2,597	415	60,408	4,832	5,237	70,477
1940	Male...........	20,618	3,385	974	137	25,114	1,825	2,712	29,651
	Female..........	12,951	2,298	643	83	15,975	898	781	17,654
	Total..........	33,569	5,683	1,617	220	41,089	2,723	3,493	47,305

American born

1900	Male	87	30	6	...	123	1	32	156
	Female	56	21	4	...	81	...	32	113
	Total	143	51	10	...	204	1	64	269
1910	Male	1,619	408	81	5	2,113	104	123	2,340
	Female	1,553	347	57	1	1,958	84	120	2,162
	Total	3,172	755	138	6	4,071	188	243	4,502
1920	Male	10,864	2,304	490	64	13,722	1,134	638	15,494
	Female	9,950	2,117	504	57	12,628	946	604	14,178
	Total	20,814	4,421	994	121	26,350	2,080	1,242	29,672
1930	Male	25,689	4,610	1,234	244	31,777	2,552	1,545	35,874
	Female	23,290	4,308	1,127	220	28,945	2,259	1,279	32,483
	Total	48,979	8,918	2,361	464	60,722	4,811	2,824	68,357
1940	Male	31,932	4,648	1,297	217	38,094	2,507	1,715	42,316
	Female	28,216	4,234	1,157	195	33,802	2,171	1,353	37,326
	Total	60,148	8,882	2,454	412	71,896	4,678	3,068	79,642

SOURCE: Obtained from decennial Population Censuses of the United States. Intermountain States comprise Montana, Idaho, Wyoming, Colorado, Utah, and Nevada.

TABLE 4
JAPANESE AMERICAN POPULATION IN CALIFORNIA, WASHINGTON, OREGON, AND ARIZONA

(by Age and Sex, 1900, 1910, 1920, and 1930; and by Age, Sex, and Nativity, 1940)

Age	1900	1910	1920	1930	1940		
					Total	Foreign-born	American-born
Males							
0–4	69	1,602	8,729	7,995	3,757	30	3,727
5–9	32	528	3,688	10,651	4,186	37	4,149
10–14	126	242	1,266	6,888	6,537	64	6,473
15–19	3,537	2,030	2,672	3,974	9,435	140	9,295
20–24	4,828	8,860	3,650	2,763	7,880	227	7,653
25–29	4,215	12,437	3,271	4,022	4,305	341	3,964
30–34	2,386	10,975	8,413	4,105	2,520	959	1,561
35–39	1,272	6,752	9,919	3,223	3,337	2,588	749
40–44	750	3,857	8,972	7,324	3,154	2,892	262
45–49	284	1,466	5,189	7,500	2,301	2,169	132
50–54	123	707	2,681	6,657	5,215	5,157	58
55–59	25	184	943	2,996	4,752	4,720	32
60–64	39	166	381	1,462	3,677	3,662	15
65–69	} 13	} 18	116	} 532	1,506	1,500	6
70–74			23		485	476	9
75+	......	8	8		161	152	9
Total	17,699	49,832	59,921	70,092	63,208	25,114	38,094
Females							
0–4	61	1,578	8,133	7,595	3,432	25	3,407
5–9	33	462	3,337	10,390	4,171	39	4,132
10–14	19	178	1,092	6,517	6,324	54	6,270
15–19	73	314	1,137	3,174	8,703	105	8,598
20–24	277	1,411	4,473	2,181	6,756	216	6,540
25–29	206	1,809	5,951	3,836	3,362	251	3,111
30–34	100	1,342	3,944	5,428	1,950	812	1,138
35–39	45	690	2,708	4,750	3,044	2,673	371
40–44	15	298	1,923	3,161	3,914	3,782	132
45–49	10	91	902	1,851	3,553	3,490	63
50–54	7	43	353	1,317	2,197	2,172	25
55–59	1	18	101	538	1,165	1,160	5
60–64	1	6	38	202	773	770	3
65–69	} 3	} 1	16	} 99	293	292	1
70–74			5		81	80	1
75+	...	1	6		59	54	5
Total	851	8,242	34,119	51,039	49,777	15,975	33,802

NOTES TO TABLE 4

Age-sex distributions of the Japanese American population resident in California, Washington, Oregon, and Arizona had to be partly estimated from U. S. census data for all years except 1940. The 1940 data, used here, are the U. S. census tabulations as published by the Western Defense Command and Fourth Army. (Statistical Division, *Bulletin 12*, San Francisco, March 15, 1943.)

For 1900, age-sex data were published by the Census Bureau for the continental United States as a whole but not for separate states; whereas data for Arizona were unavailable for 1910, 1920, and 1930. The distributions for 1900 were, therefore, reduced to 75.8 per cent for males and to 86.4 per cent for females, these being the ratios of total Japanese males and females, respectively, in the four states to those in the continental United States. Inasmuch as the three-state totals in 1910, 1920, and 1930 represented 99.3, 99.4, and 99.2 per cent of the males and 99.8, 99.5, and 99.3 per cent of the females in the four states, the three-state distributions for these years were raised by dividing each age-sex class by the appropriate percentage. The data for 1930 (obtained in photostatic form from the Census Bureau) had further to be adjusted by breaking 10-year age classes for ages 35 and over into 5-year classes. This was accomplished by applying survival coefficients (see tables 7 and 9, below) based on 1919–1921 life tables to the 1920 age-sex distribution for 25 years and older and reciprocals of survival coefficients based on 1939–1941 life tables to the 1940 age-sex distribution for 45 years and older, averaging the two estimates for each resulting five-year class as of 1930, and adjusting the estimates to the ten-year recorded totals.

TABLE 5

JAPANESE AMERICAN EVACUEES IN WRA CAMPS, 1942, BY AGE, SEX, AND
GENERATIONAL-EDUCATIONAL CLASSES

Age	Males				Females			
	Issei	Kibei	Nisei	Total	Issei	Kibei	Nisei	Total
0–4	18	.....	4,165	4,183	13	.....	3,860	3,873
5–9	25	.....	3,584	3,609	34	.....	3,520	3,554
10–14	36	27	4,737	4,800	41	28	4,626	4,695
15–19	68	525	7,379	7,972	64	346	7,387	7,797
20–24	120	1,848	6,069	8,037	139	1,348	6,601	8,088
25–29	147	1,755	3,116	5,018	129	1,503	3,265	4,897
30–34	303	911	1,452	2,667	274	703	1,240	2,217
35–39	1,652	405	706	2,763	1,625	211	406	2,242
40–44	2,812	127	302	3,241	3,336	61	125	3,522
45–49	1,896	37	93	2,026	3,792	21	59	3,872
50–54	3,415	25	25	3,465	2,725	7	14	2,746
55–59	4,851	2	5	4,858	1,529	.....	6	1,535
60–64	4,339	1	3	4,343	960	.....	1	961
65–69	2,429	.....	⎫	2,433	464	⎫	⎫	473
70–74	810	.....	⎬ 4	810	130	⎬ 1	⎬ 8	130
75+	290	.....	⎭	290	54	⎭	⎭	54
Total	23,211	5,663	31,640	60,514	15,309	4,229	31,118	50,656

NOTES TO TABLE 5

Based on data collated from tables 28, 30, and 37, in U.S. Department of the
Interior, War Relocation Authority, *The Evacuated People* (Washington, 1946),
Issei are the Japan-born, *Nisei* the American-born who had had no schooling
in Japan, and *Kibei* the American-born who had had some or all of their education in Japan. Inasmuch as most Nisei and Kibei were second-generation, that
is, children of Issei, these classes are termed "generational-educational" in
this and following tables.

TABLE 6

AMERICAN-BORN JAPANESE IN WRA CAMPS, 1942

(By Age-Groups under 20 Years of Age and by Nativity of Parents)

Age in 1942	Number					Per cent			
	Both parents foreign	Father foreign, mother American	Father American, mother foreign	Both parents American born	Total	Both parents foreign	Father foreign, mother American	Father American, mother foreign	Both parents American
1) All ages..........	58,607	6,635	1,125	5,965	72,332	81.0	9.2	1.6	8.2
2) Under 20.........	26,911	6,285	1,003	5,826	40,025	67.2	15.7	2.5	14.6
3) 20 and over......	31,696	350	122	139	32,307	98.1	1.1	0.4	0.4
4) Under 3.........	626	1,506	94	2,888	5,114	12.2	29.5	1.8	56.5
0-1..............	176	467	27	1,201	1,871	9.4	25.0	1.4	64.2
1-2..............	215	523	36	929	1,703	12.7	30.7	2.1	54.5
2-3..............	235	516	31	758	1,540	12.2	13.7	2.6	8.4
5) 3-19............	26,285	4,779	909	2,938	34,911	75.3	13.7	2.6	8.4
6) 3 and over......	57,981	5,129	1,031	3,077	67,218	86.3	7.6	1.5	4.6

NOTES TO TABLE 6

Lines 1 to 3 were obtained from *The Evacuated People*, (U.S. Department of the Interior, *op. cit.*), table 34. 318 cases in which nativity of one or both parents was unknown were excluded.

Line 4 was obtained by special tabulation, U.S. Bureau of the Census, of live births by sex and parent nativity for California, Washington, Oregon, and Arizona for 1940, 1941, and 1942. Percentages based on these tabulations were applied to WRA population by sex for one-year groupings up to three years of age as of January 1, 1943 (*The Evacuated People*, table 36), and summed to obtain the estimated nativity groupings for the population under three years of age.

Line 5 was obtained by subtracting Line 4 from Line 2.

Line 6 was obtained by subtracting Line 4 from Line 1.

The columns headed "Both parents American born" represent Sansei.

TABLE 7
AGE-SPECIFIC DEATH RATES AND SELECTED LIFE-TABLE VALUES: JAPANESE AMERICANS, IN CALIFORNIA, WASHINGTON, AND OREGON, BY SEX, 1919–1921, 1929–1931, AND 1939–1941

(A and B) Age interval x to $x + n$ (C) Age x	Males			Females		
	1919–1921	1929–1931	1939–1941	1919–1921	1929–1931	1939–1941
A. Age-specific death rates ($_nm_x$)						
0	0.10973	0.06592	0.05000	0.08754	0.05909	0.03652
1–4	.01377	.00752	.00380	.01264	.00714	.00322
5–9	.00565	.00265	.00127	.00391	.00223	.00103
10–14	.00397	.00263	.00122	.00644	.00201	.00084
15–19	.00576	.00431	.00162	.01326	.00381	.00164
20–24	.00791	.00620	.00266	.01153	.00462	.00188
25–29	.00760	.00526	.00309	.01120	.00420	.00318
30–34	.00909	.00589	.00476	.01129	.00408	.00256
35–39	.00799	.00661	.00479	.01039	.00609	.00352
40–44	.00946	.00739	.00507	.01134	.00484	.00409
45–49	.01183	.01045	.00882	0.00969	.00756	.00684
50–54	.01588	.01402	.01042	......	0.01237	.00819
55–59	0.02318	.01933	.01705	......	......	.01459
60–64	......	0.03136	.02701	......	......	.01850
65–69	......	......	.04250	......	......	0.03413
70–74	......	......	0.05299	......	......	......
B. Number Surviving to Age x out of 100,000 Born Alive (l_x)						
0	100,000	100,000	100,000	100,000	100,000	100,000
1–4	90,661	94,131	95,474	92,378	94,701	96,647
5–9	86,030	91,438	94,073	88,027	92,125	95,443
10–14	83,631	90,234	93,478	86,322	91,103	94,952
15–19	81,986	89,055	92,910	83,584	90,192	94,554
20–24	79,656	87,155	92,160	78,209	88,489	93,781
25–29	76,562	84,492	90,942	73,818	86,467	92,903
30–34	73,703	82,297	89,547	69,789	84,668	91,437
35–39	70,422	79,906	87,439	65,951	82,957	90,274
40–44	67,660	77,305	85,368	62,606	80,466	88,698
45–59	64,529	74,497	83,229	59,148	78,540	86,901
50–54	60,815	70,697	79,633	56,346	75,622	83,975
55–59	56,159	65,898	75,582	52,924	71,076	80,600
60–64	49,987	59,805	69,386	48,358	64,944	74,914
65–69	43,254	51,076	60,575	42,516	57,098	68,272
70–74	34,684	40,956	48,890	34,762	46,685	57,485
75–79	24,698	29,165	37,405	25,460	34,192	44,799

TABLE 7—*Continued*

(A and B) Age interval x to $x + n$ (C) Age x	Males			Females		
	1919–1921	1929–1931	1939–1941	1919–1921	1929–1931	1939–1941

C. Average Number of Years Remaining at Age x $(\overset{\circ}{e}_x)$ or Expectation of Life

0.........	51.2	57.5	63.2	50.7	60.4	67.1
1.........	55.4	60.1	65.2	53.9	62.8	68.4
10.........	50.8	53.5	57.6	47.7	56.1	60.6
20.........	43.1	45.2	48.3	42.0	47.6	51.3
30.........	36.2	37.6	39.6	36.5	39.5	42.4
40.........	29.0	29.7	31.2	30.1	31.3	33.5
50.........	21.6	22.0	23.1	23.0	23.0	25.1
60.........	15.1	15.0	15.7	15.8	15.8	17.4

NOTES TO TABLE 7

The life-table values shown in the second and third sections of this table were computed by the Reed-Merrell method (See Margaret J. Hagood, *Statistics for Sociologists*, Reynal and Hitchcock, New York, 1941, pp. 857–866), on the basis of the age-specific death rates shown in the first section, which were computed on the basis of official death statistics (U.S. Census Bureau) and the population estimates of table 4, above. For terminal ages, $_nq_x$ values for whites in the U.S. death registration area, 1919–1920 were substituted in the 1919–1921 and 1929–1931 computations, and $_nq_x$ values for whites in California, Washington, and Oregon in 1940 were substituted in the 1939–1941 computations.

Comparable tables prepared for whites in Washington, Oregon, and Arizona as of 1919–1920 and of 1940 yielded the following values for expectation of life at birth (age 0):

	Males	*Females*
1919–1920..............	55.7	59.2
1940..................	62.0	68.3

The following values are presented for the population of Japan in the League of Nations, *Statistical Year Book*, (1941–1942):

	Males	*Females*
1921–1925..............	42.1	43.2
1935–1936..............	46.9	49.6

TABLE 8

AGE-SPECIFIC BIRTH RATES, TOTAL FERTILITY RATES, AND GROSS
REPRODUCTION RATES

(Japanese Americans in Washington, 1921–1922 and 1940–1941; and in California,
Washington, and Oregon, 1940-1941)

(Birth Rates per 1,000 Women)

Age of women	Washington		California, Washington, and Oregon
	1921–1922	1940–1941	1940–1941
15–19.................	185.9	4.0	6.5
20–24.................	440.0	64.3	96.0
25–29.................	380.0	169.6	198.8
30–34.................	317.7	117.9	115.6
35–39.................	209.3	26.2	44.8
40–44.................	97.1	11.9	16.2
45–49.................	6.5	0.0	2.3
Gross reproduction rates (daughters per woman).............	3.98	1.02	1.17

NOTES TO TABLE 8

The gross reproduction rates shown above were computed directly from age-
specific fertility rates, the latter based on data made available for 1940–1941,
in photostat form, by the U.S. Census Bureau and from tables published by the
Bureau for the State of Washington for 1921–1922.

For 1920 and 1930, it was possible to compute gross reproduction rates by an
indirect method (see David Glass, *Population Policies and Movements*, Oxford
University Press, 1940, pp. 387–393). In these computations, fertility schedules
for 1940 were used to obtain "expected births." They are shown below, in
comparison with directly computed rates for whites in California, Washington,
and Oregon and for rates reported for Japan in the League of Nations *Statistical
Year Book* (1941–1942):

California, Washington, Oregon				Japan	
Japanese		Whites			
Year	G.R.R.	Year	G.R.R.	Year	G.R.R.
1920	3.41	1920	1.14	1925	2.60
1930	1.67	1940	.97	1937	2.14

TABLE 9

NET MIGRATION OF JAPANESE AMERICANS TO AND FROM CALIFORNIA, WASHINGTON, OREGON, AND ARIZONA, BY AGE AND SEX, 1910–1919, 1920–1929 AND 1930–1939

(Estimated by Comparisons between Population Resident at Given Census Year and Expected Survivors of Residents at Preceding Census and of Intercensal Births)

Males

Age	1920 Residents	1920 Expected survivors of births 1910–1919 and of residents in 1910	1910–1919 Net migration	1930 Residents	1930 Expected survivors of births 1920–1929 and of residents in 1920	1920–1929 Net migration	1940 Residents	1940 Expected survivors of births 1930–1939 and of residents in 1930	1930–1939 Net migration
0–4	9,046	11,781	−2,735	8,166	9,840	−1,674	3,858	4,141	−283
5–9	3,688	4,765	−1,077	10,651	14,477	−3,826	4,186	5,273	−1,087
10–14	1,266	1,554	−288	6,888	8,585	−1,697	6,537	7,925	−1,388
15–19	2,672	505	2,167	3,974	3,556	418	9,435	10,437	−1,002
20–24	3,650	228	3,422	2,763	1,203	1,560	7,880	6,681	1,199
25–29	3,271	1,898	1,373	4,022	2,513	1,509	4,305	3,817	488
30–34	8,413	8,176	237	4,105	3,409	696	2,520	2,641	121
35–39	9,919	11,362	−1,443	3,048	3,038	10	3,337	3,825	−488
40–44	8,972	10,072	−1,100	7,499	7,805	−306	3,154	3,881	727
45–49	5,189	6,134	−945	7,616	9,088	−1,472	2,301	3,009	−708
50–54	2,681	3,417	−736	6,541	8,013	−1,472	5,215	6,671	−1,456
55–59	943	1,243	−300	3,076	4,449	−1,373	4,752	6,593	−1,841
60–64	381	564	−183	1,382	2,161	−779	3,677	5,506	−1,829
65–69	116	136	−20	532 }	1,005 }	−473 }	1,506	2,229	−723
70–74	23	120 }	−89 }				485	923	−438
75+	8						161	266	−105
Total	60,238	61,955	−1,717	70,263	79,142	−8,879	63,309	73,818	−10,509

(Continued on next page)

TABLE 9—*Continued*

Females

Age	1920 Residents	1920 Expected survivors of births 1910-1919 and of residents in 1910	1910-1919 Net migration	1930 Residents	1930 Expected survivors of births 1920-1929 and of residents in 1920	1920-1929 Net migration	1940 Residents	1940 Expected survivors of births 1930-1939 and of residents in 1930	1930-1939 Net migration
0-4	8,428	11,347	− 2,919	7,758	9,380	− 1,622	3,527	3,998	− 471
5-9	3,337	4,627	− 1,290	10,390	13,918	− 3,528	4,171	5,116	− 945
10-14	1,092	1,536	− 444	6,517	8,044	− 1,527	6,324	7,599	− 1,275
15-19	1,137	431	706	3,174	3,188	− 14	8,703	10,221	− 1,518
20-24	4,473	159	4,314	2,181	1,016	1,165	6,756	6,356	400
25-29	5,951	278	5,673	3,836	1,047	2,789	3,362	3,072	290
30-34	3,944	1,259	2,685	5,428	4,138	1,290	1,950	2,106	− 156
35-39	2,708	1,620	1,088	4,794	5,507	− 713	3,044	3,695	− 651
40-44	1,923	1,205	718	3,117	3,642	− 525	3,914	5,200	− 1,286
45-49	902	620	282	1,866	2,495	− 629	3,553	4,512	− 959
50-54	353	264	89	1,302	1,742	− 440	2,197	2,943	− 746
55-59	101			543	787	− 244	1,165	1,665	− 500
60-64	38			197	297	− 100	773	1,128	− 355
65-69	16	132	34	99	117	− 18	293	425	− 132
70-74	11						81	190	− 50
75+							59		
Total	34,414	23,478	+10,936	51,202	55,318	−4,116	49,872	58,226	−8,354

A constant correction factor of 13 per cent was applied to ages 0–1 to allow for underenumeration. This was derived by comparing the "expected survivors" of the 1940 population under one year of age, and aged 1–4, by sex, with the population enumerated at 3 years of age and at 4–7, respectively, in the War Relocation Authority's census of January 1, 1943. (See tables 10 and 11.) There was, apparently, almost no underenumeration of children aged 1–4.

Expected survivors of births occurring during each decade preceding the 1920, 1930, and 1940 censuses were estimated as described in table 10, and are shown here in rows for ages 0–4 and 5–9.

Expected survivors, at each census, of residents aged 5–9 and over at the preceding census are shown in rows for ages 15–19 and over. They were estimated by applying 10-year survival coefficients, derived after direct interpolation of 1_x values for the midpoint of each quinquennial class in the life tables. (See table 7, above.) The procedure is essentially that described by E. P. Hutchinson, "The Use of Routine Census and Vital Statistics Data for the Determination of Migration by Age and Sex in the Absence of Continuous Registration of Migrants," in D. S. Thomas, *Research Memorandum on Migration Differentials*, Social Science Research Council, New York, 1938, pp. 387–398. It can be clarified by an example: The interpolated 1_x value for males aged $7\frac{1}{2}$, according to our 1919–1921 life-table, is 84,461 and for those aged $17\frac{1}{2}$, 80,934. The ratio of the latter to the former (0.9562) is the proportion of males aged 5–9 in 1920 who would, on the basis of the mortality experience represented in the life-table, be expected to survive to ages 15–19 in 1930. But, since Japanese American mortality rates declined rapidly between 1920 and 1930, allowance should be made for changing patterns. This was accomplished by averaging 0.9562, the coefficient derived from the 1919–1921 life-table, and 0.9720, a coefficient similarly derived from the 1929–1931 life-table. The expected survivors aged 15–19 in 1930 of the 3,688 male residents aged 5–9 in 1920 are, therefore, 3,556, the product of the number of residents and the average survival coefficient. All classes of expected survivors over 15 years old in 1930 were similarly based on average survival coefficients of the 1919–1921 and 1929–1931 life-tables, and those for 1940 were derived from averages of 1929–1931 and 1939–1941 values.

Since adequate data for the construction of life-tables before 1919–1921 were not available, values from this table alone were used to estimate survivors in 1920. If, as is probable, mortality declined between 1910 and 1920, expected survivors computed in this manner are overestimated.

Estimates of survivors aged 10–14, based as they are on residents aged 0–4, presented special difficulties, for deaths of children under one year of age predominate in the latter class and are distributed quite unevenly throughout the first year of life. Moreover, concentrations within the first month of life tend to be disproportionately high for populations with high survival patterns, where "preventable" deaths in the later months of infancy have been reduced to a minimum and the residual infant mortality is heavily weighted with neonatal deaths. For these reasons, a 1_x value, interpolated for age $2\frac{1}{2}$ for the quinquennial class 0–4 would have little meaning, if used with the value for age $12\frac{1}{2}$, to compute a ten-year survival coefficient. To minimize distortion due to uneven distribution of deaths during the first year of life, survival coefficients were computed for the tenth year in ratio to the first, the 1_x value for the latter taking account of the probable distribution of deaths under and over 6 months of age. Lacking information on the distribution of Japanese American deaths under one year of age, we used approximations based on other life-tables, where the patterns of survival, in general, conformed closely to those of Japanese Americans. Two of the life-tables presented by T. N. Greville (16th Census of the United States, *United States Life Tables and Actuarial Tables*, 1939–1941) were acceptable, from this standpoint. The high survival patterns of Japanese Americans on the West Coast, 1939–1941, approximated those of U. S. whites for the same period; the low survival pattern of Japanese Americans in 1919–1921 is similar to that of U. S. "other races" (i. e., all "racial" groups except whites and Negroes) two decades later (1939–1941). On the assumption that the life-table deaths (d_x or the difference between successive values of 1_x, shown in table 7) under one year of age could be distributed by months of life as were those of U. S. whites (Greville, *op. cit.*, p. 51) and that those for 1919–1921 could, similarly, be distributed as were those of U. S. "other races" in 1939–1941 (*ibid.*, p. 53), we obtained 1_x values for six months of age. Survival coefficients were then computed as ratios of the interpolated 1_x values for age $10\frac{1}{2}$ to those for age $\frac{1}{2}$, and were applied to residents under one year of age. Ratios of 1_x values, interpolated at age 13, to those interpolated at age 3 were similarly applied to residents aged 1–4. Combining the corresponding products of coefficients and residents, we obtained expected survivors aged 10–14. The 1_x values for age $\frac{1}{2}$ for 1929–1931 were obtained by weighting the 1939–1941 values 0.72 for males and 0.57 for females, against weights of 0.28 for males and 0.43 for females for the 1919–1921 values. These weights reflected the proportionate improvement at age 1 in life-table survivors between 1919–1921 and 1929–1931, as compared with the improvement between the latter date and 1939–1941. The 1_x values for $\frac{1}{2}$ year, compared with those for 1 year, are shown below:

NUMBER SURVIVING TO SPECIFIED AGE OUT OF 100,000 BORN ALIVE

Age	1919–1921		1929–1931		1939–1941	
	Males	Females	Males	Females	Males	Females
$\frac{1}{2}$ year.....	92,539	94,081	95,022	95,692	95,987	97,064
1 year......	90,661	92,378	94,131	94,701	95,474	96,647

Many of the classes of expected survivors are small, and are undoubtedly subject to errors too large to warrant presenting them, as we do, as apparently accurate to the last digit. This was done solely for manipulatory convenience.

Although "exact" coefficients (i.e., those obtained, without further manipulation, from the life-table values shown in table 7) were applied to all resident-groups up to ages 60–64, an "arbitrary" value of 0.50 was applied to age-groups 65 and over.

The difference between residents enumerated at a given census, and the survivors expected among residents younger by ten years at the preceding census, gives an approximation of intercensal gain or loss by migration. If residents exceed expected survivors, the difference is attributed to a gain by migration; correspondingly, if expected survivors exceed residents, the difference is attributed to a loss by migration. It is a useful approximation, and yields valuable data on the age-sex patterns of migratory gains and losses, but it has serious limitations, which must be noted.

In the first place, being a residual figure, it will reflect errors inherent in the application of survival coefficients. The assumption is implicit that losses of the basic population, due to death, have been eliminated. In fact, however, the difference between the basic population and expected survivors 10 years later, gives "expected" rather than actual deaths.

In the second place, its relationship to the magnitude of gross migration is quite variable. High or low gross migration may result in the same amount of "net migration." Under some circumstances, it will tell as little about migration streams as would data for "natural increase" alone tell about births and deaths. Migrants entering after one census and departing before the next are counted neither as residents nor as expected survivors. The number of migrants entering, compensated by the number of migrants departing, will have no influence on the net figure. If, however, the streams of migration tend to be unidirectional, net migration will approximate gross migration. This was true of some age-sex classes among the Japanese population, for example, many American-born children under 10 years of age were sent to Japan and most of them did not return to America until in adolescent years. Since few Japanese-born of these age groups entered or left the country after 1924, gains and losses, respectively, up to about age 20 reflect the Kibei movement. The number of elderly aliens leaving the United States was only slightly compensated by immigrants of these age groups at any time. Losses over age 50 approximate the stream of return migration to Japan. Among other classes, and particularly during the period of relatively free entrance of immigrants, streams of young adults entering the country were however heavily compensated by counter-streams of young adults returning to Japan, and net migration probably represents a narrow margin between heavy streams inward and outward.

In the third place, migration gains and losses are systematically underestimated as well as overestimated. The direction of the biases can be suggested, but their amounts cannot be determined accurately. Hutchinson (*op. cit.*, pp. 397 ff.) points out that there is underestimation to the extent that immigrants enter after one census and die before the next, and overestimation to the extent that residents at the first census have been counted as "expected deaths" though they have, in fact, emigrated before the age for which their "death risks" were computed. Since the streams of immigrants from Japan to the United States were composed of persons of ages of low mortality risk, the underestimation of gains is probably of slight importance. The overestimation of losses during the last two decades considered may, however, have been appreciable, since emigrants departing were old, and appreciable numbers may have been erroneously estimated as "expected deaths" of residents when they were in fact subject to the imputed mortality risk after they had ceased to be residents of this country.

TABLE 10

Births to Japanese Americans in California, Washington, Oregon, and Arizona 1910–1942, and Expected Survivors of These Births in 1920, 1930, 1940, and 1943 by Sex

Year of birth	Males					Females				
	Births	Expected survivors				Births	Expected survivors			
		1920	1930	1940	1943		1920	1930	1940	1943
1910	492	412	396	379	374	465	402	379	366	363
1911	678	571	550	527	521	642	557	529	512	507
1912	997	843	813	780	772	943	820	783	758	751
1913	1,500	1,277	1,232	1,185	1,174	1,418	1,239	1,189	1,152	1,140
1914	1,939	1,662	1,602	1,543	1,529	1,833	1,609	1,549	1,503	1,489
1915	2,246	1,938	1,866	1,801	1,785	2,123	1,875	1,808	1,757	1,741
1916	2,493	2,169	2,082	2,013	1,995	2,358	2,099	2,021	1,966	1,950
1917	2,742	2,413	2,304	2,235	2,217	2,593	2,331	2,238	2,182	2,169
1918	2,805	2,513	2,375	2,309	2,291	2,652	2,424	2,305	2,252	2,238
1919	2,971	2,748	2,542	2,478	2,458	2,782	2,618	2,443	2,392	2,380
1920	3,290	...	2,869	2,803	2,783	3,153	...	2,803	2,750	2,736
1921	3,526	...	3,099	3,034	3,016	3,323	...	2,971	2,918	2,903
1922	3,341	...	2,963	2,904	2,887	3,092	...	2,783	2,738	2,724
1923	3,298	...	2,955	2,899	2,885	3,061	...	2,776	2,734	2,720
1924	2,854	...	2,591	2,542	2,529	2,822	...	2,585	2,546	2,533
1925	2,956	...	2,708	2,654	2,643	2,776	...	2,562	2,521	2,511
1926	2,356	...	2,168	2,122	2,114	2,172	...	2,013	1,979	1,973
1927	2,004	...	1,856	1,813	1,806	1,962	...	1,829	1,792	1,787
1928	1,837	...	1,718	1,668	1,661	1,632	...	1,536	1,498	1,494
1929	1,463	...	1,390	1,336	1,332	1,505	...	1,440	1,390	1,387
1930	1,423	...	...	1,309	1,305	1,276	...	...	1,189	1,187
1931	1,265	...	...	1,168	1,164	1,200	...	...	1,122	1,120
1932	1,141	...	...	1,058	1,055	1,096	...	...	1,029	1,027
1933	937	...	...	873	870	959	...	...	905	902
1934	922	...	...	865	862	916	...	...	871	868
1935	879	...	...	828	824	888	...	...	848	845
1936	846	...	...	799	794	775	...	...	742	738
1937	852	...	...	807	801	806	...	...	774	769
1938	907	...	...	863	854	857	...	...	826	819
1939	879	...	...	844	830	832	...	...	808	797
1940	904	...	...	...	856	820	...	...	...	787
1941	967	...	...	...	921	935	...	...	...	901
1942	963	...	...	...	924	863	...	...	...	838

NOTES TO TABLE 10

The four-state series for births by sex had to be partly estimated, as follows:
(1) For 1910–1918 and for 1937–1939 the only series available was that for total
births, by years, for California (Bulletins of the California State Department
of Health). Japanese women of childbearing ages (15–44) in California represented 74.6 per cent of Japanese women of these ages in all four states in 1910 and
77.3 per cent in 1920. But California women were apparently more fertile than
those in the other states, inasmuch as Japanese births in California in 1919–1921
accounted for 77.8 per cent of the births in the four states. California births
were, therefore, assumed to represent 75.1 per cent of the total in 1910 and 77.8
per cent in 1920, and estimates for intermediate years were obtained by linear
interpolation. Four-state totals for 1937–1939 were estimated on a similar basis
by dividing California births by 86.6, and for 1940–1941, by 86.7 per cent. Sex
proportions of 51.4 per cent male and 48.6 per cent female, representing an
average for all years in which the sex distribution of births was known (1919–
1936 and 1940–1942) were applied to total estimated births for 1910–1918 and
1937–1939. Finally, the series was adjusted for data missing for Arizona by
dividing by 99.5 per cent in 1919–1921, 99.4 per cent in 1922–1923, and 99.3 per
cent in 1924–1925. Sources for the three-state totals by sex for 1919–1925 and for
four-state totals by sex for 1926–1936 were the annual reports on vital statistics
of the U.S. Bureau of the Census. For 1940–1942, photostatic copies of unpublished tabulations were obtained from the Census Bureau through the
courtesy of the War Relocation Authority.

The rationale for estimating expected survivors of births was the same as that
developed for estimating expected survivors of the population (see table 9)
except that estimated L_x and L_{x-10} values, interpolated from l_x values shown in
table 9 were used and that the survival coefficients so computed were weighted
by years of exposure to the mortality patterns prevailing at successive life-table
periods. (See E. P. Hutchinson, *op. cit.*, pp. 378–381.)

TABLE 11

AMERICAN-BORN JAPANESE EVACUEES (AS OF JANUARY 1, 1943), WHO WERE BORN IN CALIFORNIA, WASHINGTON, OREGON, OR ARIZONA, BY SINGLE YEARS OF AGE AND SEX; EXPECTED SURVIVORS (AS OF JANUARY 1, 1943) OF BIRTHS TO JAPANESE AMERICANS IN THESE STATES AND ESTIMATED NET MIGRATION OF SURVIVORS, BY SINGLE YEARS AND SEX, 1910–1942

(Hundreds of persons)

Year of birth	Age (x to x+1)	Males				Females			
		American-born evacuees enumerated by WRA (1)	Estimated C-, W-, O-, A-born enumerated by WRA (2)	Expected survivors of births in C, W, O, A (3)	Estimated net migration of C-, W-, O-, A-born (4)	American-born evacuees enumerated by WRA (5)	Estimated C-, W-, O-, A-born enumerated by WRA (6)	Expected survivors of births in C, W, O, A (7)	Estimated net migration of C-, W-, O-, A-born (8)
1942	0	9.9	9.8	9.2	+ 0.6	8.8	8.7	8.4	+ 0.3
1941	1	8.8	8.7	9.2	− 0.5	8.2	8.2	9.0	− 0.8
1940	2	8.0	7.9	8.6	− 0.7	7.4	7.3	7.9	− 0.6
1939	3	7.6	7.5	8.3	− 0.8	7.3	7.2	8.0	− 0.8
1938	4	7.8	7.7	8.5	− 0.8	7.0	6.9	8.2	− 1.3
1937	5	7.5	7.4	8.0	− 0.6	6.7	6.6	7.7	− 1.1
1936	6	7.1	7.0	7.9	− 0.9	6.3	6.2	7.4	− 1.2
1935	7	7.0	6.9	8.2	− 1.3	7.2	7.1	8.5	− 1.4
1934	8	7.3	7.2	8.6	− 1.4	7.5	7.4	8.7	− 1.3
1933	9	6.9	6.8	8.7	− 1.9	7.3	7.2	9.0	− 1.8
1932	10	8.2	8.1	10.6	− 2.5	8.3	8.2	10.3	− 2.1
1931	11	8.7	8.5	11.6	− 3.1	8.7	8.5	11.2	− 2.7
1930	12	9.8	9.5	13.1	− 3.6	8.7	8.4	11.9	− 3.5
1929	13	9.6	9.4	13.3	− 3.9	10.2	10.0	13.9	− 3.9
1928	14	11.3	11.0	16.6	− 5.6	10.8	10.5	14.9	− 4.4
1927	15	12.4	12.2	18.1	− 5.9	12.4	12.2	17.9	− 5.7
1926	16	14.4	14.0	21.1	− 7.1	13.7	13.4	19.7	− 6.3
1925	17	16.0	15.6	26.4	−10.8	16.2	15.8	25.1	− 9.3
1924	18	15.9	15.4	25.3	− 9.9	16.4	15.9	25.3	− 9.4
1923	19	18.5	17.9	28.9	−11.0	17.2	16.7	27.2	−10.5
1922	20	18.6	17.6	28.9	−11.3	16.8	16.1	27.2	−11.1
1921	21	19.6	18.3	30.2	−11.9	17.7	16.9	29.0	−12.1
1920	22	15.6	14.6	27.8	−13.2	16.0	15.1	27.4	−12.3
1919	23	11.4	10.6	24.6	−14.0	14.8	13.9	23.8	− 9.9
1918	24	10.7	10.0	22.9	−12.9	12.3	11.5	22.4	−10.9
1917	25	10.4	9.6	22.2	−12.6	11.3	10.5	21.7	−11.2
1916	26	10.2	9.4	20.0	−10.6	9.9	9.2	19.5	−10.3
1915	27	10.0	9.2	17.9	− 8.7	10.2	9.2	17.4	− 8.2
1914	28	8.4	7.6	15.3	− 7.7	8.5	7.6	14.9	− 7.3
1913	29	8.0	7.1	11.7	− 4.6	6.6	5.7	11.4	− 5.7
1912	30	6.4	5.5	7.7	− 2.2	5.5	4.8	7.5	− 2.7
1911	31	5.3	4.5	5.2	− 0.7	4.4	3.8	5.1	− 1.3
1910	32	4.2	3.3	3.7	− 0.4	3.3	2.7	3.6	− 0.9
1910–42	0–32	341.5	325.8	508.3	−182.5	333.6	319.4	491.1	−171.7

Colums (1) and (5) were derived from table 36 in *The Evacuated People* (U.S. Department of the Interior, *op. cit.*, pp. 96–99); columns (2) and (6) by applying percentages interpolated graphically from the following, which were derived after reconciliation of table 20 in *The Evacuated People* (*Ibid.*, pp. 67–68) with table 36 from the same source:

PER CENT OF AMERICAN-BORN EVACUEES WHO WERE NATIVES OF CALIFORNIA, WASHINGTON, OREGON, AND ARIZONA

Age	Males	Females
0–14	98.5	98.4
15–19	97.2	97.4
20–24	93.4	94.6
25–29	91.2	90.9
30–34	81.1	82.2
35–39	41.5	51.7
45–54	14.2	21.9

Reconciliation of the two tables was necessitated by variation in definitions in *The Evacuated People*, table 36 being composed of all residents of WRA camps on January 1, 1943, all persons evacuated to WRA camps at any time during 1942, and also a contingent of almost 1,000 who entered from Hawaii, some of them as late as March, 1943. Thus, the former is a net figure, reflecting entrances, departures, births, and deaths, whereas the latter included entrants only. Table 36 was corrected by subtracting small numbers of Hawaiians and Alaskans who entered camp during 1942; and table 36 was corrected by adding births (609), and subtracting deaths (67) and net departures on indefinite leave (816), whose age and sex distributions were estimated by collating data from the following tables in *The Evacuated People*: table 14, p. 50; table 88, p. 190; table 91, p. 191; table 53 a, p. 139; table 57, p. 146. In reconciling tables 20 and 36, on the basis of these other data, the following assumptions were made: (1) that all births in WRA camps during 1942 were to preëvacuation residents of the four western states and could, therefore, be added to the category "born in California, Washington, Oregon, and Arizona," and, correspondingly, that all deaths under one year of age could be similarly allocated. Due to the late entrance of evacuees from Alaska, the fact that most of the Hawaiian evacuees entered WRA camps in 1943, and the implication that the remainder of the evacuees who were natives of other states must have been residents of California, Washington, Oregon, or Arizona in order to be evacuated from these states, these assumptions seem reasonable. (2) That deaths, except infant deaths, and net departures on indefinite leave could be assigned to each age-sex class of the American-born in proportion to the population in the four-state and other-state birthplace categories in this age-sex class. The most questionable of these assumptions is that outmigration (as measured by net departures on indefinite leave) was unselective, by nativity, inasmuch as natives of inland states may well have had superior opportunities to find homes in these states and to relocate immediately. The numbers involved were, however, so small that the maximum change possible in the percentage of the American-born who were natives of the four states would have raised the percentage shown for males aged 20–24 from 93.4 to 95.5 and for those aged 25–29 from 91.2 to 92.8

Columns (3) and (7) were computed by applying the same survival coefficients as were used in Table 11, above, to the data in columns (2) and (6). Columns (4) and (8) equal column (2) − column (3), and column (6) − column (7), respectively. As an estimate of net migration, these computations are subject to the sources of error indicated in table 9, above.

TABLE 12

Japanese-operated Farms by Tenure, California and Washington, 1910–1940

Tenure	California				Washington			
	1910	1920	1930	1940	1910	1920	1930	1940
	Number of farms							
Tenants..........	1,547	4,533	1,580	3,596	312	667	244	511
Managers........	36	113	1,816	249	3	5	180	10
Part owners......	} 233	} 506	70	293	} 1	} 27	12	62
Full owners......			490	997			87	123
Total........	1,816	5,152	3,956	5,135	316	699	523	706
	Per cent							
Tenants..........	85.2	88.0	39.9	70.0	98.7	95.4	46.7	72.4
Managers........	2.0	2.2	45.9	4.9	1.0	.7	34.4	1.4
Part owners......	} 12.8	} 9.8	1.8	5.7	} .3	} 3.9	2.3	8.8
Full owners......			12.4	19.4			16.6	17.4
Total........	100.0	100.0	100.0	100.0	100.0	100.0	100.0	100.0

Source: Derived from decennial agricultural censuses of the United States.

TABLE 15

NUMBER OF FIRMS BY INDUSTRY AND TYPE IN THE JAPANESE COMMUNITY IN SAN FRANCISCO, 1909, 1929, AND 1939; LOS ANGELES, 1909, 1928, AND 1939; AND SEATTLE, 1909, 1930, AND 1936

Industry	Type of firm (or occupation)	San Francisco 1909	San Francisco 1929	San Francisco 1939	Los Angeles 1909	Los Angeles 1928	Los Angeles 1939	Seattle 1909	Seattle 1930	Seattle 1936
Construction	Carpenters, painters, plumbers, etc.		14	18		19	24		11	11
Manufacturing	Newspapers	6	8	11	7	19	13	12		7
	Food and kindred products	2	4	7	0	16	19	0	7	6
	Others	12	8	6	3	21	30	7	4	5
Transportation	Taxicabs, trucking, etc.	5	10	5	10	18	11	10	11	10
Wholesale and Retail Trade	Import-export	5	38	14	0	28	18	0	24	11
	Oriental art	42	54	51	15		15	12		
	Fruit, vegetables, groceries, etc.	37	40	22	53	526	542	31	193	211
	Produce dealers			4		38	149			
	Drugs, books, confectionery, soda fountains	18	31	23	8	75	50	9	28	16
	Restaurants and bars	57	44	40	88	221	264	89	68	64
	Flower shops, nurseries, etc.	4	12	8		143	192		20	20
	Dry goods and specialties	13	35	35	0	10	38		51	50
	Fertilizers and farm implements		4	4		27	21			
Finance, Insurance, and Real Estate	Insurance		16	16		28	50		10	12
	Others		3	5			16		5	5
Business and Repair Services	Auto repair, sales, etc.		11	5		35	50		11	12
	Employment agencies	24	4	6	7	9	11	17	9	9
	Others	8	14	16	5	13	20	7	11	9
Personal Services	Hotels, apartments, rooms	51	46	35	90	221	361	72	157	177
	Cleaning, dyeing, repair	52	114	122	16	94	133	45	95	107
	Laundries	19	17	13	7	12	22	37	33	32
	Barber shops	18	15	15	44	107	60	46	52	39
	Beauty shops			4			18		3	7
	Bathhouses	13	14	4	26	18	7	26	5	3
	Shoe repair and shoe shops	76	23	12	17	14	15	5	20	20
	Photo studios	8	9	8	6	12	13	5	5	5
	Others	3	10	13			9	0	8	6
Amusement	Theaters, etc.	0	4	4	1		3	0	4	2
	Billiards, pool, shooting galleries	28	9	6	33	20	17	25	3	2
Professional and Related Services	Attorneys and legal advisors		13	4		19	20		6	4
	Dentists			11			28		12	12
	Physicians			4			37		8	6
	Others			5			24			1
Total		501	624	556	436	1,763	2,300	455	874	881

SOURCE: The data presented were collated from the sources listed in footnote 39, p. 28, above.

TABLE 14

Japanese Americans 14 Years Old and Over, by Labor-Force Status, Major Occupation Group of the Employed, Nativity, and Sex, Compared with Population Norms, California and Washington, 1940

California

Labor-force status and occupation	Foreign-born Japanese		Population norms for (1) and (2)		American-born Japanese		Population norms for (5) and (6)	
	Male (1)	Female (2)	Male (3)	Female (4)	Male (5)	Female (6)	Male (7)	Female (8)
Population 14 years old and over	20,530	12,863	20,530	12,863	21,115	17,980	21,115	17,980
Not in labor force	1,780	7,777	3,675	9,193	8,732	12,417	7,737	13,269
On public emergency work	21	3	743	118	46	22	589	197
Seeking work	502	102	1,766	290	439	232	1,822	708
Employed	18,227	4,981	14,346	3,262	11,898	5,309	10,967	3,806
Farmers and farm managers	3,901	233	1,050	32	1,584	79	227	5
Farm laborers (wage) and foremen	4,370	546	834	14	2,490	301	970	38
Farm laborers (unpaid, family)	222	1,240	17	21	1,537	960	154	29
Total employed: agricultural	8,493	2,019	1,901	67	5,611	1,340	1,351	72
Professional and semiprofessional	527	164	1,114	553	270	198	671	451
Proprietors, managers, etc	2,756	413	2,293	303	891	161	690	84
Clerical, sales, etc	985	469	2,100	979	1,983	1,175	2,077	1,631
Service (excluding domestic)	1,014	605	1,261	462	334	471	1,235	561
Skilled labor (craftsmen, etc.)	356	30	2,609	39	269	27	1,501	22
Semiskilled labor (operatives, etc.)	787	553	1,845	412	1,019	361	2,290	428
Unskilled labor	2,407	86	1,063	14	1,078	40	997	23
Domestic service	808	599	77	403	370	1,475	51	487
Total employed: nonagricultural	9,640	2,919	12,362	3,165	6,214	3,908	9,512	3,687
Occupation not reported	94	43	83	30	73	61	104	47

Washington

Labor-force status and occupation	Foreign-born Japanese		Population norms for (1) and (2)		American-born Japanese		Population norms for (5) and (6)	
	Male (1)	Female (2)	Male (3)	Female (4)	Male (5)	Female (6)	Male (7)	Female (8)
Population 14 years old and over	3,360	2,278	3,360	2,278	3,221	2,759	3,221	2,759
Not in labor force	282	1,126	481	1,761	1,589	1,828	1,334	2,090
On public emergency work	1	—	169	18	14	10	147	35
Seeking work	94	7	268	36	90	29	276	97
Employed	2,983	1,145	2,442	463	1,528	892	1,464	537
Farmers and farm managers	554	51	334	10	222	19	56	1
Farm laborers (wage) and foremen	224	55	89	2	101	15	129	2
Farm laborers (unpaid, family)	27	244	6	5	238	187	48	4
Total employed: agricultural	805	350	429	17	561	221	233	7
Professional and semiprofessional	81	31	136	75	32	32	64	73
Proprietors, managers, etc.	712	148	357	47	112	43	76	10
Clerical, sales, etc.	165	147	261	136	209	218	227	217
Service (excluding domestic)	376	205	169	76	135	90	178	82
Skilled labor (craftsmen, etc.)	128	12	463	5	36	9	162	2
Semiskilled labor (operatives, etc.)	242	194	312	48	153	98	282	39
Unskilled labor	423	13	296	3	235	5	221	4
Domestic service	37	35	4	51	36	161	3	94
Total employed: nonagricultural	2,164	785	1,998	441	948	656	1,213	521
Occupation not reported	14	10	15	5	19	15	18	9

Columns (1), (2), (5), and (6) were obtained from the 16th Census of the United States, *Characteristics of the Nonwhite Population by Race*, pp. 106–108. These are the "observed" or enumerated distributions of the Japanese population 14 years of age and older in 1940 by labor-force status and by occupation of the employed. Columns (3), (4), (7), and (8) show "population norms" for each sex-nativity group of the Japanese in California and in Washington, and represent the occupational distribution that this sex group in the general population would have had in terms of its own age-specific labor-force and occupational rates if its age structure had been identical with that of the Japanese group under comparison. The meaning of these norms can best be shown by an example, where some of the calculations needed to determine the population norm for American-born Japanese females in the State of Washington are carried through. Section (A) in the schematic table on the facing page gives a truncated distribution of the general female population in Washington for three age classes, four labor-force categories, and three occupational classes of the employed. Section (B) shows per cent distributions or "age-specific rates" of labor-force participation and occupation for each of the three age classes. In Section (C), the complete age distribution of American-born Japanese females in Washington is presented, along with an "expected" distribution of the general female population, obtained by multiplying the observed number of Japanese females in each age class by the appropriate age-specific rate in Section (B). This is interpreted as follows: If there had been only 414 females aged 14–15 in the general population, as there were in the American-born Japanese segment, 410 of them would not have been in the labor force (414 × .9902 = 409.94), 3 of them would have been employed (414 × .0073 = 3.02), and so on. Data were, of course, available for similar computations for other age classes and for the occupational classes that have been omitted from this example. Summation over the whole age range for each column gives the "population norm" for the specified category, which when totaled for all rows equals the sum of the American-born Japanese females. The next to the last row shows the truncated norm (rounded) with which this sex-nativity group of the Japanese in Washington is to be compared, and the last row gives the actual or "observed" Japanese American distribution by labor-force status and occupational groups of the employed. These two distributions are shown in full in columns (6) and (8) of the Washington section of table 14.

Labor-force and occupational data for the general population were obtained from Volume III, *Population*, 16th Census, and the age distributions of Japanese Americans used here were obtained from U.S. Census tabulations published by the Western Defense Command and Fourth Army (Statistical Division, *Bulletin 12*, San Francisco, March 15, 1943, p. 10.)

(A) FEMALE POPULATION OF THE STATE OF WASHINGTON: NUMBERS OF PERSONS BY AGE

Age	Total	Not in labor force	On pub. emerg.	Seeking work	Employed Total	Farmers, etc.	Clerical-sales	Dom. service
14–15.........	26,562	26,302	6	59	195	—	26	106
....	.	.	.	.	.	.	.	.
20–24.........	72,600	43,914	984	3,515	24,187	26	10,793	3,308
....	.	.	.	.	.	.	.	.
75+..........	20,710	20,295	1	11	403	57	24	92

(B) FEMALE POPULATION OF THE STATE OF WASHINGTON: PER CENT DISTRIBUTIONS BY AGE

14–15.........	100.00	99.02	.02	.23	.73	—	.10	.40
....	.	.	.	.	.	.	.	.
20–24.........	100.00	60.49	1.36	4.84	33.32	.04	14.87	4.56
....	.	.	.	.	.	.	.	.
75+..........	100.00	98.00	.00	.05	1.95	.28	.12	.44

(C) AMERICAN-BORN JAPANESE FEMALES IN THE STATE OF WASHINGTON

	"Observed" totals	"Expected Distributions" (based on section B and on "Observed" totals)						
14–15.........	414	409.94	.08	.95	3.02	..	.41	1.66
16–17.........	493	458.98	5.72	8.09	20.21	.00	3.06	11.39
18–19.........	509	341.79	16.29	37.97	112.95	.05	40.77	33.49
20–24.........	821	496.62	11.17	39.74	273.56	.33	122.08	37.44
25–34.........	474	345.59	1.61	9.53	117.27	.38	47.73	9.24
35–44.........	31	23.57	.19	.47	6.77	.08	2.34	.53
45–54.........	14	10.86	.13	.21	2.80	.09	.67	.35
55–64.........	1	.82	.01	.01	.16	.01	.02	.03
65–74.........	—	—	—	—	—	—	—	—
75+..........	2	1.96	.00	.00	.04	.01	.00	.01
Total........	2,759	2,090.13	35.20	96.97	536.78	.95	217.08	94.14
"Pop. Norm."	2,759	2,090	35	97	537	1	217	94
Observed.....	2,759	1,828	10	29	892	19	218	161

TABLE 15

PERCENTAGE DISTRIBUTION OF THE JAPANESE AMERICAN AGRICULTURAL EM-
PLOYED LABOR FORCE, BY MAJOR OCCUPATIONAL GROUPS, CALIFORNIA AND
WASHINGTON, 1940, COMPARED WITH THE POPULATION NORM FOR THESE STATES

Major occupational groups	Japanese	Population norm
Farmers and farm managers...............	34.2	42.0
Farm laborers: unpaid family..............	24.0	7.0
Farm laborers: wage......................	41.8	51.0
(Number of persons)....................	(19,400)	(4,077)

SOURCE: Computed from table 14.

TABLE 16

PERCENTAGE DISTRIBUTION OF THE JAPANESE AMERICAN NONAGRICULTURAL
EMPLOYED LABOR FORCE, BY MAJOR OCCUPATIONAL GROUPS, SEX, AND NATIV-
ITY, IN CALIFORNIA AND WASHINGTON, 1940, COMPARED WITH POPULATION NORMS
FOR EACH SEX-NATIVITY CATEGORY IN THESE STATES

Major occupational groups	Foreign-born Japanese	Population norm	American-born Japanese	Population norm
Males				
Professional.....................	5.2	8.7	4.2	6.8
Proprietor-managerial............	29.4	18.5	14.0	7.1
Clerical-sales...................	9.7	16.4	30.6	21.5
Skilled labor....................	4.1	21.4	4.3	15.5
Semiskilled labor................	8.7	15.0	16.4	24.0
Service (excl. domestic).........	11.8	10.0	6.5	13.2
Unskilled labor and domestic service......................	31.1	10.0	24.0	11.9
(Number of persons).............	(11,804)	(14,361)	(7,162)	(10,725)
Females				
Professional.....................	5.3	17.4	5.0	12.5
Proprietor-managerial............	15.1	9.7	4.5	2.2
Clerical-sales...................	16.6	30.9	30.5	43.9
Skilled labor....................	1.1	1.2	0.8	0.6
Semiskilled labor................	20.2	12.8	10.1	11.1
Service (excl. domestic).........	21.9	14.9	12.3	15.3
Unskilled labor and domestic service......................	19.8	13.1	36.8	14.4
(Number of persons).............	(3,704)	(3,606)	(4,564)	(4,208)

SOURCE: Computed from table 14.

DISTRIBUTION OF A SAMPLE OF JAPANESE AMERICAN EVACUEES FROM SAN FRANCISCO BY INDUSTRY, EMPLOYMENT STATUS, AND GENERATIONAL-EDUCATIONAL CLASS AS OF APRIL, 1940

Industry	Issei			Kibei			Nisei			Total		
	Self-employed	Employees	Total	Self-employed	Employees	Total	Self-employed	Employees	Total	Self-employed	Employees	Total
Wholesale trade												
Oriental art	2	4	6	..	1	1	1	7	8	3	12	15
Japanese provisions	2	12	14	..	6	6	..	10	10	2	28	30
All others	7	6	13	1	8	9	..	14	14	8	28	36
Total	11	22	33	1	15	16	1	31	32	13	68	81
Retail trade												
Oriental art	21	25	46	1	3	4	..	67	67	22	95	117
Restaurants and cafés	18	22	40	2	3	5	..	12	12	20	37	57
Groceries	5	5	10	2	1	3	..	4	4	7	10	17
All others	26	21	47	1	8	9	2	31	33	29	60	89
Total	70	73	143	6	15	21	2	114	116	78	202	280
Personal services												
Hotels and apartments	11	30	41	..	4	4	1	4	5	12	38	50
Cleaning and dyeing	65	34	99	10	18	28	6	18	24	81	70	151
Laundries	11	22	33	..	21	21	1	13	14	12	56	68
All others	47	12	59	8	1	9	2	5	7	57	18	75
Total	134	98	232	18	44	62	10	40	50	162	182	344
Construction	6	1	7	..	..	..	..	2	2	6	3	9
Mfg. and transportation	9	37	46	..	11	11	1	24	25	10	72	82
Finance, insurance, real estate	5	12	17	1	2	3	1	4	5	7	18	25
Business and repair services	11	5	16	2	4	6	5	2	7	18	11	29
Amusement services	3	4	7	..	1	1	1	4	5	4	9	13
Professional services	33	13	46	3	3	6	3	16	19	39	32	71
Government	..	1	1	..	..	..	..	2	2	..	3	3
Grand total	282	266	548	31	95	126	24	239	263	337	600	937

TABLE 17, b

DISTRIBUTION OF A SAMPLE OF JAPANESE AMERICAN EVACUEES FROM SEATTLE BY INDUSTRY, EMPLOYMENT STATUS, AND GENERATIONAL-EDUCATIONAL CLASS AS OF APRIL, 1940

Industry	Issei			Kibei			Nisei			Total		
	Self-employed	Employees	Total	Self-employed	Employees	Total	Self-employed	Employees	Total	Self-employed	Employees	Total
Wholesale trade												
Fish		6	6		2	2	1	3	4	1	11	12
Fruits and vegetables	5	3	8		1	1		10	10	5	14	19
All others	4	22	26		2	2	3	18	21	7	42	49
Total	9	31	40		5	5	4	31	35	13	67	80
Retail trade												
Florists	7	5	12		1	1	1	3	4	8	9	17
Groceries	30	12	42	2	4	6	13	24	37	45	40	85
Fruits and vegetables	12	7	19	3		3	1	11	12	16	18	34
Restaurants and cafés	18	46	64	1	7	8	4	13	17	23	66	89
All others	18	32	50		7	7	8	26	34	26	65	91
Total	85	102	187	6	19	25	27	77	104	118	198	316
Personal services												
Hotels, apts., rm.-bd. houses	40	40	80		3	3	5	9	14	45	52	97
Cleaning and dyeing	25	15	40	1		1	2		2	28	15	43
Laundries	1	5	6		2	2		2	2	1	9	10
All others	19	2	21				5	3	8	24	5	29
Total	85	62	147	1	5	6	12	14	26	98	81	179
Construction	1		1							1		1
Mfg. and transportation	5	33	38	2	5	7		18	18	7	56	63
Finance, insurance, real estate	3	3	6		1	1		6	6	3	10	13
Business and repair services	4	2	6					3	3	4	5	9
Amusement services		2	2					1	1		3	3
Professional services	9	19	28	1	2	3	9	13	22	19	34	53
Government		1	1		1	1					2	2
Grand total	201	255	456	10	38	48	52	163	215	263	456	719

TABLE 17, e

Distribution of a Sample of Japanese American Evacuees from Los Angeles by Industry, Employment Status, and Generational-Educational Classes, as of April, 1940

Industry	Issei			Kibei			Nisei			Total		
	Self-employed	Employees	Total	Self-employed	Employees	Total	Self-employed	Employees	Total	Self-employed	Employees	Total
Wholesale trade												
Florists	1	4	5	..	..	..	1	6	7	2	10	12
Fruits and vegetables	30	28	58	2	12	14	4	66	70	36	106	142
All others	11	21	32	..	3	3	3	15	18	14	39	53
Total	42	53	95	2	15	17	8	87	95	52	155	207
Retail trade												
Florists	10	6	16	..	3	3	1	8	9	11	17	28
Groceries	40	23	63	3	6	9	4	19	23	47	48	95
Nurseries	15	14	29	3	4	7	7	7	14	25	25	50
Fruits and vegetables	63	71	134	17	57	74	23	126	149	103	254	357
Restaurants	57	109	166	4	17	21	5	15	20	66	141	207
All others	34	54	88	4	10	14	7	42	49	45	106	151
Total	219	277	496	31	97	128	47	217	264	297	591	888
Personal services												
Hotels, rooms, boarding	39	41	80	..	2	2	1	4	5	40	47	87
Cleaning and dyeing	26	17	43	2	2	4	1	6	7	29	25	54
Laundries	..	10	10	..	5	5	..	3	3	..	18	18
All others	36	5	41	5	1	6	4	16	20	45	22	67
Total	101	73	174	7	10	17	6	29	35	114	112	226
Construction	1	..	1	1	1	2	..	..	..	2	1	3
Mfg. and transportation	6	23	29	1	21	22	6	24	30	13	68	81
Finance, insurance, real estate	5	5	10	..	1	1	..	4	4	5	10	15
Business and repair services	11	3	14	1	4	5	9	16	25	21	23	44
Amusement services	6	16	22	..	2	2	..	2	2	6	20	26
Professional services	22	19	41	1	6	7	6	10	16	29	35	64
Government	..	1	1	..	..	..	..	5	5	..	6	6
Grand total	413	470	883	44	157	201	82	394	476	539	1,021	1,560

NOTES TO TABLE 17, *a–c*

Table 17, *a–c*, is based on analyses of WRA census schedules (WRA Form 26), copies of which were made available to us through the courtesy of the War Relocation Authority. The census was taken in all camps during the fall of 1942 and covered, among many other items, date of birth, birthplace, prewar residence, education (in Japan and in the United States), and the occupational history of every evacuee.

The analyses in the three parts of table 17, are limited to these categories for samples of persons born in 1921 or earlier, working full time in any nonagricultural occupation except domestic service as of April 1, 1940, in San Francisco, Seattle, or Los Angeles. They were classified in terms of the industrial grouping of their 1940 occupation, crossclassified by generational-educational groups (Issei, Kibei, Nisei) and by occupational status (the self-employed, that is, owner-operators and independent professional persons; and employees, that is, paid managers and other wage and salary workers).

The census schedules had been bound in volumes, by camps, in the order of interview, which normally proceeded block by block within each camp. Inasmuch as most of the prewar residents of Seattle were in Minidoka or Tule Lake camps, most San Franciscans in Topaz, and most nonagricultural workers from the Los Angeles area were in Manzanar, Gila River, Poston, Heart Mountain, or Granada, our sample was selected from "books" for these camps only. Because the camps had, in general, preserved the ecological pattern of prewar residence, a crude sort of area sampling was readily accomplished. For each of the specified camps, books containing appreciable numbers of residents of the city under consideration were located, by inspection, listed in numerical order, and every *nth* listing selected, in accordance with varying sampling ratios. From these books, every case fulfilling the age, occupational, and residence conditions listed above was abstracted. Neglect of books having few residents of the specified cities in the camps under consideration and of the residents of these cities who were scattered throughout other camps may have introduced a bias, but, unfortunately, no test of the nature or extent of this bias was made. It seems unlikely that it would be sufficiently large to distort seriously the patterns of observed differentials.

TABLE 18

DISTRIBUTION OF A SAMPLE OF JAPANESE AMERICAN EVACUEES WORKING IN WHOLESALE OR RETAIL TRADE AND IN PERSONAL SERVICES IN SAN FRANCISCO, LOS ANGELES, AND SEATTLE BY GENERATIONAL-EDUCATIONAL CLASS, BY EMPLOYMENT STATUS, AND BY "RACE" OF EMPLOYER, AS OF APRIL, 1940

Generational-educational class	San Francisco				Los Angeles				Seattle			
	Self-employed	Employees		Total	Self-employed	Employees		Total	Self-employed	Employees		Total
		Working for Japanese employer	Working for Caucasian employer			Working for Japanese employer	Working for Caucasian employer			Working for Japanese employer	Working for Caucasian employer	
Number of persons												
Issei	215	145	48	408	362	337	59	758[a]	179	135	60	374
Kibei	25	67	7	99	40	120	2	162	7	26	3	36
Nisei	13	170	15	198	61	310	23	394	43	96	26	165
Total	253	382	70	705	463	767	84	1,314	229	257	89	575
Per cent												
Issei	52.7	35.5	11.8	100.0	47.8	44.4	7.8	100.0	47.9	36.1	16.0	100.0
Kibei	25.2	67.7	7.1	100.0	24.7	74.1	1.2	100.0	19.5	72.2	8.3	100.0
Nisei	6.6	85.8	7.6	100.0	15.5	78.7	5.8	100.0	26.0	58.2	15.8	100.0
Total	35.9	54.2	9.9	100.0	35.2	58.4	6.4	100.0	39.8	44.7	15.5	100.0

[a] Excluding 7 whose employers could not be identified.

NOTES TO TABLE 18

The analysis in this table is based on the trade and services categories shown in tables 17–a, 17–b, and 17–c. The "race" of each employer of a Japanese employee was determined by a name-by-name check by former residents of these cities, supplemented by a check of available Japanese American directories (*Nichi Bei, Rafu Shimpo,* and *Hoku Bei*).

TABLE 19

YEARS OF EDUCATION IN JAPAN: KIBEI AND ISSEI EVACUEES
IN WRA CAMPS IN 1942

Years of education in Japan	Kibei		Issei	
	Number	Per cent	Number	Per cent
None..............	.....	....	2,478	6.5
1–2................	497	5.1	717	1.9
3–5................	1,174	12.0	5,865	15.3
6–9................	4,940	50.4	18,397	48.0
10 and over.........	3,187	32.5	10,839	28.3
Total............	9,798	100.0	38,296	100.0

SOURCE: Adapted from table 32 in *The Evacuated People*, (U.S. Department of the Interior, *op. cit.*, p. 87)

TABLE 20, *a*

RELIGIOUS DISTRIBUTION OF EVACUEES 17 YEARS OF AGE OR OLDER, IN WRA
CAMP AT TULE LAKE, OCTOBER, 1943, BY PREWAR RESIDENCE, GENERATIONAL-
EDUCATIONAL CLASS, SEX, AND OCCUPATIONAL CLASS

Prewar residence, generational-educational class, sex	Occupational class	Number of persons	Per cent		
			Christians	Secularists	Buddhists
Northwest					
Nisei males.........	nonagr.	376	43.9	18.9	37.2
	agr......	417	36.5	15.3	48.2
Nisei females.......	nonagr.	595	50.1	9.1	40.8
	agr......	251	30.7	13.1	56.2
Kibei males.........	nonagr.	149	12.7	19.5	67.8
	agr......	74	13.5	18.9	67.6
Kibei females.......	nonagr.	127	25.2	8.7	66.1
	agr......	45	17.8	2.2	80.0
Issei males.........	nonagr.	550	16.2	10.2	73.6
	agr......	534	15.9	6.2	77.9
Issei females........	nonagr.	319	27.9	6.9	65.2
	agr......	420	17.1	3.1	79.8
California					
Nisei males.........	nonagr.	692	31.5	15.5	53.0
	agr......	747	22.1	12.6	65.3
Nisei females.......	nonagr.	1,051	36.1	4.7	59.2
	agr......	326	19.0	5.2	75.8
Kibei males.........	nonagr.	264	15.5	14.4	70.1
	agr......	309	4.8	9.4	85.8
Kibei females.......	nonagr.	237	14.8	6.8	78.4
	agr......	130	4.6	5.4	90.0
Issei males.........	nonagr.	658	23.4	8.7	67.9
	agr......	1,230	7.8	6.1	86.1
Issei females........	nonagr.	589	24.8	3.6	71.6
	agr......	493	11.4	1.2	87.4

TABLE 20, *b*

RELIGIOUS DISTRIBUTION OF EVACUEES, 17 YEARS OF AGE OR OLDER IN WRA CAMP I AT POSTON AND WRA CAMP AT MINIDOKA, BY GENERATIONAL-EDUCATIONAL CLASS, SEX, AND OCCUPATIONAL CLASS

WRA camp, generational-educational class, sex	Occupational class	Number of persons	Per cent		
			Christians	Secularists	Buddhists
Poston: Camp I					
Nisei males.........	nonagr.	686	49.1	20.7	30.2
	agr......	636	32.2	20.6	47.2
Nisei females.......	nonagr.	888	48.0	13.0	39.0
	agr......	326	31.6	14.1	54.3
Kibei males.........	nonagr.	186	15.6	22.0	62.4
	agr......	202	9.4	17.8	72.8
Kibei females.......	nonagr.	216	31.5	10.6	57.9
	agr......	116	16.4	7.7	75.9
Issei males.........	nonagr.	581	28.9	15.8	55.3
	agr......	1,205	17.4	12.6	70.0
Issei females........	nonagr.	517	38.1	8.7	53.2
	agr......	533	26.2	5.1	68.7
Minidoka					
Nisei males.........	nonagr.	1,027	54.4	20.0	25.6
	agr......	300	33.3	24.7	42.0
Nisei females.......	nonagr.	1,103	57.1	7.0	35.9
	agr......	179	38.6	11.7	49.7
Kibei males.........	nonagr.	215	19.5	18.6	61.9
	agr......	64	14.1	15.6	70.3
Kibei females.......	nonagr.	199	22.1	6.0	71.9
	agr......	37	2.7	8.1	89.2
Issei males.........	nonagr.	1,737	26.0	11.2	62.8
	agr......	469	15.5	9.0	75.5
Issei females........	nonagr.	1,187	34.3	4.0	61.7
	agr......	282	16.3	2.8	80.9

Table 20, *a* and *b*, is the first of a series, others of which will be shown in following pages, based on case-by-case analysis of WRA population records obtained in three camps, Tule Lake, Poston (Camp I), and Minidoka. The two parts of this table present the basic population of these camps, as of March, 1943, and include all of the 23,474 persons who were in camp at this time and who were 17 years of age or older as of December 31, 1942.

The population records were transcribed on to cards from WRA census schedules (Form 26) in terms of the following categories: sex, date of birth, prewar occupational class (agricultural or nonagricultural), generational-educational class (Issei, Kibei, Nisei), religious preference (Buddhism, Christianity, secularism), and for Tule Lake, prewar residence (California or the Pacific Northwest). In respect to occupation, persons in the active labor force at the outbreak of World War II were classified by the last full-time job they had held, whereas students, housewives, widows, retired persons, and others not in the active labor force were classified according to the occupation of the head of the family. Issei are, by definition, the Japan-born; Nisei the American-born who had had no schooling in Japan; and Kibei the American-born who had had some or all of their education in Japan. In the religious categories, small numbers of acknowledged Shintoists and adherents to other Oriental sects were included with Buddhists; and persons who refused to answer the preference question were included, along with those who said they had "no religion," among secularists. Because of the nature of the census—that is direct and if necessary repeated questioning of a "captive" population—there were no "unknowns" in other categories.

For the analysis in the present table, the cards were first sorted by four camp groups, to differentiate Californians from Northwesterners. Poston was considered a California unit, inasmuch as almost all of the residents of Camp I had been evacuated from Los Angeles and Orange counties, and Minidoka a Northwestern unit, for its residents had formerly resided in Seattle, Portland, and contiguous areas. The Tule Lake population, however, came from diverse origins and had to be divided into two locational samples, approximately two-thirds of the total representing former residents of Sacramento, Placer, and contiguous counties in California, whereas the other third was from Tacoma, Seattle and its hinterland, and scattered rural communities in Oregon.

Each locational group, so defined, was sorted by sex, by generational-educational class, by occupational class, and by religion. For analysis of patterns of religious preference, Table 20, *a* and *b*, therefore, includes 48 "net" groups of evacuees, each of which is homogeneous with respect to prewar location, sex, generational-educational class, and occupational class. Because of the slight overlapping in the age distributions of the three generational-educational classes, it was impossible to cross classify by age, but because of the relatively discrete distributions, this factor may be considered to have been adequately if indirectly controlled in the analyses.

TABLE 21

SCHOOL ATTENDANCE, AMERICAN-BORN JAPANESE AND TOTAL POPULATION
AGED 5–24, CALIFORNIA AND WASHINGTON, 1940

Age	American-born Japanese		Total population	
	Number of persons	Per cent attending school	Number of persons	Per cent attending school
5–6................	2,902	60.3	217,803	56.2
7–15..............	20,281	98.4	1,071,783	97.4
16–17..............	6,882	93.2	267,287	85.1
18–19..............	7,099	57.0	292,864	41.2
20................	3,310	28.0	139,906	19.6
21–24..............	10,293	13.5	583,891	8.1
5–24..............	50,767	67.9	2,573,534	61.7
16–24..............	27,584	46.3	1,283,948	32.9

SOURCE: Computed from U.S. Census data. (For American-born Japanese, as
reported in *Bulletin 12*, Western Defense Command and Fourth Army, *op. cit.*,
pp. 16–18).

TABLE 22

AMERICAN-BORN JAPANESE 25 YEARS OF AGE AND OVER, CALIFORNIA AND WASHINGTON, 1940, BY YEARS OF SCHOOL COMPLETED AND BY SEX, COMPARED WITH NORMS FOR THE TOTAL POPULATION IN THESE STATES

Years of school completed	Males						Females					
	California		Washington		Calif. and Wash.		California		Washington		Calif. and Wash.	
	American-born Japanese (1)	Population norm (2)	American-born Japanese (3)	Population norm (4)	American-born Japanese (5)	Population norm (6)	American-born Japanese (7)	Population norm (8)	American-born Japanese (9)	Population norm (10)	American-born Japanese (11)	Population norm (12)
	Number of persons											
None	78	60	3	3	81	63	96	30	4	1	100	31
Grade school, 1–4	163	186	11	8	174	195	116	86	10	4	126	90
Grade school, 5–6	185	263	13	17	198	280	169	138	16	9	185	147
Grade school, 7–8	1,131	1,227	92	169	1,223	1,396	877	683	80	91	957	774
High school, 1–3	941	1,347	99	154	1,040	1,501	676	991	64	119	740	1,110
High school, 4	2,251	1,637	306	196	2,557	1,833	1,753	1,476	283	202	2,036	1,678
College, 1–3	610	664	70	64	680	728	279	483	31	61	310	544
College, 4 or more	534	512	71	54	605	566	212	299	30	32	242	331
Not reported	60	57	4	4	64	61	29	21	4	3	33	24
Total	5,953	5,953	669	669	6,622	6,622	4,207	4,207	522	522	4,729	4,729
	Per cent											
Grade school 0–6[a]	8.2	9.5	4.6	4.7	7.8	9.0	9.7	6.5	6.5	3.3	9.4	6.2
Grade school, 7–8	19.0	20.6	13.8	25.3	18.5	21.1	20.9	16.2	15.3	17.4	20.2	16.4
High school, 1–3	15.8	22.6	14.8	23.0	15.7	22.7	16.1	23.6	12.3	22.8	15.7	23.4
High school, 4	37.8	27.5	45.7	29.3	38.6	27.7	41.7	35.1	54.2	38.7	43.0	35.5
College, 1–3	10.2	11.2	10.5	9.6	10.3	11.0	6.6	11.5	5.9	11.7	6.6	11.5
College, 4 or more	9.0	8.6	10.6	8.1	9.1	8.5	5.0	7.1	5.8	6.1	5.1	7.0

[a] Including "not reported."

NOTES TO TABLE 22

The rationale for determining "population norms" in respect to educational distributions is the same as that described for labor-force and occupational distributions in table 14, above. Age-specific educational rates for the general population of each sex in California and in Washington were applied to quinquennial age distributions of American-born Japanese, 25 years of age and older, in these states, to obtain, by summation, educational distributions that would have prevailed if sex-specific age distributions of the general population had been identical with those of the Japanese groups under comparison.

The actual, or "observed" distributions for American-born Japanese are shown in odd-numbered columns, and the computed population norm for each observed class is shown in the immediately following even-numbered column. Data needed to compute the norms were derived from Volume III, *Population* (16th Census of the United States), that is, age-specific educational rates for the general population, and from U. S. census tabulations published in *Bulletin 12* by the Statistical Division of the Western Defense Command and Fourth Army, (*op. cit.*, pp. 10–12) that is, age and sex distributions of American-born Japanese. The latter publication (p. 20) is also the source for educational distributions of American-born Japanese.

TABLE 23

EDUCATIONAL DISTRIBUTION OF NISEI EVACUEE POPULATION AGED 20 YEARS AND OLDER IN 1942, IN WRA CAMP I AT POSTON AND IN WRA CAMP AT MINIDOKA, CLASSIFIED BY BROAD AGE GROUPS, SEX, PREWAR OCCUPATIONAL CLASS, AND RELIGION

Sex, age, and occupational class	Religion	Poston: Camp I				Minidoka			
		Number of persons	Per cent			Number of persons	Per cent		
			With less than 4 years high school	With 4 years high school	With 1 year or more college		With less than 4 years high school	With 4 years high school	With 1 year or more college
Males, 20–24 years									
Nonagricultural..........	Chr. & sec.	154	7.1	42.9	50.0	295	9.9	52.9	37.2
	Buddhists	78	14.1	50.0	35.9	98	17.4	62.2	20.4
Agricultural..........	Chr. & sec.	117	6.0	67.5	26.5	72	11.1	72.2	16.7
	Buddhists	102	14.7	69.6	15.7	36	11.1	80.6	8.3
Females, 20–24 years									
Nonagricultural..........	Chr. & sec.	216	1.9	50.9	47.2	325	10.2	68.0	21.8
	Buddhists	143	8.4	68.5	23.1	186	12.9	80.1	7.0
Agricultural..........	Chr. & sec.	44	13.6	65.9	20.5	31	22.6	64.5	12.9
	Buddhists	67	22.4	74.6	3.0	38	15.8	84.2	0.0
Males, 25 years and over									
Nonagricultural..........	Chr. & sec.	206	16.0	40.3	43.7	266	12.8	55.6	31.6
	Buddhists	61	36.1	32.8	31.1	90	38.9	43.3	17.8
Agricultural..........	Chr. & sec.	101	29.7	49.5	20.8	46	23.9	60.9	15.2
	Buddhists	86	47.7	44.2	8.1	41	24.4	70.7	4.9
Females, 25 years and over									
Nonagricultural..........	Chr. & sec.	167	11.4	49.1	39.5	205	12.7	63.4	23.9
	Buddhists	104	39.4	51.9	8.7	102	23.5	73.5	3.0
Agricultural..........	Chr. & sec.	34	41.2	52.9	5.9	16[a]			
	Buddhists	45	68.9	31.1	0.0	8[b]			

[a] Percentages not computed; numbers were, in horizontal order, 2, 13, and 1.
[b] Percentages not computed; numbers were, in horizontal order, 2, 6, and 0.

NOTES TO TABLE 23

Data on education were transcribed from WRA census forms on the cards for Nisei aged 20 years and older in Poston (I) and in Minidoka. This analysis is thus based on a subsample of the larger sample used in table 20. Christians and Secularists are here combined into a single religious-preference category.

TABLE 24

NISEI AND KIBEI EVACUEES IN WRA CAMPS, WHO HAD COMPLETED THEIR
EDUCATION BEFORE EVACUATION IN 1942, BY YEARS OF SCHOOL COMPLETED
AND FOR KIBEI BY COUNTRY WHERE COMPLETED

Years of school completed	Nisei	Kibei Education completed in	
		U.S.	Japan
Number of persons			
Grade school 0–6...............	647	114	570
Grade school 7–8...............	1,381	276	1,941
High school 1–3...............	2,903	796	1,464
High school 4 (or 5)...........	14,153	763	2,320
College 1–3	2,749	278	170
College 4 or more..............	1,128	102	44
Total.....................	22,961	2,329	6,509
Per Cent			
Grade school 0–6...............	2.8	4.9	8.8
Grade school 7–8...............	6.0	11.8	29.8
High school 1–3...............	12.6	34.2	22.5
High school 4 (or 5)...........	61.7	32.8	35.6
College 1–3...................	12.0	11.9	2.6
College 4 or more..............	4.9	4.4	0.7

SOURCE: Collated from data in tables 25-27, *The Evacuated People* (U.S.
Department of the Interior *op. cit.*, pp. 80–82.)

TABLE 25

OUTMIGRATION FROM WRA CAMPS, BY MONTHS, JUNE, 1942–MARCH, 1946

(Net Increase in "Indefinite" and "Terminal" Departures)

Month	Number of persons and year				
	1942	1943	1944	1945	1946
January	...	431	1,278	1,200	2,277
February	...	552	1,384	2,076	2,258
March	...	906	1,813	2,316	2,806
April	...	2,114	2,066	2,860	
May	...	2,537	1,943	3,702	
June	...	2,183	1,987	5,331	
July	18	1,591	1,766	5,013	
August	67	2,160	2,033	8,547	
September	188	1,824	1,355	15,126	
October	206	1,160	976	14,053	
November	193	877	1,009	8,792	
December	194	643	535	5,348	
Total	866	16,978	18,145	74,364	7,341

Total 1942–1946.............117,694

NOTES TO TABLE 25

These data are from table 10, *The Evacuated People* (U.S. Department of the Interior, War Relocation Authority, Washington, 1946).

"Indefinite Leave and Terminal Departure refers to departures for relocation purposes, armed forces, institutions, internment camps, and repatriation to Japan" (*ibid*, p. 27). "Net change in indefinite leave and terminal departure refers to the net increase in any particular period due to departures, less admissions and transfers to other centers, plus conversions from short-term and seasonal leave" (*ibid*, p. 27).

In table 4 (*ibid*, p. 13), the "population accountability" of WRA is broken down into the following classes (some of which are further subclassified):

```
Indefinite leaves for relocation.......................34,471
    Armed forces......................................  2,076
    Institutions......................................    323
    Internment camps..................................    973
    To Japan..........................................    318
    Other.............................................      3
Terminal departures for relocation....................82,324
    Armed forces......................................    273
    Institutions......................................    241
    Internment camps..................................  2,147
    To Japan..........................................  4,406
    Other.............................................      1
Deaths................................................  1,862
```

In addition, 27,964 were transferred from one WRA Camp to another during this whole period, and final leave status was assigned arbitrarily to 899 persons who had not been admitted to the center of assignment (for the most part, seasonal workers released by WCCA). Table 3 (*ibid*, p. 11) indicates that 109,730 persons were admitted to WRA camps from WCCA camps; 17,915 came by direct evacuation from their homes; 498 came from institutions; 826 from seasonal releases by WCCA; 1,118 from Hawaii; 1,735 from Department of Justice Internment Camps; 219 persons became "voluntary residents"; 20 came from "other institutions"; and births in camps accounted for 5,981 "admissions."

TABLE 26

EVACUEES OUTMIGRATING FROM WRA CAMPS BEFORE JANUARY 1, 1945 (*Salvage*),
RESIDENT IN TULE LAKE SEGREGATION CENTER AS OF JULY 1, 1944 (*Spoilage*),
AND RESIDENT IN ALL WRA CAMPS EXCEPT TULE LAKE AS OF JANUARY 1, 1945
(*Residue*), BY AGE AND SEX

Age	Outmigrants (Salvage)		Segregants (Spoilage)		Residents in camps, 1/1/45 (Residue)	
	Males	Females	Males	Females	Males	Females
0–4........	875	806	801	902	2,899	2,653
5–9........	580	556	713	633	2,500	2,323
10–14......	530	501	785	638	2,874	2,978
15–19......	2,503	1,958	1,086	955	3,149	3,654
20–24......	6,264	4,823	1,825	1,076	1,586	2,988
25–29......	3,425	2,833	1,226	854	1,149	2,503
30–34......	2,019	1,018	595	399	985	1,632
35–39......	1,002	466	437	288	1,067	1,197
40–44......	874	509	571	546	1,954	1,949
45–49......	559	533	522	525	1,702	2,768
50–54......	436	481	407	397	1,393	2,361
55–59......	907	267	762	204	3,525	1,430
60–64......	627	135	661	111	3,532	864
65–69......	} 394	} 108	441	67	2,644	514
70–74......			156	27	866	137
75+........			64	4	303	65
Total....	20,995	14,994	11,052	7,626	32,128	30,016

NOTES TO TABLE 26

The age-sex composition of outmigrants (*Salvage*) was obtained from table 14
of *The Evacuated People* (U.S. Department of the Interior, War Relocation
Authority, Washington, 1946). It covers "cumulative net departures as of
December 31, 1944," with "age tabulated as of date relocated" (*ibid.*, p. 50).
The age-sex composition of the population segregated at Tule Lake (*Spoilage*) is
from table 43a; that of the population resident in other WRA camps as of January 1, 1945 (*Residue*) is from table 45b (*ibid.*, pp. 107, 109). The nativity-sex
composition of the three groups was as follows:

	Salvage	Spoilage	Residue
American-born:			
Males..	17,161	7,304	15,833
Females..	12,758	5,479	19,427
Foreign-born:			
Males..	3,834	3,748	16,295
Females..	2,236	2,147	10,589
Total..	35,989	18,678	62,144

TABLE 27, a

EVACUEE POPULATION 17 YEARS OF AGE OR OLDER, MARCH, 1943, IN WRA CAMP AT TULE LAKE; SEGREGANTS MARCH–SEPTEMBER, 1943; AND OUTMIGRANTS, MARCH–SEPTEMBER, 1943; CLASSIFIED BY PREWAR RESIDENCE, GENERATIONAL-EDUCATIONAL CLASS, SEX, RELIGION, AND OCCUPATIONAL CLASS

Generational-educational class, sex, religion	Occupational class	Californians			Northwesterners		
		Pop. March, 1943 (1)	Segregants March–Sept., 1943 (2)	Out-migrants Mar.–Sept., 1943 (3)	Pop. March, 1943 (1)	Segregants March–Sept., 1943 (2)	Out-migrants Sept., 1943 (3)
Nisei males:							
Christians	Nonagr	218	27	106	165	9	76
	Agr	165	25	44	152	13	46
Secularists	Nonagr	107	17	44	71	4	29
	Agr	94	32	14	64	7	15
Buddhists	Nonagr	367	114	74	140	28	34
	Agr	488	240	44	201	36	34
Total		1,439	455	326	793	97	234
Nisei females							
Christians	Nonagr	380	66	134	298	19	109
	Agr	62	15	15	77	7	22
Secularists	Nonagr	49	16	18	54	10	17
	Agr	17	4	3	33	5	8
Buddhists	Nonagr	622	204	75	243	42	64
	Agr	247	145	9	141	37	18
Total		1,377	510	254	846	120	238
Kibei males							
Christians	Nonagr	41	10	7	19	3	8
	Agr	15	8	3	10	2	5
Secularists	Nonagr	38	21	2	29	14	5
	Agr	29	16	1	14	7	1
Buddhists	Nonagr	185	117	11	101	46	8
	Agr	265	209	4	50	28	2
Total		573	381	28	223	100	29
Kibei females							
Christians	Nonagr	35	7	12	32	5	12
	Agr	6	2	0	8	3	3
Secularists	Nonagr	16	10	2	11	4	2
	Agr	7	4	2	1	0	0
Buddhists	Nonagr	186	123	8	84	41	6
	Agr	117	82	2	36	18	3
Total		367	228	26	172	71	26
Issei males:							
Christians	Nonagr	154	31	18	89	15	19
	Agr	96	34	7	85	12	22
Secularists	Nonagr	57	30	1	56	24	8
	Agr	75	47	6	33	9	3
Buddhists	Nonagr	447	251	16	405	164	23
	Agr	1,059	706	16	416	133	18
Total		1,888	1,099	64	1,084	357	93
Issei females:							
Christians	Nonagr	146	31	16	89	14	10
	Agr	56	19	5	72	6	14
Secularists	Nonagr	21	13	0	22	8	4
	Agr	6	3	0	13	2	2
Buddhists	Nonagr	422	243	5	208	62	12
	Agr	431	253	1	335	97	22
Total		1,082	562	27	739	189	64
Total Nisei		2,816	965	580	1,639	217	472
Total Kibei		940	609	54	395	171	55
Total Issei		2,970	1,661	91	1,823	546	157
Grand total		6,726	3,235	725	3,857	934	684

TABLE 27, b

EVACUEE POPULATION 17 YEARS OF AGE OR OLDER, IN WRA CAMP I AT POSTON, MARCH, 1943, OCTOBER, 1943, AND DECEMBER, 1944; SEGREGANTS MARCH–SEPTEMBER, 1943; AND OUTMIGRANTS MARCH–SEPTEMBER, 1943, OCTOBER, 1943–DECEMBER, 1944, CLASSIFIED BY GENERATIONAL-EDUCATIONAL CLASS, SEX, RELIGION, AND OCCUPATIONAL CLASS

Generational-educational class, sex, religion	Occupational class	Pop. March, 1943 (1)	Segregants March–Sept., 1943 (2)	Outmigrants March–Sept., 1943 (3)	Pop. Oct., 1943 (4)	Outmigrants Oct. 1943–Dec. 1944 (5)	Pop. Dec., 1944 (6)
Nisei males:							
Christians	Nonagr	337	6	142	202	147	55
	Agr	205	1	53	176	124	52
Secularists	Nonagr	142	1	47	100	64	36
	Agr	131	2	34	105	65	40
Buddhists	Nonagr	207	17	35	166	102	64
	Agr	300	31	42	261	138	123
Total		1,322	58	353	1,010	640	370
Nisei females:							
Christians	Nonagr	426	1	158	289	129	160
	Agr	103	3	25	96	37	59
Secularists	Nonagr	116	5	38	75	21	54
	Agr	46	1	10	40	11	29
Buddhists	Nonagr	346	27	34	299	90	209
	Agr	177	11	16	182	47	135
Total		1,214	48	281	981	335	646
Kibei males:							
Christians	Nonagr	29	5	2	22	11	11
	Agr	19	4	1	14	5	9
Secularists	Nonagr	41	7	6	28	9	19
	Agr	36	17	6	13	6	7
Buddhists	Nonagr	116	35	7	75	23	52
	Agr	147	63	3	82	20	62
Total		388	131	25	234	74	160
Kibei females:							
Christians	Nonagr	68	1	16	51	13	38
	Agr	19	2	0	17	1	16
Secularists	Nonagr	23	3	4	16	2	14
	Agr	9	1	0	8	0	8
Buddhists	Nonagr	125	19	12	94	15	79
	Agr	88	16	3	70	8	62
Total		332	42	35	256	39	217
Issei males:							
Christians	Nonagr	168	5	17	146	26	120
	Agr	210	6	13	191	21	170
Secularists	Nonagr	92	4	4	84	15	69
	Agr	152	17	5	130	12	118
Buddhists	Nonagr	321	27	11	284	25	259
	Agr	843	102	19	722	41	681
Total		1,786	161	69	1,557	140	1,417
Issei females:							
Christians	Nonagr	197	7	16	174	32	142
	Agr	140	3	6	131	10	121
Secularists	Nonagr	45	1	0	44	4	40
	Agr	27	2	0	25	1	24
Buddhists	Nonagr	275	12	7	256	3	243
	Agr	366	29	12	326	14	312
Total		1,050	54	41	956	64	882
Total Nisei		2,536	106	634	1,991	975	1,016
Total Kibei		720	173	60	490	113	377
Total Issei		2,836	215	110	2,513	204	2,299
Grand total		6,092	494	804	4,994	1,292	3,692

TABLE 27, c

Evacuee Population 17 Years of Age or Older, in WRA Camp at Minidoka, March, 1943, October, 1943, and December, 1944; Segregants March–September, 1943; and Outmigrants March–September, 1943, October, 1943–December, 1944, Classified by Generational-educational Class, Sex, Religion, and Occupational Class

Generational-educational class, sex, religion	Occupational class	Pop. March, 1943 (1)	Segregants March–Sept., 1943 (2)	Out-migrants March–Sept., 1943 (3)	Pop. Oct., 1943 (4)	Out-migrants Oct. 1943–Dec. 1944 (5)	Pop. Dec., 1944 (6)
Nisei males:							
Christians........	Nonagr......	559	1	300	312	234	78
	Agr..........	100	0	53	73	50	23
Secularists.......	Nonagr......	205	1	92	114	69	45
	Agr..........	74	0	31	51	39	12
Buddhists........	Nonagr......	263	3	76	205	127	78
	Agr..........	126	0	33	106	66	40
Total.........	....	1,327	5	585	861	585	276
Nisei females:							
Christians........	Nonagr......	630	3	263	402	211	191
	Agr..........	69	1	18	61	24	37
Secularists.......	Nonagr......	77	1	19	59	27	32
	Agr..........	21	0	4	18	8	10
Buddhists........	Nonagr......	396	9	77	340	110	230
	Agr..........	89	2	20	81	18	63
Total.........	....	1,282	16	401	961	398	563
Kibei males:							
Christians........	Nonagr......	42	3	16	23	13	10
	Agr..........	9	0	2	7	3	4
Secularists.......	Nonagr......	40	3	6	31	14	17
	Agr..........	10	1	2	7	3	4
Buddhists........	Nonagr......	133	25	16	94	33	61
	Agr..........	45	11	6	28	8	20
Total.........	....	279	43	48	190	74	116
Kibei females:							
Christians........	Nonagr......	44	2	8	34	14	20
	Agr..........	1	0	0	1	0	1
Secularists.......	Nonagr......	12	1	0	11	2	9
	Agr..........	3	0	0	3	1	2
Buddhists........	Nonagr......	143	12	9	123	17	106
	Agr..........	33	5	2	26	2	24
Total.........	....	236	20	19	198	36	162
Issei males:							
Christians........	Nonagr......	452	10	45	397	103	294
	Agr..........	73	0	3	70	16	54
Secularists.......	Nonagr......	195	7	20	168	26	142
	Agr..........	42	5	0	37	7	30
Buddhists........	Nonagr......	1,090	76	31	985	81	904
	Agr..........	354	9	14	331	30	301
Total.........	....	2,206	107	113	1,988	263	1,725
Issei females:							
Christians........	Nonagr......	407	7	35	367	80	287
	Agr..........	46	0	2	44	5	39
Secularists.......	Nonagr......	48	1	6	42	7	35
	Agr..........	8	0	0	8	2	6
Buddhists........	Nonagr......	732	40	22	671	35	636
	Agr..........	228	6	8	214	7	207
Total.........	....	1,469	54	73	1,346	136	1,210
Total Nisei........	....	2,609	21	986	1,822	983	839
Total Kibei........	....	515	63	67	388	110	278
Total Issei........	....	3,675	161	186	3,334	339	2,935
Grand total.......	....	6,799	245	1,239	5,544	1,492	4,052

NOTES TO TABLE 27, *a–c*

Column (1) of table 27, *a–c* represent the basic population, as described above in notes to table 20, of four camp groups in March, 1943, subclassified by generational-educational, religious, and occupational groups, and by sex. Column (2) shows, for each of the 144 net groups of evacuees, those who, after Registration, remained in or were transferred to the Tule Lake Segregation Center. They were identified through a name-by-name checking of the basic cards with a roster of segregants. Column (3) shows, for each of the 144 net groups of evacuees, those who outmigrated between Registration and Segregation. They were identified through a name-by-name checking of leave permits in each of the camps listed. Postsegregation analyses were limited to Poston (I) and Minidoka, inasmuch as outmigration from Tule Lake had become virtually impossible. Column (4) in parts *b* and *c* shows for each of 72 net groups of evacuees, those of the "basic" population of March, 1943, who were still in camp in October, 1943, after subtracting segregants, outmigrants (March–October), deaths and transferees to another WRA camp (October, 1943–December, 1944), and adding the net cohort of those who became 17 years of age during 1943. Column (5) shows, for these same 72 groups, the numbers who outmigrated from camp between October, 1943 (Segregation) and December, 1944 (Recission). These, too, had been identified through a name-by-name checking of leave permits and rosters. Column (6) is the difference between columns (4) and (5) and is that part of the basic population (with the additions and subtractions noted above) which was still in camp when exclusion orders were rescinded in December 1944.

TABLE 28, *a*

POPULATION 17 YEARS OF AGE AND OLDER IN MARCH, 1943, *Spoilage* (PER CENT SEGREGATED AS "DISLOYAL"), AND *Early Salvage* (PER CENT OUTMIGRATING, MARCH–SEPTEMBER, 1943), WRA CAMP AT TULE LAKE, BY PREWAR ORIGIN IN CALIFORNIA OR NORTHWEST, AND BY GENERATIONAL-EDUCATIONAL CLASS, SEX, RELIGION, AND OCCUPATIONAL CLASS

Generational-educational class, sex, religion	Occupational class	Californians			Northwesterners		
		Population March, 1943 (1)	Per cent segregated as "disloyal" (2)	Per cent outmigrating Mar.–Sept., 1943 (3)	Population March, 1943 (1)	Per cent segregated as "disloyal" (2)	Per cent outmigrating Mar.–Sept., 1943 (3)
Nisei Males							
Chr. and sec.	nonagr.	325	13.5	46.2	236	5.5	44.5
	agr.	259	22.0	22.4	216	9.3	28.2
Buddhists	nonagr.	367	31.1	20.2	140	20.0	24.3
	agr.	488	49.2	9.0	201	17.9	16.9
Nisei Females							
Chr. and sec.	nonagr.	429	19.1	35.4	352	8.2	35.8
	agr.	79	24 1	22.8	110	10.9	27.3
Buddhists	nonagr.	622	42.4	12.1	243	17.3	26.3
	agr.	247	58.7	3.6	141	26.2	12.8
Kibei Males							
Chr. and sec.	nonagr.	79	39.2	11.4	48	35.4[a]	27.1[a]
	agr.	44	54.5[a]	9.1[a]	24	37.5[a]	25.0[a]
Buddhists	nonagr.	185	63.2	5.9	101	45.5	7.9
	agr.	265	78.9	1.5	50	56.0	4.0
Kibei Females							
Chr. and sec.	nonagr.	51	33.3	27.5	43	20.9[a]	32.6[a]
	agr.	13	…[b]	…[b]	9	…[b]	…[b]
Buddhists	nonagr.	186	66.1	4.3	84	48.8	7.1
	agr.	117	70.1	1.7	36	50.0[a]	8.3[a]
Issei Males							
Chr. and sec.	nonagr.	211	28.9	9.0	145	26.9	18.6
	agr.	171	47.4	7.6	118	17.8	21.2
Buddhists	nonagr.	447	56.2	3.6	405	40.5	5.7
	agr.	1,059	66.7	1.5	416	32.0	4.3
Issei Females							
Chr. and sec.	nonagr.	167	26.3	9.6	111	19.8	12.6
	agr.	62	38.5	8.1	85	9.4	18.8
Buddhists	nonagr.	422	57.6	1.2	208	29.8	5.8
	agr.	431	58.7	0.2	335	29.0	6.6

[a] Percentages based on 20-49 cases.
[b] Percentages not computed where base is less than 20 cases.

TABLE 28, b

POPULATION 17 YEARS OF AGE AND OLDER IN MARCH, 1943 AND IN OCTOBER, 1943, *Spoilage* (PER CENT SEGREGATED AS "DISLOYAL"), *Early Salvage* (PER CENT OUTMIGRATING, MARCH–SEPTEMBER, 1943), AND *Late Salvage* (PER CENT OUTMIGRATING, OCTOBER, 1943–DECEMBER, 1944), WRA CAMP I AT POSTON, BY GENERATIONAL-EDUCATIONAL CLASS, SEX, RELIGION, AND OCCUPATIONAL CLASS

Generational-educational class, sex, religion	Occupational class	Population March, 1943 (1)	Per cent segregated as "disloyal" (2)	Per cent out-migrating March–Sept., 1943 (3)	Population Oct., 1943 (4)	Per cent out-migrating Oct., 1943–Dec., 1944 (5)
Nisei Males						
Chr. and sec........	nonagr.....	479	1.5	39.5	302	69.9
	agr.........	336	0.9	25.9	281	67.3
Buddhists..........	nonagr.....	207	8.2	16.9	166	61.4
	agr........	300	10.3	14.0	261	52.9
Nisei Females						
Chr. and sec........	nonagr.....	542	1.1	36.2	364	41.2
	agr.........	149	2.7	23.5	136	35.3
Buddhists..........	nonagr.....	346	7.8	9.8	299	30.1
	agr........	177	6.2	7.0	182	25.8
Kibei Males						
Chr. and sec........	nonagr.....	70	17.1	11.4	50	40.0
	agr.........	55	38.2	12.7	27	40.7[a]
Buddhists..........	nonagr.....	116	30.2	6.0	75	30.7
	agr........	147	42.9	2.0	82	24.4
Kibei Females						
Chr. and sec........	nonagr.....	91	4.4	22.0	67	22.4
	agr.........	28	10.7[a]	0.0[a]	25	4.0[a]
Buddhists..........	nonagr.....	125	15.2	9.6	94	16.0
	agr........	88	18.2	3.4	70	11.4
Issei Males						
Chr. and sec........	nonagr.....	260	3.5	8.1	230	17.8
	agr.........	362	6.4	5.0	321	10.3
Buddhists..........	nonagr.....	321	8.4	3.4	284	8.8
	agr........	843	12.1	2.3	722	5.7
Issei Females						
Chr. and sec........	nonagr.....	242	3.3	6.6	218	16.5
	agr.........	167	3.0	3.6	156	7.1
Buddhists..........	nonagr.....	275	4.4	2.5	256	5.1
	agr........	366	7.9	3.3	326	4.3

[a] Percentages based on 20-49 cases.

Table 28, c

POPULATION 17 YEARS OF AGE AND OLDER, IN MARCH, 1943, AND IN OCTOBER, 1943, *Spoilage* (PER CENT SEGREGATED AS "DISLOYAL"), *Early Salvage* (PER CENT OUTMIGRATING, MARCH–SEPTEMBER, 1943), AND *Late Salvage* (PER CENT OUTMIGRATING, OCTOBER, 1943–DECEMBER, 1944) WRA CAMP AT MINIDOKA, BY GENERATIONAL-EDUCATIONAL CLASS, SEX, RELIGION, AND OCCUPATIONAL CLASS

Generational-educational class, sex, religion	Occupational class	Population March, 1943 (1)	Per cent segregated as "disloyal" (2)	Per cent out-migrating March–Sept., 1943 (3)	Population Oct., 1943 (4)	Per cent out-migrating Oct., 1943–Dec., 1944 (5)
Nisei Males						
Chr. and sec........	nonagr.....	764	0.3	51.3	426	71.1
	agr.........	174	0.0	48.3	124	71.8
Buddhists..........	nonagr.....	263	1.1	28.9	205	62.0
	agr.........	126	0.0	26.2	106	62.3
Nisei Females						
Chr. and sec........	nonagr.....	707	0.6	40.5	461	51.6
	agr.........	90	1.1	24.4	79	40.5
Buddhists..........	nonagr.....	396	2.3	19.4	340	32.4
	agr.........	89	2.2	22.5	81	22.2
Kibei Males						
Chr. and sec........	nonagr.....	82	7.3	26.8	54	50.0
	agr.........	19	....b	....b	14	....b
Buddhists..........	nonagr.....	133	18.8	12.0	94	35.1
	agr.........	45	24.4a	13.3a	28	28.6a
Kibei Females						
Chr. and sec........	nonagr.....	56	5.4	14.3	45	35.6a
	agr.........	4	....b	....b	4	....b
Buddhists..........	nonagr.....	143	8.4	6.3	123	13.8
	agr.........	33	15.2a	6.1a	26	7.7a
Issei Males						
Chr. and sec........	nonagr.....	647	2.6	10.0	565	22.8
	agr.........	115	4.3	2.6	107	21.5
Buddhists..........	nonagr.....	1,090	7.0	2.8	985	8.2
	agr.........	354	2.5	4.0	331	9.1
Issei Females						
Chr. and sec........	nonagr.....	455	1.8	9.0	409	21.3
	agr.........	54	0.0	3.7	52	13.5
Buddhists..........	nonagr.....	732	5.5	3.0	671	5.2
	agr.........	228	2.6	3.5	214	3.3

a Percentages based on 20-49 cases.
b Percentages not computed where base is less than 20 cases.

NOTES TO TABLE 28, *a–c*

Column (1) in table 28, *a–c* includes the same data as the corresponding column in table 27, *a–c*, except that Christians and Secularists are combined into a single religious category, and the number of net groups is, for this reason, reduced from 144 to 96. Columns (2) and (3) in table 28 show the percentage relation of each of the 96 net groups of segregants and of outmigrants during the period March–October, 1943, to its counterpart in the basic population of March 1943. In parts *b* and *c*, column (4) again reduces the net groups in the population of 1943 to 96, but otherwise corresponds to the same column in the table 27-series; and column (5) shows the percentage relation of each of the 96 net groups of outmigrants during the period October, 1943–December, 1944 to its counterpart in the population of October, 1943.

TABLE 29

NISEI EVACUEE POPULATION AGED 20 YEARS AND OLDER IN 1942, IN WRA CAMP I AT POSTON AND IN WRA CAMP AT MINIDOKA, AND OUTMIGRANTS, MARCH–SEPTEMBER, 1943 (*Early Salvage*), AND OCTOBER, 1943–DECEMBER, 1944 (*Late Salvage*), CLASSIFIED BY BROAD AGE GROUPS, SEX, PREWAR OCCUPATIONAL CLASS, RELIGION, AND EDUCATION

Sex, age, and occupational class	Religion	Education	Poston: Camp I				Minidoka			
			Pop. March, 1943	Out-migrants March–Sep. 1943	Pop. October, 1943	Out-migrants Oct., 1943 Dec., 1944	Pop. March, 1943	Out-migrants March–Sep. 1943	Pop. October, 1943	Out-migrants Oct., 1943 Dec., 1944
Males, 20–24 years										
Nonagricultural	Chr. and sec.	H. S. or less	77	30	47	35	185	95	89	65
		College	77	33	40	31	110	68	42	34
	Buddhists	H.S. or less	50	8	38	27	78	31	45	29
		College	28	5	19	11	20	7	13	11
Agricultural	Chr. and sec.	H. S. or less	86	17	68	52	60	30	30	22
		College	31	9	22	14	12	6	6	6
	Buddhists	H.S. or less	86	11	66	45	33	9	25	20
		College	16	3	10	5	3	2	1	..
Females, 20–24 years										
Nonagricultural	Chr. and sec.	H. S. or less	114	35	68	32	254	101	152	66
		College	102	50	50	29	71	40	30	23
	Buddhists	H.S. or less	110	17	87	29	173	44	127	44
		college	33	4	24	9	13	6	7	6
Agricultural	Chr. and sec.	H. S. or less	35	7	27	11	27	7	20	8
		College	9	5	3	1	4	2	2	1
	Buddhists	H.S. or less	65	8	52	10	38	13	24	5
		College	2	..	2	2	..	..	..	..

(Continued on next page)

TABLE 29—*Continued*

Sex, age, and occupational class	Religion	Education	Poston: Camp I				Minidoka			
			Pop., March, 1943	Out-migrants March–Sep., 1943	Pop., October, 1943	Out-migrants Oct., 1943 Dec., 1944	Pop., March 1943	Out-migrants March–Sep., 1943	Pop., October, 1943	Out-migrants Oct., 1943 Dec., 1944
Males, 25 years and over...										
Nonagricultural.........	Chr. and sec...	H. S. or less..	116	50	64	45	182	83	98	57
		College......	90	48	41	31	84	55	29	23
	Buddhists.....	H. S. or less..	42	12	30	17	74	18	55	30
		College......	19	6	13	6	16	3	13	6
Agricultural.........	Chr. and sec...	H. S. or less..	80	23	56	34	39	20	19	15
		College......	21	10	11	9	7	4	3	2
	Buddhists.....	H. S. or less..	79	16	54	23	39	9	30	17
		College......	7	2	5	5	2	1	1	..
Females, 25 years and over										
Nonagricultural.........	Chr. and sec...	H. S. or less..	101	38	70	25	156	47	109	50
		College......	66	32	34	16	49	29	19	12
	Buddhists.....	H. S. or less..	95	8	80	17	99	9	88	25
		College......	9	1	8	2	3	..	3	2
Agricultural.........	Chr. and sec...	H. S. or less..	32	7	23	6	5	5	10	4
		College......	2	1	1	1	1	1	..	..
	Buddhists.....	H. S. or less..	45	5	37	5	8	..	7	1
		College......	..	..	..	..	..	..	..	..

SOURCE: See notes to table 23.

INDEX AND
GLOSSARY

Note.—The index and glossary include: (1) complete author coverage; (2) selective subject references, designed merely as a guide to the more extensive or significant treatment of various topics; and (3) translations or definitions of some Japanese and slang phrases and of terms not explained fully in the text.

Yes-Yes [affirmative replies on questions 27 and 28; *same as* "Double Yes." *See* Registration]

Zaibei Nippon-jin Shi. See Japanese Association of America

Zone 2 [*same as* Free Zone]

F